SOME ENCHANTED EVENINGS

Also by David Kaufman

Doris Day: The Untold Story
of the Girl Next Door

Ridiculous! The Theatrical Life
and Times of Charles Ludlam

SOME ENCHANTED EVENINGS

The Glittering Life and Times of Mary Martin

DAVID KAUFMAN

St. Martin's Press ☙ New York

www.stmartins.com

Frontispiece: Photograph by Alfred Eisenstaedt / Pix Inc. /
The *LIFE* Picture Collection / Getty Images

Library of Congress Cataloging-in-Publication Data

Names: Kaufman, David, 1951–
Title: Some enchanted evenings : the glittering life and times of Mary Martin /
David Kaufman.
Description: First edition. | New York : St. Martin's Press, 2016. | Includes
bibliographical references.
Identifiers: LCCN 2015047863| ISBN 9781250031754 (hardcover) |
ISBN 9781250031761 (e-book)
Subjects: LCSH: Martin, Mary, 1913–1990. | Singers—United States—Biography.
Classification: LCC ML420.M332 K38 2016 | DDC 782.1/4092—dc23
LC record available at http://lccn.loc.gov/2015047863

Our books may be purchased in bulk for promotional, educational,
or business use. Please contact your local bookseller or the Macmillan
Corporate and Premium Sales Department at 1-800-221-7945,
extension 5442, or by e-mail at MacmillanSpecialMarkets@macmillan.com.

First Edition: July 2016

10 9 8 7 6 5 4 3 2 1

To Ken,
who taught me how to love
all over again

CONTENTS

SOME ENCHANTED EVENINGS

Chapter 1

"A STAR IS BORN"

It was my first taste of show business and I found it
delightfully habit-forming.
—MARY MARTIN

At the turn of the twentieth century, the frontier town of Weatherford, Texas, had seven churches, several schools, a courthouse, three banks, four hotels, and a single theater for cultural entertainment. The Haynes Opera House was located at the top of a steep staircase, above the R. W. Bonner Grocery Store, in a two-story building in the center of town. With their wives and their children, farmers and ranchers would come from miles around to see minstrel shows, melodramas, Shakespearean plays, and, later, touring vaudevillian acts. In 1889, the Order of Knights of Pythias held their twenty-fifth anniversary ceremony at the Haynes Opera House.

Billing himself as the "most wonderful brain and eminent thought reader living today," Charles F. Haynes performed mind-reading feats at his father's opera house. According to an extant handbill announcing his performance, the junior Haynes offered a "$1,000 Forfeit! For His Equal in the World." He lured paying customers by providing "free street tests," avoiding any obstacles in his path while, blindfolded, making his way around the public square.

Known as the Buzzard's Roost, the last few raised rows of the auditorium were reserved for foot-stomping, whistle-blowing, catcalling patrons. As the audience assembled, they could gaze at the house curtain, which depicted a Greek temple graced by three muses cavorting in the foreground. Then, before the show began, a second curtain appeared to display advertisements for local merchants: "Robert H. Johnson: Tinner and Plumber," "TURP the Tailor—North Side Square—Good taste and good tailoring go hand in hand," "Merchants and Farmers State Bank: Small Accounts Cheerfully Accepted."

Since it was the only game in town, the Haynes Opera House became a "splintery-floored barn of a place," still functioning even after it was declared "unsafe." Weatherford native Ellen Bowie Holland recalled being told by her father to get tickets whenever a performance was imminent: "But go first in the grocery store and see where Mr. Bonner has the flour stacked and buy the tickets exactly above. I don't want to fall into a barrel of herring when the building collapses."

For more than a decade after Weatherford was incorporated as a town in 1858, nearby settlers continued to flock there to escape Indian raids. There was, of course, no electricity; telephones and automobiles were conveniences of the future. And, like Charles Haynes, your neighbor would just as soon con or rook you as lend a helping hand. Here was the true American West of old, in all its absence of any glory. And here is where Preston and Juanita Martin made their home, before bringing their second daughter, Mary, into this world.

With roots planted firmly in the southern United States, Mary Martin could boast of a predominantly Scottish lineage. Her father, Preston Martin, the third of nine surviving children, was born on April 6, 1872, in Poplar Creek, Mississippi. Preston's grandparents were plantation owners. His father, James Albert Martin, was a schoolteacher and a farmer who fought with Forrest's Cavalry for the Confederacy in the Civil War. Preston's mother, Geraldine Hearon, was also from Alabama, and also the child of a plantation owner. She married James when she was twenty years old, in 1867, two years after the Civil War ended. The Martin family settled in Long Creek, "woodhouse country," fifteen miles southeast of Weatherford, where James farmed and ranched until moving into town in 1905. Preston Martin was, by then, a prosperous attorney in Weatherford, but everyone referred to him as "Judge" Martin.

Of Scotch-Irish descent, Mary Martin's mother, Juanita Pressley, was born in Brenham, in east central Texas, in 1878, but grew up in Fort Worth. She was the youngest of six surviving children whose father, William B. Pressley, a publisher from South Carolina, was forty-seven at the time of her birth. Juanita's mother, Mary Robinson Pressley, from Georgia, was forty-one. After her parents perished in an accident under mysterious circumstances, Juanita (called "Nita") was raised by her two eldest sisters, Ida and Mary. According to a descendent's transcribed 1880 census report, Mary (or Mattie, as she was known), the eldest, was twenty-four years older than Juanita and also, apparently, a "famous violinist" who "played before all the crowned heads of Europe"—but this may be only family lore.

The refined and cultured Juanita was teaching violin at Weatherford College when she married Preston Martin on August 10, 1899. Their first child, Geraldine, named after Preston's mother, was born two years later. Weatherford was, at the time, still a horse-and-buggy town with a population of five thousand, far smaller than Fort Worth, thirty miles to the west. As depicted in an early, colorized postcard with a watermelon larger than a person propped up on a wooden stand, Weatherford proclaimed itself "The World's Greatest Watermelon Center." The Weatherford High School yearbook was named, appropriately, the *Melon Vine*.

With their frequently bedridden daughter Geraldine in tow, the Martins moved into a house built in 1894, at 414 West Lee Avenue, in 1907. The house featured a multipillared wraparound porch and a sizable property, including stables and an orchard. The Martins added a second story before Mary Virginia was born at noon on December 1, 1913, a Monday— "first Monday," the day set aside every month for ranchers to sell their livestock in town. "My father always insisted that they traded off a horse and got me," claimed Martin, who entered this world in "papa's library," a sunny and airy downstairs front room with a southern exposure that opened onto the porch. (The family would move nine years later to a more colorful gingerbread-style Victorian house at 314 West Oak Street, only a few blocks away.)

When Mary was born, her eleven-year-old sister still suffered from a heart condition that had kept her confined to her bedroom for much of her childhood. Geraldine's fragile state may have been inherited from Juanita's own delicate constitution. "Doctors told [mother] she could never safely have another baby, but she wanted a son so much that she just had to try once more," Martin wrote in her memoir, though she failed to mention that Juanita had, in fact, already lost a son two years before Mary's birth, when he was only a couple of months old. Intending to give his next child every possible advantage and, presumably, hoping for another boy, Preston Martin even joined the Weatherford school board while Juanita was pregnant with Mary. "I must have known that [mother] really wanted a boy," continued Martin, "because all the time she was trying so hard to make me feminine, I wanted to be a boy. I climbed trees, hung by my heels from the trapeze, ruined all my lacy dresses, and lovingly *un*dressed all my beautiful dolls on Christmas morning, never to play with them again."

Mary would, in a sense, live the life of three children: in addition to thriving as a child herself, she had to make up for the son her parents had lost and also for her considerably older sister, Geraldine, whose illness denied her a normal childhood. Even after Geraldine recovered from a leaking valve in her heart, her younger sister continued to stand in for her. When Mary was eight years old, Geraldine had been crowned Princess of the Cotton Palace—Weatherford's own version of Mardi Gras—and when photographers came by the house that morning to take snapshots of "Jerry" in her "royal attire," everyone was caught off guard as Mary marched into the living room wearing her sister's costume. Mary also used to take her bedridden sister's lunch to her on a tray, only to stop on the stairwell, sometimes, and devour it herself.

Unlike many others who turn to the stage for the attention they lacked at home while growing up, Mary was adored by both her parents. If Mary had, in a sense, lived a life for three children, she had, in another respect, three parents: in addition to Preston and Juanita, for whom she could do no wrong, Mary was raised by Billie Jones, the Martins' black maid, who always wore a starched white uniform. Mary came to expect from the whole world the undying attention and affection that were hers from the very beginning, as if they were a birthright. What's remarkable is the extent to which she would receive them. But she would also prove uncomprehending whenever they weren't forthcoming.

All Mary had to do was step outside onto the streets of Weatherford to have the town's adoration showered on her. "It was all joy," proclaimed Martin about her childhood. "Mother used to say she never had seen such a happy child." "Everyone loved her because she was 'the judge's' daughter," recalled Harvey Schmidt, a Texan himself, and the composer of what would become Mary Martin's final Broadway musical, *I Do! I Do!* "Mary told me that when she was growing up, she just loved going around the town square, where the courthouse was, singing real loud and so proud, knowing that her father was inside."

The tall, handsome, and thriving Preston Martin had his four-room attorney's offices on an upper floor of a building overlooking the town square. "Daddy had time for everyone," Martin wrote. "I have seldom known anyone who had the depth of feeling for other human beings that my father had. No problem was ever too small to bother with, no problem so big that he wouldn't tackle it."

"It was a very wealthy community," recalled Joyce Hayes Gertz, who was born in Weatherford when Mary was twelve years old. "Most people had ranches, and a lot of them had oil. It was great cattle country, and the farmers had watermelons and peanuts in those days. There were also many churches in Weatherford, but only one movie house"—the Princess Theater, which opened in 1912. In fact, the larger Palace Theater, which

opened the year Gertz was born, was probably where Mary Martin became a fan of a British songwriter, playwright, and actor named Noël
Coward, with whom she would work during the heights of their respective careers.

"You wouldn't stop in Weatherford for anything but gasoline in those
days," continued Gertz, "because there wasn't any place to eat that was
decent." Weatherford was also an alcohol-free town within the dry Parker
County, which is part of the reason nearby Mineral Wells became a
popular spot for tourists, serving not only local spring waters, with their
supposedly curative powers, but alcoholic libations as well. "My mother
and my father both came from Mineral Wells," said Gertz. "I grew up
with Mary. Our families knew each other. Her father was a very prominent man in town, very comfortable, and I met Mary somewhere along
the way. In Weatherford, people had get-togethers a lot. My mother and
Juanita were close friends. Though this was a dry county, my mother used
to have parties, where they'd drink and have fun."

Mary had a first beau when she was five years old: Ford White, with
whom she sang "When the Apples Grow on the Lilac Tree" at a firemen's
ball. Looking back, Ford saw himself as a rather reluctant, preadolescent
beau. "Mary was always pretty much of a tomboy when she was small,"
White would say in an interview, nearly four decades later. "She'd always
want to hang around with the rest of the boys. We'd always go about
three blocks from home, where there was a hill called Oyster Hill. The
kids used to like to go up there and dig in these Indian graves for trinkets
and arrowheads. . . . Well, Mary always wanted to tag along. Three of us
boys started up there one Saturday morning, and Mary came along, saying, 'I'm going, too.' We didn't like it at all. We were just kids and naturally we were all barefooted, and we told her that if she didn't go back
home, why, we'd pick up a rock and throw it on her feet. And we did
throw several practice rocks, but it didn't faze Mary at all. Finally I picked
up one that I could barely lift, and I said, 'Mary, if you don't go home, I'm
gonna throw this rock on your foot just as sure as we're here.' And she
didn't go home. And sure enough, I dropped that big, heavy rock on her
right big toe. And to this day, there's a scar on it."

Mary had a best friend in the full-faced Bessie Mae Sue Ellen Yeager,
who lived in Mineral Wells and had been primed to become a friend for
life. "When Juanita Martin was teaching violin at Weatherford College
[before she married Preston Martin], she lived with my great uncle and
his wife," recalled Yeager, who was a year older than Mary. "So there's
always been a family connection." When the girls were in the third or

fourth grade, they started seeing each other every Saturday, riding don-keys together or attending movies in the afternoon and sleeping on a screened-in porch in Weatherford or in Mineral Wells whenever Juanita drove her daughter there to spend the weekend. Eventually, the two friends became members of a local girl's club and, later, of a high school sorority, Beta Sigma. (It's telling that Bessie Mae's father, a physician, took to calling Mary "boy.")

Martin would also call herself the "best customer" at the Palace, the larger of Weatherford's two movie houses when she was an adolescent and talkies were first appearing. It was here that Mary saw Al Jolson and Ruby Keeler and taught herself to imitate comic player Zasu Pitts. "They were my babysitters," said Martin, recalling how Juanita would drop her off early in the day and she'd sit through the same films four or five times, dreaming of becoming a star herself. "My ambition to be part of the world of make-believe was born right there," Martin would say. "To me those people on the screen were live." Dancing up a storm, Mary even won a Ruby Keeler look-alike contest sponsored by the movie house, gar-nering a year's worth of free passes—and setting in place her lifelong knack for imitating others.

While Mary derived her confidence and her congenial, jovial manner from her father, she inherited her musical ear and her love for perform-ing from her mother. Whether breaking out in song while skipping around Weatherford or dressing up in her sister's clothes, little Mary was always giving a performance. With her artistic eye and her sewing ma-chine, Juanita encouraged her daughter's natural bent for entertaining. "My mother would tackle anything," recalled Martin, who added that Juanita "could have been a great designer or costumer. Once when I was a little girl she made me a butterfly costume, of many shades of silk and lamé, that would stand up to the best of [famed theatrical costumers] Mme. Karinska's or Irene Sharaff's. She also constructed a cocoon of burlap from which I emerged, became a butterfly, and then died."

In addition to appearing at a firemen's ball when she was only five, Mary was one of three little girls who sang at the Weatherford band-stand, in the middle of town, on Saturday nights: popular songs such as "Moonlight and Roses" or "When the Red, Red Robin Comes Bob, Bob, Bobbin' Along." "Her mother pushed her," observed Mary's cousin, Don Martin, who also grew up in Weatherford. "As a little kid Mary performed all the time, but her mother was behind that."

According to the adult Martin, Juanita was "marvelous" about letting her offspring decide which religious sect most appealed to them. While

Juanita and Geraldine became Methodists, "Daddy I'm not sure ever made up his mind, but he went with them to the Methodist church every Sunday." Though there wasn't a single synagogue in Weatherford when Mary was growing up, there was a Jewish family (the Haases), and Mary apparently spent a lot of time in their kitchen. She also "loved" Sunday school at the Methodist church, but eventually chose to attend the Episcopal, "which finally had everything I was looking for: beauty, formality, pageantry, singing, and a great minister." During her childhood, Mary sang "from morning till night," including "in any church that would turn me loose. I also sang for the ladies of the Garden Club, the Music Club, the DAR, and the Eastern Star. Then I graduated to the men's clubs: Lions, Rotarians, Elks, Shriners, and the Knights of Pythias."

In her memoir, Martin would cite only two books that she read as a youth, specifically when she was eleven years old—even though one of them, *The Well of Loneliness*, wasn't published until Mary was fifteen. (The other was *The Life of Isadora Duncan*—a noted bisexual.) Written by British author Radclyffe Hall, *The Well of Loneliness* would come to be considered a classic lesbian novel of the twentieth century. Shortly after its arrival in 1928, the controversial work was "attacked in several courtrooms" for its suggestion that "inverts" should be tolerated. Though she was sure to add that she "didn't have the remotest idea what these books were all about," Martin's taking the trouble to name *The Well of Loneliness*—without even bothering to bury it in a much longer list of books—might be viewed as an intended message to her readers that she grew up with a definite and unequivocal lesbian influence.

Mary was *verifiably* eleven years old when she saw the silent film version of *Peter Pan*, James M. Barrie's classic tale of the boy who refused to grow up. Chosen by *The New York Times* as one of the ten best films of 1924, it was directed by Herbert Brenon and starred Betty Bronson, who was only six years older than Mary and who, in keeping with the stage tradition of the original Barrie play, portrayed a boy in the film.

"I wanted to be Peter Pan the first time I saw him—before I ever thought of being an actress," Martin would tell a reporter thirty years later, in 1954, when her musical version of *Peter Pan* was about to open on Broadway. Thanks to the live TV version that followed and became a perennial favorite, Peter Pan would become the role most identified with Martin, both during her lifetime and beyond.

Given an innate eagerness to please and to draw attention to herself, Mary became one of the most prominent members of her sophomore high school class. The 1927 *Melon Vine* singles out her name on a page that also contains descriptions of that year's junior and sophomore socials: "MISS MARY MARTIN ENTERTAINS: The night that Mr. Craddock's light opera was presented the second time, Miss Mary Martin gave a party to the cast. The pirate costumes were discarded, but traces of cosmetics [i.e., stage makeup] were left on the faces of the bold pirates. A small orchestra . . . furnished music along with Victrola and radio. Dancing and numerous games furnished entertainment for the guests. On departing, the entire cast declared Miss Martin a charming hostess and expressed their hope of another good time in the future." The following year, Mary was elected vice president of her junior class, whose group motto was "Always Rowing Never Drifting." On a page headed "FUN AND FOOLISHNESS" in the *Melon Vine* the following year, Mary Martin said, "If I sang I would smoke Luckies," as if she were already a celebrity sought after for commercial endorsements.

Eager to convey that her hometown fostered interest in show business as well as agricultural concerns, the adult Martin would proudly tell an interviewer for a Hollywood magazine that Weatherford produced one of the original Flora-Dora girls—pre-Ziegfeld showgirls. "She did all right by herself, too," added Martin. "She went up North and married a Yankee—a millionaire."

Perhaps because her birthday was in December, Mary was fifteen when she was a junior. It was also during her junior year in high school that Mary and Bessie Mae put on a two-person show, in which Mary sang, danced, and performed a dramatic "play": "Mary sent China Rose [her character]—in costume and fan, no less—to her tragic death," reported Laurence Schwab in an extensive *McCall's* cover story on Martin in 1949, describing the first third of her life with vivid details. "A full hour and a half she held the stage, with only her bosom friend, Bessie Mae Sue Ella Yeager, to play the violin during costume changes as doubtful relief from Mary's histrionics."

"After my show being such a success," Martin told Schwab, "Momma took me to Fort Worth to see Mizzes [Helen] Cahoon and told her she could have the opportunity of teaching me [vocal lessons] before I went into the Metropolitan Opera. But when I sang she said my voice wasn't settled yet and I should take piano lessons. But I couldn't do *that*. You couldn't stand up and be seen at a piano. Heck, I remember hating that haughty lady, making a double-dare oath I'd get back at her someday." Mary would indeed go on to receive vocal instruction from Helen Fouts Cahoon, who became one of the more influential figures in her life. As it happened, within the small town that was Weatherford, Cahoon had known both Preston and Juanita Martin before they even met each other.

"That girl," exclaimed Cahoon in 1949, referring to Mary, who would resume her voice lessons with Cahoon after she became a Broadway star, "she's just got the most remarkable ear. She's never off-key. Never needs a pitch to start, even. Nobody can claim credit for making Mary Martin sing. Nobody but God and her awful, wonderful, frightening, adorable stubborn nature. . . . You know, I think Mary was always a trifle afraid of me," continued Cahoon, who was a coloratura soprano. "She'd known me as Professor of Music at Texas University, and I used to be a concert singer and—anyway, she always called me Mrs. Cahoon. . . ."

Although Mary was a mediocre student at school, her personality was so radiant that, in April 1929, she was voted the most popular girl in her junior class. As Martin herself would say, "I was never known as a good student and everyone (except me) worried from the first to the last day that I went to school." Also that year, Mary likely saw a new musical film, *Sally*, based on "one of the most magical of all American musicals" of the same name, originally produced by Florenz Ziegfeld in 1920 and starring Marilyn Miller in the title role. "With this show [Marilyn Miller] became Broadway's undisputed queen of musical comedy," wrote theater scholar Gerald Bordman. Though the film version radically simplifies the story, it still showcases "the entrancing" Marilyn Miller, as Bordman puts it, in one number after another (from "an incandescent Jerome Kern score"), dancing up a storm and singing in her beguiling, forthright manner. Though Mary might have dreamed of one day being like Miller, little did she know that in two decades, more than one reviewer would put her in precisely the same category.

With the onset of the Great Depression, there wasn't enough money for Mary's senior class to finance a Weatherford yearbook for 1930. But on May 20 and 21, the senior class presented *Come Out of the Kitchen* in the high school auditorium. Admission was twenty-five to thirty-five cents. Mary starred as Olivia Daingerfield, alias Jane Ellen in this three-act comedy by A. E. Thomas, which was directed by Mrs. Flo Hutcheson, Mary's elocution teacher.

"This is the play in which Ruth Chatterton, now noted screen favorite, starred on Broadway for two years," explained an advance story in the *Daily Herald,* the author of which invented a rather unsavory metaphor to claim that "Mary Martin can take the sole of your shoe and make it melt in your mouth." In her memoir, Martin recalled that she had to perform the play on crutches, following a swimming accident during the senior class picnic at Lake Mineral Wells, when she "landed on a broken Mentholatum bottle which promptly cut my right foot almost [in] half."

The *Daily Herald* reported on May 24 that 111 seniors—the largest graduating class in the history of Weatherford High School till then—received their diplomas on Friday. After the processional and two "excellent" speeches, "the next number was a beautiful song, 'The Wind's in the South,' [sung] by Mary Martin. . . ."

When she was fourteen, Mary had met nineteen-year-old Swedish-American Benjamin Jackson Hagman, a strapping, 240-pound football player and law student at Texas Christian University, in Fort Worth. They started dating in the summer of 1930, when Mary was sixteen and Hagman twenty-one. "That may have been one reason why my parents packed me off to Ward-Belmont [School for Women]," Martin would conjecture in her memoir. Another was that Bessie Mae had already spent the previous year at the same finishing school in Nashville, Tennessee, and Mary was more than willing to join her best friend there in the fall. She proved less happy than she expected to be once she found herself away from home, however; she especially missed Juanita. "I had never been away from mother for such a long time before, I never realized how close I was to her, what an integral part of my life she was."

Ward-Belmont marked, for Mary, the awkward and rude awakening that awaits all youths when they first discover the larger world beyond the protective cocoon of their childhood home. As the daughter of the well-to-do and beloved Preston Martin, Mary had always been the town's darling, one of the bigger fish in the small sea of Weatherford. She naturally yearned for all the privileges her birthright bestowed as soon as they were denied her.

According to scholar Mary Ellen Pethel, "Ward-Belmont still reflected the values of a traditional girls' school for the majority of its students and patron families. However, the school developed legitimate academic programs, attained junior college accreditation in 1925 . . . (first in the South), and solidified its reputation as a center for aspiring musicians." Indeed, the school's catalog in 1927 claimed that Ward-Belmont had ninety pianos, ten of which were Steinway grands.

The school's emphasis on music training would have appealed to Mary, who studied voice with Dr. Stetson Humphrey and his wife, Irene. But the school's otherwise rigorous academic and comportment standards did not. "For Nashville's young women, behavioral expectations reminiscent of antebellum culture and the Victorian era shifted to a more active, self-reliant 'Gibson Girl,'" wrote Pethel. "Girls at Ward-Belmont were al-lowed to bob their hair or cut it short, a punishable act before 1923. By 1933, sailor tops, bloomers, long stockings, and lace-up boots had been traded in for tennis shoes and lighter clothing, including navy blue wool shorts and white shirts. Students were also allowed to wear skirts that revealed their legs. While smoking by students was strictly forbidden on campus, some students smoked when they traveled off campus or out of town. However, girls *could* be expelled if caught drinking alcohol or smoking. . . . When going out in groups for non-school activities, girls were required to wear long dark dresses, gloves, and matching dark hats."

Like all other Ward-Belmont students, Mary was compelled to study math, English, and history. (Unfortunately, no records of her two or three months at the school can be located.) There was no theater depart-ment, and no plays were performed. Though there were no local branches of national sororities at the school either, Mary was pledged by the Penta Tau club. "She made them a box-office smash at the Sunday open houses, by singing so memorably that the rush captains of the rival lodges kicked themselves for not snagging her first," claimed the first extensive account of this significant period in Martin's life. Also according to this suspect report (by Hendon Holmes in *Radio and Television Mirror,* published in March 1940, a decade after the fact), while most of Mary's friends went home for Thanksgiving, she remained in Nashville to work on a loath-some term paper. During the break, she was paid a visit by Ben Hagman.

There would turn out to be many conflicting stories concocted to account for Mary Martin's marrying Ben Hagman, ostensibly late in 1930, while she was a student at Ward-Belmont. And when contradictory reports surround a significant development in a celebrity's past, it's difficult not to blame the subject for the muddle. In this case, the swirling smoke of confusion suggests the fire of invention to cover up what is commonly known, in and out of Texas, as a shotgun wedding.

"Mary kept the story of that marriage a secret from all the world. . . . Only recently did news of it break out, and only here has the full story been told," continued the presumably fabricated yarn in *Radio and Tele-vision Mirror.* "The honeymoon was Utopia on wheels. They burned up a thousand miles over the week-end [*sic*] and Ben had to sprint to make Nashville in time for [Mary] to begin classes again. For a month she lin-gered [at Ward-Belmont], like a girl lost in herself."

"When her best friend [Bessie Mae] wriggled out of writing a term paper by going home with an infected foot, Mary decided to wriggle out of it by getting married," claimed a slightly later report in *Life* magazine, which seems to have presented as valid a reason as any for Mary's marriage to Ben Hagman. "They were married in a church, but there wasn't any music," claimed yet another item in the *Hollywood Citizen News*. "Then she went back to school, to attend a French class, and he drove away. They didn't have a honeymoon. She didn't see him until three months later." "Three months later" would make it February 1931, when, according to still other stories, Mary met with Ben and his parents in Fort Worth on her way back to Weatherford, and when, under any circumstances, she would already have been pregnant with her son-to-be—Larry Hagman was born on September 21, 1931.

As perpetrated by Martin's own persistent contradictions, confusion and uncertainty circumscribe her marriage to Ben Hagman. According to all versions of the story, Hagman drove to Nashville to spend some time with Mary when she was at Ward-Belmont, in the course of which they were married in Hopkinsville, Kentucky, seventy miles from Nashville; the earliest accounts claim it was during the Thanksgiving holiday. According to most subsequent versions of what happened, Juanita accompanied Ben on the trip, which happened a month or so before Thanksgiving, and sanctioned the marriage.

In fact, the Christian County clerk's office in Hopkinsville, Kentucky, has on file a marriage bond between Ben Hagman and Mary Virginia Martin, issued by the Commonwealth of Kentucky, purportedly on November 3, 1930, with Mrs. Preston Martin serving as surety, or guarantor, but, significantly, not as a witness. Nor does Mary Martin's unmistakable signature appear anywhere on the document. To add to that, the age of the wife is listed as eighteen (Martin was sixteen on that date), and her place of residence appears as Fort Worth, Texas, as opposed to Weatherford. Such evidence contributes to the possibility, if not the likelihood, that the form was created and filed sometime after the date indicated. (Martin's age and residence on the form are perhaps clues that the document was actually created in December of 1931, or sometime thereafter, when she was, in fact, eighteen and living in Fort Worth with Hagman.)

Indeed, while realizing that the marriage bond is specifically not a marriage license, the section on the bond for the "Date of License," including "Subscribed and sworn to before me by," is conspicuously and entirely blank. The "Record of Marriage Certificate" at the bottom of the document claims that Mary and Ben were married on the same date, November 3, 1930, by an Episcopal minister, Burgess W. Gaither; but it, too, is filled out entirely by the same hand, making it equally suspect and possibly specious.

Perhaps one of Ben Hagman's first concrete acts as a full-fledged attorney was to see to it that this evidently bogus marriage bond was created, legitimizing the birth of his son for the forseeable future. But the problem is that the forged nature of this spurious document and its clear status as a planted decoy make this public record of the marriage legally irrelevant.

According to some subsequent reports, the marriage occured at an Episcopal church and Mary sang "Oh Promise Me" at her own wedding ceremony. But none bothered to point out that November 3 is considerably before Thanksgiving or to explain why Mary and Ben crossed the Tennessee border to be married in Kentucky, since, as Martin herself claimed, she had Juanita's consent, rendering it an unnecessary maneuver. For that matter, why would she have lied about her age, claiming to be eighteen on the marriage certificate, when she was actually not quite yet seventeen years old? (As Martin herself would later characterize it, "How hillbilly can you get?")

In truth, nobody, including Martin herself, has ever been able to explain satisfactorily why such an unlikely event took place. Perhaps the most vexing question is why Juanita would have brought Ben Hagman with her to visit Mary at Ward-Belmont, when she admittedly sent her daughter to the school to dissolve the budding romance in the first place, and when, as Martin would also claim, Juanita did the driving herself. As Martin would write in her memoir, "Ben and I talked Mother into letting us get married. Through the years, I never stopped wondering why [Mother] gave her consent. She could have prevented it, but she didn't."

Mary would also say, "I got married so I wouldn't have to write that term paper," referring to her assigned theme of "Flower Decoration in the Genteel Home," which itself sounds fraudulent, or like something one might expect at a finishing school, but not at the more seriously academic Ward-Belmont. "Our marriage was not consummated for a week or so," Martin added, "but almost from the moment it was, I was pregnant." This also raises the question: If Ben Hagman came to see Mary only for the Thanksgiving holiday or for some previous weekend, how could their marriage have been consumated "a week or so" later?

In his remarkably candid memoir, *Hello Darlin'*, Larry Hagman corroborates that his mother and father were married in Kentucky on November 3, 1930, which would make it a couple of months before his conception, as opposed to the mere "week or so" before, as his mother would claim. But in recalling the circumstances, Larry alludes to the irrational and inexplicable behavior they entailed: "*For some reason*, my grandmother brought Ben along [to Ward-Belmont]," wrote Hagman, who also said, "[Mother] had married and become pregnant almost the moment her marriage was consummated. She had no idea about sex. Nor did she have much of a clue about motherhood."

Laurence Schwab, the producer who would later play a prominent role in Martin's life, would later write a more thorough account of her first marriage for *McCall's* in November 1949, referring to "big Ben Hagman, a football player from her home town, who drove Mrs. Martin over to see her daughter at Thanksgiving. I cannot imagine what Momma was doing when the kids ran off and got hitched while on a date, but they were wed in name only because the bride just had to get back to class. Big Ben must have been a silent cuss, for he drove Mrs. Martin all the way back to Texas with his mouth tight over the wheel." A decade after Schwab's report, Martin would tell Pete Martin, for the *Saturday Evening Post*, that "we married much too soon" and "neither of us was ready . . . aside from the fact that our marriage was miles too soon, we were miles apart in other ways."

Anxious to become a practicing attorney-at-law, Ben Hagman had a very clear-cut motive for wanting to marry the daughter of one of the most prominent and prosperous lawyers in the area, and, in fact, he joined Preston Martin's office as a lawyer soon after impregnating and marrying Mary. But no one, including Martin herself, could ever account for why she married the burly and crass Ben Hagman, who defined the notion of a "redneck," nor why Juanita would have permitted let alone condoned it.

Left to their small-town devices, Weatherford busybodies invented their own version of what had transpired, which would also appear to be the accurate one: Mary was pregnant before she got married, but told her parents she didn't love Ben Hagman. Preston assured his daughter that she didn't have to do anything she didn't want to, but the more proper Juanita was adamant that Mary marry the father of her child-to-be.

"Mr. Martin didn't want the marriage at all, he wanted Mary to stay in school," said Joyce Hayes Gertz. "But Juanita pushed the marriage. Everybody suspected that it was because she was pregnant, and so her mother insisted that she get married. So she left Ward-Belmont, came home and got married, and gave birth shortly thereafter. But she was not going to give up her life because she was married and had a baby. So Juanita took over the baby." Having insisted on the marriage for her daughter, who was clearly too young and unequipped to be a wife or a mother, Juanita was compelled to raise the child herself.

Whatever questions remain regarding Mary Martin's marriage to Ben Hagman—when and where or even if they were actually married, for instance—their brief life together as husband and wife proves equally enigmatic. Before Ben joined Preston Martin's office, the couple moved to the groom's hometown of Fort Worth, where Ben was "doing legal work for an insurance company. [But] things didn't go so well in Fort Worth," Hendon Holmes wrote, by way of dismissing this little-known period in Martin's life. According to Martin biographer Ronald L. Davis, Mary's parents bought a small house for their daughter and son-in-law in Fort Worth, where Juanita made several trips a week to give Mary lessons in homemaking—something at which she would never prove adept. Juanita even took the Hagmans' dirty laundry home with her every week, for the maid, Billie, to wash.

"Mary had a watermelon party for me in her yard," recalled Bessie Mae of this murky chapter in her friend's life, "and she invited all of the friends we'd known in Fort Worth. We had a really wonderful time, but I think Mary was beginning to realize that she was a married woman, pregnant, and that she was removed from this group of people that she'd danced with from the time she was in junior high school. Her life had changed and she was fighting the adjustment." In her memoir, Martin recalled playing a lot of card games: bridge in the afternoons ("when I wasn't throwing up") and poker at night with her husband and his friends. "But I never really liked games," she said.

Martin effectively withdrew from the world she had known growing up. Shortly after giving birth to her son, on September 21, 1931, the seventeen-year-old Mary became so removed and unlike herself that Juanita asked Bessie Mae's father, a doctor, to examine her daughter. Dr. Yeager prescribed rest and recuperation for the brand-new mother, who was proving incapable of taking care of herself, let alone an infant son. "Mary just bore him," said Bessie Mae about Larry Hagman, but Juanita raised him as if he were her own—"until he was twelve years old," Martin would acknowledge.

"She was a kid herself," wrote Larry Hagman in his memoir when he was seventy years old—"too young to be a wife, too young to be a mother, and too full of ambition to settle down." Juanita also confided in Bessie Mae that she didn't think sex would ever be a significant component in her daughter's life. "It was perhaps the most perceptive statement one could [ever] make about Mary's sexuality," claimed Ronald L. Davis.

Such an impression would be reinforced by Martin's eldest grandchild, Kristina Hagman: "I think that for my grandmother, sex was secondary," said Hagman, recalling an intense conversation she had had with Martin, probably in 1979. "When I decided to try and be an actress, there was a lot of pushing from Grandmother—she really wanted me to be an actress. She gave me a lecture about how important it was for me to sublimate my sexual drive and put it into my work. She said if you want to be in the theater, you have to give all of your energy to the audience. You have to save that for the public."

At some point in 1931, the Hagmans left Fort Worth and moved in with Mary's parents in Weatherford, where little Larry would be raised. Given her severe depression, Mary followed the doctor's orders and spent two weeks at the Yeagers' home in Mineral Springs, away from her husband, her parents, and her son. But it was Mary's sister, Geraldine, who provided the real cure when she suggested that Mary become a dance instructor.

Before Larry was even one year old, his eighteen-year-old mother opened Mary Hagman's School of Dance in what had been her father's brother's feed store at 101 South Main Street, on the second floor. "She said to her father, 'I want to have a dancing school,'" recalled Joyce Hayes Gertz. "So he gave her one." It was a block up from Corcanges Drug Store, where soda-jerk Borden Seaberry made many a malted drink for Mary's students. (Seaberry would later become Ben Hagman's law partner.)

"It was enormous and drafty, but it was on my beloved square," Martin wrote in her memoir. "We swept out the remains of corn and wheat which Uncle Luke had stored there, managed to get a piano up the steep, shaky stairs, put up a barre for ballet training and I was in business."

Martin taught her first group of students Sister's Waltz Clog, a simple step she had learned from Geraldine. The fee was two dollars for eight group classes a month and twice as much for private lessons. But it was also the middle of the Depression, and the enterprising instructor resorted to bartering to increase her enrollments. "The grocer would give me four dollars' credit for his little Jackie's lessons, the filling-station man gasoline in return for his son's instruction," said Martin, who also wrote that it was "better than playing cards" and that she "was doing something I wanted to do—creating."

The biggest difficulty for the teacher was how to keep ahead of her

students. "I began to make up ballet steps, becoming a choreographer before I had ever heard the word. At night I drove about twenty-five miles to
Fort Worth to learn as many routines as I could from a young man there.
He taught me the Shim Sham, the Shuffle Off to Buffalo, and a triple
time-step with break." During her trips to Fort Worth, Mary also resumed
private singing lessons with Helen Fouts Cahoon.

In 1932, when she was nineteen, Martin went to one of the country's
most famous dance schools, Fanchon and Marco, in Hollywood, to take
a teachers' course in order to advance her techniques. "Mary told her
father 'I can't continue this unless I take lessons in singing and dancing
in Los Angeles,'" Joyce Hayes Gertz said. "'I have to get more lessons so I
can come home and teach them.'"

"Usually they put me in the front row at Fanchon and Marco's because
I was younger than most of the other students—and although perhaps I
shouldn't say it, I was cuter," recalled Martin. "After all, some of them
had been teaching for years. But I kept working my way to the back row,
so I could copy the experienced students in front of me."

While Martin was studying dance in Hollywood, Preston built his
daughter a new studio at 303 West Oak, just down from their home and
across from the high school. "It was a redbrick house, with mirrors and
the ballet bars—the whole thing," recalled Gertz. "In the back was a little
bedroom. In the front was a little reception room. And that's where I
took lessons from her. I was nine or ten."

Martin also opened a second, branch school at the Crazy Water Hotel
and Health Spa in Mineral Wells, named after the supposedly curative
powers of the local mineral water. In exchange for use of the hotel
ballroom, she sang with a "hillbilly band" on noon radio broadcasts.
"I was called the Crazy Girl—after Crazy Water Crystals, you know—
and made things like 'Hand Me Down My Walking Cane' come
twanging out of my nose in a way that drove Mizzes Cahoon into
stitches, I remember. But the farmers and the ranchers loved it."

By 1935, Martin was running three different dance schools in surrounding hamlets, with her first in Weatherford as the center of operations, the second in Mineral Wells, and a third in Cisco, Texas. "To begin
with, I had five pupils," Martin would recall in 1959. "At the end of the
first month I had thirty. In three years I had three hundred in three
schools in three different towns. I also had a dance assistant, a woman
who kept books for me, and an accompanist."

Martin's most significant helper was the take-charge, roly-poly Mildred Woods, a schoolteacher's daughter from the neighboring town of

Peaster, who was two years older than Mary and slated to be "friend, companion, chaperon, boss, secretary for years to come," as Martin would write. "At first she helped out with Larry. I had become so busy that I couldn't help Mother handle the house and 'our' little boy."

A local religious fanatic ("some crank who thought dancing was sinful," according to Martin) set fire to the Weatherford school: he was convinced that dancing was an abomination and a temptation for young- sters. Five years or so later, Martin recalled responding with characteristic optimism: "That's how it is in small towns; at least, that's how it was back in Weatherford. . . . It really didn't matter very much because I had the place insured. We built it up again real pretty." Later still, Martin ex- plained, "When I first started teaching, a lot of my friends weren't sure dancing was proper. They stopped me on the street and told me, grim- lipped, 'I'll let my child study tap, but no ballroom.'"

As her advanced students required new steps, Martin returned to the Fanchon and Marco School in Los Angeles, where "one day I wandered into the wrong class," she recalled. "There were hundreds of students in that room singing a song, 'How red the rose, how blue the sky, how sweet the morning dew . . .' I thought, *My goodness, this is interesting. I'll just sit here and listen and watch.* Then suddenly somebody said to me, 'You're next,' and by this time I'd learned the song. So I thought, *I'll just get up and sing it*, which I did. Then I went back to my class. At the end of it I was told, 'Miss Fanchon wants to see you in her office.' I'd never met Miss Fanchon and I was terrified. I was sure I'd done something wrong, but I went anyhow. There, behind a desk, was a lady I'd seen listening to the auditions of *How Red the Rose.* 'What's your name?'

" 'Mary Martin,' I told her. 'I come from Weatherford, Texas. I'm tak- ing a dancing teachers' course.' She asked, 'Then why were you singing?' 'Well, I got into the wrong class, and since I was there I thought it would be fun to stay,' I explained, 'but I didn't mean to do anything bad. Won't you please forget I was there?'

" 'I'm sorry, but you won the audition,' she said firmly, 'and you leave at seven-thirty in the morning for San Francisco with a Fanchonette stage unit. You will sing that song while they dance.' There were twenty-four Fanchonettes in the unit who did precision routines like the Rockettes. I was supposed to sing over a mike while they danced.

"For a week I sang, 'How red the rose, how blue the sky, how sweet the morning dew,' with the Fanchonettes. It was my first taste of show busi- ness and I found it delightfully habit-forming. So much so that when I went back to Weatherford, teaching dancing wasn't exciting any more."

During her second stint at Fanchon and Marco, Martin learned more than just the latest dance steps. Using a dozen of her best students and calling them the "Martinettes," Martin put together her own act. "Then, in 1936, they had the Texas Centennial Fair in Fort Worth," recalled Joyce Gertz. "That's where [Broadway producer] Billy Rose had his first major show at a theater-in-the-round, Casa Mañana [a night club theater]. And some of Mary's students went to audition for it. He selected two of her girls to be in his show. Mary wanted to be in his show, too, but he turned to her and said, 'Honey, forget about you. Just go back home.'"

"So I went to father and told him I wanted to go back to California and continue my studies," recalled Martin. "He said, 'All right, Poog, honey, if that's what you want most'; so away I went again."

Chapter 2

FINDING A VOICE

It takes twenty years to make an overnight success.
—EDDIE CANTOR

With great expectations, Mary Martin drove to Los Angeles in the autumn of 1936 in a "bright, new, yellow convertible" her father had given her, along with her sidekick Mildred Woods and five hundred dollars "as stake money on the strict understanding that as soon as that was gone, she'd come back home." Six years after the fact, Martin would recall her first year in Hollywood: "I had just chucked up my dancing school in Texas to take a stab at the cinema village, and what a run-around I got," Martin told *Hollywood* magazine in April 1942. "No one would give me a chance. Casting directors told me my chin was too long, my nose was too wide, and my eyes too this and my figure too that."

She specifically regretted her screen test for Universal. "When I think of it now I shudder," recalled Martin. "In my inexperience I sang too close to the microphone and blasted into it. To complete my doom, I wore a pair of extra long false eyelashes that made me blink and weep from the black stuff that dripped down my cheeks. My test showed me as a female [Al] Jolson who shrieked like a hog-caller."

There was at least one Hollywood insider, however, who recognized Martin's potential: Hedda Hopper. Beginning life with the unlikely name of Elda Furry, Hopper had been a chorus girl and silent movie actress before becoming an NBC radio personality in 1936, around the time she met and instantly seemed like a "second mother" to Martin, who was twenty-two years Hopper's junior. Forever vying with Louella Parsons for recognition as the top Hollywood gossip columnist, Hopper had influence that would benefit Martin's career in both obvious and hidden ways. In the early days, Hopper was called upon to look after little Larry, and she readily complied.

According to Hopper, Frank Whitbeck at MGM also felt that Martin had possibilities. "[He] was crazy about her and tried to persuade producer Jack Chertok to make a short with her," claimed Hopper. "Chertok replied, 'She can't be photographed and [she] has no talent.'" In what would become one of the earliest anecdotes regarding the callow Martin, Hopper also wrote about the would-be star's first encounter with the towering musical comedy lyricist and book writer Oscar Hammerstein, at his house on Benedict Canyon: "She tried out for a chorus job in the St. Louis Civic Opera, and before performing for Hammerstein said, 'I'm going to sing something you've probably never heard before: "Indian Love Call."' Hammerstein listened, then said quietly, 'I wrote the lyrics.' She didn't get the job."

Leaving her young son Larry home with her parents in order to pursue her Hollywood dream, Martin had no fewer than three agents and five screen tests in the course of a year—without getting anywhere. Since Preston had had a stroke, Martin decided she couldn't write her father any longer asking for money for herself and Mildred Woods, her friend and chaperon. Instead, she took on what singing jobs she could, avoiding hotel bars at her parents' insistence: such proximity to customers' bedrooms would be tempting fate, they believed, if not their daughter.

Hoping to persuade the tenacious Mary to face reality and finally return home, Juanita made another visit to Los Angeles. "She arrived to find practically nothing was happening," Martin recalled, several years later. "It was then she decided that maybe, after all, it *would* be all right for me to sing in one of the hotel bars. Before this, she'd cast her eyes heavenward, secretly thinking anyone doing this was going to the dogs— but fast! Well I began in the Roosevelt Cinegrille and, after my opening night, Mother packed up and headed for home. If I was going to rack and ruin, she wasn't going to stick around and watch it."

Built in 1927, the deco-Moorish Roosevelt Hotel helped define the country's new film capital—a fantasy land for both hedonistic fun and hard work. The very first Academy Awards ceremony was held there two years later, on May 16, when Janet Gaynor, who would figure so prominently in Martin's later life, won the Best Actress Award for three different pictures: *Seventh Heaven*, *Street Angel*, and *Sunrise*. Rudolph Valentino reportedly rode a horse, bareback, through the lobby of the Roosevelt Hotel, where Martin was now receiving forty dollars a week for singing in the lounge—"at teatime for the ladies"—and in the bar at night. Martin had no idea that Juanita, before she went back to Weatherford, had made a special arrangement with the manager of the bar. "Each time I sang [in the bar] the manager stood nearby with his arms folded and watched me. Gee, at first I thought the guy was protecting the patrons from me! I wasn't permitted to sit at any of the tables or drink with the guests. . . . Well, later on I found that it was Mother's idea—not his!"

It was at the Cinegrille that Hollywood agent Colton Cronin first heard Martin sing—"Indian Love Call," as he recalled. Cronin managed to get Martin movie assignments "ghost voicing," or dubbing, for Margaret Sullavan in *The Shopworn Angel* and Gypsy Rose Lee in *Battle of Broadway*, but little else. "One black day I heard in Central Casting they were looking for someone to talk for Lassie," claimed Martin, a decade later, with her tongue decidedly poking through her cheek. "I tried, but I couldn't bark. I just couldn't."

Buddy DeSylva, head of production at Universal, also employed Martin to teach French star Danielle Darrieux to sing and dance in her upcoming film, *The Rage of Paris*, costarring Douglas Fairbanks Jr. But apart from Martin's hanging around the studio long enough to get a taste of what making a movie was really like, Darrieux had her upstart mentor banned from the set.

Though Preston Martin was loathe to do so, he arranged for his daughter's divorce from Benjamin Hagman "by proxy," while she was in Los Angeles and her husband back in Weatherford. "Ben agreed gallantly, and agreed also to my custody of Larry," recalled Martin. "By this time he had his own law office and a secretary. His secretary was a lovely young woman named Juanita, whom he later married."

But Martin's new freedom did nothing to mitigate her parents' concern about her behavior. As soon as Juanita Martin learned that Mary daughter was supplementing her income by singing late shows at the Club Casanova—and was sometimes out until six or seven in the morning—she returned to California, getting a speeding ticket on the way.

With Larry in tow, Juanita Martin moved in with Mary and Mildred in their Highland Towers apartment near the Hollywood Bowl, and Mary suddenly had to earn still more money to maintain her expanded brood. "From the Casanova I went back to another bar, Gordon's, which offered me four hundred dollars a week. I thought I was so rich I enrolled Larry in a private school, the first of about eleven that poor boy went to. I was so afraid he would grow up a sissy, surrounded by women, that I put him in a military school. He loathed it."

In her memoir, Martin would claim that singing in the Cinegrille "was one of the most rewarding experiences of my entire life." But her breakthrough performance occurred at the Trocadero nightclub on the

Sunset Strip, in the spring of 1938. It was probably on May 8 when Ivan Kahn, a talent scout for Twentieth Century–Fox, saw Martin at the Trocadero and wrote, in a memo to casting director Lew Schreiber: "I can really use the word 'Terrific' [to describe her.]" Few of the subsequent reports referred to that legendary Sunday evening as what it was then called: an "amateur night." "The Trocadero always showed off some young talent that had come to LA," claimed Marge Champion, the pixie-ish Hollywood dancer, whose husband Gower would become a major figure in Martin's later career. "And that's when I first heard Mary Martin sing. She didn't dance, but she sang."

"I'd prepared two encores, since I only had a five minute spot," Martin recalled. "Well, I didn't get off for forty-five. I'd exhausted everything, including myself." Wearing a black taffeta skirt with a red velvet sash, a white blouse and a bolero jacket, Martin was introduced by the comic (and alcoholic) Joe E. Lewis. With large-rimmed glasses, Martin first sang a suggestive number, "The Weekend of a Private Secretary," including the lyric, "I went to Havana on one of those cruises...." This was followed by her startling rendition of "Il Bacio" or "The Kiss," which, given her mid-song shift from a classical to a jazz interpretation, had a conversation-stopping impact. "For half a chorus she poured out her golden, dramatic-soprano," reported a follow-up story. "All of a sudden she turned on that impish smile. Her eyes danced. Her body began to sway. And for the first time on record 'Il Bacio' was in the groove, swinging like mad."

Martin's unexpected treatment of the song went over so well, it led to numerous encores and a two-week engagement. Indeed, Ivan Kahn returned the following Sunday, May 15, and confirmed his own, glowing, original impression of the Texas spitfire. It also prompted various studios to offer Martin screen tests, apparently oblivious of the fact that she had already tested for each of them at one point or another during the previous year and a half.

As Martin explained some years later, "Il Bacio" is "slightly operatic, and I don't do it very well that way, but I sing it because it's one of the first songs Miss Helen [Cahoon] taught me," adding that her father "thought it too highfalutin, so for him I'd start singing it the way it was written; then, halfway through I'd swing it. Father liked that and he said to me, 'Poog'—that's what he called me—'it's all right to sing seriously, just don't ever take up serious singing.'"

"I started it straight," Martin also said, "then, because I was afraid everybody would get up and leave, I began to swing it the way I'd swung it for my father. Apparently they had never heard anybody swing classical music, and it wowed them. Instead of leaving, people stood up and yelled. [The next day] I had more agents than friends."

Looking back at that all-important night, Martin further recalled, "I was there singing. I saw people at their tables looking, listening—but they also seemed to be waiting. For what? I didn't know—but the space between the tables and the place where I was standing seemed to grow and grow until it seemed we were almost not under the same roof. It was at this moment that all the words of Helen Cahoon and Stetson Humphrey [a voice teach at Ward-Belmont] crystalized into one thought: 'To thine own self be true.' And suddenly I was no longer singing in a high soprano voice, or like Kate Smith or anyone else I'd ever heard. For the first time, the voice I heard sounded like me.

"It felt completely natural," Martin continued. "I was having fun. The room that had seemed so huge and cold suddenly became small and warm. A wave of excitement swept through me from head to toe. And then I had finished. In the next minutes I experienced a variety of emotions. Fright: there must be a fire, because people were screaming. Panic: people were standing on tables and chairs. Bewilderment: the people were staying right there. It was literally minutes before I understood that I was hearing applause—a kind I never knew existed."

The list of people who were reportedly in attendance for Martin's breakout performance at the Trocadero begins to stretch credulity. "You see, it was one of those Sunday nights when everybody that was anybody in the movie industry was present," Martin herself said. In addition to Marge Champion, Jack Benny, Tyrone Power, Don Ameche, Robert Taylor, Darryl Zanuck, and Joe Pasternak were all ostensibly in the audience that Sunday night, but this was probably pure publicity hokum. In her memoir, Martin would erroneously claim that theatrical producer Laurence Schwab ("one of the most important men in my whole life") was also in the audience that career-making night, when in fact she auditioned for Schwab at his Beverly Hills home one afternoon a couple of weeks *before* her Trocadero debut.

"Colton Cronin, our casting director before I left Broadway to produce movies for a change (quite a pile of it), introduced the girl," recalled Schwab a dozen years later, "and I hoped she wouldn't mind if my wife, my fifteen-year-old son and three friends who had dropped in listened to her." The friends included movie writer Nunnally Johnson, *New Yorker* correspondent Joel Sayre, and *McCall's* editor Otis Wiese—none of whom thought much of Martin's presentation. It was Schwab's wife,

Mildred, rather, who said, "I think she's *good*, honey. . . . Of course, her hair needs fixing and her teeth. . . ."

"For the rest of the afternoon I couldn't remember one good thing about the skinny kid," continued Schwab. "But that night I did, between snatches of sleep. That simplicity, that clarity of delivery, that unfailing sense of rhythm. . . . The next day I signed Mary Martin to a two-year contract."

According to Martin, her first substantial contract was for $150 a week for a year, with a jump to $300 a week—"if I had a leading role." It was her surprising rendition of "Il Bacio" that prompted Schwab to envision her in a Broadway musical he was putting together with Oscar Hammerstein, *Ring Out the News* (also referred to as *Ring In the New*), in which she would play "the talented but swing-mad daughter of a longhaired musician who turns his classical string quartet into a jazz jamboree." Martin also accepted a thirteen-week contract to appear on the *Good News* radio program.

But first, after performing at the Trocadero for a couple of weeks, Martin had to work on her physical appearance. "In Hollywood I discovered drive-ins where I could eat chocolate sundaes day and night. I shot from one hundred to one hundred and thirty pounds in six weeks." She now proceeded to lose fourteen pounds in two months, and Cronin, her agent, referred her to a dentist, Dr. Gordon Pace. It was while Martin was having her teeth capped that Oscar Hammerstein had her audition for his collaborator, the great composer Jerome Kern. (A decade before Martin was introduced to them, Kern and Hammerstein had written what many consider the greatest American musical of all, *Show Boat*.)

"Oscar had rented a studio for the audition," according to Hammerstein biographer Hugh Fordin. "Mary . . . arrived straight from the dentist who had put temporary caps in that day. As she danced, putting her all into it with strenuous leaps and turns, suddenly a cap flew out of her mouth and landed on Oscar's thigh before bouncing to the floor. Oscar was so embarrassed that he sat perfectly still, not knowing what to do. Mary was upset, but she picked up the cap, put it back in her mouth and finished her dance."

As Martin recalled, she sang for Kern "Les Filles de Cadix," a famous Lily Pons number "with high trills." Though Oscar Hammerstein would become one of the most significant figures in Martin's career, she never would work with Kern.

Despite her need for a makeover, Martin had a meaningful suitor at this exciting time in her life. Though she herself would never go on record about Val D'Auvray, the young Larry Hagman developed a lasting friendship with this European entrepreneur, which he discusses in his memoir. "He loved mother and, I think, saw himself as her Svengali," wrote Larry Hagman about D'Auvray. "She didn't give him the opportunity. However, for a time he did fill the space in my life that was denied to my father, taking me to the doctor, to amusement parks, and one time to Errol Flynn's yacht, which he said he'd once owned."

After visiting Weatherford, Martin and Mildred embarked from Galveston on a "cattle boat" for New York. "We were living in Houston temporarily at that point, because my sister was sick with a lazy eye and she had exercises to do," recalled Martin's erstwhile dancing student, Joyce Hayes Gertz. "Mr. Martin called my mother and said, 'Could you please drive us from Houston to Galveston, because Mary wants to take the boat to New York?' During the trip, he told my mother, 'If Joyce wants to enter show business you better have a lot of money,' because he was paying all of Mary's expenses."

Martin and Mildred arrived in New York City on September 13, 1938, and checked in at the St. Moritz Hotel. Along with the date, that their room was on the thirteenth floor gave rise to Martin's small-town superstitions. But then she was terribly intimidated just by being in the big city. With her heavy Texas drawl and Southern colloquialisms, Martin felt like she was speaking a foreign language in New York: "The taxi man said he couldn't understand me," she recalled years later. She also visited the Central Park Zoo and expressed her disappointment: "It's like the one in Dallas. Same animals and all." When Martin finally met up with Laurence Schwab some weeks later, it was her zoo experience that made him realize just how "difficult" her transition to New York was going to be: "Cinderella expected even the animals to be different in New York," he wrote.

Martin's self-image had been brutally wounded during her predominantly unsuccessful years in Hollywood. "When I was in Texas I never thought about whether I was beautiful or not because I always had plenty of beaux," she told a reporter for the *Los Angeles Times* in 1954. "But the studio people here made me feel inferior. They said I wouldn't photograph and kept wishing I was better looking. When I went to New York I had lost some of my confidence, but [the British character actress] Constance Collier said to me, 'In my life I have never seen one door close that another didn't open.'"

"I remember Mary Martin when she came to call on me on the very day of her arrival in New York," recalled gossip columnist Radie Harris, probably with more than a bit of chronological hyperbole. "A mutual friend of ours had suggested Mary look me up as she knew no one in the Big City. . . . She had taught dancing at home and had gone to Hollywood three summers ago to study the newest steps with Fanchon and Marco. She had no screen ambitions, and her ultimate goal had always been New York and a Broadway show. . . . She told me that she gave voice lessons too, and that her first break in Hollywood was singing over a local network. . . . Finally, [she was] signed as a soloist on the *Good News* program at $250 a week. . . . When Mary Martin was first on *Good News*, Robert Taylor was master of ceremonies."

Shortly after she arrived in New York, Schwab phoned from out of town, saying he wasn't going to be producing *Ring Out the News* after all: "The show I had been working on with Oscar [Hammerstein]—the one intended to introduce her to Broadway—it hadn't jelled. We had abandoned it. I had nothing definite for my contract player to do at the present." But Schwab also gave Martin some hope: "I've lost too much on the show I'm with now," he explained. "In fact, we're folding it out of town. But don't worry, I'll be back soon. Something will turn up."

Within two weeks, Schwab picked up his budding star at her Central Park South hotel, gave her a cerise velvet dress and hat to wear, and took her to an audition at the Ritz Tower. "We got off an elevator into a room filled to the walls with people," recalled Martin. "As a result of previous auditions, I had learned if I sang one song, then stopped, I never got another chance, which was a shame because I sang so many different ways— blues, sweet, high, low—so when I went into that room I said, 'I will sing four songs for you. If I can't sing all four, I don't wish to sing at all.'"

Martin proceeded to warble the bawdy "A Weekend in the Life of a Private Secretary," her winning version of "Il Bacio," the swinging "Oh, Rock it for Me," and, finally, a quiet ballad whose title has been lost to the ages. Bella Spewack, who with her husband, Sam, wrote Broadway plays (including their most famous, *Kiss Me, Kate*), approached Martin, asking her if she had "ever been on the stage before?" A timid Martin evaded the specific question by responding, "Whatever it is, I can do it. I know I can do it." Spewack introduced Martin to others who had been milling around during her audition: producer Vinton Freedley, performers Sophie Tucker and Victor Moore, and songwriter Cole Porter. "I'd sung for all those famous people and I hadn't known it," said Martin. "I thought, 'This is the end. How stupid can one girl get!'" But that afternoon, she was asked to come to the Imperial Theatre to "test on the stage."

Only later did Martin learn that the people she had just met were involved with a show called *Leave It to Me!* which was already well into rehearsals; that their featured singer, June Knight, had just quit to marry a Texas oil magnate—"For one thing, he thought her main song, 'My Heart Belongs to Daddy,' was slightly on the suggestive side"; and that they needed an immediate replacement before opening in a few weeks. But any focus on the lascivious nature of the song doesn't entirely meld with Schwab's memory of what actually transpired. Schwab was among the first to learn that Knight was leaving the show, when he took her to lunch at Sardi's and asked her about her songs: " 'There's only one, Larry,' " Schwab recalled her saying, in a reconstruction of their conversation that could have been penned by the hardboiled detective novelist James M. Cain. " 'I don't think it's even written. Cole Porter keeps promising to play it for me. But, honey, you don't have to wait on oil. It just keeps gushing and, *goodness*, what comes out of that messy ground! Furs and diamonds and . . .' "

Martin was amazed and befuddled when she arrived at the Imperial Theatre later that afternoon. "It was the first time I was ever scared in my life," she later told Schwab. There, on the otherwise bare stage, was a naked lightbulb on a lone pole—the "ghost light," as theater people call the light left on when the show's done for the night. Martin was still in a daze when she was handed some lines and told to stand next to a man with a hat slanted over his eyes, gangster-like. He told her, "It doesn't matter how you say [your lines], just say them so loud they'll reach to the balcony." The man was Billy Gaxton, one of the featured players in the show.

"My first line was, 'I'd like to renew my subscription,' " recalled Martin. "I said a few more lines, and Sam Spewack came down the aisle and said, 'Come back tomorrow morning, but never, never change that reading. Say it exacty the way that you have just said it.' On the opening night in New Haven, when I stepped out on the stage and said my first line, the audience howled," Martin continued. "I thought my dress had fallen off, or something equally dreadful had happened. I didn't know my line was funny because I didn't know what had led up to it. They'd been very careful to show me only the lines I had to say; not the lines the other people in the cast were given. The idea was to make sure that I sounded like the dumb bunny I was supposed to portray, I guess."

The Spewacks based their libretto for *Leave It to Me!* on their own 1932 play, *Clear All Wires,* set in "a once elegant Moscow hotel suite that has fallen into disrepair under the Soviets" and concerning a corrupt American journalist. With updated references to the nascent but burgeoning Nazi regime, the new plot concerned an easily manipulated millionaire (Victor Moore), whose ambitious wife (Sophie Tucker) secures his ambassadorship to Russia, after playing a prominent role in Roosevelt's election. (When *Leave It to Me!* opened on Broadway, America and Russia were still on friendly terms. After Russia signed a non-aggression pact with Germany during its run, a disclaimer was added to the program for the national tour, renouncing any resemblance to current events.) Martin portrayed a "doll"—named Dolly Winslow, no less—who recently broke up with her "guy," Buck Thomas, a newspaperman assigned to undermine the ambassador. Her first line was Dolly's attempt to renew more than just a newspaper subscription. "I'm afraid some of the earthier souls in that audience read a double meaning into that statement," said Martin. "Then I sang 'My Heart Belongs to Daddy'; that really did it. I was surprised, and so was everybody else when it stopped the show."

In the number, Martin was surrounded by six chorus boys, dressed as Eskimos, who "would pick me up, sling me around, pass me from hand to hand," she recalled. One of them was Gene Kelly, making his Broadway debut. "I've never known anybody who worked so hard perfecting his art," added Martin. "I couldn't anticipate, then, that he was going to change the whole look and spirit of Hollywood musical films—but I knew his drive and his determination were boundless."

In keeping with musical comedy conventions of the day, Martin's character and her song had little or nothing to do with the rest of the plot. Nevertheless, the impact of Dolly Winslow and "My Heart Belongs to Daddy" cannot be overestimated, even on audiences filled with sophisticated New Yorkers who prided themselves on being one step ahead of world events but who were still able to be wowed by a risqué song and an ingénue making her debut. Nor should the song's impact on Martin's career be underestimated.

With the trials and travails that typically beset a career in show business, it can be difficult to isolate any single development as making a performer a star. Not so with Mary Martin. *Leave It to Me!* opened at the Imperial Theatre on Broadway on November 9, 1938. Barely clothed in a waist-length, white fur jacket, straddling a trunk at a Siberian railroad station, and all but performing a striptease, Martin sang "My Heart Belongs to Daddy," the song that would be identified with her ever after. It was an immediate sensation, catapulting Martin to overnight fame. (British theater critic Sheridan Morley would call it "the most starry overnight debut in the history of Broadway to date.") Her innocent-yet-teasing rendition of the number would help shape and define Martin's persona both on stage and in life: one of studied innocence, cultivated naïveté.

"Mary Martin, you know, is probably the most basically naïve person I've ever met," claimed Cole Porter. "I'm convinced she never had any idea about the many meanings of 'My Heart Belongs to Daddy.' But then, neither did the radio networks at first. They played it for quite a while before they discovered that some of the lines to 'Daddy' weren't quite proper."

Radio listeners, too, fell in love with the song without necessarily understanding its meaning. "People don't realize now what a major hit that was," claims Harvey Schmidt, the composer of *The Fantasticks* (the longest running musical in New York history), who grew up in Sealy, Texas, fifty miles outside Houston. "We all knew every lyric: 'While tearing off a game of golf. . . .' I never knew what that meant. Most of the lyrics were too sophisticated for me and my ten-year-old friends. But we knew them all." According to Kristina Hagman, even later in her life her grandmother said that she still didn't really understand all the lyrics to the song that made her famous.

It was one of the most calculating show business pros of the era who taught Martin how to put over the song. During a rehearsal, Sophie Tucker asked Martin, "Kid, do you know what you're singing?" Martin replied, "Well, as a matter of fact, I don't."

"I had a hunch you don't know what your lyrics mean," said Tucker. "Always remember this, kid, when you're asked to sing a dirty line—I've been singing them for years—look straight up to heaven when you sing it. Never look at the audience."

"That was Sophie's theory, and she was right," added Martin, recalling this pivotal development in her career two decades later. The extra air of innocence it lent Martin's delivery of the shrewdly naive lyric captured the insouciant attitude of the era, when the country was finally beginning to recover from the Great Depression. On November 14, talent scout Ivan Kahn wrote a memo later found in his papers, to an unidentified reader, about Martin's impact: "[She] made a terrific hit in Vinton Freedley's show in NY. . . . Winchell spoke about her last night on the radio."

"I think I was one of a handful of people that memorable night at the Imperial Theatre . . . that knew Mary Martin personally," recalled Radie Harris seventeen years later on an NBC radio program devoted to Martin's life to date. "For the rest of the audience, she was an undiscovered talent. But I don't think any of us, even those closest to her, dreamed that she would have this absolutely fabulous success that night. I've never seen a number stop the show cold [like that]. And the next morning, she was everybody's valentine: by the time I got backstage to her dressing room, instead of being the six forlorn friends who knew her, we were practically shunted aside. In the mob scene was Elsa Maxwell and Jules Glaenzer, and Winthrop Rockefeller and this man in a tuxedo who kissed her on either cheek, and said 'Darling! You were absolutely marvelous.' And Mary turned to me and said, 'Who was that?' And I said, 'That, was Noël Coward.'"

Martin continued to exhibit her naturally innocent bent off stage as well as on. "It took Mary a while to realize how instantaneous and solid her success had been," claimed a later report in *Cosmopolitan*. "After the opening night performance, Jules Glaenzer, the jeweler, took her to supper at El Morocco. When she entered the restaurant, everybody applauded her. It never occurred to Mary that she was being acclaimed. She took it for granted that the people who went to El Morocco always passed their time there clapping their hands and cheering. 'My, isn't this a noisy place?' she said to Glaenzer.

"'After all, she was hardly the El Morocco type in those days,' says a man who knew her during her *Leave It to Me!* period. 'She was a real hick. She had never heard of Main Bocher or Hattie Carnegie [two leading fashion courturiers] and she had a lot to learn about fixing her hair and her make-up. But she certainly knew how to handle herself on the stage.'"

Martin also realized that she still required vocal training to maintain, if not improve, her voice. Helen Cahoon, her childhood vocal coach, had a studio in New York and saw how her student was progressing by attending the opening night of *Leave It to Me!* "I sent her a congratulatory wire, and the very next morning she telephoned me," recalled Cahoon. "'I need singing lessons, Mizzes Cahoon.' It was that same scared Texas voice that always made me smile. And I asked when she'd like to start. 'I'll be right over to your studio, Mizzes Cahoon, if you can take me.' And, you know, over she came, that very morning after her big success, and took [lessons] from me all through her engagement. We started working on developing tones, getting back her high register that had suffered so with those years of what I call singing in the cellar. . . .

"Well, all her time in that first show she came to me at nine-thirty every morning and took her lesson. That was fine. But soon a gentleman—a middle-aged gentleman who might have posed for that sugar-daddy she was singing about—started ringing my bell. I'd say Mary wasn't here yet.

But he'd say 'That's all right' and come in and wait till she came and take up my time talking about her and then interrupt and fidget all through her lessons. I told her to tell him to stay out, but she's so sweet, and wouldn't, and, well, that man—a bachelor, he was—nearly drove me wild.

"Then one afternoon she came in alone and sat down in that chair—way down in it. 'If you had the chance, Mizzes Cahoon, to get a fur coat or a diamond cluster which would you take?' she almost whispered. 'Well,' I'm afraid I said, 'If I'd wasted as much time as you have on that old buzzard I'd take both.' As a matter of fact she didn't take either. But ever since that day Mary calls me Helen."

The greatest indication of Martin's achievement with *Leave It to Me!* was her appearance on the cover of *Life* magazine—an honor widely perceived as the pinnacle of fame and success. It was an honor beyond even what Preston Martin could afford to procure, though, according to Joyce Hayes Gertz, it was Preston Martin who paid for his daughter's penthouse at this early stage in her career.

"Her penthouse apartment is banked with flowers, her desk piled with telegrams, her door haunted by Hollywood scouts," explained the story inside, proclaiming Martin, "the hit of the season, the find of the year." There was special praise for her "burlesque strip-tease" and her "exceptional pair of legs." Even the all-powerful columnist Walter Winchell sent his latest subject a chair, after interviewing Martin in her dressing room and finding he had no place to park his derriere.

"The cover of *Life*, in fur coat and underwear, radio guest shots, an unending series of publicity articles syndicated to every corner of the country, parties, flashlight photos, nightclub offers . . ." Thus began Martin's "overnight" success and the unstoppable career that would continue to surprise everyone but Martin herself.

On December 20, while the issue of *Life* was still on the newsstands, and only six weeks after *Leave It to Me!* opened, Martin's father died at his Weatherford home from bronchial pneumonia and hypertension. "As soon as the news came ticking over the wires from Texas that Preston Martin was dead we in the audience and all members of the cast . . . entered into a conspiracy of silence against Mary Martin," wrote Harry Ferguson, a United Press correspondent. In fact, the late editions of the daily papers had been barred from the theater to prevent Martin from learning of her father's death before she performed her come-hither number about her "daddy." "There was a brief meeting of the cast . . . last night," continued Ferguson. "It was a serious meeting, called to decide who should notify Mary. And the choice fell on Victor Moore, the roly-poly comedian whose job is to spread laughter, not sorrow."

Martin decided not to attend the funeral, since she had been to Weatherford "only a week or so ago"—on December 3, to be exact—to see her father, following a cerebral stroke he had had. According to Hedda Hopper, Preston Martin "went to his grave believing that 'My Heart Belongs to Daddy' was written especially for him." The sixty-six-year-old Preston had at least lived long enough to see his beloved daughter-who-could-do-no-wrong become a national success story.

Martin's lavish success led to her performing late-night serenades at the new and popular Rainbow Room, the capstone of the Rockefeller Center complex, where, remarkable for 1938, the "comedienne" was "working with a mic [as] a defense mechanism to preserve her voice," according to *Variety*. She was allotted all of a dozen minutes to sing three songs—"Il Bacio," "Hometown," and "Listen to the Mockingbird." Though she already "owned" "My Heart Belongs to Daddy," the song was off limits to the singer who made it famous—except onstage at the Imperial Theatre. She was also supported by a gang of chorus boys, "Eight Young Men of Manhattan," which included Hollywood-star-to-be Van Johnson.

During her two-month stint at the Rainbow Room, Martin also began dating wealthy scion Winthrop ("Winnie") Rockefeller. They made a promising start on their first date, dancing at the El Morocco club, where they were voted "Handsomest Couple." Rockefeller made his affections tangible with an extravagant necklace and earrings, set in diamonds and emeralds. Their budding relationship was abruptly terminated by Martin, however, when, following a radio show performance and without any explanation, she returned home instead of attending a dinner party held in her honor by Rockefeller.

Martin found a stronger contender for a relationship in an older man, Frederick Drake, who had already been married twice and had a son nearly Martin's age. As the publisher of *Harper's Bazaar*, Drake was certainly an influential figure on her overcrowded dance card. While Drake handled Martin's business affairs in addition to his publication and had bouquets of violets sent to her every day, Martin became, as she herself put it, "officially, if not emotionally, engaged" to him. "Perhaps he was a father figure, I don't know, but I found him fascinating, magnetic," Martin explained in her autobiography.

Martin had also been receiving "masses of flowers" every night in her dressing room at the Imperial Theatre, "always with a note in poetry, signed, 'Daddy.'" She finally had an opportunity to discover who her secret admirer was when he said in his note that he would be "watching you tonight" at the Rainbow Room. Following her act, the headwaiter took Martin to a table where a wizened old man was seated in a wheelchair. He took Martin home that night to her apartment, "in the longest, blackest limousine you ever saw in your life." When she asked who he was, he told her he was "Mr. Guggenheim, the tycoon, and he sent me flowers until the day he died. Every time the note was signed, 'Daddy.'"

The girl who had been voted the most popular in her junior class in Weatherford, Texas, may have lost her real father. But with Val D'Auvray waiting in the western wings back in Hollywood, and so many admirers in New York, Martin suddenly had more "daddies" than she ever could have dreamed of.

Chapter 3

THE UNLIKELY MOVIE STAR

Strange to say, I was the only executive at Paramount who voted against signing Mary to a picture contract.
—RICHARD HALLIDAY

Wouldn't you just know that I'd marry a man who had cut his teeth on Duncan Phyfe, and done his homework on Chippendale.
—MARY MARTIN ON RICHARD HALLIDAY

Perhaps the most obscure chapter in Mary Martin's career concerns her early stint as a contract player at Paramount Pictures, where she was immediately presented as a featured actress and then as their newest budding-star songstress. Given her numerous attempts to break into Hollywood prior to Paramount, Martin had become known as "Audition Mary." She had also employed her wide vocal range and her knack for creating different voices by dubbing for other stars, including Margaret Sullavan and Gypsy Rose Lee. Songwriter Robert Wright had advised Martin to pick one type of voice or style, in order to win a part of her own in a picture. But as she indicated at her all-important audition for *Leave It to Me!* Martin was proud that she could sing in so many different ways.

Martin's natural mimetic skills had prompted her to emulate other female performers during her formative years, when she was, ironically, discovering and creating herself. "When I was 16 and 17, my family knew where to find me," Martin said in 1956. "By the phonograph, listening to records of singers like Kate Smith and Frances Langford. I played them over and over until, so far as I could tell, I sang each song just as they did (and therefore, I thought, just as well). I even found I could duplicate every sound Bing Crosby made. But I wasn't happy with *me*—the singer I wanted to be."

Unsurprisingly, given the remarkable similarities in their appearance and bearing, Martin became obsessed with Hollywood star Jean Arthur,

the sprightly, fast-talking, harebrained livewire, who is perhaps most famous for her Frank Capra films, *Mr. Deeds Goes to Town* and *Mr. Smith
Goes to Washington*. Martin patterned her vocal and physical mannerisms on her idol, who, according to rumors at the time, may have become
more than just an intimate friend. The same rumors have been raised
about the relationship between Martin and Janet Gaynor, who won the
first Academy Award for Best Actress and whom, later in life, Martin
would call her "dearest friend in all the world" and "my closest most special friend." While Martin was woefully insecure about her appearance,
she gravitated toward and copied two colleagues whom she resembled
and, increasingly, identified with.

In her memoir, Martin would recall turning on the television in the
mid 1970s and discovering herself in an old movie: "I had missed the
credits and I didn't recognize the story line, but I watched. I was bouncing around in a chic little dress looking cute—kinda. Then came a close-
up of 'me' and it was—Janet Gaynor. . . . I guess they must have tried to
make me look like Janet Gaynor, too, in the Hollywood days. . . . It's
rather typical of Hollywood, that story. We were all interchangeable."

Even though Martin never would become the movie star that either
Janet Gaynor or Jean Arthur was, it's surprising to discover from internal
memos in the Paramount archives just how much the studio kept trying
to mold Martin into one as well—and the extent to which Hollywood
magazines cooperated with such intentions. More than one story referred
to Martin's resemblance to both Arthur and Gaynor, as well as to Ginger
Rogers. It's almost as if, for a brief window of time in the early 1940s,
Martin was actually a movie star. But today, only a handful of her nine
Paramount pictures even bear watching.

In 1966, failed Broadway lyricist Paul Rosner published a novel, *The
Princess and the Goblin*, offering what insiders believed to be a scandalous
roman à clef or exposé of the strange *All About Eve*–like relationship
that Martin and Arthur shared over the years. While both actresses had
a fascination with Peter Pan, whom they would each play on Broadway, it
seems especially telling that during the period when Martin was making
films at Paramount, Arthur made *Arizona* for Columbia in what could
be considered masculine drag, wielding a shotgun and dressed as a cowboy, with recurring lines referring to her male garb. Part of Martin's attraction to Arthur may have hinged on mutual, masculine aspects of
their personae.

"Just how close Arthur and Martin became, and the exact nature
of their relationship, was to become a topic of Hollywood speculation for

years," wrote Arthur's biographer, John Oller. "It was rumored within the film colony's inner sanctum that they were romantically involved. Private speculation was only encouraged by the fact that the two boyish-looking women began to resemble each other increasingly over time." Though it may seem scurrilous to retail the long-held rumors that Martin and Arthur were lesbians and lovers, there is no disputing the fact that both women would revel in portraying the boy Peter Pan. They were also both quirky, unique individuals, whose real-world success seemed to defy their unusual natures.

Looking back, Martin's film career was doomed to failure, since it compelled her to deny her unique personality: in order to become another female movie star, Martin was forced to rein in her more natural tendencies to be kooky or eccentric, the very outsized and endearing behavior she would eventually thrive on throughout her subsequent stage career. Even the majority of hard-core Martin fans fail to appreciate the degree to which she was initially perceived as a comedienne, which was always a safe category or label for zany types such as Martha Raye, Betty Hutton, and Gracie Allen. (As theater scholar Ethan Mordden would write, Martin brought "a goofy verve, a rural gaucheness, not before encountered in a heroine" of Broadway musicals.) But in most of her pictures, Martin seems somewhat dazed and slow to respond, confirming her own sense that she was suppressing herself and felt outside of her element.

In her memoir, written nearly forty years after her arrival in Hollywood, Martin herself was extremely dismissive of her film career, claiming that she "actually never [even] saw" some of the pictures she made. Nearly two decades earlier she said, "I couldn't stand the pictures I was in. I wept every time I saw one, and I did everything in the world to get out of my contract."

Equally significant, Martin became a motion picture figure during a time of upheaval for the country, which was finally recovering from the Great Depression and on the verge of going to war. In 1939, the year that Martin joined Paramount with a contract arranged by Laurence Schwab, Y. Frank Freeman was still establishing himself as the recently appointed vice president in charge of studio productions at Paramount, the home of Cecil DeMille epics, Mae West sex comedies, and Bing Crosby musicals. In 1936, Paramount had released a whopping seventy-one pictures; if part of Freeman's mission was to make "fewer but better" movies, he achieved at least half of his goal by releasing only nineteen films a decade later. But if Martin's films were any indication, it would be much more difficult to argue that Freeman oversaw the creation of "better" pictures.

Martin's first film for Paramount, *The Great Victor Herbert*, was in some respects her best. It was certainly the most expensive picture she made at Paramount and arguably the most dramatic film role she would ever undertake. The diminutive Martin was all of five feet, four-and-a-half inches tall and weighed 118 pounds, with brown eyes offset by her reddish-brown hair, which she increasingly touched up to appear more blonde. Though not even Hollywood cosmeticians could disguise Martin's excessively high cheekbones or lack of a chin, with her richly expressive voice she was, inevitably, cast in the role of Louise Hall, the noted soprano who sings a number of Victor Herbert's classic operetta songs in the movie, beginning with "Ah, Sweet Mystery of Life." She also sings "A Kiss in the Dark" for a birthday celebration for Victor Herbert (Walter Connolly) at Luchow's, New York's top German restaurant of the day.

Loosely based on fact, the biopic *The Great Victor Herbert* might have served as inspiration for the classic tale of *A Star Is Born,* where a male star boosts the career of the woman he loves only to have his popularity overtaken by her rise to fame. Louise Hall is introduced to Victor Herbert's musical world by John Ramsey (Allan Jones), presented as "the biggest star in New York." After the couple is secretly married, Herbert reluctantly accepts Hall as Ramsey's costar. She eventually receives top billing, as Ramsey's career fizzles.

Under the working title "The Gay Days of Victor Herbert," production began on August 14, 1939, and concluded on September 30, with a final cost of $782,500—$37,500 over budget. Martin received $16,722 for her first picture, compared with Connolly's $30,000 and Jones's $27,604. Whether it was due to director Andrew L. Stone's uncertainty about working with a novice or Martin's own insecurity, he rehearsed with her every day: "long before the picture went into production," Martin told Hollywood journalist Radie Harris, "so that by the time we began shooting, I felt perfectly at home in the part."

But in an interview prepared for the studio pressbook, Martin divulged both an enthusiasm for and some trepidation about her Hollywood breakthrough: "I'm a new Mary Martin now," she said, while making the film. "I feel the same, I look the same, I talk the same and even weigh the same. But still everything's different. . . . In New York I sang swing, I tap danced, and I did musical comedy. In Hollywood all of a sudden I became a singing soprano. I did ballet and did serious acting all over the place. It's awfully far from Broadway to Hollywood but I love it!"

In truth, Martin would never feel at ease in pictures. She had her second chance for a Broadway-bound show as soon as she finished work on *The Great Victor Herbert* and went back east to star in *Nice Goin'*, Laurence Schwab's latest musical, based on his own hit play of 1933, *Sailor Beware!* Seventy-five years later, when it usually takes years to launch a Broadway musical, it's hard to imagine that one could be thrown together in a matter of weeks. But, then, *Nice Goin'* failed to coalesce into anything viable and never made it to New York.

As written and produced by Schwab, with music and lyrics by Ralph Rainer and Leo Robin, *Nice Goin'* opened in New Haven on October 21, 1939, and closed exactly two weeks later in Boston. Its disappearance into the record books was more or less predicted by a review in *Variety* that was specifically critical of Martin, "[who] is handed her initial assignment as a musical lead but it is in the dramatic rather than the vocal department that she showed best at the preem. . . ." With a glamorous photo of Martin and some sprightly cartoon characters decorating the sheet music for the show, the song titles alone begin to suggest a shipwreck waiting to happen: "The Wind at My Window," "I Shoulda Stood in Bed," "That Sarong Number," "I've Gone Off the Deep End," and "Blow Me Down."

Paramount's expectations for *The Great Victor Herbert* were immediately apparent to movie exhibitors from the unusually large, thirty-two-page pressbook. The studio's ambitions for their budding star were also evident by the way they treated the film's premiere in Martin's Texas hometown, where it played at both Weatherford's first movie house, the Princess, and the newer Palace Theater. Seemingly all of Weatherford spruced up to celebrate their "favorite daughter" in her first motion picture, which from their perspective could have been called, "Local Girl Makes Good."

"She rode into town behind a whooping parade with banners and a band playing the song that made her famous on Broadway a year ago," reported a two-page picture spread in *Life* magazine. "When Weatherford sang it, they sang 'My Heart Belongs to Mary.'" One of the photos shows Martin cuddling up with Ralph Kindel Jr., "The Boy Next Door with whom Mary played as a child." In an accompanying photo of the couple, Kindel looks remarkably like Martin's husband-to-be, Richard Halliday.

"It was a really big deal with its premiere in Weatherford," recalled Weatherford native Joyce Hayes Gertz. "The whole town turned out.

They even closed the schools. My father picked her up in Dallas and half of Paramount showed up."

"With arc lights flooding the streets, and the population for miles around crowding the sidewalk, Mary, swathed in a full-length ermine coat drove up in an open touring car," reported Radie Harris. While adding that Martin's piano teacher ("Aunt Nona") and her "expression" instructor ("Auntie Flo Hutchinson"), were in attendance, Harris wrote: "But perhaps the proudest person in the theatre, with the exception of Mary's mother, was 'old Billie,' her colored mammy, who sat in a special reserved seat upstairs."

The publicity campaign for Martin paid off with her appearance on the cover of various movie magazines, including several British journals. The review in the *New York Times* by Bosley Crowther featured a photo of a coy Martin and played up her introduction to films: "Mary Martin develops unexpected resources in the role of an actress as well as that of a frivolous chanteuse, and a charming juvenile songstress." Though she seems, at times, alienated and decidedly not her naive self, Martin is nonetheless moving in her first attempt at a dramatic part.

One person who definitely recognized Martin's potential from the beginning of her Paramount days was Richard Holman, the studio's advertising manager, who became head of the story department in New York. The following year, and after two intervening films, Holman would claim in an internal memo: "Martin, as we knew in advance, was 50% miscast in 'Victor Herbert.' The fact that she clicked as big as she did in the picture shows what a great piece of show property she is. Playing her own exciting 1940 self, singing her own type of music, wearing clothes that sell rather than conceal her shapely chassis and putting over that intriguing combination of Texas tomboyishness and Broadway swing-sophistication for which she's famous, Martin in the right modern vehicle should be terrific."

Martin's experiences at Paramount would be marked by the repeated attempts to turn her into something she wasn't. As another new contract player at the studio, Patricia Morison, would recall, "When we were first at Paramount, they were trying to make her into a glamour girl, and she was not a glamour girl. She was Mary Martin." (Morison herself would become more famous on stage, as the female lead in the original production of Cole Porter's *Kiss Me, Kate*.)

While Holman had apparently compensated for Martin's physical flaws mentally, a colleague who failed to, at first, was Richard Halliday. Another story editor at Paramount's New York office, Halliday transferred to the West Coast in the fall of 1939. "Strange to say, I was the only executive . . . who voted *against* signing Mary to a picture contract," claimed Halliday some years later. "I wasn't interested in meeting her." According to Halliday, he and Martin had "mutual friends" in New York, and during *Leave It to Me!*, when Martin was also singing at the Rainbow Room, "many of these friends tried to arrange a date." Indeed, Halliday would claim he attended the opening night of *Leave It to Me!* with his mother, his grandmother, and his aunt. This all-powerful female triumvirate subsequently told Martin that their "darling" boy had slept through the entire show.

It was later, in Hollywood, that agent John McCormick threw a dinner party for Jean Arthur and her husband, Frank Ross, a producer. "I wanted to go to the dinner because I was an admirer of Jean Arthur," recalled Halliday, who added that Arthur and Martin were "enthusiastic admirers" of each other. "But the moment I was introduced to Mary and we shook hands it was that old, wonderfully old story of love at first sight," continued Halliday. "Although John McCormick had arranged to take Mary home, I arranged it so he didn't. The group broke up and Mary and I sat outside her house and talked without stopping until six a.m."

Though Martin was still seeing Frederick Drake at the time, she naturally gravitated toward the obviously gay Halliday. She instantly recognized that she had an ally in Halliday, as opposed to in any heterosexual such as Drake—or Ben Hagman, for that matter—who would impose on her libidinal energies, which needed to be preserved for her career, her mission in life. (Several years later, Martin claimed that Halliday had "the soul of a press agent.") For the time being, though, Halliday had to content himself with writing Martin letters while she was on tour with costar Allan Jones, publicizing *The Great Victor Herbert*, and went on a brief holiday with Drake in Nassau.

Once back in Hollywood, Martin found herself at many of the same parties and gatherings as Halliday, including a "progressive" party at serial locations, hosted by celebrated party giver Elsa Maxwell, which began and ended at Mary Pickford and Douglas Fairbanks's home, Pickfair. The scatterbrained Martin later recalled wearing a short, silver fox-fur jacket that night, only to return home in a full-length coat, which she later discovered belonged to Norma Shearer. Martin also recalled attending another late-night party hosted by Myrna Loy and her husband, where everybody else—including William Powell—went skinny-dipping in the ocean. Martin was at first too demure to participate, though reluctantly, eventually, she did.

At least part of what Halliday found attractive about Martin was that she was a woman who, like his mother and his sister, Didi, required guidance and supervision. If the women in Halliday's life were like live dolls that he could primp and dress and fuss over, the fact is, every quotidian care and need of Martin's had been taken care of as far back as she could remember, and she saw no reason for that to stop now, when she was nevertheless trying to break out on her own.

Following a lunch some days after Elsa Maxwell's party, Martin and Halliday jointly admired a "clasped-hands" ring they noticed in a jewelry store window. Martin explained that such items were known as "friendship rings": "But whatever you call them," she said, "I like them better than anything else because they say so much and mean so much. They are inseparable—two."

"I couldn't get that moment or that ring out of my mind for weeks—not until I suddenly realized that I wanted to buy that for Mary more than anything I'd ever wanted," claimed Halliday. "The day I got it, Mary and I had dinner together and during dinner I proposed even before giving her the ring. It was that night that we [decided to get] married and the ring served as a clasped-hands ring, a friendship ring, an engagement ring and a wedding ring."

After phoning Richard's mother and then stopping by Juanita's on their way out of Los Angeles to announce their plan, the couple eloped to Las Vegas and married at 3:00 A.M. on Saturday, May 4, 1940. Since Martin was scheduled to start working on *Ghost Music*—which would ultimately be released as *Rhythm on the River*—they had to return to Hollywood by the next morning. "When Mary finishes work in the film, we'll take a trip to Honolulu," Halliday told a reporter for the *Hollywood Citizen News,* who added, "They will reside at Halliday's Beverly Hills home on Canyon Dr."

"The first night we began our love life together I didn't even have a wedding nightgown," recalled Martin, who was accustomed to sleeping in old-fashioned pajamas. But her new husband had a fresh supply of nightwear for her to choose from, since he was accustomed to outfitting the three women in his life up until then (his mother, his sister, and his aunt). "The next thing Richard did was throw out all my clothes," Martin continued in her memoir. "He made me over, a whole new image. Even my hair was done differently. I wondered why on earth this man had married me, if I needed so much redoing."

Thus began the long and irreversible process of Martin's turning herself over to her husband. Halliday was, in a euphemism of the day, a mama's boy. (A movie magazine described him as resembling "a monk out of the Middle Ages—sensitive, fine-cut, almost ascetic.") Surely no one, at least on the surface, could have been more diametrically opposed to the crass and macho Ben Hagman. Perhaps the greatest benefit in having married Hagman, in retrospect, was that it spared Martin from making the same mistake twice in marrying someone else who, like him, would have interfered with her career. On the contrary, Halliday nurtured and reveled in the career he helped his wife create, living vicariously through her the life he wanted for himself but that was denied him.

Destined to become the most important figure in Martin's life, Halliday would serve as her father, her husband, her best friend, her gay/straight "cover," and, both literally and figuratively, her manager. "Halliday's becoming Martin's manager masculinized him by legitimating his 'feminine' interest in clothing, food, and style, and by providing him with a high-status, business-oriented substitution for 'masculine' work outside the home," writes scholar Stacy Wolf. "She becomes the flighty star and he the reasonable controlling force of the household and of her career."

Over the coming years, Halliday would cajole and coerce his wife—who had viewed herself as unattractive—to feel like a beauty. He also recognized and cultivated Martin's inner strength, her innate belief that, despite her gangly and somewhat askew appearance, her joyous personality made her radiantly attractive to the entire world after all.

Richard Halliday was born on April 3, 1905, in Denver, Colorado, where his father, John Craig Hammond, was a reporter for the *Denver Post*. His cultural aspirations were fostered in New York City, where he grew up. "My parents attracted creative people," recalled Halliday in a feature story by novelist Irving Stone for *The American Weekly*, in 1956. "Nora Bayes, William Beebe, Isadora Duncan, Montague Glass. The house was full of music, of people singing." Halliday was raised in a predominantly matriarchal environment. Halliday's mother, Hope Harvey Hammond, was twenty-eight years old at the time of his birth, an interior designer who specialized in fine antique furniture and worked, at some point, for *Women's Home Companion*.

When Hope Harvey left her husband John Craig Hammond, their son Richard, christened John Hope Hammond, was still a boy. Hope was a take-charge woman, who did "not believe a man should have to pay alimony" and who "lived up to her principles and set out to support herself, Richard, and his sister, Mary. With a small sum of money, she went to Huntington, West Virginia, to join her family. She thought Huntington could afford a fine decorating shop and approached a local bank for a large loan. The bank let her have the money. She made a sensational go of her shop, putting Richard and his sister through college." It was Richard's sister Mary (nicknamed "Didi") who changed her surname from Hammond to Halliday when she decided to become an actress. For reasons that remain unknown—but perhaps to disassociate himself from his absent father—Richard adopted her new name as well.

Following his brief involvement with a theater troupe at Washington and Lee University in Lexington, Virginia, Halliday was a reporter for the United Press and, when he was twenty-four years old, a theater critic for the *New York World-Telegram*. He also became a secretary at a new general interest magazine, *Liberty*, which was first published in 1924. "It was a great vantage point," Halliday told Stone, "for I learned that our publisher had been trying, without success, to get [the famous novelist] Edna Ferber to write for them." Halliday tracked down Ferber, who was in the midst of a meeting, and he fell over a chair. "Miss Ferber went on her knees to comfort him," reported Stone, "and signed an agreement to write for his magazine."

But as Halliday also told Stone, he was "crazy about movies," and he became the movie editor of the magazine as well as a personal publicist for Gloria Swanson. This led, in short order, to Halliday getting a job in the publicity department at Paramount Studios, which he left to write a novel, *Fanfare*, followed by a second book. "I lost my luggage coming back from Jamaica and my [second] manuscript with it," he said. "I said to myself that this was the hand of God telling me, 'Richard, stop this silliness.'" He returned to Paramount for more gainful employment, this time as a story editor.

When Martin told her eight-year-old son, Larry, which of her recent beaux she had just married, Larry had a rather indifferent reaction. (As Martin would candidly characterize their relationship, "My son and I were more like brother and sister, or perhaps very close friends who sometimes got to play together. We didn't have mother-son discussions.") Juanita Martin was not only raising grandson Larry at the time, but she also started selling real estate in the booming hills of Los Angeles. ("Earned my first check at sixty-three," Juanita proudly told a movie magazine reporter, "and got the thrill of my life.")

At Juanita's suggestion—and doubtlessly at her expense—Larry gave his mother and stepfather a white wolfhound as a wedding present. The sleek and loveable pet was named Princess Olga, and she found a more hospitable place in the Hallidays' new home than Larry ever would.

As if to emphasize just how much Hope Harvey continued to dominate her son well into his adulthood, she planned on moving to the West Coast shortly after Halliday relocated there. Within three weeks of the Hallidays' marriage, they moved into a ten-room, white stucco frame house, with a multi-gabled, shingled roof, in Bel Air, which Harvey had chosen for herself but relinquished to the newlyweds. Costing $35,000, the house had once belonged to Paramount stars Jeanette MacDonald and Gene Raymond—and it had the hidden virtue of being close to Jean Arthur's home. Situated on a sloping hill with birch, pine, and sycamore trees dotting the front yard, it featured terraced gardens in the rear, making it more suggestive of New England than Southern California. It was also reminiscent of Martin's childhood home in Weatherford and, in that respect, instantly welcoming to her.

The familiarity of the place didn't prevent Martin from deferring, in the subsequent months at least, to her overbearing mother-in-law. More than that, the new bride would seek Hope Harvey's advice in all domestic matters, beginning with the furnishings. "Mary got as far as roses and white ruffled curtains in her bedroom, then called her mother-in-law in New York crying: 'Can't you come right away? I don't think Richard will speak to me, and I know he won't speak to the decorator!'" Harvey "loaned" her son and daughter-in-law an eighteenth-century Venetian piecrust table, a Chippendale table, and a chest of drawers that the Hammonds had cherished "ever since the Mayflower docked."

"Wouldn't you just know that I'd marry a man who had cut his teeth on [furniture designer] Duncan Phyfe, and done his homework on Chippendale," Martin told a reporter, trying to make light of her ignorance of the finer things in life. "And I don't even know Duncan Phyfe and Chippendale from Barker Brothers." As Martin also recalled, "The only thing I knew how to do when I got married was to buy a piano. . . . We had a piano before we had a bed," a statement that begins to suggest how important a sexual relationship was for the newlyweds.

"As soon as I got six dining room chairs," reported Martin, "I invited Vivien Leigh and Larry Olivier and Jean Arthur and Frank Ross to dinner. I was so pleased having a place for them to sit that I forgot all about preparing cocktails for them. My butler's from Texas (so's my cook, I have to get my servants from Texas because they are the only colored people who can understand the way I talk)." The butler's name was Jack, the cook's Melissa, and their work was supervised by yet another take-charge, African American woman, who oversaw all doings at the new Halliday manse. The Hallidays' monthly expenses ran up to $1,500, including five servants. Once everything was organized, the Hallidays took a belated, two-week honeymoon by chartering a boat. Since it coincided with Larry's ninth birthday, he and Juanita joined them for the first few days.

Rhythm on the River, Martin's second film for Paramount, would emerge as one of her rare delightful pictures. Perhaps its impact is related to how easy she found it to work with her costar, Bing Crosby. "Making movies with Bing almost made Hollywood worthwhile," Martin would later write in her memoir. "He is the most relaxed, comfortable, comforting man. No matter what happens he can ad-lib, cover up, carry on." An internal studio memo exclaimed that Martin and Crosby were viewed internally as a "dynamite combination." While shooting the film, they made an astonishing discovery: Crosby used to regularly visit the Club Casanova, the small Hollywood night spot, to hear a girl sing "Shoe Shine Boy." Only now, on the set, did he realize that it was Martin.

Based on a story by Billy Wilder and Jacques Théry, *Rhythm on the River*'s working title, *Ghost Music,* reveals the plot's principal conceit: Crosby plays Bob Summers, who "ghost" composes for Oliver Courtney— the "most successful songwriter today," we're told in the film's opening scene. Cherry Lane (Martin) is hired early on to ghostwrite Courtney's lyrics. Lest the audience overlook just how exploitative and underhanded such an arrangement is, Courtney was played by Basil Rathbone, in the type of villainous role he frequently played. Once Bob and Cherry learn of Courtney's dual duplicity—he thought Courtney wrote the lyrics; she thought Courtney wrote the music—they strive to break out on their own as a songwriting team. Ironically, they're turned down by a series of music publishers, because Bob's music sounds too much like Courtney's. In the end, Cherry sings their song, "Only Forever," in a nightclub, and Courtney is compelled to divulge that it was written by his "collaborators." That lilting melody is offset by Crosby's "real hep cat" version of the title song and by Martin's saucy "Ain't It a Shame about Mame." The original score was by Johnny Burke (Crosby's principal Paramount composer) and James V. Monaco, whose "Only Forever" earned an Academy Award nomination.

Though she received the same-size billing as her costars, Martin's relatively puny salary continued to demonstrate her lower-rung status at the studio: Martin was paid a paltry $20,416 in comparison with Crosby's $150,000 and Rathbone's $33,333. Helpfully, though, in addition to guaranteeing Martin $2,500 a week, her contract stipulated that she could leave the studio every Thursday at twelve thirty to attend rehearsals and broadcasts of Dick Powell's *Good News* radio program, for which she was earning nearly half as much as her film studio guarantee—that is, $1,000 per show—which, unfortunately, she was obliged as a contract player to share with Paramount. *Variety*'s response to the picture confirms that Paramount was carefully pursuing their wannabe star's potential: "[She was] more shrewdly dealt with by direction and story, and having gained much ease and sense of timing, greatly advantages herself in a piece which is right down her alley. She also has been much more attractively photographed."

Martin's third Paramount venture, *Love Thy Neighbor*, would do nothing to advance her aspirations to become a film star. While most of Martin's movies are, in a word, undistinguished, *Neighbor* seems the most trivial of all. Based on the real rivalry between Jack Benny and Fred Allen—who conducted an ongoing comic battle, humorously trashing each other on their respective Sunday night radio shows—*Love Thy Neighbor* proves utterly inane. (Having found all six of Fred Allen's films "pale, decent, and forgettable," his biographer Robert Taylor would declare *Love Thy Neighbor* "possibly [the] worst of [Allen's] screen efforts.") Unsurprisingly, reviewers would cite Martin's first cinematic rendition of her Broadway hit, "My Heart Belongs to Daddy" as the highlight of the picture. The review that appeared in *Variety* on Christmas day in 1940 claimed, "this vocalization can be rated, without qualifications, as among the top vocal interpretations on any screen, any time, anywhere." Porter's lyric for the opening verse was predictably watered down to accommodate a larger movie audience: "To go to hell—/ I mean, Hades" became "young men at Yale / and make them fail."

Though she claimed in her memoir that she "actually never saw" several of her pictures, Martin conversely wrote that she "cried after every single preview, I thought I was so awful." She had, after all, endured rejection upon rejection following numerous screen tests, having been told time and again that she just wasn't pretty enough for the movies. But her greatest attribute apart from her voice—her legs or "gams"—would become a plot point in many of her pictures.

What Martin apparently failed to understand about her movie experiences was that she needed a live audience—demonstrating their admiration and enthusiasm, breathing the same air—to feel truly appreciated, to unlock her inherent gift for connecting with others. How can a camera be expected to capture the invisible link between a star and her audience? What is ethereal and, to use a word coined by Lorenz Hart, unphotographable? What requires feedback and interaction to bubble up to the surface, simultaneously engulfing both the performer and the audience? If Martin couldn't see or feel her viewers on the other side of a camera lens, neither could her viewers in the confines of a cinema see or feel her extraordinary aura during a live performance.

Though Martin's contract with Paramount stipulated that she would receive "featured billing" for the films in which she appeared, by the time of *Kiss the Boys Goodbye*—her fourth picture—the studio was trying to promote her as a star. Based on Clare Boothe's stage spoof about whom to cast as Scarlett O'Hara in *Gone with the Wind*, *Kiss the Boys Goodbye* was a hit on Broadway, where it opened on September 28, 1938, and ran for 286 performances. (The play was directed by Antoinette Perry, after whom Broadway's Tony Awards would be named.) It was also a substantial success on the road before Paramount took notice, envisioning it as a musicalized vehicle for Martin. Along with her costar, Don Ameche, Martin would receive top billing.

"The combination of the title . . . and Mary Martin is a natural," wrote Russell Holman, in a three-page letter dated February 5, 1940, addressed to Y. Frank Freeman, president of Paramount. "It expresses the modern, stream-lined, warm Martin personality as excitingly as did *My Heart Belongs to Daddy*, [and] it arouses the imagination of the ticket buyers. Its exploitation possibilities are limitless. . . ."

The "exploitation possibilities" are immediately apparent when the film opens with Martin singing in the shower. (Even though Martin's body is not fully on view, there is no mistaking her resemblance in *Kiss the Boys Goodbye* to Jean Arthur.) In the flick, Martin portrays Cindy Lou Bethany, a "nice chorus girl" with the chops and the "gams" to become a Broadway musical star. (With more than a bit of casting irony, Holman's letter also claimed: "I understand Jean Arthur would love to play the role of Cindy Lou on the screen.") The inane plot takes Cindy Lou to her aunt and uncle's plantation, Magnolia Manor, in Georgia, where she impersonates a southern belle, described as "Half Vivien Leigh, half Deanna Durbin, half Shirley Temple"—even if three halves, in this instance, add up to considerably less than a whole.

When Cindy Lou is also described by Don Ameche's character as having "a simplicity, a charm, and an innocence," the role seems custom-made for Martin, and it was. Martin's highlight in the film is doing a striptease as she sings "That's How I Got My Start," which was clearly inspired by "My Heart Belongs to Daddy."

Any sense the studio had of Martin's having become a star was by now, apparently, shared by Martin herself. Wally Westmore, makeup man at Paramount, would recall the first day he met Martin on the Paramount lot: "I happened to tell Mary the story that I tell all the new young players who come to Paramount. And I cited an instance of one of the young players who believed all the publicity that was written about her, and had gotten a big head. So Mary said, 'Wally, if I ever get a big head, you tell me.' I said, 'Mary. You know sometimes the truth hurts, and people don't like it.' She said, 'I mean it, Wally. Please tell me if I ever do.' Well after Mary had done several pictures, I walked up to her and said, 'Mary, I'm here to tell you.' 'To tell me what?' And I recited our earlier conversation about the player who believed all of her publicity. Well, Mary turned around and walked away, without saying anything to me. Then later, she came back and said, 'Wally, I'm sorry. But everybody at the studio is always waiting on you hand and foot, and you get into a rut, and you begin to expect it. But believe me, from now on I'm cured.'"

This would appear to be the only reported instance of Martin's ever becoming tainted by any notion of fame. Whatever recognition and admiration would attend the long stage career ahead for Martin, immodesty would never become a part of her persona or emotional vocabulary. The fleeting sense of having been a star may have also been part of why Martin would come to have nothing but disdain for her Hollywood experience.

Emphasizing the extent to which Hollywood contract players were little more than factory workers, a full-page ad in the *Hollywood Reporter* featured a glorious photo of Martin in profile, with references to *Kiss the Boys Goodbye* ("Current Release"), *New York Town* ("Ready for Release"), *Birth of the Blues* ("Ready for Release") and *Happy Go Lucky* ("In Preparation"). It also featured, beneath her photo, two clasped hands, which, as depicted by her wedding ring, would become Martin's personal motif or family insignia, decorating her many different living environments.

Nearly three decades after the film of Elmer Rice's *Street Scene* established the conceit, and foreshadowing its use in Alfred Hitchcock's *Rear Window,* the opening shots for *New York Town* begin in the morning, with the camera panning across Manhattan before settling in the garret studio of two artists, photographer Victor Ballard (Fred MacMurray) and painter Stefan Janowski (Akim Tamiroff), and then swooping down to peek into various apartments before arriving at the ground floor as a man is leaving the basement.

The camera then pulls back to reveal a good deal of the city before focusing on a shop window, where a mannequin in a white fur coat is noticeably reminiscent of Mary Martin in *Leave It to Me!* As the character Alexandra Curtis, Martin will soon be staring into the same window.

We first see Alexandra from the rear, her crookedly drawn-on stockings conveying her poverty—and, yet again, drawing attention to Martin's legs. She is, nevertheless, the sort of kindhearted soul willing to share her last dime with a beggar—even though, when she opens her purse, she discovers she has none. She and Victor "meet cute." We learn that Alexandra is from Newton, Vermont, and that she's having a difficult time in the Big City. "I'm not going back," she says. "No matter what happens?" he inquires.

With many a colorful scene—albeit in black-and-white—including one set at Rockefeller Center's skating rink, *New York Town* is essentially a panoramic tale of New York during the Great Depression, in which the film is set. It's also about how the city provided many opportunities for survival. Victor introduces "Al" to free food samples at a department store and subsequently gets her on a quiz show, where she wins enough for them to celebrate in high style. Later still, he takes her on a cruise ship, where they join in the festivities before its embarkation for Rio: free champagne, hors d'oeuvres, and dancing, including a period-typical conga line with Alexandra in the lead.

This forgotten Paramount picture is actually much better than its reputation and neglect suggest. The inimitable Paramount (and first in Hollywood) writer-director Preston Sturges was brought in at the eleventh hour to salvage *New York Town*. Beginning on March 9, he spent five days reshooting the film's ending. Sandwiched in between *The Lady Eve* and *The Palm Beach Story*—two of his masterpieces—Sturges helped make *New York Town* Martin's most sophisticated if most underrated film.

According to an internal memo dated September 27, 1940, work on the picture was to begin on November 4, and Martin would receive her contractual salary of $2,500 per week, with a "six-week guarantee." The memo also said, "Miss Martin has stated that she was worked excessively in *Love Thy Neighbor* and has requested that she not be required to work more than eight hours in each day. She will be assured that this picture will not be too trying or taxing on her. . . ." Famous last words: as recalled some years later, a "mob of 500 extras" was supposed to rush toward her during a rain scene, and to "break" just before reaching her. But "the crowd got confused, knocked her down, trampled on her." "We shot [the scene] on a studio set but under real rain, in the real dark," Martin recalled. "Somebody made a misstep and suddenly it felt as if everybody in the whole parade had either walked on me or fallen over me."

In contrast, *Birth of the Blues,* Martin's next picture, in which she was paired with Crosby for a second time, is more typical of her Paramount offerings: the story is naive, trite, and predictable. Set in New Orleans in the 1890s, the film opens with a dedication that immediately reveals its intentions: "To the musical pioneers of Memphis and New Orleans who favored the 'Hot' over the 'Sweet'—those early jazz men who took American music out of the rut and put it 'in the groove.'" If the focus was on a drawn-out transition from "corny" songs of old to more modern swing and jazz idioms, the lineup of featured numbers demonstrates that the film's true spirit was planted more firmly in the past: "By the Silvery Moon," "Wait Till the Sun Shines Nellie," "Cuddle Up a Little Closer," and "Melancholy Baby"—the "biggest selling number in America today," according to the film's trailer. The new musical impulses are best on display with a novelty number by top lyricist Johnny Mercer, "The Waiter, the Porter, and the Upstairs Maid." And the film's debt to the Big Band era, in which it debuted, is conveyed in a coda, featuring cameo shots of Ted Lewis, Duke Ellington, Louis Armstrong, Tommy Dorsey, Jimmy Dorsey, Benny Goodman, George Gershwin, and Paul Whiteman.

Though Crosby was his usual, natural self as Lambert, Martin seemed at a loss to locate her character, Betty Lou. The vacancy in her portrayal may have stemmed more from some troubling strains in her personal life than from any vagaries in the script, however. For one thing, Martin was beginning to face the fact that any lingering hopes of becoming a film star had already been dashed by the reception of her earlier movies. For another, her new marriage was causing a kind of stress she had never encountered before.

"You see, Mammy, that's Richard's mother, came out, and at one time she was a decorator, and she came out and helped me because I didn't know anything," Martin would tell Peter Martin nearly two decades later, for a lengthy *Saturday Evening Post* feature he was writing on the Broadway star. "The true story was, I had made five pictures in a row at Paramount and Richard was the story editor there. But our hours were so mixed up and different, and I was very, very anxious to make a good housewife and do everything, but I hadn't the vaguest idea how to go about it. [But Richard had] been raised to it. He'd had a series of apartments and done them himself and he had excellent and beautiful taste.

"He's always said he can cook a chocolate soufflé, although I've never seen one. But he really does know how to do a home, and I felt very inadequate. So we had quite an argument one night and I had hysterics, and he left for the studio and I called his mother. . . . He didn't stalk out of the house, but he left awfully early for the studio and I stayed home that day and finally called his mother and said, 'If you want our marriage to last, come out here quickly.'[. . .] Anyway, she left everything and flew out and she was just a darling and she really did teach me a great deal, but almost everything I've learned has been from Richard. His taste is now my taste."

The truer or more complete story was that Martin ran off, leaving Halliday and her relationship behind, for roughly a week. She sent a letter to her husband explaining why she was giving up on their relationship and, in a sense, her life: "I don't remember what all the letter said," she wrote in her memoir. "It was a total outpouring about how I could never make him happy because I didn't know enough. I would love him forever and ever but I couldn't be what he wanted; he shouldn't try to find me. P.S. tell Paramount I might never come back. They could fire me if they wanted to."

The home-front pressures were exacerbated by Martin's pregnancy, which was made all the more complicated by a compromising physical condition: "I almost lost her every month, because of my blood type, Rh-negative." With the baby due in November, Martin requested a six-month leave of absence from the studio, beginning in July. In the process, she relinquished what could have been her best picture of all: costarring with Fred Astaire and Bing Crosby in *Holiday Inn*.

A cover story on Martin in the August 16 issue of *Movie-Radio Guide* reported that the recently married couple was hoping for a girl, whom they would name Mary Heller Halliday: "in Mary's native Texas, [Heller] means [a] sharp, energetic and alert youngster. . . . If it's a boy, they'll just drop the Mary part." Given Juanita's protests, the infant was named Mary at her christening, over which Jean Arthur presided as godmother. (Katharine Cornell would become a second godmother to Heller.) But the child would emerge as, and remain, "Heller" ever after.

Once World War II was in full throttle, the Hallidays moved into a more modest, nine-room house in "not-so-fashionable" Westwood, priced at

$16,000—nearly half what their original Bel Air home cost—and which cost only $500 a month to maintain, since it only required two, instead of five, servants. For their new daughter Heller, the Hallidays created a circus-like nursery in pale pink, with white candy stripes and curtains pulled back by diminutive circus figures. Martin made her final two pictures at Paramount while living in this, her last Los Angeles residence.

Happy Go Lucky, Martin's eighth picture, is a strictly conventional, Technicolor movie musical of the period, in which Martin plays Marjory Stewart, a Texan "cigarette girl" who poses as a millionaire and heads south in search of a rich man to marry. After the opening calypso number, as Marjory's boat docks at an unnamed tropical island, she admits to Pete (Dick Powell), a local loafer, that she's "a phony" who "came down here to find a rich husband." He helps her plot to land his onetime friend, Alfred Monroe (Rudy Vallee). But even as all of their schemes are thwarted, the viewer knows from the outset that Marjory's going to nab "Alfie," only to reject him for Pete in the end.

With a memorable, original score by Jimmy McHugh (music) and Frank Loesser (lyrics), the movie gave Martin top billing, and it also featured the rambunctious Betty Hutton and the eternally nerdy Eddie Bracken. Martin sings the title song early on, as a duet with Dick Powell, as well as her swing version of "Ta-Ra-Ra Boom De-Ay," with contemporary lyrics, and her most famous song from the picture, "Let's Get Lost," which features both her expressive voice and perfect enunciation. (As *Variety* would claim, "Miss Martin capably handles the ballad department.")

Martin's ninth and last picture for Paramount, *True to Life,* begins with an omniscient narrator intoning, "Someone once said, 'The movies should be more like life.' And a wise man answered, 'Life should be more like the movies.'" The film doesn't succeed very well at being either. While otherwise dismissing the "rather crass and moderately amusing comedy," the great film critic James Agee claimed, with his typical wit, "Mary Martin, I notice with some alarm, is playing Jean Arthur—a tendency even Miss Arthur must learn to curb." Nevertheless, *True to Life* was the first Martin film to include any reference to the anxious reality that America was at war, albeit in a humorous, throwaway subplot. A half-baked attempt to turn Martin's character's family life into something resembling the zany household of *You Can't Take It with You* features her father as an air-raid warden who sets off a number of false alarms in his neighborhood.

Martin's handlers devised more "real-life" ways for their starlet to contribute to the war effort. As reported in a movie magazine, "Mary is a big favorite with the boys in service, and for more than a year she has been rushing around to army camps to sing for them. But a few months ago she realized that this wasn't enough."

Beginning in the spring of 1942, Martin would ostensibly sign autographs only if they entailed monetary gifts for Uncle Sam. "[One] morning her secretary placed before her over 200 letters from fans requesting her autograph. Mary asked her to send a postcard to each fan telling them that she would autograph only War Stamp books or bonds. When a book was full, she would [return it with an enclosed] autographed photograph."

Also that spring, as part of a publicity stunt, Martin took first aid classes—"like dozens of other movie stars in Hollywood, like thousands of women all over the United States," according to a story in *Screenland* in the summer of 1942. Indeed, both Jean Arthur and Joan Blondell were reportedly in Martin's class. "It's so wonderful for your peace of mind to know that you can take care of your family and aid your neighbors if it ever becomes necessary in these uncertain times," explained Martin, a ready spokesperson for the war effort.

Given her own good fortune, Martin decided to give a leg up to would-be singers, providing a year's scholarship with her vocal coach, Helen Cahoon. She recruited a New York public relations man, Hy Gardner, to help activate the search. Gardner arranged for New York's WMCA radio station to hold live auditions on the air. One of the first two winners, Rosemary Smith, had experiences that closely resembled the young Martin's. "Like Mary, Rosemary was a dancing instructor with ambitions to be a singer," read a story in *Hollywood* magazine in April 1942. "Like Mary, she went to Hollywood and found no takers. They told her the same thing they told Mary. 'You're pretty, but you're not photogenic. Your mouth is too small, your hair is too this, your eyes are too that.'"

It wasn't only Martin's appearance that prevented her from becoming a movie star, however. If the so-called Dream Factory relied primarily on providing escapist entertainment, never did this become more apparent than during World War II, when there was that much more to escape from on every front. But given their period references and stale conventions, most of Martin's Paramount pictures are artifacts of a bygone era. Whatever might have made the majority of them entertaining in their day has been lost to the ages.

Chapter 4

A LITTLE TOUCH OF MARY IN THE NIGHT

*I'm just a natural-born worrier, but I haven't
anything to worry about.*
—MARY MARTIN

During her first year of marriage, Mary Martin felt terribly inadequate as a housewife—even just as a wife. Though her own mother, Juanita, lived much closer, it's telling that Martin recruited her mother-in-law, who was on the East Coast, to come to Los Angeles and help salvage the marriage. But then, Martin had already made great demands on Juanita, by having her raise Larry. She also knew that Hope—or "Mammy," as both the Hallidays took to calling Richard's mother—was in a far better position to provide Martin with pointers for pleasing her husband than Juanita. Like many another star of her caliber, Martin would come to feel that the whole world was her family while failing to build lasting bonds with her real one.

Though Mary Martin earned $115,000 in 1942 and Richard Halliday a mere $30,000, she deferred to her husband's wishes and agreed to leave Hollywood for New York, where Halliday had been more happily situated before their marriage. Given his obsession with tradition and propriety, Halliday was simply more suited to the East Coast than the more newfangled world of the rapidly changing West. Martin had also grown weary of her not-particularly-successful film career, which didn't seem to be going anywhere: she had, after all, made much more of an impression with her Broadway debut in *Leave It to Me!* four years before than with anything she had accomplished in her pallid Paramount pictures. "The professional climate [in Hollywood] was too frigid," explained Hedda Hopper, writing about this pivotal moment and decision in Martin's life. "Mary's personality gives out warmth and demands warmth in return. As she says, 'I beat my brains out and I like to hear the echo.'"

According to Martin, Janet Gaynor and her husband Adrian, the great Hollywood costumer, also encouraged the Hallidays to "go back to

Broadway" at the time. Since Martin had made only nine of the fifteen pictures she was under contract to make for Paramount, she technically took a leave of absence from the studio when she left Hollywood.

Wanting to reestablish Martin's career in the theater, yet demonstrating how tentative, in fact, their New York plans were, the Hallidays moved into a three-room flat in the Gorham, a residential hotel on West Fifty-fifth Street, only a few blocks away from Martin's vocal coach. Though Martin would later claim that the move east was made to provide Heller with a more stable home life, Heller was ensconced on the floor below her parents, where a nurse looked after her.

Early in 1943, the Theatre Guild approached Martin with a part in what would be that producing organization's first musical, written by a new team of seasoned songwriters, Richard Rodgers and Oscar Hammerstein. It was then called *Away We Go*. Although they entertained the offer, Halliday felt the ingénue role of Laurey would perpetuate his wife's lingering image as a naive farm girl or country bumpkin. Wanting to avoid such pigeonholing and to open up her future prospects, they chose, instead, to go with a new musical produced by Vinton Freedley, *Dancing in the Streets,* which offered Martin a more diversified role. (More than three decades later, Martin would tell Rex Reed, for his column in the *Daily News,* that *she* made the decision—by flipping a coin, which she would also allude to in her book *Needlepoint*, published in 1969.) The choice would prove to be a miscalculation, however: while *Away We Go* endured a mediocre response in Boston, only to arrive on Broadway as the immense wartime hit *Oklahoma!, Dancing in the Streets* failed during its tryouts and never went to New York. But with the sort of irony that makes delving into theatrical annals a rewarding experience, *Dancing in the Streets* actually seemed to be doing better than *Away We Go* in Boston: according to Lawrence Langner, head of the Theatre Guild, "there was quite a question as to whether we should not try to race in to New York ahead of [*Dancing in the Streets*]."

Based on a magazine story by Matt Taylor about three retired military bigwigs, the flimsy, if war-related, *Dancing in the Streets* had a book by Taylor and Howard Dietz (among others), music by the gifted Vernon Duke, and lyrics by Dietz. It opened in Boston on March 23, 1943, where it closed eighteen days later. The review in *Variety* was hopeful: "With plenty of redeeming features, of which Mary Martin is by no means least, *Dancing* is now being doctored and it's possible Vinton Freedley will have a click by the time the musical reaches Broadway." While Helen Eager of the *Boston Traveler* emphasized Martin's breakout performance as indicative of "big musical comedy stuff," Elinor Hughes was more dubious in the *Boston Herald*: "The dialogue needs a blue pencil and some more music numbers would help. . . . In its present state a Broadway visit would be hazardous."

Martin consoled herself by retreating with Halliday to his sister Didi's house in Connecticut, where they proceeded to rent a farmhouse of their own for the summer. Then another offer came along, for a role that would quickly establish Martin as "the top star of the US musical stage," according to *Life* magazine: the title character in *One Touch of Venus*, a part that, after long consideration, had been turned down by German siren Marlene Dietrich, who said, "I cannot play this play [because] it is too sexy and profane," which, given Dietrich's well-cultivated sexy image, was an utterly disingenuous remark. (As Dietrich further explained, she had a nineteen-year-old daughter: "and for me to get up on the stage and exhibit my legs is now impossible.")

One Touch of Venus was the brainchild of composer Kurt Weill. An old hand at writing sophisticated though lilting songs for musicals in his native Germany—including his best-known work, *The Threepenny Opera*—Weill was a relatively new kid on the Broadway block, although he already had a hit with *Lady in the Dark*, which introduced at least one plaintive ballad for the ages, "My Ship." Along with his wife—the expressive, throaty singer and actress Lotte Lenya—the Jewish Weill was an expatriot refugee of World War II.

Weill's music for *One Touch of Venus* was in an operetta mode and, more specifically, according to Weill biographer Foster Hirsch, "modeled after the work of one of his favorite composers, Jacques Offenbach." But as theater scholar Ethan Mordden claimed, it "was very much a Broadway musical comedy of the wartime 1940s. [In other words, it] was built around a star personality." Inspired by *The Tinted Venus*, an obscure 1885 novella by British humorist Thomas Anstey Guthrie, Weill took his idea for *Venus* to producer Cheryl Crawford, with whom he had already worked on his earlier American musical *Johnny Johnson*. Known for her mannish appearance and her "very firm handclasp," Crawford was that rarest of theatrical creatures: a female producer in a male-dominated business. "Crawford's lesbian friendships were commonly known among her professional associates in the Group Theatre and in the commercial theater as well," according to biographer Milly S. Barranger. "She [frequently] collaborated with gay and lesbian artists throughout her professional career." Crawford had recently had a huge success with a revival of *Porgy and Bess* when, according to her biographer, she set out to find "original, meaningful, and entertaining material to make her mark on Broadway."

After recruiting witty poet Ogden Nash for the lyrics and clever humorist S. J. Perelman to write the book, Crawford was ready to launch *Venus*. But if Dietrich had long courted the idea before finally rejecting it, Martin was, at first, loathe to take it on. She felt far too plain-featured to ever portray the mythical goddess of love. Though Crawford would commence a long and significant working relationship with Martin, when Martin was first mentioned for the part even Crawford had balked: "That skinny thing with a Texas accent to play Venus?" More than ever before, Halliday had his role as his wife's Pygmalion cut out for him, needing to build up her self-image and self-esteem. Whether or not he knew that Dietrich had recently studied Venus at the Metropolitan Museum of Art, Halliday now took Martin there to show her how varied artistic interpretations of the Roman goddess had been.

With Halliday's reassurance, Martin would become her own Venus, but not without the critical contributions of high-fashion designer Mainbocher. The value of finding Mainbocher at this crucial point in Martin's career cannot be overestimated: he would dress her both on stage and off for much of the rest of her life. After Richard Halliday, Mainbocher had the greatest influence on creating and maintaining the glamorous image of Mary Martin the world would come to know.

Paris couturier Mainbocher was actually from Chicago. He arrived in France with his original name, Main Bocher (pronounced "Bocker"), but combined the two parts to create the more elegant French pronunciation "Mainboshay" when he opened his first custom shop in Paris in 1930. The man nevertheless retained a rugged appearance.

"When I first saw Mainbocher I couldn't believe it," recalled Martin, who might have been thinking of her husband when she described what Mainbocher was not. "I had always thought designers would be tall, effete, very grand. Mainbocher looked like a businessman. He was stocky, sturdy, with the most clear, honest brown eyes. I trusted him on sight." Long before the term "main man" entered the vernacular, Mainbocher became just "Main" to Martin, for the rest of his life.

Having already designed the blue crepe dress that Wallis Simpson wore for her wedding to the Duke of Windsor in 1937, Mainbocher was at first reluctant to take on a Broadway show, but he was won over by Martin's simplicity when she auditioned for him in Weill's apartment. She sang "That's Him," one of the musical's loveliest songs, while sitting sideways on a chair she placed in front of the designer, who himself had

had aspirations to be an opera singer when he was younger. "I will do your clothes for the show if you will promise me one thing," Mainbocher told Martin. "Promise me you'll always sing this song that way. Take a chair to the footlights, sing across the orchestra to the audience as if it were just one person." Martin ultimately sang "That's Him" in a lace peignoir on an otherwise naked stage, against a black backdrop, leaning her arms across the back of a gold chair—"directly to every man and woman in the audience," according to one report. Although the frugal Cheryl Crawford would complain about ultimately spending $20,000 on Martin's fourteen *Venus* costumes, she couldn't argue with the winning impact they had on fashioning the new star, and on the show's success. As Crawford herself observed, "Mary's every entrance was applauded."

Mainbocher's reinvention of Mary Martin entailed more than just designing clothes, however. "In Hollywood the studio had draped me with hair; I had had curls hanging down to there," recalled Martin more than a decade later, while looking back at this special moment in her life and career. "But Mainbocher pulled my long blond hair back—or whatever color it was then; I guess it was blond—and said, 'Your hair should be up, up!' and Richard said, 'I've always told her that.' All of a sudden I was so changed that I felt attractive.

"Mainbocher also . . . revealed everything the movies had hidden. They had always covered up my neck with froth [including high-button collars]. OK, let's face it, my neck *is* too long, my nose *is* too big, my chin *is* too pointed; my cheeks *do* go in too far," Martin said, demonstrating just how aware she was of her physical liabilities, and how much she had taken them to heart. "Mainbocher had a theory about my back too," she continued. "He thought it was a good back, but nobody had ever seen it because it had been covered up. So he took everything off it."

Mainbocher designed six "notable dresses" for Martin in *Venus*. The "slit in the skirt" for her all-important close to act 1 was, according to the couturier, "a concession to the fact that after all, Venus is never a clothed lady. So as often as possible, I exposed as much of Miss Martin as I could."

There was yet another person involved in transforming the Texas tomboy into a goddess worthy of Broadway. According to Sono Osato, a principal dancer in the *Venus* company, Martin was somewhat "green" when she came to New York from Hollywood; or, more specifically, "from head to toe the color of peach. . . . We could tell she was very nervous by the way she tended to talk her way through rehearsals and continually patted down her hair."

Martin had been geared to assume a provocative look for her work in pictures—"In that same pose Betty Grable graced foxholes, airplanes, and submarines all over the world," continued Osato. "That [come-hither] stance cheered our fighting men, but it was certainly not a commanding posture for the Goddess of Love." Osato took it upon herself to coach Martin during rehearsal breaks. She began by demonstrating all of the bad habits Martin had picked up to create a "glamour-girl pose."

"Among her many talents, Mary is an incredibly quick study, receptive and grateful for both advice and suggestions," wrote Osato. "Copying my raised chest and wide-open arms, she tucked in her bottom, swelled her torso, and was soon striding across the stage with Olympian grandeur." Martin's pliability at this early juncture in her stage career was confirmed by Cheryl Crawford, who claimed that she "grew tremendously in the show, as did her voice, and she was always willing, even eager, to take helpful suggestions."

"It must have been in *Venus* that I first began to think about my acting," Martin recalled several years later. "First I developed a walk—on my toes, sort of—like an angel, if an angel could walk. I couldn't look—well, round as that marble thing up on Fifth Avenue [at the Metropolitan Museum of Art]—but I could try to look tall. In every show I start to fuss around in my head about movement first. I think that's the key to playing any kind of a person. The walk, you know. In *Venus* I was floating in those robes."

One of the most significant directors of the twentieth century, Elia Kazan, would become known for the harsh realism he brought to works for both the stage and screen, including *A Streetcar Named Desire* and *On the Waterfront.* He was, however, clearly out of his element with *One Touch of Venus,* his first musical, and it became all too easy to make him the scapegoat for any problems the show had. As far as Kazan was concerned, he quickly became nothing more than "a sort of overpaid stage manager, subservient to everyone else." He attributed the show's "enormous success" to "three marvelous women": Mary Martin, Agnes de Mille, and Sono Osato. Martin, according to Kazan, was "an extraordinary girl—'girl' at any age—full of the love of being loved" and capable of making "an audience believe anything."

As Cheryl Crawford recalled in her memoir, *One Naked Individual,* Martin and Kazan met for the first time over a lunch in the Oak Room at the Plaza Hotel, during which he asked her, "How do you think about playing Venus?" "I was afraid you were going to ask me that," said Martin, "and I haven't the vaguest idea." As relayed by Crawford, Martin went on: "Then he asked me how I approach a part. I told him I hadn't done much except films so I didn't really know how I approached a part. He looked puzzled. So I said, 'I think in terms of how I will walk. If I can get that walk in my mind, then I know how I'm going to play it.' He was marvelous. He said: 'That's very exciting to me; then I won't have to direct you really.'" (Several years later, Kazan wanted Martin to play Blanche DuBois in the premiere production of Tennessee Williams's *A Streetcar Named Desire,* without, apparently, getting any support for the idea from others.)

Cast as one of the male quartet in *Venus,* Jeff Warren was struck by the degree to which Martin seemed like just another member of the chorus when he met her on the first day of rehearsals. She was just this "sweet girl from Texas named Mary" with an unassuming manner. In other words, there was nothing grand or highfalutin about Martin—not at first, anyway.

As the nation was increasingly embroiled in a devastating world war, Broadway made its patriotic contribution by having the orchestra play "The Star Spangled Banner" at the beginning of every musical. The Broadway fare of 1943 was nevertheless indicative of the need for escapist frivolity. *One Touch of Venus* joined a number of other lighthearted offerings that celebrated, instead of surmounting, their roots in vaudeville: *Early to Bed, Laugh Time, The Ziegfeld Follies of 1943, Bright Lights of 1944, A Tropical Revue,* and *Hairpin Harmony.*

One Touch of Venus tells the story of a statue that comes to life and falls in love with a barber (played by radio singing star Kenny Baker), even as she confronts a number of other mortals in the then-burgeoning suburbs of New York City: the barber's wife, an art dealer, some thugs, and the art dealer's secretary, played by Broadway comedienne Paula Laurence. "I met Mary at Vinton and Mary Freedley's," recalled Laurence. "Vinton was an upper-class, establishment, very handsome producer, who did all the Cole Porter shows, and all the Ethel Merman shows." (Laurence had recently been in Freedley's *Something for the Boys,* starring Merman.) "And he had a show for Mary that he was producing, and there was a part in it that he hoped I would play, but I passed on it. It opened and closed in Boston. It doesn't figure largely in Mary's resume. I can't even remember the name of it." (The show, of course, was *Dancing in the Streets.*)

"Mary and Richard were very leery about what she would do next," resumed Laurence. "In the meanwhile, Kenny Baker and I had signed to do a Kurt Weill musical called, at that time, *Love in the Mist*—and a mist it was. We were about a month away from rehearsals and had no leading lady. . . . So they auditioned all sorts of people and didn't find anybody. I don't even remember whose idea it was to think about Mary." According to Foster Hirsch, Martin was proposed by Jean Dalrymple, the show's press agent. "Mary stopped short of wanting a guarantee that it would be a certifiable hit, because she wouldn't commit to anything else, and no one could blame her," continued Laurence. "She was, I thought, always very aware of her physical limitations and what she needed to do to present herself: she was short. She didn't have a very good figure actually— she was rather flat-chested, and in proportion, broad-beamed. She had regular facial features. But somehow, when she had a part to play, and when she felt she was being well-presented, she knew all of the things that needed to be done.

"She went into training the way I imagine a boxer does for a championship match. She approached that part as if she had never done anything before in her entire life. She took singing lessons. I used to meet her in the dressing room at Ballet Arts, where she was working with a ballet master. I was working with a very good dancer and performer named Everett Victor, who wanted to get me ready for all of this great choreography Agnes de Mille was going to lay on me. Well, [de Mille] never worked with me. I staged my own numbers. She had the most incredible dancers in that show. It was only the second Broadway show Agnes did [after *Oklahoma!*], and the time limits for a Broadway show were not the way she was used to working.

"Mary and I actually became friendly in the dressing room at Ballet Arts. And she knew that my experience in *Something for the Boys* with Ethel Merman hadn't been as tight as it had been with Orson Welles— let's put it that way." Laurence's first appearance on stage had been with Orson Welles in his and John Houseman's Federal Theatre Project *Horse Eats Hat* in 1937, followed by their appearing together in the same important company's *Doctor Faustus*. "And she assured me that we would just be bosom buddies and that everything would be lovely. And she was terribly sweet and we became really nice colleagues. She was indeed pert, chatty, affectionate, hospitable—all of those things. She also was a lot of other things, which she didn't show."

Without detailing those "other things," Laurence, in her well-articulated memories of working with Martin, went on to emphasize the "sort of a good-cop, bad-cop routine" that Martin had worked out with Halliday. "She'd say, 'Honey, come on in and have a little Coke,' while Richard would be out in front cutting your name out of the house boards [backstage message boards]. I found that all very amusing, because it hadn't been my ambition to be this great musical diva, anyway. Most of the musicals in those days didn't really make much sense—and they ran so long. I had been working, I suddenly realized, five straight years on Broadway, and I had only done three shows."

Still another memory of Laurence's suggests what shrewd business operators the Hallidays were from the beginning of Mary's Broadway career. "When we opened in Boston, we really had no ending to the show," reported Laurence. "Cheryl Crawford also did not have a signed contract with Mary. Cheryl was really dazzled by Mary, who could be pretty dazzling. Somehow or other, and I imagine this was a strategy, there was always something a little wrong with the contract as it was set up, and, 'Wouldn't it be better if. . . .' And here we were up and running, and the audiences loved us—they didn't particularly like the show much. But we all got good notices—especially Mary. So [the Hallidays] were operating from a position of great power. I remember, we were in a taxi going back to the Ritz Hotel after a matinee, and I said, 'Where's Richard?' 'Oh, he's meeting with Cheryl, about my contract. I haven't signed my contract yet.' I said, 'My God! Let's not tell any of the backers.' So they got everything they wanted. And I think that's the way they proceeded from then on."

A prudish side of Martin's nature would raise its awkward head at various points throughout her career. One of the first instances occurred just before the opening of *One Touch of Venus* in Boston, when Martin told Crawford that a line of hers was "just too vulgar" to be said: "Love is not the moaning of distant violins; it's the triumphant twang of a bedspring." Crawford reasoned with her leading lady, asking her to "say it tonight" because the writers already had enough problems to contend with, adding, "If you feel the slightest reaction from the audience that makes you uncomfortable, I'll talk to them tomorrow and see that it's cut." According to Crawford, "The roar of pleasure and delight from the audience that greeted that line opening night was so great that Mary never mentioned it again." There was a more serious problem on a Saturday night in Boston, when Martin "collapsed flat on her back" near the end of her performance. She had a fever of 104 degrees and had to be hospitalized for several days, causing performance cancellations.

The opening night of *One Touch of Venus* on October 7, 1943, at the Imperial Theatre, was a stellar occasion, with no less a personage than Cole Porter—Martin's first major booster—in the audience. The predominantly rave reviews welcomed Martin as a new star in the Broadway firmament. "It is one of a reviewer's keener pleasures to be able to tell the world that Miss Martin has grown into a performer of the first magnitude," wrote Robert Garland in the *Journal-American*, "that not only is she lovely, but that she can dance, act, sing, and project a serious scene . . . with the best of them." In the *New York Sun*, Ward Morehouse chimed in: "It's really Miss Martin's show all the way, as it should be. She is handsomely gowned and is disconcertingly pretty and she can be assured that she has scored another personal success in the theater." The ever-demanding critic and novelist Mary McCarthy was even more emphatic in the *Partisan Review*, finding "the radiant Mary Martin" the show's salvation, having "to come too often to the rescue, like the hostess at a teen-age party. Nevertheless, at its best, in its moments of self-laceration and parody, *One Touch of Venus* is the most interesting production of the season." A rare dissenting view was proffered by Wilella Waldorf in the *Post*: "Miss Martin is still no singer, but she talks her songs cleverly and when she does use her few vocal tones—she has a meager range—they are pleasant to hear."

"She turns in such an engaging job of acting and warbling that she had all the drama critics wagging their beans opening night and muttering, 'We can't believe it. She's so much better than she was when she left Broadway four years ago. And where has she been since? Hollywood. And she's a better actress now. Incredible!'" So observed theater reporter Harry Evans, in his long cover story devoted to Martin in *The Family Circle*, before adding, "and thus the powerful New York kibitzers muttered and moaned and wagged their learned skulls, because they have a beautiful and unshakable belief that every Broadway actress who goes to Hollywood has her talent impaired beyond recall."

A day or two after the opening, Martin spoke with Lucy Greenbaum for a feature in the *New York Times*. "The song sums up everything," said Martin, referring to the song that would become one of her biggest hit singles, "That's Him," with what Greenbaum notes is "an emphatic toss of red curls piled high on her head in defiance of Hollywood experts, who insisted her neck and face were too thin to support an upsweep." "I'm singing about a man," she explained. "Another kind of man than 'Daddy,'" Martin continued. "This is the composite of every woman's dreams. It's really the reason why I did the show."

A cover story in *Life* proclaimed Martin the show's greatest asset: "of [its] many delights, none is more endearing than Mary Martin. [S]he invests the Pygmalion myth with her enchanting personality, her poise, her lovely clear voice and her good looks. . . . Not since the late Marilyn

Miller left the stage . . . has the theater boasted of a more radiant musical-comedy heroine than this pretty, vivacious girl." Confirming her success in the show, Martin won the first annual Donaldson Award—a precursor to the Tony Awards—for giving the "Best Lead Performance in a Musical (female)."

Still another, more extensive story in *Life* just two months later asserted that Martin had become "the top star of the US musical stage." *Venus* had a top ticket price of $4.40, and Martin was earning $5,000 a week—twice what she had been making under contract at Paramount. But Halliday, who kept his wife on a short leash, gave her only a twenty-five-dollar-a-week allowance.

To emphasize the otherworldly aspect of her character, Martin had her hair dyed pink for the part at Saks Fifth Avenue. In a rare decision, Halliday chose not to accompany his wife to the salon one day, providing her with a five-dollar bill for a taxi and telling her to charge the hairdresser's fee. Having given the driver the five dollars for her ride to Saks, though, a humiliated Martin found herself forced to walk home after the procedure. Even in his absence, Halliday's controlling nature exerted a powerful influence.

Though he waited a couple of months to catch up with *Venus* at the Imperial Theatre, composer Richard Rodgers wrote Cheryl Crawford a fawning note, congratulating her for a "fine" evening: "I thought the show was awfully good to look at and Mary Martin pretty miraculous." By the beginning of 1944, Decca Records brought out *One Touch of Venus* as the second original cast recording of a Broadway show (the first was *Oklahoma!*) on five ten-inch records—including Martin's insouciant yet melancholy rendition of "That's Him"—and a young crooner named Frank Sinatra sang the show's biggest hit, "Speak Low," on the "President's Birthday Program" on the radio. "Speak Low" even made Lucky Strike's *Your Hit Parade* and remained on it for months. And while Martin was having a late-night dinner following a performance one night, Britain's all-purpose genius of the theater, Noël Coward, stopped by her table and kissed her on the forehead, telling her: "You were wonderful." Both Richard Rodgers and Noël Coward would write musicals for Mary Martin before the decade was over.

Harry Evans revisited the show in early December and was waiting in the wings at the beginning of the curtain call: "About 10 feet away, also watching the finale, was a girl. She looked vaguely familiar, but I couldn't see her face. . . . She was wearing a dark dress and a sort of Juliet cap. The curtain descended on the last act. The crowd burst into applause. The curtain rose. Miss Martin, Mr. Boles, Mr. Baker, and the other principals stepped forward and took their bows. Curtain fell, more applause, up went the curtain. And as it rose, Kenny Baker, standing onstage, reached out into the wing, grabbed the hand of the girl in the Juliet cap, and gave her a terrific heave. She flew through the air and lit right on the stage. The audience stopped applauding and gazed at the unknown gal, wondering if it was some sort of gag. Mary Martin and John Boles turned, saw the girl, and screamed with glee. The entire cast giggled and pointed. But the strange girl never hesitated. When she skidded onstage and caught her balance, she tore herself loose from Kenny, ducked her head, and never stopped galloping until she disappeared into the wings across the stage. You could hear people all over the audience saying, 'Who was that?'"

The "mystery guest" was the famously private Jean Arthur, fresh from a vacation in Nevada, where, she told Evans, she had been "getting some exercise." "Later, in Miss Martin's dressing room, Jean Arthur told us that this was the most authentic case of stage fright she had ever known," continued Evans. "'New York crowds have always panicked me,' she said. 'And suddenly to find myself out on a stage . . .' Then she added, 'Did you ever see anybody make a faster exit?'"

Evans also commented on a recent, "considerable controversy between several columnists involving Mary and Dick," which perhaps alluded to problems they were having during their first year of marriage, when Martin's insecurity as a housewife prompted her to leave Halliday for a week. "It seems that [gossip columnist] Jimmy Fidler intimated that Mary and Dick were about to part company. As some of you good readers may have noticed, this reporter does not specialize in scandal. . . . However, Mary Martin did request me to say that she and Dick are not being divorced."

As *One Touch of Venus* settled in for a long run, Cheryl Crawford arranged for certain cast members to entertain the troops at military bases, camps, and hospitals. According to Sono Osato, the highlight was always Martin's rendering of "That's Him." "Seeing the young men's unlined faces looking up at her so wistfully, I felt that she must have embodied all the girls they were leaving behind."

As a sweltering summer gripped New York and the temperature reportedly reached "112 degrees on stage for something like a week running," Martin received a more tangible reward befitting the Broadway star she had suddenly become: a new contraption was installed in her dressing room. It was called an "air conditioner." "With the war on, you couldn't get your hands on an air conditioner," recalled Crawford, who forfeited her personal model from her apartment. "I had it moved to Mary's dressing room where she could cool off while she was offstage. She played through the summer like a trouper after that, and I sweltered."

Well into the run of *One Touch of Venus*, Martin told a reporter for the *New York Herald Tribune* that she never could have taken on the role without her husband's support. "Venus must be happy, and in love with the whole world," said Martin. "It would be hard for me to go to the theater feeling that way if things were wrong at home. I'm just a natural-born worrier, but I haven't anything to worry about."

In addition to placating Martin's insecurities about playing a convincing Venus, Halliday also felt the need to cut back on her extracurricular activities. If he was to turn his unbridled wife into a topflight Broadway racehorse, he would have to train her to maximize her offstage time, first by cutting back on her helping "16 young would-be actresses on her personal worry list," as he told a reporter years later. Martin was treating any performance wannabes who crossed her path as pupils to be fussed over and mentored. "Mary agreed to a compromise; the number of protégées at any one time was not to exceed three." Halliday would also begin to limit his wife's socializing after the theater and frown upon her talking on the phone in order to preserve her voice.

With *One Touch of Venus* a huge hit, the Hallidays moved into a more fashionable apartment on Fifth Avenue, across from the Metropolitan Museum of Art. As documented by a two-page spread in *Mademoiselle,* the apartment had been done "entirely in pink, a magical color that figures importantly in [*One Touch of Venus*] and which she links with her success." (Halliday referred to it as "Venus pink.") The new home featured a large fireplace with a mirror above the mantel that opened up the cramped living quarters. There were also a large wardrobe, painted pink, a bleached-wood spinet piano—which the Hallidays stained themselves—and an antique baby buggy filled with plants. (This last item had been a housewarming gift from Jean Arthur.) Martin also kept her mother's violin resting against an antique music stand in the living room.

The heavy damask drapes over the windows gave the apartment a somber and serious feeling. And the overly elegant furnishings reflected the far-reaching influence of both Richard and his mother: there were a "pale" Louis XVI table and chairs and a bleached French provincial desk with Holbein aquatints hanging above. It would be many years before Martin's desire for a more comfortable living environment would prevail.

The Hallidays' new idyllic routine was disrupted in the summer of 1944, when Martin's mother, Juanita, suddenly took ill and something had to be done to care for her charge, twelve-year-old Larry Hagman. The Hallidays had no choice but to take the boy in. The gangly adolescent was shipped off to New York to live with them in their new Fifth Avenue apartment. "Mother and everyone else expected [Juanita] to die during [gallbladder] surgery, or soon after if she made it through, and they were right," recalled Hagman. "Nanny died. I cried for days."

Martin's mother—who time and again defied her own nature to help her daughter become a star—died in Los Angeles. Her funeral in Weatherford was attended by "hundreds of sorrowing friends," according to the *Weatherford Democrat*. "The daughter, Mary Martin of New York, was unable to visit her mother in California or to attend the services here due to the ill effects of suffering from heat prostration with which she was afflicted a few days before her mother became ill. The other daughter, Mrs. Robert Andrews of Dallas [Geraldine], who had gone to Los Angeles upon news of her mother's illness, was delayed in reaching Weatherford, due to transportation, but arrived here Monday evening," or the night before the funeral.

Martin's dedication to her work prevented her from attending either of her parents' funerals. Given her overarching commitment to her career, Martin was simply unequipped to function as the caring daughter or mother she wanted to be. Though Larry found his new East Coast prep school, Trinity, a comfortable fit, he was rather miserable living with his stepfather: Halliday became a dictator not only in the course of managing his wife's career but in running their home life as well.

While he might have expected his mother to be a welcome, soothing influence on the fraught situation, Larry hardly got to see her. Martin would still be in bed as he got ready for school, and she was preparing for the theater when he returned in the afternoon. "On Saturday, a matinee day, she slept till eleven, got up and vocalized, had a light lunch, and then went to the theater," wrote Hagman. "She had the 21 Club send over dinner between shows. With no shows on Sunday, she slept till noon, her explanation being 'Mommy needs her rest,' and then we got to see her around two if she hadn't scheduled press or fittings."

Decades later, Martin acknowledged her drawbacks as a mother: "[Larry] came from a household where all the focus had been on him, to one where it was all on me, because I was the 'star.' Why, his first week with us, his appendix burst and Dick, without letting me hear a word about it, drove Larry to the hospital and then drove *me* to the *theater*."

(Martin didn't mention that her unfortunate son had also had his wallet stolen en route to New York.) "Dick screened me from everything so I would be able to give the audience my happiest, most joyous performance."

If, as Martin claimed numerous times, Larry felt more like a brother to her than a son, Halliday filled the vacuum this left in Larry's life by being a spiteful and tyrannical parent. If Martin had little time for familial relations, Halliday had even less. But the Hallidays fully expected their charges to behave like storybook children, even though they failed to assume the responsibilities of parenting, always relying on others to do the hard work for them.

The one time the family managed to get together was for dinner on Sunday nights. But it was far from a happy experience, rather "hell," according to Hagman, "as far as Heller and I were concerned, thanks to Richard. By five o'clock he was shit-faced. By six-thirty, he was shit-faced *and mean*." Halliday was also a stickler for table manners. "No elbows on the table, he'd snap. Eat with your mouth closed. Your fork goes in your left hand, the knife in your right. No talking at the table."

Though fastidious and controlling, Halliday was, ironically, far less disciplined than his adolescent stepson, who learned to obey authority figures in military school. As Halliday would make clear to one colleague after another, he was rather ashamed of his own homosexual nature and had difficulty controlling himself, let alone anyone else. The severity of Larry's animosity toward his rigid stepfather cannot be overestimated: he even contemplated murdering Halliday with the .22 rifle that his real father had given him as a birthday present the previous year.

In one of the most shocking passages in his autobiography, *Hello Darlin'*, Hagman recalled, "One night, as Richard was taking Mother to the theater, I watched from my second-floor bedroom window as they went outside to their car. . . . [O]ne shot, that's all I need," he thought to himself. "I sat down on the windowsill and drew a bead on the back of Richard's head" with the rifle's telescopic sight. "But as I practiced my alibi, I talked myself out of actually pulling the trigger."

As young as he was, Hagman recognized that "Mother most likely wouldn't have had such a brilliant career without Richard in her life," and that "Richard was simply a goddamned necessary evil." Sadder still, Larry came to realize, "He and I would never get along, and it prevented Mother and me from having a real relationship until he died."

As soon as his contract was up, Martin's costar Kenny Baker left *One Touch of Venus* to pursue what would prove to be a rather unsuccessful career in Hollywood. He was replaced by a succession of "barbers," including chorus boy Jeff Warren, who went on quickly, one afternoon, since he knew all the lines. Though he was only eight years her junior, Martin said Warren made her look old and had him abruptly put back into the chorus. "He said that after a week, he was taken out of the part, as Mary Martin felt that she was 'making love to my own son.'"

Warren was back in the chorus when *One Touch of Venus* went on tour, beginning in February 1945, while Heller stayed with her father's mother in West Virginia. After 567 performances on Broadway, the Hallidays went with *Venus* to Philadelphia, Cleveland, Detroit, Chicago, and Cincinnati. Following a performance one night in Cleveland, "a most unexpected limousine and chauffeur were waiting to take us, not back to the hotel, but to the most comfortable and also one of the most magnificent apartments I had ever seen," Martin would recall decades later. "It was in a most unexpected place, too—the railroad station! At the very top of the Terminal Tower of the Chesapeake & Ohio Railroad. The tremendous paneled living room was three stories high, way up in the sky looking over the whole city, and it had a pipe organ and two concert grand pianos. There were two dining rooms and a cozy breakfast room, and a stainless-steel kitchen. Our bedrooms were equipped with everything thoughtfulness could imagine to make us comfortable, including our luggage which had been spirited away from the hotel." The Hallidays' hosts were Walter Tuohy, the president of the Chesapeake and Ohio Railroad, and "his dear wife, who was also named Mary." They became lifelong friends and entertained Martin whenever she came to Cleveland again.

In Detroit, the Hallidays were feted with a champagne-fueled party for Mary, hosted by opera and film star Grace Moore. According to Martin biographer Ronald L. Davis, "after they got back to their hotel the Hallidays continued their indulgence, and Mary wound up pregnant." It's more than just ironic that, only recently, Martin had advised Sono Osata on the difficulty of balancing a family life with a career, recommending that she not have any children if she was to continue in the theater, as the ballerina would recall her "talks with Mary Martin about having children," and her being told that she "was too young to give up success."

Due to problems with her pregnancy, Martin began feeling ill in Chicago, from where she nevertheless wrote a letter to her producer: "Some of the audiences have been the best we've ever had." She also stayed with her doctor, Loyal Davis, and his wife, Edith, who was herself an actress who had been on the Broadway stage. Martin formed an immediate bond with Edith's daughter from a previous marriage, Nancy Davis (a would-be actress destined to become—as Mrs. Ronald Reagan—an influential figure in Martin's future).

"By that time [in Chicago] Mary was quite ill," wrote Crawford. "It was an Rh-negative pregnancy and she lost the baby," which would have been her third child—her second with Halliday. In all likelihood, the fetus was aborted to avoid an increasingly difficult pregnancy, and Martin required a blood transfusion. Ruth Bond, who played Gloria Kramer in *Venus* and had also been in *Leave It to Me!* with Martin, rushed to the star's rescue with the correct blood type. Too weak to continue performing, Martin terminated the rest of the *One Touch of Venus* tour to the West Coast. "As much as I love Mary," added Crawford, the producer, "I always figured that she owed me at least a hundred and fifty thousand dollars for that episode." (In his idiosyncratic look at "the people who made the American musical," *Broadway Babies,* Ethan Mordden went even further, speculating that "Martin's excellence [and future unavailability] may be the reason the show has never had a major revival.")

"As soon as the show closed, Richard and I rushed [to West Virginia]—to find that Heller had been badly bitten by a dog," recalled Martin a decade later. "She lay in bed, drugged with sulfa and anti-rabies serum. My heart ached for her, but I held back my tears."

As if to give his wife a new lease on life, Halliday decided to buy an eighteenth-century Connecticut farmhouse on a six-acre estate. Overlooking Long Island Sound, the expansive grounds featured large, ancient shade trees, a "natural" swimming pool molded in the earth, and a running brook. Only an hour's drive from New York, it was an isolated, idyllic property on Ponus Avenue in suburban Norwalk that would become their home and their nightly getaway from the bustling frenzy of the big city, even during Martin's extended runs on Broadway.

"We bought the place in Norwalk because of Heller, our daughter, because we wanted her to have a taste of life in the country," said Martin. "It had a fabulous elm tree, hundreds of years old [and] the house and the grounds needed to have a lot of things done. We moved every tree on the place except that elm." Knocking down walls and enlarging some windows, Halliday transformed the abode into a sprawling, multi-gabled, clapboard house and created a winding path on the grounds, surrounded by bushes and trees. But it would be at least a year before their new home was ready to be occupied.

While the Hallidays were in Detroit touring with *One Touch of Venus,* Martin sent a letter, on Book-Cadillac Hotel stationery, to Hedda Hopper:

"It's two years since I've been out there [in Los Angeles]—time does go so fast—or something! I never cease to be amazed when I pick up a newspaper, read your column—and see my name. You have been darn generous and I am grateful. We'll be out in June (Richard, Larry, and Heller) and we want to see you—would really love to see you, please."

The Hallidays went to Los Angeles for Martin to shoot one of her more notable film roles, playing herself in a small part in what is inarguably her best-known picture, *Night and Day*. They visited with Jean Arthur and also caught up with Martin's childhood friend, Bessie Mae, whose husband, Jac Austin, was stationed with the Marine Corps in Santa Barbara at the time. It was the first time that Bessie Mae met Halliday: "He was so sophisticated and so knowledgeable that I wondered how he and Mary were drawn to each other," she recalled. "He was from a completely different world from hers."

Night and Day was made by Warner Bros., as opposed to Martin's home studio of Paramount. A typically fictional "biopic" of the period, *Night and Day* was about Cole Porter, whose "My Heart Belongs to Daddy" did more to establish Martin than anything she would ever achieve in Hollywood. Though the film did nothing to suggest that Porter (Cary Grant) was homosexual, in its own sly way *Night and Day* indicates that his marriage to Linda (Alexis Smith) was a sexless romance.

Famous for playing the curmudgeonly "man who came to dinner" on both stage and film, Monty Woolley had been Porter's friend at Yale and also plays himself in the picture. Nor is there any mistaking Mary Martin's identity: in her first scenes she's eating watermelon and says she's from Weatherford, Texas. She's also a ditzy singer, albeit with a "fine voice," reading the sheet music for her big number upside down. (Though the wayward sheet music is primarily a reference to her growing reputation for being somewhat scatterbrained, the fact is that Martin never did learn how to read music.) As directed by Michael Curtiz, with dances staged by Leroy Prinz, the film is as faithful as it can be to Martin's original "My Heart Belongs to Daddy" number in *Leave It to Me!*, as she all but does a striptease with little more than a white fur coat, surrounded by fawning and dancing Eskimos. According to Porter biographer William McBrien, "all the reviewers" had particular praise for Martin's cameo appearance.

Jack Warner, the ultimate decision maker at Warner Bros., was so impressed with Martin's success in *Night and Day* that he offered her the lead in Curtiz's upcoming picture, *Romance on the High Seas,* which she would wisely turn down to remain on the stage. It proved to be a lucky break for band singer Doris Day, who made her film debut in *Romance on the High Seas.* Though it's easy to speculate why Martin made such a decision, Hedda Hopper apparently did not see the development as Martin's choice. Michael Curtiz sent a defensive telegram to the gossip columnist on May 10, exclaiming: "It is very unfair to state in your column that I informed you that I was against testing Mary Martin and Lauren Bacall and insisted on Doris Day."

It was during this time that United Artists planned on making a film version of *One Touch of Venus,* and even negotiated with Paramount to borrow their contract player, Mary Martin. When plans for the picture failed to coalesce, the assigned director, Gregory La Cava, sued UA for his unrealized salary. But after her lackluster cluster of Paramount pictures, Martin was only too happy to walk away from Hollywood once again. On the other hand, having since basked in the afterglow of a Broadway hit, nothing could keep her away from the stage.

Chapter 5

FROM THE FAR EAST TO . . . THE FAR EAST

The toughest thing about success is that you've
got to keep on being a success.
—IRVING BERLIN

The kind of success that Mary Martin enjoyed with *One Touch of Venus* was a curse as well as a blessing. For one thing, it went to her husband's head, if not her own, and made the Hallidays feel indomitable and become imperious. For another, it included a built-in pressure to replicate itself. Though the world may have perceived it as an overnight success—something to be applauded in and of itself—Martin knew only too well that it was based on more than a decade of dedication and hard work. But given her obsessive need to draw attention to herself, the work was more of a compulsion than a burden, the success an afterthought. For Martin, success was not a goal so much as a side effect of her insatiable need to be adored, which would lead to her being celebrated throughout much of her life.

Like other stars before her, Martin devoted almost all of her time and attention to her career. Unlike most other stars before or since, such devotion was utterly natural for Martin and not to be denied. The magic she achieved onstage stemmed from her absolute love of performing: it was like a magnet that drew everyone into her orbit, an infectious joie de vivre that spread out across the footlights.

What is clear from Martin's involvement with her next venture, *Lute Song,* is that her compulsion to perform—in order to be adored—allowed no time to stop and reflect, nor did it leave room for others to try to contribute to her impact. With *Lute Song,* the Hallidays became ever more vigilant in taking charge of Martin's appearance, regardless of the input of anyone else with whom they had to work. If it was one thing to create the glamorous image that would become Mary Martin, it was quite another to protect and preserve it. Though the theater is first and last a collaborative process, the Hallidays frequently insisted on having or doing things their own way, on having the last word, as it were, and they had no qualms about ruffling their colleagues' feathers in the process. In the case of *Lute Song,* they countermanded both the director and the designer's wishes—without even telling them they were doing so. This was but the first instance of an unprofessional and unreasonable mode of behavior the Hallidays would resort to time and again throughout Martin's career.

Based on a fifteenth-century Chinese folk tale, *Lute Song* was more of a play with music than a musical. It was also a peculiar show for Broadway, even for its day. If it wasn't exactly art, it was "arty," as more than one critic would respond. In her memoir, Martin would call *Lute Song* "a lyrical, lovely thing," but later she would say it held little appeal for her. "That part scared me out of my wits," she said. "But it was a challenge, and Richard was all for my having all these challenges." Martin did, however, introduce "Mountain High, Valley Low," in Martin's opinion the show's loveliest song. Though Martin would euphemistically describe the score as "different and haunting," it was written by composer Raymond Scott and lyricist Bernard Hanighen, songwriters who had done nothing in their respective pasts to suggest they would be up to the task of writing a first-rate musical.

Martin's first producer, Laurence Schwab, recalled visiting the Hallidays in the summer of 1945: "They were staying at an estate in Connecticut lent them by an old friend of Dick's while he was in Europe. . . . Richard was telling me about the marvelous costumes Valentina was to design [and] about the wonderful starring contract he had arranged with Michael Meyerberg, the producer. And about the importance of the theme of the play. Not show, mind you. Richard was a bit art-conscious in those days. So this Martin gal was going to play a Chinese woman in pants, posturing and praying for her lost love. Why the hell couldn't she play an American girl and sing sweet and hot songs and dance and be herself—earthy, real, a joy to watch."

"[D]riving home that night I was sad," added Schwab, who might have been channeling short story and sports writer Damon Runyon, on whose work *Guys and Dolls* was based. "The Hallidays were falling for an 'ism'—a dangerous one for honest actresses. Flossism, I named it. It serves those brittle stars who, no matter what part they are playing, turn themselves into a Hapsburg princess talking to her subjects from a gilded balcony. 'Let 'em eat cake,' they seem to be saying in every line. The crumbs left over from the cake the Colony Restaurant chef had baked for Her Highness' luncheon."

While he was studying Chinese history and culture for his wife's involvement with *Lute Song*, Halliday discovered an ancient proverb that became the family mantra: "If there is righteousness in the heart, there will be beauty in the character. If there is beauty in the character, there will be harmony in the family home. If there is harmony in the home, there will be order in the nation. When there is order in the nation, there will be peace in the world." Martin would spend several years embroidering the proverb in an enormous petit point rug, "which my husband designed for our living room," she declared in 1955. "In the rug is also a view of our home in winter; the cherry tree in the yard which our . . . daughter, Heller, loves so much; and my son Larry's field of yellow mustard and red roses, and also his favorite guitar."

But *Lute Song* became most memorable for launching the career of a newcomer who would prove as unique as his name: Yul Brynner. Brynner's signature role—as the eponymous King in Rodgers and Hammerstein's *The King and I*—was awaiting him, at the time, in the not-too-distant future. (It would be Martin who would recommend Yul Brynner, her *Lute Song* costar, to star as the King in the original production of *The King and I*.) "Somebody told us about him and we invited him out to the Connecticut house," claimed Martin, who took complete responsibility for discovering Brynner. "He came with a guitar and sat on the floor, playing. We had seldom seen such an exciting man. He created a special magic around himself, and we knew we wanted him for *Lute Song*." That nameless "somebody" was *Lute Song* producer Michael Meyerberg, who had first seen Brynner "crooning Russian gypsy laments" in a New York nightclub. A real-estate magnate with a love of theater, Meyerberg would go out on an intellectual limb by producing Thornton Wilder's *The Skin of Our Teeth* in the 1940s and Beckett's *Waiting for Godot* in the 1950s. But *Lute Song* proved even more of a commercial challenge than those experimental plays, beginning with its difficult birth.

With the composer at the piano, Martin and Brynner worked on their numerous solos and duets in the Hallidays' apartment. A couple of months before rehearsals started, Martin also began studying independently with Yeichi Nimura, the show's Japanese choreographer, who stressed the importance of posture and hand gestures.

Director John Houseman put his finger on what he described as the production's "most persistent and vexing problem" during its extensive gestation period: "the successful blending of a Broadway musical with a Chinese classic." Houseman also acknowledged that *Lute Song* required particular "courage" on the part of Martin, "as a rising but not quite established musical-comedy star, to risk her career on such an exotic, unorthodox piece." It was also beset from the beginning by three things: the tragic death and, therefore, unavailability of its principal adapter, the Pulitzer Prize–winning playwright Sidney Howard; producer Meyerberg's encroaching, unidentified ailment (he became "quite literally a walking skeleton"); and the Hallidays' nervousness.

"As a couple they were fretful and insecure," wrote Houseman, "constantly wondering whether Mary should be doing the show at all, till I began to avoid conversations with them, which I found demoralizing." Houseman contrasted this with Martin's "behavior as a performer: throughout rehearsals I found her quick, receptive, hard-working, intelligent, and flexible on all subjects except her own songs, about which, quite properly, she had strong determined opinions: in all else I found her most willing to adapt herself to a style of performance that was utterly different from anything she had ever done before."

With a story as diaphanous as Martin's undulating costumes, *Lute Song* tells of a peasant bride, Tchao-Ou-Niang, whose husband, Tsai-Young, is pressed into imperial duty in the capital, where he is forced to marry a royal princess, leaving his parents and first wife behind. Tsai's parents die of hunger during a famine, and Tchao, played by Martin, is compelled to sell her luxurious hair to pay for their burial fees, becoming a lowly beggar in the process. Tchao makes a lengthy trek to the capital, where she is reunited with Tsai, who, according to the legend, lives happily ever after with both wives.

On the grounds that it was unseemly for Tsai to end up with two wives, the Hallidays had the ending altered, making Tchao the lone, victorious spouse. In the process, they denuded the story of its only interesting element, which is its ambiguous ending. Houseman was opposed to the change, however, and became understandably offended by their circumventing his own wishes on the matter. "The Hallidays decided that sharing a man was unworthy of a star of Mary's magnitude," Houseman explained. Though reluctant to agree to the new ending, Meyerberg ultimately relented. "So that's how we finally played it," continued Houseman, "with one wife instead of two—and I have never ceased to regret it."

Before work on *Lute Song* began in earnest and while work on their new home in Norwalk was being completed, the Hallidays relaxed, when they could, at a house they rented in New Canaan, Connecticut. With luxurious grounds and an Olympic-size swimming pool, the house was reminiscent of an Italian villa. "Whenever Mother's best friend, Jean Arthur, visited, she swam laps at night and I was given the job of holding a flashlight over the water to keep an eye out for frogs and snakes," Larry Hagman recalled in his memoir. "I always looked forward to her visits, since she swam in the nude."

Fully aware that she had to put some distance between her strict, unforgiving husband and her callow, impressionable son, in the summer of 1945 Martin found a brand-new boarding school for Larry in Vermont. The coeducational Woodstock Country School was in sharp contrast to the rigorous, all-girls Ward-Belmont in Tennessee, where Martin herself had spent a miserable term as an awkward adolescent nearly two decades before. There were only thirty students enrolled in the Woodstock Country School during its inaugural year, including freshman Larry Hagman and his fourteen-year-old roommate, Roger Phillips.

"My parents wanted me to go to Putney, but it was all full at the time," recalled Roger Phillips, who has vivid memories of his arrival at Woodstock, when he met Larry Hagman. "We went upstairs with my bags. My sister and mother were behind me, and there was this blond guy, sitting on the bed, and this redhead, on her hands and knees, sanding a bureau drawer—it must have been stuck or something. My mother and my sister were unusually quiet and I look back [at them], and their jaws have dropped to their chests. They realized it was Mary Martin."

In his memoir, Hagman relays Martin's awkward attempt to impart some motherly advice to him that day. "Though I'd been away twelve of my thirteen years, Mom was concerned about how I'd react to being sent away," wrote Hagman, "but I was delighted to escape Richard. She drove me there in the Cadillac, the backseat filled with my trunk." After meeting the Phillips clan, Martin took her son out in the hall and said, sotto voce, "You know that Roger and his family are Jewish?"

"I had no idea what a Jew was," continued Hagman. "I'd never thought about such things. Mother didn't know me. How could she? We'd never spent any time together. With great bravado and fake worldliness, I said, 'I know he's a Jew.'" Roger Phillips became and remained one of Larry Hagman's closest friends for the rest of his life.

Phillips recalled Larry's mother returning to Woodstock that fall and "singing songs around a bonfire." He also remembered, "Larry took some food from home, and when it was found out that he did it, without asking, Richard [Halliday] had him come all the way home from Vermont, to be disciplined." Though it's highly doubtful that permission would have been granted, the fact that Larry didn't even ask for it was the bigger offense to Halliday, who made his stepson turn around and make the five-hour trip back to the city to return the goods.

"During the first year at Woodstock, my father got a call from Richard's secretary, asking how much money he gave me as an allowance, so they could give Larry the same amount," continued Phillips. "I think it was seventy dollars a month. My father, who never got angry at anybody, was furious that Richard didn't make that call himself, that he would delegate such a personal matter to his secretary."

The Hallidays' skittishness about Martin's involvement with *Lute Song* continued to manifest itself during its extensive tryout period—in New Haven, Boston, and Philadelphia—as they interfered not only with the story but also with the costume and lighting designs. It wasn't until the final dress rehearsal that the Hallidays divulged that they had recruited Valentina to redo Martin's costumes "in a lighter and more 'becoming' style." It was nothing less than an "act of treachery," according to Houseman, which "caused deep offense and unhappiness."

Along with sixteen different sets and elaborate lighting designs, the hundreds of costumes had been the painstaking creation of Robert Edmond Jones, long considered the American theater's first designer genius. "[Jones] belonged to an earlier and simpler era in which the 'lighting-designer' was unknown," explained Houseman. "[Jones] regarded lighting as an essential element of his own design—foreseen and provided for in his original drawings." *Lute Song* would become the designer's "last significant and most admired work," according to fellow designer Donald Oenslager, who added, "With Jones, the craftsman never took over where the artist left off because with him the artist never left off." While observing that the sets "melt scene into scene with the movement of an unrolling Chinese scroll," Alan Priest, the curator of Far Eastern Art at the Metropolitan Museum, considered Jones's sets "the most beautiful and most true visual interpretation of China that has ever appeared on the Western stage."

But as far as the Hallidays were concerned, Jones's costumes and his lighting had to conform to what would best showcase Martin, as opposed to the work itself. With reinforcement from the composer and lyricist, Halliday persuaded Houseman in New Haven that a spotlight needed to be cast on Martin for her "critical" closing act 1 number. With it, "Mary was able to achieve a dramatic and musical climax that drew applause from the handful of weary people who were sitting out front in the darkened house," recalled Houseman. But this became the final insult for Jones. When he first discovered the change, Jones announced, "That's not my lighting." Houseman explained why they felt it was necessary. "Not on my set!" exclaimed Jones, as he went storming up the aisle, repeating the remark as he exited the theater, never to be involved with the production again. This would not be the last time that the Hallidays put their self-interests before the greater good of the project in question.

While burning some of their theatrical bridges, the Hallidays built a more enduring one with a woman who was destined to become the First Lady in 1981. It was specifically at Martin's urging that Nancy Davis was cast as a handmaiden in *Lute Song*—long before she married Ronald Reagan. Having stayed at the Davis's apartment for several days when she was in Chicago with *One Touch of Venus,* Martin could at least arrange a bit part for the fledgling Nancy Davis, whom Houseman would sardonically describe as "a pink-cheeked, attractive but awkward and amateurish virgin."

Other notable members of the supporting cast included Mildred Dunnock (who would make her mark in only three years as Willy Loman's wife in *Death of a Salesman*) and Augustin Duncan, the great dancer Isadora's brother, playing Tsai's ill-fated parents. The English-born stalwart character actor Clarence Derwent portrayed a conniving courtier. (Derwent's name would become familiar in theatrical circles for an annual award he established to honor the best performances by supporting players in both New York and London.) Derwent caught the flu, lost his voice, and missed several performances in Boston, which is where Houseman "tried hard to get rid of Nancy Davis, but Mary forbade it." It's noteworthy that Martin had the clout this early in her stage career to get away with such a demand.

A decade before she would perform in his quirky, groundbreaking play *The Skin of Our Teeth,* Martin received a crucial visit from the towering American novelist and playwright Thornton Wilder, after he attended a preview of *Lute Song* in New Haven. "I'm not right for this," she tearfully confided. "You are, if you'll forget that you're from Texas [and] remember that you were born in China," replied Wilder. Martin felt as if Gabriel himself had descended from heaven to give her advice. But even if Wilder temporarily calmed her jitters, Martin never would be comfortable in the part.

Despite all the false starts, misfires, and lack of communication, *Lute Song* finally opened at Broadway's Plymouth Theatre on February 6, 1946. Halliday gave Houseman a bottle of champagne with a handwritten note that in no way indicated the painful ordeal they had just put him through on the road: "Mary and I will always remember your kindness, your thoughtfulness and the enormous amount of vitality and good plain hard work you poured into *Lute Song*. Our thanks and our love." But as reflected by the reviews, nothing like *Lute Song* had ever been seen before and no one knew quite what to make of it.

George Jean Nathan, the dean of American theater criticism, more or less apologized for his critical brethren when he wrote: "More and more it becomes clear that plays of delicate charm are distasteful to the bulk of local criticism and that the producer who courageously takes a chance with them is destined often to suffer a heavy loss." Unlike the other reviewers, however, Nathan was rather critical of Martin, writing that "the dramatic phases of the role elude her and become in her hands mere dry elocution." While declaring it "the season's loveliest production and most charming failure," the anonymous *Time* magazine critic found Martin "attractive and scrupulously unself-indulgent in a role that leaves her, like *Lute Song* itself, a little lifeless."

As emphasized by Lewis Nichols in his review in the *New York Times*, the real successes of *Lute Song* were the elaborate designs of Robert Edmond Jones, which he called "the heroes of the evening." But even then, Martin received some understandable flak for the incongruity of being an impoverished figure clad in such rich garb, or as Burton Rascoe wrote in his review for the *World-Telegram*: "reduced to beggary in a gorgeous white silk gown" or "tramp[ing] hundreds of miles to the capital, arriving there without a speck of dust and pretty as a picture." Despite all the critical carping, the leading Broadway lyricist Alan Jay Lerner would come to feel that "although the play failed, [Martin's] performance enhanced her reputation."

The lavish look of the production reflected the $100,000 that Meyerberg had invested to put it on. (Even *Oklahoma!*, which was still ensconced on Broadway, had cost only $75,000 to produce.) It also coincided with the country's optimistic mood during the ongoing recovery from the hardships of World War II.

Despite the mediocre response to *Lute Song*, the show was "frozen"—meaning no more changes could be made—and Martin finally settled into a role that had disoriented and discomfited her throughout the tryout period.

It would be the first show in which Heller saw her mother perform. Since Martin was somewhat apprehensive about noticing her husband and daughter in the audience, tickets were arranged for them in the front row of the balcony. But a misguided messenger had them placed in the first row of the orchestra, instead, and Martin had to muster her greatest determination to avoid sneaking glances at them.

There was another special member of the audience on Sunday, March 31: Laurette Taylor, who, following a protracted descent into alcoholism, had recently made her legendary stage comeback as Amanda Wingfield in the original production of Tennessee Williams's groundbreaking autobiographical masterpiece, *The Glass Menagerie*. Considered by many to be the greatest American actress of her era ("Her sister actresses were unanimous in proclaiming her 'top gal,'" as Helen Hayes put it; "Ethel Barrymore, Katharine Cornell, Ruth Gordon, Tallulah Bankhead, all handed her the palm"). Taylor adored Martin and reportedly saw *Lute Song* six times. She celebrated the first anniversary of her greatest role in *The Glass Menagerie* by taking other members of the company to see Martin in the show.

"Afterward she gave a party at her apartment for the star of *Lute Song*," claimed a feature story years later in the *New York Times*. "It was their first and only meeting, and they spent much of it in Miss Taylor's bedroom exchanging stories about their childhood, stories that were remarkably similar despite the fact that Miss Taylor grew up in New York's 125th Street and Miss Martin in Weatherford, Texas. There was theater talk, too. Miss Martin said that she had never believed in studying acting, but she would rather study with Miss Taylor than anyone else. Miss Taylor smiled. Placing her hand on her heart, she said, 'But we have the same teacher. There is nothing I could teach you.'"

According to her daughter, Marguerite Courtney, Taylor often said of Martin, "that girl can do anything she wants to in the theater!" Hedda Hopper referred to Martin as Taylor's "great pet" and also wrote, "Mary has the same elfin magic as Laurette Taylor." Taylor's son, Dwight Taylor, felt that "[i]n many ways [Martin's] like mother. She has the same warmth and capacity for fun."

Despite Laurette Taylor's glowing response to Mary Martin, *Lute Song* predictably failed on Broadway, where it ran for only 142 performances and closed at a net loss of over a quarter of a million dollars. Looking back, Yul Brynner would blame both his and Martin's performances, saying they had been miscast and decrying his own lack of experience: "I did not like my part at all," he claimed. "[My character] was a very flimsy young man and very weak. I had no respect for him as a human being. . . . And, of course, I had no skill as an actor—none at all." Indeed, it was apparently more successful when it played in Chicago in the fall with Dolly Haas (the future wife of Al Hirschfeld, the most famous caricaturist of the twentieth-century stage) in Martin's role. According to Brynner, Haas had more of an affinity for the part, and the entire impact of the play improved. "It wasn't at all that Dolly was a better actress," he observed. "She was just better casting for the part than Mary."

The Hallidays returned every night to their new home in Norwalk, Connecticut, during the run of *Lute Song*, except for the nights before matinee days, when they remained in town at their apartment. While his wife was still performing in *Lute Song*, Halliday saw a new musical called *Annie Get Your Gun*, starring Ethel Merman. After attending the opening night performance in New Haven, Halliday told his wife: "Cut your throat, Mommy. This is the part you have always wanted to play." When she subsequently caught up with the show during its smash run on Broadway, Martin readily agreed, claiming it was the role she "had dreamed of" and adding that she knew she would "one day" tackle the part. They both recognized Annie Oakley as an ideal and irresistible role for Martin.

True to his word, Noël Coward sent Mary Martin a telegram on March 2, 1946, while she was still in *Lute Song* at the Plymouth Theatre, saying he was writing a musical comedy for her and asking if she would do it:

> THE BOOK IS NOT ACTUALLY WRITTEN UNTIL I KNOW
> WHETHER OR NOT YOU CAN PLAY IT STOP IT WOULD GIVE
> ME SO MUCH PLEASURE TO INTRODUCE YOU TO LONDON
> AUDIENCES.

Halliday shot back a response the next day, claiming that he had never known his wife to be "as excited and happy" by an offer and that she was "completely enthusiastic" about the prospect of working in London. Martin had already turned down a more unusual invitation to star as Cleopatra in George Bernard Shaw's *Caesar and Cleopatra*, proposed as part of the first season of a new company being formed by Cheryl Crawford, actress Eva Le Gallienne, and theater director Margaret Webster: the American Repertory Theatre. (All three of the principals happened to be known lesbians.) Though Laurette Taylor surely would have argued otherwise, Martin told them that she "wasn't an actor"; she was, instead, "a performer and an entertainer."

While Larry stayed with Richard's mother, the Hallidays—with the four-year-old Heller in tow—sailed to England on the *Queen Mary* the following September, enduring a rough crossing. They were greeted at the dock by Coward, who whisked them off in a Rolls-Royce to the posh Savoy Hotel, in the heart of the West End of London. They had a suite on the fifth floor, with two enormous bedrooms and a living room, overlooking the river Thames. Coward provided a proper British nanny for Heller, freeing up her parents' time for what Martin would come to see as a "vacation" before work began on *Pacific 1860*.

Conceived by Noël Coward as a small-scale musical, *Pacific 1860* was misguided—one might even say doomed—from the start. Though he originally had His Majesty's Theatre in mind, Coward had to reconsider his entire approach when that relatively small West End house proved unavailable and the Theatre Royal Drury Lane offered its auspices instead. Having suffered severe bomb damage during World War II, the Drury Lane had been vacant ever since. (This largest and oldest of London's musical theaters had served as an army headquarters since 1940.) But it was one thing for Coward to reconfigure his latest work to fit into a much larger theater and quite another when the Drury Lane kept delaying the renovations needed to accommodate a new show.

The story of a popular opera diva who falls in love with a young man on a tropical island (one of Coward's working titles was *Scarlet Lady*), *Pacific 1860* was a show in which Coward had an even more vested interest than usual, since his life partner, Graham Payn, was to be Martin's costar. This may also have contributed to Coward's feeling that he needed "a different kind of star" than he was accustomed to in previous British musicals: "still a romantic heroine, certainly," according to Sheridan Morley in his study of West End musicals, *Spread a Little Happiness*, "but one capable of playing in a lighter and more cheerful convention." To increase the show's chances at the box office, Coward also "decided that a breath of the new Broadway vigour was what his show most needed." But behind-the-scenes problems escalated as soon as Martin agreed to take on the part. From the beginning, she was "worried sick about her voice not being good enough for high-toned arias [or] not up to anything operatic," and she was "scared out of her wits at the prospect of London." This, at any rate, was the assessment sent to Coward in a letter from the Hallidays' friend, Neysa McMein, a commercial artist. But time and again throughout her life, it seems as though Martin was intimidated by the prospect of singing in a high style or operatic manner, unless she could offset it with a more modern approach, such as swing, or she could make fun of it at the same time.

Before arriving in London, the Hallidays seemed up to their usual negotiation shenanigans when, on August 23, Coward received an "irritating cable" from Martin, who "wants far too many options and rights and is not going to get them." (Halliday would ultimately insist on 10 percent of the gross for his wife, which was as much as Coward himself was to receive as both librettist and composer.) Halliday was involved in his customary haggling over his wife's contract, during which he had the audacity to suggest that they were still considering other offers. But once they were in London, all seemed to be going swimmingly—at first, anyway, before the actual work began.

After showing the Hallidays the Drury Lane and playing some of the music for them in his opulent mews flat, "They were madly enthusiastic and we drove them back to the Savoy in a haze of happiness," wrote Coward in his diary, on September 27. "Personally I think she has authentic magic. She is quite obviously an artist in the true sense. She is easy, generous, and humble." Heller's fifth birthday, on November 4, was celebrated with a stylish party at the Savoy, which included stalwart British actor John Mills and his daughter Hayley. In hopes that Heller would follow her mother in the business, the tot was about to be enrolled in ballet school at Sadler's Wells.

Two days after Heller's birthday party, following the first reading of the script, Coward scribbled in his diary: "Mary very nervous and read mournfully, none of which matters as she is very quick and full of talent." As late as November 14, Coward continued admiring his star: "She is a dream girl, quick and knowledgeable; she has all the mercurial charm of Gertie [Lawrence] at her best with a sweet voice and with more taste." But by December 11, Martin was *at last* showing signs of being tiresome."

There were also the ongoing problems with the renovations at the Drury Lane. The Hallidays arrived in London before learning that the permit for necessary repairs had been refused, and rehearsals had to be put off for more than two months. To help fill the time, Coward took the Hallidays with him to Paris for the French version of his *Blithe Spirit* ("*Jeux d'Esprit*"). "They were well rewarded," claimed Coward biographer Philip Hoare, with a "spectacular" party hosted by fashion designer Molyneux, which included a number of his top rivals as guests: Lanvin, Schiaparelli, Dior, and Balenciaga. They also attended a screening of Jean Cocteau's groundbreaking film version of *Beauty and the Beast*.

When rehearsals for *Pacific 1860* finally did occur, they were continually interrupted for work that needed to be done on the stage. The dilapidated seats in the auditorium were not even replaced until three nights before the first performance. All of the rehearsals took place in an unheated theater, during what was generally perceived as the coldest winter in a decade.

Coward's primary song for Martin was "Alice Is at It Again," but once she read the lyrics to this typically bawdy music hall number, Martin re-fused to sing it. "Alice was really *at* it, with the birds and bees and the beasts of the field," said Martin, years later, in her memoir. "I thought it wasn't right for a gal from Texas to make her London debut with this scandalous song." But the prudish Texan "gal" also recognized that it was a "very funny" song and came to regret her decision. For one thing, the replacement that Coward concocted for Martin ("There is nothing so beguiling as a One, Two, Three . . .") included a passage where she had to sing in several different languages, which eluded her. For another, after the failure of *Lute Song,* the Hallidays were particularly anxious about how Martin would fare with this, her next project. Indeed, with Coward and Judith Anderson bearing witness, Martin seemed particularly "ner-vous" when she and her husband attended a dinner party hosted by Vivien Leigh for Yolande Donlan, the star of the London version of *Born Yesterday,* directed by the great actor Laurence Olivier.

"From the first week of rehearsal onward, everything that could possi-bly go wrong with *Pacific 1860* proceeded balefully to do so," claimed British theater scholar Sheridan Morley. Beneath it all was Richard Halliday's interference, which had already reared its tenacious head during the creation of *Lute Song.* In their zeal to manipulate Martin's appearance, the Hallidays now objected to a hat designed for her open-ing scene, as well as to large bows adorning her period gowns.

When fueled by alcohol, Halliday's demands could turn especially ugly. At the end of the rehearsal on December 14, the costumer Gladys Calthrop and Coward "went into the dressing-room to try and persuade [Mary] to alter her hair, which is really hideous and completely out of period. Richard, who must have been drinking, suddenly started shriek-ing abuse at Gladys and calling her a bitch and both of us double-dyed fiends because we wanted Mary to be unhappy in a hat, etc. It was one of the most hideous, hysterical and vulgar exhibitions I have ever known in the theater. . . . What a sad pity, just as I was beginning to like Richard in spite of his noise and vulgarity. He has now broken the flimsy edifice into a million pieces." (Coward even wrote a private verse describing the fra-cas, which begins: "I resent your attitude to Mary. / It betrays a very ugly sort of mind. / She is innocent and pure / And her husband, I am sure, / Would consider your behavior rather rude and most unkind.")

While it might be tempting to ascribe the difficulties with launching *Pacific 1860* to two competitive "queens" going head-to-head, the prob-lems were manifold and varied. As Sheridan Morley further noted: "during the last week of rehearsals Noël and Mary Martin both gradually began to realize that, even for an entertainer of her undoubted and flexible talent, she was hopelessly miscast and was having to struggle with a part originally conceived for a heavier-voiced soprano." Charles Russell, Coward's American agent, offered a more sinister interpretation on what went wrong: "Gladys rather took a fancy to Mary. . . . But she wasn't interested in Gladys, so Gladys started getting bitchy about Mary's appearance."

"Gladys's bows eventually made a tactful exit," wrote Graham Payn in his memoir. "But then Mary's husband began to get on Noël's nerves. Richard Halliday wanted a say in everything, as 'Stage Husbands' often do in order to justify their existence." Payn became even more blunt when he added: "*Mr.* Martin never stopped complaining, and could only have aggravated Mary's already nervous condition. There were never specific complaints, he simply wanted all these hard-working people to know that his wife was used to better."

In the end, they all had to contend with merely "two hasty and sketchy dress rehearsals which served only to leave a frozen and depressed author-director with the conviction that there were still a thousand things wrong with *Pacific 1860*," observed Sheridan Morley, "and that he had neither the time nor the opportunity to get even a dozen of them right in the few remaining hours before the first night."

Given her penchant for accentuating the positive, Martin found something worthwhile to take away from her painful experience with *Pacific 1860*, including what she called "two of the most important techniques of acting," which she had learned from Coward: "first, how to really let go onstage; second, how to express emotion without feeling it so much that it absolutely destroys you." Payn had a more equivocal impression of the tutorial imposed on Martin. While working on a scene where Martin's character is required to strike her manager, Coward had to overcome her resistance. "Realizing her technical limitations, he did not apply the kid glove she was used to and expected," said Payn. "He would shock her into instinctive behavior, to make her 'let go' on stage. . . . He berated Mary in a way she'd never known before. How could she be so *dumb*? Hadn't she learned *anything*? And it worked perfectly. She hit her unfortunate colleague with such a resounding wallop that he couldn't hear straight for days."

"In Noël Coward's show in London I had to slap a man," recalled Martin. "Gosh, I didn't want to, but I did when Richard told me I ought to. And everybody said it looked real. . . . The leading man's face was red all through the run. I wanted to ease up, but Noël said it was good that way. To keep it in."

Without ever surmounting the many obstacles that had circumscribed its creation, *Pacific 1860* opened on December 19, with members of the audience huddled under blankets concealing hot water bottles. Clad in a "grown-up," black velvet, ankle-length evening gown, the five-year-old Heller attended a command performance with her father, when the king and queen were present to aid King George's Fund for Sailors. But it was tantamount to getting dressed up for a beheading, or at least a royal drubbing from the critics. "Characterized by an almost resentful disappointment," the reviews predictably reflected the show's many problems. "There is plenty of honest dullness," said the *London Observer*. "The evening flowed mildly on, and the tameness and triteness of Coward's plot became gradually manifest," responded the *London Telegraph*. "Pseudo-Viennese sentimentality in waltz-time, Noël Coward is Lost in the Pacific," quipped the *Evening News*.

But the real news on the Rialto was the feud between Coward, London's own "darling boy," and his latest leading lady. After the opening, "We were all invited everywhere in London, but never together," recalled Martin. "If we were invited to his friends' homes, Noël wouldn't be there. If he was invited, we weren't there. I wasn't even speaking to Graham [Payn] anymore, though we had to kiss on the stage [every night]."

Payn acknowledged that he and Martin never connected and that "two perfect strangers singing about the melody in their hearts just doesn't play true." In the end, "Mary remained an enigma," according to Payn. "She was talented but temperamental, in spite of her 'adorable' image. Her husband, by comparison, made her seem like sweetness and light. He was a bore and a boor, but he was also a convenient mouthpiece for the things Mary wanted known but didn't have the nerve to actually say."

Though Martin "played on doggedly" in the show for four months, it was utterly demoralizing to have made her London debut in such a flop, and especially so soon after her failure back home with *Lute Song*—and it began to show in what reportedly became an increasingly lackluster performance. *Pacific 1860* ultimately lost £28,000, or the equivalent of $75,000—a major sum in war-torn London. It would achieve the unfortunate distinction of becoming "the only Coward musical never to have been revived anywhere in the world." Martin herself would come to denigrate even the show's title: "Everybody thought it was a telephone number [exchange]." But there was, finally, an enticing beacon at the end of what had been a dark international tunnel for Martin. The Hallidays were still in London when they received a cable inviting Martin to do the latest Broadway sensation, Irving Berlin's *Annie Get Your Gun,* in England. It was being produced by the brightest new team of songsmiths, Richard Rodgers and Oscar Hammerstein, who had runaway hits with their first two shows, *Oklahoma!* and *Carousel.*

Though undated, it was clearly around this time that Martin hand-wrote a letter to Hedda Hopper, thanking Hopper for her "report of the opening" of *Pacific 1860* and accentuating the positive about the Halli-days' time in London, adding that Heller is "living in a little girl's dream-world," with ballet lessons and pantomimes, including *Mother Goose, Little Red Riding Hood, Cinderella,* and *Peter Pan.*

Martin also said she had been asked to remain in London "for a long, long time" to star in *Annie Get Your Gun* when *Pacific 1860* closes. "Can't think of anything I'd rather do—but how to get the money so I can *af-ford* to do it is another question," she wrote. "Remember when the papers reported that although Bea Lillie was getting $5,000 a week from Billy Rose that she had to move from the Waldorf because she couldn't afford it? *Well*—it is said over here that I'm getting 'the highest salary ever paid in the English theater,' *but* we sure would move from the Savoy *if* we could find four walls to move into! No, and it's true, can't afford even to buy a hat—not *one*," she pointedly added in a much longer letter to Hopper, who was famous for her outrageous chapeaus. "Such is something called taxes."

In point of fact, the Hallidays responded to the invitation for Martin to star in a London version of *Annie Get Your Gun* with a cable of their own:

WE WANT TO COME HOME. WE'VE BEEN GONE TOO LONG. BUT WE WOULD LIKE TO DO YOUR SHOW ON THE ROAD IN THE U.S.A.

Chapter 6

MARY GOT HER GUN

The show I had dreamed of was written for somebody else.
— MARY MARTIN ON *ANNIE GET YOUR GUN*

Mary Martin was the first to acknowledge that there were different memories of how she was corralled into doing an eleven-month road-show tour of *Annie Get Your Gun*. According to one version of what occurred, Halliday was initially dubious about the prospect, saying that stars never took over roles already originated by others and that the hardships of an extensive tour were beneath their dignity. According to another, Halliday was instantly in favor of her taking on the task, seeing it as inevitable. "I wouldn't have played it in New York; that was my friend Ethel's territory," explained Martin. "But anywhere else—I'd love it." (In her memoir, Martin also recalled that the Lunts, "the royal family of the American theater," told her: "If you intend to make the theater your life, you must tour.")

According to yet another version of the story, the Hallidays attended a dinner in 1946 at Richard Rodgers's home in Fairfield, Connecticut, when the famed composer played several numbers from the Irving Berlin score that he and his partner, Oscar Hammerstein, had produced on Broadway. Having seen her rival Ethel Merman in this sellout show, Martin coveted the role of sharpshooter Annie Oakley and sang the lyrics for the assembled guests. Some months later, while she was in *Pacific 1860,* the producers cabled the Hallidays, asking if she would like to play Annie in a London production. According to Martin, "Richard and I were so heartsick because of the fight with Noël that I simply couldn't stay there any longer." But as Martin would also recall, she first performed her "impromptu" song renditions of *Annie Get Your Gun* during a visit to Edna Ferber's Connecticut home, and later sang some of the songs for Rodgers and Hammerstein when they were all having lunch at Lawrence and Armina Langner's house in Connecticut. (The Langners ran the highly regarded Theatre Guild, which had already produced *Oklahoma!*)

"During a working weekend that summer at the Rodgerses' home in

Connecticut, Dick, Oscar and both Dorothys [their wives] went to have lunch at the nearby home of Armina and Lawrence Langner," explained Hammerstein biographer Hugh Fordin. "Other guests included Terry Helburn, Ina Claire, Mary Martin and Richard Halliday. After lunch the hosts asked everybody to get up and do something entertaining. Ina Claire did a brilliant job of mimicking famous people: Mary, who came next, had to think of something spectacular to top her; she let go with 'You Can't Get a Man with a Gun.' This was not the kind of song she usually sang, but she did it so well that Oscar and Dick were 'laid out cold.'"

Director Joshua Logan had a somewhat different memory of the events leading up to Martin's road tour of *Annie Get Your Gun*. As Logan recalled, Rodgers and Hammerstein were present at Edna Ferber's gathering, when Martin spontaneously serenaded the other guests with her surprisingly gutsy versions of "Doin' What Comes Naturally" and "You Can't Get a Man with a Gun." Her renditions were entirely out of keeping with the softer image she had projected in both *One Touch of Venus* and *Lute Song,* both surprising and winning over everyone in attendance.

Logan had begun to exhibit a bipolar condition that would increasingly circumscribe his life, whether he was working on a show or not. Despite his illness, Logan was more like a collaborator than a mere director, with hands-on involvement or coauthorship of every project he oversaw. In only a year, Logan would share the Tony Award for Best Play with Thomas Heggen for *Mister Roberts,* beating out Tennessee Williams's *A Streetcar Named Desire*. In two years, he would win another Tony Award for writing, with Oscar Hammerstein, the book for *South Pacific*.

Before she even met Logan, Martin was pleased to learn he would be directing the touring company of *Annie Get Your Gun,* given his success with the original production. "Logan took a break from his playwriting chores with Tom Heggen [on *Mister Roberts*] to recraft Annie's style from Ethel Merman's delivery to the very different approach of Mary Martin," claimed theater historian Laurence Maslon.

As pleased as she was about landing the role of Annie Oakley, Martin was even more delighted when Halliday secured their five-year-old daughter a part as one of Annie's little sisters. (Heller would lose her first tooth on tour with *Annie* in Omaha.) Martin used the development as an opportunity to ask Larry if he wanted to be in the show as well, when she visited him in Vermont in the spring of 1947. "I went numb," recalled Hagman. "I had no aspiration to be onstage. Worse, the thought of being with Richard for a year on the road made me dumbstruck." Without having given the idea any forethought, Larry suddenly blurted out, "I want to go live with Dad in Texas and be a cowboy."

Roger Phillips recalled having dinner with Larry and his mother the night Larry took the train all by himself from New York to Texas. "I remember we went to 21 [Club], and I'm walking behind them, and there're two guys standing behind the doors, and they closed ranks behind them, locking me out," said Phillips. "Mary had to say, 'He's with us.' That was my only entrée to 21. And the three of us had dinner. And I remember Mary was very teary. After dinner, we went by cab to Penn Station. I remember walking down the long platform and getting on the Pullman car with them and helping with the bags. . . . And then I left them—I don't remember if it was at my own discretion, or I was asked to, but she said her good-byes to him. She was crying and she was a mess.

"And then we got in a cab, and she was going to have the cab driver drop me off, but she said, 'Would you mind talking to me for a while? I'm going to ask the cab driver to drive around Central Park.' And we just drove around, and she kept asking me, 'Where did I go wrong?' I tried to explain that it wasn't her at all—that it was Richard, that he was too tough on Larry. He didn't cut him any slack, and Larry couldn't take it."

Larry's arrival in Weatherford presented him with a huge culture clash in more than obvious ways. Looking back, Hagman realized that he "didn't look anything like a fifteen-year-old from Texas. I wore a Brooks Brothers suit and tie, had thick glasses, and my hair was done up as was stylish in New York, in a big wavy pompadour." But Hagman would tell only part of the story of how his father, who was on the verge of running for state senator, helped him become a "cowboy" and a "real" man. It began with his "first big hunting trip" on November 16—a "day that many men regarded as sacred as Christmas," since it was the official start of deer season. While he wrote about shooting his first deer, "a rite of passage in Texas," he omitted any discussion of Ben Hagman teaching him how to gut the slain creature. Ben said, "Now, this is your first deer. You're gonna see something you've never seen before. Get real close, and look real deep." As his boy knelt down, Ben kicked his son in the rear, propelling him head first into the oozing entrails of the slain beast.

During the same trip, Ben took Larry to the red-light district in Piedras Negras, a Mexican border town, saying, "We're going to get you laid." In his memoir, Larry described their arrival at a dance hall: "Nobody was dancing, but there were about thirty girls sitting around the bar. After drinking about four or five Carta Blancas, my dad told me to pick one out. I still couldn't believe this was about to happen." Larry failed to add that his father demonstrated how to perform the sex act by first mounting the chosen woman himself. Three decades later, Larry Hagman would acknowledge to friends that he based his characterization for J. R. Ewing in *Dallas,* the most popular role of his life, on his father.

While Larry was learning—the hard way—how to become a cowboy, his mother and half-sister were rehearsing to become cowgirls. Looking back at the time when she embarked on a career as a child performer, Heller said the worst aspect of it was being homeschooled. "I have terrible learning difficulties," confides the seventy-two-year-old Heller, sixty-six years later. "I can't spell. I can't do punctuation. I can't do math." She was also surprised to discover from rereading her mother's memoir that "Mommy had problems with schooling too."

Martin's full-page bio in the oversize program for *Annie Get Your Gun* emphasized that the role of Annie "differs vastly from those she has portrayed in the past." But it also glossed over her recent failure in *Lute Song*—calling it a "hit both in New York and on tour"—and claimed "she has captured London in the stellar role of Noël Coward's *Pacific 1860.*"

As Logan would point out years later in his memoir, the general feeling was that *Annie Get Your Gun* "could not be put on the stage without Ethel Merman." But he quickly discovered that Martin offered an alternate, equally viable interpretation. Even though Martin would display a spunky aspect of her nature that had not been demonstrated before, she brought a gentler and warmer feeling to the role than the brassy Merman could muster. "I found myself making a change, albeit an almost infinitesimal change, in just about every line and phrase of the production," Logan wrote. "Only the very broad strokes and the actual tempo of the music remained the same. . . . For instance, Mary's singing of 'I Got Lost in His Arms' was much more of a breathless young girl's than Ethel's."

With customary candor, Martin exclaimed, "I don't think anybody can be a better Annie than Ethel Merman, but at least I was different. I was completely Merman's opposite." In her memoir, she described how her "style" differed from Merman's: "She has a pure, honest, God-given voice. Like a trumpet! . . . My voice isn't as big as hers; the timbre is different. . . . I stripped all the gears in my throat belting the big songs. [But] 'Moonshine Lullaby' became more of a lullaby in our show, for example." Ethan Mordden would weigh in on the irresoluble debate regarding Martin versus Merman by focusing on their "very different voices, Merman's the classic belt limited in range but dynamite within it and Martin's a medley of possibilities from earthy song-plugging to high coloratura . . . or in their respective characterological origins, Merman's as a sidekick on hand for songs and yoks, Martin's as a cutie destined for traditional heroine parts."

With *Annie Get Your Gun*, Martin was, in a very real sense, "doing what came naturally" for her. And while she reveled in her different approach, she wanted her audience to embrace it as well. And they did, including the great Laurette Taylor, who had so loved Martin in *Lute Song*, and her toughest critic of all—Ethel Merman. Along with the rest of the original Broadway company, Merman attended an actors' run-through performance of the touring production at the Imperial Theatre in New York the Sunday before the tour began, and Martin was heart-ened to observe her predecessor in the second row, "applauding like mad." Merman went up onstage afterward and hugged Martin before the two of them joined forces in one of the show's biggest hits, "There's No Business Like Show Business."

"[E]verything about the national company of *Annie Get Your Gun* was top-grade," recalled theater veteran Tom Ewell, who would become famous as a film star opposite Marilyn Monroe in *The Seven-Year Itch*. Ewell at-tended that special preview performance: "I remember the terrific ovation that Mary's company received from that audience of theater people. It was a marvelous, magical moment."

When the touring version of *Annie Get Your Gun* opened in Dallas, on October 3, 1947, it broke all records at the State Fair Auditorium by earning more than $250,000 in two weeks. Addressing the many rela-tives, friends, and acquaintances who had been imported from Weather-ford, Martin ended her closing number with new lyrics Irving Berlin had written for the song: "There're no Business / Like Show Business . . . / It's such fun to pack / Your bags and roam."

Martin was made an honorary Texas Ranger, and the mayor of Weath-erford presented her with a six-shooter finished with pearls and rubies. Stanley Marcus, of the famous Neiman Marcus store, threw a lavish opening night party with endless champagne and out-of-season flowers strewn about. "In the audience there were naturally hundreds who had seen the New York show, and were ready to declare that dainty Mary would be no standoff for hard-driving Ethel Merman," reported a story in the *Dallas Morning News*. "Her robustness surprised everyone. Miss Martin is an incomparable musical comedy personality, as long on com-edy as music."

While Martin was clearly in her element playing Annie Oakley, she was also becoming an overly demanding mother toward her five-year-old daughter. "Even though Mummy was working long, hard hours," recalled Heller in later years, "she kept a close watch on me and tried to bring me up in a natural, healthy atmosphere. . . . Everybody was paying a lot of attention to me during *Annie,* and Mummy thought I was being spoiled. Then I began horsing around backstage during rehearsals." Martin warned her daughter against such behavior, and even reprimanded her in front of other cast members. But Heller failed to heed her mother's advice and once, in the midst of a rehearsal of "Doin' What Comes Naturally," "[She] took me backstage, and spanked me, just as she'd said she would."

Martin's expectations for Heller became painfully obvious when they visited with Bessie Mae in Dallas, and Martin imposed on her daughter to demonstrate what she had recently learned at Sadler's Wells ballet school in London. "It was agony," recalled Bessie Mae. "Heller was so tense that she was not dancing as well as she was capable of doing, and Mary was tense that Heller wasn't performing properly. We were all nervous. It was just a complete fiasco. Finally Heller ended in tears and ran into my daughters' room and cried."

After Dallas, Martin's *Annie* toured the country extensively, with stops in Kansas City, Omaha, Pittsburgh, and, for its longest stint, in Chicago, where it opened on November 3. "Go way back in musical comedy and Martin's performance has no counterpart," responded the reviewer in the *Pittsburgh Post* on March 16, 1948. "It is a thing of such shining contagion that when the final curtain comes down, a feeling of real personal loss envelops the audience." The more grueling aspects of such an extensive tour naturally affected Martin's sense of where she was. After she was "up all night in a day coach," Martin was presented with the key to the city in Omaha, where she "smiled and said she was so happy to be in Utah."

Tommy Wonder, who played Tommy Keeler in the show, left the tour to attend his mother's funeral in New York and then rejoined the company in St. Louis. Having heard that Martin didn't believe his mother had actually died, he gave the star a box of chocolates upon his return only to discover that she had discarded it, unopened, outside her dressing room door. For years he said that he couldn't believe Martin thought he was lying. But such childish, inhospitable behavior was entirely uncharacteristic of the inherently congenial Martin, who customarily hid any ill will.

"In Kansas City an overflowing audience had to wait till 11:30 p.m. for the show to start because there was a concert at the theater that afternoon and the scenery could not be put on the stage till the pianist finished his last arpeggio," claimed a subsequent report. "They stayed till 3:00 a.m., missing the last suburban trains, but everyone said they would have slept in the streets rather than miss the treat."

Plans to play Memphis were canceled at the last minute, due to the racist whims of Lloyd Binford, chairman of the city's Board of Censors. Having recently cut Lena Horne out of local showings of both *Ziegfeld Follies of 1946* and *Till the Clouds Roll By*—as well as having Pearl Bailey's scenes removed from *Variety Girl*—Binford now felt that "the negroes' parts" in the touring production of *Annie* "looked too big" and that the integrated playing of black performers "with the white performers in the chorus and with Miss Martin" was unacceptable. With NATIONAL TOUR OF THE MOST ELABORATE MUSICAL PRODUCTION IN YEARS blazoned atop the stationery, John Montague, the press representative for the show, offered an exclusive item to Hedda Hopper, in a letter dated October 28: "Recently you wrote that the producers of a motion picture cut out a colored character because a Southern censor objected to it in association with white persons. In the case of 'Annie Get Your Gun,' starring Mary Martin, the producers acted differently. When the censor at Memphis, Tenn., ordered that several colored actors be cut out of the musical, Rodgers and Hammerstein cut out Memphis."

During the run in Oklahoma City, Martin discovered one night that she was losing her voice. Following an examination, the doctor announced that her vocal cords were "frozen," blaming it on the air-conditioning in her dressing room, when the real problem was the ongoing strain she was putting on her voice. He advised the stricken Martin to refrain from singing for several weeks, which proved impossible, since she was opening in Los Angeles in a matter of days, and the bigwigs—including Rodgers, Hammerstein, and Irving Berlin himself—had all planned on attending. After resting her voice entirely for several days, Martin recovered just in time for the important opening.

Martin's *Annie Get Your Gun* was a sellout in Los Angeles, where many a customer was turned away: "Movie producers, directors, top stars scrambled to get tickets. High premiums were offered just to see Miss Martin—the girl Hollywood had cold-shouldered. . . . She did her best to get seats for her former colleagues—but if you think it really hurt her to have the biggest names in Hollywood turned away at the box office, you're crazy."

"Richard and Mary sat in her 'Annie' dressing room at the Biltmore Theater in Los Angeles," claimed another report. "She was happy. Most

all the movie moguls had invented new superlatives to praise her performance. But the cinema was second choice with the Texas Lark now."

Film director George Sidney saw both Merman and Martin in *Annie*
and later directed the movie version for MGM, originally to star Judy
Garland, who was replaced by Betty Hutton. According to Sidney,
"[Martin] played the story so that you knew there was a character there,
and the love story worked with her"—as he felt it didn't with Merman.

While touring with *Annie Get Your Gun,* the Hallidays loaned their new
Norwalk home to Cheryl Crawford, who was, at the time, putting together
a new musical with Kurt Weill and Alan Jay Learner. "Mary seemed ideal
for the wife in *Love Life,* so I made arrangements for Alan, Kurt and me to
play it for her one November Sunday in 1947, in Chicago," wrote Crawford. "Mary decided against the show," which was just as well: *Love Life*
flopped soon after it opened with Nanette Fabray and Ray Middleton, who
had been Ethel Merman's costar in *Annie Get Your Gun.* (Crawford had a
more personally successful experience around this time than with *Love
Life*: she found "a small estate only four miles from Mary and Dick's place"
in Connecticut, and became a neighbor the following summer.)

On March 28, 1948, Martin received a special Tony Award for "Spreading Theatre to the Country While the Originals Perform in New York."
This was only the second year for the Tony Awards, however, which were
clearly still striving to find an identity and be taken seriously as an honor-
ific. Other honors in 1948 included a Special Award to Joe E. Brown for
touring with *Harvey,* to George Pierce "for twenty-five years of courteous
and efficient service as a backstage doorman," and to Rosamond Gilder,
an editor of *Theatre Arts* magazine, for "Contributing to Theatre Through
a Publication." Indeed, special Tony awards had been given the first year
to Ira and Rita Katzenberg "for enthusiasm as inveterate first-nighters,"
and to Vincent Sardi Sr. "for providing a transient home and comfort station for theatre folk at Sardi's for twenty years." Though so many "special" awards seemed to diminish the distinction, Martin was delighted
with the honor.

With or without the Tony Award, and despite her greatest original
parts yet to come, Annie Oakley would remain one of Martin's most beloved roles for the rest of her life. Consciously or not, she had to relate to
the true-life story of a country bumpkin who became a show business
star—a shooting star, at that.

Chapter 7

"SOME ENCHANTED EVENINGS"

You cannot analyze Mary Martin's charm any more than
you can analyze sunshine, but you can say that she radiates
more perfection and sheer joy per cubic foot of actress than
anyone else in recent memory.
—HELEN HAYES

She was just plain remarkable when it came to handling the
pressure of getting things together. . . .
—LARRY HAGMAN ON HIS MOTHER

If Mary Martin was an artist—and she was—*South Pacific* would become and remain her masterpiece. Martin herself claimed that "*South Pacific* was one of the most fabulous things that ever happened to me." But in her memoir, she emphasized how skeptical she was, at first, when she learned that she would be playing an army nurse. "You mean I'd have to wear a uniform all the time, one of those tacky khaki things?" she asked her husband when he first presented her with the idea of playing Ensign Nellie Forbush, the corn-fed, callow, "cockeyed optimist" from Arkansas.

Given the musical's innovations and impact, it's surprising to learn that Hollywood was offered the project first. "The big cry in our town is, 'Where can I find a good story?'" Hedda Hopper wrote in her column in the spring of 1949, in which she reported that there had been no takers. "You hear it from all sides—from stars, from producers, from directors. Yet when good stories are handed them, they turn 'em down and do a rehash of an old picture with new faces." (What may seem like an all-too-common, contemporary lament is now, in other words, at least seven decades old.)

Presenting itself as a "musical play," *South Pacific* had far more serious intentions than practically any musical that came before. It concerns a young American woman stationed in the South Pacific, where she falls in love with a French plantation owner—Emile de Becque—who had already fathered two children with his now-deceased Polynesian wife. Lest the show's message be lost on any audience members seeking mere entertainment, a subplot concerns Lieutenant Joseph Cable, who, though all but blinded by his love for a Polynesian girl, Liat, suffers from homegrown prejudice that presents seemingly insurmountable obstacles to marrying her. Cable's song, "You've Got to Be Carefully Taught," conveys the work's primary theme concerning the vagaries and destructive influence of racism, embodied by Nellie's conflict as well. ("You've got to be taught to be afraid / Of people whose eyes are oddly made / And people whose skin is a different shade. . . .")

The musical *South Pacific* came about in a circuitous fashion. James Michener had won the Pulitzer Prize for Fiction in 1948 for his *Tales of the South Pacific*. MGM turned down the property as a movie, after Kenneth MacKenna, the head of the story department (and the set designer Jo Mielziner's half-brother) brought it to their attention. But MacKenna recommended the book to director Joshua Logan, who was on the verge of going into rehearsal with *Mister Roberts,* another US Navy play, on Broadway. Logan started reading the book on a plane to Florida, where he was about to spend some time with the producer Leland Hayward, who, in turn, recognized the novel's potential as a musical. As a onetime top Hollywood talent agent whose client list included Fred Astaire, Ingrid Bergman, Henry Fonda, Greta Garbo, Katharine Hepburn, James Stewart, and his own wife, Margaret Sullavan, Hayward understood the significance of rights and royalties. He was dismayed to learn Logan had mentioned the Michener novel to Richard Rodgers and Oscar Hammerstein, after they attended his *Mister Roberts.* This prompted the great songwriting team to scoop up 51% of the rights, yielding them final say over every creative decision.

But Hammerstein had problems shaping the material. "What was blocking Oscar was the GI talk," recalled Logan, decades later. "He just didn't know what a captain did, and what a sergeant did, and whether a GI would stand up if a lieutenant came in the room. Well, of course, those things were second nature to me. I'd not only been at military school, but at all kinds of Army camps, and I'd been through the whole war in the service [for four years]. Also I was a Southerner, which meant I knew instinctively what words a Southerner would use. All I had to do was talk in a Southern accent and it all came out.

"So I dictated, and I spoke almost everything Nellie Forbush said, because she was from Little Rock and I was from Texarkana. Oscar played Emile de Becque. He'd throw the lines at me, and I'd speak them into the Dictaphone. He always did Bloody Mary, but I did all the captains and the GIs—Cable, Billis, all of them. We got it done in 10 days." Even though Rodgers and Hammerstein gave Logan cocredit with Hammerstein for the book, Logan was compelled, as part of the bargain, to relinquish any author's royalties. According to Logan, it was Rodgers who was the "hard-bitten businessman."

"[Rodgers] pretends to hate business, and yet it is my theory that [he] is only really happy making contracts, haggling about royalties, salaries, or theatre leases," observed Logan. "I often believed [Rodgers] was a bit embarrassed about the ease of writing music, as though it were too easy, too soft a thing for a man to do." Several years later, when Rodgers and Hammerstein approached Logan to direct another of their hits to be, *The King and I,* he was so bitter about the arrangements over *South Pacific* that he turned them down—only to regret it for the rest of his life.

Following their phenomenal success with their first two collaborations, *Oklahoma!* and *Carousel,* Rodgers and Hammerstein had an instant flop with their more experimental musical *Allegro,* and they couldn't afford a second failure in a row. "Something in them needed to work very, very hard to make sure the next show was going to be a success," said Ted Chapin, president of the Rodgers and Hammerstein Organization. "They took on a star, Mary Martin, and they took on a stranger from a strange land with good pedigree, Ezio Pinza. He was an opera singer, whose career wasn't over. He just got bored and was investigating this [relatively new realm—the Broadway musical]. And they took on Joshua Logan, a bona fide collaborator. And it was a contemporary story: everyone in the auditorium had some connection to the [Second World] War." (The story's relevance would hit home with an even more immediate impact in the midst of its Broadway run, when still more Americans went to fight in the Korean War.)

Martin was concluding her extensive appearance as Annie Oakley in *Annie Get Your Gun,* in San Francisco, when Rodgers contacted Halliday to tell him about *South Pacific.* Having strained her voice in *Annie* by singing, at times, an octave lower than usual, when Martin was told she'd be playing opposite Pinza, she famously responded: "What do you want—two basses in one play?"

The great opera basso Pinza had already moved to Hollywood, hoping to break into pictures. He even bought a home in Bel Air. But after testing for MGM and being told he was "too old," Pinza left his Hollywood ambitions behind—for the time being, anyway—and signed a two-year contract with the Los Angeles Civic Light Opera company, a contract that Rodgers and Hammerstein took over so that Pinza could play Emile de Becque.

Logan described his leading man: "His deep, sonorous voice, his massive

muscular bulk, his magnetic eyes, brought back from the past the matinee idol." Given Pinza's reputation, Martin let Rodgers know how intimidated she was by the prospect of sharing the stage with him. "She was
scared to death," said Rodgers. "She didn't want to get out there and be
made a fool of by a Metropolitan Opera star. She has no illusions about
her singing—she knows what it's good for, but doesn't think it's vocal."
Rodgers assured Martin "that we'd write the score without a single duet
for her." Nellie and Emile ultimately sing a mere twenty-nine bars together: the reprise of "I could say life is just a bowl of jello. . . ." And in
keeping with opera singer conventions, which precluded eight performances a week, Pinza's contract "included a clause that he not be asked to
sing more than fifteen minutes of material per performance."

Despite her initial misgivings and with her husband's prompting,
Martin signed on to *South Pacific* after hearing several of the show's
songs, including "Some Enchanted Evening," and recognizing the spectacular beauty of the score. Rodgers, as the hard-bitten businessman, required both Martin and Pinza to agree to salary cuts to maximize his
own earnings. (Rodgers was especially interested in the show's financial
arrangements since *South Pacific* was the first Rodgers and Hammerstein
musical that they themselves produced.) Though both stars would receive
$2,000 a week, Martin earned still more as one of fifty investors—
including filmmaker Billy Wilder, writer Thomas Heggen, and designer
Jo Mielziner—who put up a total of $225,000.

Even before rehearsals began, Martin gave herself a "poodle" haircut—
cropped and curly—which would become all the rage in the coming decade. "She and Dick [Halliday] announced that they had a thing about
her hair, and she could wash it on stage, and it was sort of a singular moment, because no one had ever seen anybody wash their hair on Broadway before," recalled Mary Rodgers, Richard's daughter and a composer
in her own right. It was this "singular" idea of Martin's that inspired
Hammerstein to write one of Nellie's—and Martin's—signature songs:
"I'm Gonna Wash That Man Right Outa My Hair."

"One day while Mary was taking a shower a 'crazy idea' came to her
and she ran out of the bathroom, dripping water on the floor, to share it
with her husband Richard, working at his desk," wrote Hammerstein biographer Hugh Fordin. "'Wouldn't it be a great scene for a movie or play
if sometime I washed my hair right onstage and then came out all dripping?' 'Don't you dare tell that to anyone,' he said. 'Not a soul. If you
do, they'll go for it, and then you'll have to do it onstage eight times a
week.' The first person who called after that conversation was Josh, and

Mary heard Richard say to him, 'Josh, Mary has a great idea. . . .' 'Don't you dare tell Dick and Oscar,' said Logan. 'You know what will happen.'

"Of course, they told Dick and Oscar," continued Fordin, "who happened to be struggling with a song that would convey Nellie's reluctance to marry de Becque and her decision to break off her romance with him. The scene in which she washed her hair onstage while singing 'I'm Gonna Wash That Man Right Outa My Hair' became one of the most talked about things in the show."

Yet another song, "A Wonderful Guy," was also written specifically for Martin. With Rodgers himself at the piano, she first performed it in Logan's apartment, reportedly at 2:00 A.M. "I was so excited I joined in and sang at the top of my voice and fell off the piano stool on the last high note," Martin remembered, failing to mention that the ruckus disturbed some of Logan's neighbors. "As he leaned over to help me up, [Dick Rodgers] said, 'Never sing it any other way.' "

Yet another of the show's most famous songs, "Bali Ha'i," was written out on Logan's dining-room table when Hammerstein showed up and presented Rodgers with the lyric. "It was written in about two minutes," recalled Bernice Saunders, who "just sailed in" as one of the six nurses, on the basis of a single audition. "While others were called back numerous times . . . I was the first to sing 'Bali Ha'i' in the Rodgerses' living room," continued Saunders. She met the Hallidays for the first time at the Rodgerses' apartment as well: Mary Martin "was sweet, and bubbly, but wanted to sing the songs herself."

"For all its integral specificity to the musical, 'Bali Ha'i' had a spectacular life outside of the theater," wrote Laurence Maslon in his *The* South Pacific *Companion*. "Perhaps it was born out of the late 1940s/early 1950s fascination with all things tropical and Polynesian—from the restaurant Trader Vic's and the Mai Tai cocktail to the eventual United States statehood of Hawaii—but 'Bali Ha'i' was the most commercially successful song from the score, following 'Some Enchanted Evening.' "

While the show was still being put together, Martin discovered a photo of herself taken when she was an awkward adolescent, enrolled in Camp Mystic in Kerrville, Texas. The tall, long-necked girl is seen holding an empty water pitcher in each hand, clad in a pair of men's striped shorts, a sailor hat, a white shirt with rolled-up sleeves, and a man's necktie. As if to demonstrate that nothing could embarrass her, the adult Martin gave the photo to Oscar Hammerstein, who placed it in his office with his own caption: "This proves there is hope for everyone." With the overwhelming success Martin would have as Nellie Forbush, any residual fears that she was little more than a dressed-up hillbilly had been finally allayed, left behind with the scrawny teenager she had been in Weatherford, Texas.

The Camp Mystic photo inspired Logan to come up with Martin's baggy sailor-suit costume for the "Honey Bun" number, which brought the audience to their feet at practically every performance. But it was Lieutenant Cable's "Younger Than Springtime," as opposed to one of her own songs, that Martin would single out as a favorite in the show. "[T]hat was the song I always hummed, or whistled," she recalled, "when I was making up, waiting for my cues, or just sitting around." Another Rodgers and Hammerstein classic, "Getting to Know You," was written for Cable as well, with the title, "Suddenly Lucky." (When it was dropped from the show, the songwriting duo promised Martin that she would get to introduce it in the future. But she relinquished it for Gertrude Lawrence to sing to "the children" when the subsequent *King and I* was crafted in 1951.) Still another song cut from *South Pacific*—"The Loneliness of Evening"—would show up in the 1965 remake of Rodgers and Hammerstein's made-for-TV musical version of *Cinderella*.

Rehearsals for *South Pacific* began at Broadway's Belasco Theatre on February 2, 1949 (the show would then try out in New Haven and Boston). "Logan had foregone the usual custom of sitting around a table with each actor holding his script and reading from it," recalled Jo Mielziner, the show's designer, who attended the first rehearsal and considered Logan "as hard-driving and creative" as anyone else involved with the theater. "He had insisted that they get on their feet because he had already developed his plans for the action of each scene. At the run-through the results were spectacular."

A late run-through at the Belasco entailed an unfortunate accident that almost derailed the production. At the end of "I'm in Love with a Wonderful Guy," Martin danced triumphantly across the front of the stage, culminating with a cartwheel. Blinded by a spotlight, she hurled herself directly into the orchestra pit, where she landed on musical arranger Trude Rittman, who was at the piano and broke Martin's fall, as well as brushing up against the conductor, Salvatore Dell'Isola. Hoping to make amends in a memorable way, Martin sent each of the injured parties goodwill flowers embedded in football helmets. "We had been within inches of terminal disaster," recalled Logan. "Instead of a cartwheel we substituted a good, safe high note." (The cartwheel would be reinstated for Mitzi Gaynor in the film version of the musical.)

But Logan introduced problems of his own during the rehearsal period. "Josh Logan was very sick when we were rehearsing," recalled Bernice

Saunders. "They now call it bipolar. When we were in tryouts, Josh Logan would go in to New York to see his psychiatrist. [The bisexual Logan] was so wrapped up in the boys doing the 'There Is Nothin' like a Dame' number, that he just went on and on and on with them. (One of Logan's instructions to the rehearsing Seabees was to "Feel it in your crotch!") And he ignored the six of us nurses. I mean, we hardly did anything. As a matter of fact, at one point, when we went through a run-through, he fired the ladies. I was in tears. But it only lasted about an hour. Dick Rodgers came in and said, 'He's not well. You're all fine, you're fine.'"

Before the company even left for New Haven, *Life* called, saying they wanted photographer Philippe Halsman to take a cover photo of Martin for the magazine. "This was one of the first concrete signs that, out of the air, people sensed the show would be as big a hit as we had hoped and prayed," recalled Martin. "The invitation from *Life*'s editors had a special meaning for me. They had taken their first photo of me for a cover when I sang 'My Heart Belongs to Daddy.' While we were trying out 'One Touch of Venus,' they had photographed me again (at 4 a.m., after a rehearsal!) and later ran four pages of style photos of Mainbocher's exquisite costumes. In still another issue, they had published a faithful and lengthy biography of me.

"This time, however, I had a problem," continued Martin. "I had fallen asleep in the sun. Never had my face been so burned, and now it was at the worst possible peeling stage." Halsman remedied the problem at his studio with a series of treatments involving cold cream. "I sang and danced 'Honey Bun' many times that early afternoon while Philippe clicked his shutter. He smiled. He beamed. . . . He had tried to perform a miracle and it worked. *Life* used the picture on its cover and was the first to hail the coming to New York of the smash hit called *South Pacific*."

One of the innovations of *South Pacific* was that it eschewed "the kind of choreography to which audiences had been accustomed," explained Rodgers in his memoir. "We had two strong, dramatic stories, and we didn't need extended dance routines to flesh them out in any way." "Dances were not choreographed, they simply developed," explained Hugh Fordin. "The show-within-a-show staged by the military men and women— ancient device though it was—became one of the high points of *South Pacific* because of its spontaneous quality. The act opened with a soft-shoe hitch-kick and scissors suggested by Oscar, who remembered that in his days as a stage manager such dances were so simple that he could put them on himself. Another routine was actually worked out by Mary, who had taught tap-dancing back in Weatherford. When Logan discovered that one of the actors could stand on his hands, the feat was 'choreographed' into the scene."

An adjunct to the diminishment in choreography was that the show didn't have a proper chorus, either, using, instead, only six men and six women to fulfill that purpose, and giving each one as specific an identity as possible. "There is no grass skirt business, no steel guitar or other such Hawaiian lines," Rodgers told a reporter for the *Los Angeles Times* shortly before rehearsals began. "There will be no stage numbers or line dancing, no chorus girl lines. The singers move about the stage in normal movement as if they are acting out a straight book story. Both the music and the dances will be a definitive part of the book story."

According to Bernice Saunders, the male chorus, or "Seabees," were older than the nurses, and a number of them had actually fought in the war. Also according to Saunders, Pinza was the company joker and flirt, who tended to position himself just outside his dressing room, "carrying on, telling jokes, and pinching all the girls. He just grabbed wherever he could grab." (As Martin told Radie Harris for a radio interview: "Ezio is a grandfather, but he's like an overgrown kid or a Newfoundland puppy.")

There was an immediate competitiveness between the musical's two stars. As Logan recalled, Pinza arrived before Martin for the first rehearsal and waited "in the alley." After Martin appeared, Pinza made a grand entrance with an unusually large entourage, including his wife, lawyer, arranger, accompanist, and others. "The most important must arrive last," added Logan. Any early competitive strain was quickly surmounted, however. "Everyone loved [Pinza], especially Mary Martin," wrote Logan. "Unlike the usual star, she had no jealousy; she wanted Pinza to succeed. She knew that if the audience loved Pinza, they would know why Nellie Forbush did."

Martin readily agreed: "He was the most earthy, peasant, darling man, with such an easygoing, warm personality. And the chemistry, I cannot tell you." As she described their first scene together: "Every time he started my way, with that face of his, that magnetism, that music, a spark came across like nothing that ever happened to me before and never will happen again." As lyricist and notorious Broadway womanizer Alan Jay Lerner would claim, "Pinza's part called for a man in his early fifties, and he not only became a matinee idol but gave all middle-aged men a new lease on life." (The fifty-eight-year-old Pinza was performing onstage with the thirty-six-year-old Martin.) Don Fellows, who played Lieutenant Buzz Adams, recalled, "[Pinza] used to get love letters and he'd put them on the call board. Some of them were crazy, women offering to leave their husbands for him." Pinza was also especially drawn to Patricia Northrop, "a gorgeous young girl in the company" who played Ensign Sue Yaeger, a name derived from Martin's childhood friend. "They'd both be waiting to go on stage together, and he would kiss her," continued Fellows. "One night she said, 'If he kisses me one more night I'm going to bite his tongue. I'm tired of this.' So he did, and she did, and Pinza cried out in pain; and then he said, 'Wonderful!'" As Fellows also recalled, "Pinza knew [Martin's] entrances and he'd go to her dressing room door and take her by the hand and lead her on stage. I'd hear her in the wings saying, 'Ezio, when you kiss, kiss me nicely,' and he'd be saying, 'When I kees, I kees!' She'd be singing on stage and he'd be whispering, 'Mary, I love you!' into her ear."

Looking back at her performances with Pinza, Martin would tell Hector Arce, for a story in *Women's Wear Daily,* "My back would be turned and he'd come on stage. I'd know he was there. . . . We got along absolutely marvelously. Sometimes I'd have problems with his kissing. He'd kiss me right past my song introduction, making love to the audience through me. I'd go to his wife, 'Doris, tell him to stop kissing me!'"

A helpless roué himself, Rodgers took delight in reports of Pinza's shenanigans and quipped about them in a letter to Logan: "Pinza is in fine shape and keeps the girls in a pleasant state of anxiety. They just never know what end to protect." According to Ted Chapin, Hammerstein's son Bill "told me about having lunch with Ezio Pinza during rehearsals of *South Pacific*. Having just met Halliday for the first time, Pinza said, 'What is that all about?'" referring to Halliday's obvious effeminacy and the dubious nature of his marriage to Martin.

A consummate opera performer, Pinza was actually nervous about making his musical debut. But he stopped the show on opening night in New Haven with "Some Enchanted Evening"—which arrives early in act 1—providing instant gratification and relief. Martin fared less well at that performance, with two of her late act 1 numbers, "I'm Gonna Wash That Man Right Outa My Hair" and "A Wonderful Guy." "There was no concentration in the crowd," recalled Logan. "Mary and the nurses, flecked with soapsuds, came to a big finish, sure of applause. To my horror there was none. Not a handclap. I was sickened and ashamed. I had let dear Mary down, bumbled some way in the staging."

The alarmed director quickly found a solution. "The next night, Logan moved the actual shampooing [during 'I'm Gonna Wash That Man Right Outa My Hair'] until later in the song, after Martin performed a verse or two of it. Her actual 'washing out' was underscored by some of

Rodgers' most amusing music in the show—a jitterbug danced by the other Navy nurses, as if they had just cranked up the radio." Logan also had Hammerstein turn "A Wonderful Guy" into a soliloquy; with these improvements in place, Martin "tore the house down," in Logan's words. "The ovation continued through the reentrance of the girls. From then on, the number was our highest peak. . . . Word had spread and *South Pacific* was a hit. It was a hit with the ticket buyers lined up at the box office, with the brokers who were already planning expensive vacations and new Cadillacs, and all the hundreds and perhaps thousands of people who are affected when Broadway has a new 'big one.'" Scalpers were reportedly selling $6.60 tickets for $60 each and a pair of tickets could go for as high as $500. According to one story, when Larry Hagman came to town to see the show with three friends—including Roger Phillips—his mother "told them to wait in line at the box office at six in the morning." And Martin's onetime beau, Winthrop Rockefeller, had to resort to contacting a former employee—at that point the Hammersteins' cook—to finagle a pair of tickets.

"Hayward and his colleagues were able to do something miraculous—they were able to return some money to their investors on the evening of the first preview [on Broadway]," explained Laurence Maslon. "Originally budgeted at $225,000, *South Pacific* actually cost $165,000 to open on Broadway because the out-of-town tryouts had gone so well that the money set aside to provide new sets, costumes, or orchestrations [was] not needed."

While *South Pacific* was trying out in New Haven, Martin made what appears to have been her television debut on March 7, in the premiere production of *Preview* on CBS, sponsored by the Philip Morris tobacco company. Conceived by Tex McCrary as an attempt to "bring to life" a video "magazine," the thirty-minute show began with "a sort of 'Life and Times of Mary Martin.'" It featured Martin reliving her career to date with "an endless succession of stills, cards, posters, photos, and some Tex and Jinx talk"—the last referring to McCrary and his wife, Jinx Falkenburg, who were trying to parlay their popular radio show into the new medium of television. "For human interest, Miss Martin's daughter, Heller Halliday, helped recite the story of mama's rise to stardom," explained *Variety,* which also claimed that the show "came a cropper almost from scratch," without any further elaboration.

South Pacific opened on April 7, 1949, at the Majestic Theatre in New York, with a $500,000 advance—the largest at that time for any Broadway show. The opening night guest list comprised a who's who of the

American theater: George Abbott, Jack Benny, Irving Berlin, Russel Crouse, Agnes de Mille, Henry Fonda, Yip Harburg, Rex Harrison, Moss and Kitty Carlisle Hart, Katharine Hepburn, George S. Kaufman, Elia Kazan, Howard Lindsay, and David O. Selznick, among others. Years later, it would be reported that a youngster by the name of Stephen Sondheim was introduced to Harold Prince by his friend Mary Rodgers during the intermission on opening night.

The opening night party was at the St. Regis Roof—a "full dress" event. Martin attended in a striking outfit designed by Mainbocher, "a gorgeous royal-blue satin dress with tiny black stripes, an enormous ankle-length bouffant skirt, no sleeves but a little strap that went across from one shoulder to the other." As described by Martin, the ensemble was offset by a Persian turban with an egret feather, and a diamond pin. Theater reporter Sam Zolotow appeared with the next day's *New York Times*, announcing, "It's a great notice." The songwriters had been so confident of a rave that they had preordered two hundred copies of the paper for their guests. Brooks Atkinson's review in the *Times* declared the show "magnificent . . . a tenderly beautiful idyll of genuine people." He ended his review by emphasizing the electrically charged anticipation that greeted the show's arrival on Broadway: "'South Pacific' is as lively, warm, fresh, and beautiful as we had all hoped that it would be." In a letter to her longtime friends the Rodgers, socialite and patron Mildred Hunter Green referred to the "never-to-be forgotten first night in New York—the whole town ringing bells!"

"I was a struggling actor in my fourth season of summer stock when *South Pacific* opened or rather exploded on Broadway," recalled Don Murray (who in several years would appear in Thornton Wilder's *The Skin of Our Teeth* with Martin). "There was an adrenaline that surged through nearly anyone even remotely connected with the theater that had begun even before the Broadway debut, and though the voice of Pinza was admired it was Mary Martin that impelled that surge. It was not the sweetness of Bel Canto, but a blitheful spirit of joyous energy in her voice. *South Pacific* was not only on the Broadway stage, it wafted through the streets of New York from passing cars, in restaurants and through open windows. The music was a radio medium with a wider audience and more prevailing influence than what was confined to the stage. It was and is unforgettable."

"Pearls, pure pearls," exclaimed Howard Barnes in his review of *South Pacific* for the *Herald Tribune*. "It is novel in texture and treatment, rich in dramatic substance, and eloquent in song." The anonymous reviewer in *Newsweek* was even more emphatic about Martin: "With a single exception, no member of the cast is irreplaceable. The exception is Mary Martin, and it is difficult to envision a *South Pacific* without her . . . a persuasive actress and remarkably talented performer." With Martin in her already famous "Honey Bun" pose, yet another cover story in *Life* magazine seemed as obligatory as it was inevitable. The story inside proclaimed *South Pacific* "a show to go down in theater history" and that, with it, Martin had become "one of the stage's really great ladies."

After seeing Martin in the show, her only rival, Ethel Merman, famously quipped, "She's okay, if you like talent." Even James Michener described his astonishment with Martin's performance: "Mary Martin *is* Nurse Nellie Forbush. If she were so minded she could sue me for having dolled her up in fiction for my book. It seems impossible that I could have thought of any fictional character so completely similar to a living actress I had not then met." From the beginning, Richard Rodgers recognized that he had a gold mine in Martin's performance, and said as much in a program note he wrote for the show: "Mary Martin needs no more help than thirty-two bars' worth of words and music to hit the audience with the impact of a Diesel locomotive."

Helen Hayes would include Martin's Nellie Forbush in her list of "The 10 Most Memorable Stage Performances" she had ever seen, along with Olivier (as Oedipus), Brando (in *A Streetcar Named Desire*), Laurette Taylor (in *The Glass Menagerie*), John Barrymore (as Hamlet), and Shirley Booth (in *Come Back, Little Sheba*). While claiming that a discussion of "the legitimate theater is not supposed to include musical comedy," Hayes could not help herself: "You cannot analyze Mary Martin's charm any more than you can analyze sunshine, but you can say that she radiates more perfection and sheer joy per cubic foot of actress than anyone else in recent memory. . . . The word 'routine' is a bad one to use in connection with Miss Martin, because her songs seem really to come from her heart, and her dances appear to be the logical expression of her feelings." (In his reevaluation of five decades of theater, *The Lively Years,* Brooks Atkinson would claim that the musical itself "belongs to the literature of the human race in music as well as in words.")

South Pacific not only won nine Tony Awards—including Best Musical, and Martin's second Tony for performance—but also the 1950 Pulitzer Prize for Drama. It went on to become the second-longest-running musical on Broadway, after *Oklahoma!* (It would play on Broadway for nearly five years, totaling 1,925 performances.) It was also one of the first musicals that recognized the value of tie-in merchandise for promoting a show:

there were *South Pacific* sheets and pillowcases, scarves and neckties, perfumes and lipsticks, dolls, and underwear—"even fake ticket stubs that people could leave on their coffee tables as status symbols." Columbia's original cast album sold more than a million copies, emerging as the number one album for sixty-nine consecutive weeks and remaining on the charts for four hundred weeks. Perry Como's recording of "Some Enchanted Evening" was Billboard's number one song for five weeks running and was joined on the charts by versions by Frank Sinatra, Bing Crosby, and Jo Stafford. And in an era when piano playing still filled many an American living room, the show's sheet music earned more than two million dollars in sales.

Given the shared steam pipes in the backstage corridor between their dressing rooms, there was an ongoing feud between Mary Martin, who required a colder environment, and Ezio Pinza, who preferred a warmer one. "Heat literally made me sick," recalled Martin. "I could not go from a hot room to a cold stage and sing. . . . Every time I passed the radiator I turned it off. Ezio turned it back on." Eventually, Martin removed the steam pipe knob, and Pinza brought in a wrench to control the radiator. But he frequently caught colds—or so he said—and missed performances, allowing Martin's wishes to prevail. Indeed, Pinza left *South Pacific* when his contract expired at the end of a year; whereas, between New York and London, Martin played Nellie Forbush for three and a half years, with five different Emiles.

Throughout the run of *South Pacific,* Martin slept until noon—except on matinee days. She also washed her hair three times a day: once to greet the day, once onstage, and then "after the show to get the soap out," according to a caption in a magazine article. This really meant she was washing her hair twenty-three times a week.

Martin's interest in hairstyling would emerge as a major development with *South Pacific.* Though everyone loved William Tabbert's mellifluous tenor voice, he was deemed too unattractive in New Haven to continue as Lieutenant Cable. The Hallidays went to work on him: "By this time Richard and I were pretty expert on hair and metamorphoses," recalled Martin. "When we finished he had soft blond curls that made his brown eyes stand out like anything. . . . When Josh, Richard, and I unveiled our new Bill in New Haven, the night before we opened, half the people in the cast thought he was a replacement."

On matinee days, Martin would trim the Seabees' hair in her dressing room before the evening performance. This became a matter of routine: the crew bought a barber pole to place by her dressing table and placed a makeshift barber's license on her door. But for the most part, Martin's dressing room was off-limits to other members of the cast. "When she was working, there was nothing else," said Bernice Saunders. "She was very professional: there was nothing social and no carrying on. We all found her adorable. But everyone always said, 'Was that really Mary Martin? Or was it the façade of a star, with Halliday behind her?' My feeling was that he was the backbone. But I liked her. And I thought she was sincere."

With or without Halliday, Martin was not above giving advice, however. Don Fellows, who had a problem with stuttering, asked Martin how she handled stage fright. "[I]t's very simple," she responded. "I come to the theater half an hour before the half-hour call, and get made up, and get into my costume. When they call the half hour I go into the john and I stay there until Gladys [the dresser] comes and says, 'You're on, Miss Martin.' Then I lean down, pull up my panties, and go out onstage. Well, that's the way you deal with stage fright."

The nurses and the Seabees shared a "community" dressing room in the theater basement, fashioned with sheets and resembling a large tent. They took turns using a nearby "tanning room" with primitive equipment reminiscent of a second-rate science fiction film. "It was awful," reported Saunders, who claimed that they came to rely more and more on bronze toner for the desired effect. "Freddie Sadoff, who played the Professor, was borrowing from everyone else's toner," recalled Saunders. "And they got so annoyed with him, until someone finally peed in a bottle we knew he was going to use. We were hysterical."

The cast's close-knit feeling was more thoroughly on display when, during the run, Dorothy Rodgers threw a surprise birthday party for her husband at their new country home, called Rockmeadow, in Southport, Connecticut. It was an "all-day picnic." "To start things off, the whole cast of *South Pacific,* led by Mary Martin, formed a motorcade a mile or so away," recalled Dorothy Rodgers. "Honking horns and ringing bells, they all drove up the driveway, to Dick's utter and genuine surprise."

South Pacific arrived on Broadway with every "single member of the [forty-one-person] cast" intact from the Boston tryout. "That is unusual, and they say it is all Mary Martin's doing," claimed a cover story by Louis Berg in *This Week* magazine the month after the opening. "She defends and coaches the weaker members, even rehearses her own understudy." After adding that Martin had been "a flop in pictures," Berg opined, "Since there could be nothing wrong with Mary, this would seem to indicate that there may be something wrong with the screen."

Beyond the paid-for benefits of a press rep working behind the scenes, the show's runaway success engendered its own publicity. Columnists had a field day "with the most fantastic rumors that ever surrounded a show," according to Hammerstein, who wrote Logan: "It is said that Pinza . . . and Mary are carrying on a hot backstage romance and those who hear this take it up from there and invent their own details." Saunders recalled that news of her own forthcoming marriage "made Winchell's column—it was just ridiculous! All these people calling me up to congratulate me. I remember Pinza saying, 'Bernice is getting married to a dentist: she has to be sure which end is up.'" Also according to Saunders, Pinza had difficulty sustaining his voice. "He said he could do three hundred concerts a year, but speaking his lines was hard on his throat. The night he left [in June 1950], our poor stage manager had to go out and announce it, and people left in droves."

As an opera singer, Pinza was unaccustomed to giving eight performances a week, and found it trying. "He loved basking in the adulation bestowed on him as a middle-aged matinee idol," claimed Richard Rodgers, "but he could never be counted on to show up for performances. The minute [his contract] was up, he was on a plane to Hollywood—where he made two of the deadliest bombs ever released." Hedda Hopper would echo Rodgers's opinion, claiming that Pinza "lacked [Martin's] judgment. He left the play for a movie career and they killed him off in two of the stinkingest pictures I've ever seen. Now she gets $25,000 for a guest appearance on TV any time she wants to make one, and Pinza is without a job."

Martin herself would miss only three performances during the twenty-six months she remained with the show on Broadway, before taking it to London. "From the beginning, Mary was wonderful," continued Saunders. "She was as surprised, I think, as anybody that this was as enormous as it was. She had not had the kind of personal success that she did with this, with anything else before. It was the biggest thing she had ever done. As a matter of fact, she went to Mainbocher, and had a whole new wardrobe made. She brought a load of her [existing] Mainbocher clothes to her dressing room, to see if any of us wanted anything. She knew everybody. . . . She was part of everything. . . . But she was still the star."

When she was working, Martin had little time for domestic matters. She wanted to make her own contribution to the new home in Connecticut and had Dorothy (Mrs. Oscar) Hammerstein shop for an antique table. Mrs. Hammerstein arrived backstage during a matinee with a table, and Martin gave her approval before returning to the stage. "One of the girls worked as a model at Bergdorf's," recalled Bernice Saunders, "and she would bring in boxes of things for Mary to choose from. There was a special arrangement made between the store and Mary."

Though the Hallidays lived in their new Connecticut home, on matinee eves they'd stay at their New York apartment in the Hampshire House, on Central Park South. According to Richard Rodgers's wife, Dorothy, "Mary and Dick Halliday are drawn to beige and 'the natural color of anything.' Dick recalls that the day Mrs. Charles Dana Gibson came to visit them in their first New York apartment, she stopped at the door of the living room and exclaimed, 'Oh, you darling children—you are going through the bleached-wood period.' 'She was quite right,' he admits, 'except that we started with bleached wood and still have bleached wood. We always seem anxious to get down to the natural wood of a piece of furniture, to see what it really looks like, to discover its original beauties.'"

Martin had taken up needlepoint from Leland Hayward's wife, Slim, and well into the run described how she worked at keeping her performance fresh: "I keep my mind so occupied with other things that singing, dancing, and romping through the show becomes relaxation. I've read, in my dressing room, *The Life of Gandhi,* then Tolstoy's *The Kingdom of God Is Within You,* from which Gandhi got much of his inspiration, Tolstoy's *War and Peace,* and other works." But there is little evidence anywhere else in her well-documented life that Martin was ever much of a reader, making such a claim seem specious and publicity driven. Martin rather occupied herself by resuming work on a rug in needlepoint and petit point, as designed by her husband ("my professional manager"), and with assistance during the next two years from her dresser, Gladys Hardwick, and from Heller: "It will illustrate our home life—our house in the country, our children, our flowers, our animals. It will take a great deal of concentrated work." Decades later, Martin would tell a reporter that she had previously "resisted" the notion of needlepoint "because her own mother had been so expert at it, and [she] had vowed as a child never to learn to sew anything." What began as a pastime and a hobby would eventually become a second vocation.

Martin was impressed by the show's parade of backstage visitors. Hedda Hopper, who had by then become a close friend, would see *South Pacific* five times. "Dearest Hedda," Martin wrote in a May 9 letter to Hopper, "Lots of wonderful new experiences happen in the midst of this wonderful show—but I really think that about the tops is your coming to the dressing-room—that beautiful hat—the gleam in your eyes—your taking my shoulders—your repeating 'well, I just don't believe it—.' I had to write you because it has stayed with me, and I had to thank you for the good feeling it gave me. So you really liked the show! I'm so happy—the reason I kept asking you is because I feel about it like I do about a precious child, and I just can't bear the idea of anyone not liking it." Though Hopper obviously more than merely "liked" Martin as Nellie Forbush, her admiration for the star was also tempered by a pragmatic outlook. Having recently read a script by Clare Boothe Luce for a film that would reunite Martin with Bing Crosby (though apparently called *Saint Anthony and the Gambler,* the film would never be made), Hopper sent Luce a letter, explaining why she didn't think it was right for Crosby or Martin: "I couldn't see . . . Mary playing a part where she was always angry with [Bing]. While Mary's a great actress, she's not awfully pretty, and she must have a very lively, gay part to lift the corners of her mouth. The difference between a gay part and one where you're always angry is the difference between a leading lady and a character woman; and anger puts 15 years on any woman's age. And I'd hate like anything to see that happen to Mary."

Someone else who evidently liked *South Pacific* was the young Elizabeth Taylor, who, at Hopper's suggestion, visited Martin backstage following a performance with her mother and her then fiancé, Conrad Hilton. "I've always wanted to meet her tremendously," Martin wrote in a subsequent letter to Hopper, "because, as everyone agrees, she's truly the most beautiful girl or woman of our time—and also because Larry, my son, hasn't had as much respect for me ever since years ago I had to admit I'd never met her. Now Larry seems quite proud of me—thanks to you."

Another illustrious backstage visitor was Helen Keller, who told Martin, "You are the true spirit of youth," as she ran her hands across Martin's chiseled face. Still other top-flight backstage visitors included Prime Minister Nehru of India and the grande dame of the American stage, Katharine Cornell, who affectedly asked Martin to borrow some of her makeup because she had been crying.

But perhaps the most surprising backstage visitor was Noël Coward, who came to see the show early in its run. Following the fiasco of Martin's starring in his *Pacific 1860* in London, Coward had maintained his distance and silence for three years. Their initial friendship and mutual admiration were now, however, instantly renewed. "Mary was really enchanting," observed Coward in a diary entry. "Afterwards Mary and Dick and I had a reunion. It was really touching. Mary was genuinely in tears and truly happy and relieved that we were making up. I feel as though a weight has been lifted from me. I hate quarrels and feuds, and she had a bloody time in England and I have felt uncomfortable and unhappy about it."

"Everyone in the world came to see it," recalled Martin. "People came to *South Pacific* to get married, to get divorced, to get back together again. Presidents, kings, emperors came to see it." Nevertheless, Martin usually wasn't aware of who was in the audience until they visited her in her dressing room after the performance. Nearly three decades later, Martin would recall, "They wouldn't even tell me when somebody famous was out front, [except] once. But that was because they knew how disappointed I would be if I hadn't known that my idol, Dame Margot Fonteyn, was coming to see me. . . . That was really something. Here I was flopping around in a sailor suit and doing this dumb little dance. . . . I was dancing up a storm and then I spotted Dame Margot in the third row. Well, I got so excited I fell down, right on my backside, clear in the middle of my dance. After that, they never told me if anyone I admired was in the audience again."

In an article for the *New York Times,* "My One Year of 'South Pacific,'" Martin wrote, that it was Nehru, "of course," who told her about Gandhi's book and Tolstoy's *The Kingdom of God* when he visited her backstage. "Like a bobby-soxer, I begged him to sign a program, which he graciously did. My only defense is that his is the only autograph I've ever asked for."

Having run out of superlatives during the extended run of *South Pacific,* Richard Rodgers once quipped to Martin, "You were absolutely *adequate* tonight!" The thriving star also received seventy-five to one hundred letters a day, which her secretary Marion Cazier handled, though Martin was sure to answer the more personal ones herself. Martin sent Ethel Merman an obligatory if awkwardly phrased telegram for the New Haven opening of *Call Me Madam* on September 11, 1950:

THEY MAY CALL YOU MADAME [*sic*] BUT I THINK YOU'RE VERY GREAT AND VERY WONDERFUL.

Both to get away from the frantic pace of city life and to provide the eight-year-old Heller with a semblance of a normal little girl's existence, the Hallidays spent the bulk of their week at their home in Norwalk, where Heller could romp with their three French poodles, Paris, Dites-Moi, and Honey Bun—the last two named after songs in the show.

There was almost another flare-up with Coward when he visited the Hallidays in Norwalk and discovered one of his paintings in the bathroom. "My *White Cliffs of Dover* over your potty," he bellowed. "Good

God!" "Well, Richard thought the light was best there, honey," explained Martin, which restored their newfound equanimity.

Given Larry's "total dislike" for anything theater-related and his previously telling his mother he wanted to be a veterinarian, Martin was surprised when her son just "turned up" at the Norwalk house, announcing that he had "made a mistake" and that he wanted to become an actor after all. His mother contacted Margo Jones, who gave Larry some bit parts in various shows at her theater-in-the-round in Dallas. He then enrolled in the drama department at Bard College. "Larry called and said, 'Hey Rog, where are you gonna go to college?' And I said, 'Bard,'" recalled Roger Phillips, Hagman's erstwhile roommate at the Woodstock Country School. "In those days, anyone could get into Bard, as long as they could pay the tuition. And he said, 'It sounds good. That's where I'm going.' And we were roommates at Bard as well. He stayed less than a year."

During his first and only year at Bard, Larry met one of the most significant figures in his life, Theodore Flicker, who would, in the coming years, direct him both on and off Broadway, on television, and in numerous films. "My first memory of Larry was at a drama department party," recalled Ted Flicker. "He was drunk and I was either drunk or high, and we met under the piano. We started some sort of drunken conversation. Somehow from that conversation, we knew that we were going to be 'asshole buddies.' We were very macho, and the drama department was very gay. The star of the department was a wild queen, whom we hated."

"Honestly, as long as I live I don't think I'll ever forget that morning in our New York apartment," recalled Martin of Larry's Bard days. "I was in bed, reading the paper, and when I looked at the dance review, there it was in black and white: A critic, reviewing a Bard performing-arts recital, was calling Larry—my Larry—a fantastic dancer! I couldn't believe it was the same Larry Hagman, because I hadn't even been able to get him to do the shortest timestep for me! Even though I scarcely knew the president of Bard, I just jumped out of bed to call him and thank him for what he was doing for my son."

The American Magazine ran a story on the Hallidays' home life in their June 1950 issue, emphasizing the forty-five-mile drive to and from the city. The accompanying photos showed Martin in bed with a breakfast tray, surrounded by lilac floral wallpaper and curtains and a coordinated duvet. They also featured Martin and Heller in the yard with the poodles—mother and daughter doing ballet exercises together—and Martin sitting on the edge of a bathtub, washing her hair. "At 5:45 p.m on the dot dinner is served, and at 6:15 there's a frenzied farewell at the door to Heller and the dogs, and the hour-and-15 minute drive into town," wrote Wayne Amos in the article. "Then comes the show, in which Mary sings six numbers and is off stage only about 20 minutes during the two-and-a-half-hour performance. After the curtain, she greets admirers in her dressing room. Finally, comes a postmidnight snack, and the drive home to Heller."

Clad in a Mainbocher dressing gown and resting between her matinee and evening performances, Martin was visited in her dressing room by Radie Harris for a radio interview on March 4, 1950. When asked how she managed to cope with the grueling schedule of eight performances a week for such an extended period, Martin gave complete credit to her husband. "Without him to manage me, advise me, worry for me, take care of all business—in fact, do everything—I don't know how I'd ever get along." On the subject of her eighteen-year-old son's newfound acting aspirations, Martin told Harris: "As a matter of fact, I've always suspected that he didn't particularly like his mother being an actress." While adding that he was studying drama at Bard College, Martin continued: "Now Larry is as big a ham as I am and says his ambition is to do a play with me."

But Martin was wise enough not to take any of her success for granted, maintaining weekly voice lessons with her longtime coach, Helen Cahoon. She also took off one afternoon from her carefully modulated schedule to record an album with television and radio star Arthur Godfrey, and on December 1, her thirty-seventh birthday, Martin made a duet recording with her son for Columbia Records, supervised by orchestra leader and music producer Mitch Miller. "Wearing a sport jacket and horn-rimmed spectacles, and carrying a big package ('It's my old lady's birthday'), Larry bounced into the studio first," reported a follow-up story in *Time* magazine. "We had never so much as sung 'Silent Night' together before," claimed a somewhat surprised Martin. Though it required "three hours of coaching, needling and playback," they recorded a sprightly version of Irving Berlin's "You're Just in Love" and "Get Out Those Old Records." (Given their phenomenal success with *South Pacific*, Columbia also had Martin make studio recordings of songs from *Anything Goes, Babes in Arms, The Bandwagon,* and *Girl Crazy*.)

Far more momentous was the decision for Larry to play a Seabee in the upcoming London version of *South Pacific,* bringing his mother's work and family life together in a more complete way. Working with Larry healed Martin's relationship with her son—up to a point. Nothing would ever resolve the irreconcilable differences between the brash, young, willful Larry Hagman—all bluster and bravado—and his effete, closeted, homosexual stepfather. The only things Halliday and Larry ever had in common were their hatred for each other and their mutual addiction to alcohol.

Mary Martin's final Broadway performance as Nellie Forbush seems, in retrospect, to have emphasized the degree to which *South Pacific* was like a living, breathing New York landmark. "About halfway through the last act that night, firemen and policemen from all around the Broadway theatre district started coming in to the Majestic, standing at the back of the theatre," recalled Martin. "And then people from other theatre box offices, newspaper columnists, photographers, and taxi-cab drivers came. Ours was the last curtain to go down—between 11:25 and 11:28—and gradually actors from other shows, some still in makeup, and their dressers, and even stagehands and ushers from the nearby theatres crowded in, pushing the earlier arrivals down the aisles until there were solidly packed columns of people right down to the orchestra pit.

"As Emile and Nellie touched hands and the curtain started down," continued Martin "the sound of all those thousands of voices filled the theatre and the music played and played and the curtain kept going up and down and up again. And then, unlike what had happened at any other performance, four Seebees in fatigues, with their backs to me and the packed theatre, slowly came onstage carrying a long metal pipe with one of the big mechanical props we had used—a part of an airplane engine—dangling in the middle. They reached center stage and turned around—and there were Dick, and Oscar, and Josh, and Leland! Oh! How I remember! More music and shouting and whistling and the next thing I knew, somehow a black velvet box has been gotten out of the prop and put in my hands. Someone had to help me open it. . . . I slowly lifted from the box a glittering, shimmering bracelet of gold and pearls and diamonds."

The four men who were responsible for the character that, more than any other, made Mary Martin "Mary Martin," gave her a permanent memento to compensate for the ephemeral nature of the theater. With the "unnerving, unabashed, wonderful directness" of a child, Heller, who was still up when her parents came home that night, discovered that the bracelet contained fifty-two pearls and sixty-four diamonds.

Though Martin would forever be the cockeyed optimist Nellie Forbush, when she left the Broadway production of *South Pacific* in June 1951, she was replaced by Martha Wright, whose offstage sightings with Richard Rodgers led to many an unsubstantiated rumor about the composer's carrying on with his new leading lady. It also led to a well-circulated anecdote after conductor Salvatore Dell'Isola left the show and Wright asked

Rodgers, "Wouldn't it be nice if we could get Sal back again?" to which Rodgers replied, "Wouldn't it be wonderful if we could get Mary Martin back again?"

But Martin was committed to the upcoming London production, before which the Hallidays took a brief vacation, cruising the East Coast on a rented sixty-seven-foot yacht, the *Capella,* and spending a weekend ashore on Cape Cod, where they visited Chip Chop, Katharine Cornell's home in Martha's Vineyard. Throughout the trip, Martin was more or less continually at work on the large, five-and-a-half-by-seven-and-a-half-foot needlepoint carpet, which became known as the "Traveling Rug." Then, with Heller and Larry tagging along, the Hallidays set sail on August 3, 1951, for Southampton, England, where the unlikely foursome proceeded to spend some free time on a motor trip through Ireland, Scotland, and, finally, the English countryside. They visited Castle Combe, a historic site converted into a contemporary hotel. It was here that Halliday became irate with Larry for riding a horse bareback. "Things got very heated," recalled Larry, "but I was beyond caring." Larry packed to leave, only to be confronted by his mother, who pleaded with him to stay: "She wouldn't admit Richard was a son of a bitch to me, but she emphasized that having me in the play was very important to her," said Larry. "Though she didn't say it outright, it was a way for us to have a relationship." He might have added that it was the *only* way for them to even see each other.

Since London theater tickets cost roughly a third of what Broadway charged for seats, the Hallidays had to contend with Martin's earning less than she had made in New York. But this didn't prevent them from maintaining a first-class existence. When they settled in London, the Hallidays initially moved into the Savoy Hotel, in the heart of the West End, before finding a more permanent flat at Grosvenor Square.

As part of a massive publicity campaign to promote the arrival of *South Pacific* in the United Kingdom, an *International News Photo* was taken of the four of them in the audience at London's Phoenix Theatre on September 19. While his mother's hair had grown ever shorter, Larry's became longer: he was sporting a pompadour, which was becoming popular with the in crowd of the day, which Larry longed to be a member of. His eyes glazed, the gaunt and awkward teenager seems out of place and almost out of time—as if he came from or belonged in another world. And, in a sense, he did: his military academy upbringing and hunting trips with his father provided no background for the refined, cultured environment Larry was suddenly thrust into.

During rehearsals, Larry was impressed by how "quickly drawn into her own world" his mother was. "She was so focused, so consumed with breaking in a completely new cast, doing interviews, and she was just plain remarkable when it came to handling the pressure of getting things together in less than a month. It was the first time I'd ever watched her this closely and I saw how much she loved it."

But friction quickly escalated between Larry and Halliday, who couldn't let go of the horse-riding episode, and Larry felt compelled to live separately. He moved to Belgrave Square with Archie Savage, the show's lead dancer, who was the only black member of the original cast and one of the few to accompany Martin to London. "I knew Archie from New York, where I'd once rented his Third Avenue apartment," added Larry. "He was a gay black man with impeccable taste." But within a couple of weeks, Larry joined up with his Bard colleague Theodore Flicker, who was enrolled at the Royal Academy of Dramatic Art in London and had a flat in St. John's Wood.

"We invited Mary and Richard to come to our flat," recalled Flicker, "and Richard was clearly, seriously uncomfortable with us roughneck kids. Richard said something, and suddenly Larry was on his feet: he was going to kill Richard. If I hadn't grabbed Larry, and held him back, he certainly would have hit him. I had never seen that kind of rage in Larry before or since."

The London production of *South Pacific* was installed at Theatre Royal Drury Lane, where Martin had had an unhappy run five years earlier in Noël Coward's *Pacific 1860*. That partially explains why she was distressed prior to the London opening. She was also quite thrown because Josh Logan wasn't around, at first, to fiddle with the new staging. Jerry Whyte, Rodgers's "favorite assistant," did the "preliminary block-in directing." To accommodate the raked stage at the Drury Lane, Martin's first number ("A Cockeyed Optimist") had to be restaged. Throughout her career, Martin was discombobulated whenever a show that had been "set" suddenly had changes imposed. In large part, this was due to her being nearsighted and somewhat in the dark without her glasses, having to rely more than most performers on the blocking and director's guidance during rehearsals.

From Logan's perspective, the problems stemmed from Martin herself. The director didn't arrive in London until a week before the show was slated to open. "I couldn't believe my eyes and ears at the performance of Mary Martin, who to me could do no wrong," recalled Logan. "She was still charming, pretty, vivacious, but too *carefully* so. She was strident and mechanical. She lacked her great gift—spontaneity. [But] the biggest blow to my morale came when I went over to talk to Mary Martin and saw her shrink from me." She also repeatedly said, "I don't want any changes, Josh," though Logan couldn't understand where such concerns were coming from, since he hadn't intended on making any. Nor were Rodgers or Hammerstein on hand to help deal with the situation: according to Logan, they spent most of their time at press conferences, promoting the show.

There was at least one change that Logan imposed upon Martin, when he discovered how difficult it was to either "see or hear" Wilbur Evans, her London de Becque, perform "Some Enchanted Evening." "I decided to face Mary Martin and ask her permission to move him downstage," claimed Logan. "But it meant that Mary would have to turn her face, as she had not done with Pinza, in order to be seen by the audience. She was unnerved by the idea, yet when Wilbur showed joyful enthusiasm at moving downstage she agreed. . . . But the reserved and careful Mary Martin I was directing now at the Drury Lane was still not the Mary Martin I had directed in 1949." As Logan also pointed out, it's difficult for any star of a long-running show to suddenly be working with new costars, let alone an entirely different cast: "It pulls the plank from under them and they feel they're falling. It's one of the most painful and dangerous things in our theatre."

As Martin herself recalled, "Josh, the driving perfectionist, had made changes of places where I was to stand, to walk, to turn. After playing Nellie for two and a half years, I was finding it difficult to erase his previous directions and he could see this. I was growing very nervous and beginning to doubt that I would remember all the changes."

Broadway musical performer Walter Willison recalled having a long conversation about the London version of *South Pacific* with Logan, who told him, "When we were doing *South Pacific* in London, it was the day before the opening. We were doing a dress rehearsal and Mary was a mess. She couldn't do anything right. She was just awful. Her line readings were off. She was manic." Logan was dealing with "manic" issues of his own, more and more, at the time. Finally, Logan went to Martin's dressing room, where he found her hysterical and in tears. She told him, "Years ago, when I did Noël Coward's *Pacific 1860,* the critics just hated me." So even though *South Pacific* had been a huge hit in the States, she was terrified the London critics were going to hate her again.

"Josh didn't know what to say to her," continued Willison. "Everything she was doing was wrong. How could he comfort her? She was sobbing. She had been trying too hard. He said he didn't know where it came from, but he just heard this voice and told her: 'he who doubts from what he sees will never believe. . . . Do what you please. If the sun and moon should doubt, they'd immediately go out.'" Logan was quoting the eighteenth-century British poet and artist William Blake. "Then she just put her hands on her hips and said, 'Oh, thank you, Josh. And she hugged him. And they put on their coats to leave. And it was pouring rain, but everybody was lined up with their umbrellas, waiting to buy tickets for opening night. And she was so elated: she went and got coffee and donuts for everybody. And in the rain, with an umbrella, she stood there singing, 'I'm in Love with a Wonderful Guy' for everybody." Martin also commemorated the sage advice by making a pillow for Logan with the Blake quotation done in needlepoint.

After he finally arrived, a few days before the opening, Rodgers was "shocked" when he attended a dress rehearsal. His memories contrast sharply with Logan's. "Apparently tiring of his original concept, Josh had so deliberately altered and rearranged the show that it no longer held together." But as further recalled by Rodgers, Martin was crying crocodile tears to manipulate the circumstances. "At the conclusion of the rehearsal, Mary sent word that she wanted to see Josh, Oscar and me in her dressing room," claimed Rodgers. "We found her crying hysterically. Between sobs, she told us that if the show wasn't put back the way it was originally, she wasn't going to open in it. . . . Josh agreed to her demand. But Mary was still uncontrollable. She was sitting facing her dressing-room mirror and I happened to be standing in a spot where I was the only one who could see her reflection. It was barely perceptible, but as our eyes met in the mirror, Mary winked." This was one of the few occasions when Martin didn't recruit her husband to take on an unwelcome task for her, relying instead on her considerable acting talents to get what she wanted.

There were other problems beyond anyone's control. The musical opened at the Drury Lane on November 1, 1951, and that winter proved to be one of the most severe in memory. "I would come out of the shower . . . sing 'I'm in Love with a Wonderful Guy'—and my pants would freeze. When I finished, I had real ice on my dungarees and my dressing-room maid had to crack it off to get me out of them."

But opening night was everything that Martin could have hoped for, including—according to Larry Hagman—two dozen curtain calls, and backstage visits from Noël Coward and from the most highly revered British theater couple of all, Laurence Olivier and Vivien Leigh. "Show incredibly slow," Coward wrote in his diary. "Audience wildly hysterical. Mary had a great ovation which she richly deserved." They all attended the opening night party at the Savoy, where Martin danced with Olivier and her son danced with Leigh.

Following a prolonged illness, King George VI made his first public appearance in some weeks by attending a command performance with the rest of the royal family. He engaged the star afterward with a specific question about the relative size of the theaters in New York and London, asking how it affected Martin's performance and projection. He also acclaimed "A Wonderful Guy" one of the six greatest musical comedy numbers of all time. On that all-important night, Larry flubbed his single line, announcing Nellie's arrival, by "jumping" his cue—that is, giving it too early. "The actor playing the captain stared at me like I had lost my mind," recalled Larry. "He ad-libbed. 'Tell her to wait.' . . . Mother didn't say anything. Her laugh was sufficient."

After the king died, exactly a week later, Martin was approached by many a journalist seeking an interview: as the last American who had spoken to the king, she was much sought after. But in an overly modest mode, Martin refused to speak to any of her interrogators, saying, "I'm not important, and I'm not a public figure."

There was one interview Martin gave, however, before the London opening, with her American friend, Jinx Falkenburg, for Jinx's husband Tex McCrary's NBC show, *New York Close-Up.* Jinx claimed that the London opening night displayed the same "electricity" in the house as the New York opening had. "I remember Jinx saying to me, sitting in our bedroom at the Savoy, 'Wouldn't it be funny if the London critics didn't like it?'" recalled Martin.

What was intended as an ironic, throwaway remark proved prescient. Under titles such as *South Soporific,* the London reviews were mean-spirited put-downs of the musical's more serious-minded intentions, and an obvious backlash against the hype that heralded the show's arrival. "In America, *not* to have seen *South Pacific* is a social gaffe," began a three-page spread in *Picture Post,* with Martin scampering in her sailor suit from the "Honey Bun" number on the cover. "In England, advance bookings are very advanced. But many London critics, with slightly petulant integrity, declined to caper to the swelling tune of advance publicity. . . . The show was long-winded, ponderous. . . . It was not properly a musical (bare-chested Marines, but no scantily clad girls, little glamour, hardly any dancing)." Most critics took the high road, begrudging the "vast publicity campaign" that preceded the arrival of this "interloper," as best encapsulated by the response in the *Illustrated London News*: "For Mary Martin's sake, and for the Rodgers' songs, we welcome *South Pacific*; but we might have welcomed it twice as loudly if we had not been told, from New York, that it is four times as good as it is."

As Martin summarized the response: "Not one [British] critic liked it much except Kenneth Tynan, who didn't work for a daily but for a weekly." In his rave review, Tynan went so far as to attempt "to temper the innocence of some of my colleagues, who seem to have blamed the show for not living up to the inaccurate puffs it had received in their own newspapers." He also held Martin responsible for the "huge sob of delight" he felt in the theater: "Skipping and roaming round the stage on diminutive flat feet, she had poured her voice directly into that funnel to the heart which is sealed off from all but the rarest performers."

Only with the benefit of hindsight can one see that there was a reverse snobbism at work with the other critics. While American theater had come into its own in the 1940s—with one masterpiece after another by Tennessee Williams, Arthur Miller, Eugene O'Neill, and, yes, Rodgers and Hammerstein—the Brits resented losing their long-held superiority for all things pertaining to the stage. They were also on the verge of regaining their footing with what would become known as "kitchen sink" dramas, imbued with a gritty realism, which, rare for a musical, *South Pacific* also displayed.

As Martin characterized the British critics' responses (apart from Tynan's): "All the other reviewers found it sort of racist: 'What is this message of tolerance, what is your problem?' 'Doesn't everybody know this?' 'Why sing to us "You've got to be taught to hate"?'" The British reaction also reflected a more selfish, behind-the-scenes dilemma concerning America's involvement with the recently waged war in Korea: though the Yanks had belatedly joined the United Kingdom in combating Hitler during World War II, the Brits now had no interest in coming to their rescue in Asia.

In spite of the critics' lackluster response, Martin and company didn't have to apologize for their performances. *South Pacific* instantly became as popular a hit in London's West End as it had been on Broadway, selling out its run during the year that Martin remained with it. Scalpers were quickly selling one-pound tickets for ten times that amount. Columbia brought out a "45 R.P.M. Extended Play Record" of the original London cast, featuring excerpts of "Some Enchanted Evening," "Younger Than Springtime," "Bali Ha'i," and "Twin Soliloquies."

In December, Martin sent a handwritten letter, on Theatre Royal Drury

Lane stationery, to Hedda Hopper: "It's such fun to say Merry Christmas this way to you—because I always think of you as THEATRE—and this is really a very great wonderful THEATRE.... Heller is mad about the Sadler['s] Wells Ballet School and studies so hard and exercises so much we're sure she thinks she has to take Norma Shearer's place tomorrow!—We can't help but hope business will bring you to London—and—South Pacific—again—and us—always—love—Mary (Martin is the last name)!"

A special performance was held on May 6, 1952, to be captured on 16-millimeter film, as a "Photographic record of the London presentation . . . for library purposes only." Under the best of circumstances, any filmed version of a stage work turns a three-dimensional event into a static, two-dimensional affair. There was also no audience present, which necessarily throws all the players off of their game: without any reactions, there can be no interaction, and a "live" event automatically becomes canned and stilted—not to mention, in this relatively early case, primitive. Martin's command of her characterization—her utterly real realization of the quirky "knucklehead Nellie"—is nonetheless evident in every gesture and in every word she utters or sings.

Some months into the London run of *South Pacific,* Martin finished the needlepoint carpet she had been working on for nearly three years, which would forever after be called, simply, "The Rug." "And that was the [very] night that Noël Coward came backstage before the curtain went up to tell me Princess Margaret was in the audience and that he would bring her backstage after the performance," Martin would write in *Mary Martin's Needlepoint,* published in 1969. "During intermission, I arranged the champagne and glasses; after the final curtain, I rushed to the dressing room and carefully laid the rug in front of the door sill. We, The Rug and I, were ready. The door was swung open by Noël. Princess Margaret was about to enter when Noël looked down and said in his glorious, clipped, *audible* English voice, 'Oh, no!—Not that bloody rug again!' "

It was also well into the London run of *South Pacific* when a man named Tommy Connery auditioned at the Drury Lane for the British touring production. After he was cast as a Seabee, and before the show began its tour, Tommy changed his first name to Sean, and within a year of its tour, back in Edinburgh, Sean Connery was playing Lieutenant Buzz Adams, the featured role that Larry Hagman ultimately played in London.

Noël Coward attended Martin's final London performance as Nellie Forbush on November 8: "She gave a superb performance and had a terrific ovation," he wrote in his diary, adding, "she is a great artist." Martin had sealed her renewed friendship with Coward earlier in the year by performing in his cabaret act one Sunday in January at the Café de Paris, after several hours of rehearsal on a Friday afternoon. "Really a triumph—Mary was superb—tore the place up," Coward observed in his diary, on January 13. They enjoyed themselves enough to give a repeat performance the following November.

After Mary Martin conquered London as Nellie Forbush, a well-crafted survey of her life appeared in *Coronet* magazine, touching on by-then familiar topics: "Mary's spectacular career has its puzzling side in a profession where physical beauty is the accepted prerequisite to success. For she is not a beautiful woman," wrote Charlotte and Denis Plimmer. "Mary's figure, for all its grace, is more boyish than curvaceous. In Hollywood's lexicon, she's no 'sex-boat.' Her favorite role, that of Navy Nurse Nellie Forbush in *South Pacific,* delighted her because it demanded no siren gowns, no plunging necklines."

Though she never would have advertised or even admitted it at the time, Martin did not entirely enjoy herself after inhabiting Nellie Forbush for three years. "During the last months of the run," she told journalist Harry Evans four years later, "I was so fed up with that show—with everything about it—I thought I'd go into a spin. Every performance was torture, and I'd burst out crying if anyone gave me an angry look." She smiled, as she added, "Imagine being fed up with songs like 'A Wonderful Guy' and 'Some Enchanted Evening'!"

Shortly after Martin finished her run as Nellie Forbush in London, the Hallidays took a much-needed vacation, "on a slow boat to Jamaica," she wrote in a letter to Ray Walston, who played Luther Billis in the London *South Pacific* and then, later, in the film version. They sailed on the freighter *Corrales* from the London Docks on November 11, with the announcement that they would be returning to London "for six months' holiday," and that, "While her parents are away, Heller—a student at the Sadler's Wells Ballet School—will stay in London with her nanny."

From Jamaica, they flew to New York, for Martin's participation in yet another motion picture, her second since she had left Paramount in 1943: *Main Street to Broadway.* Directed by Tay Garnett and written by playwright Robert E. Sherwood, the film may have been intended to try to win back some of the audience that the theater had recently been losing to television. But it would do nothing to revitalize Martin's previously abandoned film career. (It was dismissed by British film scholar Leslie Halliwell as a "flat attempt to show the public how Broadway works.") It stars Tom Morton as Tony Monaco ("The Writer") and Mary Murphy as his girlfriend, Mary ("The Actress"). Tony is described as "the most promising young American dramatist"—even if the story is built around his difficulties writing a play "about wholesome America," for the decidedly unwholesome Tallulah Bankhead.

Beyond its lame plot and crude production values, *Main Street to Broadway* comes across as another *Stage Door Canteen*—though it has nothing to do with any particular war. In addition to Martin and Bankhead, it also features many Broadway figures playing themselves in cameo appearances, including Ethel and Lionel Barrymore, Shirley Booth, Rex Harrison and his wife Lilli Palmer, Helen Hayes, Henry Fonda, Louis Calhern, John Van Druten, Al Hirschfeld, Cornel Wilde, Joshua Logan, Agnes Mooorehead, Gertrude Berg, Leo Durocher, and Richard Rodgers and Oscar Hammerstein, whose song "There's Music in You" is featured throughout the picture.

With Rodgers at the piano, "songstress" Martin makes her first appearance singing the lilting number with Hammerstein at her side. She sports her short poodle haircut from *South Pacific* and is on for roughly half a minute. Martin gives a richer rendition of the song much later in the film, when she's on a stage, portraying a bridesmaid, singing to her sister, the bride, as Hirschfeld sketches the two of them. The play within the play, *Callico and Lust*, stars Bankhead and is directed by playwright John Van Druten. . . . "It's theater: it makes life endurable because it reaches people through their dreams"—a claim that actually describes movies more than works for the stage, via the unconscious impact of cinematic effects.

With Martin's work on *Main Street* completed, the Hallidays returned to their "small, most attractive flat" in London, where Heller had some more classes at Sadler's Wells. While Heller was studying ballet, her mother resumed voice lessons with coach Dino Borgioli, two days a week. "Borgioli raised her voice from a frail high C to a tentative E-flat that made the C come easy," explained a *Newsweek* article devoted to the "toast" of Broadway. The Hallidays ushered in the New Year with a party hosted by the Lunts at Noël Coward's studio. "They, the hosts, left early and I was left to carry on," Coward jotted down in his diary on December 31. "Vivien [Leigh] and Larry [Olivier] were sweet—so were Mary and Dick. Drank in the New Year."

Though Martin had a lot to toast, as she was stepping into a new year and the future with Nellie Forbush a permanent part of herself, the big question was what would come next for the international star, who had time and again surmounted one obstacle after the other.

Chapter 8

A NEW DIRECTION

*Mary is obviously the greatest star the musical
theatre has produced.*
—ALAN JAY LERNER

The possibility of playing Eliza Doolittle in *My Fair Lady*—arguably the greatest role Mary Martin would ever turn down—was in the air while Martin was appearing as Nellie Forbush in *South Pacific* in London. As documented in his diary on July 28, 1952, Noël Coward was approached to turn Martin into a singing Liza: "The Theatre Guild had offered me the dubious task of doing the music, book and lyrics of *Pygmalion* with Mary Martin. It is an interesting proposition, but I must read the play before deciding."

Rodgers and Hammerstein had already decided not to pursue a musical version of George Bernard Shaw's *Pygmalion* when upstarts Alan Jay Lerner and Frederick Loewe agreed to take the project on—but only if Martin would play their Liza. "Mary is obviously the greatest star the musical theatre has produced [and] I do feel anybody after Mary is second choice," Lerner wrote in a letter, dated May 10, 1952, to Gabriel Pascal, the Hungarian filmmaker who had made a film version of *Pygmalion* in 1938. "And the cockney she can do easily. From a show business point of view it would be a great tour-de-force for her. Then, too, Mary is the only one I know who has naturally that odd combination of the little girl and the great lady. I can't think of another part when both these qualities could be better employed—or on the other side, when Mary could run more of a gamut of all her talents. This is one play that should be written *for* her and *with* her."

Though the very notion of Mary Martin as Eliza Doolittle may be difficult to conjure today, Lerner's insights into her natural gifts lend the match a certain credibility. After first approaching the Hallidays in London with the idea for a musical version of *Pygmalion*, Lerner and Loewe performed five songs for them back in New York, two years later—only two of which made it into the final show: "The Ascot Gavotte" and "Just You Wait 'enry 'iggins." Given those relatively lackluster numbers—and with their more stunning songs for both *Brigadoon* and *Paint Your Wagon* in mind—Martin told her husband "those dear boys have lost their talent," and they decided to pass up the offer.

In view of Martin's landslide success as Nellie, the Hallidays had a great deal at stake in selecting Martin's next project. Whatever that might prove to be, a musical *Pygmalion* did not seem to them to be the ticket.

Also late in the London run of *South Pacific*, Joshua Logan came up with his own answer to the question that had been gnawing away at the Hallidays for three years: How could Martin ever top, or at least equal, such success with her next venture? Logan discovered a new play by theater veteran Norman Krasna called *Kind Sir*, about an actress in love with a foreign diplomat who pretends to be married in order to evade having to marry her. It presented what seemed a two-pronged break-through for Martin: Logan phoned Halliday in London and explained that since it was a nonmusical play, *Kind Sir* would emphasize Martin's abilities as an actress, even as the specific role could surmount her calcifying, Goody Two–shoes image as an innocent ingénue. When Halliday approached her with the idea, Martin said, "All right, Dick. Anything you and Josh say." (The decision was made shortly before going onstage to play Nellie Forbush for reportedly the "2,392nd" time—which is obviously a wild exaggeration.)

Logan did not tell the Hallidays that he and Krasna had already approached Joan Crawford with *Kind Sir*, who read for the part and then turned it down. (As Crawford told Logan and Krasna: "I just wanted to know whether or not I could do it, for my own satisfaction. I could never play a long run on the stage. I'd be bored to death. But thank you for letting me make the experiment.") They also had film star Charles Boyer lined up when Martin agreed to costar. Since Boyer had been a French matinee idol, everyone involved probably hoped to recapture the same onstage electricity Martin had enjoyed with Ezio Pinza playing a Frenchman in *South Pacific*.

Before beginning work on *Kind Sir*, the Hallidays left London for a European trip, in the winter of 1953, on yet another freighter—"our favorite way to travel," claimed Martin, given the seclusion for her to work on her latest obsession, a needlepoint of her husband's hand clasping her own. Though the Hallidays and Heller were the only passengers, they were "astonished" to discover that their every need was being taken care of. "Before the end of the day, we learned we were traveling with the head steward and stewardess of the Queen Mary," recalled Martin. "This was their way of spending their vacation. . . . 'If you'll be good enough to give us your trunk keys, we will unpack while you are having tea,'" James Harvey told the grateful Hallidays.

"I remember little else except their thoughtful service, days and nights of quiet, the calm seas and sunny skies, and sitting for hours in the sun concentrating on the tiny canvas with the silk threads," continued Martin. "We touched North Africa—very colorful, but something aboard ship was more colorful. We pulled up at two ports in Spain. Oh, yes, very colorful and very exciting. But it was more exciting to get back to the ship and finish Richard's fourth finger and to progress, perhaps, on that gloriously clear day to the white cuff at my wrist. . . .

"I worked for hours with my chair turned so that the sun poured over my left shoulder onto the canvas. . . . Heller said I frowned a great deal of the time and Richard claimed my eyes were growing smaller. Finally, when I wouldn't even stop long enough for tea, he declared, 'I've heard about compulsive drinkers, but a compulsive neeledpointer is something new!'"

As Martin also recalled of the trip: "Everywhere we stopped there was a transatlantic telephone call from [producer] Leland Hayward asking us, 'When will you be back? Will you do a TV show for me?' And we kept saying, 'No.'" In her memoir, Martin explained, "I had never done television [before] because I was so afraid it would be like Hollywood: 'Stand here, stand there, don't move.'" But as she also said, "You get a feeling of timing and response working before an audience in a theater that you never get in a television studio or on a movie set." Despite any misgivings, however, Martin could resist what was as inevitable as her future for only so long.

In 1950, 3.1 million American homes had a TV set. By 1955, there would be 32 million, confirming that baby boomers and television were coming of age at the same time. "If television and radio are to be used for the entertainment of all of the people all of the time," claimed Edward R. Murrow, the most highly regarded reporter and voice of the new medium, "we have come perilously close to discovering the real opiate of the people." Though still in its infancy, television was clearly having a dramatic impact on American life and culture—just as the automobile had during the previous fifty years. Whereas highways were built in the 1940s to transport military equipment from one army base to another, the television link between the East and West Coasts was only just completed in the fall of 1951. These two strains of influence on American life were about to come together, as it were, when the Ford Motor Company decided to celebrate its fiftieth anniversary with a "TV show which would evoke the spirit of the past half century and be the biggest and best entertainment in TV history." And Leland Hayward was given an unheard-of budget of $500,000 to make it happen.

Once he learned the Hallidays were stopping in Cuba on their way home to the States, the tenacious producer and his wife met up with the them in Havana, greeting the weary couple at the dock when their ship arrived. Hayward took them to dinner but waited a decent interval before describing the television special he had in mind. "As a matter of fact," Martin recalled, "I think Leland waited almost five or six hours before he brought up the subject of the Ford television show."

Hayward did not say that the special would look back at the invention of the airplane no less than the automobile, at fashion trends and the increasing importance of films, and at the Great Depression as well as Hitler's rise to power. The top agent turned producer rather made it sound like the entire focus would be on Martin. "I know how fond you are of [Ethel] Merman, and I've been thinking, wouldn't it be nice if Merman visited you on your show and sang one song with you?" said Hayward. "It would be great," replied Martin, "but you could never get her to do it." "I think she'd love to work with you," said Hayward, adding, "Of course, the whole show [would be] yours."

With *Kind Sir* scheduled for the fall, Martin agreed to participate in the TV extravaganza, which was to be performed and aired live— simultaneously on NBC and CBS—on June 15. In May, the Hallidays went to Texas, where they visited with Martin's sister in Fort Worth and with her childhood friend, Bessie Mae, in Dallas. Martin's lovable Honey Bun character in *South Pacific* finally received a tangible, real-world credential with a dinner at the Adolphous Hotel in Dallas honoring Martin with an admiralty appointment in the Texas Navy. The new admiral's attention quickly had to turn, however, to the upcoming *Ford 50th Anniversary Show*.

To touch upon seemingly every aspect of American history and culture during the first half of the twentieth century, Hayward recruited both lyricist Oscar Hammerstein and newsman Edward R. Murrow as coanchors/emcees. A new theater and ballet choreographer wunderkind, Jerome Robbins, was to be the director. In addition to Martin and Merman, other guests, beloved of the period, would include Frank Sinatra, Marian Anderson, Wally Cox, Rudy Vallee, Bing Crosby, Lowell Thomas, Amos and Andy, and Eddie Fisher. While declaring it, two decades later, "perhaps the most memorable Special of the era," the editors of Time-Life Books found the Broadway divas' twelve-minute duet "the show-stopper" of the two-hour "spectacular," adding: "For sheer theatrical excitement, nothing yet seen on television had matched their performance; suddenly it was clear that TV could be great entertainment." "The duet was destined to become show-business legend on its first hearing," claimed Merman biographer Brian Kellow. "Millions of homes across America were suddenly converted into nightclubs."

"It was Jerry [Robbins], who had never worked in this new medium, who had to make the unlikely duo into a team," according to Robbins's biographer, Amanda Vaill. Having rehearsed "our heads off ten, twelve hours a day," according to Martin, the two of them lip-synched to an early, static-ridden vaudeville recording of The Happiness Boys (Bill and Earnest) singing "Your Folks and My Folks," each performing in male drag with wide-striped jackets, baggy white pants, boaters, and canes. (Martin even sported a mustache.) After the earthy, animated Merman belted out "There's No Business Like Show Business" from *Annie Get Your Gun* and the more ethereal Martin sang her "A Wonderful Guy" number from *South Pacific,* the two of them perched on adjacent high stools and joined forces for a medley of thirty-one American standards. A highpoint was their combining "Tea for Two" with "Stormy Weather," finding harmonic agreement between seemingly disparate songs. While Martin regards Merman intently and fondly throughout their duet, such attention was not reciprocated by Merman, who performs "out front" to the camera and appears oblivious to Martin's presence.

"Both women were in superb voice," wrote Brian Kellow, who acknowledged that the duet "revealed to a wide audience [Ethel's] dislike of looking at her stage partners." "Spontaneous it may have seemed," observed Vaill, "but Jerry had scrutinized and buffed every detail, suggesting alternatives for some of the songs, marking passages where the tempo needed quickening, adding 'together bits' to keep the alternating solos from turning into a duel." Martin gave full credit to Robbins in her memoir, where she claimed "the genius of Jerry Robbins really made the show possible." (She would find a far more tangible way of repaying Robbins in the not-too-distant future.)

Though it was clearly the two Broadway divas who won America's heart, the forty-five-year-old Merman was confined to singing and dancing, while the thirty-nine-year-old Martin was given a wider range for displaying her talents. After being introduced by Leland Hayward, Oscar Hammerstein emerges from a black background to become the narrator

in Thornton Wilder's archetypal *Our Town* and, in turn, introduces
Martin as Emily. Though far too old for the part, Martin proved remarkably moving in the scene where Emily dies and chooses to relive her
twelfth birthday on earth. And, in what many would consider one of the
special's highlights, Martin got to show off her natural bent as a comedienne in "The Shape," a brilliant, self-contained segment depicting the
changing fashions decade by decade, as narrated by an authoritative,
disembodied voice. With little more than a simple black jersey "tube,"
period hats designed by stage and screen costumer Irene Sharaff, and her
marvelous facial expressions and beanbag body, Martin twists herself
now into a Gibson Girl, then into a twenties flapper, and finally into an
emancipated, bustling woman-about-town, with traffic noises blaring
and tempus fugiting.

According to Martin, it was only when they were well into rehearsals
that the two divas compared notes and discovered Leland Hayward had
played each of them against the other to secure their respective commitment to the project. "Apparently that so-and-so Hayward said the same
thing to Merman—'Wouldn't it be nice if Mary Martin sang one song
with you on TV, although of course it would be really your show'; for it
turned out later that we both had the same contract with him, but he
never would have gotten either of us if he hadn't hornswoggled us both
with his blarney. We didn't find this out until we began to rehearse.
One afternoon Merman asked me, 'What is your understanding with
Leland?' And I said, 'What is yours?' Then we both told each other and
we died laughing, for by that time we were having a ball."

But in spite of Martin's claim in her memoir that she and Merman
"from the beginning . . . got on like gangbusters," producer Lawrence
White recalled, "they hardly spoke to each other. Jerry [Robbins] and I
and Leland [Hayward] concocted a solution, because when it came to the
billing of these two women we had our problems. They both wanted
top billing of the whole show. [So] the advertisements in the papers for
the show had a big circle, and way on the top of the circle you'd have
Merman and Martin, so they [both] had top billing there."

While a new form of commercial advertising was the fuel that drove
television's growth and development, Neiman Marcus sold 44,500 repli-
cas of Martin's simple jersey dress within a month of the *Ford 50th Anniversary Show* broadcast. "Television, which already has brought about a
small revolution in the eating, sleeping, reading and movie-going habits of
the nation, would appear now to be invading the music field, long considered the personal property of radio's entrenched legion of disk jockeys,"

added the November 13 issue of *TV Guide,* during the publication's very first year. Decca Records had recently brought out a "direct off-the-tape recording" of the show, featuring Martin and Merman's duet, or "12 minutes of some of the most inspired popular music ever to hit the airwaves," and "available in all three speeds"—78, 45, and 33. Within a month, Decca sold 200,000 copies of the recording. "The added visual impact of TV can sell a new song just as effectively as it sells a sponsor's product," continued the article.

Soon after the Ford special, the Hallidays took a well-documented trip to Madrid for the grand opening of the first Hilton Hotel in Europe. Conrad Hilton chartered two planes for his American guests—including Gary Cooper, Merle Oberon, Kathryn Grayson, George Jessel, California Governor Earl Warren, and the Hallidays. As Hedda Hopper wrote about the inauguration of the Castellana Hilton, "Guests from all over the world attended the hotel opening; but Conrad Hilton, our movie stars, and Mary Martin stole the spotlight."

While touring Madrid with Tex and Jinx McCrary, the Hallidays were introduced to Luis Miguel Dominguín, considered the world's greatest bullfighter. "Mary was hesitant about going to a bullfight, but Dominguín offered to accompany the party to the arena and explain the subtleties of the bullfighter's art." As they observed a torero being gored, Martin's "varying reactions" and "climactic" dismay were captured by McCrary's camera and reproduced in *Look* magazine several years later, when the photos were about to appear in *Gates of Fear,* a book by Barnaby Conrad.

Martin sent Hedda Hopper a Western Union telegram on September 15:

I AM GLAD THAT BULL DIDN'T GET ME IN SPAIN COULDN'T BE HAPPIER THAT YOURE [*sic*] OUR PIGEON IN NEW ORLEANS. YOUR BEING THERE WILL ADD TO THE HAPPINESS AND EXCITEMENT WE ALL ARE HAVING HERE LOVE AND KISSES ALWAYS—MARY MARTIN.

The Hallidays' "pigeon in New Orleans" was testing the waters for them in that great Southern city. *Kind Sir,* Martin's next offering, was the first Broadway-bound show to ever try out in New Orleans, relatively near Joshua Logan's hometown, Texarkana. "The city was so in awe of *Kind Sir* and its stars that I was afraid the opening night audience could not relax enough to enjoy the play," Logan wrote in his memoir. "All the national magazines did cover our opening, and I was happy to lead the reporters and photographers all over the city for local color." Indeed, *Life* magazine ran a five-page photo spread, explaining, "For the gala opening both the town and the townspeople were all dolled up. Big signs told Logan he was welcome and pink satin programs were bestowed upon the entire audience."

Logan was not the only one apprehensive about the play's opening in New Orleans. Martin was so nervous about making her acting debut in a comedy—that is, a nonmusical play—that she had trouble sleeping during the rehearsal period. Hedda Hopper claimed she did all she could to "bolster her morale." According to Hopper, Martin "poured out her gratitutde in a telegram":

ONCE BEFORE ANOTHER GREAT WOMAN SOPHIE TUCKER HELPED ME IN MY VERY FIRST SHOW STOP NOW YOU BY SOME MIRACLE WERE SENT TO ME GOD BLESS YOU AND THANK YOU MY LOVE ALWAYS—MARY.

But Hopper was a true friend who didn't just tell Martin what she wanted to hear. As the Hallidays' "pigeon in New Orleans" eventually wrote, *Kind Sir* proved a "fiasco" and "for the birds—definitely not for Mary." As Hopper also reported: "In the seat next to me, Mainbocher, who'd done [Martin's] costumes, slid down almost out of sight so he wouldn't be asked to take a bow" at the New Orleans opening. In retrospect, Martin herself would declare *Kind Sir* a "disaster." But, as she further explained, "After *South Pacific,* I would have done anything with Josh Logan."

Signs of Logan's emotional imbalance during *South Pacific* quickly became more noticeable and debilitating as work commenced on *Kind Sir,* which was on a collision course with disaster from the get-go. "We never knew what Josh was going to say next, or how he was going to ask us to play our parts," said Dorothy Stickney, who played Martin's character's sister in *Kind Sir.* "So we really ended by having very little actual direction. Josh's suggestions were so erratic at times that we just had to do the best we could on our own."

Due to his bipolar condition, Logan was in and out of hospitals during the development of the production, and the play and the players lost their way with no one to guide them. Halliday was evidently less of a behind-the-scenes presence than usual—missing in action in New

Orleans; or, more likely, losing himself in the notorious gay bars of the French Quarter.

Groucho Marx, an old friend of the playwright, went to see the production in St. Louis, where Logan underwent one of several nervous breakdowns. "Although I have no memory of the next few days, I have been told that I made many telephone calls and eventually showed up at rehearsal in Cleveland," Logan later wrote.

On the road, *Kind Sir* then played at the National Theater in Washington, DC. But by the time the show arrived in New York, Logan was in a sanatorium near New Orleans.

Kind Sir opened on Broadway on November 4, 1953 (Heller's twelfth birthday) with a $700,000 advance—the highest ever for a play—but failed with the critics and with theatergoers. "[T]here is no doubt that *Kind Sir* isn't all that it should have been under the circumstances," claimed a cover story in *Newsweek,* with customary simplicity. "There is no disguising the fact that Norman Krasna's 'romantic farce' is no great shakes either as romance or as farce."

"My great idea of pairing Mary Martin and Charles Boyer in a light romantic comedy had backfired," admitted Logan. "The public came to see a combination of *South Pacific, Algiers* and *Mayerling.* With their appetites set for a juicy steak dinner, they had been served fish." Martin, however, fared much better than the play with the critics, including Walter Kerr, who wrote in the *Herald Tribune* that she was "incontestably dazzling" and who pronounced Mainbocher's costumes for her "breath-taking stuff." In the *New York Times,* Brooks Atkinson wrote, "It quickly becomes obvious that Miss Martin and Mr. Boyer have nothing but their own charm to work with." As the anonymous writer in *Newsweek* also wrote: "The evening, however, belongs to Mary Martin. The actress is given six stunning gowns by Main Bocher and a spot of humming at the piano for a few bars of 'Long, Long Ago'. . . . Jane Kimball is strictly Miss Martin's own creation, and she plays the part with dignity, assurance, a natural sense of timing, and a nostalgic hint of the cornfed girl who was Nellie Forbush. . . . With a little more experience she may well become one of the legitimate theater's first comediennes."

The reviewers' emphasis on Mainbocher's lavish costumes suggests that *Kind Sir* was as much a fashion show as a play, like those contained in many a women's movie of the period. As described in an issue of *Pageant* magazine, "they include[d] a chartreuse dressing gown with a bustle, a full length cloth of gold coat, a negligee made of pastel Indian saris, an imperial blue ballet length dress dotted with black velvet, an oyster white satin evening gown, a lipstick red wool travel outfit trimmed in mink, and a pearl gray wool afternoon dress."

Martin put it succinctly: "When they review the clothes, you know something is wrong with the show." But the focus on Martin's costumes may have contributed to her being declared one of the Best Dressed Women of 1953. As an article in the *Los Angeles Times* proclaimed on January 4: "Duchess of Windsor Nearly Slips Off List: She Ties for 10th Place with Mary Martin." Wallis Windsor's autobiography would be excerpted in a subsequent issue of *McCall's,* which also featured Martin posing in a dozen different getups borrowed from the collection of the Metropolitan Museum's Costume Institute, capturing the "last 55 years" of "looks." The extravagant spread was prompted by her recent *Shape* segment from the *Ford 50th Anniversary Show.*

Though there had been hopes for an extension, *Kind Sir* played only its limited run of 166 performances and closed on March 27, 1954. (Far more effective than the misguided play was the 1958 film based on it, *Indiscreet,* starring Ingrid Bergman and Cary Grant.) While she only sang a few token bars in *Kind Sir,* Martin sustained her love for music by taking piano lessons at the Julliard School in New York during the run of the play. Halliday arose every day between 6:00 and 7:00 A.M., and worked until midnight, looking after their Norwalk home and managing his wife's business affairs. "These last include judgments on Miss Martin's costumes and clothes, seeing that her fan mail is answered, and keeping their lives as uncomplicated as possible by lawyers, agents, and other folk."

But not all "folk": Martin's phenomenal television success with the *Ford 50th Anniversary Show* was rewarded when NBC offered to build her her own studio in Norwalk, guaranteeing her $500,000 for twenty-seven "spots" over an eighteen-month period. Even more telling of his wife's success, Halliday turned down the offer, holding out for a better financial arrangement. "The Hallidays have found that the fewer outside jobs Mary accepts, the greater is the demand for her services. 'Mary is full of exciting contradictions,' her husband concluded. 'She has the guts of a Texas steer and yet she's a delicate and feminine human being. I want to keep it that way.'"

Indeed, Mary Martin's next television appearance aired simultaneously on all four TV networks, CBS, NBC, ABC, and Dumont, the day after *Kind Sir* closed on Broadway. Less than a year after the *Ford 50th Anniversary Show,* General Foods followed suit by celebrating its twenty-fifth anniversary with a $250,000, ninety-minute special on March 28, 1954. "Mary Martin was an effortless charmer as mistress of ceremonies, actress, singer, dancer and keynoter," claimed a follow-up story in *Time* maga-zine, on April 5. While honoring General Foods, the special was as much a tribute to its unofficial sponsors—Rodgers and Hammerstein. With Jack Benny, Edgar Bergen, Ed Sullivan, and Groucho Marx helping to introduce the performers, Martin offered her most popular songs from *South Pacific* as well as "It's a Grand Night for Singing" and "It Might as Well Be Spring" from *State Fair,* John Raitt and Jan Clayton performed their love song from *Carousel,* and Tony Martin and Rosemary Clooney sang songs from *Me and Juliet. The King and I* was represented by Yul Brynner and Patricia Morrison, and *Oklahoma!* by Gordon MacRae and Florence Henderson.

Almost exactly a year later, Martin would offer the first of three TV productions of the most memorable creation of her life, *Peter Pan.* It was estimated that one out of every two Americans saw the original broadcast.

Chapter 9

"THE FIRST LADY OF TELEVISION"

Like Peter Pan, Mary flies untouched over the negative things in life.
—HEDDA HOPPER

At various times in her life, Mary Martin claimed that Peter Pan was her favorite role, essentially the part she was born to play. She had no way of knowing that, more than half a century later, it would remain the part for which she would be best remembered. The image of Mary Martin as Peter Pan—arms akimbo, strutting her stuff and "crowing"—has become as iconic as any other produced by and for American culture.

Peter Pan is significant for Mary Martin in another, less obvious respect: nowhere does Martin's self-identificiation with Jean Arthur seem more pronounced than with *Peter Pan*. Just as Arthur had arrived in Hollywood before Martin, she performed her stage version of the boy who wouldn't grow up prior to that of her doppelgänger. As Martin herself claimed about Arthur, "One of our bonds was that we both adored Peter Pan. [We] often were invited to costume parties; and Jean and I both always wanted to go as Peter Pan. It got so bad we would call each other up to declare our intentions—whoever called first got to go as Peter." (Like Eva Le Gallienne, who beat each of them to the part of Peter Pan, Arthur and Martin may have been lesbians who enjoyed cutting their hair short and playing a boy.)

"That was my happiest role and I think my finest acting," declared Jean Arthur, whose college colleague and lifelong friend, Nell Eurich, claimed, "That role changed [Jean's] life. . . . From then on, she began to wear her hair like Peter Pan, from then on she felt like Peter Pan. She lived that role." As Martin would ultimately tell a reporter for the *Los Angeles Times*: "It's the shortest I've ever worn [my hair]. There's only one more step I can take and that is to shave my head and sing the Yul Brynner role in *The King and I*."

The unbridled smile and irrepressible glow that Martin displays throughout all three broadcast versions of *Peter Pan* stems, in no small part, from her finally feeling like she's found herself as a boy, with a true boy's haircut and spirit. Though Annie Oakley and Nellie Forbush are close runners-up, never before did she feel—or seem—more in her element.

"According to Mother, *Peter Pan* is the most important thing she ever did in the theater," claimed Larry Hagman. "Never mind [that] it was a hit or audiences smiled through the whole thing. For her it was a role that allowed her to play herself. Mother was someone who had dared to follow her dreams from Weatherford to stardom; she followed her heart; she refused to see any limitations. I figured that's as close to flying as humans get. In spirit, she really was Peter Pan."

James Barrie's classic tale of a boy's perpetual youth may have been geared toward children—with pirates and Indians, no less—but its ultimate message suggests that eternal youth is only a frame of mind, regardless of one's age. Throughout the decades, there has been a long list of famous leading ladies who have played Peter, including Gladys Cooper, Elsa Lanchester, Margaret Lockwood, Marilyn Miller, Maude Adams, Eva Le Gallienne, and Mia Farrow. "The role, although that of a boy, traditionally is feminine," explained *New York Times* journalist Gladwin Hill, "the tradition stemming from Barrie's feeling that only a woman could give it the requisite gentleness and sensitivity." In addition to declaring Betty Bronson in the 1924 silent film a major influence on her life, Martin would also claim that the first time she saw *Peter Pan* on stage was when she was in London with *Pacific 1860,* in an otherwise forgettable version starring Mary Morris and Alastair Sim (the latter of *A Christmas Carol* fame).

Though Jean Arthur introduced her Peter Pan to Broadway in 1950—four years before Martin—there would be major differences with their respective versions beyond mere chronology. Arthur's *Pan* featured a Leonard Bernstein score of mostly incidental music—as well as Boris Karloff as Captain Hook—and Arthur didn't sing a note. Indeed, copyright arrangements with the Barrie estate required that Arthur's *Peter Pan* be considered a play as opposed to a musical. Martin's musical would introduce a number of standards beloved for generations to come: "Never-Never Land," "I Won't Grow Up," "I'm Flying," "I've Gotta Crow."

Arthur's version was a highly regarded hit, offering 321 performances at the Imperial Theatre. Even Martin claimed, "I hate to admit it but she *is* Peter Pan." (Ironically, one critic responded that Arthur was "looking and sounding pleasantly like Mary Martin"—several years before Martin undertook the part.) But Martin's version would surpass it in practically every other respect, to become, inarguably, the most memorable performance of Mary Martin's life and career, and—especially thanks to several TV productions—the one for which she would be most remembered by posterity.

According to Jean Arthur biographer John Oller, the producer of Arthur's *Pan*, Peter Lawrence, planned to approach Martin first, but Martin had just opened in *South Pacific*, and her "handlers ... professed non-interest on her behalf, smugly assuming that the young producer [Lawrence] would never get his project off the ground. Lawrence nevertheless knew that 'Mary Martin was *dying* to do it.'"

Martin had to wait more than a decade for her Peter to soar in one theater or another. As early as 1944—during the run of *One Touch of Venus*—the Hallidays had approached Kurt Weill to compose a score based on the Barrie play. Though Weill considered taking on the assignment, the Disney cartoon version suddenly intervened. The Hallidays also discussed the possibility with Rodgers and Hammerstein during their early *South Pacific* days, only to learn that the rights were already taken by Lawrence. (Assuming his wife's voice in a letter he wrote in 1970, Halliday claimed: "Rodgers and Hammerstein were going to produce it with Ezio Pinza as Captain Hook and myself for special matinees during the run of *South Pacific*—but we couldn't clear the rights.")

By the time *Peter Pan* emerged for Martin in 1954, she had turned down another project, *Fanny*, which had already been cast with Martin's erstwhile costar, Ezio Pinza. Like *South Pacific*, *Fanny* was being directed by Joshua Logan and, after *Kind Sir*, Martin was unwilling to have anything further to do with his difficult mood swings.

The Hallidays were also, at the time, considering another new musical intended for Martin, based on *Friendly Persuasion*, a popular, 1945 collection of stories by Jessamyn West about a Quaker family. Tentatively titled *Eliza*, the musical was being put together by the new, first-class theatrical team of Charles Laughton (a performer) and Paul Gregory (a producer), who had already toured with their critically acclaimed stage versions of *Don Juan in Hell* and *John Brown's Body*, and brought *The Caine Mutiny Court Martial* to the Plymouth Theatre just as *Kind Sir* was closing on Broadway. Though *Friendly Persuasion* would emerge three years later as a heartwarming film starring Gary Cooper and Dorothy McGuire, the musical version evaporated as mysteriously as the lifestyle it depicted. After befriending and eventually marrying Janet Gaynor, Paul Gregory would nonetheless become a close friend of the Hallidays, beginning a decade later.

Martin was also intrigued by another simmering concept: to star as one of her idols, Laurette Taylor, in a stage adaptation of the great actress's life. Martin's interest in Taylor had recently been reignited by the arrival of a bestselling biography written by Taylor's daughter, Marguerite Courtney. When it was in manuscript form, Courtney had presented it to the Hallidays, her friends, for their advice. At the time, film studios were bidding on the property, and there was even talk of a Broadway show to star Martin—a notion that would lead, in a decade, to her biggest Broadway musical flop, *Jennie*.

The most beloved of all Peter Pans really began to coalesce in the fall of 1953, when Edwin Lester, the director of the Los Angeles and San Francisco Civic Light Opera, invited Martin to do a new musical version, with Halliday and Leland Hayward as coproducers. The Hallidays were invited to choose their own creative team. After her recent success with Jerome Robbins on the *Ford 50th Anniversary Show,* Martin was eager to work with the young theatrical genius again, and Robbins was equally keen to make his debut as a musical book director. (Robbins was, at the time, the prestigious choreographer of eight Broadway shows.) But finding songwriters proved more of a challenge, and the Hallidays only partially came up with a solution by selecting a lyricist first.

"Richard and I discovered Carolyn Leigh one night while driving home and listening to the radio," recalled Martin. "We heard a beautiful song called 'Young at Heart' and I said, 'That's the person to be a part of *Peter Pan.*'" The lyrics' principal conceit—that youth is a frame of mind or an attitude as much as it is chronology—perfectly encapsulated one of Barrie's messages.

Though the song's composer was Johnny Richards, Leigh was now working with an unknown musician, Morris (aka "Mark") Charlap, nicknamed "Moose." Like Martin and Leigh, Charlap embraced an innocent, positive approach to life. And here, at the beginning of his relatively brief career and near the end of his unsung life (Charlap was severely diabetic), he wrote three of *Peter Pan*'s most enduring songs with Leigh, which perfectly captured Peter's spirit: "I'm Flying," "I've Gotta Crow," and "I Won't Grow Up."

Though they chose their director and songwriters, the Hallidays had to cede casting choices to Robbins. This presented an immediate dilemma when Martin wanted Heller to play Wendy to her Peter. At the time, Martin had pet names for her daughter: "Madam-Queen" and "La Belle." And whether Martin was aware of it or not, she wanted to keep Heller as close to her as possible while she remained true to her first love: her work.

But even though Heller later revealed she had been rehearsing the part of Wendy in Norwalk, Connecticut, Jerome Robbins was seriously opposed to having her play such an important part in the show, on the grounds of nepotism. "Jerry had a fit," recalled Robbins's assistant, Mary Hunter. "It's inartistic, it's a rotten idea," exclaimed Robbins. When Hunter emphasized that Martin would make his life miserable if Robbins failed to use Heller, a compromise was found by casting her in the smaller part of Liza, the Darling family maid. (Having performed with her mother when she was only six years old in *Annie Get Your Gun,* the twelve-year-old Heller would still be assuming a more prominent role in *Peter Pan.*) To compensate for time away from home, Heller was enrolled in the Professional Children's School in New York, designed to accommodate young stage performers and their peripatetic schedules.

"*Peter Pan* was my first chance to sing—and dance—with Mummy," recalled Heller, less than a decade later, about a role that was enhanced to allow her to have such an opportunity with her mother. "We did the reprise, 'I Gotta Crow,' in which we both crowed like roosters in spring. . . . Just before *Peter Pan* opened in San Francisco, our director, Jerome Robbins, thought that I was ready to do a ballet. He asked Mummy and Daddy, who produced the show, if they agreed. They were both delighted."

Martin would also take credit for suggesting the elegant yet versatile Australian actor Cyril Ritchard as Captain Hook. "I had seen him perform only once, in a Restoration comedy with his wife, Madge Elliott, and with John Gielgud, who also directed," recalled Martin, "but I had never forgotten his perfect timing, his presence. He would be the ultimate Hook, and he was."

The classically trained Margalo Gillmore was cast as Mrs. Darling, lending an air of maturity and sophistication to the otherwise phantasmagoric and "panto"-like production. Though also a youngster, Kathleen Nolan was already a veteran of live TV drama when she was given the part of Wendy, the crucial figure who connects the grounded Victorian world of the Darling household to the fantasy realm of Never Land—not to mention the children to the adults. (Nolan would become better known three years later, as Kate in TV's *The Real McCoys.*) And there were at least two carryovers from the Jean Arthur version: Joe E. Marks as Smee, Hook's right hand (so to speak), and Norman Shelley as the lovable Darling sheepdog, Nana.

Having already worked with her in *High Button Shoes,* Robbins was so taken with the energetic and naturally comic Sondra Lee that he included her in the cast roster before he even knew what role she would play. With eyes as big as her personality, Lee became one of Peter's Lost Boys, but her irrepressible exuberance and her unique presence made Lee a natural to eventually take on the more unique and substantial role of Tiger Lily.

After the first of several auditions, at the Musicians Union Hall in Hollywood, "I was eliminated because I was too tall," recalled Joan Tewkesbury. But given her height, Tewkesbury was called back and cast as the Ostrich. She also doubled as one of the Indians. (Tewkesbury, who was eighteen years old at the time, would, two decades later, write the screenplay for Robert Altman's masterful film *Nashville.*)

"We had a few weeks of rehearsals just on the dance numbers, before Mary came," continued Tewkesbury. "After things had sort of gotten started, Mary came with Heller and Richard. And she was amazing, because she was a true force of nature. And Heller was this wonderfully ironic kid. Jerry devised having the Ostrich, the Kangaroo, and the Lion as a way that Liza could come to Never Land, too, and dance with the animals."

Tewkesbury recalls the Hallidays' arrival for rehearsals as an "entourage" suddenly descending on the company. "They were dressed beautifully. They were very East Coast. Looking back, you would say Cole Porter made the whole thing up: Mary had a glorious crushed beaver coat that was blonde. She was a dame. She was a real presence. Richard was elegant, in that East Coast, European, well-moneyed way: very smart. . . . Everything just sort of rolled off the tip of his tongue. [But given Richard's effeminacy,] you wondered how Heller had gotten here."

The Halliday trio had arrived by train in Los Angeles on June 16 to begin rehearsals. "The Texas-born singer-actress has been away from Hollywood for six years," ran a story in the *Los Angeles Times*. "And it was evident yesterday as she stepped off the Santa Fe Super Chief that there have been some changes. Mainly—her hair. It's carrot-colored. And butched. . . . 'Had it done in the corner barbershop back in New Canaan,' she said."

"When I first saw [Mary Martin], she had stockier legs—too stocky for someone who was going to be playing Peter Pan," recalled Sondra Lee. "Somebody had said, 'Well, you know, she's diabetic.' Then when rehearsals began, she got thinner and more lithe, and spunkier. Also her costumes were changed. They were much simpler at the beginning, and then they became creatively wonderful. They were more subtle: different shades of green . . . the suede was a better quality . . . little beads here, and they were glorious costume designs that evolved.

"The truth is, I loved Mary's voice as a singer," continued Lee. "The force of her voice was to be reckoned with: it could *part* your hair, and it happened to me; but not as an actor. Mary's speaking voice, her acting voice, didn't have as much truth in it as a seasoned actor could or should have.

"I think her Peter was a lot 'cuter' than it had to be: that's because she was far more at home in her musical numbers. But she rehearsed until she knew what she was doing; and she had energy up the wazoo. And she was always ready to work. Her work was always a positive approach to whatever she was told."

Lee also recalled that a youngster named Paul Taylor (the future famed choreographer) was in the ensemble: "But he broke his nose during rehearsals, and they had to let him go during previews in San Francisco."

The decision to telecast the show live on NBC's *Producers' Showcase* was made during the rehearsal period, while Robbins—who cobbled the musical's book together from previous versions of the story—was engaged in fast and furious changes to every aspect of the production. This added a huge gravitas, if not *gravity*, to the show's potential. Though the larger-than-life Martin was innately opposed to being reduced to a tiny moving image on a TV screen, her unbounded adoration for Peter Pan would transcend the medium's inherent limitations, even as it became her most permanent role.

A week into rehearsals, Martin's biggest fan, Hedda Hopper, gave an all-star dinner for her favorite performer. As reported in Hopper's column on June 23, the other "billion dollars' worth of talent," or guests, included Lana Turner, Liz Taylor (with Michael Wilding), Jennifer Jones, Jean Simmons, Joan Crawford, Ethel Merman, Clifton Webb, the Bob Taylors, Dick Rodgers, and Cole Porter.

"At evening's end, Mary said, 'This is the first party I've been to in years when nobdoy asked me to sing a single number.'" As Hopper also related, "the only singing voice we heard the whole evening came from a non-musical actor who wasn't present. Walt Disney just happened to have a recording of Kirk Douglas singing 'A Whale of a Tale' from his *20,000 Leagues Under the Sea*, so he brought it out and we listened. When it was over, Mary said, 'That's one of the sexiest voices I've ever heard.'"

The single most stunning aspect of Martin's *Peter Pan* was to be the extent of the flying it entailed, as overseen by Peter Foy, an aerial specialist who was imported from England. "No Peter Pan had ever flown very far—just through the window of the stage set, over to the mantelpiece, around the room, and back out the window," recalled Martin. "I was determined, instead, to fly all over the place. I wanted to fly at least sixty feet across the stage, up to the top of the wings in the back of the theater, in and out the window, everywhere. I also wanted a flying ballet with Peter and the children, Wendy, Michael, and John, all sailing around together." Indeed, the most magical moment in the show arrives in the first act, when Wendy, Michael, and John join Peter aloft in the Darling nursery, before taking off into the nighttime sky for Never Land. Martin told a reporter, "There may have been Peter Pans who could fly better than I but there was never one who enjoyed it more."

As Martin further explained, there was no secret to the technical aspects of the flying achievement or the apparatus it involved: "It was all piano wires, harnesses, ropes, and expert rope-pullers. I was hooked to a very strong piano wire which was attached to a harness that went around my waist, over my shoulders, through my legs." In one of her many unbridled statements, Martin went on to declare, "I discovered I was happier in the air than on the ground. I probably always will be." Martin was forty years old when she first played Peter, yet her indomitable attitude toward the challenge of flying would stay with her for at least two more decades.

"There was no real rigging until we got to San Francisco," recalled Joan Tewkesbury. "And when we moved into the theater, I became the flying understudy. I was the same height and the same body type. Mary was a little smaller, but in terms of where we carried our weight, it was in our butts."

Though Martin had utter confidence in the wire that held her aloft, there was one time when it failed her, during a tryout in San Francisco. She was abruptly dropped thirty feet, and just as suddenly snapped back up again. "I was stunned and dangling," recalled Martin. "The audience thought it was all part of the show. The stage manager closed the curtains quickly and made an annoucement about 'technical difficulties,' and there was a slight delay while they got the technical difficulty—me—safely back to earth."

Heller would recall a problem with her own wiring during a performance. "Just before the ballet started, the kangaroo, who was on stage, was supposed to disconnect the wire [from me]. But he couldn't get it off. 'Come off stage—quick!' whispered the stage manager from the wings. Meanwhile, Mummy, as Peter Pan, was lying on stage, supposedly asleep. The decision whether to go off stage was mine. I either had to do the dance as it was choreographed—with the wire on my back—or lose my big chance. I decided to go on with the dance and, fortunately, it went perfectly. Later I learned that Mummy had one eye open all the time, and saw the whole thing. 'Heller, I almost dropped dead!' she exclaimed. 'But I was proud of you!'"

Joan Tewkesbury remembers a dress rehearsal when Heller peeked through the curtain, before going on: "All of Richard's 'friends' came and sat in the second row, and Heller said, 'My "uncles" are here tonight.' Billy [Sumner], said, 'Yeah. . . . Right.' We got the picture, at that point. But they were charming and darling, and they loved her. Oh my god, she was taken care of by those fellows."

"In San Francisco, every day there would be a different version of the [Indians'] dance, because that was the one thing Jerry could futz with," continued Tewkesbury. "We had 11,000 different versions of the ["Ugg-a-Wugg"] dance. Invariably, someone every night would be over here doing version twenty-five, and you'd have to pull him back in."

Another memory of Tewkesbury's suggests just how makeshift the first version of *Peter Pan* was: "Richard [Halliday] thought the Ostrich costume was too heavy, so he went out and bought a *bazillion* dollars worth of ostrich plumes, and kept sticking them in the back. It was made from a rug. We were all in these very tall headdresses."

The Lyric Opera production of *Peter Pan* opened on July 19, 1954, at San Francisco's Curran Theatre, which was a tiny "jewel box" space. The cast went to Robbins's apartment that night, waiting for the papers to come out. As characterized by Bruce K. Hanson in *The Peter Pan Chronicles,* his in-depth history of the Barrie story in its many incarnations, the reviews were "polite" but not altogether positive. The *Variety* critic, as if speaking for all of them, pinpointed the major problem: "The entertainment lies chiefly in the handling of the ensembles and choruses and the occasional ballets. As a consequence, the point of interest is Captain Hook, rather than Peter Pan, and Miss Martin is in the rather curious position of functioning as a subordinate player, while Ritchard emerges as the star of the performance." The *Variety* critic further emphasized the vacancy of Martin's role by playing up Lee's contribution: "In the dance department, Miss Lee has no difficulty establishing herself as an important factor. She has a keen sense of timing and a shrewd method of establishing audience relationships."

Though Martin contractually had the right to close the show out-of-town and avoid the attention—and disgrace—that a Broadway run could bring, she had come too far to relinquish her lifelong dream to play Peter Pan on the Great White Way. But the road to Broadway is often paved with rocky terrain, and Martin's *Peter Pan* required a major overhaul before arriving there. Songs were dropped, altered, added, and Halliday had the onerous task of telling someone if their number was being deleted. Although Sondra Lee predicted it, Tewkesbury and others were shocked when Tiger Lily's showstopping "Wild Indians" was eliminated. "Sondra was always nervous about it from the very beginning," recalled Tewkesbury. "She said, 'If anything goes, this is what's gonna go.' We all said, 'Are you nuts?' Because of course we were naïve and we didn't know."

"When a show revolves around a star, that star has to be protected," said Sondra Lee, with her no-nonsense attitude. "What I did learn was that Cyril was the best protected, because in his contract, it said if they removed something they had to replace it with something: 'Oh You Mysterious Lady' and all those sort of campy and sentimental songs, not subtext songs. . . . I was too naïve to know any of the bullshit then," added Lee, "but I was having the time of my life."

Lee also remembered being called into Martin's dressing room, without any explanation. "In San Francisco, after the reviews came out—and they were extremely flattering for Cyril and for me—I got the message that Miss Martin would like to see me in her dressing room. Her light-skinned, delicately freckled dresser [Gladys Hardwick] was there. And for some reason, Mary was seated facing the dressing table, and I remember her dressing gown was open, and it was shocking to me.

"I had no idea why I was asked," continued Lee, "but I think she murmured something about my being 'precious,' and how happy she was that I was so wonderful in the show. But I didn't know what the hell I was doing there, or what it was all about. As enigmatic as Mary was to me, my success in the show was enigmatic to her. I can't say she was evil or angry. But it was definitely a thorn of some kind [in her side]."

According to Lee, though Halliday was a continual presence, she never saw him arrive or leave with Martin, nor did she ever observe him in the wings. "Jerry would have killed him," said Lee. "He would have had him barred from the theater. But Richard and Edwin Lester were always screaming and yelling in the lobby. They had knock-down, drag-out fights.

"We used to say, Richard Halliday was missing just one thing," continued Lee, "a pair of very high heels. He was like a runway model. He had that gait. He was very tall and very lean. And when we were mean kids, we'd look in the trash bin at the end of the night to see how many [liquor] bottles were there." This is one of the early indications that Halliday's alcoholism was becoming an obvious and notorious problem.

"The thing about Mary and Richard was they were good friends," said Joan Tewkesbury. "They were in mischief together, in business together. They were bonded like you only bond with another human being, out of respect. The person that was really Mary's rock was her maid, Gladys. Gladys had been through a lot, and she knew every corner of Mary's life."

The sympathetic, no-nonsense Gladys Hardwick, Martin's dressing-room attendant, had already served as Vivien Leigh's and Ruth Gordon's dresser, and along the line worked with Ethel Merman, Geraldine Page, and Florence Henderson as well, before her death in February 1970.

Looking back, Kathleen Nolan succinctly summarized the problem with the first, San Francisco version of Martin's *Peter Pan*: "If you have a vehicle for Mary Martin and Mary Martin is not getting all the reviews, then something is wrong and it has to be fixed." In her memoir, Martin conveniently omits any reference to this demoralizing development in the genesis of *Peter Pan*. As she would tell journalist Elliott Sirkin about her attitude in general, "If it was an unpleasant experience, I don't remember it."

With the evident need to "fix" *Peter Pan* to make it more of a showcase for its star, Halliday and Lester brought in Betty Comden and Adolph Green, the winning lyricist/libretto team who had already written *On the Town, Two on the Aisle,* and *Wonderful Town.* For fresh songs they also called upon composer Jule Styne, who had previously collaborated with Robbins, the choreographer of *High Button Shoes,* and had, five years earlier, written one of his most delightful scores for *Gentlemen Prefer Blondes.*

According to Comden, they thought they were going to have to close the show. But as Green recalled, "They wanted to see if we had any ideas and we all told Jerry [Robbins] afterward that the show could be saved. He got very excited and so did Mary Martin and we went to work on it."

While retaining a number of the original songs by Charlap and Leigh, the new songwriting trio had eight days before the show was to arrive in Los Angeles, and they wrote as many songs as there were days, including "Never Land," "Mysterious Lady," and "Ugg-a-Wugg." "Comden and

Green took the subtext to the true story of Peter Pan and put it into a Broadway vernacular," explained Sondra Lee. While the creators were still tinkering with the score when it opened in Los Angeles on August 16, 1954, the reviews reflected the degree to which the focus became more on Martin and her Peter. "Miss Martin's *Peter Pan* is one of the great events of theatredom and, as such, should be seen," wrote Milton Luban in the *Los Angeles Times*. "She creates an elfin atmosphere of childlike gaiety that is contagious and is almost certain to make a box office hit of the show both here and in New York." Dick Williams concurred in the *Mirror*: "Mary Martin, America's first lady of musical comedy, returned triumphantly to Los Angeles last night at Philharmonic Auditorium. First-nighters gave her a walloping ovation at the end of the performance. It is clear that she has an immense amount of fun with the role. It is equally evident that she enjoys having her cute daughter, Heller, cavorting about with her as the housemaid, Liza."

During the run in Los Angeles, Hedda Hopper visited Martin in her dressing room and read a telegram from Larry Hagman, informing his mother that he had met a Swedish girl and wanted to marry her. "Mary didn't know the girl or anything about her," reported Hopper. "Whom Larry married must have been a matter of deep concern and understandable anxiety to her. But she scribbled her answer: 'Dick and I didn't ask anyone. Love told us. Of course you have our blessing. Love and congratulations to you both. MOMMY.'"

Hagman had already dated the voluptuous Joan Collins—Ted Flicker's classmate at London's Royal Academy of Dramatic Arts—by the time he met Maj Axelsson. Maj, a clothing designer, was three years older than the twenty-two-year-old Larry. According to Hagman, "Maj had serious reservations about getting involved with a guy from a show business family." But in his memoir, Hagman proceeded to describe any hesitancy to his proposal of marriage as amounting to Maj's silence, for a matter of minutes, before she accepted. Larry Hagman and Maj Axelsson were married on December 8, 1955. Hagman claimed that "Mother"—not "Richard and Mother"—gave them an Austin-Healey as a wedding present.

By this point, Hagman had been conscripted in the US Air Force and stationed in London. According to Hagman's close friend Ted Flicker, "he married Maj because she is very shrewd—peasant shrewd. She perceived immediately what Larry needed: a mommy. She took care of Larry. She did everything for him. She made sure he felt loved and cared for. She cooked for him, and sewed his clothes.... She became the mother he never had."

Though probably apocryphal, one of the more delightful theatrical anecdotes concerning Mary Martin claims that she sent Ezio Pinza a telegram on his opening night in *Fanny*, saying: "I hope your *Fanny* is as big as my *Peter*." *Fanny* had opened two weeks after *Peter Pan*'s first Broadway flight at the Winter Garden Theater on October 20, 1954. The reviewers were rapturuous in their response to Martin, and none more so than Walter Kerr. "I don't know what all the fuss is about," began a coy Kerr from his perch at the *Herald Tribune*. "I always knew Mary Martin could fly.... Miss Martin and her musical-comedy version of 'Peter Pan' are sky-high with joy.... It's the way 'Peter Pan' always should have been, and wasn't."

In the *New York Post*, Richard Watts Jr. found it "a considerable improvement" over the Barrie original. "[The] chief virtue of the production is its air of high spirits that keeps away the curse of excessive sentimentality." While pointing out in the *Daily News* that Martin's daughter "has a nice little song-and-dance turn with her mother," John Chapman added that Martin "somehow manages to look at least as young as Heller." Brooks Atkinson got to the heart of the matter in the all-important *New York Times*: "If Mary Martin is satisfied, so are the folks out front. A lot of the exuberance of Texas has stolen into the legend now." *Time* magazine claimed that Martin "looks as boyish as can be expected of any grownup of the opposite sex. She is hard to beat at singing, she can dance, she can duel with Captain Hook; and when she flies through the air, she races and soars and dips like some Peter Pan-American."

"I'm one of the ones who did see Maude Adams in *Peter Pan*," John Chapman would also claim, a year later, in a radio interview. "I came to the conclusion . . . that Miss Martin was the best Peter Pan I have seen. There was more of a youthful, boyish, quality to Mary. She was really a real boy. As I recall, Miss Adams always was the lady. She was the great star, and so on, and she was this distant lady, and some of that perhaps made her performance a little more distant."

Though it would be nearly three decades before she would be able to see what he had to say, perhaps Martin's most significant critic was Noël Coward. After attending the show, Coward wrote in his diary on December 1, 1954: "Except for moments in the first act it had little to do with the original. [Mary] was wonderful and whenever she had Barrie's lines to speak there was a 'true' quality. Her flying was miraculous."

British musical creator Sandy Wilson (*The Boy Friend*) wrote in a letter that he saw Martin in *Peter Pan*—"a play I have always loathed. . . . Well, I was quite bowled over by her performance. I had seen her in Noël C[oward]'s dreadful 'Pacific 1860' at Drury Lane, and later in 'South Pacific' at the same theatre, and she impressed me as being enormously efficient and talented, but she didn't move me at all. But in 'Peter' she did, very much, and when I went round to meet her, I liked her instantly and we got on very well." Wilson did not, however, particularly like Halliday, "whom I didn't care for so much: he seemed rather bogus." While the show was running on Broadway, the *Los Angeles Times* named Martin Woman of the Year, adding that it was in and of "itself a special honor for one whose home base is 3,000 miles from Los Angeles."

Shortly after the Broadway opening, Robbins described some nearly harrowing accidents at different performances, in the December 11 issue of the *New Yorker*. "There's a projector just behind the top of the proscenium arch that throws the light that represents Tinker Bell . . . and one time the lens fell off, and missed Mary by a foot. Another time, it damned near eliminated Cathy Nolan."

There was a mishap of another sort when Moss Hart and Edna Ferber—longtime playwriting collaborators, who happened to be in the midst of a feud—simultaneously showed up in Martin's dressing room following a matinee. "After the show Martin received children of friends backstage where, still in her Peter Pan costume, she would sprinkle fairy dust on them at close range," wrote Hart biographer, Steven Bach. "Moss and [his five-year-old daughter] Cathy arrived at her dressing room just as Ferber [and her five-year-old grandniece] Julie did. The grown-ups ignored each other so ostentatiously that the children couldn't help but be puzzled by the chill in the air. 'Who is that, Daddy?' Cathy asked, nodding in Ferber's direction. 'That, my dear,' Moss replied, 'is Captain Hook.' "

Mary Martin won her third Tony Award for Best Actress for *Peter Pan*, and Cyril Ritchard won for Supporting Actor. Though 1955 was the last year that the Tony Awards failed to include any nominees in their roster, other potential candidates that year included Julie Andrews in *The Boy Friend*, Florence Henderson in *Fanny*, Pearl Bailey in *House of Flowers*, Hildegardd Knof in *Silk Stockings*, and—probably Martin's stiffest competition—Gwen Verdon in *Damn Yankees*.

Peter Pan ran for only nineteen weeks on Broadway, but it realized a profit by having presold the television rights. The broadcast version of

Peter Pan on Monday, March 7, 1955, at 7:30, presented itself as the first Broadway show to sidestep the more customary path of a road tour and appear directly on television. Sponsored by both Ford and RCA, it was produced by NBC's *Producer's Showcase* at a cost of $450,000, and anticipated forty million viewers. But it reportedly reached sixty-five million and appeared in half of all American households, making it "the most popular single program ever to have been televised." (It also garnered Martin an Emmy Award.) Even in a primitive kinescope recording of the live production, one can see why it was so successful. While Martin truly looks and moves like a boy who was recently hatched by some glorious bird with spindly legs, her joyous performance knows no bounds, appealing to viewers of all ages. Far beyond the imaginings of his Victorian creator, James Barrie, Peter has been magically and literally captured for all time, never to grow any older.

Following the production and some live commercials for Ford and for RCA original cast albums—including *Peter Pan,* priced at $4.98—Martin returned on camera, in costume, to share her gratitude for the event, before "crowing" again for the viewers and taking off into the nebulae of the show's credits, as it were: "Thank all you grown-up children, all you little children, and all you middle-sized children for being with us tonight and believing with us in Never Land. I can't tell you how happy we are to share this lovely land with you. And I can't think how to say 'thank you' to the Ford Motor Company, RCA, and NBC for making it possible for us to be with you. And remember this—always keep youth and joy and freedom of spirit within you. Think lovely, wonderful thoughts and don't forget to learn to crow a little, with fairy dust on you. Good night."

Declaring "NBC's *Peter Pan* . . . the biggest news of the week," *Time* magazine added: "Warm, saucy and soaring, Mary Martin made *Peter Pan* close to 100% make-believe on both color and black-and-white screens. . . . Director-choreographer Jerome Robbins shaved away sentimentality in favor of movement and laughter. . . . Ford made palatable its light-touch commercials [but] RCA tried to fob off [singer] Vaughn Monroe in a fantasy of its own and suffered by contrast." Shrewdly, the NBC network had optioned future showings. And given the number of other television specials she would appear in for them, Martin was dubbed "the first lady of television."

Following the fabulous success of the *Ford 50th Anniversary Show,* and in anticipation of the broadcast of *Peter Pan,* the Hallidays embraced the relatively new medium of television as an opportunity to be seized. But, just as she preferred working on the stage to making movies, Martin harbored similar feelings toward the smaller screen. "This television medium is fantastic," Martin told Joe McCarthy, for a lengthy cover story in *Cosmopolitan,* shortly before *Peter Pan* would air for the second time. "They tell me more children will be able to see *Peter Pan* on TV than could see it in theaters if I played it for thirty years. Now you know that's wonderful. But my heart still belongs to Broadway," which is where, after all, Mary Martin initially used the same words to express her feelings about "Daddy."

Martin did not anticipate the lasting impact her *Peter Pan* would have, via television, on future generations. She did, however, hope it would become a staple of the American theater—with others playing Peter. "My honest desire," Martin told a reporter before opening on Broadway in the part, "is to have something that will stand up so it can be put on year after year, all over the country, with lots of people playing Peter Pan, like the English pantomimes, because generation after generation have never seen Peter Pan."

As soon as Martin's work on *Peter Pan* was concluded, the Hallidays satisfied their occasional need to "get away from it all" by taking a freighter on an impromptu trip to South America. They arrived in Buenos Aires on April 7, 1955. Following a visit to Rio de Janeiro they went to Uruguay, Argentina, and then Santos, Brazil, which led to a last-minute invitation to visit movie star Janet Gaynor and her husband Adrian, the silver screen's celebrated costumer, at their new home in the middle of the vast country—or, more specifically, "the high inland state of Goyaz, fifty miles of dusty oxen-road from the nearest telephone"—not to mention nine hundred miles from Rio and an hour's drive from the nearest post office. According to Harvey Schmidt, when they finally arrived there, Martin told Halliday: "My goodness! I can't believe we've come all this distance to see a place that looks just like Weatherford, Texas." It was, of course, far more exotic than Martin's casual remark suggested.

"To get there we had to fly in a small plane," explained Halliday. "The roads are no good. The place where the plane landed looked terrible. But when we got to the valley where Janet and Adrian live, we found ourselves in paradise. It was green and lovely, full of beautiful trees and flowers. The thing that really got us was the climate. It's the same all the year round, never lower than 58 and never above 80, and the air is always dry and bracing. They say it only rains in the evening, between eight o'clock and midnight. Mary and I both suffer a lot from sinus trouble in New York. Down there we felt like Venus and Apollo."

Having designed the fabulous costumes for *The Wizard of Oz,* including Dorothy's fabled ruby slippers, Adrian now created his own Emerald City in this Brazilian Shangri-la for himself and Gaynor. Their palatial house was "a dream in marble," reported Halliday. "Vast rooms, lofty ceilings. Huge windows and large balconies and verandas—each commanding a view of breath-taking beauty: Virgin jungle, waterfalls, winding mountain streams—side by side with vistas of cultivated land that stretches beyond sight. Every stick of furniture in the house—every rug, drapery, and picture—seems to have been created for its place." The marble was quarried nearby, and what Adrian estimated would have cost more than $225,000 to build back home cost only $25,000 in this little known part of the world.

According to Martin, their hosts were still in the process of unpacking their furnishings from California, including a king-size bed, which "was big enough for the four of us to dine on"—and indeed, spend the night: "we sat there and ate and talked all night long." If Martin's early reference in her memoir to Radclyffe Hall's *The Well of Loneliness* seemed to be an umistakable announcement about her lesbian background, the otherwise gratuitous mention here of spending the entire night in bed with Gaynor and Adrian seemed to serve the same purpose.

According to Martin, she was indicating the other side of the valley when she said to Gaynor, "Why didn't you build over there instead of here? It's much prettier." Gaynor explained it wasn't available and Martin said, "Well, if it's ever for sale, let us know and we'll buy it."

Within a year, the Hallidays bought their own personal estate in faraway Brazil, which would become their private getaway until Halliday's death, nearly two decades later.

Chapter 10

BY THE SKIN OF HER TEETH

I knew I wasn't good in it, and I thought I knew why.
—MARY MARTIN ON PLAYING SABINA IN
THE SKIN OF OUR TEETH

By the mid 1950s, a new form of theater had emerged as a revolutionary, iconoclastic movement in France. As practiced by Jean Genet, Samuel Beckett, and Eugene Ionesco—among others—it would come to be known as theater of the absurd and help to transform not only the way we look at plays but also the way we look at ourselves and the world. Several English-speaking playwrights would join their illustrious ranks, including the British Harold Pinter and the American Edward Albee. Only in retrospect can we find an unintentional predecessor or forerunner for the absurd theater movement in Thornton Wilder, most famous for his perennial classic, the highly experimental *Our Town*. Wilder had an even greater, instant wartime success in 1942 with his truly absurd allegory, *The Skin of Our Teeth*, about the indomitability of the human race in the face of ongoing travails—entailing everything from the Ice Age and plagues to hurricanes and world wars. It featured Fredric March and Florence Eldridge as Mr. and Mrs. Antrobus, Tallulah Bankhead as their lascivious maid, Sabina, and a newcomer named Montgomery Clift as their son, Henry. To mention that the Antrobus homestead in New Jersey includes a dinosaur and a mammoth as household pets begins to suggest the absurdity of the proceedings.

Staged for the State Department as part of the Festival de Paris at the Théâtre Sarah Bernhardt and representing the United States in an international "Salute to France," a 1955 revival of *The Skin of Our Teeth* featured an all-star cast: George Abbott and Helen Hayes as the Antrobuses, Mary Martin as Sabina, and up-and-coming film heartthrob Don Murray as Henry. Though cast against type as the lascivious Sabina, Martin's kooky side, her being "as corny as Kansas in August," also made her a natural choice for the character. One might say Martin's quirky celebrity hinged on her celebrated quirkiness. Both on and off stage, at least part of Martin's winning effect was based on her exploiting this pronounced aspect of her personality—usually with a knowing twinkle in her eye.

Aware that Hedda Hopper was going to be in Istanbul early in the summer, Martin sent her intimate friend a letter on March 16, asking Hopper if she could "go back home by way of Paris. [We] would really adore it if you could possibly come stay with us and see *Skin of Our Teeth*." And Hopper did.

Rehearsals for the Paris premiere began in New York, at the Belasco Theatre, and at first all seemed to be going well—so well, in fact, that "everybody" in the theater world had to get in to see the show before it shipped off for Europe. "At our final run-through, we were packed with professionals," recalled the revival's director, Alan Schneider, "all of whom expressed regret that only the French would see us." The wild enthusiasm prompted producer Robert Whitehead to announce that, following their Paris venture, the company would perform the production in Washington, DC, Chicago, and New York.

Whatever bargain Martin had long ago made with herself and her husband/manager to put her career before any personal concerns, even before her family, she increasingly found ways around this by involving both Larry and Heller in her work. Heller would play Gladys, the Antrobus's all-American daughter, in *The Skin of Our Teeth*. "Heller was a lovely young girl, who behaved very professionally," said Don Murray. "She had a very good upbringing and was not a brat in any way."

Larry also went to Paris, from London, to undertake a supernumerary role as an alcoholic. In addition to his Austin-Healey, which he took on the ferry to France, Larry brought his new wife, Maj, with him, to introduce her to his famous mother. It would also prove to be Maj's brief encounter with the stage—not only did she have a walk-on part, but she helped out backstage with the costumes—a baldfaced attempt to ingratiate herself with Martin if not Halliday, who was less inclined to welcome Larry, let alone his new bride, into the fold. Given the onoing animosity between them, perhaps no one was more surprised by Halliday than Larry himself, who later reported: "Offstage, for the first time in my memory, both Richard and I were on good behavior. There were no contretemps between us."

Their second day in Paris, the Hallidays were honored with a luncheon at the US ambassador's home. As soon as they arrived, the band began to play "Dites-Moi" from *South Pacific*, and Martin delighted the assembled guests by singing along. "The whole place went gaga," according to Larry, who was in attendance with Maj.

The Hallidays spent a good deal of their two weeks in Paris as houseguests of Martin's beloved couturier, Mainbocher. One afternoon, Martin visited socialite Ginny Chambers, whose eighteen-year-old godson, Peter Duchin, was staying with her in what had used to be Cole Porter's Paris residence. Peter was playing the piano, and when Martin asked him if he knew "My Heart Belongs to Daddy," he proceeded to offer an infectious jazz version of the song.

"Your dad sure didn't play it like that," said Martin, referring to Peter's famed though deceased bandleader father, Eddie Duchin, who had accompanied her on the first runaway hit recording of her signature song. "He stuck more to the tune." Martin proceeded to ask the younger Duchin if he would play for her when she sang the song on an upcoming TV special in the fall. He readily agreed, only to have his godmother tell him, "How wonderful, darling. But don't forget, you're only eighteen and your studies come first." The always reliable Martin sent Chambers a follow-up letter in October, claiming, "It was sad to get a message that Peter would not be allowed to be a part of the program. I am sure there must be much we don't know that made such a decision necessary. . . . Undoubtedly it must have had something to do with his schoolwork."

While the Hallidays gallivanted about Paris with Hedda Hopper, George Abbott, for his part, attended a ball held by the Rothschilds, where he was unhappily obliged to dance the night away with the show's publicist, Gertrude Macy. Given these outside obligations, "Rehearsing in Paris proved more difficult than in New York," Schneider later complained in his memoir. "Everyone was always a bit late coming in from sightseeing, shopping, eating or drinking." But the Paris rehearsal period was otherwise enhanced for Martin when Hayes magnanimously relinquished Sarah Bernhardt's "ornately furnished" dressing room to her costar. (The Hallidays also acquired Bernhardt's chaise lounge, which ultimately took a position of pride in their Norwalk home.)

By opening night, everyone was more than a little hopeful about the show's prospects. When Schneider went backstage to wish his Sabina luck, "Mary kissed me warmly, gave me a gold tie clasp with 'Love, always, Mary' inscribed on it," as he later wrote. "She and Richard . . . told me that she had never worked with a director who had helped her more, and that she hoped she would never do another show without me."

But things began to change as soon the actors started performing before a public audience in Paris. For one thing, even though it was presented in English with simultaneous translation, the French had difficulty following the play, which could be challenging under any circumstances.

For another, the Paris audiences only "laughed politely" at Martin's Sabina, but "roared" at Hayes's comedic performance, according to Schneider, who added, "Suddenly I felt a hand clutching my left shoulder, a voice spitting into my ear, 'What have you done to my wife?' I turned directly into the pained countenance of Richard Halliday, whom I had just left smiling benignly at me in Sarah's and Mary's dressing room. At first, I thought Dick must be drunk; then I decided he must have mixed me up with someone else. I put my finger to my lips and turned away, my heart beating loudly. . . . It was only after the show that I was able, with [producer] Bob [Whitehead]'s help, to understand what I had done to Richard Halliday's wife. I had neglected to tell her that Helen Hayes might get as many laughs as she would. Or more."

As Schneider further emphasized, the politics on the world stage played a role in how the American entry fared in the Festival de Paris. Though Joseph McCarthy and his HUAC henchmen had by then been discredited, the Cold War between the United States and Russia was still a hot-button issue, with backyard fallout shelters selling in America at a faster pace than ever and elementary school children practicing bomb drills under their desks. (The real-world circumstances made some of Wilder's original intentions at least as relevant as when *The Skin of Our Teeth* premiered during World War II.) "French stagehands, mostly Socialists or even Communists, were determined to help the American 'imperialists' no more than they had to," explained Schneider. "They worked according to rule, managed not to understand a word of English when they felt like it, and rarely said 'hello,' 'goodbye,' or 'thank you' in any language."

Schneider had perhaps a more legitimate gripe when he claimed that the French were more favorably disposed to the Germans and the Chinese, revealing the international festival for the political contest it was— the theatrical equivalent of an international Olympics. *The Skin of Our Teeth* was scheduled after the Berliner Ensemble, "which had five years of rehearsal," and before the Peking Opera, "which had five hundred"—in comparison to their own five weeks.

But what no one, including Martin herself, seemed to recognize, was that once she chose to take on the flamboyant role of Sabina, she had an enormous challenge riding on her decision. It was only Martin's second nonmusical play; and the fact that her first, *Kind Sir,* had been a flop added to her discomfort in the part. She wanted to succeed in the course of stretching herself, but she was also noticeably insecure in the process. Maybe, this time, she could prove that she wasn't merely an expressive singer and dancer but a genuine actress as well. On the other hand, Martin's ambitions could never be assuaged: her continual aim to prove herself to herself involved proving herself to the rest of the world. Ultimately, Martin's fears were not even surmounted by her success. Every step on the boards was as if it were her first.

"I knew I wasn't good in it, and I thought I knew why," Martin recalled years later, revealing just how acutely aware (or overly self-conscious) she was of the image she projected. "The role of Sabina had been written for Tallulah Bankhead. The marvelous asides to the audience, the tough wisdom of Sabina, *were* Tallulah. . . . But our director insisted that when it was time to be 'the actress' I should be me, Mary Martin. . . . A Tallulah line coming from a Mary Martin–type character doesn't work. I argued and argued but the director was unmovable. That was the way I had to play it."

"Alan Schneider's method of direction was very personal," recalled George Abbott. "He made notes and then took each actor aside and talked to him privately." This should have worked well for Martin, who actually "asked for extra time with [Schneider] and came to rehearsals hours ahead of everyone else to work on her scenes."

But in spite of her personal misgivings, Martin remained a stalwart professional, albeit forever concerned with the impression she was making on colleagues and on audience members alike. "We rehearsed in New York and then in Paris," recalled Don Murray, who was fresh from serving in Korea when he undertook the role of Henry. "Mary Martin was a warm person, and immediately friendly. She made me feel very much at home and at ease, right at the first rehearsal."

Murray nonetheless noticed the problems Martin was having with Schneider, which entailed some ambivalence about her image and her attempts to change it. "In playing the part of the seductress, most of it was about trying to get her to be more overtly sexual," said Murray, who added that her difficulties also had to do with her acting technique. In contrast with his own Stanislavski-based training, which was "all based on reality and emotions—you get to your part from the 'inside,' from your emotions and feelings . . . this was all very different from Mary Martin, who would start from the outside, and be [only] concerned with her effect on the audience."

Martin also tried to deflect her tension by being playful with Heller backstage, as recalled by playwright Sandy Wilson, who made the trek from London to Paris to see *The Skin of Our Teeth*. "I went round afterwards at the Sarah Bernhardt Theatre," Wilson would write in a letter to

Elliott Sirkin, "and in the course of our meeting Mary and Heller Halliday, who was also in the show, did a close harmony rendition of 'My Funny Valentine' 'dans les coylisses' ['in the corridor']—I'm not sure why, but it was very effective!"

Despite any problems perceived by the Hallidays in particular, Martin was well-received by at least one French reviewer, suggesting that her reputation had by now been firmly established internationally. In *Le Figaro litteraire,* Jacques Lemarchand referred to "the brilliant Mary Martin," even though he found the production "too agitated, and lacking, it must be said, in intimacy."

But when Martin threatened to withdraw before *The Skin of Our Teeth* transferred to the States, producer Robert Whitehead reported that Kim Stanley was on hand to take over the part of Sabina. This was all the Hallidays needed to hear to commit to remain with the show—with some newfound leverage for doing so on their own terms. Though Schneider continued to direct the rest of the cast, noted TV director Vincent Donehue was brought in to supervise Martin's performance.

Following its two-week run in Paris in June, *The Skin of Our Teeth* revival opened in Washington, DC, at the National Theatre, on July 18, and then at Chicago's Blackstone Theatre, on August 2. It was during this period that Donehue told Martin to play Sabina like anyone but herself, which was exactly what the skittish actress wanted to hear. " 'Vinnie' was the kindest, wisest, gentlest man [who] appeared to rescue me from my dilemma," recalled Martin. "We didn't change one single line, we just changed the mental approach, which changed the delivery."

But bringing in Donehue to direct Martin baffled and befuddled Helen Hayes, who had never experienced such an unconventional, duo-director arrangement before, and it tested Schneider's tolerance. Though Donehue was "an old friend" and the two of them had many a dinner together during the Chicago run, Schneider was embarrassed by the situation. Schneider would also claim that he wasn't "sure whether Mary and Helen ever spoke to each other again," when, in fact, they remained the best of friends. If no one understood one diva's behavior better than another, both Martin and Hayes maintained their natural, non-diva-like demeanor with each other.

As if to emphasize that the theater was her real family, Martin was also, according to Don Murray, "a great audience." Along with an extra in the production, Murray had written a parody called *No Skin Off Our . . .* ("Ass" was the implicit end of the title). They performed it for the other cast members both in Washington and in Chicago, in hotel meeting rooms. "Mary Martin was the greatest audience I ever had," explained Murray. "She literally fell on the floor, laughing. It was so prolonged and huge and genuine, and it got everyone else to laugh as well."

As Murray recalled yet another anecdote to underscore Martin's generosity, there was a heatwave when they performed in Chicago. "Instead of air-conditioning, they had these big fans blowing backstage. One night, I had difficulty hearing and didn't get my cue to get downstairs and prepare for my entrance. I remember Alan Schneider running up and saying, 'Don! Don! You're on!' I had stranded Mary Martin out on the stage, and I felt like I deserved to be fired. But later, when I apologized, she was so warm about it. She said she had fun ad-libbing. It was amazingly magnanimous of her."

Nearly sixty years later, Heller remembered an unhappy episode during a scene she had with Helen Hayes. "She scared the shit out of me," said Heller. "I was only a child, and in the second act, I think they put fake boobs in my bra, because I didn't have any yet. And I remember sitting on the stage, on a bench with Helen Hayes, and we were looking out at the ocean, or something. All of a sudden, she was supposed to do some lines, and I thought, 'You're supposed to do your lines now.' So I started to say her line, to give it to her. And it did help her: she picked up on it. But then, when we got off stage, she started screaming at me, 'Don't you ever, ever, EVER do that again.'"

Following Chicago, *The Skin of Our Teeth* began performances at the ANTA Theater in New York on August 16, when orchestra seats topped out at $4.05, and where it joined the recently opened classics to be, *Bus Stop, Cat on a Hot Tin Roof,* and *Inherit the Wind* on Broadway. Martin's newfound comfort in the play was reflected in the critics' reactions. After pointing out that the "gala" opening featured a chamber orchestra in the lobby of the ANTA Theatre, Robert Coleman added, "Miss Martin, as the siren always threatening family ties, is saucy, sexy and electric."

Richard Watts Jr. was even more emphatic in his review for the *New York Post*. "It is Miss Martin who scored the major triumph. [She] has the role that many observers had thought only Tallulah Bankhead, who created the part, could portray in the curious comic terms in which Mr. Wilder wrote it. But Miss Martin, who has just the mocking gusto necessary to bring it within the scope of her own highly personal style, provides the enlivening quality that is necessary to both the character and the play." Walter Kerr concurred: "If Miss Martin is more wonderful at one time than another, it may be when she is simply aglow with self-admiration as she succeeds in luring the Father of the family into her beach cabana. . . . Miss Martin smiles her great Cheshire-cat grin, tosses an elegant wrist into the air, and lets a roller-coaster of sound rip from her throat." In the *New York Times,* Brooks Atkinson chimed in: "Miss Martin gives a brilliant comedy performance that weaves in and out of the story without effort—now kidding the play, now taking part in it as a full-fledged character, but never losing control of the work as a whole."

But perhaps William Peper described Martin's contribution most thoroughly in the *New York World-Telegram and Sun*: "From the moment that Mary Martin comes tripping onstage, swinging her feather duster as the raffish Sabina, the play is a delight. . . . [Martin] has the time of her life prancing about in red spangles, running up and down the aisles with a flashlight and chattering irreverently with the audience about the play. She does it all with infectious glee and cunning skill."

The production's run culminated with a highly unusual televised performance on September 11, a "special two-hour color program" to introduce NBC's brand new "multi-hued *Color Spreads*" and Sunday Spectacular series, at an estimated cost of $240,000. As captured for posterity in a kinescope of the broadcast, what's most remarkable about Martin's performance is that there is no residual awkwardness to her Sabina. She breezes through a role that seems as natural for her as breathing.

But Martin's earlier difficulties with *The Skin of Our Teeth* had at least one unforeseen and unwelcome consequence: having directly witnessed her mother's trepidations on a daily basis, and still hurt by the dressing-down that Helen Hayes had given her, Heller was prompted to tell her parents she was not going to pursue a career in the theater after all. She yearned for the relatively calming influence of an everyday, domestic existence. More specifically, Heller explained that she missed a boyfriend she had left back home in Connecticut and that she wanted to return to school—that she wanted to have, in other words, what some would call a "normal" life.

"Suddenly, all the bright lights that had dazzled me for years began to fade," recalled Heller in a *Good Housekeeping* article in 1963. "The fast pace, the famous people, the frantic traveling—I began to lose interest in it. It started with roses. Every day, for several weeks, I had received a bouquet of roses at our hotel. The card was always signed the same way: 'Your Admirer.' One day, we were all in Mummy and Daddy's room. The telephone rang, and my mother answered. She looked up smiling, and said, 'Your Admirer wants to talk with "Meez Halleeeday!"' Nervously, I picked up the phone. A smooth, French voice asked me for a date. I blurted out, 'No, I couldn't possibly,' and hung up. I never discovered who my secret admirer was. But his call made me realize that I was not dating or meeting young people and doing the things people my age were doing."

Heller enrolled in George School, a Quaker boarding school in Bucks County, where Oscar and Dorothy Hammerstein had their home. (In fact, it was Oscar Hammerstein who recommended it.) Within a year, Martin would tell an interviewer that Heller "hasn't any [stage ambitions]—no definite ones. Heller can take show business or leave it. She's not a born ham, you know, like me." Later still, after pointing out that Heller had "been with us in the theater since she was five"—from *Annie Get You Gun* to *Peter Pan* and *The Skin of Our Teeth*—Martin exclaimed, "This is what is so crazy. . . . She doesn't want anything to do with the theater now. She wants to be a nurse. How can you figure children?" When Martin reminded Heller of their "dream" for "her to play Wendy to my Peter," Heller replied, "Mother, I'm in college, and if I'm going to college I must stay there." Perhaps mindful of Peter Pan's motto, Martin added that Heller "really had grown up." (Decades later, Martin would recall that when Heller "changed her mind" and decided not to be an actress, she said, "Mother, you haven't grown up, but I have.")

Ironically, in a letter to Hedda Hopper sent several months before the Paris premiere of *The Skin of Our Teeth,* Martin divulged that casting Heller had been Helen Hayes's idea: "[D]o you know the first time I talked on the phone, Helen asked if I'd make her one promise—would I promise that Heller would play the part of her daughter in the play?!!! Can you imagine what happened to my heart, the air—our world?! Heller still doesn't know this," Martin confided to Hopper, before adding, "Helen Hayes makes all our hearts sing because she goes on and on being so dearly wonderful and I can't wait to start rehearsals at the end of May with her. What an experience! My luck is fabulous." Apart from any ambivalence she felt over her daughter's decision to leave the theater, Mary Martin's life was indeed fabulous in 1955.

Chapter 11

"TOGETHER WITH MUSIC"

I don't know of one enemy Mary has in the ruthless jungle of show business she has stalked for 20 years — a fact which, believe me, is almost unbelievable.
— HEDDA HOPPER

Though television was, in a sense, anathema to Mary Martin, it was fast becoming more than just a supplement to her lifelong commitment to live performance. As soon as she was finished with the broadcast of *The Skin of Our Teeth,* Martin began working on *Together with Music,* her first—and only—TV venture with Noël Coward. *Together with Music* grew out of the cabaret act the two of them performed at the Café de Paris on January 13, 1952, while Martin was in London with *South Pacific.* They had then repeated their two-and-a-half-hour engagement in November of that year.

Deriving its title from a song Coward wrote for the occasion, *Together with Music* marked Coward's television debut as well as the first of three CBS specials—the other two being adaptations of his *Blithe Spirit* and *This Happy Breed*—for which Coward was receiving the then-princely sum of $450,000: "This, of course, is enormous money and I shall certainly do it," claimed Coward in his diary. As suggested by a second song which Coward wrote for the show, "Ninety Minutes is a Long, Long Time," it would also prove unprecedented by featuring two performers for ninety minutes, without any backup singers or dancers to fill out the evening. And, as the liner notes for the reissued double album boasted twenty-eight years later: "There seems to have been a crazy notion in Madison Avenue echelons that if networks had a right to turn a profit they also had a responsibility to strive for the highest possible artistic achievement."

As early as March 19, 1955, Coward wrote in his diary that he had received a cable from Martin confirming her participation in the program and that he was "ecstatic about our project." In July, Martin sent a letter to Coward reaffirming her enthusiasm for the special: "We love every word we read, every picture we see of you—and every glowing word that reaches us. So maybe we're ready to face the TV together!!"

As documented in *Life* magazine, the reunited friends actually began putting the show together at Coward's "luxurious winter estate" in Jamaica, where the Hallidays arrived on September 13, two days after the live broadcast of *The Skin of Our Teeth*. Fresh from performing at the Desert Inn in Las Vegas, Coward himself had only just arrived a couple of days earlier, with his new pianist Peter Matz. Coward's US agents were also already in Jamaica and showed him the "very exciting" plans for the set: "68 feet in depth and with the series of curtains which will part and roll themselves up into pillars as Mary and I advance for our entrance. . . ."

But any preliminary optimism was somewhat diminished as soon as Martin heard the title song. "To my horror Mary took against 'Together with Music,' very firmly indeed," Coward wrote in his diary on September 14. "I admired her honesty but it was dreadfully irritating and disappointing. Actually I am afraid she's right, and so I am now in the throes of rewriting the entire number and making it more romantic." By their third day in Jamaica, Coward was complaining about his houseguests: "I was right about peace departing with the arrival of the Hallidays. They are both quite incredibly noisy. Richard never stops emitting shrill, whining screams for no reason at all. Mary has a naturally piercing voice, and between them both mealtimes are deafening. Otherwise they are no trouble at all and retire firmly to bed immediately after dinner, which is wonderful."

While they were hard at work for the next nine days, the Hallidays' visit proved far more unpleasant than even this early report indicated. Coward may have long before forgiven them the "uproar over Mary's dresses" during *Pacific 1860* that led to their long-standing feud, but Halliday's erratic, drunken behavior quickly reminded him of it. "Trouble has come inevitably because Richard, we must face it, is not only neurotic, hysterical, noisy and a bad drinker, but a bad character as well," observed Coward in one of the most damning indictments of Halliday's nature. "Fortunately Mary, over the years, has discarded her rose-coloured [*sic*] spectacles and is no longer deluded. I am deeply sorry for her. . . . She is a curious mixture of wisdom and innocence. For years—fifteen years—she has allowed Richard to order her life, run the house, deal with all business and social matters, oversee her dresses, do her hair and generally protect her from any extraneous slings and arrows. This has left her, not entirely willingly, free to develop her talent and build the triumphant career she so very much deserves. But lately she has begun to realize that she has been too assiduously sheltered. She has watched Richard over and over again in every production she has been concerned with, making sudden unpredictable scenes, losing his head and insulting people right and left, thereby not only undermining her own popularity but leaving acres of debris to be shoveled away, and a dreary trail of acrimony and misunderstandings...."

"The other evening at dinner," continued Coward in a much longer entry, "Richard suddenly turned on me with snarling, whining hatred, accusing me of cheese-paring and not be[ing] willing to spend enough money on the production, etc. All this without the slightest lead up. I turned on him in no uncertain manner and ultimately silenced him. Mary also turned on him without any compromise and altogether it was a horrid little episode. Later he wept and apologized and wrote me a long, humble letter suggesting that he withdraw from any further participation in *Together with Music*.... Two nights later he started up another drunken tirade, which Mary and I managed to calm before it got out of hand.... Personally I think he is heading for a nervous crack-up ... two drinks set him off and I really can't risk having to order him out of the television studios in front of everyone and engender a first-class scandal in all the news columns."

The night before the Hallidays' departure on September 25, there was a cocktail party at which Martin and Coward "performed so that we could get some sort of audience reaction," according to Coward. "The heat was really appalling and we and our entranced public dripped with sweat. Mary was really magical. She gave out as if she were doing a command performance."

Several weeks later Coward reported that rehearsals in New York were "going very well," perhaps because Halliday was confined to a hospital to deal with his alcoholism: "a purplish ex-drunk stands in for him, presumably to guard Mary's interests." Coward also felt that Martin was having problems with the *Madame Butterfly* "burlesque," and went on to provide some rather candid thoughts that formed one of the more succinct impressions about her overall affect and effect:

"Mary is a great performer and a very good character. She is painfully naïve and has no clue about playing comedy and never will have. She also has a strongly developed 'Rebecca of Sunnybrook Farm' quality and a desire to be perpetually sweet before the public, which is death to sharp comedy lines. She infuses our 'comedy' bickering with saccharin and shies away from any riposte which sounds as though she were being 'mean' to me. This is *not* a help in scenes which have been written on the assumption that we are having a light professional quarrel"—a quarrel that perhaps reflected the extended one that prevailed until Martin's superlative performance in *South Pacific* melted Coward's icy attitude. The highly competitive Coward continued his entry with a somewhat cryptic note: "The result will be that I shall play rings round her. None of this much matters but it is certainly aggravating."

The invited audience for the live event included a number of Coward's stellar friends: Margot Fonteyn, Clifton Webb, and Lynn Fontanne and Alfred Lunt—not to mention William Faulkner. As conceived by Coward, the show opened with a pretext or pretense of candor, as its two stars are ostensibly still preparing to begin and standing outside their adjacent dressing-room doors, resorting to some well-rehearsed banter and bickering. "You got it hopelessly wrong when you were rehearsing it yesterday," warns, on cue, a self-satisfied and typically immodest Coward to a dewy-eyed Martin. "I can't stand the idea of ninety million people looking at you doing something you're really not very good at." Coward's put-downs don't stop there and even hit a bit closer to home, when he claims that Martin's "Richard" "looks haggard. . . . He's nothing but skin and bone. . . . He's aged ten years since we've started rehearsals. My heart bleeds for Richard." Before offering their first number, "Ninety Minutes Is a Long, Long Time," Martin gives as good as she gets: "There's a dangerous note of British superiority in your whole attitude," she warns Coward. "Now that's not the way to make the American public love you." Coward's script, his whole approach to the program, seemed to be playing off the notion that television was increasingly intrusive on a celebrity's private life.

After the two of them descend a spreading staircase to sing the title number, Martin proceeds to introduce Coward to his first television audience. "Uncle Harry," his first solo, was from *Pacific 1860*, followed by his "own personal version" of a traditional Scottish ballad, "On the Bonnie Banks of Loch Lomond," which begins in earnest before being jazzed up, a la Martin's "Il Bacio." Throughout the program, Coward was clad in a tuxedo and Martin attired first in a flouncy chiffon dress and later in a sleeveless black gown—both designed by "Main Bocher" (as the credits had it), naturally.

Like their assumed attitude, their sartorial elegance belies their culturally bereft backgrounds: Coward's as a working-class commoner and Martin's as a small-town hick. (As Coward once put it, he grew up in "genteel poverty.") A large part of their mutual attraction hinged on their unspoken recognition that they had far surpassed their wildest dreams in the course of surmounting their respective roots. Coward's entire "act" was built around his sending up the very upper-crust manners he aspired to and emulated. Martin rather embraced the upper-crust manners to which she wasn't born, like a proverbial kid in a well-stocked candy shop.

Martin and Coward had something else very specific in common: one of Coward's first stage appearances was as Slightly, the Lost Boy, in *Peter Pan,* when he was all of twelve years old. The most heartfelt segment in *Together with Music* arrived two-thirds into the program, when Martin sang "London Pride," as if to, and certainly about, Coward; and Coward, in turn, delivered a rambunctious, toe-tapping rendition of "Deep in the Heart of Texas" to one of the Lone Star state's most beloved natives.

It's hard not to see how bored and affected—which is to say, above it all—Coward seemed throughout the performance. He continued to exhibit a superior attitude in his response to the show itself. "The Press notices are unqualified raves and it appears that, apart from being clever and pretty and wittier than anyone in this whole big wonderful world, I have also revolutionized television by proving that two people, without support of an elaborate production, can hold for an hour and a half." But Coward's postmortem also contained some fulsome praise for Martin: "Mary, after the first scene in which she dried up and became rather baby-talky, was absolutely superb," declared Coward. "She infused magic into 'Kick Out of You', 'I've Only Got Eyes for You' and 'Daddy.' We *just* got away with 'Butterfly' and our final medley was fine and tore the place up."

The raves included Hedda Hopper's notice in the *St. Paul Dispatch* ("The greatest entertainment I've ever seen on TV ... their everything was only great"), Ben Gross in the New York *Daily News* ("All in all, the most intelligent and captivating revue I have ever seen on television"), and Jack Gould in the *New York Times* ("The rewards were unusual and varied ... made Saturday evening at home seem like a night out"). Gould, in fact, seized the special as a sign that television was finally growing up in the straitlaced 1950s: "In his delightful patter numbers Mr. Coward went further in the realm of naughty wit on TV than perhaps any other artist. Yet the walls of Madison Avenue didn't tremble and there was no outcry from the self-appointed guardians of the medium's morals. This is progress of a high order." But in his review for the *Los Angeles Mirror-News,* Hal Humphrey grumbled that "someone should have noticed during the camera rehearsals that Miss Martin does not take too well to a full close-up on TV. Those 'third-degree' shots weren't necessary." Gould also pointed out that "at the end of his first half hour [Coward] apparently lost a substantial share of his audience, which evidently flocked over to George Gobel." This was rather like switching from champagne and caviar to hot dogs and baked beans.

While the arrival of television brought the entire world into the privacy of America's living rooms, it had, in a sense, the opposite effect on certain celebrities, making public displays of their personal environments. Put another way, long before there was reality TV there was a TV reality, in which the terms for promoting oneself suddenly had a new requirement: it was no longer enough to open one's heart and mind to scrutiny; one's home and private life became fair game as well, as epitomized by Edward R. Murrow's *Person to Person* show on CBS on Friday nights. Predictably, Martin became one of Murrow's guests during the second year of *Person to Person,* on April 30, 1954. There was a certain focus on the large needlepoint rug that Martin made, which had recently garnered first prize in a needlepoint exhibition in New Hope, Pennsylvania. Within several days of the broadcast, CBS received roughly 15,000 letters requesting copies of the Chinese proverb embroidered on the rug.

It was "both an honor and an ordeal" to appear on *Person to Person,* according to Tim Brooks and Earle Marsh in *The Complete Directory to Prime Time Network TV Shows*: "TV cameras were bulky and inconvenient to move around those days, meaning that a technical crew virtually had to take over the home of the subject several days in advance, running heavy cables from room to room and carefully mapping out every movement to be used on the night of the broadcast, to avoid tangles and confusion."

And where television led, the rest of the media felt compelled to follow. Like all other publicity seekers, the Hallidays had to open their home to a seemingly endless parade of reporters and journalists, who showed up with an entourage of photographers, editors, and art directors. This was perhaps part of what fueled Heller's decision to abandon a career in show business, and certainly part of what led her parents to locate a truly remote retreat for themselves in Brazil. (Ironically, Jack Paar would eventually follow the Hallidays to Brazil with his TV crew— as would a number of other journalists and media bigwigs.)

Though Martin would always welcome the limelight, at times she grew weary of the hard work involved in maintaining it. "During the run of *South Pacific* I told [my life story] so often I grew sick of it," claimed Martin, who also recalled when Cynthia Lowry, a new reporter on the beat, came to the house in Connecticut to interview her about *Peter Pan.* "When she walked in she said, 'I really don't know anything about you.' I asked her, 'Are you sure?' and when she said, 'Yes,' I said, 'Come with me,' and we went down to the pool and I really told her a story. I said that I'd been born on an Indian reservation and that my mother was an Indian. I've forgotten what I told her daddy was—probably a buffalo hunter—and she said, 'What a story!' Even after we'd had lunch she was still saying, 'What a story!'

"When I said, 'I'm glad you like it because I'm sick of my own,' she did a double-take and threatened me, 'I'm going to ruin you. I'm going to print it exactly the way you told it to me.' So I told her a more accurate story, and we had a lovely time."

The *Women's Home Companion* ran a cover story on Martin in their January 1956 issue. Written by Martin's trusted friend, Hedda Hopper, it was the most complete magazine biography of Martin to date, and it naturally had an emphasis on her all-important relationship with Halliday. "Where Mary is vivacious and exuberant, Dick is quiet and reticent," wrote Hopper. "Where Mary is impulsive and utterly uncalculating, Dick is cool-headed and, from long experience, a shrewd judge of scripts, shows and the esoteric ways of the theater. He not only pulls Mary down to earth when she's flying too high, but acts as a buffer between her and a world which would squeeze her limp. . . . When you talk with Mary, it's always 'we thought,' 'we decided,' 'we plan,' 'we believe.' Nor has sentiment suffered by the arrangement. The Hallidays wallow in it. Dick calls Mary 'Mommy'; she calls him 'Daddy.'"

"There is a lot of sunlight in this house and Mary has enhanced it with a warm décor dominated by sunshine yellows," added Hopper, after visiting the Hallidays at their two-hundred-year-old, idyllic Connecticut farmhouse on Ponus Avenue in Norwalk. The property included a six-acre lot, with a separate cottage studio, where Martin occasionally vocalized and Heller had an ideal playhouse. The expansive grounds also featured large and ancient shade trees, a "natural" swimming pool molded in the earth, a running brook, and a view of Long Island Sound. With a wisteria-covered terrace, the house was filled with the clasped-hands motif that had long since become the Hallidays' insignia. A pair of four-foot-high French porcelain chanticleers, or roosters—a gift from Jean Arthur—stood on the stone gateposts to welcome visitors.

As was by now customary, the Hallidays furnished their home with fine antiques, including Bristol glassware, surrounded by paintings by friends: Henry Fonda, Beatrice Lillie, Noël Coward, and Janet Gaynor and Adrian. Heller's bedroom proudly displayed a doll that Helen Hayes had given her, after Hayes's daughter, Mary MacArthur, had died from complications of polio. "Heller's baby dresses are framed on the wall of her bedroom," wrote journalist Joe McCarthy in *Cosmopolitan*. "One of them, the frock she wore on her third birthday, was designed for her by Main Bocher [*sic*]."

In addition to the main house and the studio, the Norwalk property also had a brand-new $22,000 guesthouse that was built with proceeds from *Peter Pan*. "From the entrance hall we come to the large living room, which is painted a lovely shade of blue," explained Harry Evans, in a detailed description in *Family Circle*, following *his* visit to the Norwalk guesthouse. "The first eye-catcher as you cross the threshold is the unusual picture window directly over the fireplace, which commands the opposite end of the living room. The window was Richard's idea, and it's a beaut. There is also an excellent flower still life, painted by Mary, in this room. Both the kitchen and bedroom lead off from the living room. The kitchen is a compact and handsome job with built-in appliances. The large bedroom is wallpapered in a bold flowery pattern, dominantly green. We noticed an easel with a painting that Mary had started."

Late in 1955, NBC imposed on Martin by preparing an industry promo for her upcoming second live broadcast of *Peter Pan*. While the cameras were rolling, Martin and Heller provided viewers with a tour of the guesthouse, which Martin took to calling "the Peter Pan House." The promo begins with mother and daughter poring over the countless pictures and letters children sent in following the first broadcast the previous March. They proceed to point out a number of prized possessions on the premises, including Sarah Bernhardt's chaise lounge, which the Hallidays had recently brought back from Paris; a framed Hirschfeld caricature of Martin as Peter Pan in flight; a tiny piano from Martin's youth; and a plaque that read, "Our favorite PAN in this kitchen is PETER." It's revealing to observe Martin suddenly becoming distant or vacant whenever she thinks, apparently, that the camera has been turned off.

Given her lifelong adoration for *Peter Pan*, it's surprising to discover that Martin actually intended her 1956 version to be her final incarnation of the boy who refused to grow up. According to an advance story in *TV Guide*, "[Martin's] next flight into Never Never Land, she insists, will be her last—'unless I try out as Captain Hook,'" quipped Martin. "*Peter Pan*, she feels, should be telecast every year, but the title role should be played by 'some sweet young thing. *Not* Mary Martin. . . . If I never do another television show, I can honestly say, I've had it. Two hits—one for the children [*Peter Pan*] and 'Together with Music' for the grown-ups. . . . I love 'Peter Pan,' " she added. "But I'm afraid this is the last time around for me. I refuse to end up as the world's only flying grandmother!" Martin would, of course, continue to soar as Peter Pan long after her grand-children became a welcome part of her life. She would even take pride when some of her grandchildren brought young friends into her bed-room to observe the sleeping Peter Pan.

Though a kinescope version of Martin's second live broadcast as Peter Pan seems more grainy and primitive than the first, nothing can suppress her exuberance in the part. Everyone was back for Peter's second flight on NBC on January 9, 1956, including a noticeably more mature Heller. A newcomer was Broadway composer Harvey Schmidt, who first worked with Mary Martin as a graphic designer for her second *Peter Pan*.

"I had just been hired by NBC at that point, in the graphics depart-ment," said Schmidt. "I was down to my last ten dollars when I got this job. And it was great, because it was a union job and it paid very well. NBC was trying to get people to buy color television sets—no one had a color televi-sion at that time. And so they used lots of artwork. There were two or three shows a week that were out at this huge Brooklyn studio, where *Peter Pan* was done. The center core of it was about two city blocks long. And when I went out, I was filling in for an artist who had done the original titles. This was the second year. That artist was sick or something, and I was just so pleased to go out there because I was such a fan of Mary Martin's.

"I remember coming out of the blinding sunlight, and just standing there right inside the door, in the pitch black, and there came Mary Martin flying right at me, from two blocks away. There was nobody else near except for the pianist playing. And then, there was Mary Martin, sailing right at me. And she'd fly back, and they would turn her around. And here she'd come again. And she started singing to me—I was the only person there. I couldn't believe that after all those years of being in-fatuated with her, here she was singing to me."

Given that nearly a year had elapsed since the first and last broadcast of Peter Pan, there was a run-through on January 7, two nights before the live performance, when, according to an AP report, "about 300 children from settlement houses and other charitable organizations … inundate[ed] the balcony seats." Martin's flying prompted "yells and screams of delight [only to become] uncontrollable." But perhaps no one, at the time, was more delighted than Harvey Schmidt, who was trans-ported back to being a ten-year-old who had memorized all the words to Martin's "My Heart Belongs to Daddy" on the radio.

If an unmitigated measure of celebrity is being featured—or victim-ized—in the scandal sheets, Martin was canonized in the pantheon in

April 1956, when *Uncensored* ran a story on the Hallidays' new home in provincial, out-of-the-way Brazil. As reported, they could "play" there, as they wanted, without the harsh spotlight of any media attention glowering over them—except for *Uncensored,* that is.

The Hallidays had been so eager to establish a getaway in Brazil that their first attempt proved a fiasco, when they discovered that they paid $16,000 "to an American woman who didn't even own the land she had sold them. The local authorities hushed that up [by reimbursing the money]," reported Hedda Hopper, "since they couldn't afford to have the news leak back to the United States." The Hallidays' new exotic property ultimately cost an additional $50,000. But even then, the nearest electricity was 25 miles away, which was 625 miles closer than the nearest phone.

"After months and months of delay, we were actually moving into the house in Brazil, 'Our Farm' Nossa Fazenda," Martin would write in her *Needlepoint* book. "It was small and still unfinished, but work had been done we had not yet seen. We rushed excitedly in and out exclaiming over discoveries and surprises, behaving much like the farm chickens which had been thrown into cackling confusion by our arrival."

To describe the Hallidays' new Brazilian home as remote doesn't begin to suggest the difficulties one had to endure to get there. It took a total of twenty-seven hours to travel from New York to Anápolis, the nearest town, in Goiás, Brazil. After flying first to Rio de Janeiro and then taking a smaller plane to Brasília, one had to make the far more desolate journey to the Hallidays' ranch on dirt roads, if they could be called that. Joshua Logan, who would visit some years later, described this last leg as "one of the most arid rides in the Western World," before arriving at what truly sounds like Shangri-la. "We passed vast stretches of sandy soil on which, spasmodically, a few thirsty tufts of crabgrass grew," continued Logan. "There was not a tree in sight the whole way, and nothing that resembled one—not even a bush. Along the road, no happy peasants walked carrying baskets on their heads; the roads were deserted. As we rode on and on, we saw no villages, no homes, no houses, no cars, no animals—there was nothing but the long stretch of macadam cutting those arid, sandy wastes in half.

"Eventually, three hours later, we came to a pitiful, bleached-wood town with a few dusty, ramshackle buildings looking out on backyards filled with broken bottles and rusty tin cans. This was the resting place. After a warm Coca-Cola, we took off again for another half hour's ride to the Halliday house. Suddenly, there was a patch of green in the distance, and as we approached it, we saw bamboo trees growing out of the yellow-gray sand. Over a gate were the words 'Nossa Fazenda,' Portuguese for 'Our Farm,' and I knew by the painting on the sign of their signature, two clasped hands, that it belonged to Mary and Richard. . . .

"We drove into the bamboo and were in another world immediately. Mary's and Richard's home was an anachronism. It shouldn't have been there, but it was. Everything was green: there were flowers, bushes, trees, and two small lagoons. Chickens and ducks were plentiful, and we could see quite a few cows."

"Mary Martin and Dick are at last in their farm," wrote Adrian in a four-page letter to Hedda Hopper, dated March 11, 1956. "So much has happened to them and so much is new, a language very strange to them and everything so different from their gently padded New York life that they have become real pioneers and wonderfully good sports. Mary, who never cooked before turns out delicious cakes from their Brazilian wood stove and is more proud of them than any stage performance. Dick who has never been much for horses rides like a cowboy and loves finding out how to increase his egg production (I'm speaking of his chickens now) and how to sell his avocados in the village market.

"Janet who also always crossed the street when she saw a horse coming—now loves to ride and is constantly planning the days to include riding. She is painting very well. . . . Last night we went over to the Hallidays for dinner and a Brazilian friend arrived with a monkey on a chain for Mary and a canary in a cage for us—Janet acts as interpreter for Mary very often because she has advanced the most of all of us in her Portuguese and really carries on well." (The fact that Gaynor already had a pet monkey of her own suggests that others were beginning to abet Martin in her growing tendency to imitate the retired film star in all things.)

Adrian failed to add that "everybody was in uniform for serving dinner" at the Hallidays' dining table every evening. Nor did Adrian even know, perhaps, that his wife and Martin were doing more than just applying suntan oil when sunbathing in the nude together in Brazil, as recalled by one of Gaynor's servants half a century later, in a documentary, with a certain widening of her eyes: "They are like children . . . they have no shame."

In her gossip-filled response to Adrian's letter, addressed "Dear Janet and Adrian and Mary and Dick," and dated April 18, Hopper felt compelled to share some of her latest tidbits: "Tell Mary John [sic] Logan is having quite a time with Marilyn Monroe, who has been in the hospital for ten days and out of *Bus Stop*. Josh maintains that Marilyn is a great actress. I still think she will marry Arthur Miller as soon as he gets a divorce and he is now in the midst of getting it." (Marilyn Monroe's costar in Logan's film version of *Bus Stop* was Don Murray, who had recently worked with Martin in *The Skin of Our Teeth*.)

The other newlyweds in Martin's life, Larry and his wife, Maj, were finally coming to the States for the first time in the summer of 1956. After a brief initiation in New York City, they went to Larry's mother's house in Norwalk. "Mom and Richard weren't there," recalled Hagman. "We were greeted by Richard's sister, Didi, who was the opposite of him, warm and loving. She was a friend to us until the day she died. She helped us settle into the guest house."

But not for long. . . . The aimless Larry and his wife, Maj, considered building a "small house" and managing the new Brazil estate: "Larry intends to turn the property into a self-supporting coffee plantation, as Miss Gaynor and Adrian have done with their place on the opposite side of the valley," wrote McCarthy in his profile on Martin for *Cosmopolitan*. "If the location lives up to the Hallidays' expectations, they will then build another house for themselves."

As Hagman confirmed decades later in his memoir, he and Maj fell in love with Brazil and considered staying there, or making it their home. "There was one little refrigerator, which ran on kerosene," explained Hagman. "Our food was cooked on a wood fire in the kitchen. Yet it was exactly what I'd been looking for. They had horses and ran some cattle on the land. They also had ten thousand chickens and were the biggest supplier for Brasília, the soon-to-be new capital of Brazil. I had a feel for the ranch; the unbelievable beauty really touched me. The dirt was red the way it was in Weatherford, Texas. Mother noticed the effect it had on me and said that if I liked it that much, I could take it over and run the place.

"The offer sounded good until my first blowout with Richard," continued Hagman. "Early on he and I got into one of our fights [and as] much as the ranch touched my soul, I knew it was no use. There was no changing Richard. No talking to him. He was just a pain in the ass—and that was when he was at his best. He was worse once the booze and the speed kicked in. After eleven o'clock in the morning, he was impossible. Later I found out one of the reasons Richard liked Brazil so much was that he could buy almost any medication over the counter, including amphetamines."

The Hagmans quickly moved to New York City, where Larry hoped to follow his mother in the business by becoming a professional actor. They settled in a cheap apartment on Sixth Avenue in Greenwich Village. "Larry and Maj didn't have any money," recalled Roger Phillips. "They didn't have a sou. They used to call me up all the time and ask if I could come down with a pack of Pall Malls and a quart of Ballantine Ale. I remember being there once, with Larry's father, Ben, and [Ben's second] wife, Juanita. Ben was three sheets to the wind with bourbon, and Juanita went to say something, and he looked at her and said, 'Shut up, shitface.' It was bad. It was really bad."

Apart from Larry and Maj, one of the Hallidays' earliest visitors in Brazil was NBC executive Nat Wolff, who made the cumbersome trek with a $500,000 contract for Martin's exclusive appearance on the network over the next five years. Her first offering would be a TV adaptation of Garson Kanin's delightful Broadway comedy, *Born Yesterday*. At forty-three, Martin was decidedly too old to play Billie Dawn, the proverbial dumb blonde, whose surname begins to suggest her rebirth as one smart cookie. Martin felt compelled, however, to tackle a part her idol, Jean Arthur, had attempted but failed to see through. (Before the character of Billie established Judy Holliday as a star, Arthur had originated the role on the road. After concluding her New Haven run, the temperamental and insecure Arthur became "ill" in Boston, and never went on during the Philadelphia tryout, where she was replaced by Holliday, who also played the role in the 1950 film version.)

As directed by the author, Martin's Hallmark Hall of Fame version aired on NBC on Sunday, October 28, 1956, at 7:30, with the significantly longer play reduced to three twenty-five-minute segments. Having already performed his role more than a thousand times on Broadway (but not in the movie, where he was replaced by Broderick Crawford), Paul Douglas played Harry Brock, the gangster-like wheeler-dealer with political connections, whose girlfriend, Billie, improves her mind and her outlook through the mentoring of Paul, played by Arthur Hill (who, in several years, would win the Tony Award for playing George in the original Broadway production of Edward Albee's *Who's Afraid of Virginia Woolf*).

In addition to Martin's affecting a baby voice, there's a rather silly and counterproductive attempt to make her appear younger than she was by having Billie conspicuously clutch a copy of *Seventeen* magazine when making her entrance. Though Martin failed in her memoir even to mention this chapter in her life, "It was a disaster," she claimed elsewhere. "I wanted to play that part so badly, and we came back from Brazil so I could do it. Garson Kanin wanted me to play Billie southern, and that was a mistake."

Though Kanin indeed directed Martin in the TV version of *Born Yesterday*, his involvement was cited by Val Adams in the *New York Times* as part of "the new controversy about air credits for directors of television programs," which had been stirred up by the Radio and Television

Directors Guild, reflecting the need for new rules to govern the relatively new medium of television. According to the Guild, George Schaefer, the show's producer, should be credited as director, since "Mr. Schaefer will be the one who sits in the television control room at show time and actually 'calls the shots' and switching cues. This, by the guild's interpretation, should give Mr. Schaefer credit as director of the program."

Confirming that Martin's Billie Dawn was coming too soon after Judy Holliday made her indelible impression on the role, most of the reviewers agreed with Martin's negative assessment of her own performance, as summarized in the *New York Herald Tribune,* which found her "spectacularly miscast." "It just doesn't play too amusingly when Billie's a lady," observed the reviewer in the *New York Times.*

In his review for the *Los Angeles Mirror-News,* Hal Humphrey shared his surprise that the network retained the play's adult language and situations without having "received any calls complaining about any of the dialogue, or the fact that Billie Dawn and Harry Brock were operating outside of wedlock. Not a single viewer called to object." While Humphrey considered it a strong and welcome sign that the television medium was "growing up," one person who very definitely objected was the show's sponsor: "When the whole significance of [Billie's] character dawned on him, he was not very pleased," claimed Duane Bogie, the show's producer. "I remember his phone call from Kansas City right after we went off the air. *Born Yesterday* was the only show we ever did that Mr. Hall really didn't like. He was terribly upset and he let us know that. Mr. Hall was a moral man and took quality very seriously." Founder and president of Hallmark Cards, Joyce C. Hall had befriended the Hallidays, who were his guests in Kansas City, Missouri, on more than one occasion. Apparently, Hall had just assumed that Martin, in keeping with her image, would only be involved with a project that was "cleaner" and less "adult" than *Born Yesterday* proved to be.

Critic Humphrey also appreciated "watching a comedy on TV without a laugh track" to prompt his reactions and, unlike most other reviewers, felt that Martin held her own against the inevitable comparisons with Judy Holliday: "Her Southern accent escaped her on occasion, otherwise she did the brassy, dumb blonde to a turn." Latter-day viewers are apt to agree with Humphrey's opinion and discover that Martin's natural yet studied naïveté is perfectly suited to Billie's emotional and intellectual transformation.

Chapter 12

"EVERYTHING OLD IS NEW AGAIN"

It was almost as if it was on film, because it was identical
every night. But it always seemed new. It was theater magic.
—JOHN ERMAN, ON MARY MARTIN'S
STAGE PERFORMANCE

During each of Mary Martin's three televised flights as Peter Pan, Dwight D. Eisenhower was installed in the White House, presiding over what would seem, in retrospect, like a bland and sleepy era: the fifties. While the country was increasingly embedded in a so-called Cold War with Russia, Eisenhower, who ended the Korean War upon taking office, was keen to keep the peace.

Hedda Hopper attended Eisenhower's second inauguration, in January 1957, in a dress designed for her by Mainbocher. "My dear Main," she wrote the month before, "I can't begin to express my gratitude for the sensational gown I'll have for the inauguration in Washington, D.C. I felt like a queen the minute I put it on. If I don't knock the spots off everybody there it won't be your fault. I know that Mary Martin is going to turn green with envy when she sees it. I don't suppose [First Lady] Mamie will even speak to me."

Mary Martin, for her part, decided the best way to move forward was by looking back. January brought the announcement that Martin would be re-creating her roles as Ensign Nellie Forbush in *South Pacific* and Annie Oakley in *Annie Get Your Gun* to help celebrate the Civic Light Opera's twentieth anniversary season. She would perform both works for five weeks each in Los Angeles and San Francisco, culminating in a live telecast of *Annie Get Your Gun* ("as a two-hour TV spectacular in color") on November 27. "The twenty playing weeks, plus the rehearsal time, will keep Mary Martin in California for approximately a six-month period," trumpeted an advance article in the *Los Angeles Times,* proud to have its onetime Hollywood resident back home and at the top of her game.

Shortly after the Eisenhower inauguration, Martin wrote Hedda

Hopper a letter of her own, detailing her then-current activities: "As I write I'm as nervous as though I were getting ready for my first audition. Have been working on lots and lots of Dick Rodgers songs for weeks—to get 14 of them together for an album—with Dick playing the piano. I've always adored his piano playing—(he has a simplicity, a strength and a warmth unlike anyone else)."

Recorded over a three-day period in April, shortly before the Hallidays left for Los Angeles, "Mary Martin Sings, Richard Rodgers Plays" would include only twelve Rodgers songs, two-thirds of which feature lyrics by the composer's first partner, Lorenz Hart, and only four by Hammerstein. Though her voice is still at a supple and expressive peak, Martin brought the same unvarying sweetness to each of the dozen numbers—even to Hart's wickedly acidic lyrics for the murderous "To Keep My Love Alive," and to Hammerstein's plaintive and yearning "It Might As Well Be Spring." The one exception is her heartfelt rendition of "Some Enchanted Evening," which plumbs the depths of what few realize is a truly haunting song.

In a rare display of left-wing sympathies, Mary Martin made some unusual demands before agreeing to participate in the Civic Light Opera's *South Pacific* and *Annie Get Your Gun*. "Martin Wolfson and Myron McCormick were both blacklisted actors, who had remained in the original production of *South Pacific* for its entire run, because they couldn't get any other work," said John Erman, who played the Professor in the Civic Light Opera production. "So when it came time to do the revival, she stipulated that she have those two performers. The Light Opera was a very right-wing organization. And the word came back, 'I'm afraid they would not be acceptable to our board.' And she said, 'If they're not acceptable, I won't be able to do this job.'"

In fact, practically everyone in the revival had been involved with a previous production of *South Pacific,* either as a replacement on Broadway or in a touring version. Barbara Luna, who was one of the two "Polynesian" children in the original, was now cast as Liat in the Civic Light Opera revival. The Emile de Becque was completely new, however: Giorgio Tozzi, who, like Pinza, was a notable Metropolitan Opera basso.

The Hallidays arrived in Los Angeles via train at the beginning of May, to be joined by Heller the following month, when her school term in Pennsylvania was completed. "My daughter has no interest in the stage now," explained Martin, "because she is dedicating herself with great determination to domestic science in school. So her stay with us will be strictly

[a] vacation." As Hedda Hopper had recently written, "Mary's relationship with her daughter has always been more that of big sister than mother." And it was perhaps in that spirit that Martin was no longer going to interfere with Heller's wishes to become an ordinary civilian as opposed to a show business trouper.

South Pacific would first play San Francisco, but rehearsals convened in Los Angeles, where, Martin claimed, she slipped "right back into the show as if I had never left it. Ensign Nellie Forbush was just like second nature for me." Not everyone shared her perspective or attitude, however. "We had a director [Albert Marre] who was about as inept as anybody could possibly be," said John Erman. "He had this idea to restage all of the musical numbers, because he thought he could do them better. His first concept was to rehearse at the beach [in Malibu], where he had a house. My first memory of Mary Martin was rehearsing on the beach. And, of course, none of us could hear the piano because the waves were so loud. It was about as idiotic as it could be. And I looked at this woman, who did not bat an eye. She just did exactly what he asked her to do. I didn't know much, but I knew it was a terrible idea."

"As it happened, the weather was pleasant," claimed a puff piece in the *Los Angeles Times*. "The waves breaking upon the shore in an unchanging rhythm provided an unusual background for the music being pounded out on a piano which had been dragged onto the patio from Marre's living room."

The show opened on June 3, at San Francisco's Curran Theatre, which was a jewel-box theater. According to Erman, "Richard Halliday was always present, but very much in the background: he kept his distance. He would watch, he would listen—he didn't interact directly. But he was the henchman. When we got to the Curran, we would see Miss Martin get out of her car. There was always an African-American chauffeur and she would get out, and then Mr. Halliday would get out. They would see her to the stage door and then drive off. The scuttlebutt was that Richard was going to a neighboring theatre to dress the hair of Hermione Gingold and Mary McCarty, who were doing [Noël Coward's] *Fallen Angels*." The Hallidays' all-purpose chauffeur-butler-cook was an extremely flamboyant and obviously gay man named Ernest Adams, who had previously worked for the Lunts and for journalist and writer Adela Rogers St. Johns. Though it never reached the level of scuttlebutt, Adams also apparently became Halliday's live-in lover.

Like his wife, Halliday clearly considered himself an expert hair stylist, and he kept giving notes to the nurses in *South Pacific,* telling them their hair was growing too light, for instance, and asking them to re-dye it. "But in those days, it was real dye," added Erman. "And finally, when one of them said, 'If I dye it one more time, my hair will fall out,' she was told not to worry, that in that case they'd just get her a wig."

Erman recalled Jean Arthur paying a visit backstage after a matinee in San Francisco. "I was standing on the stage, and I see this little woman in very sensible shoes and a little plaid suit. And I see Miss Martin come out of her dressing room, and they ran to each other. They embraced in such a way that even I, still a virgin, knew this was not just two friends saying 'hello.' But then, of course, there was a lot of gossip swirling around the company about the two of them.

"We closed on a Saturday, and then we opened on Monday in Los Angeles, in this enormous space," continued Erman, referring to the Philharmonic Auditorium, where they performed for what seemed like an empty audience of people sitting on their hands. "When it was over, Mary Martin turned to the company and said, 'We can't have gotten *that* bad, after only two days.' Well, the truth was we couldn't really hear the audience reactions [in so cavernous a space]. The audience loved us, but we didn't know it. We didn't have the ability to interact with them. It was like performing in a gulf."

According to Erman, "There was never a sense with Mary Martin of, 'I've played this show 5,000 times,' or 'I can't believe I'm doing this again.' Her performance was always fresh and charming and divine. She just emanated pure joy, and it was perfection! It was almost as if it was on film, because it was identical every night. But it always seemed new. It was theater magic." On the other hand, the cast was genuinely embarrassed by Martin's curtain speech on opening and closing nights. "They were so juvenile, and so out of keeping with a great theater star, that we would all hang our heads in shame. It sounded like someone at a high school graduation. We'd grab each other, saying, 'Oh, no. Here she goes again.'"

Erman's impressions regarding Martin's "magic" were elaborated by critic Albert Goldberg in his review for the *Los Angeles Times*: "You fall in love with her at once and you stay in love through all her vicissitudes to the final curtain. This is not an imitation but the real thing—as real as things ever are in the theater." Goldberg went on to write one of the most definitive descriptions of Martin's artistry as a performer: "It is hard to define Miss Martin's magic. Some of it may be because you are not only in love with her but because she is also in love with you—the audience. She takes you to her heart as you take her to yours." While singling out John Erman as one of the "lusty and vocally overpowering" Seabees,

Goldberg continued his reverie, trying to capture Martin's effect: "It is real and unreal, touchingly human and make-believe, and you can laugh with her and choke a bit at the same time. We haven't seen the like before and we are not likely to again."

There were two backstage visitors in Los Angeles who were less welcome than others. "Josh Logan was about to do the movie of *South Pacific*," recalled Erman, "and he brought Mitzi Gaynor to see the show. He took her backstage to see Miss Martin, and we got the impression from Gladys [Martin's dresser] that she [Martin] was very upset."

Though Martin never publicized her feelings on the matter, it was extremely hard for her to accept that Nellie Forbush, a beloved character she had helped to create, in one of the greatest American musicals of all time, was about to be permanently captured, as it were, by someone else—namely, Mitzi Gaynor. It's extremely telling that Martin would never even bring herself to see the film version of *South Pacific*. More than just insensitive, it was callous and cruel of Logan to confront Martin with Mitzi Gaynor while Martin was in the midst of inhabiting Nellie Forbush all over again, no less.

A decade and a half after the film was released, Logan acknowledged that casting the picture was his biggest initial problem: "Pinza was dead, and Rossano Brazzi had been signed to play de Becque," explained Ross Drake, after interviewing Logan. "Mary Martin was a stage actress, not a movie star, and besides Nellie Forbush was supposed to be 25 years younger than de Becque. Miss Martin was older than Brazzi."

"I tried to get them to use Elizabeth Taylor," Logan told Drake, "because at the time she was freckle-faced and young and very ambitious. But she went up and sang for Dick Rodgers, and she was so scared, she croaked.... Eventually, every actress in the business began contacting us to play Nellie Forbush. The favorite, outside of Mary Martin, was Doris Day." More inexplicably, if defensively, Logan also said, "Outside of my own family, I love Mary more than anyone in the world, but I felt I couldn't subject her to the endless adjustments she would have to make in putting her superb performance on film."

Doris Day was eager to take on the part, but her husband and manager, Martin Melcher, kept ratcheting up her fee; given her fear of flying, Day was reluctant to become involved with a film that was to be shot on location in Hawaii. In contrast to Ross Drake's subsequent report, Mitzi Gaynor won the coveted role even before Rossano Brazzi was cast. (Ironically, Brazzi's voice would be dubbed in the film by Giorgio Tozzi, who played de Becque in the Civic Light Opera production.)

Shortly after Gaynor was announced for the film, Hedda Hopper sent a conciliatory letter to Martin: ". . . distressed that you're not playing Nellie in the picture. I think they've gone off their rocker. Mitzi Gaynor's a sweet girl but by no stretch of the imagination is she Nellie or ever could be. You'd have thought they'd learned their lesson with *Oklahoma* and *Carousel*, (in which key roles were also recast) but some people never learn . . ."

Martin's revival of *Annie Get Your Gun* for the Civic Light Opera had an equally rousing impact when it opened at Los Angeles's Philharmonic Auditorium on October 7. In his review for the *Los Angeles Times,* Edwin Schallert declared Martin's return to Annie Oakley "in all respects inimitable." He also claimed that the way she rode a horse positioned on a treadmill made for "one of the most extraordinary devices for excitement that the stage has proffered in many a day."

After first working with Martin in *Peter Pan,* Joan Tewkesbury now returned as a dancer in the revival of *Annie Get Your Gun*—"probably at Mary Martin's request," she suspected. "She was a force of nature, she really was," continued Tewkesbury. "You could feel all this energy contained, until it just burst right out of her. There would be certain nights, performances with Cyril [in *Peter Pan*], and certainly with Mr. [John] Raitt [in *Annie Get Your Gun*], night after night, when it was stunning. You know how sometimes in the theater when everything gets so silent, you hope it never ends? She had them.

"The thing you learn from Mary was that you go on, come hell or high water. There were times when she had the flu, or her throat was bothering her." (Contrary to Tewkesbury's memory, Martin was, in fact, so ill during the Civic Light Opera run of *Annie Get Your Gun* that she missed four performances in Los Angeles, and her young understudy, Renee Guerin, had to take her place.)

"But her singularity, and the comfort of her self-isolation, was a very interesting thing to perceive," continued Tewkesbury. "Because as a young person you think, 'Oh, it's all parties and fun.' But no. She was extremely disciplined. She mentioned that she used to be a real party girl: 'And only in later life [said Martin] do I realize that Richard had put a stop to it. He really set up this thing about discipline. And it pays off. It's like being a nun, in a funny kind of a way.'"

Perhaps because the Civic Light Opera *Annie Get Your Gun* was leading up to a live broadcast, Vincent Donehue had been recruited as director. A director of highly regarded TV dramas, Donehue had previously helped Martin surmount problems she had with *The Skin of Our Teeth*. He was now making his musical debut as a director with Martin in a role that could have been custom-made for her.

"I found that when it came to identifying places in the score [while I was directing] I resorted to a form of sign language," admitted Donehue. "The musically literate members of the company would be talking about 'eights' and 'fours' but I would say, 'Well, it's where she raises her arms.'"

Mary Martin's television version of *Annie Get Your Gun* appeared on her home network, NBC. Given their success with her *Peter Pan* two years earlier, the publicity seemed even louder and more ubiquitous. When Martin showed up at the studio for a four-hour publicity shoot, she was met by four network photographers, three *TV Guide* personnel, three press agents, three network vice presidents, the design team, the technical crew, three "wranglers," and a live horse—not to mention the show's seven different sets.

The horse, "steadied only by running guy wires," was actually positioned on a treadmill to give the illusion of really going somewhere, while the photographers snapped away. Ever mindful of her appearance, Martin had a bit of an altercation with one of the photographers when she noticed him capturing her from the front: "Uh-uh, dear. No full-face shots." "It's all right. They won't use them, you know," responded the photographer. "Oh yes they will, you know. And I'll sue, you know."

Nor was Martin the only one trying to control appearances. As Donehue acknowledged, "We cut all the off-color lines that drew laughs" in the original version of *Annie Get Your Gun,* adding that if *Peter Pan* had been "a children's show that appealed to adults," they wanted this to be "an adult show that children [could] love."

The network and its sponsors certainly got their wish, as many an American family crowded around their living-room television, with all eyes glued to the set for two hours on Thanksgiving Eve, November 27, 1957. The special earned Martin her picture on the cover of *TV Guide,* slyly smiling in Western garb. A two-page ad inside billed it as "Wonderful family entertainment . . . brought to you by Pontiac and Pepsi-Cola."

Having performed *Annie Get Your Gun* 478 times onstage, Martin had newfound problems re-creating the role for television. The stages at the NBC studio in Burbank were so vast and "widely scattered" that she needed to be shuttled from one to another, to preserve her energies for the performance. Stage Manager George Lawrence became Martin's "runner," carting her piggyback in enough time to make her costume changes. During a final rehearsal, Martin slipped a bit in his arms, skinning her shin before an Indian dance, "which turned out to be the best number in a generally first-rate show," according to a feature in *Life* magazine.

In spite of her ongoing TV success, Martin's original ambivalence about performing on television continued to dog her. "I'd never wanted to do television," claimed Martin a year after the *Annie Get Your Gun* broadcast. "It was too much like the movies, and the movies had given me too much unhappiness."

In December 1957, the Hallidays announced they were terminating their contract with NBC. "Just how much income [they gave up] is not known, but it was less than $100,000 annually," reported Val Adams in his "News of TV and Radio" column in the *New York Times,* adding that, "based on a clause in her contract that she and her advisers believed afforded her a means of escape, [the Hallidays] no longer consider her long-term contract in effect. This seemingly odd turn of events was publicly disclosed last week, although it is now known the actress and singer had been seeking to terminate her contract for more than six months. . . . They just want to be free agents and make a deal for one television show at a time."

It may also be that the couple wanted more freedom to negotiate their private lives at this particular juncture. Not only was Brazil now a constant lure for the Hallidays, but the couple sought some domestic stability with a new, upscale habitat in New York: an elegant duplex penthouse in the Campanile, a prewar deco sliver of a building at 450 East Fifty-second—at the very end of a dead-end street—with two terraces commanding views of the East River. A circular staircase led up to Martin's bedroom on the sixteenth floor. (Though few people would ever know it, Richard's bedroom was on the main floor, hidden away in the servants' quarters, where Ernest also lived.) Previous residents at the Campanile included Ethel Barrymore and Alexander Woollcott, who was famously immortalized as the Man Who Came to Dinner. (With her inimitable way for spicing up practically any perception, Dorothy Parker christened Woollcott's apartment at the Campanile "Wit's End.") The Hallidays' new neighbors now included Greta Garbo, Clare Boothe and Henry Luce, and Drue and Jack Heinz, famous for their "57 Varieties" of ketchup. Perhaps less coincidentally, Joshua Logan lived directly across the street, in the more grandiose River House. The Hallidays also took a separate apartment in the Campanile for Richard's mother, and eventually another one-room apartment, on the fifth floor, also overlooking the East River, would serve as an office for their personal assistant, Lee Tuft.

The frequency of the Hallidays' moving wasn't simply a matter of expediency. Every new location provided Halliday with the opportunity to fulfill the true love of his life by decorating a new space. In less than two years, Martin would tell a reporter for the *Saturday Evening Post*: "Richard . . . and I have had twenty-two homes in our life together. At least I think it's been twenty-two. Several times I've tried to count them, but each time I came up with a different number, so I gave up."

Moving a mammoth, "emperor-size" double bed proved particularly cumbersome under their peripatetic circumstances. "It has been more trouble to us than anything in the world because every time we've moved it's been a problem," explained Martin. "We kept our Norwalk home for fifteen years, and during that time we remodeled the place, so when we moved to this apartment, we had to remove one whole side of the house to get that bed out. When we got to the new apartment, the telephone rang and the superintendent downstairs said, 'Mrs. Halliday, a man has just left your bed in the middle of the street.' I was rehearsing, Richard was talking in the office with about six people and I didn't like to tell him anyhow, because this is a very nice apartment house." There was no simple way to get that bed into their new home. Ultimately the bed frame had to be cut in half and hoisted up sixteen floors, "using a block and tackle on the outside of the building," Martin explained.

While she was involved with the revivals of *South Pacific* and *Annie Get Your Gun* for the Civic Light Opera, Martin received a call from her daughter-in-law and learned she was going to become a grandmother. In his memoir, Larry Hagman recalled being on the verge of getting small parts in two TV shows, *The West Point Story* and *Sea Hunt*. But he was still so financially hard up at the time that he and Maj helped "put groceries on the table" with money her nursing-student sister, Bebe, earned by selling her own blood to the Red Cross: "I could have asked my mother for money, but pride wouldn't let me," wrote Hagman, who, once again, wasn't even talking to his mother at that point. The desperate and enterprising Maj had fewer qualms about approaching her mother-in-law for financial support.

As reported by Hagman, Maj told Martin, "'I come from a family where, if you have a difference, you work it out.' My mother was silent. 'It's a shame that you and Larry are gonna be this way,' Maj continued. 'We're going to have a baby. You're going to be a grandma.' More silence.

'You should talk to him,' Maj said. 'It's up to him,' my mother finally said. That was the opening Maj needed. The two of them talked for about forty-five more minutes."

After Heidi Kristina Mary Hagman was born at Lenox Hill Hospital in New York City on February 17, 1958, Martin performed her first grandmotherly duty by sending her Rolls-Royce and chauffer to take Heidi and her parents home to their Greenwich Village apartment. Martin also had an ulterior motive for overseeing the naming of her first grandchild: "She gave me my name to look good on a marquee," said Kristina Hagman, more than half a century later. "Heidi Hagman—'H. H.,' just like Mary Martin, or 'M. M.' She was going to have an absolute dynasty of people who had names that she had given them on marquees—forever."

When Heidi was only a year old, her mother took her on a public tour of the White House, with a photographer on hand to capture their progress. "I was told that when Dwight Eisenhower heard that Mary Martin's granddaughter was there, they pulled us out of the line to go up to the Oval Office," recalled Kristina Hagman.

There was a great deal going on beneath the quiet and nondescript surface that characterized the Eisenhower fifties. And in a similar way, Mary Martin's relationship with Richard Halliday was certainly not what was presented to the outside world. Like the era that circumscribed their marriage, the bond between Mary Martin and Richard Halliday was far more complicated than it seemed, the terms of the bargain they made with each other beyond the realm of acceptable behavior. Their desperate connection to each other was their shield from a real world that could neither comprehend nor tolerate who they really were.

Chapter 13

HAIL MARY

She had plenty of street smarts, in terms of her own career.
And that was the only thing she seemed to care about.
—MARY RODGERS ON MARY MARTIN

All you think about is the show! You don't care about Mary.
—RICHARD HALLIDAY

Certain works of art come to represent a closing more than a start, a culmination as opposed to a new beginning. The 1961 film *The Misfits* emerges as a prime example, since it proved the swan song for both Clark Gable and Marilyn Monroe, two of the silver screen's greatest legends. In music, *The Magic Flute* stands out as Mozart's ultimate masterpiece, composed during the last year of his life. *The Sound of Music* takes its place in this pantheon as Rodgers and Hammerstein's final collaboration. It also signals the beginning of the end of what would come to be seen as the golden age of the American musical, even as it stands as a latter-day example of the form's roots in operetta.

It may be well-known in the theater world that Mary Martin, as opposed to Julie Andrews, originated the role of Maria in *The Sound of Music*, but few cultural arbiters realize that Martin and her husband were the moving force behind the creation of this phenomenally successful musical in the first place.

As the saying goes, however, success has many fathers. In his sideline capacity as a scout for Paramount pictures, Vincent Donehue saw two German movies based on the life of Baroness Maria von Trapp—*Die Trapp Familie* and *Die Trapp Familie in Amerika*—and considered them a worthy project to pursue. He recognized the universal appeal of her story, of being a young Austrian postulate who fell in love with a widowed naval commander and his ten children and who went on to develop an international reputation as part of a singing family. He even envisioned Audrey Hepburn in an American film version of the story—perhaps because the svelte beauty was already making *The Nun's Story*. But more germane to the genesis of *The Sound of Music,* Donehue brought the German films to the attention of his associates and friends, the Hallidays.

Initially viewing the material as a dramatic vehicle for Martin, the Hallidays asked Rodgers and Hammerstein to write a single song that "Mary could sing someplace in the show." Feeling this was a misguided way to proceed, Rodgers told the Hallidays that they "should do it without songs, do it as a straight play, or do it as a full musical, go all out." More privately, Rodgers told Leland Hayward, another leading creator of *The Sound of Music,* "No way am I competing with Mozart and Brahms and Austrian folksongs—all that stuff [the Trapp family sang]. Oscar and I would like to write the entire score." (But as Rodgers also noted, "The German picture had very little singing in it, was more or less a dramatic story about the Trapp family.") The Hallidays decided on taking the musical route, only to learn that Rodgers and Hammerstein were already committed to another project. "We had to explain that we would be tied up with *Flower Drum Song* for a year," recalled Rodgers, "but they came back with the two most flattering words possible: 'We'll wait.'"

The long delay proved advantageous, since the Hallidays' lawyer, William Fitelson, had to make no fewer than six trips to Munich to negotiate the stage rights. According to one version of what transpired, Baroness von Trapp was ultimately tracked down in an Innsbruck hospital, having contracted malaria when she was a missionary in New Guinea. According to another, the Hallidays themselves confronted Maria von Trapp shortly after she arrived in San Francisco: they gave her a pair of tickets to Martin's *Annie Get Your Gun* at the Curran Theatre and won her permission to embark on a musical version of her life.

In fact, Trapp had already sold the rights to her life story for a mere $9,000 to the German production company that made the earlier films, and the Germans now asked the Hallidays for a rather sizable $200,000. "Dick was a very shrewd businessman," recalled Frank Goodman, who would become the show's press agent. "He and Mary looked around for capital, and guess how they figured it all out? Mary [had] had a long-term contract with NBC Television. She'd been such a huge hit for them in *Peter Pan*. NBC could run it, year after year, and the kids loved it. . . . So Dick went over to Radio City and asked the NBC executives for an advance. . . . NBC, of course, wanted to keep their star happy, and they knew Mary would earn back that money for them in the future, so they agreed to lend Mary and Dick the $200,000 so they could use it to finish their deal with the Germans!"

Though it wasn't at all necessary for them to do so—and though no one ever could have imagined that it would amount to anything substantial—the Hallidays also gave Maria von Trapp three-eighths of 1 percent of their own royalties. Beyond being a gesture of goodwill for good luck, perhaps it was intended to secure Trapp's participation in re-telling what was basically her story.

While work on the project was stalled until Rodgers and Hammer-stein were ready to proceed roughly a year later, the workaholic Martin was not about to remain idle for such a prolonged period. The Hallidays decided to bide their time by sending Martin on an extensive road tour with a solo show, *Music with Mary Martin,* which basically traced her life to date in song, from her beginnings in Weatherford, Texas, to her Broad-way blockbusters.

Enter the elder of Richard Rodgers's two daughters, Mary, who as-pired to follow in her father's footsteps by becoming a musical theater composer. Mary Rodgers was, at the time, working with lyricist Marshall Barer on what would emerge as her most well-known work, *Once Upon a Mattress.* (The 1959 Broadway musical starred a zany newcomer by the name of Carol Burnett.)

Mary Rodgers was also working with her pianist sister Linda on a short children's musical called *Three to Make Music*—a natural out-growth of her contributing material to Leonard Bernstein's Young People's Concert series. "My mother asked me to start writing lyrics for my sister, which was nonsense," said Mary Rodgers. "The only reason I wrote lyrics was so that I could write the music to go with them." *Three to Make Music,* she explained, "was about the man who writes it, the man who plays it, and the man who hears it." By adding to this a truncated, five-minute, one-woman version of her father's latest confection, an origi-nal musical retelling of *Cinderella,* and ending with an obligatory scene of Martin flying as Peter Pan, *Three to Make Music* was expanded into *Magic with Mary Martin,* which, in turn, was introduced on tour with *Music with Mary Martin.* (Starring Broadway's latest arrival, Julie Andrews, Rodgers and Hammerstein's *Cinderella* had its first live televi-sion broadcast on March 31, 1957.)

"I ended up working on both shows [*Music with Mary Martin* and *Magic with Mary Martin*]. It was my first paying job," Mary Rodgers continued, recalling that she received a flat fee of $6,000. "I wrote some connecting music on the adult show [*Music with Mary Martin*] at the same time that I was working on *Once Upon a Mattress.* I remember Dick Halliday came up to me and said, 'How dare you work on your own stuff when I'm paying you to be writing Mary's show?' From that point on, he was very difficult to deal with. He was really a *beast.* . . . I remember someone had said, 'Mary [Martin] makes the bullets and Dick Halliday fires them.'

"My first husband was gay," continued Mary Rodgers, whose marriage to Julian Beaty Jr., known as Jerry, ended in divorce. "He didn't drink a lot [like Richard Halliday], but he had a very unpleasant personality. And then, when I was working on *Mattress* with Marshall, he had a friend and lover named Ian, who was great in bed," said the eighty-year-old Mary Rodgers, who was quick to dispel any notion that she was the well-behaved matriarch many had mistaken her for. "I once had a very interesting weekend at [agent] Flora Roberts's house on Fire Island: me and Marshall and Ian. And then, when I mentioned that Marshall wanted to marry me, Daddy did something he never did before, which was to close the door to his library and say, 'I'm not going to let you do this.'" Rodgers warned his daughter against marrying an obviously gay man. "He said those marriages don't work, not because the guys are sick, but because the guilt they live with is so painful. He ran through a list of people who had 'arranged' marriages. He said, 'Look at you and Jerry. . . . Look at Richard and Mary. . . .'"

While Richard Rodgers surely also had in mind his first collaborator, Lorenz Hart, when he thwarted his daughter's intention of marrying yet another gay man, he also got to the heart of Richard Halliday's awkward interactions. Most of Halliday's ugly and nasty behavior with colleagues can best be understood in terms of the self-loathing that epitomized homosexuality in the pre-Stonewall era, an internalized attitude that permeated practically every aspect of his existence. Bringing to mind Lorenz Hart's lyric "the self-deception that believes the lie" (from *I Wish I Were in Love Again*), Halliday's collaborations were marked by an overarching insecurity that translated into arrogance, a sense of inferiority that needed to be compensated by a superior attitude, a feeling of isolation that strained any efforts to collaborate with associates. Within the tribal community that circumscribes the theater, Halliday perpetually felt like a loner and an outsider, as he was in other aspects of his life. (He even alienated, at various points, Noël Coward.) Burying his truer impulses and living a lie made Halliday insincere and insufferable for others to contend with.

What Martin would later term her "favorite tour of all," presenting *Music with Mary Martin* and *Magic with Mary Martin* as separate events, played eighty-seven performances in sixty-four cities, from September

1958 to March 1959, beginning in remote Alaska—to celebrate its brand-new statehood—and concluding at Yale University's Poli Theatre in New Haven, with stops in relatively small cities such as Beaumont, Texas, Binghamton, New York, and Youngstown, Ohio. As directed by Vincent Donehue, the bus-and-truck road show included a twenty-piece orchestra conducted by John Lesko, featuring guitarist Luiz Bonfa and dancer Dirk Sanders of Les Ballet de Paris.

Having recently toured Alaska with Bob Hope, Hedda Hopper sent a cautionary letter to "Darling Mary and Richard": "Don't work too hard and take some of your old Mainbochers. The stages up there are very dirty. I can imagine what you are going to do to those beautiful gowns."

With hopes of televising both shows at the end of the tour—initially, apparently, with CBS, but ultimately, in fact, with NBC—Halliday was well aware of the difficult road ahead. In an undated letter to public relations agent Joseph Bleeden, Halliday wrote: "We start out next month for a tour of one-night stands and in the event the CBS deal is set, will get back just in time for Mary to start camera rehearsals for the show. She'll be 'dead' after all that traveling and performing, and there won't be a minute that she can spare for interviews or photos. That's a shame, we know it. But those are the facts. And then she starts out again for more one-night stands. Yes, we like doing things the hard way!"

She would be "staying overnight in motels, and improvising in school gymnasiums, municipal auditoriums, civic halls and a wide variety of local theatres, for one-night stands, [which] are . . . new to her varied career," claimed an advance story, which didn't mention that the vagaries of such a vagabond existence were slightly mitigated for Martin by her being transported in the 1947 Rolls-Royce that Halliday had purchased in London. They were also eased by the constant ministrations of Ernest, their chauffeur, and Martin's dresser, Nena Smith, "a beautiful Mexican-born lady whose profession is wigmaker," according to Martin.

Describing *Music with Mary Martin* as "a musical resume of my life," Martin explained, "I open with a song called 'The Song Is You,' and my theme is 'I Hear Music When I Look at You.' When I finish that song, I tell the audience, 'Truer words were never said, because my song *is* you—and it's a love song. Some people fall in love at first sight, some people never fall in love at all, but I fell in love at five when I sang 'The Lilac Tree' at the Fireman's Ball in my hometown, Weatherford, Texas. I didn't fall in love with one face in that audience—I fell in love with all of them. It's been that way ever since. So now I'd like to sing for you the first song I ever sang.'"

In the midst of the tour, the Hallidays were home in New York for Thanksgiving, after which Mainbocher wrote Hedda Hopper: "Mary and Richard came in yesterday—Mary looking absolutely divine—Not tired, but a little thinner. I think that despite the rough spots she has had a wonderful time. She surely is an exceptional gal—so outgoing and giving and such a trouper!"

Though the tour had many memorable nights, none was as notable as one performance of *Music with Mary Martin* in Newark, where the stellar audience included Vinton Freedley, who had produced Martin's first Broadway show, *Leave It to Me!,* as well as Joshua Logan and Leland Hayward—and Hollywood gossip columnist Radie Harris. Given the many old friends and colleagues in the audience that night, "I had a hard time choking back my tears," said the star.

The Hallidays opted for traversing the vast expanse of Texas in a commuter plane. In a *New York Times* feature, Martin recalled a mishap when she was performing in Lubbock, and a storm prompted a blackout. "We kept right on playing in the dark until the lights were fixed," Martin said. In the same article, Halliday proudly noted a new road sign that greeted one's arrival in Weatherford, Texas: "Home of Parker County Watermelons and Mary Martin." As Martin also recalled, the "regular dressing room" at Constitution Hall in Washington, DC, "is so far from the stage, and I had so many costume changes to make, with only a few seconds to make them in, that I had to dress in the men's room. . . . You should have seen me hanging my Mainbocher clothes over whatever I could find in there."

The tour was particularly hard on the young Mary Rodgers, who had lived a life of privilege as Richard's daughter. She was trying to break into the business herself by continuing to work on the scripts during the beginning of the tour. "Dick [Halliday] was so drunk and out of control all of the time, and he really lost it with me," she recalled. "He once fired me on the set. What a time we had, between Dick being so drunk and mean, and Vinnie Donehue drinking a lot himself and driving around the country, and Mary being pretty much a cipher. She had plenty of street smarts, in terms of her own career. And that was the only thing she seemed to care about. . . . She also had a very good sense of humor about herself. I never saw any particular form of affection between her and Richard; but, between them, they were pretty lethal in terms of getting what they wanted."

The tour culminated with both shows performed live for television on Easter Sunday, March 29, 1959, consisting of *Magic with Mary Martin,* airing from 3:00 to 4:00 P.M., and *Music with Mary Martin*, from 7:00 to 8:00 P.M. Performed in a studio in Brooklyn and broadcast in color on NBC, the two shows cost $500,000 to produce. (Martin earned $100,000.) The matinee was presented in a jewel-box theater, fashioned after the tiny playhouse at Versailles, with Mary Rodgers's narrated prologue and a puffy-pantalooned Mr. Clown perfectly conveying the pedantic spirit of the enterprise: "This is the theater, the doors open wide / And here is the audience, sitting inside. / Now this is a ticket, especially for you, / And here is the man, who will tear it in two. / Give your half to the usher, and follow his feet. / He knows where you're sitting. Oh, here is your seat." The evening performance was suitably more elegant, featuring Martin, in a black tuxedo with top hat and cane, tap-dancing to "Lady of the Evening" and, at another point, in a black sleeveless gown on a white grand piano, crooning "Tea for Two."

Richard Rodgers's displeasure with Martin's rendering of his *Cinderella* may have been a comment on his daughters' compression of the material no less than Martin's performance. And the production values for *Music with Mary Martin* seem, in retrospect, rather slipshod and thrown together. But the reviewers were, as always, dazzled by Martin: "Both productions show one of the world's great show women at the very peak of her powers as singer, dancer, actress and personality," wrote Jack Moffitt in the *Hollywood Reporter*. "*Music with Mary Martin* was a thing of excellence—dash[ing], spirited, visually beautiful, and even stirring," claimed Marie Torre in the *Herald Tribune*. In the *New York Times*, Jack Gould emphasized that much of the company was battling a "severe virus" for several days: "Miss Martin herself had run a fever as high as 103 degrees but such was her professional trouping spirit that she declined to withdraw or take the easy way out by taping the program in advance."

"Mary got sick," recalled Mary Rodgers. "She even went to the hospital with pneumonia, or something bordering on it, and her understudy had to stand in for her during rehearsals. But she insisted on doing these shows live on Easter Sunday. I don't know why, because there was tape then." As Halliday told a columnist for the *New York Post*: "Three doctors were in attendance. We had two standbys ready to go on in the event anything happened to Mary during either show. . . . She'll probably be in bed 48 hours, at least." On the verge of playing a character half her age for the next two years, Martin would be able to use whatever preliminary rest she could come by.

Mary Martin was forty-five years old when she undertook the role of Maria in *The Sound of Music*, which had a book by Howard Lindsay and

Russel Crouse—one of the most successful playwriting teams in Broadway history, already responsible for the massive hits *Life with Father* and *Arsenic and Old Lace*. Having previously worked with Lindsay and Crouse on *Call Me Madam,* it was Leland Hayward who now approached them with several ideas, including musical versions of *Gone with the Wind* and Gypsy Rose Lee's new memoir, *Gypsy*—or a musical about the Trapp Family Singers to star Martin. This last was the one they found irresistible, even though, given her age, Martin probably would not have even been cast in the part if it hadn't been written for her.

"Working with Mary Martin again made me appreciate even more what an extraordinary trouper she is," Richard Rodgers wrote in his memoir. "During rehearsals and during the run of the show on Broadway she was constantly in training, both vocally and physically. Nothing we ever suggested was considered too demanding. . . . In all the years I've known her, I have never seen her give a performance that was anything less than the best that was in her." Martin said, "It was one of the most disciplined shows I ever did." And as a ten-page coverstory in *Life* magazine depicted, Martin was in training every day with a punching bag to improve her aging vocal instrument. "[The exercise] strengthens her diaphragm action and also helps condition her body to produce big tones," explained William Herman, her voice teacher for the show.

In yet another cover story, in *This Week* magazine—a weekly insert in Sunday newspapers throughout the country—Martin introduced the writer, Charles D. Rice, to the "torture chamber" above Herman's studio: "She led us upstairs into a room that looked like an emergency ward. There were three beds—'Pilates beds' she called them—placed in a row." This was half a century before Pilates became a routine part of many a gym goer's regimen. "They did look like instruments of torture, and in a way they were, but the torture was constructive. You could row in them, lift weights, or shift the sections into a number of other hideous means of exercise." As Martin accounted for the workout: " 'I don't think people realize how loud you have to sing on stage. When I finish a song like 'Do-Re-Mi' . . . they think I'm sort of crooning. But here's the way I really have to sing it'—and she started off with a blast that nearly took the hair off our head."

Martin also fortified herself for the part by developing a meaningful and lasting relationship with Sister Gregory, a nun who headed the drama department at Rosary College in Chicago. Sister Gregory struck up a correspondence with the Hallidays after seeing the original production of *South Pacific*. And now, "everyone concerned agreed that we needed

Sister Gregory's advice," wrote Martin in her memoir. "Finnie [Done-hue], whom she had never met, flew out to Chicago to get acquainted before he started rehearsals. . . . She was the inspiration for those joyous songs 'My Favorite Things' and 'Maria,' because she told us what fun nuns have, all the happy times inside the convent or an abbey. I can still hear her saying, 'Don't make nuns sanctimonious!'"

Sister Gregory was but the first of what would become a long parade of "hundreds of priests, nuns, [and] catholic prelates who came to see the show and then came backstage afterward," according to Martin, adding that she was "blessed twice by monsignors, kissed by priests, and even received a special blessing from Pope John in Rome." Though her dressing-room table was cluttered with religious icons and figurines, as Martin further explained, her "own religious belief turned out not to be a formal, organized sort of 'go to this church' kind, but rather a belief that there is Someone there, within me, and all I have to do is call on Him."

After seeing Hammerstein's proposed lyrics for "Climb Ev'ry Mountain," the savvy Sister Gregory wrote Martin a letter, saying, "It drove me to the Chapel. (Relax, chums, I'm sure it will not affect your audiences in the same way.) It made me acutely aware of how tremendously fortunate are those who find a dream that will absorb all their love, and finding it, embrace it to the end. . . . Mr. Hammerstein's lyrics seem perfectly, yet effortlessly, to express what we ordinary souls feel but cannot communicate."

While Sister Gregory became an "unofficial technical advisor in Catholic matters," Richard Rodgers sought authenticity in his musical compositions by reaching out to another religious figure, Mother Morgan at Manhattanville College in Purchase, New York, who introduced him to Catholic liturgical music, including classic hymns and Gregorian chants. This was the "closest Rodgers ever got to musicology research for any project," claimed Laurence Maslon in his in-depth study of the making of the musical, *The Sound of Music Companion*.

The attention to detail on *The Sound of Music* proved extensive. Bruce Pomohac recalled playing Richard Rodgers's score of *I Remember Mama* for Martin in the mid-1980s, to ascertain if she had any interest in recording it. "I asked her about *The Sound of Music*," he said. "I wanted to know if they had pursued an Austrian accent." 'We made the decision that what we would do is take on a style of English, that was high English,' explained Martin. 'It was an educated family in a wealthy home. It was also a formal environment. So we thought if our English was formal, it would convey something that our accent didn't need to do.'"

Yet another influence on the development of the script was Maria von

Trapp herself. After reading an early draft of what was tentatively titled "The Singing Heart" and then "Love Song," Maria pointed out that her own character needed to be more of the tomboy she had actually been, in order to make her transformation into a bride and mother even more striking. (In the original German documentary, Maria makes her entrance sliding down a banister—much to the consternation of her sister nuns.) She also felt that Captain Trapp's severity was stressed at the exclusion of his genuine transformation into a loving husband and father. Lindsay and Crouse failed to heed the Baroness's major concern, however, regarding one Father Wasner, a seminarian professor who lived with the Trapp family and tutored the children in their singing. The seasoned playwrights understood that the story was better served by giving Maria that all-important assignment.

The Baroness von Trapp's hands-on involvement with shaping the material prompted Halliday to resort to his controlling tactics: he "did whatever he could to keep the headstrong matriarch back home in Vermont during rehearsals." (*Life* magazine ran yet another advance story and picture spread of the show, with photos of Martin romping in Vermont with the ten Trapp children—seven daughters and three sons—as opposed to the total of seven written into the libretto.)

According to casting advisor Eddie Blum, while the book for the musical was coming together "the big problem was finding someone to play opposite [Martin]. They tried to get a man with a Mitteleuropean background, even if she didn't have one herself," he recalled. "Someone would get on the phone with an idea and come up with [teenage heartthrob pop singer] Bobby Darin! It was nutty.... Naturally we went the operatic route first, looking for another Pinza. No luck. We tried a great German actor but he couldn't sing. Then we called in Leif Erickson. We heard he could sing and they loved him. But not enough."

It was Blum who recommended an Israeli folksinger by the name of Theodore Bikel. After performing two Frank Loesser songs from *Guys and Dolls* at his audition ("Luck Be a Lady" and "My Time of Day"), Bikel played his guitar and "slipped in" one of his folk songs, at which point Martin turned to Rodgers and said, "We don't have to look any further, do we?"

The Viennese-born Bikel was a character actor who had already made a number of films—most notably *The African Queen* and *The Defiant Ones*—when he was cast in this, his first Broadway musical. "I was a very good friend of Larry [Hagman]'s when he was in the Air Force, in London," recalled Bikel. "He stayed in an apartment that was literally next door to where I was living, and we hung out a lot." According to Bikel, Hagman used to attend gatherings at his flat. "Larry came and played the guitar and sang songs. In fact, he made up songs. I even put one of them in my folk song book."

But Bikel was ten years younger than Martin, which only emphasized the discrepancy in her age with that of the character she was playing. Gray highlights were added to Bikel's hair every two weeks: "They couldn't make her younger, so they made me older," he explained.

There was another challenge: casting seven children, between eight and thirteen years old. "We interviewed more than 300 looking for the right ones," recalled director Donehue. "They had to emanate health and joy and, of course, they had to sing. But we cared most [about] what kind of human beings they are." Since children grow so rapidly, they needed to be replaced with some regularity during the course of the show's extensive run. And in view of Martin's being severely nearsighted, she required that all replacements be the same height and have their hair dyed, if necessary, to resemble the originals she had grown accustomed to playing with. (In retrospect, Martin's notorious problems with making any changes to a show once it had been "frozen," or set, had as much to do with her limited visual capacity as anything else.)

Having portrayed one of the nurses in *South Pacific,* Bernice Saunders was now cast as a nun in *The Sound of Music.* "The first day of rehearsals, Mary was so sweet, saying to me, 'Oh, look. We're gonna be working together again,'" recalled Saunders. "There were only seven of us [nuns] to begin with; but then they added a whole other group and we became a chorus of fifteen. And they had their pick of 'voices' in the city; because we were so covered [by our costumes], it didn't matter what we looked like." According to Saunders, "if anything, Mary Martin was more sure of herself than before, because she now had this marvelous reputation."

Following extensive tryouts in New Haven and Boston, *The Sound of Music* was slated to arrive on Broadway at what had been the Globe Theatre, which had recently been renamed the Lunt-Fontanne when Alfred Lunt and Lynn Fontanne opened with Friedrich Dürrenmatt's *The Visit,* on May 5, 1958. According to Fontanne's biographer, Margot Peters, "[Fontanne] and Mary Martin were considered the best makeup artists in the business, following Lynn's rule: 'You make up for the orchestra, not the balcony.'"

The creation of *The Sound of Music* was tragically underscored by Oscar Hammerstein's encroaching illness. He had just learned he required surgery for what would prove to be stomach cancer, and, on September 18, showed up at the stage door of the Lunt-Fontanne Theatre and handed Martin a slip of paper. "I wrote a little couplet and I really don't know where it's going to go in the show because I haven't thought past this, but I'd like you to have it," Hammerstein told Martin, adding, "Don't look at it now. Look at it later."

The note contained the lyrics for what would become a new duet with Lauri Peters, a second-act reprise of "Sixteen Going on Seventeen," including one of the poet-lyricist's most succinct and poignant perceptions, worthy of his brilliant predecessor in partnership with Rodgers, Lorenz Hart: "And love in your heart wasn't put there to stay / Love isn't love till you give it away."

Several days later, Hammerstein was operated on. The verdict of the severity of his condition and his limited time left was kept from him. Too ill to attend the tryouts in New Haven, Hammerstein received a reassuring cable from Lindsay and Crouse:

WE ARE SIXTY GOING ON 70, YOU CAN DEPEND ON US. HOWARD AND BUCK.

It was decided in New Haven that the appearance of the Nazi officers was heavy-handed and potentially offensive: their onstage presence was downplayed by eliminating their swastika armbands, for one thing, and their brown costumes, for another. Stefan Gierasch, who played the leading Nazi Herr Zeller, was also given a new uniform. "Stefan spent a lot of time with us," recalled Bernice Saunders, "because he was carrying on with the gal I was rooming with. He came in with his new blue uniform and said, 'How does it look?' I had to point out that his private parts were far too accentuated by his tight pants."

Though Lucinda Ballard designed the costumes for the show, Mainbocher was in charge of Maria's wedding gown and party dress. A behind-the-scenes battle ensued when Martin insisted on lace and blue ribbons for Maria's underwear, until Rodgers asked Leland Hayward to intercede. "They had a big fight over the drawers," recalled Ballard, "and Leland and Dick Rodgers walked down the corridor with Dick Halliday shouting at them, 'All you think about is the show! You don't care about Mary.'"

"Richard Rodgers knew more about the theater than [Halliday] did, but Halliday was always out there protecting Mary," claimed Russel Crouse's wife, Anna. "Mary was very smart. She'd let her husband bite the paddle and, when asked, she 'didn't know anything about it.' I saw

Dick [Rodgers] lose his temper with Halliday and speak his mind [and] on a couple of occasions Dick just took off after Mr. Halliday. . . . Mary and Dick [Rodgers] didn't speak for quite a while after that. One night the wonderful man who owned the Ritz-Carlton in Boston gave a party for the company in the dining room after the show. Mary and Dick [Rodgers] were sitting on opposite sides of the room and nobody was speaking!"

It was in Boston that Oscar Hammerstein finally got to see *The Sound of Music,* his forty-fourth and last show, for the first time. "I remember he sat in a box, with his wife Dorothy," said Anna Crouse, "and Dorothy came out during the intermission to Russel, and she said, 'I have only seen Oscar'—Poppy, she called him—'cry once in my whole married life . . . and he's been crying.' Broke your heart."

As determined during the previews in Boston, there was a serious structural problem with Captain von Trapp's character getting lost in the story. "The Broadway book had not served him well," wrote Christopher Plummer about Trapp, the character he, in turn, would play in the beloved film version of the musical. "Even in the screenplay, he was still very much a cardboard figure, humorless and one-dimensional." The original creators at least attempted to address the problem, when Hammerstein, post surgery, arrived midway through the Boston tryouts, and he penned his very last song with Richard Rodgers, "Edelweiss," which became Theodore Bikel's only solo number. (As Bikel recalled, the song was so authentic sounding that an audience member once told him how much she enjoyed singing it "in the original German," when she was growing up.)

Having incorporated the name of her childhood friend Bessie Mae into practically all of her shows ("I sent her opening night flowers every time a show opened with her name in it," Martin once said), Martin finally figured out a way to do so with *The Sound of Music* when she was in Boston: they listed her in the program as yet another postulant. But what always worked like a good luck charm for Martin backfired this time for Bessie Mae, when the IRS hounded the Weatherford native for unreported earnings—which, of course, Bessie Mae never earned.

Lucinda Ballard recalled another funny offstage episode in Boston, when the nuns, on a rehearsal break, went to a nearby bar for some drinks. "[A] large crowd of very proper Bostonians were gawking in appalled horror at the sight of a dozen nuns with their shoes kicked off, their habits hiked up around their knees, their feet on tables as they smoked cigarettes, drank beer and swapped decidedly un-nun-like anecdotes containing very un-nun-like adjectives! The 'nuns' were hastily shepherded back to the safety of the theatre before a riot began."

In a case of *reverse* mistaken identity, there was a bizarre incident following a matinee when some authentic nuns had gathered backstage to meet Martin, which had been prearranged. "Before they could reach her dressing-room, however, musical staging director Joe Layton came bustling through, saw the nuns standing about looking understandably uncertain, and tore into them. 'God dammit!' he yelled, 'You girls know you're not supposed to stand out here in the hall in your goddamned costumes! Now get back to your dressing room right this minute and get them off!'" He was, of course, shamefaced when he finally realized his error, and learned that they had all gone home without meeting Mary Martin.

Referring to the "silliness, stiffness and corny operetta falseness of the script," critic Elliot Norton's response to the Boston tryout might have put a damper on the company's spirits, but most of the preliminary reviewers continued their long-held reveries for the songwriting team that had already given them *Oklahoma! Carousel, South Pacific,* and *The King and I.* And when *The Sound of Music* opened at Broadway's Lunt-Fontanne Theatre on November 16, 1959, the $480,000 musical had a record-breaking advance sale of $2,320,000.

Wearing a green satin gown that Martin had given her for the occasion, Maria von Trapp attended the opening night party, which, like the one for *South Pacific,* was held at the St. Regis Roof. Upon her entrance, Martin "pressed the hand of Helen Hayes [and] bear-hugged Claudette Colbert" before turning to Ethel Merman, hugging Marlene Dietrich, and then "kissing people right and left." Other members of the stellar audience that night included Katharine Cornell, Gypsy Rose Lee, and Kitty Carlisle and Moss Hart. Anna Crouse recalled it as a "devastating" evening as soon as the morning papers became available. Unfortunately, Norton's negative Boston notice proved a harbinger of the major New York reviews. As Martin would recall, when the reviews were read aloud, "They were all 'Oh, how boring, boring, boring, all those children, dogs and nuns!" "The scenario," Brooks Atkinson wrote in the *New York Times,* "has the hackneyed look of the musical theatre [that Rodgers and Hammerstein had] replaced with *Oklahoma!* in 1943. It is disappointing to see the American musical stage succumbing to the clichés of operetta." In the *Herald Tribune,* Walter Kerr picked up on Norton's "corny" trope: "I can only wish that someone had not been moved to abandon the snowflakes and substitute cornflakes . . . not only too sweet for words, but almost too sweet for music . . . the people onstage have all melted before our hearts do."

In his well-considered discussion for *Saturday Review,* Henry Hewes emphasized the show's sentimentality, its "compounding of the reverential," making it, in the end, "crushingly unexciting": it "drowns in perfection, and tastefulness." And, although Martin "plays Maria with authority and her usual vitality," she had also, by then, "created a public impression of extroverted goodheartedness and wholesomeness beside which the already canonized saints seem unpleasant characters." (Despite Hewes's irredeemably negative response, Martin was pictured on the magazine's cover, in costume as Maria, clutching her guitar case.)

Although he had singlehandedly defended *South Pacific* against the sour grapes and envious gripes of his fellow British critics, Kenneth Tynan was less sanguine about Mary Martin's final collaboration with Rodgers and Hammerstein. "[Martin's] buoyancy is corklike and enchanting, despite a tendency to address the members of the audience as if they, like the Trapps, were her stepchildren," he wrote, adding that she "can still brandish a note as blithely and suddenly as the best of them, though the sunlight of her voice is somewhat dimmer than it used to be." Tynan closed his already damning review with a particularly scathing quip: "To sum up uncontroversially, *The Sound of Music* is a show for children of all ages, from six to about eleven and a half." Even a puff piece in *Life* magazine was compelled to acknowledge that the show was too saccharine for its own good: "Mary Martin suffuses everything with her charm and the whole show is like a Christmas pudding, full of delights and sweetmeats— though some may wish it had a bit more spice and brandy." (Christopher Plummer would, famously, call the musical "The Sound of Mucous.")

From the beginning, the creators of *The Sound of Music* had been overly defensive about the sentimentality at the core of the story, which made its phenomenal success almost an embarrassment for them. "Sentiment has never been unpopular except with a few sick persons who are made sicker by the sight of a child, a glimpse of a wedding or the thought of a happy home," claimed Oscar Hammerstein, who added, more than a little disingenuously, that, "No incidents were invented or dragged in to play on sentimental susceptibilities of the audience as some critics seem to feel." Most of the critics' "carping" was "aimed at the book, which, predictably, was labeled too sentimental," concurred Richard Rodgers, who also said, "the truth is that almost everything in it was based on fact." "Although it's a true story, the setting being Austria seemed obviously one for operetta," added Howard Lindsay. "We had to keep the story convincing and believable, not letting it get into the never-never land that operetta lives in."

In truth, the powers that be behind *The Sound of Music* took an already sentimental page from history and made it far more so. The eldest of the Trapp children was not, in reality, a sixteen-year-old girl going on seventeen and ripe for romance, but an awkward adolescent boy. The real Maria was originally sent to the Trapp household to look after the captain's second daughter, who was bedridden, as opposed to his entire brood, each of whom had been stricken with scarlet fever when they were younger. Rather than frowning on singing, Georg von Trapp welcomed music in his home and accompanied his children on various instruments long before Maria entered their domain. And when the Trapp family escaped as Germany annexed Austria in 1938, it didn't involve a dramatic, scenic climb over the Alps but the comforts of a train ride to Italy. ("Ride any train" would hardly have had the same emotional impact as "Climb ev'ry mountain.")

But critics be damned—or at least rendered superfluous. Nothing could stop the winning combination of Rodgers and Hammerstein when Mary Martin's name was attached to theirs. *The Sound of Music* proceeded to bring joy to untold millions of theatergoers around the world. It would run on Broadway for three and a half years, and nearly twice as long in the West End, where it became the longest-running musical in London theatrical history. The Twentieth Century–Fox film version would become the top-grossing motion picture of all time, surpassing even *Gone with the Wind* during its initial release. The Columbia original cast album was number 1 on the Billboard charts for sixteen weeks, and remained in the listings for five years. The show also won six of the nine Tony Awards for which it was nominated. While all the young women playing Trapp children were competing as one against Lauri Peters and Patricia Neway, who won for Featured Actress in a Musical, *The Sound of Music* tied with *Fiorello* for Best Musical. In the most contested award of the year, Martin won her fourth Tony as Maria, besting Ethel Merman as Mama Rose in *Gypsy*. Ethan Mordden would call it "a feat of *Guinness Book* proportions." And as Merman herself would say to Cheryl Crawford, "How can you buck a nun?"

While Martin's biography in the program for *The Sound of Music* quotes Merman's more famous remark about her rival, "She's okay, if you like talent," it also includes a couple of glaring errors: *One Touch of Venus* did not run for "almost three years in New York and on tour," but for two. And the claim that "to date, the star has not had an opportunity to appear with her actor-son Larry Hagman" overlooks their having worked together for a year in *South Pacific* in London.

But as Ethan Mordden also observed, "by 1959 Martin was a phenomenally popular star of musicals, a figure whose very entrance upon a stage brought a host of associations along. Martin was Broadway's ageless gamine (to, basically, Ethel Merman's ageless "broad"), Annie Oakley merged with Peter Pan. This was especially true of Martin's Maria, ruthlessly charming with the kids and coy with the Captain, though deeply worried, inward, in her scenes with the Abbess."

Though there is no apparent connection between *The Sound of Music* and *Peter Pan,* both stories concern the forlorn plight of orphans. Rodgers and Hammerstein created a more overt connection with Martin's musical version of *Peter Pan* by echoing the sentiment of the prelude to "I'm Flying" ("Just think lovely thoughts...") with Maria's very own, "My Favorite Things."

A debilitating blizzard brought New York to its knees in snowdrifts and prevented several members of the cast and the orchestra from making it to the theater one night, when Martin, "*shtarker* that she was," showed up for another sold-out performance. She made a curtain speech at the end of the show, thanking everyone for "climbing every mountain" and "fording every snow-mound" to get to *The Sound of Music* that evening, making a lasting impression on a fourteen-year-old member of the audience, who had already fallen in love with Martin as Peter Pan: "It felt like she was talking directly to me, and I was so thrilled that when I got home, I wrote her a letter," recalled Susan L. Schulman. "And she answered. And so I wrote another letter, and she answered. And I went back to see the show again, and told her I was coming, and she left my name and I went backstage. And, of course, I was speechless." (Several years after seeing the original production of *The Sound of Music* six times, Schulman would find her voice as a theater publicist, who struck up a long-term correspondence with Martin and crossed her path several times more in the future.)

The following summer, Martin had a "brief vacation" from *The Sound of Music.* The Hallidays visited with designer Edward Molyneux and attended a bash held by Elsa Maxwell in Monaco, during which the guests were treated to impromptu entertainment by Beatrice Lillie. When Martin expressed her surprise and dismay that Lillie had not yet been to see her latest show, the wacky if elegant comedienne explained that she had indeed recently been to the Majestic, but was rushing to catch a plane home to London that night and had no time for a backstage visit. When Martin said "That's a likely story," Lillie proceeded to perform one of her famous, spontaneous pranks: "She picked up two pieces of Melba toast," recalled Martin, "put them beside her face like a nun's wimple," got down on her knees, and played my scene which began, 'Oh, Mother Abbess . . .'"

"Bea was very fond of Mary Martin and had a fun evening," according to Lillie's friend and biographer, Bruce Laffey, who also attended the Maxwell dinner. "[Bea] told her story about the priest who whispered to a nun that he loved her. The nun blushed and bashfully whispered back, 'That's all right, just don't get into the habit.'"

"The whole terrace at Monte Carlo was in hysterics," added Martin. "[Bea] wrecked the dinner, but she made the party."

But that summer brought tragic news as well. Though Oscar Hammerstein lived to appreciate the success of his last show, his death on August 23, 1960, prompted Broadway theaters to dim their lights for the first time, commencing a tradition for honoring the contributions and passing of significant members of the theater community. Having created the character of Nellie Forbush for Martin with both her warmth and zaniness in mind, Hammerstein's demise was a real blow to the star.

"When he died it was a matinee day," recalled Martin, who had received a call from Dorothy Hammerstein: "Do the two shows, Mary," she said, "and do them well, because that's what Oscar would want." According to Martin, "It was just ghastly, but we all did it. I think I broke down on every second line." A sedative Martin had taken before the evening performance no doubt contributed to her breakdowns. "Mary wept through the second act," reported Bikel. "Whenever she turned away from the audience, joy left her face as if she wiped off old makeup." Following the performance, Martin collapsed in Bikel's arms.

"I had just returned from a tour of Europe, which my parents had given me as a graduation present," reported Heller. "Three days before I arrived, Oscar Hammerstein died. It was a stunning blow to Mummy, who deeply loved and respected him. I found her almost completely drained of her amazing energy."

Heller pursued a new vocation that fall by enrolling in a nursing school in Boston. That same fall, Hollywood's soon-to-be number one female star, Doris Day, attended *The Sound of Music* with her soon-to-be assistant Barbara Flicker, who recalled Mamie Eisenhower sitting across the aisle, "sound asleep throughout the performance." Following a lunch Hedda Hopper had with "Mrs. Eisenhower" (and "Mrs. Raymond Massey" and "Mrs. Charles Brackett"), she sent Martin a letter relaying that the former First Lady "spoke affectionately about you and told about your coming to the White House when you were playing [in *The Skin of Our Teeth*] in Washington."

There was an even more significant encounter with another former First Lady when a limousine arrived at the Lunt-Fontanne to fetch Theodore Bikel following a matinee. "I had no political discussions with either Mary or Richard, except when John Kennedy was running for president, and I kept making campaign speeches for him," recalled Bikel. "Management really gave me a hard time about that, including Halliday and Hayward, until they saw Eleanor Roosevelt in the same car that came to take me to a campaign."

Bikel offset his more serious-minded political activism with a playful and ironic attitude, as when he was rehearsing a scene with Kurt Kasznar, who played Max, and they delivered all of their lines in German. "It was hysterical," recalled Bernice Saunders, the "nun," who also remembered receiving a humorous but sweet telegram from fellow Semite Bikel on opening night: "What kind of a job is this for a nice Jewish girl?" As Bikel would also point out, "almost all the actors who would play Nazis or Nazi sympathizers in the second act were Jews—Michael Gorrin, and Stefan Gierasch. . . ."

But according to Saunders there was a noticeable aloofness between Martin and Bikel throughout the run: "I don't think she really liked him very much. It was not a warm relationship. But then, he could be a pain in the ass. Whenever there was a party he wanted to go, and he always took along his guitar. He never stopped playing—he was attached to the damned thing."

True to form, Martin kept her distance from colleagues both during rehearsals and throughout her two-year run in the *The Sound of Music*. Bikel came to feel that "it wasn't her choice," however. "She was far more willing to open up. But Richard Halliday was calling the shots, and it was like an edict from Richard: he insisted on putting her on a bed of cotton and preserving her [like a butterfly specimen], until it was time to take her out to be on stage." Bikel illustrated his point with a telling memory of his appearing on *The Tonight Show* during the run of *The Sound of Music*. "One day I said to her, 'You know, today after the show, I'm going over to the NBC studios to be on Johnny Carson's show.' She said, 'Oh good! Richard's out of town—I can stay up and watch you.'"

More than just being out of town, Richard Halliday was seeking medical help for his alcoholism by checking himself into a hospital and "drying out"—a cure that, unfortunately, did not last very long. (As Lucinda Ballard observed, Halliday had been "drunk all the time and not making too much sense" during this period.) "In addition to being domineering, Richard's being gay made him bitchy," continued Bikel. "It was a byproduct of that. But even though we all knew that he dominated her life, in public he was kind of obsequious: deferring to her and almost fawning over her, as if he were not her husband but a fan. But we all knew it was an act. She was a genuinely sweet person. I had compassion for her, and sometimes even pity, because she was so carefully guarded and shielded from the world. It seemed to me that on stage she kept playing these little, simple people, but she hadn't met any in years: she was whisked from the theater in a limo to her penthouse every night. She hadn't been in a bus or on a subway in years. It seemed to me the only thing she could play was her memory of simple people, when she was growing up in Weatherford, Texas."

In contrast with Saunders's impressions, Bikel has certain memories suggesting that Martin got as close to him as she ever did to any of her costars. He recalled, for instance, when she first began wearing contact lenses in the midst of the run. "She was unaware of the effect they had on her and on her performance," said Bikel. "She was supposed to play a frightened little thing, very bravely marching up to the martinet that I played. . . . And at that particular performance, she kept on smiling through all of our scenes together. I was so puzzled.

"The first chance I had to talk to her was at the intermission. I went to her dressing room, and I said, 'Mary, is anything the matter?' She said, 'No. Why?' I said, 'Your performance is quite different tonight.' She said, 'It is. What am I doing?' I said, 'You're smiling—all the time.' She said, 'I am?' I said, 'Yes, you are.' She said, 'Oh! Oh! I know why that is. I went to the doctor this afternoon, and he gave me those 'things.' I said, 'What things?' She said, 'Those things for your eyes.' I said, 'Contact lenses?' She said, 'Yes. And you were so lovely. You were always just a blur before tonight.' "

Martin attended the final run-through of the touring company of *The Sound of Music,* starring Florence Henderson. "I remember that the night before the company left New York to open in Detroit was a Sunday," recalled Anna Crouse. "So it was decided to use the Lunt-Fontanne sets to do a run-through, and they invited a preview audience, including Mary, who, of course, had never seen the show from the front of the house. And at the intermission, we couldn't find Mary. She was down on all fours, feeling around the floor where she'd been sitting. Russel said, 'Mary, what is the matter?' And she said, 'I've cried my lens out.' Isn't that wonderful? Because she'd been playing it night after night, and she never knew what the effect was on the audience."

The go-to publicist for a Broadway show at the time was Frank Goodman, who, with his new partner Ben Washer, was simultaneously handling the original productions of both *The Sound of Music* and *Gypsy*. "And because I was low man on the totem pole, they told me I had to get new pictures of the stars, on two successive Wednesday matinees," recalled David Rothenberg, who began his career as an apprentice in the Goodman/Washer office on West Forty-eighth Street, "I had to go to Mary's dressing room, and to Merman's. And everyone said, 'Oh Mary's the sweetest person in the world, but don't let Merman eat you up.' I went to see Merman first, and knocked on the door, and she said, 'All right, kid, let's see 'em. . . . This one. . . . This one. . . . This one.' She was gruff, but direct and professional [as she approved each picture]. Then, when I went to see Mary, she said, 'Oh, Darling, come in. Let me see the pictures. What beautiful photographs. . . . No. . . . No. . . . No. . . . No. . . . I think we'll have to have another photo call.' But she never stopped smiling. . . . Well, I dined out on that story for months."

Born in Louisville, Kentucky, in 1906, Washer was rather a Southern gentleman, more refined and considerate than the blustery Goodman. (He was also a graduate of the University of Michigan who became a theater editor for the *New York World-Telegram* and a critic for the *Philadelphia Record*.) There were unconfirmed rumors that Washer and Halliday had been more than just friends when they both started out as journalists. "Ben Washer was living with a guy and he would come and cry on my shoulder, because his 'friend' was running around a lot," recalled his secretary, Lee Tuft, who came to play almost as important a role in the Hallidays' life as Ben Washer would.

A "red diaper baby" and longtime left-wing activist, Tuft had originally been a secretary for the Theater Division of the WPA during the Depression and then for the Group Theatre. She knew where all the theatrical bodies were buried, in other words, when she became Cheryl Crawford's personal secretary. The Hallidays increasingly relied on Tuft to help out with their business matters, until she finally became their personal secretary in the 1960s, with her own office in the Campanile. "I had a separate room on the fifth floor, overlooking the East River," said Tuft. "Mary was around all the time. She was very warm, very friendly. She was a woman who was completely dependent on Richard. He kept her in cotton batten. But whenever he went away, she would get together with all these friends, people she wouldn't see otherwise. She would always get together with Cheryl and Ruth, Cheryl's sidekick, and other gay gals."

A year and a month into the run of *The Sound of Music,* NBC was reviving *Peter Pan* for its third telecast—on Thursday, December 8, 1960—its first to be made and preserved on tape. (There were plans to repeat the broadcast at Christmas "for the next two years, at least.") It was also to be directed by Vincent Donehue, instead of Jerome Robbins. "Frankly, I didn't want to do it this year," Martin said at the time. "Not while playing *The Sound of Music,* which by itself is a full-time job. But the mail from parents and children requesting *Peter Pan* has been terrific. So many children have grown up since we did it last. . . . And to be doing it for Christmas is ideal. When NBC came along and said it had a sponsor and a time and everything else all set, I just couldn't say no."

Nor could Martin say no to a pretty rigorous rehearsal schedule, since the original Lost Boys had outgrown their roles and new children had to be cast. (One of them, Luke Halpin, would enjoy greater fame four years later as the young star of TV's *Flipper.*) To maximize Martin's time, rehearsals were held at the former Helen Hayes Theatre, across the street from the Lunt-Fontanne, on nonmatinee days, from 11:00 A.M. to 6:00 P.M., when the star would have a quick dinner in her dressing room before going on as Maria. According to a feature in *TV Guide,* NBC paid an extra $7,000 "just to make life easier for the star of *Peter Pan,*" including $6,000 to rent the Helen Hayes for three weeks, and the remaining $1,000 for two apartments in Brooklyn, near the NBC studios, where most of *Peter Pan* was being taped: one for the Hallidays and the other for their personal staff, including Martin's hairdresser and maid. The first act, set in the Darling nursery, was taped at the former Ziegfeld Theatre on West Fifty-fourth Street. And while *The Sound of Music* was continuing its sell-out run at the Lunt-Fontanne Theatre, Lynn Fontanne herself taped the voiceover narration in London for this new version of *Peter Pan.*

There was a major mishap during a rehearsal one afternoon at the Helen Hayes Theatre, when a new assistant in charge of the flying apparatus missed a cue and Martin crashed into the theater's brick wall. "There was a sound like a rifle shot when I hit the wall," she recalled. Though her left arm was in great pain, Martin felt compelled to keep it from the newcomers whose understandable fears about flying would only be accentuated if they knew she had injured herself.

"It was feared at first that she had broken her arm, but it was just badly bruised," according to a follow-up report on the episode in *TV Guide.* After some fluid was drained from her elbow, Martin went on that night as Maria, with her arm in a sling. "As the postulant my arms were folded meekly most of the time, and the audiences I don't believe ever noticed the sling which held my broken [rather, injured] arm," recalled Martin in

her memoir. "We had slings in the color and material of every other costume in the show." It became a bigger problem when Martin played a
guitar during the "Do-Re-Mi" number: "I stuck my guitar between my
sling and left side, and pretended to strum with my right hand while a
musician in the orchestra pit filled in the guitar music," recalled Martin.

When she resumed rehearsing *Peter Pan* at the Helen Hayes Theatre,
Martin noticed that some clever stagehands had placed a "huge mattress"
on the wall; as she flew closer, she discovered a sign that read: "Mary
Martin *slapped* here."

"NBC was smart enough to store all the sets from the original [*Peter
Pan*] production," Halliday explained at the time. "They need just a little
repainting. We also have available a kinescope print of that show. We cut
the 'kinnie' into 17 different scenes and play each scene before we rehearse
it. That way we can time and play the show as before." While underscoring
that the latest version would be able to exploit technical improvements
with television lights and camera work, Halliday added that his wife's
flying would also be more impressive this time: "Originally she had to
limit her flying to a small space because the studio was crowded with so
many sets. Now she can fly all over that Brooklyn studio."

"The sound stage in Brooklyn was as big as a football field," recalled
Joan Tewkesbury. "And it was hung with blue scrim all the way around,
and little twinkling lights, and the floor was painted with clouds. You
really had the sense of flight. And she took off like a rocket. When she
sang, 'I'm Flying,' it was heaven."

But if the intention was to try to retain the magic that Jerome Robbins
brought to the enterprise from the beginning, Sondra Lee, for one, felt
that it didn't entirely work: "Vincent Donehue," she said, "left out all of
the little, special moments." There were also problems because AFTRA
(the American Federation of Television and Radio Artists) was threatening to strike, so the actual taping was rushed through more rapidly than
originally planned. "Everything was pretty much done in one take," recalled Edmund Gaynes, who was thirteen years old at the time and played
Slightly, "the most boastful of the Lost Boys," in 1960, earning $400 a
week. To put his salary into perspective, Gaynes's father "was working for
the Brooklyn Navy Yard and making $90 a week. Everyone was under
the gun [and] many mistakes were left in, simply because they had no
time to do things over." The most "glaring" error occurs when Martin sings
". . . *we're* like a rooster" instead of ". . . *just* like a rooster" in her duet of "I've
Gotta Crow" with Liza.

On the other hand, Martin's third version of Peter Pan has, if anything, *grown up*: she seems more assured and confident. Her rendition of "I've Gotta Crow" is more cocky than even before, her "Neverland" more heartfelt, and her "I Won't Grow Up" more defiant. Any sense that the forty-five-year-old Martin was too old to be playing twentysomething Maria von Trapp did not carry over to what had already emerged as her most beloved role, as the boy who would not grow up.

Having just sent a color TV to Mainbocher so he could watch the latest *Peter Pan* in all of its visual splendor, Hedda Hopper followed up with a letter, addressed to "Dearest Main" and dated December 20: "Wasn't Mary superb? This was the best of the lot. We will never change her and I am never going to try again. She is Peter Pan and believes in fairies—and do you know?—I am beginning to take on her outlook. I can hear you scream with laughter at this and say, 'Imagine Hedda's going soft.'"

In their contract negotiations with the Hallidays for a "two-show agreement" that included *Peter Pan,* NBC was also "smart enough" to invest $20,000 in *The Sound of Music* as a pledge of good faith, "thus giving [the network] a 5 per cent interest" in the Broadway show, according to Val Adams's report in the *New York Times.* Adams further claimed that NBC, apparently aware of Martin's hesitation, had considered Shirley MacLaine and Nanette Fabray for this *Peter Pan* before coming to terms with Martin, who, given the television broadcasts, would seem to own the role in perpetuity no matter who else would play it.

In April 1961, the Peter Pan Company issued royalties from "stock performances" and "the record album" to Martin for $22,842, and to the Light Opera Association for a relatively paltry sum of $1,418. A cover letter explained that "Mary Martin graciously deferred virtually all of her own compensation from the [original] telecast. . . . Mr. Halliday and Miss Martin felt that they would like to make a further deferment of monies due to Mary in order that the company could pay a dividend to the investors."

Though it was perceived as generosity for other members of the *Peter Pan* team, the Hallidays may have deferred some of their royalties to avoid a higher marginal tax rate, which in that era was as high as 91 percent. And at the time, *The Sound of Music* was an even bigger cash cow for them. The "authors' royalties" for the December 1960 telecast of *Peter Pan* were $15,000, which the Hallidays also chose to defer.

In a little more than two years, the Hallidays would sign yet another agreement with NBC, allowing the network to rebroadcast the "current 'classic' version" of her *Peter Pan,* as it was taped in December 1960.

Despite any and all impressions to the contrary, Theodore Bikel felt particularly close to Martin when, after twenty-five months, they both left *The Sound of Music* at the same time. (In twenty-six months, including tryouts, Martin had missed only a single performance.) "We couldn't wait to be free, finally," said Bikel. "But when the day came, we were devastated. During the good-bye scene at the end, we cried [not as the characters], but as who we were. I remember talking to Mary, saying, 'You know, Monday will be easy'—because we never worked on Mondays. 'But Tuesday is going to be hell.'"

As soon as Martin put *The Sound of Music* behind her, she spent several weeks in Bermuda with her childhood friend Bessie Mae. While Martin's place in the theatrical firmament had been firmly established long before, and she could easily afford to take a vacation, Richard Halliday remained back home, trying to get a new, *sober* lease on life by producing a play that wouldn't involve his wife. Based on his novel of the same name, Morris L. West's *Daughter of Silence* had what can only be deemed a quiet reception when it opened at Broadway's Music Box Theatre on November 30, 1961. Even its known stars, Rip Torn and Emlyn Williams, could do nothing to salvage the convoluted story about a teenager who killed a man who had participated in the rape and murder of her mother during the war. (The teenager was played by Janet Margolin, who was on the verge of her fifteen minutes of fame two years later, playing another psychologically challenged youth in the acclaimed art-house film *David and Lisa*.)

Halliday hired the Goodman/Washer office to handle publicity for the show. "I was still an apprentice in the office," recalled David Rothenberg, "and it was one of the shows I was working on with Frank." Indeed, Rothenberg had to take over the show once Rip Torn refused to deal directly with Goodman, given the publicist's stormy nature.

"I remember, we were out of town in Philadelphia, and Mary was with Richard Halliday, doing interviews," continued Rothenberg. "And when I met her, I said, 'There are so many people that want to talk to you. How can I reach you?' She said, 'I'm in the [phone] book.' And she was, too, on East Fifty-second Street. She was very responsible about helping Richard to promote the show, and I found Mary extremely gracious—she couldn't have been nicer. I had just no issues with her whatsoever."

Rothenberg went on to recall the opening night party for *Daughter of*

Silence at the Hallidays' New York apartment, with Larry Hagman, Adrian, and Janet Gaynor in attendance. "Richard was not the most masculine man I ever saw. In fact, he was positively *floating,*" said Rothenberg. "But he was a gentleman. It was that whole era of men who were gay and married to actresses: Guthrie McClintic [the theatrical director married to Katharine Cornell], Chuck Bowden [the theatrical producer married to Paula Laurence], Alfred Lunt [the famous actor married to Lynn Fontanne]. . . . I remember I walked in on Janet [Gaynor] and Mary, holding pinkies and mooning with each other. I sensed there was definitely something going on there," referring to their obviously furtive behavior. Rothenberg also sensed that the Hallidays were not altogether taken with Martin's *Sound of Music* costar: "Whenever Bikel's name came up, they would raise their eyes and smile knowingly."

Having sold their Norwalk home as trips to the Brazilian getaway were becoming more routine, the Hallidays now leased a small house in rural Connecticut for some much-needed rest and recuperation for Martin. Martin occupied herself with her beloved needlepoint and painting: "She loves to paint with oil colors, and is pretty good," claimed Heller, "although she always paints people from the back because she doesn't know how to paint faces." While Martin also started thinking about a much longer project—her memoir—Halliday remained in the city during the week to look after their business affairs with a recently formed company, Halomar Productions, located at 75 East Fifty-fifth Street. He was particularly busy putting together what they thought would be Martin's next Broadway musical, *Blood and Thunder,* based on a novel by Dwight Taylor, about his theatrical producer father, Charles, and his mother, Laurette, considered by many to be the greatest actress America ever produced.

Martin was also involved in planning a large New York wedding for Heller's upcoming marriage to Anthony Weir, an advertising man, on January 20, 1962. Martin gave a lengthy account of the whole affair after the fact to Hedda Hopper, who devoted her entire column to the story on February 13.

"This chapter in my book-to-be," claimed Martin, "is called 'Take Her, She's Mine'"—referring to the new Broadway hit comedy of the same name. What started out as a church wedding with a reception at the River Club for 365 people—"and this without inviting anyone from Texas as the entire state might come," Martin joked—was finally aborted when the bride and groom to be said they didn't want a big wedding: "that kind of money would send two children through college for a year."

What was then called an "elopement" was hardly that, however, since a good many members of both families attended the weekend festivities, beginning with a late-night breakfast at the groom's parents' home in Pennsylvania on a Friday.

Plans for the marriage to take place in Elkton, Maryland, had to be abandoned: "In Maryland one must be a resident of the state for 48 hours, which we knew, but somehow we'd forgotten about Sunday," explained Martin. With twenty-six people bearing witness, "our darling elopers" were married in "the first Methodist Church in America" in Leesburg, Virginia. "The minister was a dear thirty-two-year-old Southerner. Heller's daddy gave her away; Tony's daddy was best man, Tony's sister maid of honor, and both mothers cried," said Martin, who also told Hopper, "I sat on the wrong side of the church, the groom's." "Mummy loved the whole trip and, since we had not yet ordered rings, even gave me hers to wear at the ceremony," Heller recalled. Heller did not, however, wear the wedding dress Mainbocher had made for her. Looking back, Martin had to confess, "What started as a quiet little elopement ended up costing much more than any wedding would have—the story of our lives."

Within a week of their marriage, the Weirs settled into their new home on East Eighty-fifth Street, near the East River, thirty-three blocks north of Heller's parents, who came by for the occasional dinner. Though she had given up any acting aspirations, Heller did not completely relinquish her taste for attention: she became a model. "I modeled at Elizabeth Arden," she recalled. "All the Kennedy men would come in, and we'd put on negligées for them, so they could give them to their girlfriends. Luckily, I didn't end up with one of them," added Heller, referring to the "Kennedy men" as opposed to the frilly nightwear they purchased.

After opening in a Broadway musical flop, *The Nervous Set* (as cowritten and directed by his good friend Ted Flicker), Larry Hagman became a regular on the daytime soap opera *The Edge of Night*. With Larry well on his way to becoming a show-business star in his own right and Heller establishing a home life of her own, Mary Martin was finally free to focus completely on herself. This makes it all the more ironic, and sad, that, at this moment of personal liberation, she turned down both *Hello, Dolly!* and *Funny Girl*—two of the last great musicals of Broadway's golden age—to star in the same season's *Jennie,* which would prove to be Martin's biggest flop.

Chapter 14

"POOR JENNY, BRIGHT
AS A PENNY"

*For more years than a gentleman should mention
my heart has belonged to Mary Martin. But Jennie does
not make it easy to remain faithful.*
—HOWARD TAUBMAN

There is no agreed-upon measure for gauging the greatness of a performer or a performance. The ambition to capture a transcendent performance with mere words is, almost by definition, self-defeating. It's the equivalent to Virginia Woolf's mandate for herself to pin down a moth; tantamount to Oscar Hammerstein's attempt to phrase, if not solve, the problem that is Maria with his customarily brilliant lyrics: "How do you keep a wave upon the sand? How do you hold a moonbeam in your hand?" This is partly why, when attempting to describe what is ephemeral by nature, critics tend to circumnavigate the phenomenon without ever arriving at their destination.

Consider the well-wrought observations of both Stark Young and Harold Clurman, two of the deans of American theater criticism: "Technique, which is always composed of skill and instinct working together, is in this case so overlaid with warmth, tenderness and wit that any analysis is completely baffled," wrote Young in 1945. "Only a trained theatre eye and ear can see what is happening, and then only at times. . . . She is the real and first talent of them all. [Her] special gift . . . is impossible to convey with anything like the full, wonderful truth."

"A luminous confusion composed her aura," wrote Harold Clurman, the following year. "It warmed us deeply because it was generated from the unrhetorical sources of an ordinary woman's being rather than from any studied glamour. There was always something surprising about it. . . . Her face was always suffused with a look of startled wonder, at once happy, humorous, frightened, and innocent."

Both Young and Clurman were describing the sublime Laurette Taylor, who became a national treasure as the initial Amanda Wingfield in

Tennessee Williams's *The Glass Menagerie*. But they might just as well have been writing about Mary Martin.

Looking back at the life of Mary Martin, the biggest challenge is to try to comprehend her technique, to attempt to capture her effect on an audience. What was it about Martin that made her unique, that imbued any theater she played with her special gift, her aura that seemed to transcend time and space even while reveling in them? Every performance was the same only to the extent that it was different. By living and acting in the moment, Martin pinned down what was effervescent, making it seem everlasting.

While working on her portrayal of the legendary Taylor for her next Broadway musical, *Jennie,* in 1963, Martin told a reporter for *Look* magazine that Taylor had been a friend as well as an actress she idolized. The admiration was clearly reciprocal: Taylor saw Martin in *Lute Song* six times the year before she died. According to Halliday, when his wife told Taylor that "she was really an amateur at serious acting and was going to take lessons," the grande dame of the American theater responded, "You and I need no lessons. Our hearts tell us what to do."

But any hopes that Martin harbored of resurrecting Laurette Taylor in *Jennie* went up in flames. The creation of the show was comprised of misguided side trips, unresolved intrigues, aborted attempts, and enough players to fill an old-fashioned address book. The saga of *Jennie*'s journey to Broadway all but defies explication.

Nine years after Taylor had died, her daughter, Marguerite Courtney, started sending chapters of a biography in progress she was writing about her mother to the Hallidays, explaining that "Laurette Taylor would rather share this with Mary Martin than anyone else." Viewing it as a vehicle for Martin, the Hallidays optioned the book. But "unable to find a producer, a director or an author who agreed with their feeling that the focus should be on Miss Taylor's early years," they let the option lapse after several years.

Laurette resurfaced in a stage adaptation of the same name, which opened on September 26, 1960, in New Haven, written by Stanley Young, a longtime literary critic for the *New York Times,* and produced by Alan J. Pakula. Theater aficionados all but salivate when learning that the cast for this woebegone production featured Patrick O'Neal, Joan Hackett, Nancy Marchand, and Bibi Osterwald *and* that it was directed by José Quintero (who had become best known for reviving neglected plays by Eugene O'Neill). It starred film great Judy Holliday, of *Born*

Yesterday fame, but, reportedly, "Holliday's insecurity [about making her dramatic stage debut] was further undermined by the lack of direction by José Quintero and the New Haven opening of the play was a shambles." The play closed less than a week later, after a single preview in Philadelphia, when Holliday "suddenly took ill."

Alan J. Pakula went on to produce, write, or direct classic films such as *To Kill a Mockingbird, All the President's Men,* and *Sophie's Choice.* But he also held on to his personal obsession with Laurette Taylor: as soon as Taylor's son, Dwight, wrote *Blood and Thunder,* a novel about his parents' involvement with the rough-and-tumble world of early American melodramas, Pakula approached Cheryl Crawford with his idea for a musical version. With Richard Halliday's enthusiastic support, Crawford seized it as a perfect showcase for Martin's talents.

Pakula wrote Halliday on December 12, 1961, that he had the hot playwright George Axelrod (*The Seven Year Itch*) in mind for the adaptation: "I had a general talk with him regarding the elements that excited us about the project and also reassured him that we were not concerned with an actual account of the true story of Charles and Laurette Taylor. . . . He mentioned that [songwriter] Arthur Schwartz had been trying to get in touch with him on the phone. I imagine it was about our project."

In less than a month, Pakula turned instead to Max Shulman, whose recent comic novel *Rally Round the Flag, Boys!* had been a bestseller. "Attached is a rough outline of the Mary Martin book [for the musical]," Schulman wrote Pakula on January 4. "I'm going to work with Schwartz and Dietz on Jan. 5 . . . meanwhile your associates will be kept apprised of all developments." (Howard Dietz and Arthur Schwartz were eminent songwriters, responsible for such classics as "Dancing in the Dark" and "That's Entertainment," the beloved 1931 musical *The Band Wagon,* and, later, *The Gay Life,* which was a critical success but financial failure, starring Broadway musical comedy ingénue Barbara Cook.)

Pakula's "associates" here included Cheryl Crawford and Richard Halliday. Thanks to Halliday, Vincent Donehue was quickly brought on board to direct the show. At this early stage, musical film star Dan Dailey's name was advanced as Martin's costar, and Halliday also recommended auditioning previously nonsinging movie star John Payne: "I'm told that [he] has an excellent singing voice." But whatever trail can be reconstructed from Pakula's private papers simply vanishes after Shulman was about "to begin working on dialogue" on March 2, 1962.

In her memoir, Crawford failed even to mention Pakula in relation to

Jennie. "Mary chose Arthur Schwartz and Howard Dietz to do the music and lyrics after she fell madly in love with a [trial] song of theirs, 'Before I Kiss the World Goodbye,'" recalled Crawford. (If only Martin had remembered that Dietz wrote the lyrics to her first dismal failure, *Dancing in the Streets,* which never even made it to Broadway, she may have thought twice about using him as her latest lyricist.) To write the book, Martin "accepted" a man recommended by Crawford, Arnold Schulman, whose first Broadway play, *A Hole in the Head,* had become a popular 1959 film starring Frank Sinatra.

But, clearly, Laurette Taylor proved too hagiographic a figure for Martin to maintain any equanimity about this project. Martin's ambition to pay homage to one of her most highly beloved heroines may have been undermined by that regard from the beginning: Martin said as much when she was on the road during tryouts of *Jennie,* acknowledging that she had grown "leery of playing Laurette" and explaining why she had to distance herself from the "character": "She was the greatest actress in our theater and if I thought I was playing her, I'd never be able to get on the stage. *Jennie* is sort of her life story at the beginning but it's really someone else. I think in terms of myself in projecting the character. But there's a heart and warmth in Jennie that's Laurette Taylor."

Martin had difficulty even using Taylor's name and considered renaming her character after a Texas friend, Myra. "Then I saw something in the *New York Times Book Review* about Jenny Jerome, who was Winston Churchill's mother. It's such a beautiful name! I said, 'Let's call her Jenny Jerome.'"

As Crawford stated even more boldly in her memoir, "*Jennie* turned into the toughest production I ever tackled." And in retrospect, Martin more or less agreed with her.

"Richard and I believed in it passionately, at first," recalled Martin. "We plunged in with real joy. [But] no matter what we thought up, how hard we worked, how long we rehearsed, the show just wouldn't come together. It was too complicated, in plot and script. Constant changes in cast, songs, dialogue didn't help. It became more and more a patchwork quilt." Worse yet, "It all got very tacky," which was Martin's euphemism for *ugly.* "Things were so strained that no one spoke to anyone else for years."

After years of putting shows together on their own terms, the Hallidays simply failed to appreciate the degree to which theater was, first and last, a collaborative art. Early in the development of *Jennie,* they "uninvited" the distinguished Lucinda Ballard (who had won a Tony Award for her work on *The Gay Life* in 1961) from doing the show's costumes, in favor of Irene Sharaff, even though Ballard's husband, Howard Dietz, was one of the show's three principal creators. Such a self-defeating maneuver makes one wonder what, if anything, the Hallidays had learned about the business they had been in for more than two decades.

Before work on *Jennie* began in earnest, Martin gained a second grandchild, when Preston Benjamin Axel Hagman was born in New York, on May 2, 1962. Martin also recorded the *Bing Crosby Christmas Show* for ABC, which aired on the following Christmas Eve. It was Crosby's first color TV show and, since they had made three Paramount films and done "countless" radio programs together, it marked a reunion for Martin and Crosby as well as being their first time on TV together. Sponsored by Clairol, the special preempted the popular, weekly *Ben Casey* show. ("*Casey*," claimed Hal Humphrey in his TV column, "can't kick, because Bing is boss of the film company which turns out the *Ben Casey* series.") Crosby's only other named guest for the special was André Previn, who was in the process of establishing himself as a top-flight film composer, conductor, and jazz pianist. But, according to Humphrey, "By the time Bing got through paying Mary's salary, the show's budget was pretty well depleted."

The Christmas special opened with a familiar duet, "This Is a Lovely Way to Spend an Evening," featuring Martin in a simple black sleeveless dress and pearls, her hair in an upswing curl. The duet led into a song medley including "I Hear Music," and the pair dancing "Cheek to Cheek"; Crosby, for his part, seemed listless and aloof. Martin made her second appearance solo, singing a sequence of novelty numbers in a blue sleeveless gown. Contributing to an array of rainbow-colored TV hues, Martin next appeared in an orange-patterned, blowsy dress for a "Coffee Time Medley" with Crosby, consisting of "What's New?," Noël Coward's "Mad About the Boy," "Singing in the Rain," and "Wait 'Til the Sun Shines Nellie." She wore a gold brocade suit when she sang "You're Nearer"—a song included on the album she had made with Richard Rodgers two years earlier—but that number was omitted from the broadcast.

"Bing Crosby seemed subdued and almost uncomfortable in his Christmas Eve special," observed Cynthia Lowry in her review of the program. "Costar Mary Martin, an energetic performer, appeared to be carrying the major burden in the low-key show."

Jennie's misguided trek to Broadway proved to be far more dramatic than anything that occurred onstage. Many of its difficulties were detailed in a dozen lengthy letters that Bernice Saunders wrote to her husband, Hank, back home in New York, first from Boston and then from Detroit, where *Jennie* kept undergoing far more changes than most shows had to endure on the notoriously bumpy road to Broadway. (Having already worked with Martin in both *South Pacific* and *The Sound of Music,* Saunders was now a member of the "singing ensemble" in *Jennie.*)

"They asked me if I wanted to be in the new show, and I was delighted," recalled Saunders. "Everybody thought this was going to be the next big thing for Mary. Everybody, in fact, was clamoring to put money into it, including my husband and myself. But we were just a little bit too late—luckily."

In her first letter, Saunders's emphasis on the technical aspects of the production is an ominous indication of the show's ultimate impact: all smoke and mirrors without ever becoming emotionally involving. "We've been working all day and night—we're now on a 12-hour schedule—so there's really not much time for much else but meals and sleep," wrote Saunders in her missive, which cost eight cents to send via airmail from Boston to New York. "You will not believe these sets [designed by George Jenkins] and effects and gimmicks—Each scene is so fantastic—huge—realistic—absolutely spectacular. There's no traveler curtain—nothing closes—it's all done with two turntables and drops and lights.

"We couldn't believe it—one set was heavier and more involved than the other. The opinion is that this is about the heaviest show anyone has seen. Of course the rain missed the trough that's supposed to catch it. . . . We have our first preview Sat. nite, the 25th [the 27th of July, actually] and it's for the Democratic Party (a benefit) or the Kennedy Foundation—nobody seems quite sure. But at any rate Bobby Kennedy is to be there—and a slight chance that [President] JFK might be too."

Martin personally added to the technical extravaganza onstage by contributing an exercise machine from her home at the Campanile, in which she would spin around and around. A huge Japanese contraption Martin originally discovered at Hammacher Schlemmer, the luxury novelty store, the rotating wheel was "tall as a room, 12, 15 feet high" and painted gold for *Jennie,* in which it was used as a melodramatic torture device for the distressed title character in one of her set pieces.

By Thursday, July 25—two nights before the first preview—Saunders sent her husband a remarkably objective and perceptive assessment of just how badly things were going: "The show—production wise—is almost a shambles. The sets and technical problems are so huge and ridiculous that they can't get them to work—and a sort of mild hysteria is setting

[in]. It was all going so well when we got here—Mary was delighted at the ease and time—no sense of urgency but we open two days from now—and they can't get the sets on—the rain floods the pit and the stage—and there are such quick changes everyone is exhausted. I am now in all the musical numbers—but we spend all our time changing—tights, wigs, hats, etc. (everything is impossibly tight and hot and impractical) and running on for staging that lasts two minutes (just enough time for Miss M. to change). Fortunately, I have a fairly easy second act—but a hectic finish—the whole production is so overproduced—and as it stands now it's really not a good show—dead spots and no comedy and just not coming off.

"Of course they're rewriting every day and I'm sure it will all shape up but a strange realization is creeping in—so you can imagine the comments and the discussion ... it is fascinating to see how people can lose sight of an overall picture and how they have all these gimmicks and ridiculous detail that's so unnecessary.

"All the costume people are here—Irene Sharaff with a staff of about ten people—four music copyists—two laundresses—pianists—dressers—and on and on—and these are some of the people who have been watching and not being very impressed. Of course they all expect a masterpiece, so again it's relative but I see weeks and weeks of work. Even after we open we can rehearse five hours every day—There's even a rumor that we may not get to Detroit because of the massive move of scenery, and play ten weeks here [in Boston]—I doubt that."

According to musical scholar Ken Mandelbaum, while the *Playbill* cover for the Boston production of *Jennie* at the Colonial Theatre depicts Martin in an offstage photo, "beginning to look her age," the cover for the Broadway production would wisely show Martin in costume and in character, or "the ageless Mary audiences loved."

On July 31, two days after the Boston opening, Saunders observed: "Today we had the day off because this show is going to have a great overhauling. They say they're not going to do bits and pieces but try to really re-do where it needs it. . . . The [enclosed] reviews as you can see were not too much to be happy about. Mr. [Elliott] Norton [the most highly regarded of Boston critics] I think was hard because of Mary Martin and the supreme effort . . . we here know the [performances] are really more in the hands of the director who has not done all he should—and that's mild. . . . All his effort goes into Mary and everyone else suffers."

Nearly half a century later, Saunders also recalled that Vincent Donehue kept on saying, "Show me your heart" during rehearsals. "And nobody knew what he was talking about." But it became a backstage mantra, frequently used to introduce some levity to the otherwise grim proceedings.

At the time, Saunders considered herself "fortunate to be part of a small group" invited to visit the book writer, Arnold Schulman, and his wife at their "fancy" hotel in Swampscott, with a "little terrace overlooking the ocean. He's a delightful little guy . . . who can't care less for all this 'grand' carrying on—and didn't want to go to the Hallidays for all the rehashing with the select group . . . he has a fairly clear idea of what he has to do and wants to do—and now will do—without all the interference and humiliations that go with a star vehicle—One thing he said that was very interesting is that Mary would like to break away from her image of [a] 'sweet thing' and play this more like Laurette Taylor—aggressive, ambitious, etc., but that V. J. Donehue is holding her down—and he wants to write that way for her—so that the play would be less [a] soap opera about a woman and two men in her life and more of an interesting character study. He also said . . . that the songs, particularly the lyrics (which are terrible) are no help in evolving any scenes or situations so that there have to be lots of little talky [expository] scenes, which slow down everything. The score is really mediocre and Mr. Schwartz is really the most humorless, almost ridiculous man. . . . Incidentally Arnold Schulman also said that Halliday was a most clever—shrewd—capable man who is still a bit inexperienced as a producer but knows just how to handle everyone with sugar—or threats—or even blackmail—but he does it and is a whiz. . . . Last night someone said that [*Sound of Music's*] Lindsay and Crouse who were here for the opening—are still in town and maybe going to work on the book—I almost fell over—it can't be true!"

Saunders enclosed the *Variety* review of the Boston tryout, which was merciless in its criticism: "Everything's not all right about *Jennie,* a nervous item and nervous performances for the most part," it began. "Show is in rough shape and needs rigorous polishing, rewriting, fitting and cutting if it's to jell. Mary Martin stands out as the bright spot in a sea of conflicting plots, subplots and mechanical effects without one big, big song number. Yet, when she's onstage her elusive magic makes the role of Jennie sizzle, but there's not enough to back her up at present."

The day after the opening in Boston, Saunders complained, "And we've been told that there will be lots of changes and cuts and WORK. I'm very annoyed—and I know you'll be upset with me—but I can't help it. My whole little bit has been cut. It was a cute bit with Mary and we did it so well it came off *too rude* for her. So Vinnie cut it."

Saunders finally had some hopeful words to share with her husband three weeks later, near the end of the Boston run: "Tonight we put in a new number—which is what we've been working on—a waltz which Mary sings—and dances—and we're all in it. It comes in the first act just before she meets [actor] Robin Bailey at the stage door—when she gets her part and it's called 'Born Again'—It's busy and pretty and schmaltzy which is what we need and it went very well. Thank goodness." But, Saunders added, "We've been working so darn hard these last few days that we're all pooped. And the colds and one-day virus and swollen glands have hit this group." Worse yet, she reported, "we understand thru [sic] the grapevine Mr. Schwartz is a real cry baby about his music and insisted on shaving down the scene preceding 'New York Town' because he was afraid it was affecting the song."

Saunders's letters from the time fail to mention the many animals used in the show—perhaps, along with the busy sets, to distract the audience from the book problems—and the trouble they presented. "There were birds and dogs and a donkey—and a cheetah," Saunders later recalled. "Dennis O'Keefe said he would not work with a cheetah, because it was too dangerous. . . . So they got a St. Bernard, and made a head for it. And of course the dog came on and shook his head, and it was just a riot. There was also a pony, in a scene when we were all on stage: Dennis came in with a gift for [Jennie]—a huge big box, and out came the pony. One night, he opened the box, the pony came out and dumped right on the stage. And Kirby Smith, who was the husband of Nena Smith, who took care of Mary all the time—he played the sultan. He was all dressed up in that gorgeous outfit. . . . He walked off stage, came back with a broom, cleaned up the mess, and took a gorgeous bow to the audience, who went crazy."

As Cheryl Crawford so aptly put it, the company "limped" its way to Detroit: "Fortunately, business there was good, since the public was devoted to Mary. But there was a terribly disagreeable meeting." With so many bruised egos and strained relations, Crawford did her best to act as mediator: "Soon I was the only contact among the various parties, spending nights until three a.m. going up and down in elevators [in the hotel] to the various rooms trying to effect a compromise about what should be done."

Dated September 3, Saunders's first letter from Detroit described the two-day train ride from Boston before imparting the momentous news that Martin's costar, Dennis O'Keefe, had been replaced, "and the fellow was here yesterday—George Wallace (that's what I said too—who's he?

He [previously] did *New Girl in Town* with Gwen Verdon) . . . and they didn't tell Dennis till yesterday afternoon that they had someone—Let him make that rotten trip on the train—I guess they feel that since it's going to cost them almost $100,000, they weren't going to worry—his contract goes to next October and they have to buy him out."

Indeed, O'Keefe apparently bore no ill will toward his executioners, as Saunders wrote in her next letter, four days later: "He sent George Wallace a welcoming telegram and gave a party for us all Wednesday night which was fun and a nice change. . . . Mary had a couple of days vacation and is much happier—securer I think with this fellow who will give her no problem and not detract—that alone may keep them happy with him." There was also significant news that dancer Carol Haney—who came to prominence with her steamy dancing in *The Pajama Game*—was introduced to help out with the choreography, albeit without credit.

After the opening in Detroit on Monday, September 9, Saunders sent her husband the latest batch of reviews: "which I would say are even worse than Boston considering the fact that we've been out and fixing all this time," she wrote. "But the word is (among us 'in' people) that there is something up—something *big*—as they say. The situation seems to be this: when we were in Boston Jerry Robbins told Mary that her dramatic scenes were good and what she had was not bad (the show that is)—so she has been insisting that her things—except for minor points—not be changed. She's being the star, and taking the reins and has been putting a stop to any drastic changes Arnold Schulman wants to do—Halliday seems to be floundering—Schwartz is a maniac—and the show (mostly second act) just sits [there] and everyone has been saying, where are the new changes?

"So we hear now that Arnold has a new second act which Mary has not accepted—everyone else has—thinks it will work. So he finally said to Mary (who wants to revert to the original Boston show—she feels that the show you start with should be the one you bring in—polished, played well, etc., and all changes do nothing—which is a point—but not here, I think) that she could not do [the] old show. He [Schulman] would not allow it—and there was a moment of, the hell with it—we won't even go into New York!!! Of course that's ridiculous because there's too much at stake not to try—but you can imagine the tension around here.

"So the idea now is—and the decision was to be reached last night—that someone be brought in to sort of referee—to produce sort of and just say 'this goes—this stays,' and 'Mary can do this'—and everyone must listen. And guess what the name is that is being tossed about—you're right:—old R[ichard] R[odgers]. Of course all of this is hashed over talk—but much of it did come from Arnold [Schulman] who is a dear as we've said and just presents a situation—but can you imagine? I can't really see why Dick [Rodgers] would want to get involved in this—altho [sic] he must have said he might at one time if they're even thinking of him. You remember they sort of parted during 'S of M' [Sound of Music]—and what a blow to [Martin's] ego to have to call him—and what a bouquet for him—Also the fact that he's not really working on a specific project now—Soooo how's all this for news—and isn't this all too much? I think I'd have had much less fun if everything went well and we had a big hit. . . . Carol Haney seems at a standstill too. It's as if everyone is holding their breath."

In retrospect, what was most remarkable about the Hallidays' attitude was how clearheaded they were about the show's dismal prospects. Halliday, at least, had been disabused of any notion that his wife's name alone guaranteed a triumphant success. He was not blindsided by the apparent feeling many others had that she could do no wrong.

Producer-writer Paul Gregory—Janet Gaynor's fourth and last husband—recalled attending a rehearsal when Jennie was in tryouts. "Donehue was sitting in the front row of the theater, and they were trying to figure out how to make a scene work," recalled Gregory. "Richard was almost having a fit, with his usual deep breathing, and walking back and forth. And Donehue turned to me and said, 'For God's sake, take this man for a walk, will you?' So I got Richard out of there, and he was just a mess. He said, 'It's not going to be a success.' And it wasn't. It was a very sad story, because Laurette Taylor's was not a happy life. But it had been Richard's idea to do the show in the first place."

Given all the turmoil and conflicting recommendations, the Hallidays made the most draconian decision of all—to fold Jennie in Detroit and not bring it into New York, even though it would mean losing their considerable investment in the show, not to mention Martin's weekly salary of $5,200 and the $2 million advance.

A few hours after the announcement of their decision, "we were told we would be sued for $2 million if I did not open with the show in New York," Martin recalled several years later. "I had forty-eight hours to decide whether to continue to perform and ask the audiences to share my disappointment or go to court and be forced to work the rest of my life to pay out an enormous sum of money." As Martin more specifically recalled in her memoir, Dietz and Schwartz's lawyers "told us if we didn't permit the show to open they would sue us for the whole sum." So they decided to proceed to Broadway.

Looking back at this major disappointment in her career, Martin would summarize the situation with a level head: "The author said he was writing a serious play. The composer and lyricists insisted they were writing a light, entertaining score. It was my conceit . . . that I could bring their opposing purposes together to make a successful whole. What followed was my most torturous and frightening experience."

According to Howard Dietz, the show's biggest problem was Martin, who "grew more proper as her role in musical comedy became more certain." More specifically, Dietz blamed the religious figures who had, previously, carefully monitored *The Sound of Music*: "There was always a nun or two or a priest watching rehearsals [for *Jennie*] and Mary fell under the spell of one of the nuns. The nun couldn't act, sing, or dance but she could influence Mary," he complained in his memoir. Though Dietz felt that "Before I Kiss the World Goodbye" was one of the best songs he ever wrote with Arthur Schwartz—and Martin originally agreed with him—she now found the lyric too suggestive, in a lascivious way, and beneath her dignity, refusing to sing the "couplet that roused her ire": "Before I go to meet my maker / I want to use the salt left in the shaker." "Mary's nun had triumphed," said Dietz.

"Mary Martin was a great performer and fun. [But] she was victimized by her lack of trust in anyone but herself." Dietz further griped that "after Arthur and I had written some entertaining songs for the version of *Jennie* we thought we were working on, it transpired that Mary and Vinnie Donehue, a TV director who was totally under the Halliday thumb, had decided that there were to be no funny songs." Dietz also recognized that, with the Hallidays as producers, he and Schwartz "were not protected contractually [and] we would have little to say . . . our choice of Oliver Smith [as set designer] was passed over for George Jenkins."

Dietz was ultimately dismissive of *Jennie* in his memoir, writing that it "had more operations than I did, but despite the surgery it had trouble talking, walking and being entertaining. To flatter it, one would call it a flop."

Schwartz took an even more dire position by suing Boston critic Kevin Kelly for writing in the *Boston Globe* that the score "poaches on the melodies of other composers, from Rodgers and Hammerstein to Meredith Wilson, Frank Loesser, and Bob Merrill." Indeed it did, but Broadway composers had long since grown accustomed to borrowing from their predecessors in their efforts to fashion something new. Though presented in more extreme language, Kelly's response was really just another way of saying the music for *Jennie* was an old-fashioned pastiche, a deliberately familiar score.

Marguerite Courtney visited Martin in her dressing room on opening night at Broadway's Majestic Theatre to present her with the same "lucky rose quartz" that Guthrie McClintic had given to Laurette Taylor for the opening of *The Glass Menagerie*. But when *Jennie* opened on October 17, 1963, it was far beyond any help a good luck charm could bestow. Anticipating the embarrassing reviews, the Hallidays pointedly failed even to attend the opening-night "wake" at Sardi's.

Many reviewers seized *Jennie* as an opportunity to reiterate their unequivocal love for Martin, along with their disappointment with her latest offering. "For more years than a gentleman should mention my heart has belonged to Mary Martin," Howard Taubman confessed in the *New York Times*. "But *Jennie* does not make it easy to remain faithful."

"Imagine having Mary Martin play an entire show with the corners of her mouth down," wrote Walter Kerr, in the *Herald Tribune,* where he declared the show "a woeful tale of some woeful people told in a woeful way." After describing the physical perils awaiting the eponymous heroine, Richard Watts Jr. said in the *New York Post* that "when *Jennie* confronts [Martin] with such minor ordeals, she is unconquerable but the accompanying libretto presents difficulties insurmountable for even her boldly adventurous spirit." "The only way to walk out of *Jennie* in a satisfied frame of mind is to flee about ten minutes after the overture," wrote the reviewer in *Newsweek*. "For all hands—with the exception of Miss Martin who stays commendably in charge of herself—this is a theme that seems to have numbed talent."

After seeing the show a week into its run, Noël Coward pronounced it "ghastly." Perhaps Coward's British colleague Sandy Wilson put it most succinctly when he wrote that *Jennie* "seemed like a terrible self-indulgence on [Martin's] part." Despite the more-or-less universal responses, Martin's hard-core fans had to be sure to catch the show during its two-and-a-half-month run.

At least two people who would become involved with Martin in the coming years remembered attending *Jennie* shortly after President Kennedy's assassination, when the whole world seemed to come to a standstill and most of Broadway was dark. "My mother and I attended the Saturday matinee, [the day] following the assassination," recalled James Kabel, who would tour with Martin as her dresser in *Legends* in the mid-

1980s. "Mary Martin came out in front of the curtain before the overture and told the audience that no one backstage really wanted to do the show, but they felt the audience would benefit by having a distraction from the grief for a couple of hours." Long before befriending Martin, journalist Elliott Sirkin remembered seeing the show, two days after the tragedy: "Before the show, she came out, wearing her robe, and made a little speech applauding Jacqueline Kennedy for her courage."

"We in show business are schooled in the discipline that the show must go on," Martin told the audience, according to Frank Rich in his memoir *Ghost Light*. "I cannot ask you to forget, but perhaps we can help each other for the next few hours."

Unfortunately, Martin herself would not soon be able to forget the painful experience that *Jennie* had been. Predictably, it closed after only eighty-two performances on Broadway, emerging as one of the few blemishes in her illustrious career.

Chapter 15

THE REAL THEATER OF WAR

You can really get tired from too much glamour!
—MARY MARTIN

Still wounded by the grueling and unrewarding experience that *Jennie* had been, Mary Martin retreated with her husband to their getaway in Brazil in 1964. As theater scholar Gerald Bordman would write, with *Jennie* "Miss Martin learned to her dismay that she was not the powerful drawing-card she had believed [herself to be]." But in Brazil she could revel in the freedom to sleep as late as she wanted, in seclusion (which made the sprawling natural environment all the more relaxing), and in not having any professional obligations. "I slept 10, 12, even 13 hours a night," she recalled. "I was not thinking of the past or the future. I was very much living in the present."

Martin had recently turned down the opportunity to play Ziegfeld star Fanny Brice in an upcoming musical called *Funny Girl*. Mindful of just how trying her last Broadway outing had been, she next rejected a more suitable role that had been customized for her, based on Harold Brighouse's *Hobson's Choice*. (As produced by Cy Feuer and Ernest Martin, who even, in vain, visited the Hallidays in Brazil, the musical version would arrive on Broadway in November 1966 as *Walking Happy*.) But in spite of the glorious sunsets, the comforting isolation, and her newfound sense of freedom, the itch—or the *need*—to perform eventually got the better of Martin.

Martin had an even more conscious and compelling motive for throwing herself back into the work arena. While she flourished away from the hustle and bustle of eight performances a week and found respite from the failure she had suffered with *Jennie,* her husband's drinking problems were only exacerbated by so much leisure time—as was his less obvious addiction to amphetamines. As Halliday himself would later write about their Brazilian hideaway in a letter to Lee Tuft, their personal secretary in New York, every "Eden" has its "snake."

Martin was more than a little intrigued by an upcoming musical based on Arthur Laurents's 1952 play, *The Time of the Cuckoo*. With a score by Richard Rodgers and lyrics by Oscar Hammerstein's protégé Stephen Sondheim, *Do I Hear a Waltz?* concerned an unmarried, middle-aged woman who finds romance while vacationing in Venice. Anne Bancroft was reportedly under consideration as the lead, which Martin wanted to play. But according to Laurents, Rodgers felt Martin was too old for the part. Then too, some unresolved turbulence with Richard Halliday during the creation of *The Sound of Music* may have contributed to Rodgers's ambivalence about working with Martin again, just as it apparently prevented him from helping to try to improve *Jennie* during its tryout period.

A subtle sign of Mary Martin's greatness was her willingness, this late in her career, to tackle groundbreaking musical roles that others had originated—as long as she could relate to the part and make it her own. Nearly two decades after bravely following Ethel Merman as the title character in the national road company of *Annie Get Your Gun,* Martin, in 1965, embarked on an international tour of *Hello, Dolly!* The proposal for Martin to play Dolly came from Marge and Gower Champion— director of the smash Broadway hit, starring Carol Channing—when the famous dancing couple visited the Hallidays in Brazil.

Based on Thornton Wilder's *The Matchmaker, Hello, Dolly!* was a standing-room-only phenomenon at Broadway's St. James Theatre, where it opened in January 1964 with its ebullient star, Channing, and where it would continue to run for the next five years on Broadway with one replacement following the other, including Ginger Rogers, Martha Raye, Betty Grable, Bibi Osterwald, Pearl Bailey, Phyllis Diller, and Ethel Merman. But Martin was the first to take such a daunting assignment on the road.

The shrewd yet eccentric impresario David Merrick quickly recognized he had struck Broadway gold with *Dolly* and further mined it by conceiving of the international tour with Martin as his leading lady—yet another role she had originally turned down. But after lolling around their Brazilian ranch for several months, the Hallidays were eager for Martin to work again. Like so many in and out of the business, they had already seen Channing "knock Manhattan on its left ear as Dolly Levi," as Martin put it in her inimitable Texan style. What's more, if no one had been more surprised than Martin to discover that her name alone could not fill a house—with *Jennie*—*Dolly* seemed an ideal comeback vehicle.

Martin was particularly enticed because she knew she could bring something different to the irresistible force at the center of *Hello, Dolly!*

She saw her own sister Jerry as vital, as the proverbial live wire. Like Dolly Levi, Jerry "loves everybody," claimed Martin (who may have been describing herself when she added that her sister was "also the con woman of all time"). Martin thus had a model for seeing Dolly as more real than the colorful caricature Carol Channing had drawn.

As packaged by Merrick, Martin's version was planned to tour the United States and Canada for nearly half a year. Then it would venture off to Tokyo and, more boldly still, Russia, where it would play in both Moscow and Leningrad at the height of the Cold War—at a moment when President Johnson, newly installed in the White House, was overseeing a huge escalation of US troops fighting in Vietnam. Martin's *Dolly* was to culminate its run in London, where it would be ensconced at her old haunt, the Theatre Royal Drury Lane.

Though Martin is dismissive of her American tour of *Dolly,* relegating it to only a two-sentence reference in her memoir, its impact would rather confirm just how far her stature and her fame had spread—in sharp contrast with her experience with *Jennie.* "We opened in Minneapolis [on April 17]," recalled John Sheridan, who played the young hayseed clerk Barnaby in Martin's *Dolly* and who, at seventeen, was the youngest principal in the company. "Then we played Kansas City, Missouri; and on my birthday, May 9, we were on a train to New Orleans. . . . Then Dallas, Memphis, Indianapolis, Toronto, Cleveland, where we got all of our injections." (The inoculations against foreign flora and fauna would prove necessary in ways that no one could have anticipated.)

With Gower Champion at the helm, rehearsals for the international touring company commenced in March 1965 at the Variety Arts Studios on West Forty-sixth Street in New York. "The first rehearsal we did was '[Put on Your] Sunday Clothes' in the feed store and Miss 'M' stood next to me," said Sheridan. "Once we got to know her, we called her Miss 'M.' You didn't want to call her 'Mary,' because you didn't want her to be like everybody else. You wanted her to be the star.

"She was dead center, and I was to her right. She was this petite woman, and she always wore this kerchief around her head and her neck [during rehearsals]. She was holding my hand, and I remember how huge her voice was—coming from this tiny woman. She was blasting, and my ears were aching, and I kept thinking, 'She's as loud at least as Miss Merman,'" said Sheridan, who, under his childhood name, Johnny Beecher, had been a replacement in the original *Gypsy,* when Ethel Merman was still belting out Mama Rose. "Miss 'M' wore black slacks and a poncho. She smelled great. She was fantastic and funny and full-out all the time . . . and so kind to everybody else."

Perhaps most famous for introducing "Aba Daba Honeymoon" with Debbie Reynolds in the film *Two Weeks with Love* in 1950, Carleton Carpenter was now playing Cornelius, the senior clerk, in Martin's *Dolly*. "Gower's secretary called me when I was in Boston with *Your Own Thing*"—a rock musical version of Shakespeare's *Twelfth Night*—recalled Carpenter. "And she said, 'Give your notice, because you're gonna be in *Hello, Dolly!*' I never even had to audition for it.

"I really fell in love with Mary Martin when we started rehearsals," continued Carpenter, "because it was the first time she hadn't learned the score with the composer: she learned everything along with the rest of us, and I was so impressed with her starting from scratch, like everybody else. But I never worked with a bigger star, before or since, who was so wonderful onstage to work with. And I [ultimately] did *Hello, Dolly!* with three ladies, including Ginger Rogers and Carol Channing. . . . But there was a huge difference between the three ladies I played with. [Martin] was right there, every minute, in the place she was at. She was just a sensational actress, as well as a wonderful singer, and it was just a joy to be onstage with her."

On the persistent and irresolvable question regarding who was the greatest musical comedy performer of the twentieth century, Mary Martin or Ethel Merman, Carpenter comes down firmly on the side of Martin. "When I first started in 1944, there were two big names in New York," said Carpenter. "Mary Martin and Ethel Merman, and I was pretty solidly in the Merman camp. But then, when I saw Mary Martin in *One Touch of Venus,* it really swung me from Merman to her. She all of a sudden was an actress to me. And I began to think Merman was not an actress: she was a vaudevillian, or a showoff, or 'camp,' you would say today."

Though Carpenter had little memory of Richard Halliday, John Sheridan recalled that Halliday was a constant presence at the theater. "I remember him leaning against the mirrors during rehearsals, always saying, 'Mary, save your voice.' I just assumed he was her voice coach, because he hadn't been introduced to us yet."

Martin displayed her customary magnanimity to Judith Drake, who played Ernestina the milliner in the touring *Dolly*. "She had been told that I was from Oklahoma, which may be why she especially took me under her wing, right from the start," recalled Drake. "We were in rehearsal and I did my take *to* her, and she reached over and took my chin and turned it to the front, saying, 'Darlin', say that to the audience and you'll get a laugh every night.' It was my realization that she wanted the entire show and everybody else to be good—not just her."

The final week of rehearsals took place at the St. James Theatre, working with the original set, which was to be replicated throughout this "Class A" tour of *Dolly,* as were the original costumes and practically every other technical element of the production. "We had no audience rehearsal-staging and treated it as a brand new production, which it basically was," said Willard Shaffer, Merrick's electrician and all-purpose manager for touring productions. "It was a pretty elaborate set, with nothing cut back. And during that first week, Richard [Halliday] was around backstage all the time: he'd hang around the switchboards, which is where I was. I probably talked to him more than he talked to anybody else. Then, when we opened a week later, he took me into the dressing room to formally meet Miss Martin. And she was just charming. Nobody called her Mary—it was always 'Miss Martin.'"

Martin's different approach from Channing's original Dolly was emphasized in *Variety*'s review of the opening in Minneapolis, in which "[Martin] proved that Dolly isn't Carol Channing's exclusive property. [She] gives [the] title role her own interpretation, and Miss Martin has never been known to take a backseat to anybody." Martin's variation was more specifically described by John Rosenfield, the *Dallas Morning News* critic, who got a head start on the production's arrival in Dallas by covering it first in Kansas City: "Miss Martin . . . is a comedienne rather than a screwball, a not inconsequential actress and the more musical songstress," wrote Rosenfield. "By the sheer thrust and breadth of her Dolly Levi, [Martin] appears to have absorbed the part histrionically as well as musically." In other words, she presented more of a viable character and less of a cartoon.

There was one technical way in which Martin modified her performance on the basis of Channing's experience. As she told John Sheridan, her contact lenses had become uncomfortable and she had stopped wearing them. But after learning that Channing had taken a spill off the runway during a performance, she always wore a lens in one eye onstage to avoid such a mishap.

While the company was in New Orleans, John Sheridan got food poisoning from a restaurant dinner prior to a performance. "They didn't know if I could go on for the second act," said Sheridan, "but Mary came into my dressing room and snapped a thing under my nose, saying it would make me feel better. It was poppers [amyl nitrate]. I was on the floor with my head over the toilet. I threw up and felt better, and I went on."

Following the performance on May 5, Martin was in her dressing room visiting with some friends, when the stage manager rushed in to say he couldn't keep the autograph hounds at bay much longer. She went back onstage, where the entire cast was awaiting her arrival for a surprise celebration of the Hallidays' twenty-fifth wedding anniversary.

With 3,700 people in the auditorium, *Dolly* opened in Dallas on May 18 at the State Fair's Music Hall, for an unprecedented two-week out-of-season run—a sixteen-performance engagement. More than one hundred citizens of Martin's native Weatherford, Texas, had been bussed in to attend the grand opening. Following the gala event was a clambake, during which Martin gave a rousing rendition of "Hello, Dallas!" before chatting with a Weatherford delegation.

"From the same stage where Tebaldi and Kirsten were bravoed in countless operatic curtain calls a few days earlier, Mary received a 5-minute standing ovation by merely appearing onstage as the curtains parted on the first act," wrote Pericles Alexander, the Amusements Editor of the *Wichita Falls Times,* in a letter to Hedda Hopper dated May 21, 1965. "The Texas star's sun-drenched, warm soprano gives a lyrical dimension to the characterization," Alexander continued. "Mary makes Dolly her very own role with individual characteristics and a fetching personality to defy comparison with Carol Channing."

As Merrick's longtime press agent, Harvey Sabinson, recalled, "During her curtain speech in Dallas, [Martin] pointed out that her black nursemaid [Billie] was in the audience, and that she no longer had to sit in the balcony but was sitting in a choice seat in the orchestra." (This was a year after the Harlem riots in 1964, and only several months before the weeklong Watts riots in Los Angeles.)

While President Johnson was at work on the landmark legislation that would transform civil rights in the United States, he attended *Hello Dolly!* in Dallas, in his home state of Texas. Judy Drake recalled an onstage mishap during that particular performance: "There's a number where I pick up a gun and give it to Dolly to aim at the boy to [make him] take the girl. Well, I always check my props, and the gun was there. But then, when I went on, my gun was missing. I went on pretending to hold a gun, and she pretended to take it and then pretended to shoot with it." Given the recent Kennedy assassination and President Johnson's attendance at the performance, the Secret Service had carefully inspected the backstage premises and removed the prop gun.

The Hallidays further celebrated their silver wedding anniversary while *Dolly* was in Dallas, when the Hagmans and Heller and her husband—and Martin's three grandchildren, including Heidi, Preston, and little Tony Weir—made an unexpected visit following the matinee on June 7, prompting the first photo of "Mr. and Mrs. Richard Halliday and all the members of [the] family assembled at one time"—according to the photo credit. It's very telling that everyone seems to be looking off in another direction, except for Martin and Heller, both of whom knew how to pose for the camera.

The visit gave rise to the same animosity that had long existed between Larry Hagman and his stepfather, and now with Hagman's wife, Maj. Only this time, the friction was visible with Hagman's mother, as well. Halliday thought he was protecting his wife from the endless wrath of her abandoned son, and Martin wanted nothing to do with it. She simply didn't like dealing with the aggravation and had to wonder why the couple had come. But then Larry's career was burgeoning—in only two months, *I Dream of Jeannie* would premiere on NBC, launching the longest run of his career thus far; and perhaps he saw this as a perfect opportunity for a good deal of advance publicity.

The Dallas engagement was followed by Memphis, Indianapolis, and then Toronto, where Martin learned of the death of her first husband without shedding a tear. (Larry Hagman's fifty-six-year-old father had had a sad, lingering demise, following a series of strokes.)

In yet another demonstration of her commitment to her work, Martin took lessons in Japanese from a private tutor in Toronto. She wanted to be prepared for the company's upcoming trip to Tokyo.

A special visitor at the troupe's next whistle stop, in Cleveland, was NBC producer Lucy Jarvis, a highly regarded documentary maker, who had already won an Emmy Award for *The Kremlin,* an insider's look, and was on the verge of winning her second for *The Louvre.* NBC wanted Jarvis "to chronicle the trials and triumphs of Mary Martin and *Hello, Dolly!* overseas" in a sixty-minute documentary.

"I was the first woman producer and first woman executive in all the networks, beginning in 1958–59," a justifiably proud Jarvis proclaims today. "The Russians called me the 'field marshal,'" adds Jarvis. "I was the only one ever allowed to do a film of the Kremlin [in 1962]. President Kennedy had introduced me to Khrushchev, in Vienna, and said, 'This lady wants to do a documentary on the Kremlin.' And Khrushchev said in Russian, 'Why not?'"

While the company took their *Dolly* to Vancouver, Portland, and finally Seattle, Jarvis went ahead to Russia, only to discover that the Soviets had cancelled the State Department's plans for the *Dolly* tour behind the Iron Curtain. In her memoir, Martin would claim no one ever knew why Russia had cancelled *Dolly*. But Jarvis says, "The Russians sent word to me: 'Because of what you are doing in Vietnam, we will not allow. . . .' So David [Merrick] said, 'In that case, let's go to Vietnam, and she'll entertain the troops. . . . I'm going to contact the president. By using *Hello, Dolly!* as his [campaign] song, [Johnson] owes me.' David contacted the White House and said, 'We want quid pro quo. And what's more, we're sending a lady from your [Texas] backyard: Mary Martin. You owe us. You owe her. You owe me.' And Johnson said, 'It'll cost a fortune. I will have to put you on a government plane.'

"There were 2,000 soldiers allocated to guard this troupe," said Jarvis, "Mary and the cast, and me and my people from NBC. It was one thing to transport the show. It was another thing to worry about a television crew. We shot this in 35-millimeter color film."

It wasn't until they were performing in Portland, Oregon, that the company learned of the Soviet cancellation—from a TV news broadcast. That the company manager hadn't told them directly dismayed them even further. And it wasn't until they were in Japan that they learned they would be going to Vietnam as a replacement for the Russian trip. "It was entirely up in the air when we went to do three weeks in Japan," recalled Sheridan.

On their way to Japan, the seventy-one-member troupe stopped in Honolulu, where they were greeted by Bea Lillie, the dotty though beloved English comedienne. Both in her memoir and in the hour-long NBC TV special devoted to the tour (Hello, Dolly! *Round the World with Mary Martin*), Martin would refer to her experience in Tokyo as a high point of her life. By the midsixties, the Japanese were enthralled by all things American, and, as emphasized in the documentary, Martin was treated like royalty by the Japanese empress, as well as the crown prince and his wife. She also attended Kabuki theater and visited Kyoto, the onetime capital of Japan, in addition to an orphanage in Tokyo, where the children sang Martin's own *Sound of Music*'s "Do-Re-Mi" to her in Japanese. Martin, in turn, did her Japanese-language version of "Hello, Tokyo, I'm so glad to be here in your town" at every performance of *Dolly*.

The royal Japanese reception was presented with great fanfare, including a mounted, life-size version of Martin as Dolly descending the stairs, in the lobby of the Takarazuka Theater, where it played. "She met the emperor, but we weren't allowed to film that," recalled Jarvis, who also remembered, "She was very phony when she was out in the real world. But when she was herself, she was a down-at-home girl. She could curse. . . . She could be angry. . . . She could lose her temper. She wasn't that fancy person she showed to the rest of the world. She was very simple."

A duplicitous aspect to Martin began to express itself in new ways to the company as well, once they were in Asia. "We started getting these odd notes from the stage manager, saying, 'Look at Mary, look at Mary,'" recalled Sheridan. "And it was so unlike the situation before: she was so giving, and everybody was looking at her all the time because we loved her. But Richard ended up being out front, instead of just being friendly backstage. So all of a sudden, he became like Gower Champion and David Merrick. And you would say something to him, and suddenly he was very different. Instead of clowning around with people backstage and grabbing your shoulder, Richard was standing there [out in front], inspecting us all the time. You'd start getting these funny notes from the stage manager, but you knew that they were really coming from Richard. And all of that started to turn people off."

Martin also became noticeably less friendly. Instead of making some jovial remark, as she often did, or even making eye contact, as she always would, "She started looking down at the floor, when coming from her dressing room, to get on the stage," continued Sheridan. "And you could tell that she was embarrassed by the whole thing. We just knew that the notes were coming from Richard. Especially the boys in the 'Dolly' number started to turn off to her. So instead of playing things spontaneously and keeping everybody on their toes, and making it more fun for her, all of that spontaneity was cut back and they were just doing what they were told to do. And she just wasn't as present anymore. Now, it was like she was performing on her own and everyone was there to support her."

Beneath it all was the anxiety of not knowing where they would be going next on their international tour. It proved far from a relief when they learned it was to be Vietnam.

The war in Vietnam was famously the first to be waged in American living rooms via television images, leading to seismic shifts in cultural and revolutionary politics, with repercussions that continue to unfold to this day. This horror was embedded in the fearful and furious response when the company learned they would be taking *Dolly* to the war zone. For President Johnson, of course, it was a PR maneuver: placing two American icons, Mary Martin and *Hello, Dolly!* in the midst of the fray.

It wasn't only the controversy surrounding US involvement with Vietnam that unsettled the company, but also the idea of performing in the midst of a war, as well as the discomfort they would undoubtedly have to endure. The bulk of the troupe protested vociferously, and Martin, who had reservations herself, gave them a pep talk: "We have to do this for our country, for our soldiers," adding that, "We're in this together." "Mary reassured us," recalled Sheridan, "saying 'I'll be with you every step of the way' and adding, 'In World War II we performed for the troops.'"

"Marilyn Lovell and Coco Ramirez [who played Mini in the show] and I had just bought all these winter clothes for Russia," recalled Judith Drake. "So we were especially disappointed to discover we didn't need them now, because it was going to be warm [in Vietnam]."

While the company continued to perform in Tokyo, Halliday made three advance trips to Saigon with Willard Shaffer, Merrick's all-purpose technical assistant, to better prepare for what would inevitably be a fraught journey. "Mary Martin and Richard took a liking to me," recalled Shaffer. "Every show I toured with Mary Martin, I'd do a day run, ahead of time, to the next city we were going to play; and Mary sent Richard with me. But it was probably Richard who said to her, 'I should go with Willard and check it out.' Richard loved his cocktails, but he couldn't drink around her. So he would come with me on the plane, and he would toss them down. And I'd go to the theater and he would disappear for a couple of hours, before I'd meet up with him again, later.

"Richard would also get his way by being a little outrageous," continued Shaffer. "He was always coming on to me. Everybody knew he was gay, but nobody talked about it. On the plane, he'd put his hand on my inner thigh, and I'd have to push it away. But he was so drunk at the time, he could hardly stand up."

Though Shaffer was himself homosexual, he presented himself as straight to Halliday. And with his brawny physique, Shaffer could just as easily have been cast as a Seabee by Joshua Logan as he was a technical assistant by David Merrick. And what there was to see of Shaffer was often visible: "Switchboards in those days were called resistance boards," explained Shaffer. "The dimmers worked by heating coils, which generated a lot of heat. Summer or winter, I would strip down and work in my underwear. Mary saw that, and for Christmas she had half a dozen shorts made and embroidered *Hello, Dolly!* over the ass: red on white shorts. She was always doing needle work, as was Richard."

Shaffer did not necessarily hide his sexual persuasion from the rest of the troupe, however. "I remember going to a bar when we were in New

Orleans—even though I was underage," recalled Sheridan. "It was open to the street, and it had a 90 percent gay clientele. We were at the Vieux Carré Motel. And I remember thinking it was odd that this big butch guy [Shaffer] was in a gay bar. I knew my story. But at that point, the gays I knew were mostly dancer boys. And here was this guy with his spiky hair [a military buzz cut]. I remember having one conversation with him about that, when a couple of us had dinner in Vancouver, and we were eating between shows, and we were saying, 'It's not how you look or what your job is, but what you're comfortable with.'"

There were more than 140,000 American troops in Vietnam when Mary Martin took her *Dolly* to entertain at least 12,000 of them. The company was flown from Tokyo in "a drab, windowless troop transport," according to Shana Alexander, in a seven-page cover story about the tour for *Life* magazine. "As we prepared to let down in Saigon, our escorting officer advised us that our arrival had been preceded by the most massive security precautions ever undertaken in that city, and that we would now make a 'speed penetration landing to avoid picking up any small-arms fire.' . . . When we landed, the door was yanked open, and out of the streaming tropical downpour on the field leaped a tanned, handsome general to plant a dashing kiss on Mary Martin's cheek. At the same time, a flock of exquisite girls in graceful floor-length gowns and white gloves appeared out of the rain and started entwining fresh flower garlands around everybody's neck."

More than Martin, more than even Merrick, it was Willard Shaffer who looked after the company and created a family feeling. Throughout the *Dolly* tour, Shaffer acquired aluminum pans, which he placed on top of his large lighting boxes backstage, where he cooked hot dogs for the cast to enjoy during the performance. And in keeping with the military atmosphere, he also had cold beers on hand.

"When the company finally arrived [in Vietnam], I threw a rooftop party, with a bar and some music," recalled Shaffer, "while bombs were going off in the distance. And everyone was saying, 'This is terrible. We didn't want to go to war.' They were afraid. But Mary Martin had saved the day. She said, 'The President of the United States wants us to go, and we can't say no.'" A number of the cast members were further upset when they learned that they were to be provided camouflage uniforms for protection in lieu of soldiers, and some refused to wear them.

The first performance of *Dolly* in South Vietnam was given on October 9, a Saturday, at Bien Hoa Air Base, twenty miles northeast of Saigon.

"'Opening night' came at high noon in sweltering weather and suffocating humidity inside an Air Force maintenance hangar," reported Ruben Salazar in the *Los Angeles Times,* where he went on to describe "the fighting men [sitting] on sandbags, and the cast, wearing high-collared and heavy 1890 clothing . . . in danger of wilting, and the sound system failed at times."

General William C. Westmoreland began the proceedings by reading two telegrams. The first was from President Johnson, thanking the cast:

THE FOOTLIGHTS MAY BE DIMMED AFTER THE SHOW BUT THEY WILL NOT BE DIMMED IN THE HEARTS OF THE SERVICE-MEN WHO SEE YOU PERFORM.

The second was from Defense Secretary Robert S. McNamara, relaying that the president was recovering after gall bladder surgery. Johnson had also sent a more personal note to Martin:

YOU ARE A FRONT LINE PATRIOT IN THE WORK YOU ARE DOING. YOU ARE MAKING YOUR PRESIDENT AND ALL OF WEATHERFORD, TEXAS, DEEPLY PROUD OF YOU.

In addition to the extreme heat and technical problems, the cast had to contend with a wide variety of other makeshift tactics. There were only four musicians, for instance; the rest of the music was prerecorded on tape in Tokyo and piped in, under Willard Shaffer's supervision. "[This] meant we had to follow the music," explained one disgruntled chorus member, "instead of the musicians following us."

And then there were the makeshift accommodations. "They had built a four-story building in Saigon, but it wasn't yet complete," recalled Shaffer. "For one thing there was no electricity. We got the army to lend us a generator, and I hooked it up to the power and had my gang hook it up to the house power. And it was so hot. . . . We found a room that had a whole bunch of ceiling fans, and my crew installed them in all of the rooms. But then, we couldn't move in until they brought lizards for each room, to eat the insects."

The onerous, eleven-performance tour of duty in the midst of war entailed any number of unusual circumstances for the troupe. They were called upon to visit hospitals and USO clubs after performances. Soldiers were recruited as stagehands to carry the heavy equipment from one makeshift venue to another. There was an unplanned felicitous moment at Nha Trang Air Base when a soldier discovered his girlfriend was a dancer in the company; Martin delivered the equally unexpected, perfect ad lib as they embraced: "Dolly Levi is a matchmaker, after all."

Given the strenuous conditions and poor food, Martin lost considerable weight. And though it went unremarked at the time, she recalled that she arrived in Vietnam with a "terrible cold" and that she had an even worse allergic reaction to the penicillin she was given by a medic. "My face was bloated like a cream puff, my eyes were swollen. [Though] the swelling had gone down enough so that I could at least fit into my costumes and use my hands." Martin described walking through that particular performance in a total blur, performing like a robot, until "the second act, after more shots, [when] I began to realize where I was and what I was doing."

US Ambassador Henry Cabot Lodge honored the visit of *Hello, Dolly!* with a party at his residence, beginning with a string trio playing "Some Enchanted Evening," sung, somewhat painfully, by none other than Lodge himself. The party was perceived as a terrible slight, however, since the ambassador invited only four of the principal players to mingle with "all sorts of minor officials and press representatives of the most obscure origin," according to producer David Merrick. Merrick added that "all the ambassador did was get himself some free entertainment." Considering how well reported the event was, master of promotions Merrick garnered some free publicity of his own when he refused to join the line to shake the ambassador's hand. Merrick pointed out just how controversial the politics of Vietnam were, as he added: "I cut the ambassador dead, left him a floating ice island in his sea of protocol. I have more to do with my time than shake hands with washed up Republicans."

Lodge's oversight deeply offended the cast, who had placed themselves in harm's way—not to mention great discomfort—only to be dismissed by their ambassador to Vietnam. It also accentuated the growing feeling that they were mere peons commandeered to support Martin. When they arrived in Vietnam and asked if their makeshift hotel was air-conditioned, they were told, "Only a few rooms." "We know who those are for," responded a chorus member. "Mary, David Merrick . . ." According to a report in the *New York Times,* "the whole bus burst into song: 'Foxhole Mary is the girl we love' "—to the tune of "Bloody Mary" from *South Pacific.* Their truer feelings were reflected by a ditty they invented to the same tune, traveling by bus during their tour of Vietnam while Martin was flown in a helicopter: "Foxhole Mary said she'd ride with us. Foxhole Mary is not on this bus. Foxhole Mary hovers over us. Now ain't that Peter Pan!"

"It's a long jump from Texas to London," says Martin, who alone narrates the sixty-minute NBC documentary, which aired on February 7, 1966. "Tokyo: a world of color and sound," she adds by way of introducing the contrast with their next stop: "Vietnam: gray, grim. Vietnam was a shock. . . . October 6, 1965: Operation Rehearsal. . . . At twelve noon, our military audience descended. . . . They came by plane, by jeep, by foot. They sat on rows of sandbags. They leaned on rifles. What a miraculous transformation: a hanger one minute, a theater the next. . . . A most unusual opening night: that noon . . . that gray day. The theater brought color and magic back to the lives of our men.

"Using Saigon as our base, we were always convoyed through the danger zones. . . . But only after the area had been cleared of mines and booby traps. . . . This was the real theater of war. . . ."

The special also shows Martin and Westmoreland visiting the wounded soldiers in field hospitals, at least one of whom had seen the production several days before. "My heart belongs to all seventy-one of the company—they showed no fear and never complained." It also depicts Martin in costume onstage, singing the title song with newly minted lyrics for the occasion: "Hello, fellows. It's so nice that we could come to where you are. . . . Here's our hat, fellows. We're glad we're where we're at, fellows. . . ."

"Mary was not a great beauty, but I think we made her look great," claimed Lucy Jarvis, nearly fifty years later. "Cameras don't lie, but our cameras lied. We had great people working on her all the time: we had our makeup people, but they had their makeup people, too. She was not a pretty woman, but we made her look pretty.

"Richard would drive the costume people crazy with his attention to detail," continued Jarvis, who implicitly confirms that Halliday's reputation for being bossy and interfering preceded him. "Richard was very difficult. He was a pain in the ass, and she was Lady Bountiful. I had to be very close to Mary, otherwise we couldn't have done this. I had to have direct access to her. I had other people on my team deal with Richard. I did as little as possible with him. I didn't like him. If I started to deal with him, then I would have been stuck with him. I didn't want anything to interfere with my relationship with Mary, which was a good one.

"She used to have big fights with Richard, too," continued Jarvis. "You were in places in Vietnam where you couldn't hide. . . . Richard was very angry that she had this very close relationship with me, and that she would never let him get between her and David [Merrick]—except in matters of finance. Otherwise, she had to have access to David. But David respected her. It was his ace in the hole. David was not one to spit in his own soup."

As they were nearing the end of their Vietnam ordeal, Martin had prepared a speech, hoping to regain some of the camaraderie she had lost with the company during this leg of the tour. "It was ridiculous," said Lucy Jarvis. "She started out by saying, 'This whole thing [the war] was such a mistake: all those good boys, and all those wonderful people. We're all in the same boat together.' And I'm listening to this, and I said, 'If Lyndon Johnson hears this, he's gonna kill us. We'll all be in jail.' I said, 'Mary you're out of your cotton-pickin' mind. You can't say that. It sounds like a communist speech.' She got hysterical. She said, 'But it's all about peace.' I said, 'You can't say we're all in the same boat. We're not, unfortunately.' So we rewrote the speech for her."

Following Vietnam, the company took *Dolly* to Okinawa and Korea, briefly, neither of which was included in the documentary. "We cut out Korea because NBC wasn't interested, and I *certainly* wasn't interested," recalled Lucy Jarvis. "I thought that it would diminish what we did in Vietnam."

It was in Korea that Halliday's drinking had serious consequences, when he had a mild stroke. "Richard came to the airport in a wheelchair," recalled Sheridan. "This was when they were leaving Asia and before we went to London—there were two weeks in between." Prior to opening with a predominantly English cast in London—given Equity rulings, only the principals were allowed to remain with the show—the Hallidays took a much-needed vacation to Hong Kong, Bombay, Beirut, and Rome. While Halliday spent most of his time in bed recuperating, Martin gallivanted on her own. Once they were in London, rehearsing with the predominantly English cast, Martin told John Sheridan, "Richard said 'Yes,' to everything. And I had the charge cards. I just went shopping everywhere and nobody knew me. I could do whatever I wanted. I could go to bed whenever I wanted. I could get up whenever I wanted. I ate whatever I wanted. It was the most fantastic two weeks in years."

"But then when she got to London, she was in jail again," Sheridan said.

Though London was the last stop of a long and at times arduous journey for Mary Martin as Dolly Levi, the NBC documentary of the tour be-

Learning to pose at an early age: Mary Martin was a two-year-old child of privilege, when this photo was taken in the spring of 1917, in her hometown of Weatherford, Texas. (*Author's Collection*)

"This proves there's hope for everyone," responded Oscar Hammerstein, when Martin gave the lyricist this summer-camp photo of her gangly, awkward, adolescent self. (*Author's Collection*)

Martin sang on CBS Radio in 1937, the year before she became an overnight sensation introducing "My Heart Belongs to Daddy"—and essentially performing a striptease—in Cole Porter's *Leave It to Me!* on Broadway. (*Author's Collection*)

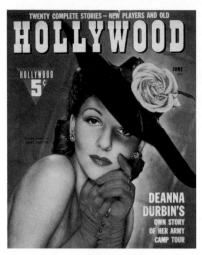

Two of the countless Hollywood magazine covers featuring Martin, published during the three-year period when she made nine movies as a contract player at Paramount. (*Author's Collection*)

This publicity picture puts Martin beside Robert Preston, shortly before they made *New York Town* together, in 1941. The two would be paired again, twenty-five years later, in Martin's final Broadway musical, *I Do! I Do!* (*Author's Collection*)

Another Paramount publicity shot of Martin, here with her mother, Juanita, who raised her daughter's son, Larry Hagman, while Martin launched her own career. (*Author's Collection*)

May 16, 1940: Martin with her brand-new, second husband, Richard Halliday, who became her manager and transformed his plain-Jane wife into a sultry temptress. Given the good-cop, bad-cop relationship they developed, Mary Rodgers relayed being told: "Mary Martin makes the bullets and Dick Halliday fires them." (*Author's Collection*)

It's hard to say who is who in this 1942 photo of Martin (L) visiting Jean Arthur (R) on the set of Columbia's *The Talk of the Town*. More than just "palsy-walsy," as the photo's original caption would have it, the two were rumored to be lovers. "We were all interchangeable," claimed Martin, of Hollywood studios' attempts to duplicate their stars' success and appearance. (*Author's Collection*)

Martin as the "cockeyed optimist" Nellie Forbush, on the cover of the April 11, 1949, issue of *Newsweek,* with her *South Pacific* costar, lothario Ezio Pinza. (*Cover photograph © Zinn Arthur / The Image Works*)

The Hallidays with daughter Heller and Martin's nineteen-year-old son, Larry Hagman, in the summer of 1951, setting sail for Europe and an extensive West End run of *South Pacific.* (*Robert Kradin / A.P. Images*)

Martin on the steps of the Theatre Royal Drury Lane, where she greeted "the press and her public" for the London premiere of *South Pacific.* (*H. Palmer / Author's Collection*)

Peter Pan sniffs out the enemy pirates, with the irrepressible Sondra Lee as Tiger Lily. "Dearest Sondra," reads Martin's inscription: "Precious things come in small packages—they say—I know you are very precious to us—to me—Love, Mary Martin." (*John Engstead / Sondra Lee Collection*)

Martin getting made up as a boy, for her most beloved and coveted role: Peter Pan. (*Photofest*)

Taking in Martin's remarkably lofty view of the audience as she soared atop the proscenium as Peter Pan. (*NBCUniversal / Getty Images*)

The two presiding queens of Broadway, Ethel Merman (L) and Martin (R), in male drag on *The Ford 50th Anniversary Show*, which was directed by newcomer Jerome Robbins and aired simultaneously on all four TV networks (including Dumont) on June 15, 1953. (*Author's Collection*)

The cast of the 1955 revival of Thornton Wilder's *The Skin of Our Teeth*, which played Paris, Washington, D.C., and New York before airing live on NBC. L to R: George Abbott, Martin, Helen Hayes, Heller Halliday and Don Murray. (*Author's Collection*)

An archetypal image of Martin as Maria von Trapp teaching the children to sing "Do, Re, Mi" in *The Sound of Music,* the smash-hit musical which Martin had commissioned Rodgers and Hammerstein to write for her. (*Friedman-Abeles © The New York Public Library for the Performing Arts*)

Martin loved the Brits as much as they loved her. That's Martin and Noël Coward at Sir Noël's Jamaican retreat, rehearsing for *Together With Music,* their two-person, CBS-TV special, in September 1955—eleven years after Coward wrote the (flop) West End musical *Pacific 1860* for Martin. (*Author's Collection*)

The eccentric English performer Bea Lillie (L) and Martin (R), adoring one another. While Coward developed a more meaningful—if fraught—relationship with Martin, he once proclaimed Bea Lillie "the world's greatest comedienne." (*Author's Collection*)

The entire clan made a surprise visit to Dallas, where Martin was touring with *Hello, Dolly!* before she took the show to Vietnam, Tokyo, and London, in 1965. L to R: Maj, Preston, and Larry Hagman, Martin (in her "Dolly" costume), Heidi Hagman, Richard Halliday (with grandson Tony Weir in his arms), Anthony and Heller Weir. (*Author's Collection*)

Having epitomized the Golden Age of the Broadway musical, Martin (L) and Ethel Merman (R) revisited the transformed and sleazier Times Square of the 1970s. (*Author's Collection*)

Martin (R) embracing Janet Gaynor (L), backstage after Gaynor's opening night in the Broadway version of *Harold and Maude*, February 8, 1980. One can see that Gaynor was, as Martin put it, "my closest most special friend." (*David LeShay*)

gins there. "That was the bookending of it," explained Lucy Jarvis. "She starts in London, reminiscing."

Martin is clad in Dolly's brocaded red dress, donning Dolly's wildly feathered hat and sitting at her own makeup table. With a huge sitting room, a dressing room, a kitchen and a bath, it would prove the most opulent star treatment Martin ever received at the Drury Lane. She described the environment in a letter to her sister Geraldine: the room was filled "practically from floor to ceiling with plants—flowers—cakes (one a replica of the ramp Dolly walks on), another huge one with 'Happy Birthday Mary—Happy Opening' and the complete stage of Drury Lane with Dolly standing stage center—all done in spun sugar! They really do things big here!"

In another, handwritten letter dated Friday, December 13—"NBC arrives tomorrow to finish shooting the documentary," it read—Martin wrote Hedda Hopper that actor and photographer Roddy McDowell had sent her a "huge print of your photograph," inviting Martin to describe Hopper for his forthcoming book of celebrity photographs, *Double Exposure*: "Yours is the only [photo] I have in my huge 'Receiving Room' at the Drury Lane—except I do have photos of the children and grandchildren." The predominantly black photograph depicts the upper right quadrant of Hopper's face, presenting her right eye in stark focus. "That eye was on this sparrow for many a year," begins Martin's response to the McDowell photograph, which inexplicably employed the past tense, as it continued: "A seeing eye—filled with compassion. A mixture of wanting to know all the facts of lives and being disappointed when they did not live up to her tremendous standards. I knew. She had been my son's unpaid babysitter. A kind, tough, wonderful, innately sensitive woman who always had my admiration, my gratitude and my love."

Given the horrible experience she initially had at the Drury Lane with Noël Coward's *Pacific 1860,* Martin had been terrified the night before opening with *South Pacific* at the same theater and had to be pampered by her director, Joshua Logan, who had had problems of his own. Now, however, Martin was returning to her London theatrical home with an unmitigated sense of enthusiasm and exhilaration.

There was one unfortunate accident during the first day of rehearsals in London, however, when Carleton Carpenter fell off the stage at the Drury Lane. "I didn't realize it was a raked stage," recalled Carpenter. "They hadn't put the runway on properly." He broke his pelvis and spent ten days in the hospital. "I flew home with Gower and Marge, the morning after the opening. My picture was in the paper, saying, 'Goodbye, Dolly!'"

Hello, Dolly! in London gave new definition to "taking a town by storm": the Queen Mother's night was a benefit "in aid of [the] Historic Churches Preservation Trust," two nights before the opening. Princess Marina attended the following night, on Martin's fifty-second birthday. She asked "the white wigged attendant to fetch champagne" with which to toast Martin onstage and sang "Happy Birthday," with all of her party and the cast joining in. Opening night reportedly entailed twenty-six curtain calls: "From the opening curtain you could feel the electricity—going off like fireworks," Martin wrote to her sister. Martin introduced Gower Champion from the stage, "and he got the bravos he so deserves." The queen then came on Monday night, with Lord Mountbatten "and party."

Each night they were there, following the curtain calls, the royals would come down to the stage and first greet Martin, who in turn introduced them to the rest of the cast. "The queen shook hands and talked with each member of the cast, saying something personal to each one—as did the Queen Mother, Princess Marina and, last night, Princess Margaret and Lord Snowdon! They did not sit in the Royal Box but in the dress circle which is the center of Drury Lane and [commands] a much better view of the stage."

The Snowdons had recently returned from the States, prompting some controversy in Parliament over the expenses of their trip, and Martin interpolated some fresh lyrics that night to show her support: "You were great—dear Snowdons . . . In the States, dear Snowdons—they're still glowin', they're still crowin'—that you're goin' strong." On December 10, the Duke and Duchess of Gloucester, and Princess Alexandra and her husband, attended. As Martin wrote her sister, "You can really get tired from too much glamour!"

The "darling" Queen Mother told Martin: "All through the performance tonight I could not help but think of our last meeting." It had been when she had seen *South Pacific* with the king by her side the week before he died.

"They say it's the first time in history that the entire Royal family have come to this extent." It was the acme of Martin's parvenu ambitions. "Oh, dear," Martin told, Hedda Hopper, "for a little girl who wanted to go on stage at the age of five to the old gal who sings 'Wow-Wow-Wow, Look at the Ol' Girl Now,' I've really [arrived]."

Despite all of the hoopla—or perhaps because of it—the reviewers tended to be snooty about the show itself: "*Dolly* is just the thing for ten-year-olds," sniped one. "After all, no musical has ever failed at Drury Lane just because it's corny," quipped another. Despite the reviews, both Martin and the show were a huge success. On some nights, a regular two-pound ($5.60) ticket was going for ten pounds ($28) on the black market. Indeed, the show was viewed as a vehicle for Martin, as proclaimed by the review in *The Times* of London announcing that it was "single-mindedly bent on mobilizing public enthusiasm for Mary Martin." Such an attitude was potently reinforced by Hugh Leonard's description of the title song's impact: "It is the show-stopper of all time; and Miss Martin—whose business it is to be irresistible—has cemented her own legend forever."

Shortly after the reviews appeared, Hollywood columnist Sheila Graham nabbed an interview with Martin for her syndicated column. "Imagine, me a girl from Weatherford, Texas, meeting five royals in one week," exclaimed Martin, revealing her lifelong humility and uppity ambitions at the same time. Graham also reported, "There is now some question of whether Carol Channing will follow Mary into the Drury Lane. . . . Carol is peeved that she was not chosen to be the first Dolly in London." (But as Willard Shaffer emphasized, Merrick had wanted Martin to play Dolly in the first place. "He pursued her for years," claimed Shaffer. "He wanted her even before Carol Channing. But she wasn't interested.")

Behind the scenes, Martin was well aware that she was not in her best voice. After the heat in Okinawa, the rain in Korea, and now the cool damp in London, she had recently come down with a cold—like most of the principals—and was sounding huskier than usual. Via her husband and David Merrick, she even prevailed upon RCA to postpone the recording of the London version of *Hello, Dolly!*, hoping for her voice to improve. But Christmas was fast approaching and the record producer was willing to stall for only so long.

On Christmas day, the Hallidays invited all the principals, including director Gower Champion, to their tiny low-ceilinged cottage on Hays Mews—one of the rare times they mingled with the other major players. Then, "when the album finally came out, we were doing a picture call onstage," recalled John Sheridan, "and Mary came out and set up a little Victrola that she travelled with, and she kept playing the album over and over again. She was so excited that the show was recorded. It was recorded at a studio out in the middle of nowhere."

Despite any vagaries in her voice, the recording indeed reveals that Martin's Dolly was more human—more caring, more vulnerable, more *real*—than Channing's. Far more of a vocalist, Martin's Dolly also eliminated the quotation marks and exclamation points that Channing relied on to create her character. There was also a special treat for the principals when, one night following a performance, they remained onstage at the Drury Lane to watch a private showing of the NBC documentary of their tour.

There was a funny incident during the curtain call on February 9, when Drake, as Ernestina, slipped and fell on her back, revealing her undergarments. "Mary announced that it was my birthday and that I had had too much birthday cake," recalled Judith Drake. "And the whole audience sang 'Happy Birthday' to me."

When Sheila Graham interviewed Martin shortly after the London opening of *Dolly,* she also spoke with Halliday, who told her that his wife hadn't been as excited about a new show since *South Pacific* as the one coming next. As fine as Martin was as Dolly Levi, Gower Champion's real gift to her would be *I Do! I Do!,* in which she would create her final great role: Flaming Agnes.

Chapter 16

"LOVE ISN'T EVERYTHING"

She never behaved like a diva, but she was one.
— WILLARD SHAFFER ON MARY MARTIN

Mary Martin returned from her world tour of *Hello, Dolly!* saddened by the recent death of Hedda Hopper, who passed on February 1, 1966. More than just a witness to Martin's meteoric rise to stardom, more even than a friend and a confidant, the famous Queen of Gossip had been a constant and influential supporter. With the death of Sophie Tucker in early February as well (not to mention the death of Richard Halliday's mother in May), mortality was looming large in Martin's thoughts—especially in view of her husband's latest physical maladies.

Though there was nothing typical about Martin's relationship with Halliday, she was about to embark on a project that, at its core, defined what it was that made all marriages alike—even if, as Tolstoy suggested in his famous remark about "unhappy" families, no marriage really can ever be mistaken for another. Whatever understanding Martin and Halliday initially had with each other when they set out in 1940 to spend their lives together, it was becoming more and more difficult for Richard to hold up his end of the bargain. Richard, the overseer, the vigilante, the manager, the caretaker, was increasingly ailing and in need of care himself. He divested himself of a good deal of his daily workload by increasing Lee Tuft's responsibilities, beginning in August, to handle all of the Hallidays' business and financial matters.

When Martin had been working with Noël Coward on *Together with Music* a decade before, she had acknowledged that Halliday's drinking made him, at times, more of a hindrance and a liability than an asset—and a problem that needed to be remedied. More recently, TV documentarian Lucy Jarvis made it clear that Halliday's reputation as a difficult manager of his wife's professional affairs had spread beyond the confines of the theater world. But even in this respect, Halliday was slowing down: he would prove far less of a haggling participant during the creation of Martin's next and—though, of course, no one had any way of knowing it—her final Broadway musical. "Richard did not interfere with *I Do! I Do!* at all," said the show's composer, Harvey Schmidt. "I heard about him, in the earlier years. None of that was in evidence, at all. He couldn't have been more supportive, in every way. I just found him lovely."

Though it must have seemed strange at the time, NBC aired *Mary Martin at Eastertime with Radio City Music Hall* on Easter Sunday, April 3, 1966, while Martin was still performing at the Drury Lane in London, portraying Dolly Levi every night. But Martin had filmed the sixty-minute TV special long before it was broadcast. First announced in August 1964, the show was actually prepared in time to be broadcast on Easter 1965 but then held up for a year. "It was discovered that NBC's contract was with one union and the Music Hall's with another, so the show could not be performed in the Music Hall as planned," explained journalist Aleene MacMinn in a Seattle paper. As cumbersome as it sounds, Radio City Music Hall's enormous art deco stage was re-created in NBC's Brooklyn studio, which cost a huge amount of time and money. "That's where another problem arose. Musical specials don't come cheap, and this one was particularly expensive and by the time NBC got around to looking for a well-heeled sponsor last year, one was not available."

Martin was made an honorary Rockette for the event, and the show incorporated the Music Hall's annual Easter pageant. Martin performed songs from three of her Broadway hits—"There Is Nothing Like a Dame," "The Sound of Music," and "Put on Your Sunday Clothes"—plus a host of standards, including "Blue Skies," "Look for the Silver Lining," and "Spring Will Be a Little Late This Year." But delaying the broadcast by a year did not help the impression of the show as being rather archaic in the midst of the turbulent 1960s, when, worse than just old-fashioned, a TV variety show seemed irrelevant—as confirmed by the response in *Variety*: "the creeping squareness that infects virtually all variety efforts was felt."

The Hallidays may have assumed they were leaving the London theater behind when they returned to New York in the spring of 1966, but it seemed to be following them. While the Beatles would begin their final American tour in August, the Broadway season was marked by a so-called British "invasion," with new plays by Harold Pinter (*The Homecoming*), Frank Marcus (*The Killing of Sister George*), and Peter Shaffer (*Black Comedy*) adorning marquees.

Martin's own offering would be a two-character musical, without any supporting players, dancers, or chorus—an idea so novel, it seemed positively avant-garde for Broadway. But after the extravagances of the over-produced *Jennie* led to such an embarrassing failure and steep financial loss, the unprecedented simplicity of *I Do! I Do!* held a special appeal for the Hallidays—not to mention for its notoriously thrifty producer, David Merrick. Based on Jan de Hartog's *The Fourposter,* a 1946 hit that propelled the joint careers of husband-and-wife team Hume Cronyn and Jessica Tandy, *I Do! I Do!* portrays the history of a marriage during the first half of the twentieth century. It also seemed a rather quaint and benign throwback to outmoded notions of normalcy in the midst of the countercultural and revolutionary 1960s.

Looking back, Marge Champion felt that Martin's involvement with *Hello, Dolly!* was conceived by producer David Merrick "to fill the time until *I Do! I Do!* would be ready. That's why we went to Brazil," she added, referring to Marge and Gower Champion's visit with the Hallidays at Nossa Fazenda in 1965, to sell them on Martin's starring in both musicals. According to Merrick biographer Howard Kissel, the producer's "longest creative partnership" would prove to be with Gower Champion, beginning with another innovative and highly successful musical, *Carnival!*, in 1961, and including their biggest hit together, *Hello, Dolly!* "The two were a splendid match," added Kissel. "Champion was as tough, even as cruel a taskmaster as Merrick but much better at concealing it beneath a wholesome all-American charm."

"Gower had always wanted to do something with us," recalled Harvey Schmidt, who, with his partner, Tom Jones, had written the longest running musical in Off Broadway history, *The Fantasticks,* and the more recent *110 in the Shade,* yet another Merrick offering on Broadway. Champion had lunch with the songwriting duo in the fall of 1964 at the New York Athletic Club, where he presented each of them with a copy of Ludwig Bemelmans' noirish Paris novel *The Street Where the Heart Lies,* with hopes of adapting it as a musical. Shortly thereafter, Schmidt rented an Italian villa "about a hundred miles north of Rome," at Porto Santo Stephano. The villa belonged to classical pianist Mario Braggiotti, "a big radio star on WQXR," according to Schmidt, who would go on to compose the bulk of the score for *I Do! I Do!* on the maestro's highly prized Blüthner grand piano, over the better part of a year.

"We had only been there about a week and a half when Gower called from David Merrick's office," recalled Schmidt. "At that time, it wasn't so easy to place an international call, and it was downright exotic to be sitting in Italy and having Gower Champion call us from David Merrick's office. He said, 'I want you to stop thinking about *The Street Where the Heart Lies*. David Merrick wants you to turn *The Fourposter* into a Broadway musical, but with two stars in it.'

"At first, we both secretly thought it was a terrible idea, that it was going to be too difficult for a Broadway musical. But we didn't tell him that," continued Schmidt. "Then, the more he talked about it, the more interesting it started to sound—especially when he mentioned Mary Martin and Robert Preston. And with David Merrick producing, of course, and Gower directing, we suddenly felt it was something we could do, and we got very excited about it."

Schmidt, who had developed a childhood crush on Mary Martin when he was ten years old and heard her sing "My Heart Belongs to Daddy" on the radio, became a little boy all over again, seventy-some years later, as he recalled working with her in the mid-1960s. "Tom was going into Rome that weekend to get some books, I remember. But we talked a little bit about how the important thing would be to open [the story] up, in some way. We figured out if we could set it up with the opening wedding and everything. . . ."

In a fit of inspiration, Schmidt conceived what would become the show's biggest hit single, "My Cup Runneth Over," in Italy. "The day I wrote it on that fabulous Blüthner piano, I just started playing it, right off—the music just kind of wrote itself. I was searching for something that would be spellbinding, and it seemed too mechanical, to me. But Tom loved it. He thought it would be wonderful for that spot [in the show]. And he turned out to be right, because everybody responded to it that way."

The protracted creation of *I Do! I Do!* became something of an international affair. After working on songs for the show in Italy, Schmidt eventually played some of them for Martin while she was touring with *Hello, Dolly!* in the States before taking it abroad. The Hallidays were staying, at the time, with their friends Walter and Mary Tuohy in their grand aerie at the top of Cleveland's Terminal Tower. *Dolly* had just given its final performance in the city that was referred to, at the time, as "the biggest mistake on the lake."

"It was a Sunday afternoon, in that big building in the heart of Cleveland, where all the trains come in," recalled Harvey Schmidt, who, with Jones and Merrick, met the Hallidays there to perform the score for them. "It was a gorgeous triplex. We had to go up to some floor, and then through this tiny little door. We had to bend over, and then enter this fantastic apartment—huge, ballroom-size. And it had a fabulous piano, a Steinway. Whenever you'd meet with Mary, you would first be met by

Richard: he'd take care of the drinks and chitchat. And then, Mary would always make her entrance at just the right moment. In Cleveland, it was on an upper balcony: she opened her arms to greet us before coming down the stairs. It was all sort of like *Citizen Kane,* but in a good way—high ceilings everywhere, and this long, long table, with a huge banquet. We were all seated at one end, with David Merrick.

"That's when Mary was very enthusiastic about the new stuff we had done," continued Schmidt. "And they were really definite about it. It was a very exciting afternoon. She was in a great mood, touring with *Dolly.* They were travelling all over with their cook and driver, Ernest, who had worked for the Lunts for many years. He was a terrific guy. Their Rolls-Royce was taupe, which was my favorite color. That dinner was very celebratory for all of us. And then the very next day, it was [announced] in the *New York Times* that Mary was going to do the show."

Schmidt put the preliminary, working songs on a relatively new device called a "cassette tape," so Martin could hear them at her convenience while touring with *Dolly* in Asia and London. "Portable recorders had just come out," recalled Schmidt. "This guy from London had sent Mary something on one. And she asked if I could put this show on a tape. Tom and I both did, but I did most of Mary's stuff. And she was very pleased to get it."

During its protracted development, Martin's commitment to *I Do! I Do!* proved occasionally precarious, however. She particularly vacillated whenever Robert Preston wavered about his own involvement, which, according to Gower Champion, was hard-won in the first place. "We finally got Mary to agree, but couldn't persuade Preston for another six months," claimed Champion. "After he turned me down four times, I gave up. But Merrick doesn't take no for an answer."

Though Martin and Preston had nothing but fond memories of working with one another at the beginning of their respective careers at Paramount in 1940, when they made *New York Town* together, Preston's own sense of self-worth had recently been shaken. Broadway's most famous Music Man had flopped in *Ben Franklin in Paris,* before more recently completing a run on the Great White Way in *The Lion in Winter* with Rosemary Harris as his costar, who received a Tony Award as well as the lion's share of thunder and attention. As far as Tom Jones was concerned, "[Preston] didn't want to be in another show where the woman was going to take all the notices from him again."

"He had been walking at his country place up in Connecticut," added Schmidt, "and he got something caught in a tree and really injured his eye." (As later reported, "a low hanging tree branch scratched the retina of Preston's eye while he was walking his dog.") "But I also think he was just tired. He said he needed to take time off."

Long after the *Dolly* tour ended, Schmidt played some of the *I Do! I Do!* songs for Martin again in person. It was after the Hallidays had made yet another rejuvenating trip to Brazil in the spring of 1966, when Robert Preston was suddenly out of the project—again. "And Mary was very disappointed," recalled Harvey Schmidt. "There're very few musical men whose name could match Mary Martin's. That's what was so perfect about Robert Preston: they were like 'twin towers,' you know. So Gower was exploring other people. One of them was Howard Keel, who Gower knew from MGM. So they brought Mary up from the jungles of Brazil to New York." The Champions had made *Jupiter's Darling* with Keel at MGM a decade earlier, which proved to be a costly dud.

The Champions were, then, living in another "fabulous apartment," a recent gift from producer Lester Osterman, on East Seventy-ninth Street, overlooking Central Park. "It was just south of the Metropolitan Museum," recalled Schmidt. "The producer gave it to Marge and Gower, just because Gower had stepped in to try and help him salvage a show [*High Spirits*]. Gower said it was like winning it, instead of money. I remember the first time we were over there . . . and the big living room . . . and Marge coming down the stairs. It had a really high ceiling, and a very dramatic stairway to make your entrance on. The setting was like in an MGM version of a show being written in New York: you could look out at Central Park; and you could picture Howard Keel and Mary Martin there, with me on the piano. It's been a picture-book episode in my mind ever since, from that one day we were there."

Though Sister Gregory, Martin's friend and advisor, had recently arrived in Brazil, the Hallidays dropped everything to rush to New York in order to see if Martin was able to do *I Do! I Do!* with someone other than Robert Preston. Martin would recall the event in her memoir, without identifying Howard Keel. "David Merrick asked us to fly to New York for one day and night to hear another actor. This man could act, he had a beautiful voice, but there just wasn't the special astringent quality of Bob [Preston]." According to Schmidt, Champion also felt there was too much of an age difference between Keel and Martin: "Howard was a lot more youthful and robust in the part," added Schmidt. "But with Robert Preston, somehow you didn't question what age he was."

Feeling "pretty glum" after the audition, Martin also remembered Champion asking her how badly she wanted to do the show. "I said very badly indeed, but only with Bob," she wrote. "We were all sitting around as at a wake when all of a sudden David Merrick walked in and said, 'I've got Bob Preston.' . . . Richard and I were so happy we could have flown back to Brazil without a plane that night."

They returned to Brazil and the houseguest they had left behind. Sister Gregory went to work helping Martin learn her role of Agnes, the happy bride turned expectant mother, then middle-aged, and finally contented wife. This was before Harvey Schmidt made the all-day trek to Nossa Fazenda, to work some more with his beloved star.

"I didn't even know that I was going to go to Brazil until I read it in the Sunday [*New York*] *Times*," said Schmidt. "It was set up in her contract that any composer was to be sent down there by David Merrick to work with her on the score. And I was thrilled about that, because part of my long fascination with Mary Martin and her husband was that they were living this very beautiful lifestyle. I loved the idea of just going down there to work on the songs. And it was arranged for the composer to go first class—everything they did, at that point, was first class.

"I got to Brasília around noon," he continued, "and they told me I'd have to take a jeep all the way to their ranch. I had instructions to give the driver, but he knew where it was. It still took all day. There wasn't even a real road. Finally, we knew we were at the right signpost when the driver flashed his flashlight and there was a brass pair of clasped hands right on the wooden gate. So we drove up the path and came to a couple of dark buildings. He killed the engine and we sat there for a moment. Then I heard this familiar voice coming out of the dark: 'Haavee? Haavee, Darlin'? Is it really you?'"

After they showed Schmidt to the guesthouse, "we just stood there talking for quite a while, and Mary and Richard were facing me," said Schmidt. "It was a very warm feeling. And I noticed behind them on the wall was this huge sculpture of some kind of spider—it was green-black. I didn't say anything about it. And they showed me where the candles were, and the bathroom. We were tired at that point, and they said they would send out my breakfast. Ernest was a fabulous cook. It was all served on Royal Dalton China, you know. I woke up the next morning and I looked at the wall and I saw that the sculpture wasn't there. And I then realized it had been a live tarantula. I asked them about it, and they were quite horrified. But they were quite common down there. Where it had gone, I didn't know. But I kept looking for it the whole time I was there."

Apart from his understandable paranoia about the wayward tarantula, Schmidt had nothing but fond memories of his Brazilian adventure. "It was all so primitive, but that was the charm of it," he recalled. "There were these very dry hills, but then the valleys would have monkeys and macaws, and all these jungle sounds going on. It was very environmentally pleasant on the plateau areas. Richard was also doing a series of terraces off the back of the house, or fountains, with water cascading down. And the house had a porch on it, which is where Mary and I would rehearse. There was an upright piano. And we would rehearse every afternoon. I'd have my fabulous Ernest breakfast, and then I'd practice by myself, and then she'd come out early afternoon, and we'd work for several hours. I'd just sing along with her.

"Mary always had a drink at the end of the day: a frozen daiquiri," continued Schmidt. "She'd spend most of her days already practicing what kind of look she wanted for this musical: her hair and her costumes. It's so odd about her looks: they could go in so many different directions. But [costumer] Freddy Wittop even came down with some materials for Mary to make selections."

As he recalls Martin driving him into town once, "in this old, beat-up pick-up truck," Schmidt's description evokes a scene out of *South Pacific,* with Nellie Forbush at the wheel. "She was just wearing overalls, and sandals, which she took off. So she was driving with her toenails painted an immaculate, bright red. And we got to talking about driving. She said that she had an aunt, growing up in Texas, and people would pray that she would stop driving. And then Mary started doing an imitation of how her aunt drove, because there was no real road or ditch. We were just careening around this prairie land, laughing hysterically. She was laughing as loud as I was."

According to Schmidt, Martin learned her part as Agnes "by doing it many times. I was just there two weeks in all. But then she insisted that I come back to Rio, to work some more with her. When I said, 'David Merrick's not going to pay for that,' she said he would. And he did, too."

Schmidt also worked individually with Robert Preston back in New York, before rehearsals began. On the first day of rehearsals, Martin showed up with a special gift for all the principal creators: lobby cards from *New York Town,* featuring a still photo of herself and Preston. "Mary is handing him a horseshoe," said Schmidt. "We all got the same picture, but she prepared them for each of us in a special way. They were beautifully finished off."

Champion quickly turned the rehearsals into something of a closed shop for himself and his two stars, however, ousting even Merrick from the proceedings. "Gower was sort of at the peak of his powers," observed Schmidt. "It was a real love affair between Mary and Bob and Gower. But Gower told us that he didn't want us around at every rehearsal. He thought it would be smoother and easier for them, because it was such a small group."

He was also, in other words, more focused. "Gower was at his best as a director with that show, because he had two very experienced people," claimed Marge Champion. "I know it was the happiest time he ever had in directing a show, because there was no chorus to take his attention away from the stars. From his nightclub experience, [in other words, helping individuals develop their act], he always found if he let people go a little bit, he would find things." Martin recalled one of those "things" in her memoir, when she added some levity one afternoon by suddenly riding one of the offstage kid's tricycles for a lark. Champion noticed her genuine glee and told her to leave it in the show. As Martin put it, "Our entire rehearsal time was like a three-way tennis game, a love match. Bob would suddenly do something which Gower and I loved. Gower would think up something we couldn't wait to try. I stayed awake nights dreaming up things to please them. I can't ever remember having such concentrated fun while working." Preston readily and succinctly agreed with her sentiments: "I may never work for anyone else as long as I live."

There were five weeks of rehearsals, beginning in late August, at Broadway's 46th Street Theatre, later renamed the Richard Rodgers. Tom Jones recalled how, during rehearsals, Halliday would bring his wife's lunch in a picnic basket, "and they would set it up very formally in her dressing room." There was one person who, uninvited and unannounced, attended some of the rehearsals. "I wrote to Mary and said I had been standby for so many leading ladies, and that 'It would be my crowning joy to be your understudy in *I Do! I Do*! She told me to call David Merrick," recalled Iva Withers, who was a prominent understudy or replacement in many a musical comedy in the middle of the twentieth century, including *Carousel*, *The Unsinkable Molly Brown,* and *Oklahoma!* "It presented a real problem, though, because neither Mary nor Robert Preston would allow anyone to watch them rehearse," continued Withers. In fact, Merrick had no understudies for his two stars. "But I was a sneak. I had done *Guys and Dolls* at the 46th Street Theatre, so I knew every way in and out of the theater. And I sneaked in and watched them rehearse from the gallery."

Despite Champion's dictate regarding rehearsals, David Merrick also did what he could to maintain some behind-the-scenes control. "Merrick would secretly have people dropping in on rehearsals," recalled Willard Shaffer. "He wouldn't let them do anything, but he'd want their thoughts and opinions." Later still, during the tryouts, "Merrick would come to rehearsals and watch them from the back of the theater, but nobody ever even knew he was there," added Shaffer. "Then he'd fly home, and call me that night with his suggestions."

Following his careful ministrations during the *Hello, Dolly!* tour, Shaffer learned that the Hallidays were directly responsible for his involvement with *I Do! I Do!* "I found out later from the company manager that it was in Mary Martin's contract that the electrician would be Willard Shaffer," Shaffer recalled. Though it hadn't occurred to Shaffer, Halliday may have been more responsible for the stipulation than his wife, however. "He would use me as his 'escape,' to go on drinking binges. Every time I had to go somewhere—even to go ahead and scope out the next city for *I Do! I Do!*—he had to go with me." Shaffer also discovered that he was making considerably less than the other technicians involved with the show. "Had I known it was in her contract, I would have demanded more money. But Jack Schlissel, Merrick's general manager, conned me into it."

Though Halliday evidently did not intervene during the developmental phase of *I Do! I Do!*, as his health improved he made his presence more apparent during the rehearsal period and, then, throughout the run. While looking back on working with Martin and *I Do! I Do!* for nearly two years, Shaffer said: "She never behaved like a diva, but she was one. Richard was the bad guy. She never complained about anything directly, but she would complain to him, and he would, in turn, complain to me, and I'd take care of it. Some men on the fly floor were talking once, and she could hear them. She'd tell Richard and I'd get them to stop talking, saying Richard had complained."

"Even with Gower Champion, she and Robert Preston would laugh and chuckle with each other during rehearsals, when they were doing blocking, and things like that," continued Shaffer. "And she would do what she was told. But then, when she didn't like something, Richard would go to Champion. I was able to see this going on during *I Do! I Do!* Gower would tell me that the designer wanted one thing, but she'd want a different color—things like that. But her sense of what was right or wrong was extremely good. Whether it was for lighting or blocking, her instincts were always right on the money. And as far as doing what was right for her, boy was Richard good at it. If he got any resistance from anybody, he could get very nasty: 'This won't do. We can just get on a plane and go home.'"

There was one number in the second act, "Thousands of Flowers," which everyone—including, ostensibly, Martin herself—loved. But it was eliminated during the Boston tryouts at the Colonial Theatre, which began on September 26. While claiming in her memoir that it was "a lovely number," Martin added that "it was too lyrical for that spot in the show." According to Willard Shaffer, there was an even more specific reason for its removal. "Every show we ever did with Gower Champion, there was always a scene that never worked," said Shaffer, who became Merrick's chief electrician for plays as well as musicals. "We had a number called 'Thousands of Flowers': it was lovely sounding, with Mary Martin singing it. But she didn't particularly like it. During the number, there were these huge, artificial flowers that came flying in, and they took all the attention away from Mary Martin singing. So it just went away."

Martin came down with a severe case of gout in Boston and had to be hospitalized, so performances were suspended. "Whenever Gower visited her in the hospital, it was no surprise to find her sitting up in bed with a violin crooked under her chin, sawing away," claimed Champion biographer John Anthony Gilvey. She was practicing for a new duet, "When the Kids Get Married," which was a last-minute replacement for "Thousands of Flowers." Champion jazzed up the number—and the show—by having Martin play the violin and Preston the saxophone.

It was also in Boston that Martin confronted Shaffer directly, instead of calling upon Halliday to carry out some unpleasant business on her behalf. "I made a bad lighting mistake at the end of the show one night, which kind of clipped her applause," recalled Shaffer. "It was a slow fade to just a head shot, and I went down too fast, and it cut the audience response. So I was summoned to her dressing room—the only time ever—for a mistake. She said, 'Willard, you know better than that,' as she was smiling at me. And she was right."

But also, according to Shaffer, Martin was making mistakes of her own during the tryouts. "She had trouble with her lines," he said. "It was painful getting through rehearsals, 'cause she just couldn't get them down, and Gower was concerned. When we were doing previews, she would mess up and forget where she was and Preston would bail her out. But she had it pretty darn pat before the critics came."

"Mary was a very, very slow study, spending six to eight months, even at that point in her career, learning the lines," confirmed Tom Jones. "It wasn't like we could do a new number for the juvenile, the ingenue, or the dancing chorus. It was *just them*. So even though we were writing, it took at least three weeks to get in a new number." But once she finally learned her part, Martin was consistently flawless. "She never had an 'up' or a 'down' performance," Shaffer recalled. "Never walked through it. If you would have filmed her first and last performances and compared them frame-to-frame, you would see no difference. Her attitude was always, 'This is what I do, and I'm gonna do it right.'"

Arriving at that point required more time, however. Establishing a pattern that would mark the show's progress no matter what improvements were made during the extended tryouts, the Boston reviewers wrote love letters to the two stars while criticizing the material. A nervous Merrick brought in some top guns to fiddle with the score, including Jerry Herman. (Ironically, Merrick had introduced Charles Strouse and Lee Adams to embellish Herman's score for *Hello, Dolly!* during *its* tryouts.) But unlike some of the producer's other collaborators, Schmidt and Jones "were able to withstand Merrick," according to theater scholar Steven Suskin. "When he arrived at the stage door of the Colonial [Theatre in Boston] bearing Comden, Green, and Styne interpolations in his fist, they just said no. (Merrick usually got his way by threatening to close the show, but with *I Do!*'s stars and tremendous advance sale, Schmidt and Jones were able to out-bluff the master bluffer.)"

It was also in Boston that Shaffer's mother and aunt came to see the show, and Martin gave them a full forty-five minutes in her dressing room afterward. "She showed them what she was working on with her needlework," recalled Shaffer. "Then a couple of years later, she sent signed copies of her needlepoint book to each of them for Christmas," he added, referring to the bestselling *Mary Martin's Needlepoint,* published in 1969.

As scheduled, *I Do! I Do!* continued its pre-Broadway tryouts in Washington, DC, where it opened at the National Theatre on October 19 and played for three weeks. Merrick remained anxious over ongoing expressions of dismay from the critics: "after an enchanting first act the musical finds itself with nowhere to go," wrote Cecil Smith in the *Los Angeles Times*. But according to Shaffer, it was Champion who asked for more time to "get it right." "Merrick found that the Schubert [Theater] in Cincinnati was available, so we went there for a few weeks to give Gower more time to work on the show," recalled Shaffer. "Gower had a Thanksgiving dinner for everybody involved. Even though the show only had two actors, there were ninety people behind the scenes, including the musicians, stagehands, personal chauffeurs. . . . He arranged this big Thanksgiving dinner at the hotel, where each table had its own turkey. Gower made a party out of it, because everybody was tired, and had thought they were going to be home in New York for the holiday. It was also in Cincinnati that Robert Preston got Mary Martin drunk as a skunk backstage, the night when the *Life* cover photo [of the two of them in costume] was taken."

With a kind of retrospective outlook that only the distance of time can provide, Martin would claim that *I Do! I Do!* "seemed a culmination to me." She went further, in her memoir, to say, "Just as the subject matter ... was a culmination of my life, so the challenge of performing it was to my career," and she emphasized how taxing the show was to do. "Gower plotted the production like a wartime invasion," she wrote, "every moment, every prop, every second. One of us, Bob or I, had to be on stage the entire time, singing or talking, while the other ran off to make necessary costume changes. I had fifteen costumes and five wigs, so I had to hustle my bustle. ... This sort of thing takes not only stamina but also choreography. Gower is a master of that. Every move, every change, was made on a beat of the music."

I Do! I Do! opened on Broadway at the 46th Street Theatre on Monday, December 5, 1966, two weeks later than originally planned, after more than two months on the road—an unusually long time frame for tryouts. The opening night party was at Rockefeller Center's snazzy Rainbow Room, where the soon-to-be-divorced Champions impressed the black-tie guests by doing what they were best known for, taking over the floor as a famous dance team. As it had been throughout its extended tryout period, the show was greeted as a vehicle for its stars—a musical built for two. Walter Kerr in the *New York Times* centered his review on a metaphor appropriate to the season: "[A] Santa Claus who shall here be known as David Merrick has hitched a very high-powered Donner and a very high-powered Blitzen to a very low-powered One Horse Shay [sic]." While adding in the *World Journal Tribune* that "Mary Martin will have the gift of youthfulness as long as she lives," Norman Nadel concurred: "What makes *I Do! I Do!* unique is the fact that you are always watching two of the most talented and entertaining performers in the American musical theatre."

"Mary Martin exists to be wooed," wrote the reviewer for *Time,* which resorted to some unusually lofty language for the popular weekly: "She focuses light, as a magnifying glass brings the sun to a pinpoint of burning stillness. When she sings, one may imagine that the choir of the seraphim pauses to take rehearsal notes." Perhaps the critic for the *Saturday Review* was the most perceptive, saying, "There is never the illusion that we are seeing Agnes and Michael. We are quite obviously seeing Mary and Bob, which under the circumstances may be a good thing. For it takes the curse off the compound sentimentality of the story." After catching the show at the beginning of its run, Noël Coward wrote, more simply, in his diary, "Both of them superb."

Though they were playing Agnes and Michael, Martin and Preston were very much aware that the audiences were coming to see them. They were, in other words, really playing theatrical versions of themselves—an approach that was built into the original metatheatrical conception of Jones and Schmidt and accentuated by Champion's highly presentational staging. The play opens on a bare stage, before pieces of furniture begin floating in. The twenty-five-piece orchestra performs behind a scrim, which was illuminated to reveal the musicians at the beginning of the second act. Agnes and Michael suddenly become old, near the end, when Martin and Preston apply their makeup and change their costumes in full view of the audience.

Given how grueling it was for its two middle-aged stars to perform such a demanding piece, they would only commit to seven performances a week, eschewing Wednesday matinees, which were practically mandatory on Broadway. "We had a gentleman's agreement to do Saturday matinees as long as we were physically able," explained Martin. "Bob and I did them for the first six months of the run, then we had to stop." (Stalwart musical performers Carol Lawrence and Gordon MacRae started performing matinees at the 46th Street Theatre on October 18, 1967.) And given that everyone was paying specifically to see Martin and Preston, Merrick adopted a "no understudies" policy from the beginning: if one of them couldn't go on, there would be no show.

The toasts of Broadway, Martin and Preston were a natural choice to cohost the 1967 Tony Awards, the first to be televised nationally, on March 26. The couple performed "Nobody's Perfect," one of their more sprightly numbers from I Do! I Do!, which would unfortunately lose the Tony for Best Musical to Cabaret. However, Robert Preston won for Best Actor in a Musical. Though nominated, Martin lost to Barbara Harris, who had a distinct advantage by playing three very different characters in The Apple Tree. (During her acceptance speech, the preternaturally shy Harris was accosted onstage and rendered speechless by a gatecrasher, who kissed her before dashing offstage.) As Time magazine reported on the awards telecast, "the new Tony—poised, polished, brimming with talent—arrived at Manhattan's Shubert Theatre and in one swinging sweep, made Emmy and Oscar look merely like tired vaudevillians. . . . The show itself, aired on ABC, won the ratings sweepstakes over NBC's Bonanza and CBS's The Smothers Brothers Comedy Hour." After Marian Seldes won for Featured Actress in a Play that year (in Edward Albee's A Delicate Balance), Martin struck up some backstage small talk with a customary faux pas, telling the perfect, elocutionary American actress, "I bet you can't wait to take your award home to London."

Having toured with Martin in *Hello, Dolly!*, Judith Drake went to see *I Do! I Do!* one night with her aunt. "We had house seats," recalled Drake, "and Mary Martin knew just where we were sitting and threw her bouquet to my aunt." But according to Martin, such archery was really something of an accident: "Because I always threw the bouquet from the same spot, with the same gesture, the flowers landed in practically the same place every night. By chance, the area I hit happened to be our own house seats, though I didn't know it." Larry Hagman reportedly went to see his mother in *I Do! I Do!* a couple of times. "Mary said that he absolutely loved the show," recalled Shaffer. "And it really meant a lot to her, that he had loved it so much."

The top ticket price for *I Do! I Do!* was $9.90, the same as for *Fiddler on the Roof* (in its third year) and for *Hello, Dolly!* (in its fourth), versus $6.75 for a ticket to *Barefoot in the Park* (also in its fourth year). Neil Simon had three additional shows running simultaneously on Broadway that season: *The Odd Couple, The Star-Spangled Girl,* and the musical *Sweet Charity*, earning Simon a percentage of weekly grosses averaging $200,000. Producer David Merrick bested the playwright with his weekly combined gross of $325,000 for *Cactus Flower, Don't Drink the Water, Hello, Dolly!,* and *I Do! I Do!* Martin was personally earning $7,500 a week for her portrayal of Agnes, or basically ten percent of what it cost to initially produce the show.

There were, however, some rare weeks when Merrick earned a bit less for *I Do! I Do!* On Thursday, May 11, 1967, Sam Zolotow reported in the *New York Times* that there had been no performances since Monday, and wouldn't be, "until Miss Martin recovers from a virus infection affecting her nose, throat, larynx and vocal cords. . . . The management is insured against canceled performances whenever either star is ill, effective after the second night of such a cancellation." The following October 6, a Friday, the *Times* reported that, having already missed two performances earlier that week, Martin "sang her way through all but 15 minutes of last night's performance . . . before she bowed out reluctantly, weary with the flu and medication." The announcement of the cancellation reportedly brought "energetic and sympathetic applause [from] the audience."

The immense strain of such a difficult role over so many months led to ongoing health problems for Martin. Carol Lawrence and Gordon

MacRae took over for the show's two stars on December 4, shortly before Martin was hospitalized for a hysterectomy. Before beginning a difficult, eight-month national tour with Preston of *I Do! I Do!*, Martin recuperated at Nossa Fazenda for several months.

The Hallidays found their Brazilian hideaway somewhat changed since they had first colonized it thirteen years earlier. The nearest electricity, which used to be twenty-five miles away, was now only three, and the nearest phone was twenty miles away, instead of six hundred and fifty. The Hallidays were still dependent on kerosene lamps, but increasingly comfortable in what would soon become their primary residence. In a story in the April 1968 issue of *Esquire,* Martin described her relatively sedate life in Brazil at the time: "I learned to cook at long last on our wood stove. Also, at this late date I learned to sew. . . . My husband designed and had built a studio of red brick and white tile that reaches to the top of the highest tree above our house—where I can enjoy myself for hours at a time, painting, learning, experimenting without interruption. At night I can read or do needlepoint by the kerosene lamp—or learn more about the Portuguese language. We can listen to music we have wanted to hear for years—or I can study a Portuguese song. Friends drop in now and then from faraway for a visit."

The two of them went horseback riding every day. "[W]e can ride until we are hungry and stop by a stream under a shading tree and eat our picnic," explained Martin. "Or we can ride for four or five hours, making discoveries of new roads, new jungles that we have never seen before." They also looked after what had become a Brazilian industry: "We have a small herd of cattle, five thousand chickens, a citrus grove, acres of vegetables, banana and avocado groves. We have built six houses where six families live and work on the farm. There are usually two dozen men working on the place—we have had as many as sixty. We have designed and built dams, bridges and roads, as well as barns. We grow our own corn for the chickens and cows. We grow cotton; the women pick it, clean it, spin it, dye it, and weave upholstery fabrics or rugs for the bedside."

This was all in preparation for their agreement to spend at least two years in Brazil, away from the fray and the frazzle of working in the theater. But first came Martin's commitment to take *I Do! I Do!* to twenty-six cities over the course of a year. It started with a week in Rochester, New York, on April 4, 1968, followed by Indianapolis and Minneapolis, before two months each in Los Angeles (from April 29 to June 22) and San Francisco (from June 25 to August 17). According to Willard Shaffer, no matter what hotel they stayed in, the Hallidays always had adjoining suites with separate doors, so Martin could get her sleep and Richard could have his privacy and his male escorts.

As was her custom, Martin also became essentially a prisoner in her dressing room. "Robert Preston and Gower would walk around with the crew and everybody, as they were setting up," recalled Shaffer, "asking them how they were, and all those nice things. And she'd never even show her face, until it was, 'Places, please.' Preston was a glad-hand, keeping peace in the family. He was the pal of the crew."

But also as usual, Martin maintained a positive outlook toward the ordeal of touring. "The Road," Martin told Aleene MacMinn, for a story in the *Los Angeles Times,* "keeps me alive in a show. There's the thrill of each new city and the challenge that every Monday night is an opening. When you go on the road, you discover that people come to the show because they love to go to the theater—they have to, to pay those horrible prices. In New York, they go because it's the thing to do. They're saturated with it." But Martin refused to talk about her recent health problems, underscoring how important it was to keep any offstage difficulties from the public. "They're there to enjoy themselves," she told MacMinn. "The illusion would be spoiled if they were aware of any work or any problem. They should be aware of nothing but the show. During *Peter Pan,* people were always wanting to come backstage to take pictures of the flying and I always said no. If they photographed that, the illusion would be gone."

Martin also told MacMinn about the needlepoint book she was working on with her husband, "scheduled for publication next year." The biggest surprise was her pronouncement about their future. "After this tour, we have no plan in the theater. Richard and I are looking forward to spending two years in Brazil. People talk about doing things like that, but never do." In a parenthetical aside, MacMinn suggested that this was "a decision made for her by her doctor last winter," without explaining Martin's circumstances any further.

Theater publicist Bob Ullman was employed to go on the road with *I Do! I Do!* for six weeks. "I first met Mary Martin at Dorothy Rodgers's gorgeous apartment, filled with antiques," recalled Ullman. "I had seen her in *Leave It to Me!* and *One Touch of Venus,* and we got on like a house on fire. She said it was going to be wonderful, and it was. I didn't have to do anything as a press agent: I'd take out an ad, saying Mary Martin and Robert Preston, and it was sold out. They both said they'd like to do joint press conferences, preferably at the airports. I remember, for two weeks, in the Twin Cities, all I did was go antiquing."

The show's aging stars did not have as easy a time of it, however. What had been difficult from the beginning became, increasingly, an endurance test. "Bob and I were both coming apart at the seams, but we didn't know it," recalled Martin in her memoir. "Bob began catching colds which he never acknowledged, and having troubles with his voice. I had diverticulitis and didn't know it—the cortisone I was still taking [ever since Vietnam] masked it." They nonetheless continued the tour: from Vancouver, Seattle, and Portland to St. Louis, Kansas City, Omaha, St. Paul, and Phoenix.

In Dallas, in November, just how badly Martin was faring became apparent to her childhood friend, Bessie Mae, and her husband, Jac Austin. "As soon as the Hallidays arrived in Dallas, the Austins got a call from Richard," according to Ronald L. Davis. " 'I don't have time to be polite,' Halliday said. 'We need a doctor right away. We're at the Stoneleigh Hotel, and could you send us a doctor?' Bessie Mae and Jac contacted their family physician, and he managed to get Mary well enough to perform on Monday. 'I could tell by the look of Mary's face that she was ill,' Bessie Mae said. 'There was a puffiness, and I think it was a reaction to the medication she was taking.' Also, Mary was depressed and crying a great deal, which was not like her at all." But as with most negative aspects of her life, Martin kept her feelings to herself. Her whole life had been so blessed and charmed that she was simply unequipped to comprehend such feelings, let alone to share them.

Despite Martin's apparent problems, the troupers valiantly soldiered on for another two and a half months—Houston, Memphis, Charlotte, Greensboro, Richmond, Washington, DC, Baltimore, Cleveland. . . . They finally came to a halt in Detroit, in February 1969. "We were all spared the sight of a burst abscess right on stage at the theater in Detroit by the fact that I woke up one Saturday morning absolutely unable to move," Martin wrote. The remainder of the tour was duly canceled by a doctor's ultimatum: "If you want to live," he said, "then my word is law. Stop working."

While Richard's health had recently seemed so precarious, Martin's own iron constitution had begun to fail her. She was treated for six weeks for a bleeding ulcer, and reportedly "wound up in a Chicago hospital." Following the doctor's orders, the balance of the *I Do! I Do!* tour was canceled and the Hallidays retreated to Brazil. It would be nearly a decade before Mary Martin would undertake another role in a Broadway play.

Chapter 17

DEEP IN THE HEART OF . . .
BRAZIL

I told Richard that I have heard people say
"I love you so much—I'll buy the Brooklyn Bridge."
But no one but him has done it!
—MARY MARTIN

When the Hallidays moved to their South American home in July 1969, they had a pretty clear idea of what their lives would be like at Nossa Fazenda. Ironically, they had less of a sense of what they were leaving behind. The summer of 1969 marked not only "one giant leap for mankind," when Neil Armstrong set foot on the moon, but also a huge cultural turning point for the so-called love generation, as encapsulated by Woodstock, which was billed, at the time, as "Three Days of Peace and Music." A *New York* magazine columnist named Gloria Steinem had just, in April, published an article, "After Black Power, Women's Liberation," upending clear-cut, calcified gender roles that had seemed unquestionable as recently as the decade before. Judy Garland died at the end of June, setting the mood for drag queens to fight back when a New York bar known as the Stonewall was raided by the police, signifying the beginning of the gay and lesbian revolution. In certain respects, the Hallidays were leaving the States just when they should have found it more hospitable to who they really were.

Though the Hallidays were removing themselves from the scene of many social and political upheavals, they would continue to be troubled by the behavior of their children—that is, by Heller's protracted divorce from her first husband, Tony Weir, and by Larry's becoming an outspoken hippie, denouncing his mother's and stepfather's ways. They were also baffled by the turmoil they thought they were saying good-bye to in New York. In only a year, Halliday would write from Nossa Fazenda: "We are deeply unhappy—because—the newspapers and magazines here are full of the most—shall we say?—shocking photos of this and that

in L.A., New Orleans, San Fran., N.Y., Chicago, New Haven, etc., etc.—
and the folk here are sad-alarmed-frightened [*sic*] for us in the U.S. . . ."

For the Hallidays, however, Brazil was still a place to heal their various
ailments with rest and relaxation—and with many a visitor. They flew
to São Paulo with Agnes, their new white French poodle (a gift from *I
Do! I Do!* stagehands), on a Pan Am flight on July 20. When they arrived
in Brasília, they were greeted by Ernest, their butler, with a new Ford
Galaxie: "avocado green with a black top." "Customs were marvelous,"
Halliday wrote in a letter. "The new car and friends awaited us—the
home-coming sensationally successful. Have only seen Dona Maria
[i.e., Mary] as elated two or three other times in twenty-nine years. Yes,
this durn place for some reason again surpasses our hopes, our dreams.
We are healthy and happy." Only some days later, however, Halliday observed that "Dona Maria found the changes too thrilling to easily digest
and oh so much to do that she has had forty-eight hours of collapse. . . ."

What letter after letter would make clear was that, more than just a
gentleman farmer, Halliday had become a rather industrious one, with
lime, garlic, coffee, and pine trees, 4,000 "baby chicks," as well as a growing herd of cattle and twenty-nine workers. As he would write in a subsequent letter, Halliday was "up at 5:30 a.m., which is no problem at all
after eight hours of sleep—and—we've seeded 25,000 more banana plants—
hundreds more avocado trees of eight different varieties that will produce
twelve months of the year. . . ."

In many of his letters, Halliday alludes to his wife as "Madame." (For
that matter, their personal secretary Lee Tuft is, more than once, called
"Miss Smarty-pants.") Though they rarely refer to each other in the third
person, both Halliday and Martin write like very good friends who saw
each other regularly but lived apart—certainly not in the next room.
And in the larger sense, that's just what they were: each other's best friend
and confidante, but nonetheless confined to or contained by his and
her own private world. The Hallidays' clasped-hands logo or insignia—
recognizable to anyone who knew them, and only recently added to their
stationery—was more a symbol of what they hoped to convey than a
representation of their real relationship.

Martin's routine activities were independent of her husband's. A
studio had been added above Martin's bedroom, where she would paint,
design clothes, and generally keep active: "I don't know how to design,
but I'm having a ball," Martin relayed. In addition to collecting "three or
four dozens of roses from her garden each morning before sunrise," in
which 350 rose bushes had been planted, Martin would devote a good

deal of her newfound freedom to her second greatest passion, doing nee-dlepoint, which had long been an obsession. *Mary Martin's Needlepoint,* including many reproductions in full color, an oversize, utterly personal book on the subject, was published by William Morrow in the fall. (Martin had received a $12,500 advance for the book, which practically paid for their acquisition of new adjoining land, at $84 an acre, when, fifteen years earlier, they had paid just $52.)

As Lee Tuft, the Hallidays' secretary, wrote them on July 31, "Berg-dorf's will have a window display—all the Fifty-seventh St. windows de-voted to the book. They have bought 500 books, 250 autographed and are really going all out including a very expensive ad shared with William Morrow. They will also use the shoe windows on Fifth Ave." Six weeks later, Tuft wrote: "The book is doing very well. They originally sent out 8,000 copies—they have orders for 15,000. . . . Bergdorf reordered 300 so they sold out their original order. Book of the Month Club is not offering your book until January," when, it was later reported, they took 10,000 copies.

Though the Hallidays would get much of their news in Brazil from *Time* magazine, which arrived "two weeks after publication" and which they devoured "cover to cover," they were also kept abreast of both private and public matters by Lee Tuft. For more than three years, beginning in the summer of 1969, Tuft wrote more-or-less daily letters from her one-room office in the Campanile, with its view of the East River. (The rent for her small abode was seventy dollars a month.) The thousand-plus pages of correspondence between Tuft and primarily Richard Halliday document this particular period in the Hallidays' life with vivid details, while re-counting political and economic developments of the day as well.

However, it is Tuft's letters that often prove both revealing and enter-taining, nearly half a century after they were written. A hard-core Green-wich Village denizen who spent what free time she could rousing the leftist rabble at Union Square, Tuft brought her revolutionary zeal to revolutionary times. (Pulitzer Prize finalist Amy Herzog's play *4000 Miles* was basically an homage to Lee Tuft, her grandmother.) Tuft's canny intelligence and compassionate humor inform many of her letters, which are necessarily filled with quotidian matters—such as the Halli-days' perpetual need for prescription drug renewals as well as specific books and recordings—but also laced with cultural and gossipy bulletins that transcend merely personal concerns.

Many of Tuft's letters seemed geared to convince the Hallidays that they were fortunate to be so far removed from the social upheavals back

home. She also evinced, perhaps, more than a tad of envy over the Hallidays' relatively peaceful existence. "Tomorrow is 'Moratorium' Day," Tuft
wrote on October 14, 1969. "The whole country is involved in protesting
the war in Vietnam. Hal Prince is closing down *Fiddler* [*on the Roof*] for
that night and Woody Allen isn't going to perform [in his play, *Play It
Again, Sam*]. . . . So if you don't mind, am taking the day off to do my
bit." Tuft was occasionally even more overt about the Hallidays' safety
and happiness. She was also slightly sardonic, when she waxed poetic on
March 26, 1970: "Oh, but you both are the luckiest people, you are oh so
wise—so prescient—so practical—to find yourself in such a healthy environment with nothing to disturb your tranquility but the cackle of
chickens laying eggs, the crow of the cock heralding the morning, the low
of the cows giving forth milk and the silence of nature growing with the
sighs of the wind and the heat of the sun; with the pleasure and excitement of fulfilling yourselves with projects of your own choosing. You
don't even have to know of the horrors of our city, in contrast—such as:
    "The strike of the mailmen which lasted ten days and seeing the Army
and National Guard taking over; or the slowdown of the airports as the
controllers are dissatisfied so that the Easter week-end fouls so many
people up, or the threatened railroad strike, or all the bombings that have
been taking place in department stores, buildings, night clubs—some
politically motivated, some Mafia directed and some, just cranks. But so
it goes!"
    But life in Brazil for the Hallidays was not quite as carefree as Tuft
portrayed it. Their existence "down there" was conveyed by Martin in
one of her "family" letters, dated September 19, 1969. In a handwritten
cover note to Tuft, Martin allowed: "You'll be the first to read this M. M.
masterpiece. You lucky girl," before adding that, "Our new cow had a calf
last night," and signing the letter, "I am terribly sincere." The six-page
typed letter itself described Dorothy Hammerstein's recent visit of three
weeks as "pure joy," encompassing a side trip to São Paulo "for two days
and nights" and then a visit to Bahia "about 1,000 miles from Sao Paulo,"
where the American ambassador had been kidnapped, but the consul,
Reed Bird ("of all names") gave the three of them a private tour in an
"Embassy car" with a police escort ("two huge men in plainclothes").
"The consul had a phone call from a friend of his daughter's—saying HE
was next on the LIST to be SNATCHED! SUCH fun—like James
Bond stuff." This was followed by an excursion to Rio, where they stayed
at the Palace Hotel in Copa Cabana and the manager said he had a "surprise" for them: "There was a knock on the door. I opened—and there on

the floor—clear across the hall was—Larry, Maj—Heidi and Preston . . . singing 'SURPRISE'!!!"

Martin continued, "That was the beginning of the week that should NEVER [have] HAPPEN[ed]!!," while proceeding to focus on the hippie-like appearance and behavior of the Hagman crew: "My son longish hair—beads—Mexican shirt—levis—moccasins—bag over shoulder—huge bamboo horn—and playing a bamboo flute (at ALL times—even in elevators and restaurants!) Maj in Mexican mini dress (all ruffles—that came to her . . . well let's say MILES above knees) beads—bags over shoulder. . . ." The described events that followed do nothing to prepare the reader for the final assessment: "Oh! DEAR— such screams—scenes—Larry saying such things to me—I can NEVER print—most sick-making. I still can't understand their coming 1,000s of miles for him to get something out of his system that has apparently been there for thirty some odd years. Well, at least they didn't go off into the night—as they did before, but they did LEAVE—after being with us seven days. You know I didn't ASK them to come—actually would rather they hadn't at this time—but they did and they've left—and it's all very sad—but I can NEVER feel the same again. . . . Someday—maybe some- day, I will 'feel' again about Larry—but not now, NOT NOW."

The night before they left, the Hagmans had a confrontation with Martin, while Halliday went to bed. But exactly what was said was not shared by Martin in her long letter, in which she also wrote about her taking Portuguese lessons "three times a week" and about Halliday's "bad foot" ("a calcium deposit in his heel"), which prevented him from walking and required three days of treatments. She ultimately signed off with, "from Me and Daddy."

"Your wife's letter got here in six days," Tuft wrote Halliday, in re- sponse. "As you can see—even the mails fly for her! How very sad for Larry to carry such hostility for so many years and not have the maturity that comes with age, experience and particularly being a parent him- self." Also, "Talked to Heller today. . . . She finally has insisted that the divorce be put on the calendar and is waiting to hear—tomorrow—if it has been done. She obviously feels that she's not as good a daughter as she might be!"

Larry Hagman's "hostility" toward his mother and stepfather increas- ingly became a matter of public record. "That sick man who thinks he's still a boy," claimed Halliday in a letter on November 22. "People around the country have been sending us columns of interviews [with Larry]—none of 'em less than hurtful and all making him sound like a silly jackass. [It's especially] hurting since Heidi has been deluging M. M. with letters and I've wondered why. Now we know—that Larry doesn't mind involving his young daughter unnecessarily in a sad situation—nor does he mind copying Peter and Jane Fonda—washing their dirty linen in public [about *their* father, Henry]. Very sad to both of us. Several letters with columns from strangers saying, 'Without your permission, I'm going to cut this young man's throat!' 'He couldn't be your son!' 'Wait till I get my hands on this guy. . . . Etc., etc.' "

Regarding Heller's wavering decision to divorce Tony Weir, Tuft would write, "She says she has learned a lot over this period and feels that she has matured a lot. One of her comments was that she thought all husbands operated like her daddy who was so devoted and she was constantly comparing Tony to her Daddy and when he didn't measure up—well he wasn't a good husband and didn't love her. Now she understands that his involvement with his work is no reflection on her."

Heller was, at the time, receiving a thousand dollars every month from her parents, and Halliday was also, every so often, having a thousand- or two-thousand-dollar check drawn for Didi, his sister, from their late mother's estate. Even from afar, Halliday kept a watchful eye on other expenses back in New York, signing off, for instance, on Christmas gifts to the building staff at the Campanile and deciding which individuals would receive ten dollars, which five.

For Martin's fifty-sixth birthday on December 1, celebrated with a visit from Ward-Belmont vocal coach Irene Humphrey, Halliday gave his wife an extravagant bridge—"An IRON BRIDGE," she wrote in a "family" letter the next day. "It's 170 feet long and will cross the water of our new lake. It's Japanese and beautifully, gracefully done! We are going to paint it 'Chinese red!' Oh! What fun. Did anyone ever have a bridge given them? Not even Elizabeth Taylor can boast of that. I told Richard that I have heard people say 'I love you so much—I'll buy the Brooklyn Bridge.' But no one but him has done it! WHAT A MAN—what marvelous imagination. Irene nearly died from the fun of it all."

Though it would go out over both their signatures, Halliday wrote another "family" letter, dated December 27, describing their celebrations on Christmas day. Halliday did not mention in his letter that Heller failed to visit for Christmas, as scheduled, but that her new boyfriend, Rick, came without her. Nor did he allude to the fact that Heller, like her mother, was undergoing psychotherapy. "Between you and Rick we know 99% more than [Heller] is able to get out," Halliday would write Tuft, a month later. "One point she did make though was that Dr. S. told her not to be anxious, feel guilty about not writing us, and so—well, we under-stand that—since Heller was three years old she's felt overly guilty, overly anxious to please us. We've never been able to fathom from what it started—we've lectured her on this quality without success. So we don't disagree with the Dr.—but—Heller has picked a hell of a time to start a new relationship."

This was followed six weeks later by Tuft's well-taken advice: "Sure wish you wouldn't be so unhappy about Heller. She is and has been much too dependent on you—and she's trying terribly hard to grow up and not be a child." Halliday's response suggests that Tuft was having a salutary effect on her employers' emotional well-being: "We are gradually realiz-ing it's Heller who has been too dependent on us and not the other way around."

Despite ongoing travails with his daughter, Halliday rang in the new year on an ecstatic note: "We are having more joy than we even ever dared dream was possible and wish we could share it with one and all during 1970," he wrote on January 12. On February 9, Halliday expressed his conviction that they had made the right decision to move to Brazil; first, by saying others confirmed it ("Cannot get over the fact that every letter we receive, almost without exception, says 'you'd be idiots ever to come back'"), and second, by emphasizing how well his wife was doing ("within the last ten days there has been a major improvement in Mary's health"), adding that the doctors had originally "said it would take six to twelve months."

Given her newfound strength, Martin wanted to be every bit as indus-trious as her husband, as confirmed in the same letter by the first refer-ence Halliday made to a surprising development: "Shall I tell you [Mary] returned form Anápolis Friday to announce, 'Richard. I've been looking at business property in town with the idea of buying—you know—and opening a needlepoint shop!" This new venture especially made sense in terms of Halliday's having written, "As M. M. said recently—'Would be such a waste of time to be in the theatre,'" and despite their hearing about "talk" of Martin being considered as Katharine Hepburn's replacement in the Broadway musical *Coco*. Even though it was home to 100,000 people, Anápolis had no beauty parlor and no clothing boutique, when the Hallidays decided to open what they would call "Nossa Loja," or "Our Shop," to fill both those vacancies.

While Martin was noticeably better, Halliday's health was deteriorat-ing. He was particularly beset by a spur in the heel of his right foot, which required a series of cortisone shots: "It's hard to know . . . which is more painful—the spur or the shots." Two weeks later, the inflammation had become as "hellish" as any pain he had "ever known." A month later, a "cortisone infection" led to an emergency operation, though the infection was worse still in April, requiring long-term antibiotics.

The idea of a boutique quickly became more of a reality for Martin, however, as described in Halliday's family letter of March 29: "Madame-Miss-Mrs. [sic] Dona Maria exclaimed, 'Oh! It's going to be such fun to have a little shop—and—Richard, you won't have to become involved at all!' I'm still not clear what she meant," he added, with a typical lament from a husband who feels his wife doesn't entirely appreciate all he does for her. "Have just completed the ninth set of drawings—inside-outside and all the planting too. After each one, delightful, beaming, charming Dona Maria has said, oh so dearly, 'Yes, that is what we were talking about—wasn't it, Richard? . . . And so, I've started translating her ideas about feet into meters."

The Hallidays went to São Paulo on May 21 on their "first shopping spree" for the new store. This may have also been when they saw a Portuguese production of *Hair,* the Broadway musical sensation, which both proclaimed and represented "the dawning of the Age of Aquarius." (For a story in *Women's Wear Daily,* Martin would tell Hector Arce how much she admired "the complete freedom of amateurs" exhibited by the show and extol the pleasures of being anonymous in Brazil, as opposed to being back home in New York, where she couldn't leave the apartment without being recognized.)

In a letter addressed "Dear Mr. Nicotine-less, tarless, caffeine-less, willpowerful, Illustrissimo Senhor Richard Halliday," and dated June 15, 1970, Lee Tuft wrote that after her recent visit in late April, "Aunt Jerry" told Heller her father was "quite ill and had tentatively planned to come up to Chicago to see Dr. [Edward] Bigg"—a development that apparently did not come to pass; though, five months later, "the Biggs from Chicago" came to Nossa Fazenda. Halliday's "having some problems" during this period was confirmed by his sister Didi, following *her* visit in July.

Despite Halliday's health problems and the amount of time he had to devote to managing the farm, he was spending more and more of his energies on the creation of their boutique, Nossa Loja. By September, Halliday realized that neither he nor his wife had written a family letter for some months and wondered aloud if "we have bitten off more than either of us realized and we must be serious and we must make a go of it."

After "five full-time sewing ladies giving ten hours per day" preparing for some months, the shop was finally ready for business on October 31.

"There is so much curiosity about the building, we've had to hire guards 24 hours a day to keep people out," Halliday wrote Tuft, a month before the grand opening. "When engaging the night guard, he asked seriously, 'How many people can I kill each night?' " A countless number of excited Brazilians attended the opening, including visitors who made the four-hour plane trip from São Paulo, when a "four-man combo of local Mormon missionaries" serenaded them. Built to resemble a Japanese pagoda, with vibrant red, white, and black columns and sliding doors, the unusual store was "a combination of haute coiffure and couture." "For the beauty shop, I got together with a Japanese ironmonger and Brazilian sink maker, and I had them build an armchair you can tip back to wash your hair. It took three months but when it was finished, I felt like Edison," Martin told Dennis Redmont for an AP story. She was also, perhaps, thinking of Neiman Marcus and her Texas roots when she added, "This has been such a gas, that I think I'll have to put out a catalogue."

"[The store] really is the most hysterical success," Halliday scribbled in a note on one of Tuft's typed letters—"like a fire sale at Gimbels or Macys. We had no idea this could happen—not a dress left—ten sewing ladies using up all material left to fill orders. . . ." The shop also sold curtains, shoes, hats, and costume jewelry.

After visiting Nossa Fazenda, Hector Arce ran a feature on his experience in *Women's Wear Daily* on December 11. While explaining that Halliday had agreed to a "contract" to spend two years with his wife at their Brazilian getaway, ending in July 1971, the report confirmed they were far from idle. "Richard has become an excellent farmer," said Martin. "Everything we serve at our table comes from our land. It's a working farm, and it hasn't been a commercial payoff, because we keep improving. Brazil is like an insurance policy." As Arce emphasized, one of the "improvements" was Nossa Loja, selling needlepoint items and women's clothing, the latter made "exclusively" from Brazilian fabrics.

"Nossa Loja started as a hobby, but it has become as exciting to Mary as a Broadway show," wrote Arce, "just as making money off the farm is as thrilling to the Hallidays as any of their royalties from show investments." Martin also relayed that "a publisher talked me into writing my autobiography," adding that she had already "written one hundred pages and I haven't [even] been born yet."

With her customary wisdom, Lee Tuft seemed to have the final say on the significance of Nossa Loja: "Do I remember your saying you were going to Brazil for R & R? (Rest and relaxation to you)?" she wrote on December 23. "Oh well, never did figure Dona Main Maria in the role of recluse. In any event, there must be many moments of gratification and pleasure—and if you start making a profit—well that's icing on the cake and it sure sounds as if you're well on the road. So when will the first Nossa Loja branch store be inaugurated?"

Primarily from investments ("Oppenheimer-cash" for $73,358 and "Ogden" for $50,000), the Hallidays' total income in 1970—Martin's first full year of retirement—amounted to $323,996, including $68,750 from *I Do! I Do!*, $34,186 in royalties for the *Needlepoint* book, $22,425 from *The Sound of Music,* "Record Royalty" of $19,875, and $36,000 for rent of the New York apartment. The expenditures amounted to $309,472, including a whopping $108,509 to the government for taxes, $131,921 for living expenses and farm maintenance in Brazil, $9,150 to Heller and $6,027 to Lee Tuft. (Ernest Adams also received $2,739.)

When Dr. Edward Bigg visited Nossa Fazenda in February 1971, he noticed that an "indentation" on Martin's lower left cheek had grown larger, and said it urgently needed to be examined. Within a month the Hallidays spent a week in São Paulo, where they had dinner with Dr. Fernando Gentil, and his "very American" wife, who had spent "their honeymoon, two decades before, holding hands watching Martin and Pinza" during a performance of *South Pacific,* and had "seen Martin in everything she's ever done since." According to Halliday, Gentil was considered "the greatest [plastic surgeon] in Brazil—if not Latin America," and he was elected to perform the necessary surgery on Martin's face.

What was planned as a three-hour operation ultimately consumed seven, involving five doctors and costing approximately six thousand dollars. "The operation was for skin cancer," Halliday later explained, in a fairly graphic report. "We were told there are ten different kinds . . . and M. M. had three. Two of them spread across the forehead, both cheeks and the chin and had increasingly roughened the skin and in some places were sensitive to touch. The third kind appeared in three different places and was more serious. Two places bled frequently. . . . The other places were near corner of right eye, and just below left nostril."

In addition to accommodating Martin's surgery, the Hallidays had to fit in two sets of guests in the first half of the year. Richard Barr, Edward Albee's regular producer, was seeking Martin's participation in a musical adaptation of Truman Capote's quirky Southern novel, *The Grass Harp,* which had already failed as a stage play, adapted by Capote himself, in 1952. The new musical version had a book and lyrics by Kenward Elmslie and music by Claibe Richardson, both of whom, along with Barr, visited Nossa Fazenda in mid-May. "The authors could not have been more ideal guests—professionally and personally they were superb," Halliday wrote on May 21. "We are really sad that the part [in *Grass Harp*] didn't have anything of interest for M. M." Halliday was not surprised to learn from his attorney, Bill Fitelson (who was "Barr's lawyer too"), that they "are having trouble raising money." With Barbara Cook as its lead, *The Grass Harp* would open at the Martin Beck Theatre on November 2, only to close, promptly, a week later. It would nevertheless achieve a cult status via a much-beloved original cast recording.

After their houseguests' departure, Martin responded to a letter from *Hello, Dolly!* colleague John Sheridan, telling him: "two composers from N.Y. were just here to play new score—saying they heard I was in a wheelchair cause I wouldn't come back for Tony Award T.V.!" Sheridan having written that he was in a brand-new Broadway revival of *No, No, Nanette* starring Ruby Keeler, prompted Martin to tell him, with her customary graciousness toward other performers: "But to think you're in a show with my favorite gal cum laude dancer, singer-actress and plain wonderful woman—whom I've never met—but oh! Want to someday, when I can tell her I won a contest in Weatherford for looking like her and sorta dancin' like her. . . . Oh! I love life's beautiful patterns."

Shortly after the Richard Barr group left Nossa Fazenda, Jack Paar and his wife arrived in June to make another TV documentary about the Hallidays' Brazilian home. "Jack Paar has been here after eight years and done another TV," Halliday would write his *Peter Pan* coproducer, Edwin Lester, looking back on Paar's visit. "This time of both the Fazenda and the Loja. In fact there hasn't been a moment we either haven't had or have been preparing for family, friends or the U.S. Ambassador or suddenly serving tea to the biggest potato or beet or tomato growers of the U.S." Halliday was sure to explain that he wasn't complaining about the abundance of their activities, rather reveling in them: "It's altogether pleasant and there isn't a question in our minds but that we do live in the greatest climate to be found anywhere in the world. Mary's sister has been down twice and so has my sister. They enjoy it as much as we do."

The Hallidays spent three weeks in July, shopping for Nossa Loja, "covering 10,000 miles by plane landing in twelve cities and fourteen towns and villages through the north, the central and eastern Brazil," Halliday also detailed to Lester. "Among other things we bought some of

Brazil's famous hammocks for Bonwits. Oh yes people want us to export to there and to spread out to Brasília and Sao Paulo here, but it's already taking too much of Mary's time and somehow we have to find the way to leave her more time and release her from so many pressures."

Both Hallidays were bedridden late in the year: Richard with a stomach bug and Martin after a fall from a stepladder. For the first time, Martin prepared her family Christmas letter orally on a cassette tape, addressed primarily to Bessie Mae: "I'm trying to do something and I'm getting so tricky with this tape-recorder business," she told Lee Tuft in the beginning, "because you know Jack Paar brought me one down when he came, the ones like the astronauts took to the moon." With cinematic-like details, she proceeded to describe their spending Christmas Eve at Nossa Loja, which "was ablaze with white, Christmas carols playing like mad—and rain pouring like, well rain pouring like God had decided that all the world should cry. . . . And I must say, it really looked like Neiman Marcus when it was a small store, back when we were growing up, Bessie. We bought all kinds of decorations from Sao Paulo, silver and crystal, and golden fruits, and brass handmade things, and silk-stone and jewels. . . . I could just go on and on. But I think it's just nice to tell you that we have been selling like crazy. We doubled last year's business. That's a lot of cruzieros for a small town. . . ."

With amused pride and awe, Martin also boasted about her husband's latest project. "Richard never stops," she said. "At the moment, he's taking a rest after our huge turkey lunch for two, after we opened our goodies for Christmas morning. He is designing a hundred and seventy-five bathrooms for a hotel. Our best friend in Anápolis, Jibram, who's been our greatest friend down here, all these years . . . you realize we've had this farm for eighteen years. . . . He's building a seventeen-story hotel in Brasília. And he just thinks that Richard is the king—he knows everything about design. You should see the way he puts everything together down here. So Richard said, I'll think about it.

"My dear, idiot husband not only plays store, he plays hotel now all the time. . . . I keep telling him he's a little boy, playing with [toy] trains. . . . Of course, Jibram is going to rue the day that he ever hired Richard to do this, because if it's done the way Richard wants—and he won't do it unless it is—it will just be the dadburnest [sic] hotel anybody ever saw in the whole world!"

In a letter to her employer dated January 5, 1972, Lee Tuft included a list of the latest economic and political woes in New York: "The subway fare has gone up to 35 cents. . . . There's a 2½% surcharge on state income tax. . . . All the bridges and tunnels have gone up considerably. . . . There's a three-cent tax on cigarettes and a bigger tax on liquor and gas. . . . There are now 10 contenders of the presidency in the Democratic Party. . . . And Brazil and Russia are getting pretty cozy!"

Ben Washer—Tuft's erstwhile boss and Halliday's early colleague—also appears in many a Tuft letter, especially after "it seems every P.R. office around town is suffering because of the depression here and they laid off a number of people in Ben's office—he was one." A number of Tuft's regular allusions to Washer demonstrate that he was overly and persistently concerned with how he was perceived by the Hallidays. He should have rested assured, since Washer was the one person Halliday trusted to pinch-hit for Tuft whenever she and her husband took a trip. (The Tufts went to Mexico, Europe, and even the Soviet Union, but, apparently and remarkably, never to Brazil, despite an open invitation to visit Nossa Fazenda.)

Tuft also kept her employers abreast of other odd developments back home, including news from Gloria Swanson, who phoned to say that she "stayed up til 4 a.m. reading and loving" Martin's needlepoint book, and Tennessee Williams, "who did the weather on Channel 7 news the other night." An interesting postscript on February 21, 1972, reported: "Walter Winchell died. That's an end to an era, isn't it?" And it was.

But still other members of the old guard continued to figure prominently in the Hallidays' life, and none more so than Richard Rodgers. In March, the Hallidays made their first visit to New York in more than two years for two very distinctive and contradictory reasons: for Martin to participate in a celebration of Rodgers's seventieth birthday at the Imperial Theatre, and for Halliday to appear in court regarding an ongoing lawsuit against Rodgers and the Hammerstein estate over rights to *The Sound of Music*.

Though Leland Hayward and Richard Halliday were the original co-producers of *The Sound of Music*, it had become apparent in 1967 that they weren't receiving any money for the lucrative sales of the RCA soundtrack recording of the film version. In a letter to her childhood friend Bessie Mae, Martin revealed that it was Rodgers himself who, during a lunch with Hayward, inadvertently opened "the kettle of fish" concerning royalties for the soundtrack: Rodgers had exclaimed, in a comradely fashion, "What about that check we received for the first picture recordings?" only to discover that Hayward hadn't gotten any money. And according to Hayward, before the arbitration began in

August 1967, Rodgers told him, "Let the lawyers fight, but we'll remain friends."

As Martin further explained in her letter, it was during the creation of the original stage production of *The Sound of Music* that Rodgers and Hammerstein "asked to have their names first in the billing, in name only—not to receive additional money. Well, all went well until the picture came out and grossed more than any of all time!" While the Hallidays imagined that the late, "darling" Oscar Hammerstein "truly didn't ever know any of this," Martin added, as a vindictive aside in her letter, that Rodgers "*really* does like money!"

According to a story in the *New York Times,* Hayward and Halliday received an arbitration award of $1,076,795, which was based on the sales of eight million copies of the RCA soundtrack album, and which "was the largest amount [ever] awarded in a commercial arbitration case." Better still for Halliday and Hayward, royalty payments would continue to be made in perpetuity from future sales of the soundtrack album.

In spite of any adversarial friction, Richard and Dorothy Rodgers gave a dinner party for the Hallidays a night or two after they arrived in New York on March 10, 1972. "I think we kissed in about 1,000 pictures," Martin would write Bessie Mae about the dinner. "In the middle of kiss 500, a man from the press asked who was writing my next show. I like an idiot replied, 'He is,' pointing at Richard Rodgers. After he got his eyebrow down, he said, 'Oh?' I said, 'Aren't you writing *Arsenic and Old Lace* as a musical for Ethel [Merman] and me?'" Indeed, Rodgers was eager to score *Arsenic and Old Lace,* as confirmed on the night of March 26, 1972, when the Museum of the City of New York sponsored *A Celebration of Richard Rodgers,* a benefit at the Imperial Theatre.

As produced by Anna Sosenko, singer Hildegarde's longtime partner and manager, and directed by the suave dancer/choreographer Donald Saddler, *A Celebration of Richard Rodgers* was primarily a concert of the great composer's songs, featuring Mary Martin, Celeste Holm, Richard Kiley, Gordon MacRae, Helen Gallagher, Gene Nelson, Tony Randall, Bobby Short, Benay Venuta, and Walter Willison—among others.

The evening ended with Leonard Bernstein playing a plaintive piano rendition of "Nobody's Heart Belongs to Me," followed by Martin singing a six-minute medley of "I Could Write a Book," "Honey Bun," "I'm Gonna Wash That Man Right Outa My Hair," and "A Wonderful Guy." (It was both significant and noticeable that she did not, for obvious reasons, include a number from *The Sound of Music*.) Martin then introduced Rodgers himself, for his brief thank you. "I don't know what to say, except to thank these wonderful artists," Rodgers stammered, indicating Martin as he added, "Some came a long distance—I can't imagine who. . . ." During the presentation, the guest of honor was supposed to be seated in the center of the front row, but changed his seat at the last minute to have easier access to the stage. This flummoxed both Bernstein and Martin, who, during their presentations, gazed vacantly in the direction of his assigned seat. (Bernstein even said, "wherever you are.")

Walter Willison, who sang his heartfelt "I Do Not Know a Day I Did Not Love You" from Rodgers's *Two by Two,* recalls Anna Sosenko coming up to him after the show, saying, "They're talking about you," as she escorted him to Martin's dressing room. "That was the first time I heard that Rodgers was writing *Arsenic and Old Lace* for Mary and Ethel to star as the Brewster sisters, me to play Mortimer Brewster, and Tricia O'Neil to play the girl next door," claimed Willison, who had opened the Rodgers's celebration that evening with a medley of duets with O'Neil. "Hal Prince was going to direct. I forget who the book writer was going to be."

Though a Richard Rodgers musical version of *Arsenic and Old Lace* would never come to be, the Hallidays also apparently met with Josh Logan while they were in New York to talk about *his* latest project, a musical based on Emlyn Williams's 1940 play, *The Corn Is Green,* about a spinster schoolteacher named Miss Moffat, as a starring vehicle for Martin. (Williams was an actor as well as a playwright who, in fact, had costarred in Morris L. West's *Daughter of Silence,* which Halliday had produced on Broadway a little more than a decade before.)

News that the Hallidays were going to be in town also prompted Alexander Cohen ("that great impresario") to invite Martin to participate in the upcoming Tony Awards on April 23, which gave a special award to Richard Rodgers that year for his fifty years in the theater. According to Lee Tuft, Cohen "also speculated on whether you would be interested, I mean MM, in a TV Special," which may have been a TV version of *Do I Hear a Waltz?* as refered to in yet another Halliday letter.

The Hallidays instead spent five days in Palm Springs, where they visited with Janet Gaynor and her fourth husband, Paul Gregory. From Los Angeles they flew to Mexico City, where Halliday inspected some marble and stone tiles for his hotel bathroom designs, before returning to Nossa Fazenda.

"Particularly after Adrian died, I went with Janet down to Brazil to help settle things, never, ever, ever, imagining that I would end up marrying

Janet Gaynor," recalled producer Paul Gregory, who became best known for a series of touring productions starring Charles Laughton and for the 1955 film *The Night of the Hunter*. Gregory, who married Gaynor in 1964, was also one of the few friends of Martin who formed a lasting, negative impression of her. "I just thought Mary treated Richard so badly. He was hiding out in this little hut in Brazil, and he was drunk all the time, and I had many personal conversations with him. I don't have any desire to beat up on Mary Martin—their relationship was their relationship. But he told me, 'I would have left her years ago if I had some place to go.' She was a monster. Her sweetness was all an act, I can tell you.

"I think Richard saw himself in her," Gregory said. "I think he saw what he wasn't able to do. Richard was very bright, but he was trapped. He had such funny mannerisms, and said such strange things, and they were all very amusing to me. But she just devoured him. She had him on a leash."

With or without the leash, Halliday's health problems were becoming more and more intrusive during the summer of 1972. In addition to coping with hypoglycemia, which was only exacerbated by his drinking and prompted an angiogram, Halliday had a serious infection in late July or early August, when he was running a temperature of 104. "Had five nurses out here! And intravenous feedings four times per day!" he wrote Lee Tuft on August 13. "And first day out of bed fell from weakness and tore ligaments of left knee! Obviously I was on wrong train. . . . In fact I find myself dizzy and a little bewildered." Halliday was clearly thinking about his mortality when he asked Tuft to track down an article "about cremation in Brazil," which he had read some months ago in a "Brazilian news sheet you send each month."

But he recovered well enough to help oversee a great many guests at Nossa Fazenda in early August for shooting, on August 9, an episode of the television show *This Is Your Life,* built around Martin. Heller and her children made a surprise visit to participate in the show. "Yes, M. M. was really surprised re [*sic*] the TV show [*This Is Your Life*]," Halliday wrote Tuft on August 21, "and assume you know Aunt Jerry, and Bessie Mae and her husband, Jac Austin, were all here, plus Janet [Gaynor] and Paul [Gregory] and Ralph Edwards and his wife and a crew of twenty-three—No Larry nor any of his family were asked—Aunt Jerry still here. Josh L[ogan] and that group will be here this time next week."

The show itself contains any number of revelations. With a false mustache and a pidgin-Portuguese accent, host Ralph Edwards first showed up at Nossa Loja, where Martin, wearing a powder blue shirt jacket and white pants, was stationed with Janet Gaynor, expecting "a Rio travel-ogue company" to stop by and take some footage of the boutique. The bulk of the episode was filmed outdoors at Nossa Fazenda, with lawn chairs to accommodate the surprise guests, beginning with Halliday and then "Sister" Jerry Andrews, followed by Bessie Mae—who arrives with a homemade cake—and an extremely tanned and long-haired Heller. A group of local children sing "Do-Re-Mi" to Martin, including Heller's boys, Timmy and Matthew, who emerge to cavort with their grand-mother. Sounding quite a bit like a cross between Bessie Mae and the el-derly Jerry—not to mention Truman Capote—Halliday describes various rooms in the house, as previously shot: "Adrian's African Room," "The Ecclesiastical Room," and "The Green Room." The entire episode unfolds so quickly that Martin barely seems to have time to catch her breath—or her equilibrium. Though Gaynor's husband does not ap-pear on the show, Paul Gregory, in fact, produced it.

There was a heated exchange of letters in September, which demon-strates how upset Halliday was becoming over circumstances beyond his control and also, from Tuft's perspective, how her boss had, perhaps, as-sumed more responsibilities than he was capable of fulfilling, given his deteriorating health. After many letters detailing repairs to the Campa-nile apartment, looking after the vacating tenants (Ernest, who had been working for them, "insisted . . . that they were taking some of your silver"), and preparing the place for new ones, Halliday misguidedly accused Tuft of doing "nothing I have asked you to do."

The "much maligned" employee responded, "You must understand, Mr. Halliday, that whatever motivates my action has always been in your interest and I really cannot deal with [such accusations]." After adding that "the apartment is rented with an option to buy," Tuft volleyed some accusations, couched as advice, of her own: "I suppose in retrospect you would have been better off not designing hotels and not getting involved in Nossa Loja and just enjoying the leisurely life that the Fazenda affords you both—and perhaps even getting involved in a musical will present all sorts of hazards not worth the effort in the long run. But then, perhaps it is just as difficult to retire and do nothing." In view of her overseeing so many improvements at the New York apartment, Tuft wrote, in a subse-quent letter: "Gee, Mr. Halliday, being an interior decorator certainly has its problems and headaches."

But no matter what difficulties Halliday was facing, it seems clear that he would have preferred to remain in Brazil during this period in his life, when he was not only managing a constantly expanding farm and a store, but now designing a large number of hotel bathrooms as well. Nevertheless, according to Josh Logan, Halliday also detected that his wife wanted—or was it needed?—to return to the stage, an impression shared by Tuft, who would write, earlier in the year, that after reading Martin's description of the Hallidays' doings in Brazil, and despite Martin's involvement with Nossa Loja, she got "a sense that there's not quite enough for her to fulfill herself." Without first discussing the matter with Martin, Halliday had phoned Logan from Brazil, asking him to "find something for Mary. She's dying to work, and I'm dying for her to work. She's only happy when she's busy, and I'm sure you can find a story that she'll like. Please do it, and call me if you get any ideas at all."

In his second volume of memoirs, *Movie Stars, Real People and Me*, Logan claimed it was Halliday's phone call that prompted him, in due course, to recommend *Miss Moffat* for Martin. Though the call apparently occurred before the Hallidays' then-recent trip to New York, it was soon after their return to Nossa Fazenda, on May 16, 1972, when Halliday wrote Logan a promising letter concerning the project: "Mary and I join you and [your wife] Nedda in admiration and enthusiasm re: Emlyn's *Miss Moffat*," Halliday claimed, before explaining that they had no idea, at first, who was responsible for the lyrics. "We were bewildered, amazed, puzzled, yes excited, happy, frustrated, curious about who had written the fabulous lyrics. Certainly not any of the men who've worked with Mary—Rodgers"—who had, following Oscar Hammerstein's demise, become his own lyricist with his haunting score for *No Strings*—"and definitely not Alan Lerner—they seemed to have poured out of Emlyn, but an Emlyn who had had years of experience writing musical lyrics. We were pleased and impressed to read he had actually written them."

While allowing that "we agree it doesn't get started as quickly as it should," Halliday focused on the even bigger question (the "all-important, major need") of a composer, suggesting "Richard Rodgers, of course— and recently when we were in Palm Springs Fritz Loewe played his new score for *The Little Prince* [for us] and he still has that special, magical, musical talent that makes all these [new] kids sound exactly as they are— second, third, fourth rate piano players. Burton Lane is, of course, a real composer. . . ."

Martin added a note of her own to her husband's more detailed letter, claiming that, "when I read the original play, I didn't cry at [the] end," even though she "felt" the play's emotional undercurrent more deeply when she saw Ethel Barrymore in the original stage production. But now, with "Emlyn's new scenes . . . I started weeping and wept til the end. . . .

Richard's reaction was exactly the same! So we both wept at some place (that's good). I guess you and Nedda and us go for the same type of sentiment—when it's real!"

Logan would find his composer for *Miss Moffat* in Albert Hague, who had previously scored both *Plain and Fancy* and *Redhead* for Broadway. With Emlyn Williams already slated to do a South American tour of his one-man re-creation of Charles Dickens's readings, Logan scheduled a visit for the three of them with the Hallidays in Brazil, a trip that he also financed.

Upon their arrival in late August, Martin ran out to greet and embrace her guests, before welcoming them into her home. According to Logan, the Hallidays' Brazilian abode "wasn't a house, exactly; it was a doll's compound. Each room seemed to have a separate roof. One house was a living room. It was all charming, open, and terribly original, an atmosphere only Richard and Mary would create." Though the environment was casual and comfortable, dinner was something of a formal affair, observing rules of etiquette worthy of Amy Vanderbilt.

Dinner was served by "three of their twenty-nine servants," after which the potential collaborators went to the "wicker music room," where Hague played some songs he had written for *Miss Moffat*. The wicker cover for the keyboard had to be propped up with a wire hanger, and a makeshift rack fashioned to hold the music.

"Finally, Albert sat down to play," continued Logan, "and suddenly I saw pink blotches appear through the pallor of his cheeks. He whispered to me that there was no action whatsoever as he pressed the pedals." Worse yet, were the "strange and discordant" sounds that emanated from the piano. As Martin explained, "I've tried to have it tuned, but of course it's awfully difficult because the mice have eaten all the felt off the hammers."

After Halliday served drinks, he and his wife "listened to the first song as though they were in a catatonic trance," Logan recalled. Whatever they felt about what they proceeded to hear, the Hallidays failed to share any reaction before they all retired for the night. Only when Logan confronted them after breakfast, the following morning, did Martin say, "We would like you to go on working on it, but we can't say yes or no in the present condition of the score. There's just not enough of it yet to hold on to."

With "semi-hopeful hearts," Logan, Williams, and Hague further worked on the show in New York, where more songs were written. The Hallidays next met with the *Miss Moffat* contingent the following

February, at a hotel in Rio de Janeiro, "with a very good piano and a room to work in," recalled Logan. "We played the score again. Mary sang several of the songs. We could tell how exciting she would be in the part."

The five of them planned on next getting together at Emlyn Williams's home in Corfu. But Logan found it more than a little ominous that Halliday would stop talking in the middle of his sentences. "He just has to hold his breath a moment because of the pain [in his stomach]," explained Martin. When Logan said the obvious, that Halliday should see a doctor, Martin added, "Oh, God, if he only would. I'm sick with worry. But you know how strong-willed he is, and he can be very stubborn about anything concerning his health." Within two weeks, Walter Willison was visiting Logan at his apartment in River House, when a call came through from Martin in Florida, reporting that she wouldn't be able to do *Miss Moffat* because Richard Halliday had died.

At the time of his death, Richard Halliday's thousand-acre farm in Brazil had 10,000 chickens, 250 dairy cows, and enough memories to make it difficult for his wife to move forward for the next couple of years.

Chapter 18

AN ICON SPEAKS

My dear, my son is a star. I am an icon.
—MARY MARTIN

"Mary Martin is the most natural, unspoiled actress or woman I have ever met," claimed Jack Paar, a pioneer of TV talk shows, who sometimes went on location to interview his subjects or guests. "She can ride a horse, herd cattle, drive a truck and still sit like a queen in a Rolls-Royce. She's equally at ease with Noël Coward or a Brazilian cowboy. She loves people: a theaterful or only a few at a church wedding in the forests of Brazil. Of course, Mary also sings, dances, paints—and we all know she can fly. She is, by any standard, one of North and South America's most valuable resources."

Thus begins Paar's narration for a TV documentary he made about Martin, a twenty-minute segment of *Three Remarkable Women,* which also included primatologist Jane Goodall and doyenne Ethel Kennedy, and which aired on ABC on January 20, 1973. Paar's opening remarks were actually written seven years before, to accompany Roddy McDowell's striking photo of Martin in *Double Exposure,* a collection of celebrity portraits with captions by other celebrities.

"You will not find this road on the map of Brazil, but the locals call it the Doña Maria Highway," Paar also says at the beginning of the documentary, referring to a road that was built for and named after Martin herself. Paar goes on to explain that the road was cut through a former Brazilian forest, and that the Hallidays' house was more than nine hundred miles from Rio de Janeiro, as well as a two-hour drive from the capital of Brasília. Seventeen years after they had the house built, Nossa Fazenda still had no phone or television. Electricity had, finally, been introduced only ten days before Paar's arrival; the house had been lit before then with thirty-four kerosene lamps.

Paar visited Brazil and shot his footage for the documentary in June 1971. Martin had, by then, been removed from the public eye for two years. In the documentary, Paar dispels the persistent rumor that Martin was "critically ill" and wheelchair bound. The Hallidays had, after all, retreated to Brazil in the summer of 1969, after a series of setbacks required Martin to cancel the final stops on her *I Do! I Do!* tour—and on doctors' orders, no less. But by the time the documentary aired a year and a half after Paar's visit, Halliday himself *was* critically ill. The farm to which he had devoted the last four years of his life had finally become a profitable operation in November 1972. Halliday had by then been beset by so many different ailments that his regular correspondence with Lee Tuft, his personal secretary back home in New York, had become a trickle. He also seemed to be losing his grasp on chronology—if not reality. On November 16, Tuft began one of her lengthy letters, saying, "You keep dating all your letters October—you must have lost a month somewhere along the way—but it really is November!"

November was also when Halliday's sister Didi was coming for another visit, and when Heller's divorce from Tony Weir was to become final. The month before, the Hallidays' Nossa Loja was permanently closed, a sign of Martin's ultimate lack of enthusiasm for keeping it going. Despite many declarations to the contrary, a small boutique in a provincial town just didn't generate the same sort of excitement Martin had known during extensive runs in any number of shows, either on Broadway or on tour. But Halliday clearly hoped that he and his wife would remain in Brazil: he even arranged for them to negotiate the great distances in central Brazil by having their own plane—with tragic consequences.

"As we left Brasília the front page of the newspapers announced that Mary Martin's new airplane had crashed on her land at Nossa Fazenda," Halliday wrote in a letter dated November 17, apparently his last, in the voluminous files of letters Lee Tuft kept for more than half a century. Considering the tragic events he was describing, Halliday was remarkably matter-of-fact with his words: "As we arrived home the police, the doctors, the wrecking crews were taking away the last of the remains of the airplane, and a 30-year-old American who had been forced to land without any gasoline left and he'd landed safely, until one wheel suddenly sank into a soft spot newly made by the heavy rains—and threw the plane upside down and a spear of wood went clear through the young man's head."

In what appears to be Tuft's last letter to her boss, dated December 29, 1972, she wrote, "Saw a note that the Champions are getting a divorce after all," which may have been the reason Gower and Marge Champion did not revisit Nossa Fazenda the previous month, as planned. But Halliday's faltering health may have been another. Janet Gaynor and Paul

Gregory were, however, staying at Nossa Fazenda at the end of February, when Halliday was ill with what they thought was a bad cold—severe enough to keep Halliday confined to the guest house. After taking him to a hospital in Anápolis, he was flown to a better-equipped facility in Brasília, where, following a hernia operation, the sixty-seven-year-old Richard Halliday deteriorated rapidly. The doctors recruited Martin to try to get her husband to cough during his final hours, but he was too weak to comply. He died on March 3, 1973, a Saturday, with severe intestinal blockage. "In the end it was pneumonia that took him away," Martin said. "Everything stopped functioning—his lungs, kidneys, his brilliant brain." Time and again, Martin would note that *Peter Pan* had its sixth television broadcast the night before Halliday's death.

"When Richard was dying, I was told he kept asking for Bibi, my aunt, my mother's sister," recalled Kristina Hagman. "She was very sensitive to him, and to how much of his own identity he gave up, to live through Mary. He felt comfortable with her, because she didn't condemn him [for his homosexuality]."

Heller went down to be with her mother, as did David Warshaw, the Hallidays' lawyer. In keeping with her husband's wishes, Martin set out to have Halliday cremated in Brazil, but the Catholic customs simply made his instructions too difficult to be executed. With a bitter irony, Martin must have felt that only Halliday could have achieved such a Herculean task. Martin flew with Halliday's body to Florida. It was from here that she phoned Joshua Logan to tell him that Halliday had died. She was clearly feeling too estranged from her son to give him the news directly, and she had Ben Washer contact Larry Hagman on her behalf. "He told us that Richard had died," Hagman would write in his memoir. "I paused for a moment, then turned and told Maj and the kids the news. I felt sorry for Mother and sent my regrets, simple and sincere."

Harvey Schmidt recalled having breakfast at the Plaza Hotel one morning, when Josh Logan and David Merrick arrived. "They looked so serious and solemn," recalled Schmidt. "And later, they came over and said that Josh had just spoken to Mary and found out that her husband had died."

"Mary decided to bury Richard in Weatherford, Texas," said Joyce Gertz, Martin's onetime Weatherford dance student. "He would be spinning in his grave if he knew that's where Mary buried him, because he just hated Weatherford." Within a week of Halliday's death, the *New York Times* announced that "the bulk" of his "$650,000 estate will be used to set up a trust fund for his widow."

After returning to "that very silent farm" in Brazil, Martin said that, "as soon as possible I went away, as far as I could get from the memories. I ran to sister and her comfort in Fort Worth. Didi went with me." In what is perhaps the single most candid and revealing passage in her memoir, Martin would confide, "While I was in Fort Worth, and even now when I have the long nights, when I question my innermost self about our life, my guilts, my regrets for many things, I wonder if I ever really knew my husband. Does anyone ever completely know a person even after three decades together? Richard was a very private person."

In a heartfelt letter to Cheryl Crawford, she wrote, "It is just almost impossible for me to imagine life without Richard—because he is half of me. The half that is left is not the vital, 'radiant,' fun loving person he knew. But I know I must come back to life someday. Otherwise all the years [of] his love, devotion, and sacrifice of the things he didn't do would be in vain. I can only thank God that he had at least three-and-a-half years of joy in the land, the earth, that meant so much to him."

Following Halliday's death, Martin didn't really reenter "the wide warm world" until Heller's marriage to business executive Bromley DeMeritt Jr., on July 14, 1973, at Katharine Cornell's home in Martha's Vineyard, where Martin had rented a house of her own that summer and stayed with Nena Smith, her longtime dresser. The fact is, Martin had several people taking care of her from the minute she was born in Weatherford, Texas, and there was never a period when she lived alone. The loss of Richard Halliday created a void and a vacancy that quickly needed to be filled.

"For thirty-four years it was *our* career," Martin would tell Paul Rosenfield for a story in the *Los Angeles Times,* looking back on this traumatic period in her life. "He edited me, planned everything three to five years ahead. I couldn't settle down after Richard died. I went to Martha's Vineyard, Munich [where she visited Mainbocher], Greece and London for three months where Margot Fonteyn got me in a ballet class at Sadler's Wells. But my mind couldn't concentrate. I couldn't read anything but want ads." Any sense Martin ever had that Halliday may have harmed as well as helped her career died with the man. Once Halliday was gone, the only thing Martin could see was his absence, which became palpable in the vacuum he left behind.

Martin was, at least, being well looked after throughout this peripatetic time of unrest. A personal letter typed to "Darling Lee" Tuft on October 10, 1973, when Martin was back at Dorothy Hammerstein's at 101 Eaton Place in London, demonstrated just how much her inner sanctum mobilized to keep the new widow preoccupied: ". . . am trying to pretend I am my darling Richard, and am dictating my first letters [to you]," Martin wrote, before explaining that she had recently returned from Paris, where she had a "very grand dinner" with Josh and Nedda Logan at Versailles, and where she "saw collections of beautiful clothes" and visited "the lovely chapel Saint Chapelle," boutiques, cafes, Montmartre, and the famous Paris flea market. Richard's sister Didi then spent a couple of weeks with Martin in London, before returning to the States, when Martin went on to Greece to "be with" Nancy (aka Slim or Lady Keith) in Greece. "Went by plane, changed planes, met by boat, then horse and carriage, finally arriving at her lovely simple home on the island of Spetsai," Martin continued. "My first venture of travelling alone, and that was one whirl of boat to boat, swimming with Nancy, Alastair Keith (her stepson), Truman Capote and friend, and me. Oh, how the other half lives!"

Lady Keith returned with Martin to London, where they had plans to see Jerry Robbins's new ballet at Covent Garden—"with Jerry, whom I haven't seen in so many years. I can't wait to see his work as I have missed so many of his glorious moments through the years."

Martin further explained her busy activities in London, with some newfound self-introspection: "I have started ballet and voice lessons again, just to have a normal routine, as I love being social but it really isn't my thing, and I find I miss being on a routine. Life is still difficult without Richard so keeping busy is the only solution. . . . So far have seen only *Crown Matrimonial* with Wendy Hiller and the Alec Guinness show—absolutely mad about both of them. Oh, what great artists they are!"

According to Joyce Gertz, it was shortly after Halliday died that Martin began looking for a place in Palm Springs, where she would be near her "best" remaining friend in the world, Janet Gaynor. "And she told me that she took the first place the Realtor showed her," added Gertz, "and that she knew that's where Richard wanted her to be, when she later discovered that the next-door neighbor was somehow related to Richard." Martin also imported the daughter of the Hallidays' foreman at Nossa Fazenda to handle all household matters in Palm Springs—though Lucy, as she was called, was loath to leave the comfortable life she knew in Brazil for the unknown and frightening world of the United States.

Built in 1936, the large, 3,500-square-foot home was located at 365 Camino Norte West. Martin had the battleship-gray house with its red-tile roof painted pink. As she told journalist Paul Rosenfield, she "turned the back of the house into the front, and turned my life around." Retired Hollywood star William Powell lived directly across the street. "The first day I moved in, he came out to get his mail, and he waved to me," recalled Martin. "And then he said the loveliest thing. He said, 'Welcome home, Mary.' It was so dear—I almost passed out." Other neighbors included Alice Faye and William Holden, whom Martin also said she saw often.

Also according to Gertz, "Ben Washer was really Halliday's friend, who was more than just a friend. And before he died, Richard asked Ben to take care of Mary." Though he started taking over for Lee Tuft while Halliday was still alive, Washer gradually began to manage Martin's life and career—to replace Halliday, as it were, even if no one ever truly could. Washer was himself something of a lost soul, whose long-term, live-in partner had left him, according to Lee Tuft. Before then, his "room-mate" had been "running around a lot" with other men, which was a continual irritant and source of dismay for the mild-mannered Washer.

One of Washer's first assignments had been to call Larry Hagman with the news that his stepfather had died, and he now moved in with Martin in her Palm Springs home and remained with her until his own demise nearly a decade later. "I just never moved out," Washer would say. "Mary is not the kind of dame who can be alone." As Martin herself was the first to say, Washer, when asked, defined his job as being "Baby-sitter for the oldest baby in captivity."

"Every morning and night when Ben and I go in the pool, with the palm trees and the moon," Martin wrote, in a letter to Cheryl Crawford, "we feel we are Nelson Eddy and Jeanette MacDonald (very old ones!). I just had two speakers installed on the outside, so now we even have music everywhere. Ben has been sensational, and we have fun cooking outside, both trying to stay on diets."

Martin would spend the next two years focused on finishing her memoir, which was a constructive way of dealing with her grief when she was flooded with innumerable memories of her late husband. During the course of promoting the book, Martin conveyed that she had, actually, been working on it for well over a decade, in "three bursts of creativity." "The why of her authorship, mainly, is because a lot of people kept asking her to write one," claimed Allen MaCaulay, a staff writer for the *Bergen Record*. "The urging started during the run of *South Pacific*."

"But that was a little early," said Martin. Her preliminary work on a memoir began in earnest following a dinner in Philadelphia with author Morris West (whose play, *Daughter of Silence,* was being produced by Halliday) and his agent, Paul Revere Reynolds, who said, "Mary, you're always yakking and telling stories about this and that. Why don't you write them down?"

"My reply," said Martin, "was that I didn't know how to write, but he said, 'Well, you certainly know how to talk and tell the stories, just write the way you talk and the way you think.'" Then, after Martin finally finished her two-year run in *The Sound of Music,* she went on a vacation with Bessie Mae to Bermuda, where she suffered insomnia. "I was going mad," she recalled. "But when I left for Bermuda, Richard handed me a great big yellow pad and lots of pencils and said, 'If you get restless, write . . .' So I started writing, and I wrote and I wrote and I filled up the entire pad. I kiddingly say—but not too kiddingly—that I wrote a hundred pages and I hadn't even been born yet. I thought this would be the longest book ever, longer than *War and Peace* and *The Brothers Whatever* combined, longer than the Yellow Pages," Martin continued.

"The early parts just rolled out. I have total recall, so that part was easy. But other parts were very, very, very difficult and painful. It was like analysis, like being on the couch. I used to blame my mother for a lot of things, but after I finished writing about them and read them back later, I realized it was no one's fault but my own."

Halliday sent the pages to Reynolds, who replied, "This is not only good. It is very, very good. Keep at it!" "Well, of course, I was delighted . . . and never kept at it again." Not until five years or so later, when the Hallidays beat a fast retreat to Brazil following the dismal failure of *Jennie,* and Martin's memories took her up to the point in her story where she met Halliday. But she didn't really focus on her memoir until Reynolds contacted her again—when she was in London following Halliday's death—telling Martin, "If you don't do it now, you never will." The final section was the hardest for her to write. "She felt adrift after her husband's death," claimed Allen MacCaulay. "The void that Halliday's death left was truly huge." "Richard had run everything," Martin told MaCaulay. "He was boss. He was always first. I ran, and ran, and ran," she explained. "I couldn't settle down."

"When I got to the part about Richard," Martin told yet another interviewer, "I couldn't write it. I put if off and put it off and finally didn't come through with it until the last minute, in fact until spring of last year [1975]." Martin claimed the breakthrough came when she was riding on the Merritt Parkway with her new son-in-law, Bromley DeMerritt Jr., and was instantly reminded of the countless times she had made the same car trip with Halliday—from their Connecticut home to one Broadway theater or another. "We used to do all our talking on the Merritt Parkway," recalled Martin. "Well, there I was with Bromley, and suddenly I looked out the window and everything had burst into bloom. I looked—and absolutely dissolved. Tears just poured down, the first time I had allowed that to happen.

"It was suddenly brought back that this was spring, the time of new life, and Richard wasn't there to see it. I composed myself and when we arrived in New York I went right into my room, closed the door and wrote about Richard's death, which I had not faced before. It took something as dramatic as seeing a new tree in bloom before I could finally do it."

Martin did not really write at least the last third of her memoir, however, as much as she relayed her memories to a tape recorder, every day, in Palm Springs, where Dora Jane Hamblin was on hand to transcribe them. Seven years Martin's junior, Hamblin, who was known as "Dodie," was a longtime contributor to *Life* magazine. "How this dear lady by the name of Dodie Hamblin (who is transcribing the book) can hear me by tape all day and by night . . . while she transcribes the same bloody voice by banging away at her typewriter is beyond my comprehension," Martin wrote Bessie Mae. "We do, at intervals, swim in the heated pool while still taping."

In the book itself, Martin would indicate her substantial debt to Hamblin, following her primary dedication to Halliday: "I am enormously grateful to Dora Jane Hamblin, without whose help this book would not have been written."

Only four or five months after they brought out Doris Day's bestselling memoir, *Her Own Story*, William Morrow was hoping for another blockbuster with Martin's *My Heart Belongs*. One of forty-five titles Morrow had on their spring list in 1976 (Margaret Truman's *Women of Courage* was another), *My Heart Belongs* had an initial print run of 50,000 copies, indicative of the publisher's enormous confidence in the book's prospects. By the first week of publication, in April, there were 70,000 copies in print, with two more printings to follow. (Its list price was $8.95.) A five-week tour was lined up to promote the book, with stops in twenty cities. "It will be like the old Paramount days, mostly one-night stands," Martin told Eugenia Sheppard for a story in the *New York Post*. "I'll enjoy it because it's so easy for me to yak, yak, yak."

"When they sent out the itinerary, I'd never seen anything like it," Martin told Aleene MacMinn, for the *Los Angeles Times*. "It's like doing five weeks of one-night stands with eight shows a day. This is all new to me. . . . I've never done any talk shows before because I was always having to save my voice for a show. Somebody said am I nervous and I replied I'm only nervous that they'll stop me in midsentence, that they'll turn me off."

Martin kicked off the tour by taping a segment of the *Merv Griffin Show* on April 15, just before she left Los Angeles, to be aired on May 10. The New York leg of the tour was timed to accommodate the Tony Awards on Sunday, April 18, during which Martin honored the American Theatre Wing, which produced the Tony Awards itself. (The landmark musical, *A Chorus Line,* swept the Tonys that year.) Early the next morning, Martin appeared on the *Today* show, followed by a smattering of radio and magazine interviews. Then, on that Monday night, Morrow threw a large book party at the Majestic Theatre, where Martin had starred in *South Pacific* for two years. "I looked at that Monday schedule and said, 'I don't see anyplace on here for lunch . . .' to which a friend replied, 'I told them you didn't eat lunch.' "

Famed fashion columnist Eugenia Sheppard also reported on Martin's book-signing event at Altman's "for several hundred of the millions who, for years, have been idolizing her." The bestselling author was clad in "a Venus pink dress printed in white hearts." It was during the tour that Martin unveiled Ronald Thomason's statue of herself as Peter Pan, in Weatherford, on the bicentennial, July 4, 1976. In a letter addressed to "Very Dear Everyone" at the unveiling, Martin wrote: "I can say: 'I'm Flying' and 'I Gotta Crow'. . . . To think that Never-Land was right there in Mary Martin's back yard! To think that her dreams were born, and that a time such as this was not on any chart but happened because so many hearts from her beloved home town . . . believed in a Never-Land." The statue was given a place of honor "in a garden in memory of her parents" in front of the Weatherford Library.

Martin found the tour more difficult than she had anticipated, particularly at the start, when she had to face Barbara Walters on the *Today* show, on April 19. "I feel like I know you intimately, because I wake up with you in my bedroom every morning," Martin said to Walters, striking a gracious note at the beginning of the interview. But in keeping with Walters's penchant for digging up personal revelations, the interviewer kept asking leading questions, in this case insinuating that Halliday was gay.

"What people know the least about you is your private life, I think, and since you do deal with it in the book, I thought we might talk a bit [about] your very special marriage to Richard Halliday," Walters said, early in the conversation. "That he and you made 'you' your career. That he decorated your homes and your dressing rooms—he did your hair. I used to hear that he did your hair. I never believed it."

Her face aglow and dressed in the same all-white suit with a red ker-chief that she sported on the cover of *My Heart Belongs,* Martin gave a relatively innocuous, straightforward response: "We did it at home you know—I would do the front and he would do the sides—because I had to have a permanent every three weeks, in *South Pacific,* to keep it that madly curly." But Walters resumed her homosexual implications, like a dog with a favorite bone. "How does a man, when the woman is the career . . . he made life very sweet for you: he took care of all the troubles," said Walters, "but also in doing your hair, and decorating the office, your dressing room. . . . How does a man like *that* retain his ego and his masculinity?"

"Well, I think, for instance, he never wanted to get married," replied Martin, who began to consider her words more carefully and to stumble over them in the process, "his career was the most important. He was story editor at Paramount when I married him. And I never wanted to remarry. So we married. And there we were. And the first time we went out, I can remember Frank Freeman, who was the president of Para-mount at that time, he said, 'Who wears the pants in the family?' And I said, 'We buy two pair of pants with every suit.' Because, the thing is, Richard was the boss. He was the captain of the ship. I—and I loved it that way. And I—he gave me so much, you know, so much love and warmth and security, that through the years I never missed—and I never saw another man in thirty-four years that I thought was as attractive. Nor have I seen one since."

Walters's line of questioning is perhaps best appreciated in the con-text of "outing" gay-but-closeted individuals, which was becoming more prevalent by 1976, when the stigma of being homosexual had begun to be offset by a celebratory mood, as reflected by a colorful gay pride parade every year in New York, the last Sunday in June, commemorating the Stonewall uprising seven years before. Walters might have also asked Martin why she chose to refer in her memoir to Radclyffe Hall's lesbian novel, *The Well of Loneliness,* as a specific influence on her growth and development as a person. But, then, no other journalist or media reporter seemed to pick up on the reference either.

There was a miniature press conference or group interview one morn-ing with several reporters, held in Martin's upscale suite in the Plaza Hotel. Martin emerged from her bedroom casually dressed, in a blue turtleneck pullover, white slacks, and Moroccan slippers. "She writes like she talks," Ben Washer had warned the journalists: "No punctuation, no paragraphs."

Washer quickly slipped into the background, as was his wont. "He almost might as well have not been there," recalled Elliott Sirkin, who was assigned to review *My Heart Belongs* for the *Village Voice*. "He was just there for an emergency. . . . He was a raunchy old goat—very cheerful. But he was the help, and she treated him like the help—in a high-class way."

"It was a memorable interview," continued Sirkin, "because one of the reporters with whom I shared the interview was a truly awful man, who tried to upset her and make her cry, the way he'd done with Doris Day a few weeks earlier. He was using this sort of prosecutorial style: Why wasn't there any politics in this book? She said she despised politics: she didn't think politicians needed a performer's words of wisdom." Despite her hostile interrogator, Martin proved unflappable. In the end, she insisted that everyone "crow" along with her, as she demonstrated how to vocalize it.

In his review of *My Heart Belongs* for the *Los Angeles Times,* Seymour Peck wrote, "The self-portrait may be altogether accurate; the prose is so relentlessly gushy as to be cloying. . . . It is a saga that unfolds pleasantly, but not much of it is unfamiliar. And the actress provides no searching insights into her techniques, her pursuit of her art . . . she is not one to go the big confessional route to achieve a best-seller." Peck withheld his kinder remarks for "the best parts [which] are to be found in the scenes that take place offstage, as Miss Martin remembers Mr. Halliday and their life together on their large, idyllic farm in Brazil to which they went to rest and refresh themselves between engagements" and for "her reflections on the joys of living away from the limelight, on the pleasures of privacy, on marriage, on raising children, on illness and death, [which] are quietly touching, graced by a simplicity that is missing from her earlier chapters."

With a headline that encapsulated *his* response to the book ("Mary Martin seems to think that she really is Peter Pan"), Foster Hirsch was somewhat more critical in his review for the *Chicago Tribune.* "Unlike Doris Day in her wonderfully frank memoirs," wrote Hirsch, "Mary Martin is careful not to tarnish her reputation or to give her fans the lowdown on her private life; and in her book the great musical star never really steps offstage." While writing that "the relentless cheeriness gives the book an inspirational tone, a kind of *Reader's Digest* uplift that contains only hints of the woman who's hiding beneath the aura of the star," Hirsch claimed that "[it's] a glossy celebrity book, in which the star treats us graciously, with the same warmth that she has always communicated to audiences; but she maintains her distance. . . . The book is filled with many tantalizing parenthetical statements that indicate that she is a more complex and contradictory personality than she wants to let on. . . . [She] is, on the evidence of this book, a deeply private woman."

Perhaps the most succinct yet accurate assessment of *My Heart Belongs* was provided by Martin's "bio-bibliographer," Barry Rivadue: "Though the memoir avoids being a fully honest purge, it remains highly readable as an often insightful, intelligent look at a remarkable life in the theater."

Best known as Mrs. Howell on the popular TV show *Gilligan's Island,* actress Natalie Schafer was a Palm Springs neighbor who became a good friend of Martin's. ("[Schafer] has that caustic wit, just like Noël [Coward]'s, which I adore," Martin told Sirkin.) After reading *My Heart Belongs,* Schafer said to Martin, "You don't hate anybody. I have a mission now, Mary, to find someone you dislike." Martin responded: "I have no time for hatreds and dislikes. Life is not long enough—it's too short as it is." This may conform with the always-cheerful attitude Martin cultivated and some felt made her insincere. But as Martin's *Hello, Dolly!* and *I Do! I Do!* colleague Willard Shaffer reported: "I always thought this lady was too sweet. I mean, it was sickening: it was like too much sugar in your coffee. But then, I had stomach cancer in 1977, and I was just out of intensive care when Mary Martin called me from California. In fact, she was my first phone call. Then, four or five weeks later, I had just gone back to work. Merrick lent me to somebody else for an Irish play starring Jason Robards. [A revival of O'Neill's *A Touch of the Poet* opened on December 28 at the Helen Hayes Theatre.] She was in New York, staying at the Plaza. She said, 'Why are you working? You shouldn't be doing that.' I said, 'I have to do what Mr. Merrick tells me.' She said, 'No you don't.' She also asked about my mother and my aunt. She used to send Christmas cards to the three of us every year, too."

Though it seems to fall in the category of too good to be true, it may be that Martin actually was the original "cockeyed optimist" long before Rodgers and Hammerstein wrote the song of that title for her. Apart from an apparently unwanted marriage to Ben Hagman near the beginning of her life, any adversity that Martin had ever known was either short-lived or quickly sublimated by some other welcome development—except of course, for the death of Richard Halliday, from which she would never fully recover.

Martin spent Thanksgiving in Brazil, where she was overwhelmed by her memories of Richard Halliday. She gazed upon the hill where Halliday had once planted a fresh grove of avocado trees, looking forward to seeing them bear fruit, a decade later, but he didn't live long enough. "The avocadoes were the size of footballs," Martin reported. "But three days there was all I could stand." Indeed, Martin had anticipated just such a response, telling Aleene MacMinn several months before making the journey, "I love it so, but it's so far, and it's tough to go back because it's now everything Richard said one day it would be, but he's not here to enjoy it." Martin put the Brazilian property on the market for $550,000, only to change her mind and hold on to it for some years afterward.

Though Martin's next theatrical venture would not be a musical per se, one of the hardest tickets ever to come by, on Broadway, was for a one-night-only event the following spring, on Sunday, May 15, 1977, when Mary Martin and Ethel Merman joined forces for a benefit for The Friends of the Theater and Music Collection of the Museum of the City of New York. When Arnold Weissberger, theatrical lawyer and chairman of the board of the Museum, phoned Martin, inviting her to make her first stage appearance since *I Do! I Do!* nearly a decade earlier, she responded, "I'll do anything with Merman!"

Long before they knew what they were going to be doing—or even which Shubert Theater they'd be doing it in—Martin and Merman announced their shared comeback on *Lifestyles with Beverly Sills,* the opera diva's afternoon talk show on NBC. "My guests today are the two superstars of the American musical comedy stage," said Sills. "You two are in a sense the living clichés of show business, because you were young hopefuls who walked out on a stage . . . and woke up the next day stars." The conversation predictably focused on the duo's first and last joint performance, on the *Ford 50th Anniversary Show* in 1953, when producer Leland Hayward had perpetrated "a con job" by telling each of them that they would be the focus of the TV special.

Together on Broadway was also newsworthy enough to warrant an advance segment on the *Today* show, for which the frizzy-haired, bushy-mustachioed Gene Shalit interviewed the two stars sitting next to each other on a yellow sofa in Merman's apartment. Hardly the gracious hostess, Merman proceeded to monopolize the first half of the nine-minute interview. But then, more than being merely deferential, Martin seemed somewhat lost, displaying none of her customary verve or vitality. When Shalit asked if they were going to be "nervous" on May 15, Martin, who was evidently already nervous, responded, "She won't be. I will," before adding that she hadn't appeared on a stage in five years, referring to her participation in a 1972 tribute to Richard Rodgers. "I wouldn't be doing this if she weren't going to be there," said Martin, with Merman at her side. Anticipating a kind of pandemonium, Merman allowed, "I'm liable to cry," explaining, "When we walk down there, what's going to go on in that audience. . . . Believe me, I don't think we'll be able to go into the first number."

After Merman relayed how, well into the run of a show, she might be thinking about what she needed to be purchasing from the store while "mechanically" performing a number, Martin was appalled, saying, "I can't even bear to think of her thinking about something else." Shalit's rather ponderous, final question, "What do you have in your life now that you would find most difficult to give up?" prompted Martin to reply: "I wouldn't want to give up my newfound life, which has been difficult to come by, with my husband having gone away. And I must say that . . . having this second chance to be with my family. . . . I would hesitate ever letting anything come in front of that again. It's been an utter and complete joy. And I don't deserve it. But I'm very, very lucky and I'm very proud to have this second chance."

While the top ticket price for a musical was, at the time, twenty dollars and, in only a few months, Liza Minnelli would command the all-time high of twenty-five dollars for an orchestra seat to *The Act,* tickets for *Together on Broadway* at the Broadway Theatre were an unheard-of $150 each. Nevertheless, the museum never dreamed how many "friends" it actually had: the benefit made the museum $145,000, and the theater even had to return an additional $35,000 for orders that couldn't be filled.

"They could have sold tickets for a thousand dollars a seat," recalled Donald Saddler, the elegant dancer and choreographer, who staged the event. "Sinatra wanted to come, but couldn't get in." According to a report in the *New York Times,* various celebrities who weren't in the show tried to serve as "ushers and usherettes just to see the performance." "Donald F. Smith, who was in charge of tickets, said he felt like 'cutting my veins' as he sent back hundreds of checks."

As put together by producer Anna Sosenko, *Together on Broadway* opened with the "two First Ladies of the theater"—as Mayor Abe Beame would refer to them on stage that evening—bursting through large paper hoops and costumed in their respective signature roles as Mama Rose and Nellie Forbush, singing "Send in the Clowns," Stephen Sondheim's bittersweet song and number one hit from *A Little Night Music.*

"They came through to such applause that it was at least five minutes before they could even continue," said Saddler, who also recalled the difficulty of handling two divas' rivalry, given that star billing traditionally begins on the left. "In the billing, so one didn't precede the other, their names appeared in a circle: 'Merman-Martin-Merman-Martin-Merman-Martin.' " Indeed, the program was ingeniously conceived to have no rear cover, but two fronts, so to speak: depending on which side was opened first, it featured either Martin or Merman in a luxurious black fur ad for Blackglama, popular at the time, with the byline, "What Becomes a Legend Most?" (Martin's dresses for the event were designed by movie-star clothier Jean-Louis.) Early in the developmental process, Sosenko had "cornered" Saddler, saying to him, "Now, listen, you have to tell Mary that Ethel always wants to be on stage right.' According to Saddler, "I thought to myself, 'How am I going to tell a big star like Mary Martin that she'll always have to be on stage left?' "

After first getting together with the stars in Merman's Manhattan apartment, Saddler had a more in-depth meeting with Martin at her home in Rancho Mirage. The choreographer found Martin's home "exactly what you would have expected: one of the loveliest ones in Palm Springs I had ever seen—with a beautiful pool. She was very homey, and always made you feel like it was special to be with you—she had that quality." During their private tête-a-tête, Saddler raised the issue of the two stars' positions on stage. "I was explaining that there were going to be these nine-foot circles [hoops], covered with white paper, and each of them would burst through. Then Cyril Ritchard, the compere of the evening, would come out. And then one lady would go stage right and the other stage left. And Mary looked at me very sweetly and said, 'And Donald, I suppose you would like for me to go stage left.' And I said, 'That would be lovely.' She said, 'Well, I know it's important to Ethel, and it doesn't mean that much to me. But I do know that "right" is the star's side.'

"Then, on the first day of rehearsals, they went through the sequence of songs and sang it through," continued Saddler. "And then I brought out two stools near the piano and I said, 'Would you like to sit on the stools and recap any of the gestures or moves you remember doing on stage?' So they both sat down like sweet little girls. And Ethel went right over to the one on the right, and Mary smiled at me, and winked, as she went to the one on the left." (When Saddler once asked Martin what defines a star, she replied: "When all the heads [in the audience] look up at you at the same time.")

Martin was, however, understandably nervous about making her comeback on a stage after such a long absence—so much so that she insisted on wearing a body mic for the performance. Though Lena Horne first wore one as early as 1957 (in *Jamaica*), body mics had only become conventional on Broadway since Martin last appeared in *I Do! I Do!* But once Martin chose to use one for *Together on Broadway,* Merman decided to as well.

In her *Broadway Ballyhoo* column, Radie Harris pronounced *Together on Broadway* "one of the greatest shows ever to hit Broadway" and "a night that will live forever as a flight to the stars on [Cole Porter's] gossamer wings," beginning with a standing ovation "that lasted for more than five minutes." Although Sinatra reportedly failed to get a ticket, seemingly everyone else involved with New York theater did: Claudette Colbert, Mike Nichols, Jerome Robbins, Brooks Hayward, Yul Brynner, Nedda Logan, Robert Fryer, Lillian Gish, Jack Paar, Kay Thompson, Millicent Martin, Jule Styne, Mabel Mercer, Hermione Gingold, Gloria Vanderbilt, Joel Grey, Bill Blass, Julie McKenzie, Margaret Truman, Arthur Laurents, Dorothy Hammerstein, Tammy Grimes, and Betty Comden and Adolph Green. Lauren Bacall, Ginger Rogers, and Phyllis Newman were among those wait-listed who managed to secure house seats at the eleventh hour.

Also, according to Radie Harris, "It was Mary who conceived the idea for their joint entrance, and it was terrif." Harris also credited Martin with the winning idea for both of them to descend separate staircases as Dolly Levi—each resplendent in Dolly's red-sequined gown and plumed hat—greeted by all-star Harmonium Gardens waiters: Barry Bostwick, Yul Brynner, Peter Gennaro, Joel Grey, Larry Hagman, Geoffrey Holder, John Lithgow, Burgess Meredith, Cyril Ritchard, George Rose, Donald Saddler, and Bobby Short.

"There were two Dollys and two staircases with a dozen dancers," recalled John Sheridan, who had been in the touring company of *Hello, Dolly!* with Martin. Sheridan was recruited by Saddler's assistant director, Mercedes Ellington, to show the illustrious chorus boys the waiters' steps. (As Joel Grey said later, "After all those years, we're finally in the chorus.")

According to Bob Ullman, the event's press rep, when a stagehand in the wings said of Martin, "Isn't she great!" Merman replied: "Yes. She certainly is. She's a dyke, you know."

"Ethel Merman is the bonfire and Mary Martin is the smoke," said Walter Kerr in his write-up of *Together on Broadway* in the *New York Times.* "It was Ethel the Eveready who opened up first (and second, and third, and after that I lost count)," Kerr continued. "I think of [Miss Martin] as smoke, not just because everything about her curls, such as her apricot smile and the peach-tinted fringe of auburn hair that sneaks out from under her sailor cap like seafoam. It's a matter of elusiveness. Smoke is always changing shape, so that you can't be sure from moment to moment just what it most resembles; heaven knows you can't catch it."

Kerr went on to report that Martin began the evening "with a slight vocal mishap [when] she somehow slipped off pitch and stayed there until her next time around. Next time around, though, she knew where she was: down at the footlights, subtly weaving magical patterns made of near-whispers and visual slipperiness. You see, she starts off like a stray feather rising unbidden from the floor to undulate gently in midair, lazily doing the bidding of any breezes that happen to be around, and then just as you've got used to her easy-going little-girl charms, you notice what a very dirty sound the lady manages to produce during one of the breaks in 'My Heart Belongs to Daddy.'

"At which point you realize that you've got a much more complex proposition on your hands than you thought. Meantime, she's up and taken off like a hummingbird gone ice skating. And opened her throat, as well as her arms, to skip as deliriously as ever through 'Wonderful Guy.' "

Theater publicist Josh Ellis, who was fortunate enough to secure a ticket for that legendary night, recalled: "Ethel was raring to go and in great shape, but Mary clearly wasn't—there was a lack of energy, with diminishing returns. There was also supposed to be a commercially released recording of it, but Mary Martin killed it, because she knew she wasn't at her best." Though she apparently had not been at her best vocally, Walter Kerr's well-wrought description of Martin's overall effect powerfully suggests she still had that ineffable quality that makes a star a star.

An after-theater supper for six hundred members of the audience was held at the United States Steak House Company in Rockefeller Center. Martin arrived looking like a "two-toned sprite in pink and green," while telling Enid Nemy for the *New York Times,* "Darling, it was the most beautiful night ever for me." When Radie Harris asked Larry Hagman if Martin was really his mother, he replied, "No, there's too little age difference between us."

Following a rehearsal for *Together on Broadway,* Martin and Merman were riding home in a limousine through the Great White Way—which they as much as anyone had made great—but now found noticeably degraded, with sex clubs and porn houses visible everywhere. "Jesus," said Merman, "Just look how they've fucked up Times Square." Indeed, during her *Today* show interview with Gene Shalit, Merman also said, "People don't take an interest in their appearance going to the theater [anymore]. They come in blue jeans cut up to here. . . . The girls look like a strip-act, or something. And these are the people that sit down in the second and third and fourth row in the orchestra. You look in the orchestra pit, and the musicians have got white shirts on, up to here, not even a summer jacket on. It's all disappeared. It's not the theater that Mary and I knew."

Beyond the seedy appearance that now seemed to define Broadway—along with so much else in the culture—Martin was equally dismayed by the changes that had taken place inside the theaters since she last strode the boards in *I Do! I Do!* "I think what's happened to Broadway is devastating," said Martin. "The only interesting musicals are revivals."

While a number of old-fashioned and freshly minted musicals had arrived in the intervening years—including *Follies, A Little Night Music, Chicago,* and, a true landmark, *A Chorus Line*—the avenue was increasingly dominated by rock and roll's influence, beginning with *Hair,* followed by *Godspell, Two Gentlemen of Verona, Pippin, Jesus Christ Superstar, The Wiz,* and *The Rocky Horror Show. Beatlemania,* which was an out-and-out rock concert, albeit a highly successful one, grossed more than seven million dollars at the Winter Garden Theatre in the 1977–78 season alone, which seemed a diminishment in so many respects. If there were fifty-four new productions on Broadway the previous year, theatergoers now had to content themselves with only forty-one.

Martin's one-night return to Broadway was like a proverbial shot in the arm, however, that truly exhilarated her for the first time since Halliday's death, four years before. Whatever doubts or anxiety she had had about setting foot on a stage for the first time in nearly a decade, the outpouring of love and appreciation that surrounded *Together on Broadway* made Martin crave more sustained attention—the kind that could only come by appearing in a new Broadway show.

Any consideration of Mary Martin's next Broadway project, *Do You Turn Somersaults?* must nevertheless begin with the question, Why? Why did she decide to make her comeback with such an inauspicious vehicle? An overly sentimental two-hander by Russian playwright Aleksei Arbuzov, *Do You Turn Somersaults?* is set in a sanatorium in Riga, where a retired performer (Martin) embarks on an autumnal romance with a resident doctor (Anthony Quayle). Titled *Old World,* the initial English version was produced by the Royal Shakespeare Company and featured Peggy Ashcroft and Quayle. With an eye on bringing the play to Broadway, Cheryl Crawford encouraged Martin to catch the London production, when she was there promoting her memoir. (W. A. Allen brought out *My Heart Belongs* in the United Kingdom, where Tisha Browne, for one, found it "riotously funny and surprisingly uncloying.") Hoping to make the play more palatable for an American audience, Martin thought it might be reset in Boston and Cape Cod or even redone as "a small musical" for herself. Though nothing ever came of either suggestion, the odd if formulaic comedy arrived in the States with a new title slapped on.

"This play is about age and loneliness and two people finding each other," Martin told Aljean Harmetz for a feature story in the *New York Times*. "It's the age I am and the way I feel about life at this moment." After explaining that she had turned down offers to do *Life with Father, Life with Mother,* any number of plays by Noël Coward, and a musical version of *Arsenic and Old Lace,* Martin described her vacant frame of mind, which hardly seems like a good position for making any sort of a career decision: "In the four years since Richard has gone, I've been in limbo, my brain dormant. I've been living on the surface, not allowing myself to go into depths. I haven't even wanted to read a book in four years. I was afraid to go back on the stage, and I've never been afraid of anything in my life. Except death. I've always been afraid of death. I wasn't with my mother or my daddy when they died and I've never been to the cemetery, to their graves." In fact, Martin hadn't even attended either of her parents' funerals.

While costly pre-Broadway tryouts were becoming a thing of the past, *Do You Turn Somersaults?* initially avoided the Broadway spotlight by beginning life on August 6 with a "break-in" run at the University of Tennessee in Knoxville. During a technical rehearsal in Knoxville, in "the darkness backstage," Martin fell off of a revolving platform and had to go on with her leg in a cast. "I'm always hurting myself," Martin told Harmetz. "It may not be my image, but I've hurt everything from my head to my feet and all the stops in between. I never travel without ice bags and liquid freezing medicine.

"When I fell off the platform, I thought I had reinjured the ankle I hurt in *I Do! I Do!* About midplay, my knee began to hurt. And at 5:30 the next morning I called a friend [presumably Ben Washer] and said, 'You'd better get me to a doctor.' Six hours later the doctor said he had 'good news and bad news.' The leg wasn't broken, but I had torn the ligaments. He told me I would have to be in a cast unless I wanted it to be immobile for the rest of my life." Martin nonetheless demonstrated her tendency to accentuate the positive even in the midst of misfortune. "Since you have to step down with the leg that's in a cast and up with the leg without a cast," she told Harmetz, "I've finally learned left from right at a most advanced age."

Do You Turn Somersaults? opened later in August at the Kennedy Center in Washington, DC, for a five-week run, before embarking on an eleven-week road tour of Wilmington, Chicago, Fort Lauderdale, and Boston. It was at Martin's suite at the Ritz Carlton Hotel in Boston that journalist Elliott Sirkin met up with her for a feature he was writing for *After Dark* magazine. "I'm happy in this part," Martin told Sirkin, while adding, "it's the hardest acting I've ever had to do. . . . Don't use this if you don't want to, but Shirley Booth came down from Cape Cod to see the matinee on Wednesday. I didn't know she would be there, but when she came backstage, she told me something I'll never forget. She said, 'You're a little bit like Lynn [Fontanne], but you can do things she can't do. And you're a little bit like Laurette [Taylor], but you can do things she couldn't do.' I was so thrilled. I knew Laurette Taylor, and I worshipped her."

Martin also told Sirkin that she was "mad about" Anthony Quayle, and, after turning down a number of requests to perform in Noël Coward's *Tonight at 8:30*, "now that I found Anthony, I think I'm gonna do it with him."

In interview after interview to promote the play, Martin emphasized that she had been at something of a loss without Halliday telling her what to do. (Unfortunately, having chosen *Do You Turn Somersaults?* seems to confirm just how lost she actually was.) Though she had completed her bestselling memoir and devoted more of her time to her grandchildren—perhaps trying to compensate for the family life she never really had before—Martin had problems negotiating the logistics it entailed. Finally free of Halliday's interference and able to welcome into her life the family she never knew she had, Martin still needed a Halliday to handle the practical arrangements. She complained to Rex Reed, for instance, about recently being a captive in her son's car, after she agreed to accompany the Hagman brood on an outing to Aspen, only to discover that the resort was 750 miles from her Palm Springs home, and "not just around the corner."

After meeting with her to talk about *Somersaults,* Reed described Martin as a character straight out of a play by Tennessee Williams: "one of those defenseless Southern belles buffeted by fate and unable to cope with simple realities . . . charming her way through a world of men by exaggerating her own defenselessness." He added, however, that such an impression differed from "her reality." "She is no pixyish Peter Pan androgyne but a strong, solid figure of a woman, more of an Annie Oakley."

But was she? The vulnerable aspect of Martin's nature, which was always present, simply became more pronounced once Halliday was no longer there to protect her or tell her what to do. And for the most part, not even "Uncle Ben," as Washer quickly became known, could ever truly fill those aspects of what had been Richard Halliday's job description: Washer was constitutionally incapable of giving orders or even making any weighty decisions for himself or for anyone else. The image everyone conveys of Washer finds him timidly lurking in the background during interviews—as well as in Martin's life.

By the time it finally began performances on January 9, 1978, at Broadway's 46th Street Theatre—where Martin had performed in her previous two-hander, *I Do! I Do!* with Robert Preston—*Do You Turn Somersaults?* had become an embarrassment that closed in less than three weeks, or considerably shy of what had been preannounced as a limited, ten-week run, losing its entire $400,000 investment. "This kind of bittersweet old folks' romance is one of the hoarier commonplaces. . . . Arbuzov's plotting and dialogue come across creakier than a crone's bones," observed John Simon in his review for *New York* magazine. After he attended the play, Rex Reed spoke for many when he asked why Martin had chosen such a "dreary and vapid" work for her return to Broadway. "It is discouraging to contemplate the number of first-rate musicals Mary Martin has cancelled[,] postponed or said 'no' to in the past dozen years. It is even more dismaying that she said 'yes' to such drivel."

On the other hand, the critics tended to be overly kind and respectful of Martin, honoring her for her work in the past if not the present. Saying that it easily could "have dissolved into a soup of mawkish sentiment," Frank Trippett, in *Time* magazine, claimed that its two stars "souffleed [it] into an amusing and often touching entertainment." Adding that their "arthritic Charleston . . . would vindicate the evening if nothing else did," Trippett ended by saying Martin's "one ditty is a wistful circus song that proves that at age 63, her heart wisely belongs not to memories of her glittering past but to a riper, richer present."

In her review for the *Los Angeles Times,* Sylvie Drake wrote that it was geared "for an audience that deeply *wanted* to feel sentimental anyway," and that "What makes [it] work to the considerable degree that it does is the expertise of the pros involved—not just the actors and director, but the technical team as well, [including] Ann Roth who drapes Miss Martin in an array of costumes far too stunning for the character of Lidya, who after all, was only a circus cashier following an earlier career as actress and artist."

Joshua Logan would seize *Somersaults* as an opportunity to write, in his second memoir, that, "Mary is a great lady of the theatre. To me, artists are aristocrats of today, and Mary is an aristocrat of aristocrats. A production is already blessed to have her as the star." But no one was as defensive about the play as Martin, who insisted that she could relate to the role. She told Elliott Sirkin, "Honey, this play is longer than *Hamlet,* and I have to do most of the talking. But I want to age gracefully in the theater, as in person—not that I ever do anything gracefully in person—and here was this play about a woman my age, and it was a contemporary story."

Martin would ultimately claim that *Do You Turn Somersaults?* presented her with "the first closing notice I've seen in my forty years in the theater," adding that "it's not a New York show" and "I didn't want to bring it here," when the record clearly indicates otherwise. But then, Martin would deflect the difficulties all performers have with negative notices by resorting to the oldest alibi of all, claiming that she never read any of her reviews. "If they are too good I get a little nervous," she told Richard Lee for the *New York Post.* "If they're bad, well, there you are, you've opened, and you've got to do another performance that night, and you keep remembering what they said. I stopped reading them after *Sound of Music.*" She also explained how she had turned down far loftier projects in the intervening years: "because I'm not at my top anymore, and I know it, and I wouldn't want to take on that responsibility."

Though Martin's next venture would take her on the road every so often for the next few years, it had nothing to do with the stage. "I have entered into a deal with Fieldcrest, designing sheets! and their executives have all been here [to Palm Springs] en masse," Martin wrote in a letter to Elliott Sirkin, on March 9. "NOW, three rooms of my home are being torn asunder, madly, getting ready to be re-done in sheets and towels, hurled willy-nilly throughout in behalf of being photographed in order to SELL SHEETS! I have found that, at least in my case, writing a book necessitates going on the road, one night stands, to sell it; and now [it's] the same with designing sheets."

When Fieldcrest first approached Martin to become its representative, they told her they had been looking for someone from the musical world. "I don't quite understand how we're going to manage singing sheets or pillowcases," she responded. "We finally decided we could use designs that are representative of the shows I've done. I've always worked on needlepoint backstage, so there's a needlepoint pattern and there's 'Enchanted Evening' from *South Pacific.* For the flying pattern, we couldn't incorporate Peter Pan himself—no one should sleep on top of Peter Pan, after all, he's a spirit—so we chose the balloon, which evokes the kind of freedom he represents."

As announced with a full-color, photo-rich four-page spread in an issue of *House Beautiful,* "Mary Martin's new collection for bed and bath" was even given a name by Fieldcrest: "Some of My Favorite Things." "Colors are soft and muted, well-suited to the living and dining rooms as well as bed and bath," explained Victoria Erin Towns in the accompanying text. "Even the patterns are chosen with an eye on versatility—Mary is a firm believer in—and practitioner of—decorating with sheets. . . . In true Renaissance-woman spirit, Mary did all of the decorating [of her Palm Springs home] herself. Throughout the house, wicker and pastel carpets combine with an eclectic mix of Oriental and antique furnishings to highlight her new bed and bath designs. And her mementos are everywhere. . . . Tabletop still-lifes display her memorabilia: photos of kith and kin, antique friendship symbols, porcelains galore."

Since Martin's involvement with Fieldcrest coincided with her son's becoming more and more recognizable as the reprobate J. R. Ewing in *Dallas,* she reveled in the discovery of just how famous he was. "I was appearing at a mall on a Sunday [for Fieldcrest]," she recalled, before the all-important episode in which J. R. was shot. "Would you believe there must have been 1,000 people there, coming up to me and saying 'Would you mind signing "J. R.'s mother" for me?' I got the biggest kick out of it." On the other hand, as reported by Hagman himself, when she was asked at a press party for *Dallas,* "What's it like to have an icon for a son?" Martin paused before responding, "My dear, my son is a star. I am an icon."

Susan L. Schulman was handling press for CBS television when *Dallas* was "at the height of its glory," and recalled an "event for the TV critics" at the Hagmans' house in Malibu: "Larry had T-shirts made that said, 'I Slept with J. R.,' and dollar bills printed with, 'In J. R. I Trust.' I said something to the effect that I knew his mother a little bit and I could see where he got his skills for working a room. He looked at me and said, 'Oh, darlin', I can't hold a candle to her, in that department.'"

There was another story regarding their comparable fame, and how it intersected, which both Martin and Hagman enjoyed telling. "Joel Grey, a close friend of Larry's, was opening in Las Vegas, and he invited Larry to come with his wife and daughter," Cheryl Crawford wrote in her memoir. "Mary was asked too. When they all left their hotel to go to the one where Joel was to perform, a large crowd of teenagers spotted Larry, surrounding him with squeaks and squawks, begging for his autograph, trying to hug and kiss him. Mary stood aside with a friend [Ben Washer], unnoticed. The doorman hastened to put Larry and family into a taxi. As it departed, Larry leaned out of the window, waved to his mother and called, 'See, Mom! This is show biz.'

"At the opening they all sat together at a table. When Joel appeared, he announced, 'I don't usually do this, but I have a great friend here tonight whom I would like to introduce, Larry Hagman.' There was great applause. Then Joel continued, 'And there is someone else here. You may have seen her in *Peter Pan* or *South Pacific*. . . .' "

"As she rose and waved, people went nuts," recalled Hagman. "They stood, with some climbing on their chairs for a better look, and clapped so long the house lights went up. Despite Mother's efforts to quiet the house, the applause wouldn't quit. It was literally a showstopper. Finally, after blowing kisses to all sides, she sat down. Then I felt a rap on my knee. There was Mother, leaning toward me. With a twinkle in her eye, she said, 'And that's show business too, baby!' "

Clearly, Martin was not entirely ready to relinquish the limelight—not yet, anyway. Despite the dismal failure of *Do You Turn Somersaults?*, Martin continued to try to find relevance in her golden years with a made-for-TV movie, *Valentine,* which aired on ABC on December 7, 1979, and proved to be another misfire. With its focus on leftover hippie notions and other EST-like phenomena that seemed to define a West Coast sensibility at the time—albeit for the senior set—it struck many viewers as being as saccharine and vapid as its title—even though it won a prestigious Peabody Award.

In the film, the sixty-six-year-old Martin plays the seventy-one-year-old Grace Schwartz, a Jewish widow who lives in an assisted-living retirement home on the beach in Venice, California. Though Grace's days have been numbered by her doctors, she finds romantic respite with the Irish Catholic Pete Ferguson (Jack Albertson) and even runs off with Pete for some golden-ager bliss in Lake Tahoe, where, following two weeks of rehearsals, the movie enjoyed some location shooting. Grace's highly disapproving daughter, Emily, considers Pete "sleazy" and resists all the life-affirming verities her mother represents, even in the midst of her approaching death.

"While Miss Martin is delightful in the role," wrote Arthur Unger in the *Christian Science Monitor,* "the script is insistently cloying and over-romanticized to the point that it borders on advanced-age immorality. It is calculated to be cute, poignant—and sexy. While the idea of mature passion may have a certain validity, the presentation cries out for subtlety and sensitivity rather than the tearful soapy treatment it receives. . . ."

When Unger asked Martin if she had any future plans for the theater, she claimed, "I won't do another musical although I might do something with songs. But not a big musical because it now costs over a million dollars and I would never leave any show until it had paid off its investors and made a lot of money. And I don't want to be tied up that long. I want to spend more time with my family now that I've discovered them again."

"I missed a lot," Martin also told Unger. "But I didn't know I missed it. Theater was my lifestyle, and that was the way it had to be." She was quick to add, however, that things had changed during "the past six years"—or ever since her husband's death.

For Hagman, of course, it was a very different story. "One of the reasons Larry had been so mad at Richard was that Mary should have been doing more satisfying things with her life than hooking rugs," said Barbara Flicker, who with her husband, Ted, saw the Hagmans along with Martin any number of times. "I mean, it was dull stuff. And he really resented it." As Flicker further recalled, when she and her husband first met the Hallidays with the Hagmans, "Mary was ignoring them. They had cut Maj out of their life, and then Larry threw them out of his life." But years later, when the Flickers visited the Hagmans at their Malibu beach house, "There was Mary, sitting there, being demure-like, the grandmother of the kids, and this darling old lady. If anything, she became very close to Maj, who was running her life for her: showing her how to do things and how to organize her life. It had become a totally different relationship than the one we had been hearing about all of those years. I remember thinking, wasn't it a shame that they had lost so much time? And I think Mary was very aware of that. But I'm not sure Maj or Larry was."

Hagman's lifelong friend Roger Phillips shared Flicker's impressions. "After Richard died, Maj and Larry really took care of her," said Phillips. "They took over her assets. Whenever I saw her at their place in Malibu, she couldn't have been nicer. When she would see me, she would make me feel like it was the greatest thing that happened to her that year. But she made everybody feel that way. It was a talent she had. She and Maj were not that close until later in Mary's life, when Maj became very protective of her."

Chapter 19

"SUNNYSIDE UP"

*I never saw myself on stage, so there really is no need for me
to see myself now, or I might never go back on television.*
—MARY MARTIN

For baby boomers born before 1955, Mary Martin epitomized Peter Pan and seemed to own the role, even though Martin herself appreciated that others would come to play "the boy who refused to grow up." When she saw Sandy Duncan enchanting a new generation of youngsters in a hit revival of *Peter Pan,* Martin envied the upstart's ability to fly out over the audience, which was something Martin had always wanted to do: Martin's flights for live audiences had been confined to the proscenium stage in theaters.

While Duncan was making her nightly flights at the Lunt-Fontanne Theater in 1980, the seventy-four-year-old Janet Gaynor made her Broadway debut in *Harold and Maude.* A misguided stage version of a beloved cult film of the same name—about an eccentric elderly woman and her young, loner friend—*Harold and Maude* opened on February 8 at the Martin Beck Theatre, where it closed two days later.

"It was originally to star Glynis Johns as Maude," recalled Josh Ellis, who handled the show's publicity. "But Glynis quit after a couple of weeks of rehearsals." According to Ellis, Gaynor and her husband, Paul Gregory, were staying at the time at the Mayflower Hotel, on Central Park West. "And a prominent feature in their hotel room was a large picture of Mary Martin, which they put on a bureau. By this time, I had heard endless rumors about the two of them," he added, referring to Martin and Gaynor. Indeed, with the caption, "Hug for Janet's First Night," *The Star* tabloid ran a photo of Martin embracing Gaynor, as if to both confirm and fuel the rampant rumors that the two stars had been more than just good friends.

"On opening night of *Harold and Maude,* everything went wrong," Ellis continued. "It was a disastrous night. The show had a turntable; and, ten minutes into the show, the turntable froze and there was no moving it at all. They would hand parts of the set to Janet to bring on, including, for instance, a tree. It was a horrible, horrible experience.

"At the end of the show, we made room for Mary Martin to be the first guest back [in Janet's dressing room]; and I would even hold the photographers back. And before we let the press photographers in, Mary Martin said to Janet, 'I don't know how you ever got through it. It was the most embarrassing opening night I have ever experienced, and I just don't know how you had the presence of mind to get through it.' Janet said, 'Mary. Remember what you told me about doing a Broadway show? You said that doing a Broadway show would be an adventure. Well, tonight was an adventure.'"

A new Broadway show was not the sort of adventure Martin herself was about to embark on anytime soon. She spent much of the summer of 1980 at the Hagmans' home in Malibu, in a room that Maj prepared especially for her mother-in-law, "all white and organdy, with floating curtains facing the Pacific Ocean." On October 27, at Beverly Sills's final opera performance, Martin was one of a number of other divas—including Ethel Merman and Leontyne Price—who appeared in the second-act party scene of the New York City Opera's *Die Fledermaus,* where guest artists famously interpolate their favorite numbers or arias. "Walking off with the whole show were Mary, with a stunning rendition of 'My Heart Belongs to Daddy,' and Ethel, with 'There's No Business Like Show Business,'" claimed Merman biographer, Brian Kellow.

When Larry Hagman was invited to London in November to perform at a special benefit celebrating the eightieth birthday of the Queen Mother—an enormous fan of *Dallas,* as were a great many of her English subjects—he took his mother along as a surprise guest. Martin was "tucked into his dressing room" at the Palladium, until her son broke out in a rousing chorus of "There Is Nothing Like *This* Dame," at which point Martin emerged on stage, in her *South Pacific* sailor costume, singing "Honey Bun" "at the top of my lungs and stopping once to look up at my big Baby Boy— 'Get a load of Honey Bun tonight,'" recalled Martin. "We had a ball. We even did 'The Eyes of Texas.'" This was in spite of Hagman, famously, forgetting his lines and failing to tell the queen what seemingly the whole world wanted to know, at the time: "Who shot J. R. Ewing?"

Martin would perform "Honey Bun" yet again with Bob Hope for his seventy-eighth birthday celebration at West Point on May 25, 1981. Martin was also, by then, visiting a dozen or so cities twice a year for her sponsor, Fieldcrest, "talking and appearing on TV and in department stores," she recalled. "It was another form of show business, but this was bringing me really close to people." She even went to London and Dublin to promote her line of linens for Fieldcrest, and then as far as Australia for the opening of the company's new mill there, and eventually to Hawaii.

While dividing her time between her newly discovered family and taking promotional trips as a representative for Fieldcrest, Martin also, in tandem with Janet Gaynor, agreed to endorse Velvaderm, an expensive skin lotion, at the posh I. Magnin department store in Los Angeles and in well-placed advertisements in various magazines. During this, the last decade of Martin's life, there were requests for her to endorse an endless number of products as well as tributes for her to participate in—including many dedicated to herself. Martin and Ben Washer were invited by Lady Bird Johnson to stay at the LBJ ranch, after the opening ceremony for a new library in Houston, commemorating the "Most Famous Women in Texas," and Martin cut the ribbon. Martin was also present in September 1981, when the forty-nine-year-old Larry Hagman was inducted, with his own star, on the Hollywood Walk of Fame, "imbedded next to that of his mother." When Hagman said, "Looks like I'm going to get top billing," Martin replied, with a Gracie Allen–type logic, "It all depends on which way you walk down the street."

Martin found relevance as an elder spokeswoman in her twilight years, however, by becoming the cohost of a syndicated afternoon TV talk show called *Over Easy*. As sponsored by a grant from the US Department of Health, Education, and Welfare, *Over Easy* was produced by Jules Power and Richard Rector for San Francisco's KQED. The show actually began life in 1977 with host Hugh Downs, who, three years later, was joined by his erstwhile *Today* show partner, Frank Blair. It eventually aired on 235 public broadcast stations nationwide, including PBS in New York, every weekday at noon.

Power came to feel that it was important to have a woman cohost, and an older one at that: "to break down entrenched social attitudes," by featuring "an older female host and a younger male host . . . rather than the stereotypic kindly gray-haired male star of 55 or 60 and some 23-year-old dippy girl." In the past, *Over Easy* had been "strong on content and outstanding guests," Power told Aleene MacMinn of the *Los Angeles Times,* "but if we were going to take a new direction for its fifth year, it needed more of a humanistic touch, a personal involvement. It needed anecdotes and observations and off-the-cuff kind of feelings about things."

Power was sure to add that Martin had already been on the show as a guest, when she sang Kern and Hammerstein's little-known, plaintive "Walking Hand in Hand," for instance, on September 25, 1979, accompanied by Isaac Stern on the violin. "Here is a woman who's got life," Power said of Martin. "She's ingenious, she's curious, inquisitive, outspoken in her observations, very compassionate . . . all the qualities that ought to go into a show like this, the ones you think you're building into it, but they still need to come out the small end of the funnel with someone. I thought Mary would be ideal."

As far as Martin was concerned, her involvement with *Over Easy* was destined to happen. In a religious-oriented magazine called *Possibilities,* she recalled wanting to move to her "favorite" city, San Francisco, but imagining how difficult it would be. "I went for a walk in the park [in the Palm Springs mountains] and sat on a park bench to talk to God about my problem. Of course, if you sit on a park bench talking to God, people think you're crazy, so I called him 'Ephraim,'" she explained, referring to Dolly Levi's tendency, in *Hello, Dolly!,* to talk to her late husband of the same name, before making any momentous decisions. (According to Kristina Hagman, her grandmother "used 'Ephraim' as her way of saying 'thank you' to God. Throughout the last twenty years of her life, she was always talking to Ephraim.")

That same day, Ben Washer phoned Martin with the news that Hugh Downs had called, wanting her to cohost "a PBS talk show designed for an over-forty audience," adding that it would be filmed in San Francisco. "She immediately put the phone down and went into the privacy of her bedroom and said, 'Ephraim, I didn't mean this soon!'"

With another new cohost, the forty-one-year-old former *Today* show anchorman Jim Hartz, Martin made her *Over Easy* debut on September 29, 1981, featuring Pearl Bailey as their guest. They had already taped a total of sixty-five segments over the summer, with Bob Hope, James Stewart, Milton Berle, Josh Logan, Ethel Merman, Joel Grey, Janet Gaynor, and many others. Since hosting a talk show was an entirely new experience for Martin, she recalled having to be prompted by Hartz during the first few tapings: "He would press one finger into my back to remind me to ask another question," she claimed. "Two fingers meant 'shut up.'" This was before she became comfortable with a more customary teleprompter.

"I did it because I thought I could be helpful," Martin told Judy Klemesrud for an in-depth report in the *New York Times*. "I know so many older people who just sit back and say, 'Oh, my life is over.' Then they start getting afraid to do things, to try things, which is a tragedy. I've watched it with people I love. They're afraid of breaking a hip or something."

The interview took place in the Berkshire Place Hotel, with the grandmother of six looking "elegant" in a brown silk tunic over black silk pants.

Though she was "the picture of good health," Martin claimed to have pesky problems with arthritis and with a cataract in her left eye. She credited being in basically fine shape, however, to regular exercise (swimming, walking three miles a day, and "practicing transcendental meditation"), careful diet ("eating mainly fish, chicken, fruit and vegetables"), and a regimen of six "potent" vitamins each day.

"I never retired," Martin continued, when Klemesrud asked about the loss of her husband in 1973. "After Richard's death I was tired, but not retired. For about two years I just sort of ran and wouldn't face anything. I went to London and other places. Then one day I thought I saw Richard standing there saying, 'Don't indulge your sadness.'"

When Aleene MacMinn asked Martin if she intended to watch the shows as they appeared each day, she replied, "Maybe, maybe not," before demonstrating just how critical she could still be of her appearance. "The only tapes I've seen are five shows I did in New York, interviewing Lillian Gish, the Cronyns [Jessica Tandy and Hume Cronyn], Eva Le Gallienne and Maureen Stapleton. I thought they weren't all that bad, but not all that good, either." As she continued to explain her feelings on the matter, Martin touched upon what must be viewed as her lifelong insecurities with seeing herself, as captured by any kind of a camera: "So I said to myself one day in the shower—that's where I get all my famous ideas, like washing that man right outta my hair—I never saw myself on stage, so there really is no need for me to see myself now, or I might never go back on television."

While announcing that she planned on celebrating her upcoming sixty-eighth birthday in Brazil, Martin allowed that she might continue with *Over Easy* the following year, because "I'd certainly like to live in San Francisco, so we'll see." She also shared her personal philosophy with MacMinn, which was essentially her motivation for doing the show: "So many elderly people tend to close doors instead of opening them to new challenges. You might retire from a certain job when you're sixty-five, but you never, never retire from life. I've said that five dozen times on *Over Easy*. Keep busy 'til your last breath." Once her ties to San Francisco became more definite, Martin rented a pied-à-terre in the Pacific Heights section, at the northeast corner of Broadway and Pierce Street, for four months each year.

Janet Gaynor had already been a guest on *Over Easy* when she made the fateful decision to be on the show again, in September 1982, with her husband, Paul Gregory. The couple was staying with Martin and Ben

Washer and, on September 2, they taped their second segment of *Over Easy*, focusing on "their late-in-life love and marriage." When Gaynor said, on the show, "Paul really knew my affairs" and Martin responded, "How wonderful," Gregory piped in, "I knew what I was getting," to laughter all around.

On Sunday, Labor Day, September 5, Martin, Gaynor, Gregory, and Washer got into a taxi and headed for dinner at Kan's Restaurant in San Francisco's Chinatown. With Gregory in the front seat, Martin was in the back, directly behind the driver, Gaynor to her right and Washer on the far right, when the cab, heading east on California Street, was hit by a van, traveling north on Franklin, at 7:20 P.M. (According to some reports, Washer was in the front seat, Gregory in the back.) It was still light at the time. "The impact sent the cab skidding for more than 80 feet before it smashed into a tree on the opposite side of California Street," according to a police report.

Washer was pronounced dead at Mission Emergency Hospital, and the survivors were taken to San Francisco General, where Gaynor immediately underwent a five-hour operation to repair serious abdominal injuries, involving a ruptured bladder and a severely damaged kidney. She also suffered multiple pelvic fractures, eleven broken ribs, and a right collarbone fracture. The diminutive and seriously compromised Gaynor received ten pints of blood during the first twelve hours after her admittance.

Martin had fractured two ribs and her pelvic bone, as well as injured a kidney and punctured a lung. Gregory had broken several ribs and bruised a kidney. He remained in intensive care with an irregular heartbeat. The driver of the van, Robert Cato, was jailed after being treated for minor injuries. The forty-six-year-old cab driver, Ronald Drury, was also treated and released.

"Jules and I were already in bed when we got a call about the accident," recalled producer Jules Power's wife, Dorothy. "So we got dressed in about two seconds, and we went to San Francisco General immediately." "They were still working on Mary when I saw her and her first words to me were, 'Ben's gone, isn't he?'" claimed Jules Power, "and I thought all that night how much of an extension of her life Ben had been. Then she said, 'I'm sorry; I'm sorry that this is going to disrupt so many people....' That's Mary," added Power. "Mary Martin and Janet Gaynor are American originals. Looking at them that night, I wouldn't have given odds on [their] survival but these are two very strong ladies and the trauma team at San Francisco General is the best. They will pull out of this, physically and emotionally."

"I checked with hospital officials a few minutes ago, and they say there is no change in the condition of either woman, and that's encouraging news," claimed reporter Doug Murphy the next day, on Channel 5, KPIX, the CBS affiliate in San Francisco. "They are both awake, and they are both alert. Mary Martin is listed in serious but stable condition, and Janet Gaynor is listed in critical but stable condition. They're happy about that simply because of her age and the seriousness of her injury, that she's not getting any worse. Her husband, Paul Gregory, is listed, tonight, in fair condition. . . .

"Police say the driver of the van that ran the red light, and struck their cab, has been released on bail," Murphy continued. "Robert Cato is charged with felony drunk driving, reckless driving, and vehicular man-slaughter. Martin's son, Larry Hagman, visited his mother early today. The hospital switchboard has been jammed with calls from fans from around the world. . . . Officials here say that Martin could be out of the hospital in as short a time as two weeks. Because Gaynor is in so much more serious condition, nobody here has mentioned, yet, when she can be released from the hospital."

"Maj and I flew to be with her immediately," recalled Larry Hagman. "I was distraught and more upset than I realized. . . . By then, Mother and I had learned to appreciate each other in ways that had been impos-sible when we were younger." Hagman obviously felt closer to his mother than ever before, as doubtlessly colored by an accident with such fatal consequences, but Paul Gregory's negative views of Martin have calcified in the decades since. "I tried to get Janet to realize that Mary was only exploiting her," he recalled. "Because that's all Mary ever did with any-one. It was all 'me, me, me.' If it wasn't 'me,' then there was no 'you.' Mary was the most unoriginal human being I ever knew. She copied everything Janet Gaynor did, and didn't have a thought of her own in her head. It used to annoy Janet, because Janet would get something, and then turn around, and there would be Mary, wearing what Janet had."

Perhaps with some justification, Gregory even came to blame Martin directly for the accident. "If she wasn't using Janet, we would never have been in San Francisco," he continued, "and my little girl wouldn't have been crushed to death in a cab, when Mary was trying to cut the cab-driver's hair, and he wasn't paying any attention to where we were going." Gaynor, who never completely recovered from her injuries, died two years later.

As Martin herself would claim: "The cab driver had the longest hair, and I thought if I had scissors, I'd snip it right off. That's the last I remember until I woke up in the hospital and my children were standing over me." According to Gregory, Martin, in fact, had a pair of manicure scissors in her purse, and started to clip a wayward curl on the driver, who, distracted by the clipping, had the collision.

But apparently Martin's barbering techniques did not figure in the judge's decision, following a two-week court case in February. "Paul Gregory asked her to testify in court," said Susan Grushkin, who half a decade later became Martin's live-in aide and companion. "She refused, and he never forgave her for that. And the reason she refused was because she truly didn't remember. She had had a concussion. She was a very honest person and didn't feel she could give her testimony. And then Paul stopped speaking to her: he wouldn't even tell her where Janet was buried [after she died], or give her anything of Janet's to remember her by, which was very painful to her, because they had been such close friends."

After determining that the thirty-six-year-old truck driver, Cato, had been drunk on September 5, "tailgating, weaving and speeding and had run at least one other red light before he careened through a stoplight and hit the taxi," the superior court judge, Raymond Arata, admonished him, "It was as if you took a gun and shot it down Franklin Street." Cato was sentenced to the maximum of three years in prison, and Martin ultimately accepted a $100,000 insurance settlement for her injuries.

In view of the extent of her injuries, Martin's recovery in the hospital proved slow but methodical. "I started by raising myself to a sitting position in bed," she recalled a couple of years later in *Guideposts*. "It took a while before I could get to the point that they would let me put my feet on the floor. And then I was unable to straighten up. I was given a walker and taught how to push it ahead of me, then shuffle my feet after it. It took a week to learn how to push my way six inches at a time, but little by little—push, shuffle; push, shuffle—I began to get somewhere. And then one day I shuffled all the way to Janet's room [in the hospital]."

Following her nine-day recovery, Martin was released from San Francisco General Hospital amid much fanfare. She was taken downstairs in a wheelchair and then transferred to a walker. Along the way, the hospital staff was "hanging out windows" and urging Martin on, shouting, "We believe! We believe!" as if restoring Tinker Bell to life in *Peter Pan*. "That really got to me," said Martin. "I burst into tears."

Given the accident and recovery period, Martin canceled a scheduled appearance with Ethel Merman on the Emmy Awards broadcast that September. "Millions of people will miss seeing us on the 'Emmys,'" Merman wrote Martin, "but I will miss us most of all—I was anxiously looking forward to our duet together. Get well, we'll do it again. Much love, Merman."

In the coming months Martin displayed, yet again, her indomitable spirit, reflecting upon the accident. "I've never known anything in my career to equal it," she told Victor Merina, a reporter for the *Los Angeles Times*. "If out of this tragedy, something good can happen, that would be the loveliest part of all." Martin was eager to take her own advice as a talk-show host, by returning to work the last week in September. "With 'Welcome Back, Mary' buttons and signs popping up everywhere and confetti showering her, the veteran actress was cheered by about one hundred fellow workers as she returned to television station KQED," Merina reported.

Though Martin had already taped fifty-two of the season's sixty-five programs before the accident, Jules Power felt it "would have looked ludicrous" to open "without acknowledging that the accident took place." A special edition of *Over Easy* was made on October 1, to be aired the following week. "For a change it's Mary not only as cohost but also as role model for much of the audience," said Power. "Within a week she suffered many of the changes that all of us do through the years: her own physical changes because of the accident, the loss of Ben Washer, an extremely close friend and associate, and Janet's impairment and probable long hospitalization."

"Her return [episode] is a homecoming, a family reunion and a thank-you note to the thousands who wished her well," claimed Ed Bark of the *Dallas Morning News,* who explained that she was joined on the program by Larry Hagman and Heller. "Dr. James Peterson, a soothing old-timer, also is on hand to talk about the importance of 'grief work' after a loved one is lost," continued Bark. "There are no deep revelations forthcoming, and Hagman at times seems to be uncomfortable. Martin, 68, says she remembers 'thankfully nothing' about the accident. Determined to recover quickly, she managed to block out the death of 'Uncle Ben' Washer until her hospital stay was over."

Ben Washer's last real job for Martin had been moving the two of them into a smaller home in the greater Palm Springs area, a three-bedroom condominium at 82 Princeton, in Rancho Mirage, where Washer had fixed up his own "suite." Martin would name the bar, in a corner of the new living room, "Uncle Ben's Saloon": "He always thought it was one of the prettiest words in the language," Martin explained.

"The house was in a new development, on a golf course, with a pool," recalled Louis Magor, who became Martin's musical director during this period. "It was a very nice tract house, with a big living room and an understated elegance—with just the 'right' pictures on the piano, of Mary with Queen Elizabeth and with Noël Coward. In the garage were cut-outs of her as Peter Pan. She was a real presence throughout. Over the bar was a large object made out of Ben's bow ties.

"There were also a couple of original Hirschfelds in the house, including one for *The Skin of Our Teeth,*" continued Magor. "And Heller's young daughter had taken a Crayola and written on it. And when Heller saw it, she went berserk. Mary said, 'just calm down.' Mary added a mitten of hers, and glued it to the poster, and then wrote [about what just happened], and signed it, 'Mary Martin.' She saw in children something that not many people see: she saw their potential. She was also a decorator. She knew how to wear stuff. She also knew how other people should dress."

The young Mary Martin, who did not know how to keep house or even make herself presentable when she married Richard Halliday more than forty years before, had, in other words, learned his lessons well and become very nearly the stylist her husband had been. "I remember once, in New York," continued Magor, "she had given Heller a lounging outfit. And Heller went up, put it on, and came down. She said, 'Ma, it looks *terrible!*' Mary just touched her, here and there, saying, 'cha-choo, cha-choo,' and repositioning a couple of things. And then it was exactly right."

A well-organized surprise party, originally planned by Washer, was held by a group of friends to celebrate Martin's sixty-ninth birthday, on Sunday, November 28, 1982, at her new home. The ruse involved taking the guest of honor to the opening of a new art gallery in Palm Springs, while others, including her nurse, Bea Kilgore, and neighbor Nelda Linsk, went to work decorating the house and arranging the catered food. Asked to arrive at 6:30, the prestigious guests included philanthropists Walter and Lenore Annenberg, wine merchants Robert and Margaret Mondavi, Jinx Falkenberg, Natalie Schafer, Mrs. Bob Hope, and Mrs. William Powell. Instead of "Happy Birthday," pianist Peter Mintun played "Hello, Dolly" on the piano as everyone sang "Hello, Mary" when she arrived at 7:00. Later in the evening, Martin and Alice Faye sang "Side by Side"—among other songs.

"As Mary said later, 'Well, I just felt like going home and putting my feet up and having a bowl of soup,'" recalled Mintun, who befriended Martin during this period. "But when she walked into her house, with all her friends there, singing, 'Hello, Mary . . . Well Hello, Mary . . . It's so nice to have you back where you belong,' she greeted every single person, warmly. And then she excused herself and went to her bedroom; and she came out with a Marc Jacobs quilted bed-jacket, looking refreshed, with a little powder and paint on her face.

"She said, 'You know, I just wish I were turning seventy, because sixty-nine just sounds so tacky.' Then, it was just hors d'oeuvres and buffet drinks, and I played the piano. Donald Corren, who eventually played the lead in *Torch Song Trilogy,* played the piano with me. We just met that night and became great friends. Alice [Faye] did some singing. And someone suggested Mary sing 'Never Land.' It almost seemed sacred. But she did. And here she was, she had recuperated from this fracture, and she actually sank into this yoga position on the carpet, and sang 'Never Never Land.' No one could have left that party without feeling like they had gotten some gift from Mary. It was a glorious event."

Despite the festivities, after many years of being haunted by her husband's death, Martin was now weighed down with relentless memories of the more recent taxi accident and its aftermath. "The worst comes around 3:30 in the morning," she told Bob Thomas of the *Philadelphia Inquirer.* "That's when I wake up and all the memories come back again. So I read or do needlepoint until I can go back to sleep again."

Martin also turned to work as a positive way to offset the grief and the natural fears that coincide with aging. Within three weeks of her surprise birthday party, she began shooting an episode of ABC's popular TV series, *The Love Boat,* which was designed for celebrities to make guest appearances in comedy vignettes. In the episode, called "So Help Me, Hanna," Martin portrays Hanna Harvey, a San Francisco boutique owner, who's described as "quite a whirlwind" and "Hurricane Hanna," with "a need to help everyone on the face of the earth." Hanna meets a former paramour, Jarvis (Max Showalter), on the "love boat," the *Pacific Princess,* and helps him reconcile to the fact that his son, Kent, wants to be a professional pianist, as opposed to a businessman. She also sings Cole Porter's "It's De-Lovely" and offers a jazzy, scat rendition of Chopin. But the episode proves little more than an opportunity for Martin to show up in one colorful ensemble after another for each of her half dozen or so scenes.

While she was shooting *The Love Boat,* Martin was approached by Lissa Levin, the producer of a new TV series, *Gloria,* which was a spin-off of *All in the Family,* starring Sally Struthers and character actor Burgess Meredith. Levin was all of eight years old in 1960 when she fell in love with *The Sound of Music* album and wrote Martin a letter, addressed to "the Lunt-Fontanne Theater." "I received a package in the mail including a lovely letter," recalled Levin, "production stills from the show, a picture of her in her dressing room and of her and Maria von Trapp. I remember taking it to show-and-tell." After she became a writer of *WKRP in Cincinnati*, Levin sent Martin another letter: "It basically said I had not given up my love of musical theater, and that the work I was doing was in part inspired by the humor and joy she brought to people in musical theater, and that she was my muse."

According to Levin, it was during a weekly Monday meeting for *Gloria* that "Burgess Meredith, out of the blue, said, 'You know, I'm an Irish tenor, and it's always been a dream of mine to sing a duet with Mary Martin.' And all the heads at the table turned to me, because my obsession with Mary Martin was very well known. And I said, 'Why don't we see if we can do a half-hour *musical* version of our show?'

"Mary Martin had recently had the accident and wanted to prove she was still active, so she was doing an episode of *The Love Boat*," continued Levin. "So the casting people at Embassy Tandem got in contact with her manager, and the manager conveyed that Mary Martin was interested. I went to what was then Twentieth Century–Fox [where *Love Boat* was being made], and I go to the soundstage, where I was waiting for a break in her rehearsal. When they were done, she came over to me and remembered full well that we had corresponded. . . . There was an area with a warehouse full of couches, from various sets. I sat down on one, and she gets upside down on the couch, with her legs hanging over the back, and her head hanging upside-down, very close to the floor. And she said, 'This is very good for me, to stretch my back.' And then she said, 'Okay, go. Tell me the story. What will the plot be for this half hour? And everything else about the songs.' I explained the plot line, and that she would sing a duet with Burgess, and that she would have a solo. And I described the nature of what the duet and the solo would be. And she loved everything about it.

"And she said, 'Done. Let's do it.' Then by week's end I found out that she had to back out, because, incredibly and coincidentally, Burgess Meredith lived next door to Larry Hagman in the Malibu colony, and Larry was building some kind of extension that was blocking out the sun over Burgess's deck; and Burgess was suing him for his 'place in the sun.' Mary Martin, who had had an estranged relationship with Larry Hagman for years but currently had a very nice relationship with him, did not want to compromise that. And she conveyed profuse apologies for not being able to go ahead with this."

Shortly after Christmas, Martin visited Janet Gaynor in the hospital. "When I saw her last week, she had pneumonia and a temperature of 104 and didn't remember that I had been there," Martin told Bob Thomas of the Associated Press. "But today [on the phone], she sounded just like Janet, and she talked about working with her walker. She said it pained her so much she had to bend over at a 90-degree angle. I assured her that I felt the same way when I started. But now I've thrown the walker away, and eventually so will she."

Though Martin had felt compelled to turn down the offer to appear in an episode of *Gloria,* the new year brought more tributes and invitations to which she could agree more readily. The erstwhile Nancy Davis was First Lady, and the Reagans invited Martin to cohost a special event at the White House with *Annie Get Your Gun* costar John Raitt and premiere violinist Itzhak Perlman. *In Performance at the White House* was held on the South Lawn on June 6, 1983, and featured "young" performers, including Judith Blazer, Liz Callaway, Michael Ross, and K. T. Sullivan.

Martin had a special fondness for Nancy Reagan, ever since she had gotten her a part in *Lute Song.* But according to Martin, she "stayed away" when Ronald Reagan first ran for the presidency in 1976. "I have stayed out of politics as much as I could, throughout the years," she explained. Then, after Reagan became president in 1980, "I had a special request from Nancy to come to a White House dinner for the president of Brazil and his wife," claimed Martin. "That was my first official visit to the Reagan White House [in 1982], and it was all because of my long love affair with Brazil, and our home there."

On September 15, 1983, Martin was Peter Mintun's special guest on his weekly WALW radio program in San Francisco, *Music in the Air,* featuring "original music of the 1920s and 1930s from the 'Top of the Mark' Hopkins Hotel." When Mintun played one of her early recordings of "My Heart Belongs to Daddy," Martin was prompted to talk about Sophie Tucker's providing pointers on how the song should be delivered. "For the rest of my life, Sophie came out of town, whenever I was trying out a show," Martin told Mintun. "She'd sit up in the balcony, and I wouldn't [even] know that she would be there. And then she'd come back[stage] and see me after, and say, 'Okay, you do this. You don't do that.' And she was always there, all her life."

When cued by Mintun, Martin made the surprising announcement that she was about to become an honorary Boy Scout. After actor Jimmy Stewart and his "darling" wife had been guests on *Over Easy,* she explained, Stewart sent Martin a letter, saying, "We want this to be a first: we want to make you a Boy Scout." "And having never wanted to be a Girl Scout, I just thought, what a marvelous idea," Martin told Mintun.

Martin's parents, who were counting on a son when Mary was born in 1913, would have been both elated and astonished when their daughter was made a Boy Scout, with James Stewart—the archetypal all-American Boy Scout himself—presiding at a special event in Los Angeles on December 1, her seventy-first birthday. The following month, in New York, Martin was declared an honorary Girl Scout, during a tribute to Mainbocher, who had designed the troops' outfits—as well as uniforms for the WAVES and the Women's Auxiliary of the Marine Corps. The Museum of the City of New York provided Martin with her wedding gown from *The Sound of Music*, also designed by Mainbocher, for her to wear at the Girl Scout Council of Greater New York's dinner "salute to the designer."

That same week Martin picked up an award for achievement in the arts, presented by the Northwood Institute and the Institute for Advanced Studies in Theater Arts at the famed Players Club in New York's Gramercy Park. She also made a side trip to Vermont to be with Maria von Trapp for the reopening of the family lodge, following a devastating fire. "She and I are very much alike," said Martin, to commemorate the occasion. "We're both accident-prone."

While she continued to cohost episodes of *Over Easy,* Martin found a new summer home at 480 Vallejo Street, on Russian Hill, where she resided from July through October, in 1984. "The apartment had wonderful bay windows, overlooking the hill," recalled Peter Mintun. "It belonged to Bob Lansdon and Ray Jones, who had moved to San Francisco from New York in the 1970s. They were always entertaining, and they liked to drop people's names a lot. Very often they would recruit people like myself, or Steve Ross, to play at their parties. They became very social as retirees. They had been in the PR business, in New York. They were avid cabaret and theatergoers." They also, according to Mintun, simply vacated the premises to make it available for Martin.

"She said she won't use a walking stick ('not until I have to') and she reported that four or five times a day she climbs five flights of San Francisco stairs for exercise," wrote Peter Stack in the *San Francisco Chronicle*. "I live four flights up," Martin explained. "The fifth flight is the hill I must walk up. I decided to live in San Francisco because of the hills. A person can always walk on the flatlands like in Palm Springs, but since I determined that the only way I was going to walk again was to go out there and walk, I figured I wanted to enjoy uphill, and downhill."

Martin was feeling fit enough to contact the Smithsonian and have them send her original Peter Pan harness and costume so she could fly again at a special benefit for the Trauma Center of San Francisco General Hospital. Featuring Robert Preston, John Raitt, Larry Hagman, Florence Henderson, Sammy Cahn, Billy Daniels, Arsenio Hall, Van Johnson, and Dolores Hope, *Mary Martin at Davies Hall: An Evening with Her Friends,* was months in the planning, for a single night of merriment, mishaps, and a mind-boggling Martin finale on October 22, 1984, in San Francisco's symphony space. The event raised $200,000.

While claiming that *Peter Pan* would be the "theme of the evening" ("via our advertising, lobby decorations, invitations, programs, plus certain elements in the show itself"), an internal memo for the event planners, dated June 11, claimed, "We have reason to believe that Janet Gaynor's health is such that she will be able to attend—and appear." Despite such a positive prognosis, Gaynor died on September 24, from injuries she sustained in the accident two years before.

"My assignment on the program was solely to create a musical tribute to Gaynor," recalled Peter Mintun. "First we played Max Steiner's *A Star Is Born* theme from Janet's movie of the same name. I spoke about Janet and her relationship to silent movies. Next the orchestra and I played 'Diane,' while a clip from her favorite film, *Seventh Heaven,* was projected above the orchestra. We also played the cheerful 'Sunnyside Up' from Janet's very successful, 1929 musical film of the same name. After I exited the stage, Bob Preston returned and announced that the San Francisco General Hospital would honor Gaynor's memory by naming a wing after her."

As directed by dancer and choreographer Miriam Nelson, the Monday evening, black-tie event opened with a dramatic and winning effect, when the entire orchestra rose on an elevator lift from the pit to stage level, with Martin in the middle. "When the glee club started singing, 'Cause it was Mary, Mary, Mary is a Grand Old Name,' Mary began appearing [first] to the audience in the balcony," recalled Nelson, in her memoir, *My Life Dancing with the Stars.* "They started applauding and yelling, which built tremendous excitement. . . . By the time Mary was in full view, the audience was on its feet, going wild. The orchestra started vamping 'My Heart Belongs to Daddy' . . . for quite a while before the audience had quieted down enough that Mary could start singing. When she finished, of course, the audience was back on its feet."

"As soon as she sang it, all worries about whether she can still sing flew out the window like Peter Pan," wrote Gerald Nachman, in his review of the evening in the *San Francisco Chronicle.* "The answer is an unapologetic yes. It's much the same voice—clear, winsome, warm, twinkling. . . . This wasn't just a love-in, it was a comeback."

Though Martin's "Honey Bun" number with Larry Hagman also went over "terrifically" well, "both she and John Raitt had problems with 'Anything You Can Do,'" according to Peter Mintun. Martin also, according to Louis Magor, the event's musical director and orchestra conductor, "had a hell of a time trading lines" with Florence Henderson on "My Favorite Things," since they both "had to break up a song they had done hundreds of time, and do it differently this time, sharing the lyrics." "It was quite a glamorous night, made no less memorable for the fact that much of it played like a dress rehearsal, with cast, orchestra and chorus frequently in the dark on how to proceed," responded Murry Frymer, in a review for the *San Jose Mercury News*.

"Mary had been concerned that Sammy Cahn might go on too long, because he'd written so many songs and had so many versions of them," Magor recalled. "But then, when it came to the show itself, she got the wrong series of costumes in the wrong order. There was a long stage wait, and it was Sammy Cahn who saved the show, by coming out and doing all of this material, and driving the audience crazy—they got a real treat. I remember saying to the audience, 'Mary will be right out,' and thinking to myself, 'God, I hope so.' It was this huge production for her, with no intermission, and only one rehearsal, that day."

Though what was announced as a ninety-minute event went on for nearly three hours, any missteps were more than forgiven when the stunned audience beheld Martin flying overhead and, sprinkling fairy dust on them, singing, "I'm Flying." Six weeks shy of her seventy-first birthday, and two years after the major accident that caused serious injuries to her pelvis, Martin defied more than just gravity. She defied family and friends—and perhaps even her own expectations—by taking to the air and flying as far as the balcony. For Martin, it was the proverbial dream come true. For everyone else, it was a monumental moment that, like the most special in life, transcended time and space. Once again, Mary Martin found that place in Never Land, "where dreams are born and time is never planned," for anyone fortunate enough to witness her remarkable flight.

Chapter 20

WHAT BECOMES A
LEGEND LEAST?

If once upon a time I was Audition Mary, now I am
Benefit Mary, going everywhere, meeting people, singing and
talking for causes.
—MARY MARTIN

"I have never been so happily busy in my life," Mary Martin wrote in
1984. "I have six grandchildren now, to fly with me through the many
exciting windows of our lives. The oldest, Heidi Kristina, was married
October 29, 1983, and I look forward to one day becoming a *great* grandmother. The youngest is Geoffrey DeMeritt, four, who manages to be as
busy all the time as his father, Bromley, is and his grandfather, Richard,
used to be. . . .

"In many ways the past ten years of my life have been like a roller
coaster—big, big highs and then deep, deep lows, like the automobile accident that took away my beloved friend Ben Washer and left my Janet,
Janet Gaynor, so hurt and ill. Partly because of that, partly because of all
I learned being cohost of the television program *Over Easy,* I am now into
causes. If once upon a time I was Audition Mary, now I am Benefit Mary,
going everywhere, meeting people, singing and talking for causes."

Martin's words here appeared in the first of five new chapters she wrote
for an updated edition of her memoir, *My Heart Belongs,* which William
Morrow brought out as a Quill trade paperback edition in 1984. Martin's emphasis in these chapters on developments in her personal life reflected the importance that her family now had in her day-to-day
thoughts and existence. It's telling that, in thirty-nine new pages of text,
she didn't even bother to mention that she had costarred in a Broadway
play (albeit a flop, *Do You Turn Somersaults?*) since her memoir was originally published in 1976.

Like the song that was written with Martin in mind—and the phrase
that, perhaps better than any other, described who she really was—in
true "cockeyed optimist" fashion, Martin simply chose to ignore the

more unpleasant developments in her life. She certainly didn't dwell on unhappy memories—especially when her life was overflowing with so many fortuitous ones.

It is also revealing that younger people, whom Martin was now working with, viewed her in more of a parental role than anyone had tended to before. In the absence of Richard Halliday telling her what to do, or how to do it, and in the course of embracing the roles of mother and grandmother, it was as if Mary Martin finally, well into the sixth decade of her life, grew up. "Mary Martin was so incredibly gracious and funny and motherly," recalled Louis Magor. "She would hold you in a special way when you took a picture with her. You felt like she was protecting you and taking care of you. Whenever I stayed with her in Palm Springs, I felt taken care of.

"We went swimming all the time after dinner in Palm Springs," continued Magor. "The first time I went swimming there, she gave me Ethel Merman's robe, from their [recent] performance together. When we would go to a restaurant, she would always be sitting facing the restaurant, so people could see her. At hotels, she would take periodic walks, so people could visit with her. I remember once, in Rancho Mirage, a lady from the Midwest came over and was just bowled over that she was talking to Mary Martin: they had been chatting like old girlfriends. And afterwards, when I said, 'Mary, do you know how good you made that woman feel?' she said, 'Do you know how good that woman made me feel?'"

Magor also remembered a specific development when he was putting together the event at San Francisco's Davies Hall, on October 22, 1984, which demonstrates just how much Martin had evolved as a take-charge person. Having discovered the orchestral score for some of the evening's songs in Martin's personal files, Magor realized, the day before the performance, that he only had the parts for the viola and percussion and needed to get the rest of the thirty-piece orchestra's sheet music transcribed—"on my own dime," he said.

"Well, I had wanted to get this done without bothering Mary.... When I went to her dressing room the next day, Mary said, 'Oh honey, I'm so sorry. You should have come to me first.' She said, 'When you make a mistake, always come to me, because, first of all, I can tell you whether it's important or not. Second of all, I can fix it, if it is.'" This was not the Mary Martin of yore, who, flustered by any disturbance or upset, had Richard Halliday, and then Ben Washer, see to every problem.

With Louis Magor helping to put it together, Martin gave a concert in

Milwaukee, on May 30, 1985. "As a matter of fact, the Milwaukee Symphony tried to cancel the performance, because it wasn't selling," recalled Magor. "They want me to cancel," Martin told Magor. "I will not cancel, because I do not do that. But if they insist, I'll see to it that no one I know, or who knows me, will ever work there, either."

Though the Milwaukee Symphony proceeded with the concert, there were a good number of unsold seats when, the day or so before the event, Martin discovered a useful way to unload them. "We were staying in the Hyatt, and we were rehearsing that morning, when a very attractive woman came up to her and said, 'Peter Pan—we love you,'" recalled Magor. "She was the wife of a well-known TV personality, and she was there as a guest of the 'Battered Women of Wisconsin.' She was about to go in and give a lecture on how to improve their lives. We had seen these women in the elevators: these were down-and-out people who were searching for an answer to their troubles."

When they learned that there were 250 people in the group, Magor and Hampton conferred with Martin and her assistant, Gene Kilgore, who arranged for the tickets to be given to the women. "After the concert that night, Mary waited and signed all those women's programs," recalled Magor. "That's what happened when you were with Mary Martin."

Martin was back in New York three days later, in time for the thirty-ninth annual Tony Awards, on June 2, where she presented a special Tony to her *Lute Song* costar, Yul Brynner. While clearly reading the teleprompter, Martin sang "Getting to Know Him" to the tune of "Getting to Know You," as Brynner was specifically being celebrated for his 4,600th performance in *The King and I*. Though he was in failing health, Brynner looked every bit the king, and his acceptance was remarkably succinct: "I'm not going to make a long speech. I just want to thank Mary Martin—for everything," he said, prompting hints of laughter from the audience. "And Dick and Oscar, Rodgers and Hammerstein. I also want to thank Yul Brynner: he turned out all right, after all. Thank you very much."

Though Bea Kilgore's brother Gene had come to serve as a temporary aid for Martin, the loss of Ben Washer, who had made all arrangements and looked after things for her after Halliday's passing, proved a particular blow to Martin. Feeling like a widow all over again, Martin found comfort by spending her summer of 1985 in London with Dickey Quayle and Electra Biggs, two other well-heeled widows, who related to suddenly being on their own, as it were, and having to learn to manage quotidian matters they always used to take for granted.

A year older than Martin and sixteen years older than Dickey Quayle, Electra Waggoner Biggs was a Texas-born sculptor, socialite, and heiress, whose family ranch would sell for $725 million in 2014. "Because of the fact that she was such a wealthy woman who had servants all her life, she expected everyone to do everything for her," reported Dickey Quayle's daughter, Marky. "The 'Electra Buick' was even named after her. Anyway, she expected Mom to be her personal aide when they were traveling."

For their London vacation, Martin rented a house on Clabon Mews, off of Cadogan Square, in Belgravia: "As smart as you can get, in London," claimed Christopher Kyd, who ran a "car-hire" business and became Martin's regular driver during her stay that summer. "It had been stables for horses and for the grooms. Now, of course, they're very chic houses. It was very nice. Not glitzy at all, but a very nice three-bedroom house."

With London as their home base, the three widowed musketeers made side trips to Venice and Belgium, and toured the West Country of England for four or five days. In the West End, they saw Lauren Bacall in *Sweet Bird of Youth* as well as Vanessa Redgrave in a revival of *The Seagull*. They also visited with Martin's *Do You Turn Somersaults?* costar, Anthony Quayle. "Mary took a picture of my mother and Anthony Quayle at his house in London," recalled Marky Quayle. "He was a distant cousin of my dad's—they both came from the Isle of Man. When Mary took a picture of my mother hugging him, Anthony said, 'We Quayles have to stick together.'"

"I remember, when I had to pick her up, I had been told it was Mary Martin," recalled Christopher Kyd, the chauffeur. "But I wasn't going to say anything at all about who she was. She was quiet. But then she said, 'Do you ever go to the theater?' And I said, 'As a matter of fact, I saw you the first night of *South Pacific* at Drury Lane,' whereupon she warmed to me, and we then got on very well, indeed. She told me that she had stayed at the Savoy Hotel when she was in *South Pacific*. And she told me how she used to love the fruitsellers shouting out to her at Covent Garden, when she was going back to the theater on her matinee days, 'Hi, Mary. How are you, darling?' They all recognized her."

"As with all divas, she was quite self-centered, but she was very nice," continued Kyd. "She got along absolutely fine with her friends, but she was definitely the boss, even if she wasn't bossy. Still, she had to be looked after. They had to do everything, handling the money, booking me. . . . She wasn't used to doing anything for herself."

Shortly after she returned to the States, a major tribute for Martin's life and career was held on Sunday, October 20, at Broadway's Shubert Theatre in New York, where *A Chorus Line* had been ensconced for more than a decade. Martin arrived the previous Wednesday in New York, where she stayed in a canary-yellow suite at the Wyndham Hotel. ("She always stayed in 1101," said Louis Magor. "She loved the service there.") Martin appeared the next morning on the *Today Show,* heralding the upcoming tribute. When Jane Pauley said, "But the most exciting thing, I hear you're coming back to Broadway in a new play!" her guest would only go so far as to allow, "Well, we're talking about it," without even mentioning that it was a comedy called *Legends,* by popular novelist James Kirkwood, best known as the book writer of *A Chorus Line.*

That afternoon, Martin taped her contribution to a PBS documentary on Irving Berlin. She also had dinner at Petrossian, an upscale Russian restaurant on West Fifty-eighth Street at Seventh Avenue, with Heller and Maj. Larry Hagman was directing an episode of *Dallas* that weekend, which precluded his attendance at either the dinner or the upcoming tribute to his mother.

Our Hearts Belong to Mary cost $300 a ticket, with the proceeds benefiting the Friends of the Theater Collection of the Museum of the City of New York. The show opened with a spotlight on Martin and her *Lute Song* costar, First Lady Nancy Reagan, in a stage-left box, kissing and embracing as their picture was being taken. In addition to singing "Before the Parade Passes By," Martin performed duets with Heller (Cole Porter's "True Love") and with Nancy Reagan ("Mountain High, Valley Low," from *Lute Song*). John Raitt offered "Some Enchanted Evening" and Robert Preston "My Cup Runneth Over" from *I Do! I Do!* Carol Channing performed a takeoff of "My Heart Belongs to Daddy" with songwriter Jerry Herman, who wrote new lyrics for the occasion. There were also filmed interludes of Martin's brilliant fashion spoof, "The Shape," from the 1953 *Ford 50th Anniversary Show,* and of her flying as Peter Pan.

Other performers and participants that night included Sandy Duncan, Lillian Gish, George Abbott, Van Johnson, Mayor Koch, and Maureen McGovern, who sang "Never Land." Josh Logan recited a poem, and Helen Hayes reminisced about strolling in Paris with Martin, where they were performing together in *The Skin of Our Teeth,* when an overhead bird made an unwelcome deposit on her companion. "I was very frightened," Hayes recounted. "I thought, 'What do I do when she faints?' And I looked at her and she turned and looked at me and said, 'For some people, they sing.'"

Though he was unable to participate in the event in person, Larry Hagman prepared a filmed "salute" to his mother. Dressed in a suit, delivering a more-or-less formal tribute, he introduced some levity by falling face-forward into a pool of water at the end. Though it required a lot of behind-the-scenes subterfuge, Maria von Trapp was presented as a surprise to Martin. "We had to keep her from Mary," recalled Louis Magor, the program's musical director. "We sequestered her in one of the dressing rooms. She arrived in a dirndl. And after I did that, I thought to myself, 'My God. I just asked Maria Von Trapp to hide—again.'"

While Martin was in New York for *Our Hearts Belong to Mary,* she met with Carol Channing to talk about *Legends,* the upcoming play about rival stars they would be doing together. Martin also got together with her new friend Susan Grushkin. Claiming "there's a huge difference between being a fan and having admiration for someone," Grushkin shuns the notion of having been a "fan" of Martin's. But regardless of terminology, Grushkin was a major Martin enthusiast when she was studying ballet at New York's High School of the Performing Arts and injured her back.

"I needed something to keep me sane," Grushkin recalled. "I happened to be in a bookshop with my mother, and I found the needlepoint book that [Martin] and her husband Richard had written. And it was only because her name was on it that I bought it. I taught myself to stitch, thanks to the instructions in her book. I sent her my first pillow, as a thank-you, and she sent me a beautiful letter in return. I didn't know it, but it was just at the time that Richard had died. It was just the most beautiful letter, telling me what a comfort the pillow was."

Grushkin first met Martin at a book signing in New York, when *My Heart Belongs* was initially published in 1976. It was after Grushkin heard about Martin's taxi accident that she decided she had to make something special for her. "I wanted her to know that I was thinking of her," said Grushkin. "I decided it had to be needlepoint, and I knew she loved to read. So I put them together, in the form of a book: scenes from shows she had done, and words to her favorite songs and to mine, in needlepoint and petit point. Having gotten a little carried away, it took [me] nine months to complete. The first book had twelve 'pages,' including the two covers. And there are two more volumes that she wanted some day to be in the Smithsonian. For *South Pacific,* I stitched a bottle of Prell [shampoo] and a bar of Ivory soap, with which she used to wash her hair. . . . For *Annie Get Your Gun,* I did her on the horse. For *One Touch of Venus,* I did her in the chair, with the Mainbocher negligée. . . . I stitched the bed from *I Do! I Do!*"

Grushkin sent her first volume of needlepoint "pages" to Martin in Palm Springs. "She called me, on Christmas morning, when she got it," continued Grushkin. "She was with Max Showalter [Martin's *Love Boat* costar]. She and Dorothy Hammerstein were the only women who were there. But that's what really brought us together, officially."

Two years later, Martin invited Grushkin to have breakfast with her and her conductor, Louis Magor. "She was here in New York, for *Our Hearts Belong to Mary.* She wanted to talk about the book *Only the Best,* by Stuart Jacobson [which featured Grushkin's needlepoint book], and my book as well. She asked me if I wanted to go on the road with her and *Legends.* I said, 'But I've never done anything like this. I'm trained as a dancer.' She said, 'You'll learn as you go.' And I thought for a second, and I said, 'Sure. Why not.' I mean, how could you give up a chance like that? I had no idea what I was getting into, but I wasn't about to say no."

Susan Grushkin became Martin's live-in helpmate and companion for the rest of Martin's life. "I've always felt like she wanted to make me over," Grushkin further recalled. "Because I had this long braid, long hair parted in the center. We were on the road [with *Legends*] when she made it shorter."

"It wasn't work," Grushkin also said. "We were having fun together. We were making each other's lives work. She had a housekeeper watching everything while we were away. I would keep in touch with all that. I rehearsed some lines with her, but she had somebody else really working full time on that. In the beginning, my responsibilities were very limited. But then it all grew, as time moved on. In addition to working as her assistant, Mary treated me as a friend and second daughter. She helped me to believe in myself and taught me so much, for which I will always be grateful."

"I don't think Suzy knew what should happen or shouldn't happen, at first," recalled James Kabel, wardrobe supervisor and Martin's hairdresser throughout the upcoming *Legends* tour, "because she was so young. She was 'Suzy.' But then, as the show progressed, over many, many weeks, Suzy's hair got shorter and more blonde. She got rid of the frumpy clothes and started dressing more chic. That was all very apparent. As was Susan's managing of Mary: the finesse became better and better. It was really quite remarkable."

Martin took pride in refashioning Susan Grushkin—if not exactly in her own image, at least in the ways that Richard Halliday had remade and, in a sense, manufactured Martin. It was, perhaps, Halliday's second greatest lesson and legacy, after Martin herself.

While reminding more than one commentator of the off-camera feud between Bette Davis and Joan Crawford, James Kirkwood's play *Legends* concerns two has-been movie icons and archrivals who are invited to make their comeback by costarring in an Off Broadway show, called, no less, *Star Wars: The Play*. This means that, for the first time in their lives, the bitchy and crass Sylvia Glenn (Carol Channing) and the Goody Two–shoes Leatrice Monsee (Martin) have to get along with each other. "I hope she looks like Sam Jaffe in *Gunga Din*," Sylvia says of Leatrice, whose name alone suggests prim and proper airs as well as the moral high ground. After Leatrice arrives in an elegant, fur-trimmed cape, offset by a large black feathered hat, sporting an orange crop of hair underneath, Sylvia asks, "What is that color—Greer Garson pink?"

Leatrice, of course, has another side that belies her refinement. In a typical exchange, when Sylvia says, "You were forever playing nurses and nuns and saints and I was stuck playing tramps," Leatrice replies, "That was not my fault. It was typecasting." Or as Leatrice, when asked if she wants a drink, also says: "Gin, on the rocks. But please, don't make it too strong."

Legends would prove something of an embarrassment for all concerned, not because two real Broadway *legends* were playing over-the-hill stars eager for a last hurrah, but because the play is so flimsy, the dialogue so predictable and banal. Nothing can disguise or compensate for the inevitable conclusion that the script is a one-note bitchfest trying to fashion a full-length play out of occasionally witty, if relentlessly catty, remarks and rejoinders.

As conceived by Kirkwood, *Legends* is a vehicle for two aging actresses with nowhere to go. Perhaps because it evokes a poor man's version of Neil Simon's *The Sunshine Boys*, Martin kept saying no to Kirkwood and *Legends,* until Larry Hagman finally, in the fall of 1985, compelled his mother to go ahead with the project. "I really think it's funny," he told Martin. "I think it's touching, and I think it's time you got back to work. I think you've been off long enough." Hagman even became a behind-the-scenes producer, "which is rare," Martin would divulge a couple years after the fact, "because one thing Mr. Larry Hagman is very careful about is where his money goes."

In his early attempts to woo Martin, Kirkwood resorted to a highly theatrical gesture by dipping the palm side of his hand in stage blood, and then imprinting the script's title page with his handprint, conveying to Martin the depth of his passion for her participation. "She didn't know it was fake blood," claimed Elliott Sirkin. "She thought he really had cut his own palm open for her, and that really got to her. The impression she gave me is it was one of the reasons she agreed to do the show."

Only later would Martin also confide that, after seeing Claudette Colbert and Rex Harrison in a Broadway revival of Frederick Lonsdale's *Aren't We All?*, she thought to herself: "If Claudette could do it, I could go back to work, too." According to Kirkwood, Colbert specifically encouraged Martin to take on *Legends*. In retrospect, the Colbert connection seems something other than mere coincidence in at least two respects: the English Clifford Williams, who directed the revival of *Aren't We All?*, was also the director of *Legends,* and, during her two years as a contract player at Paramount at the beginning of her career, many felt Martin was, in fact, made to look like Colbert.

But at various times in recent years, Martin claimed she would never do another Broadway show: "I'd want to be in top form and I couldn't be," she told a reporter in 1980. "The idea of pushing that hard doesn't intrigue me." Two years later, when she appeared in an episode of *Love Boat* and there was "talk that her character might be expanded to create a new series," Martin told Bob Thomas for an Associated Press story, "I don't know about doing a series. . . . That's not child's play. Nor is going back to the theater. I don't think I would be able to face a show every night and twice on Wednesdays and Saturdays."

Though she probably never made the connection, Martin's reluctance to take on *Legends* became something of a self-fulfilling prophecy for failure. "My mother always told me, 'Let your conscience be your guide,'" she said to Arthur Unger for a feature story in the *Christian Science Monitor* in 1979, echoing a sentiment she had recently included in her memoir. "I'm sure everybody had a mother like that who said things like that," she also told Unger. "But I took mine seriously. And it was just in me all my life. Every time I've gone against what my conscience told me, what's inside my head, something I knew I shouldn't be doing, it has been wrong."

Martin's involvement with *Legends* was doomed, in other words, from the beginning. But even if the part of Leatrice had been custom-made for her, as James Kirkwood claimed, when Martin first read the script in April, inexplicably and ironically she assumed she would be playing Sylvia, whose dialogue is riddled with the type of four-letter words that Martin refused to say off or on any stage. As soon as Martin shared her mistaken assumption with Kirkwood, he told her: "Well, you've always had a rather sweet image, an image of a total professional, who doesn't swear or carouse but who's still been rather canny about her career, and that's Leatrice."

Yet another observation of Kirkwood's suggests that the more complicated and contradictory impression Martin made at the very beginning of her career, with "My Heart Belongs to Daddy," remained until the end: "Mary struck me as being down to earth, eminently likable, fun; beneath the exterior and the reputation, there seemed to lurk a slight bawdy streak. My mother would have described it as 'Naughty—you know, underneath she's got a naughty little something and it's delicious.'"

Such was Kirkwood's claim in *Diary of a Mad Playwright,* a delectable chronicle of the fraught development of *Legends* and of its tormented, yearlong tour of the United States on its turbulent road to Broadway. As many a theater insider observed, when it was published in 1989, Kirkwood's *Diary* was one of the most telling books about the funny and tragic business of putting on a play, made all the more harrowing because the play, about the clash of two theatrical titans, starred two theatrical titans. With Martin cast as Leatrice, Kirkwood considered Ginger Rogers, Eve Arden, Maggie Smith, Elizabeth Taylor, and Irene Worth as her co-star, before going with Martin's own choice of Carol Channing for Sylvia. (As Martin would tell Janice Arkatov of the *Los Angeles Times*: "They kept sending me the play—and finally just wore me down. I said, if they could just get my good friend Carol. . . . Whether we like it or not, by this time, we *are* legends.")

But then, true to the characters they were playing, Channing would sometimes do all she could to undermine Martin's tenuous grasp on her part during the stressful tour of *Legends.* After opening in Dallas, on January 9, 1986, when Martin was still grappling with her lines and when they were about to move on to the Ahmanson Theatre in "beautiful downtown Los Angeles," the following appeared as a "Page Six" item, via Cindy Adams, in the *New York Post*: "Sunday, while being honored by the city of Dallas, Carol was asked, 'Where is Mary Martin?' Quicker than you could say 'putdown,' she quipped: 'She is in her hotel room learning her lines.'"

As early as December 13, when they were still in rehearsals in Los

Angeles, Martin told Janice Arkatov, "I wanted to learn the script before we started, but there wasn't time. We're on *constantly,* and learning the words, figuring out where to move is like patting your head and rubbing your stomach: 'Where do I move now, what's the word?' It annoys me not to have it at my fingertips."

In view of her continuing problems with her lines even after opening in Dallas, Martin threatened to quit early in the tour. She later claimed Helen Hayes was instrumental in her decision not to: "She called the minute she found out what trouble I was having and said, 'Don't quit now, just keep on exercising your gift,'" Martin claimed. "Helen told me how much she regretted having stopped acting on the stage; now, having been away from it so long, she doesn't feel she can ever go back." Larry and Maj also gave Martin "a pep talk" and Maj even "stayed with me at my hotel for an entire week."

"Gossip about *Legends* was everywhere," claimed playwright Terrence McNally, "and, as gossip goes, it was pretty heady stuff." Martin's problems with memorizing her lines became the biggest news on the Rialto in years. It also led to Martin wearing a hearing device to feed her all of her lines during the performance. "It was Nancy Reagan who recommended the ear bug to Mary," recalled James Kabel. "According to Mary, Nancy said, 'This is what they use on Ronnie.' Prior to that, they had announced that Ronald Reagan was going to start wearing a hearing aid. Well, within a day, the equipment was flown in to Dallas. They put it in Mary's ear, and it was like a bird suddenly taking to flight. She knew the lines, all she needed was the first word or two."

The hearing device created problems of its own, however: once, in Los Angeles, during the second act, "her ear bug cut out and she was not able to get her lines," recalled Kirkwood. "I cannot describe what a muddle ensued. Mary dipped back into the first act for a while; Carol got that wild look in her eyes as she tried to keep the train on the track. And when the insults between the two ladies are supposed to fly at the end of the play, it was incredible. Mary would take the beginning of one insult and tack it on to the end of another, so that it made no sense at all. The play came completely unglued."

Even more incredible was a performance in Phoenix, half a year into the tour, when, "toward the end of the first act, Mary started receiving taxicab dispatch calls in her ear," Kirkwood also reported. "The frequencies got all mixed up and she was getting calls to send out *taxis*! The crew did everything they could to try to change or fix the frequencies, but nothing worked, so they just had to take the goddamn thing out of her ear in the intermission."

"Yes, she heard the taxi calls one night, and threw the earpiece at me to hold," recalled Susan Grushkin. "But isn't it wonderful that she made it work with the most positive attitude towards everybody and having to deal with all the nonsense going on?"

"Sure enough, Mary was getting those taxi calls during act 1 in Phoenix, and you saw her reach up and take the thing out of her ear," added James Kabel. "She was flying solo for the first time, and she was nailing it. And you could see the hurdle, the achievement of 'I got it now.' They flew the prompter home that night. They essentially said to her, 'If you could do it now, you're gonna do it.' She took the leap off the diving board, and from that point the performance level shot so high, because she was really in the moment. And the old magic was suddenly there, in Phoenix."

But also, according to Kabel, from the very beginning, "Once she hit the stage with the audience out there, there was the real *legend* at work," he said, referring to Martin's delayed entrance in the play, about ten minutes into the first act. "The magic of how she embraced the audience—it's almost like she was winking at them and saying, 'We're all one. We're all together.' Somehow, she got them within her first few entrance lines. The transformation was marvelous."

Explaining that "this is one of the old girls' road techniques," Martin traveled with her personal trifold makeup mirror. "Each week if you get a different mirror, you don't know what you're looking at," she told Kabel. "If you travel with your own, that sits eighteen inches away from you every week, you know exactly what you're getting." Martin's makeup table also always displayed the same photo of herself nestled in Halliday's arms. "She occasionally commented about it," said Kabel: "How much she missed him . . . the sadness of his not being there anymore to take care of her on this journey of *Legends*. There's something about being a hairdresser on a show. It's a very intimate moment with most stars, and they tend to let their guard down and become very intimate with you."

Since the reviews that greeted *Legends*—in practically every city it played—were at best tepid, James Kirkwood felt compelled to rework the script during much of the tour. When they reached San Francisco, where *Legends* opened at the Curran Theatre on April 25, "Larry Hagman was suddenly around a lot," according to James Kabel. "That's when the arguments about replacing Clifford [Williams] as the director surfaced. Clifford was working on a show in London, and couldn't make it over for more stagings, so Larry Hagman took over and worked the new dialogue into the production. And I remember Carol saying backstage, 'Thank God, we've got a real director now.' And Larry was beaming."

In her memoir, Channing wouldn't even deign to refer to Clifford Williams by name. "In rehearsal we had an English director," wrote Channing, as she went on to corroborate Kabel's memory of Hagman taking over. "But you know who we got later for a director? Mary's son, Larry Hagman, and he was superb. He played no favorites with us. He has a fine divining rod as a director. It comes from being basically an actor. We all know those are the best live theatre directors."

"San Francisco was a crucial opening because it was Carol's hometown and Mary's adopted town," Kabel continued. "So the energy going in was crucial. There was great anxiety about getting it opened in San Francisco, and what the reviews would be. I also remember [the female impersonator] Charles Pierce coming by backstage, probably in San Francisco, to meet and greet the girls. And Carol asked him, 'How do you do your Bette Davis?' So here was this famous drag queen teaching Carol Channing his Bette Davis mannerisms, so she could use them in the show."

According to Kirkwood, when he read the notice in the *San Francisco Chronicle,* "Gerald Nachman said the show had improved since he'd seen it in Los Angeles but he was still not strewing roses in my path. The other reviews were mixed, but some from surrounding cities were very heartening."

Also according to Kirkwood, it was in San Francisco that he began "hearing rumors that Mary and Larry Hagman were grumbling about my royalties," prompting him to write the following letter, addressed to "Dear Mary": "Just a brief note. There seems to be a lot of talk going around about my royalties. So you and Larry understand, I came down from my contracted ten percent to eight percent when you wished to do only seven performances a week instead of the usual eight. In addition to this I either waived or deferred royalties for the last three weeks of the Los Angeles run and I have also agreed not to take anything in San Francisco until we have passed our operating costs. I believe I have been entirely fair and hope this will set to rest all this talk of unreasonable pay for the author."

In the absence of Halliday or even Ben Washer to negotiate Martin's contract, Channing and her husband and manager, Charles Lowe, reportedly looked after her concerns. "Being the shrewd business people they are, Carol and Charles knew that if Mary left the show, there would be no show," claimed James Kabel. "So they said, 'Let's do what we can to take her under our wing and help in the process of surviving this event.'

"Carol had signed a 'favored nations' deal with Mary," Kabel further explained. "Whatever one star would get, the other would get. Most big stars were getting around $15,000 to $20,000 a week at the time. And when the contract came to Carol, it was for only $10,000, plus, I think, two percent of the royalties. But then the producers were ruthless with the ladies, and they weren't getting their royalty payments, which is the big reason they ultimately left the show. But they started to realize that if they joined forces together, 'united they stand, divided they fall.' So they really became trusted friends."

During the extended tour of *Legends,* there were, of course, any number of funny if harrowing moments offstage as well as on. In Portland, Oregon, the theater had a fifth-floor rehearsal room where Martin was warming up one day. When Grushkin went to fetch Martin and walk her down to her dressing room prior to the performance, there was no sign of Martin. Martin had inadvertently exited via the fire exit, only to have the door close and lock behind her, forcing Martin to wend her way down the fire escape to the street, where she had trouble locating the theater entrance. "We eventually found her roaming around and got her inside," said Kabel.

In Boston, when Martin learned they were cutting Leatrice's lengthy, motivational mastectomy monologue ("It was a character speech to allow Leatrice to have some real heart, as to why she was who she was," explained Kabel), she said, "I don't need to work. I don't ever have to work again. I wanted to quit in Dallas, but I stuck with it and I worked on and on and now I know it and I like doing that speech, it means a lot to me. . . . This is a very rare moment in my professional career. Not only is the speech ruined for me, but also the play is ruined for me. . . . I will not play London and I will not come to New York. I'll fulfill my contract, and then you can get someone else and cut anything you want."

"Mary essentially said, 'If the speech is cut, I'm cut,'" according to Kabel. "She went into her dressing room and locked the door. I got there about six thirty to do the wigs, and Suzy [Grushkin] came down to commiserate, saying 'Bad day. Bad day.' Nobody knew if she was going to do the show or not. Well, they called 'half hour,' and I went up with the wig. I knocked on the door, and she said, 'Who is it?' 'It's James.' 'Come in.' The door unlocked and they let me in. They locked the door. I said, 'Mary, are we doing the show tonight?' 'Oh yes, of course. But don't tell them.' She was going to keep them waiting." Though reports would emerge that

Martin quit *Legends* because the monologue had been cut, it remained in the show for the duration of the tour—the following four months.

Kabel also said that an ongoing problem was that Martin and Channing "had two very different techniques of comedy. The first several fights they had were over costumes and comic timing. Carol believes you have to wait for the laugh to go down, so that the audience can hear the next line. Mary's style was skipping a stone across a pond—always at the peak of a laugh, you keep them laughing—you don't let the laugh die. . . . There's the famous story, when they both had their body mics on, and Carol turned to Mary, right in the middle of the show, and said, 'Well you killed that laugh.' And Mary said, 'Is that a line?'"

"Toward the end of August, just before the move from Washington [DC] to Philadelphia, I got a report," recalled James Kirkwood, "that Carol was once again correcting Mary on stage. . . . Mary swore she'd leave in January and said she would never think of coming to New York 'with that woman.'"

Though Martin's difficulties with her lines evidently returned on occasion, once she was without her hearing device, there was every expectation that the show would get a boost in national attention when "Ron and Nancy, old friends of Mary's" would attend the opening night in Washington, DC, on August 13, 1986. But following Boston, word had reached the White House that both Martin's and Channing's characters inadvertently get high on hashish brownies during the play's second act. And since Nancy Reagan had "only a month or so before this" launched her notorious—and, many felt, self-defeating—"Just Say No" to drugs campaign, the Reagans felt they had to stay away. "So they were not only not coming to the opening night," Kirkwood would write in his *Diary of a Mad Playwright*, "they were not coming, period. Instead, Mary was going to have breakfast at the White House."

Nor was it lost on many of the Reagans' critics at the time that Nancy's censorious antidrug crusade coincided with her husband's shameful neglect of the impact AIDS was having on the country, not to mention the world. (Playwright and number one AIDS activist Larry Kramer was even inspired to write *Just Say No,* a scathing, satirical play on the matter.) Sadly, as James Kabel would point out several decades later, the *Legends* company "lost four or five people to AIDS, including the producers and Kirkwood," whose *Diary of a Mad Playwright* was, in fact, published posthumously.

"Legends was a very *Rashomon* experience," claimed publicist Josh Ellis, who worked for the firm Solters and Roskin, which managed Carol

Channing, and who caught up with the production in Philadelphia, New Orleans, and San Francisco. "We'll never know what really happened or how. Kirkwood had his version of it. Carol had her version of it. But it wasn't a good choice. Carol and Mary's temperaments don't match. Their ways of learning a script don't match. It was very different from one city to the next. As two personalities, they didn't mesh. . . . They had very different modes of comedy: their tempos weren't working. It was never a good volley, and that's really both participants' problem. It was the combination of not being able to volley and not having particularly funny lines with which to volley. Some of the lines were just deadly. And I imagine both actresses were trying to figure out 'how.' How are we going to make something that's not particularly funny funnier? And how do we take two people who are vicious to one another and still [have them] be liked by the audience?"

Elliott Sirkin recalled sending Martin a letter after meeting with her in Philadelphia, where he saw *Legends,* and where she mentioned that she had considered quitting the show instead of bringing it in to New York. "Basically, I told her that while I thought the audience in Philadelphia was glad to see her, and that the way she used pantomime made me think a bit of Keaton and Chaplin, the play itself was—like the author's hand—a bloody mess. I concluded by telling her how much I had enjoyed our recent time together, and that whatever decision she made about staying in the play or leaving it, I was sure it would be the right one. The decision she made to get out, I think, really was the right one, but I also thought it was very important that she make the decision for herself. I was blown over by the emotion and the ecstatic gratitude of her letter in reply. It wasn't until then that I really realized how deep her emotions ran, and how easily they could swallow you up if you weren't another Ezio Pinza or Noël Coward.

"She may have discussed her decision with other people," continued Sirkin, "but I'm really pretty sure I was the catalyst, and I've never regretted it. It would have been catastrophic to end such a distinguished career in such misogynistic drivel."

Following Philadelphia, *Legends* played Cleveland, Chicago, St. Louis, and Atlanta, before culminating its tour in the producer "Zev Bufman's circuit" in Florida, including Orlando, St. Petersburg, Miami, Fort Lauderdale, and Palm Beach. Once Martin announced she would be leaving *Legends* after her final contractual obligation in Florida, James Kirkwood wrote both of his stars a joint letter, imploring them to continue on to New York. "Everybody I talk to in the theatrical community here—and that's a lot of people—is saying: 'What the (excuse the F-word, Mary, but that's what they say) fuck is the matter with you/them/it/the producers?' Why do they say this: BECAUSE this is the one season you'd clean up in New York. There is nothing to see. People come to town and there's ME AND MY GAL, and a couple of others—A COUPLE—coming in and that's it. Empty theaters up the kazoo and people dying to be entertained. I'm now beginning to get requests for house seats for *A Chorus Line* AGAIN after twelve years! . . . So what if some of the critics jump on the playwright. No one ever gives a flying hoot in hell about him anyway. I don't even. I'm up for it—only because I know they wouldn't dump on you two. That would be like defecating on the crossed flags of Britain *and* the United States in front of the White House with the Supreme Court looking on."

According to Dena Kleiman, who spoke to both of the stars for a story in the *New York Times,* after the show's closing was announced, "Miss Martin and Miss Channing admit their stylistic differences but insist that their affection and admiration for each other continue and that tensions between them have absolutely nothing to do with their decisions to leave the show."

In the end, *Legends* failed to fully pay back its initial one-million-dollar investment, but it would appear as if there might have been some creative bookkeeping involved in accounting for the weekly profits and expenses throughout the tour. (In Portland, Oregon, reportedly $120,000 was "stolen from the box office.") Also in the end, Kirkwood would put the blame on Martin for only giving seven performances a week: "If we had played eight performances a week at a lo-ball [*sic*] figure of $25,000 per each eighth performance, that would have added up to $1.3 million, which would easily have brought us into profit." There can be no doubt that Martin had grown too weary of the work and the worrying, and too tired of the touring, to continue.

An item in the December 22 issue of *Time* claimed that *Legends* had grossed nearly $10 million since beginning its twenty-three-city tour the previous January and that the stars were leaving after their stint in Palm Beach next month. "I was seventy-three the other day," Martin told the *Time* reporter. "My body doesn't have the resilience [it used to]. People think it does because that's all they see. But the next day. . . ."

"The legends may be leaving, but *Legends* will go on, perhaps even to Broadway in the spring," continued the story in *Time*. "Alexis Smith is among those being considered for the task of following one of the ultimate hard acts to follow." Three decades later, *Legends* has yet to appear on a Broadway or Off Broadway stage in New York—and it proved something of a failure all over again during a thirty-week tour that began in Toronto, in September 2006, costarring two more ladies who were famously at each other offstage as well as on: Joan Collins and Linda Evans.

A week or so after their final performance in *Legends,* Martin and Channing had dinner at Elaine's, the fashionable eatery on New York's Upper East Side, with Charles Lowe, Susan Grushkin, and Josh Ellis. "For all the talk of their not getting along with one another, they couldn't have been better buddies that night," recalled Ellis. "Now, were they really buddies that night? Was it only an act? If so, an act for whom? It wasn't like there were photographers at Elaine's. It was just dinner with them. . . . I think they were both very relaxed."

Ellis also remembered riding home in a hired car on Central Park West after dinner, when they happened upon the scene of an accident, with flashing police-car lights and blaring ambulances. Ellis was struck as he observed Martin cover her ears, put her head down to her chest, and go into a mantra: "Ugh-a-wah, Ugh-a-wah, Ugh-a-wah," a carryover from her duet with Tiger Lily in *Peter Pan,* now meant to tune out an unpleasant occurrence that doubtless reminded Martin of her own life-changing taxi accident six years before. "It was heartbreaking to witness," recalled Ellis. "It was obvious that the trauma of the San Francisco accident involving Janet Gaynor and Ben Washer was still with her."

Chapter 21

BENEFIT MARY

*Mary's unique magic has been a source of constant wonder
and envy of all of us who work in the musical theater.*
—BERNADETTE PETERS

The fiftieth anniversary of Martin's theatrical career in 1988 was marked by several notable events. Along with Michael Feinstein and Nancy Wilson, Martin was Phil Donahue's special guest for a cabaret-type evening at the Rainbow Room in the spring, which was subsequently televised. "And now, ladies and gentlemen, this is our big surprise," announced Donahue. "She opened this room fifty years ago. And she's still knocking 'em out: as a singer, as an artist. And, yes, she's very proud of her son, too. Ladies and gentlemen, please welcome Mary Martin."

Elegantly costumed in a black top, with a skirt of wide, black-and-white horizontal stripes, Martin talked her way through "Before I Kiss the World Goodbye" (from *Jennie*) before blending in "Before the Parade Passes By" (from *Hello, Dolly!*), with a musical reference as well to "My Heart Belongs to Daddy." Michael Feinstein followed, accompanying himself in a rendition of the Gershwins' "Our Love Is Here to Stay," and then Nancy Wilson sang "Angel Eyes." As she roamed around the room, inviting others to join in, Martin finally sang the song Rodgers and Hammerstein promised she would introduce, when they originally eliminated it from *South Pacific* and before they inserted it into *The King and I*: "Getting to Know You."

Far more people would ultimately see *In Performance at the White House,* which took place on April 24 and then aired on PBS on May 18, 1988. Hosted by President and Mrs. Reagan, and directed by David Deutsch, Martin was the key participant, with Marvin Hamlisch serving as the master of ceremonies. Musical Director Louis Magor was also on hand as Martin's pianist.

"We focused on a particular kind of magic," explained Nancy Reagan, during her scripted introduction. "The showstopper, when audiences jump to their feet and applaud, because—well, no one really knows why, but they know it when they hear and see it. . . . I'm very pleased that today we have with us five ladies who've been knocking them dead, [including] someone who is very special to me, Mary Martin."

With Heller and her husband seated in the front row next to the Reagans, the ladies performed on a raised platform, in front of two grand pianos, a ballroom chandelier overhead. The program begins with an atypically subdued and elegant Dorothy Loudon, singing Sondheim's "Broadway Baby" from *Follies,* and then her signature number, "Fifty Percent," from *Ballroom.* Jennifer Holiday followed with her breathtaking, breakthrough number from *Dreamgirls,* "And I Am Telling You I'm Not Going," before Hamlisch offered a piano solo of Sondheim's "Send in the Clowns." Next came Bea Arthur speaking her way through "Back on Broadway," followed by Cy Coleman's "It Amazes Me." Elaine Paige then made her American debut on the show, belting out "Don't Cry for Me, Argentina" from *Evita* and "Memory" from *Cats,* two of her famous anthems, which Paige had originally introduced in London's West End.

But, as Hamlisch emphasized, the evening belonged to Martin. "Tonight we have with us a true living legend," said Hamlisch, by way of introduction. "Now this is the first time I've ever worked with Mary Martin and I have to tell you, it hasn't been work at all. . . . A truly remarkable Broadway lady, who has had a love affair with American audiences, as well as audiences all over the world, now get this, for the last fifty years—she told me I'm allowed to say it. What an honor just to be on the same stage with a national treasure—Mary Martin."

"What keeps one going for fifty years?" Martin rhetorically asked, before fitting in the debt she still felt she owed her departed husband. "Well, having some of the most talented, creative people in the world, like Richard Rodgers, Oscar Hammerstein, [and] Josh Logan helps a great deal. And to be married to a man named Richard Halliday, who produced *our* career for thirty-three years. . . ."

Wearing a white sequined top and gown, with a pearl necklace adorning her neck, Martin proceeded to sing "Cockeyed Optimist." Then, sitting sideways on a chair, "That's Him," from *One Touch of Venus,* after which she left the stage for a moment and returned in a white mink, to sit on a piano and offer "My Heart Belongs to Daddy." Martin couldn't reach her high notes anymore and she even sings flat for some passages. But as noticeable as her vocal limitations are, they are quickly surmounted by a regained confidence and a sassy attitude she hadn't displayed in well over the decade since Halliday's demise. After all else—after the death of her husband, the traumatic taxi accident, the loss of Ben Washer, and then Janet Gaynor, and the horrible daily pressures of performing in an unwelcome play for a year—it was as if Martin had finally found contentment and, through contentment, happiness.

Martin continued to celebrate her fiftieth anniversary in New York, on Sunday, June 12, when she was part of a tribute to Cole Porter, "A Cabaret for Cole," at Town Hall, which was, in turn, part of the First New York International Festival of the Arts, including many other celebrants, such as Celeste Holm, Michael Feinstein, Julie Wilson, Barbara Cook, Barbara Carroll, Sylvia Syms, Steve Ross, Margaret Whiting, and Liliane Montevecchi. "A startlingly spry 74, Miss Martin seems to burst into a room as if shot from a cannon, rather than entering it like a normal mortal," wrote Leslie Bennetts in an advance story about the event in the *New York Times*. "One has the feeling she might zoom into the air and fly around the ceiling at any moment."

"[Cole Porter] taught me more about lyrics than anybody in my life," Martin told Bennetts. "He said, 'Every word is important; it must be heard.' One time we rehearsed all day and all evening, till 2 in the morning. He called me at 3 a.m. and said to me, 'I did not hear the word maul. I don't want that to happen again.' . . . And it didn't. Years later, Oscar Hammerstein said to me 'I have never in my life heard anybody pronounce every word so clearly.'"

The following day, June 13, Martin was at the Equitable Theatre on Seventh Avenue for the Museum of Broadcasting—later renamed the Paley Center—where she introduced a restored version of *Peter Pan*, which had already been the museum's annual Christmas show for a number of years. Clad in a green pants suit, Martin arrived on stage—*crowing*. "It is so joyous to know that it always holds its own," Martin candidly said about the show that she knew would outlive her. Martin also said that she and Cyril Ritchard discovered they had the same birthday once, when they were simultaneously presented with birthday cakes.

"After she finished her introduction to the screening, she took a seat in the row in front of me, and one seat over," recalled Jane Klain, remembering a special moment six years before Klain joined the Paley Center as a senior editor. "With rapt attention, I watched Peter Pan watching *Peter Pan*. And when Peter said, 'Clap, if you believe in fairies,' Mary Martin was clapping enthusiastically—she seemed transported by the moment. And then, when everyone else clapped, I noticed a tear falling down her cheek—which is when I lost it, and started crying uncontrollably."

As requested by a member of the audience, the presentation ended with Martin giving a lesson in crowing. "The person who got up in the

audience and said 'Would you teach us to crow?' was me," recalled theater publicist Susan L. Schulman.

With Susan Grushkin, Martin spent time, that summer, in London,
where they attended a revival of *South Pacific* at the Prince of Wales
Theatre, featuring Gemma Craven as Nellie Forbush and produced by
Ronald Lee, who was the understudy for the Crocodile in Martin's original *Peter Pan*. They also went to San Miguel de Allende, Mexico, where
they met up with Bessie Mae and her husband, Jac Austin.

The peripatetic duo was home in time for a gala evening on August 30
at the Hollywood Bowl, where Martin was on the bill with Placido Domingo, Carol Channing, Bea Arthur, Elaine Stritch, and Dolores Gray.
According to *Los Angeles Times* critic Dan Sullivan: "It is news that Mary
Martin still makes 'My Heart Belongs to Daddy' sound bawdy. . . . For the
first chorus, one can believe that the girl in the song doesn't understand
what the words mean. Then it becomes clear that you, the listener, are the
naïf. This is conveyed with perfect daintiness, the Martin hallmark. Then
we had a reprise of Martin's Nellie Forbush in *South Pacific,* stuck like a
dope with a thing called hope. And then the twin soliloquy from that
show, with Domingo playing DeBecque, the planter. Domingo, a little
nervous in Pinza's shoes, went off pitch. Not Martin."

Committed to attend the American Bankers Convention in October,
in Hawaii, Martin turned the trip into something of a personal affair by
having Heller accompany her. "Mary presented the slide show she had
put together of her life, which she also presented for IBM and on other
occasions," recalled Grushkin.

On January 9, 1989, Martin was back at New York's Museum of
Broadcasting for a tribute to the television work of Richard Rodgers.
"She plans to catch a preview performance of *Jerome Robbins's Broadway*
this week as well," reported Jeremy Gerard in the *New York Times,* referring to a musical anthology of the great director and choreographer's
shows, including a flying scene from *Peter Pan*. Martin's visit coincided
with NBC's announcement that it would rebroadcast *Peter Pan* on
March 24, for the first time in sixteen years. Though it had "seemed a
natural to become a TV perennial, like *The Wizard of Oz* and the traditional holiday classics . . . after three more airings (1963, 1966, and 1973)
it vanished," observed Aleene MacMinn in the *Los Angeles Times*.
"Everyone who ever read the Barrie play is a fan," Martin told MacMinn.
"Barrie had this dream of perpetual childhood. He didn't want anyone
to grow up, and that intrigues certain kinds of people. . . . I happen to be
one of them. I'm still not real grown up."

"It is Miss Martin's conviction that Mr. Robbins—who staged and choreographed the original production—and not she, was the show's hero," Jeremy Gerard also reported. "It would never have been the way it was if it hadn't been for Jerry," claimed Martin. "Jerry is Peter Pan and always will be. He'll always be a Lost Boy."

In March, Martin would tell Jeanne Wright of *USA Today,* "I don't feel seventy-five," and also that she turned down an offer to replace Barbara Bel Geddes in Larry Hagman's hit TV show *Dallas,* because "she didn't want to tread onto her son's territory." Martin was, at the time, close to deciding that she would make her Broadway comeback as the Stage Manager, or narrator, in *Grover's Corners,* Tom Jones and Harvey Schmidt's musical version of Thornton Wilder's classic American play *Our Town.* "She said yes, she said no, she said yes, she said no," claimed Jones, who had already played the Stage Manager in the show's world premiere in Chicago in the summer of 1987. "This is very different from anything she's ever done, because she's not the active verb in the piece. That's troubling her. She likes the piece, finds herself very moved by it, and connects with it. I think it would be a wonderful finale to her career."

"It worked very well in Chicago," recalled Harvey Schmidt, the show's composer. "It ran for several months and we had time to really work on it there. During that period, the producers were saying they needed a star, and it would have to be [to play] the Stage Manager. Unfortunately, only movie stars seemed to matter: they explored everyone—even Burt Lancaster. But no one was willing to leave the golf course and tour around the country. Then it closed at the Lincoln Marriott Theater [in Chicago], but there was still talk about what to do next. I remember they were saying how terrible it was that a woman can't do it; and then somebody said, 'like a Mary Martin.' And we jumped at that.

"I called her," continued Schmidt. "She was back home in Palm Springs, and she was just thrilled with my call. She got very excited about a musical version of *Our Town,* telling me she did scenes from the play on the *Ford Show* [in 1953]: she really talked lovingly about that experience with Oscar Hammerstein. She also adored the fact that it was Tom and I [her *I Do! I Do!* team] doing the musical, adding she would love to hear the songs. Then she turned the phone over to her new assistant, saying, 'One of the best I've ever had. I turn everything over to her,'" referring to Susan Grushkin.

Grushkin arranged for Schmidt to introduce Martin to the score "in a couple of weeks" at his apartment on West Seventy-fourth Street in New York. "Mary and I went to Harvey's apartment to hear the music and lyrics," said Grushkin. "We fell in love with both. I remember having lunch at the Oyster Bar at the Plaza Hotel afterward and discussing how moved we were by them."

"We went out to Mary's in Palm Springs a couple of times—once, early on, just for the producers to meet her," Schmidt said. "I remember Marge Champion was going to do the choreography, and she came too. Then, when it got more serious, Mary wanted us to come and see her lawyer. So we met him. She told us that she'd been having dreams recently in which Oscar Hammerstein appeared, saying, 'Mary, you've got to see the theater up here. You've never seen a theater this gorgeous.' She told it very nicely and excitingly." Martin's recurrent dreams about Oscar Hammerstein inviting her to perform in a big theater in the proverbial sky were clearly coinciding with her encroaching mortality.

Also in March 1989, Martin went on a two-week cruise of the Pacific Ocean aboard the *QE2*, as sponsored by the Theatre Guild, with other guest stars—Helen Hayes, Patricia Neal, and Richard Kiley—all singing for their supper—or, rather, for their cruise. "Before the cruise, she noticed that one of her legs was swollen," recalled Susan Grushkin. "We went to see several doctors, each of them saying they were unable to find the cause, that it wasn't anything serious, and not to worry about it." Grushkin also remembered one doctor recommending a colonoscopy, and Martin saying, "When we get back . . ."

Martin and Grushkin flew first to Hawaii, where they had dinner with Helen Hayes, her son, James MacArthur, and his wife. "Once we were on the ship, Mary just wasn't herself," said Grushkin. "She didn't have much of an appetite and she was very tired. We didn't know until we were back home that she had already lost a lot of blood. If she indeed was aware of what was happening, she kept it to herself. She was determined to fulfill her commitment and complete the cruise"—like the veteran trouper Martin was.

Grushkin also recalled a "large storm in the China Seas" over two consecutive days, causing "many of us to feel quite uncomfortable but also giving us a few good laughs. During one of the performances, midway through 'Some Enchanted Evening,' sung by Richard Kiley to a seated Mary Martin, her chair began moving towards the edge of the stage with Richard trying inconspicuously to move with it. Barely able to finish the song, they both burst into laughter," said Grushkin. "Helen Hayes had to hang on to the piano to stay upright. . . . By the time we reached Hong Kong, the last stop on the cruise, Mary knew we needed to get home."

As announced in *Variety,* Martin had agreed and planned to star in

Grover's Corners on Broadway, beginning with a national tour in November. Designed by Schmidt, a full-page ad for the show in the trade weekly depicted a larger-than-life Martin with her raised, open arms embracing the viewer, as it were, with a host of other figures peeking out from behind her, their arms open wide as well.

Schmidt recalled showing the ad to Martin, before it ran, during one of his visits to Palm Springs. "Mary said, 'You know, my breasts don't come out that far,' and I said, 'I can take care of that.' Mary then invited us all out to a restaurant, run by a little French couple. She and Marge were talking about having been to their doctors. Mary was saying how she had a problem, but they couldn't find anything. Then, shortly thereafter, when they were getting ready to sign the contract, she found out that she had cancer."

According to Larry Hagman, his mother had developed severe back pains that spring, prompting him to take her to a "renowned sports doctor," who, on the basis of X-rays, said she needed to see an internist. As soon as it was discovered that Martin had colon cancer, she was admitted to Cedars-Sinai Medical Center in Los Angeles, in early June 1989, when Dr. Leonard Makowka performed a three-hour operation on her. Makowka discovered that Martin's cancer had metastasized, and "Mother's prognosis wasn't good," according to Hagman.

Martin recovered from her surgery by spending the rest of the summer in Martha's Vineyard, staying in the same house she had rented sixteen years before, for Heller's wedding. "It's right on the beach where I walk almost every day," she wrote, in a letter to Peter Mintun, on September 30. "Am doing everything those wonderful doctors at Cedars-Sinai have told me to do and am getting along extremely well. Leaving tomorrow—will stop in Dallas for a few days to see my brother-in-law before heading home [to Rancho Mirage]. Then I plan to stay a while and make some decisions about what to do next."

Martin agreed to be honored during the twelfth annual Kennedy Center Awards on December 3, 1989, which aired on CBS twenty-six days later. The other four recipients that year included singer Harry Belafonte, actress Claudette Colbert, ballerina Alexandra Danilova, and classical composer William Schuman. "She was and is and always will be Peter Pan," said Gregory Peck, introducing Martin. "If we didn't have musicals, we'd have to invent them for her." *Peter Pan* lyricist Betty Comden referred to Martin as a "great artist and a great star who has that rarest of qualities—bundles of charm." In her presentation during the black-tie tribute, Broadway musical star Bernadette Peters claimed "[Mary Martin] makes us believe not just in the wonders of Never Never Land, but in the magic of the world we see every day. Mary's unique magic has been a source of constant wonder and envy of all of us who work in the musical theater. . . . She makes us believe in the magic of the theater and in the magic of ourselves, because she believes it, too. When Captain Hook asked his spirited adversary, 'Pan, who and what are you?,' the boy replies, 'I am youth. I am freedom. I am joy.' He might just as well have said, 'I am Mary Martin.'" And, typical of the competitive but loving, ironic banter that had come to define his relationship with his mother, Larry Hagman said, "I taught her everything she knows."

Wary of becoming too ill to attend the ceremony, Martin postponed her first chemotherapy treatment until after the Kennedy Center tribute. Susan Grushkin recalled driving Martin to Cedars-Sinai Hospital in Los Angeles from Rancho Mirage, when, yet again, the accident-prone Martin endured another injury, so late in her life. "The day before, I noticed something didn't feel quite right when stepping on the brake, so I brought the car into the repair shop. The repairman drove it, felt exactly what I had felt, but said not to worry about it, that it was nothing serious and not to bother renting a car as I had suggested perhaps doing. It was obviously not the correct diagnosis, because suddenly, in the middle of the highway, something went terribly wrong and I had no control over the brake or gas pedal. Thank goodness we had our seatbelts on because we ended up hitting the center divider and landing upside down. Mary's ankle was severely broken and we were taken to a hospital in San Dimas, where, fortunately, we met a wonderful doctor and nurses who took great care of us both."

But it was her body's reaction to chemotherapy and the spreading cancer that forced Martin to cancel, at the last minute, her scheduled appearance at the seventy-fifth anniversary celebration of the Shubert Theater in New Haven on May 12, 1990, when she was to offer yet another version of "My Heart Belongs to Daddy," the song that had made her famous. Martin then felt strong enough, however, to spend much of the summer in London, including a side trip to Scotland, during which she continued chemotherapy treatments.

"She had no professional commitments to fulfill and therefore had time to reconnect with friends," said Grushkin. "She knew she didn't have much longer to live and was, in a way, trying to recapture a special time in her life in those two places. We first rented an apartment in Knightsbridge, but because of construction noise, moved to a two-bedroom suite in the Howard Hotel, with a view of the Thames. I remember being in touch with Dr. Howard House, who came to visit and to see the hotel that 'had been named after him.' Friends Bob and Ray flew in from San Francisco—I can't remember their last names but they were not the comedy duo. And we visited with John Ross, a producer, and John Taylor, a songwriter—both very dear men, who had previously spent a special Christmas with us in Rancho Mirage. We also spent time with friends in Manchester, attended the Queen Mother's birthday celebration, and saw about ten shows."

Once she was home in Rancho Mirage, Martin's condition quickly deteriorated. In October, she was admitted to a two-room suite in the Eisenhower Medical Center in Palm Springs for more tests, when she was put on an IV drip of Demerol to help control the pain and ease her way during her final weeks. As Susan Grushkin recalled, televangelist Robert Schuller came to visit Martin in the hospital, "which meant a lot to Mary," Grushkin said. "She used to watch his TV program every Sunday morning and drew inspiration from his positive words. She even appeared on one of his programs, reciting the words to 'Never Land' from *Peter Pan*."

Other visitors included Heller, Dolores Hope, and Dr. Howard House. When Larry Hagman was asked by reporters that fall about his mother's condition, he would say she was doing fine. But he knew better. Despite his involvement directing an episode of *Dallas* in Irvine, California, and his mother's telling Hagman that his work was more important than his spending time with her, Larry visited her in the hospital. He was dismayed to discover that "a prominent television pastor was sitting on her bed, holding her hand and praying for her. His regular visits had started to concern me. Call me cynical," Hagman explained in his memoir. "I'm from the South, and every pastor I'd ever met while growing up made deathbed visits in an effort to get their church 'remembered.' I made sure Mother didn't remember his church at all."

"She didn't follow any one religion in particular," claimed Susan Grushkin, looking back on how Martin coped with her mortality near the end. "She said that she had tried them all while growing up. Although she had chosen the Episcopalian faith, she wasn't in church every Sunday—rather, it was more of a 'spirituality.' She told me of her dreams about Richard, and about Oscar Hammerstein and the theater. We spoke about why and how we had come together. She said maybe we had known each other in a previous life, but added, 'Who knows what happens when we go on from here?' She obviously thought about things like that but didn't dwell on them. She was going to try everything to get well, but then thought of death as the greatest adventure and didn't want to continue in this world if she wasn't healthy and able to live a full life. She knew and accepted that she wouldn't be here much longer."

"Mary's dying wish was that she didn't want Larry to see her pass away," said actress and friend Natalie Schafer. "The wait for death was the hardest thing. Mary wasn't worried about how it affected her . . . but she didn't want her family and friends to suffer." After all, if Martin had been too busy to be with either of her parents at the time of their deaths—or even to attend their funerals—why should it be any different for her own son now?

Larry Hagman last saw his mother on October 28, 1990, a Sunday, the day he set aside every week to refrain from uttering a single word, to preserve his voice for work the week ahead. "She'd never liked Bach, yet she knew I enjoyed whistling Bach Inventions," recalled Hagman. "So she started whistling one of my favorites. I did counterpoint. We whistled while holding hands until she grew too tired. I sat for a while longer, then kissed her good-bye."

Heller also visited her mother in Palm Springs, during Mary's final days. "I was living in Houston at that point, and had kids," recalled Heller. "But I just knew that the time had come where it was important for me to go by myself and be with her. She was in the hospital. It was sort of known that she wasn't going to make it. I was staying at her house. I love to garden, and there was an archway at the entrance, with these huge flowerbeds going up either side of the walkway. It wasn't a very bright, sunny situation. So I planted a lot of flowery plants that loved shade—impatiens, that sort of thing.

"Then, when she came home, I stayed with her for a few days. We cuddled in bed. But I realized I had to get home, because I had been away a long time from the kids. I just remember saying to her, 'Now, Mommy, you just listen to the doctors and do everything they tell you to. Okay?' And she said, 'I will, I will. . . .' I said, 'We'll talk every day, and maybe in a month or so, I can come back.' That was really our last conversation.

"I remember, I went out into the alcove with my suitcase, waiting for the cab to come pick me up and take me to the airport. And I remember saying to myself, 'Heller, you're not going to see Mommy again. You just have to know that.' And I just stood there. And all of a sudden, this little hummingbird came down. And it started going from one side to the other, to the flowers I planted. And then it went out and came back and went around my head about three times. Then it stood in front of me—I could almost feel its breath—and shook, shook, shook. And then it flew off. My interpretation was, this was Mommy coming down to me, saying, 'I love you. I'm giving you kisses. But I gotta go. I gotta fly away.'"

Shortly after Martin had returned home to die, Carol Channing was one of the last to see her alive, though unable to speak. "I said, 'I love you, Mary,' and she tried to answer me," recalled Channing. "Then she squeezed my hand and I knew she heard."

Mary Martin died in bed, at her Palm Springs home, on November 3, a Saturday. "I remember calling Heller," recalled Susan Grushkin. "It would have been around 6:15 P.M., Eastern Standard Time. Larry and Maj were there as well. They flew out the next day and I picked them up the next evening at the Palm Springs airport." It was Hagman's publicist, Richard Grant, who notified the world of Martin's demise.

"She thought death was the biggest adventure ever," claimed Grushkin. "She said I can always talk to her, even after she's gone, and I can always talk to her, like she talks with Richard and Janet and Dorothy and all the people she loved, who have gone on."

"We're not going to dwell on this illness or the fact that I'm not going to be here much longer," Martin had told Grushkin some weeks or months before her death. "I want to believe that we have this connection with people we loved in this world that goes on."

Chapter 22

"WHAT A WAY TO GO!"

*I'll keep living until it's time. Then I'll just go
on to another stage.*
—MARY MARTIN

"More than any of her peers, she was what she played and she incarnated the songs that she sang," wrote theater critic Mel Gussow in his front-page obituary of Mary Martin for the *New York Times,* which appeared on November 5, 1990, accompanied by a photo of Martin in her *South Pacific* sailor costume. "Her voice was never the strongest instrument. She was not beautiful (though she could be radiant). Through determination, pluck, charm, self-mocking humor and a profound sense of self, everything converged to create an exhilarating theater artist. . . .

"While Ethel Merman was an entire brass section and Carol Channing was a parade, Miss Martin remained natural and exactingly true to life—and it was poetry. . . . For fifty years Miss Martin projected the vitality of someone who loved her work and knew precisely how to make other people share in her happiness," Gussow also observed, as he further relayed that Elia Kazan, who had directed Martin in her first Broadway starring role, in *One Touch of Venus,* said that she was "full of the love of being loved."

Befitting the icon that Martin had become by the time of her death, the *New York Times* also ran, the following day, an unsigned editorial devoted to her legacy. "Little kids are lucky," it began. "They can see as well as hear her joyous 'I'm Flying' in the videotape of *Peter Pan.* But we older kids know what they don't, that Mary Martin had a life in the theater before she played the boy who never grew up. . . . We wish we could stick a cassette in the VCR and see her, all legs and innocence and bunny fur, caroling that her heart belongs to Daddy. In a sailor suit that was thrice too big, singing about a girl named Honey-Bun who was 'A hundred and one pounds of fun.' In governess garb teaching the von Trapp children their do-re-mi's."

The *New York Times*'s Sunday critic, David Richards, weighed in with his own appreciation the following weekend: "If Martin . . . was the most airborne of musical comedy performers, her stardom depended as much on the no-nonsense pragmatism that audiences perceived in her. . . . What she did literally in *Peter Pan*—fly out into the arms of the audience—was really what she did in all her musicals. . . . She was a born extrovert. . . . She didn't come on strong so much as she came on gregarious."

In the *New York Post,* Clive Barnes claimed that "her special charm was an innocence that was never sugary, a voice that never cloyed and a personality that happily combined the indomitable with the vulnerable on a spectrum that made it possible for us all to identify with." It was Oscar Hammerstein's son, William, whose comments suggested that Martin would live on beyond herself: "The bright light and good cheer that Mary brought to the world will not fade merely because of her absence."

As sponsored by London's Hospital for Sick Children, which controlled the rights to James M. Barrie's *Peter Pan,* an ad in *Variety* seemed to have the last word, referring to Martin as Peter's "greatest portrayer" and suggesting that Barrie's legacy would always be entwined with her own: "Wherever she has flown, her bright light will be forever visible to millions of children who, because of her, will never grow old."

According to Mary Martin's wishes, Larry Hagman had his mother cremated, and he planned on burying her ashes in the family plot in Weatherford on the Saturday following her death. But Hagman was distracted by his commitment to direct an episode of *Dallas* that week and forgot to have the Palm Springs mortuary send Martin's ashes to his home in Malibu.

In the blurred circumstances that often attend funeral arrangements, Hagman also forgot which particular Palm Springs mortuary had taken care of the cremation. He had to phone several before finding the right one. "I'll never forget saying, 'Hello . . . Larry Hagman here,'" recalled Hagman. "'Do you have my mother's ashes there?' Neither will I forget the man's response. 'Yes, as a matter of fact Mr. Weasel is just walking out the door with them. He's going to mail them to you.'"

Mr. Weasel's name alone was enough to put Hagman ("punch-drunk from sleep deprivation and anxiety") in stitches. "I was waiting for instructions on what to do with [the ashes] and decided I better mail them to you," Weasel told Hagman over the phone. "I was laughing so hard I couldn't speak," recalled Hagman. "He thought I was crying." "I'm sorry you're taking this so hard," Weasel responded.

According to Susan Grushkin, Hagman next contacted her, to have her bring his mother's ashes to the cemetery. "Larry called me, saying he had forgotten to pick up 'Mother,' asking if I would do that and bring her to Weatherford," Grushkin recalled. Martin's ashes had been placed in a metal container, which triggered the alarm when Grushkin went through security at the Palm Springs airport. "It was only appropriate, given the fact that often while traveling Mary would set off the alarm by a belt or necklace she'd be wearing."

As Grushkin further recalled, the airline upgraded her to a first-class seat, "since it wouldn't have been right to have Mary flying coach." Nor did Grushkin feel it was seemly to place Martin on the floor beneath her seat: "She remained on my lap for the flight home [to Dallas]. Bessie Mae, her daughter, and I were going out for dinner and thought about taking Mary with us, but, in the end, [we] decided it would be best to leave her in the room. I guess one had to be there to appreciate the humor of the situation. But typical of Mary, she still had us laughing even on this sad occasion, which was exactly how she would have wanted it."

Martin also managed to have the final word on both where she and her husband were buried. "Weatherford wasn't necessarily Richard's favorite place in the world," said Kristina Hagman, Martin's eldest grandchild. "But grandma wanted to go home and she wanted to be with him. So she got everything she wanted. Richard was so good at controlling everything when he was alive, and here was something that grandma finally got to control"—from the grave, as it were.

In his memoir, Larry Hagman described the "whole family" congregating in Weatherford for "a tearful good-bye" to his mother. "Many of Mother's old friends spoke. We put pictures of the family in her ashes. . . . Heller added a miniature bottle of Kahlua, her favorite drink. It was a fitting memorial to a life well lived."

A suitable container had to be found for interring Martin's ashes. "My dad said, 'You know, we have to find a proper receptacle,'" recalled Kristina Hagman. "They had discussed what would be appropriate for Mary and it wasn't going to be dark and heavy or depressing in any way. Mom selected two or three absolutely gorgeous, cut-crystal containers, and dad chose the sparkliest one."

Kristina Hagman also remembered the family whooping it up that evening, with a "big drunken dinner" at the Mansion in Turtle Creek, a famous resort hotel in Dallas, where Hagman used to live part of the year in a penthouse apartment, later to be known as the J. R. Ewing suite. "We celebrated her so thoroughly by dancing the night away," claimed Kristina.

"And Susan was shocked, saying, 'Oh, my God. You're going out danc-ing?' Dad turned to her, and said, 'That's exactly what Mother would have wanted.'"

With an enormous line of people circling the block in midtown Manhat-tan and hoping to secure a seat, the public memorial for Martin was held at 2:00 P.M. on January 28, 1991, a Monday, at the Majestic Theatre, where *South Pacific* had its initial, three-year run. Larry Hagman and Heller Halliday DeMeritt introduced the program, which included John Raitt, Carol Lawrence, Jerome Robbins, and President and Nancy Reagan, who contributed their remarks via videotape.

"She was the greatest figure we're ever going to have in musical com-edy," said Helen Hayes, who spoke at the memorial, before quickly cor-recting herself: "Mary would rap me over the knuckles in heaven when I got there," if Hayes failed to even mention Ethel Merman in the same breath. Claiming that Martin was "truly the purest soul that I have ever known," Florence Henderson further explained, "She was so generous; she always let people into her circle of light." Henderson was also sure to relate what had become Merman's most famous, off-the-cuff remark about Martin: "Oh, she's all right, if you like talent."

Carol Channing sang "My Heart Belongs to Daddy" with fresh lyrics written to honor Martin: "She played a nurse / She played a nun / She played a boy who was a fairy / She stopped the show when she had to crow / And our hearts belong to Mary." Van Johnson, who was originally a backup dancer at Martin's late-night show at the Rainbow Room, atop Rockefeller Center, in 1938, recalled more recently performing with her at Davies Hall in San Francisco. When he noticed the seventy-one-year-old Martin harnessing up to fly as Peter Pan, he said, "Mary, you're *not*!" re-called Van Johnson, "and she said, 'Oh, yes I am, and I may not come back.' And she zoomed up to the roof and sprinkled gold dust all over our hair."

"The memorial was a spectacular event," recalled Kristina Hagman. "My father was very glad that it was so beautifully pulled off—that the people he hoped would be there were there, and that it was in a beautiful venue, and it was done just the way grandmother would have liked it to be done. I specifically remember being backstage with Helen Hayes, this tiny person, who was just so sparkling and so wonderfully irreverent. She was of a considerable age—I think ninety or ninety-one—and she was complaining that everybody was celebrating her birthday too frequently. She said, 'I've been given three birthday cakes, and I'd just like to get on with it.'

"The only sad part of the memorial for me," continued Kristina, "was also one of those aha moments about fame, when, afterward, we went to Sardi's. This was my grandmother's special moment, but nowhere on the walls was there a picture of Grandmother. And I thought, 'You know, it had always been there'—her most recent show had always been up on the wall. And it wasn't anymore. I thought, 'Okay, now I get it. It's fleeting.' I shared it with my father, and he said, 'That's show biz, honey.'"

In the midst of all the encomiums, quips, and anecdotes that were shared at Mary Martin's memorial, perhaps Van Johnson's memory of her harnessing up for her final flight as Peter Pan came closest to approximating something Martin was thinking near the time of her death. Though it's impossible to know what her final thoughts actually were, it's likely that Martin achieved, in some fashion, one of her wishes for how she would depart this world.

"My dream is to fly in Madison Square Garden," Martin told Leslie Bennetts for an article in the *New York Times,* two years before her demise. "I flew a few years ago in San Francisco—down from the third balcony, throwing fairy dust onto the audience," just as Van Johnson, who had been there, recalled that special moment at Martin's memorial. "You see, the further the length you fly is, the faster you can go," Martin continued to tell Bennetts. "I want Madison Square Garden to build a window that goes outside. I love to go fast; I have no fear." After a significant pause, during which Martin was clearly contemplating any mortal's concept of eternity, she said, "And then I'll just fly out that window and not come back. . . . What a way to go."

ACKNOWLEDGMENTS

While clearing out the house of my youth in a suburb of Cleveland, Ohio, I came upon a 1958, black-and-white photograph of my seven-year-old self standing in front of the family Christmas tree, dressed as Peter Pan, in a green felt costume my mother made for me. I had already fallen in love with Mary Martin as Peter Pan when I saw her on TV, with my friend Debbie Nathanson. Debbie and I met in kindergarten and spent many an afternoon growing up together, singing along with Broadway shows, including *Peter Pan*, *South Pacific*, and *The Sound of Music*—we even took acting lessons on Saturday mornings and performed in school productions together. Though I imagine I didn't know, at the time, what a biography was, I'm certain that the seeds for this one were planted during those salad days, recalled now as vivid memories—and with a mature gratitude to Debbie, for helping shape the lover of musicals I became.

In the course of delving into the past for the sake of this biography, Mary Martin's New York became my New York. It was a glorious empire at the height of its cultural splendor—radiant and vital in ways that, today, can be recaptured only through the living and breathing memories of those who contributed to its vivacity, even as they contributed to the making of this biography.

Though being an author is a solitary occupation, my experience as a biographer has also been something else, with a rich parade of collaborators who became friends. While working on *Some Enchanted Evenings* for the past seven years, I became particularly grateful for the warm and meaningful relationships I have formed with Sondra Lee and Walter Willison, each of whom introduced me to many other players who are part of Mary Martin's story. Walter was also tireless, from the beginning, in making me superbly packaged DVDs and CDs of rare Mary Martin movies, TV shows, and recordings—and in obtaining for me, from seemingly all over the globe, obscure magazine articles, photographs, programs, and other Martin memorabilia. Fellow author James Gavin also supplied me with a number of homemade DVDs of Martin's television shows.

Jane Klain, a friend who became an impassioned collaborator, used her powers of detection to help me track down any number of people to locate still more Martin rarities, including Martin's journalist friend and correspondent Elliott Sirkin, as well as Jim Parish, who provided me with *Kiss the Boys Goodbye*, and Dennis Payne, who helped me obtain a copy of *The Great Victor Herbert*. Jane's assistant at the Paley Center, Richard Holbrook, was also helpful, as was the Museum of Modern Art curator Charles Silver, who screened *Main Street to Broadway* for me and also supplied a personal file of Martin articles.

And then there's *Vanity Fair* photo editor Ann Schneider, who, as always, helps define what it is to be a friend. Ann came on board in the first few months of 2016, using her professional eye and talent to help search through a thicket of photos and come up with the most crucial and finest images, making Ann an artist in her own right. I am also grateful to certain other friends and aquaintences, whose friendship deepened in the course of their ongoing encouragement, including Jim Baldassare, Kaye Ballard, Lois Battle, Mark Beard and Jim Manfredi, Jill and Irwin Cohen, Bob Colacello, Douglas Colby, Tony Converse, Graham Dennie, Michael Feingold, Howard Green, Martha Green and Stephen Chodorov, Harry Haun and Charles Nelson, Robert Heidi and John Gilman, Robert Gutman, Foster Hirsch, Bryan James, Louis Jordan, Wilson Kidde, Linda Kline, Miles Kreuger, George and Rosemary and Luke Lois, Howard Mandelbaum, Kenny Nassau and Lee Hebner, Alix Nigian, Richard Osterweil, Robert Ray, Lenore Rosenberg, David Samples, Lester Shane, Barbara and Scott Siegel, Ken Siman, Jeffrey Tuller, Nicholas Wright, Sherman and Joan Yellen, Bill Young, and Roberta Zlokower. Charles and Anne Wright led me to Anne's brother Clay Bailey, who in turn contacted Jess Hill, Director of the Upper School, Harpeth Hall School. Jess referred me to Mary Ellen Pethel's then-forthcoming book on Ward-Belmont, and also to Mary Tanner Bailey and Linda Barnickel of the Nashville Public Library, and to Judy Williams, Research Librarian, Lila D. Bunch Library at Belmont University in Nashville.

When I set out to write this biography, I believed that Mary Martin was a collection of contradictions that needed to be sifted and sorted before I could understand who she was. For their help in making me appreciate that Martin's contradictions often coexisted and, in fact, helped define her, I am grateful to the many people who knew and/or worked with her, and who shared their memories with me: Carleton Carpenter, Marge Champion, Ted Chapin, Don Dellair, Judith Drake, Josh Ellis, John Erman, Barbara and Ted Flicker, Joyce Gertz (and her daughter Barbara Humphreys), Paul Gregory, Susan Grushkin, James Kabel, Kenneth Kantor, Christopher Kyd, Paula Laurence, Sondra Lee, Lissa Levin, Louis Magor, Peter Mintun, Patricia Morison, Don Murray, Sono Osato

(who "spoke" to me via Bernie Carragher), Roger Phillips, Bruce Poma-
hac, Dorothy Power, Mary Quayle, Mary Rodgers, Howard Rogut, David
Rothenberg, Harvey Schmidt (and his assistant John Schank), Susan L.
Schulman, Marian Seldes, John Sheridan, Richard Sherman, Elliott Sirkin, Joan Tewkesbury, Lee Tuft, Bob Ullman, and Walter Willison. I am
especially grateful to both Bernice Saunders and the late Lee Tuft for
permission to publish from their letters. Heller Halliday and Kristina
Hagman, respectively Martin's daughter and granddaughter, also helped
set the record straight in various ways—as did George Dansker, one of
the world's great authorities on all things pertaining to Martin. George
read certain portions of this manuscript during its early development and
provided guidance.

For supplying me with a home-away-from-home during research trips
to both Los Angeles and Dallas, I am indebted to Daniel and Katharine
Selznick and to Cynthia and Lester Melnick. The Melnicks' daughter,
Leslie Diers, made an adventure out of driving us all to Weatherford, Texas,
one warm, autumn Monday in 2011—two days after Lester's eightieth
birthday—where we discovered Mary Martin's past together, with the
added help of Cynthia and Lester's friends, Linda and Michael Lindsey
and Wendy Jenkins. Our tour of Weatherford was enhanced by Danielle
Felts and Tyler Sievert at Weatherford City Hall, and by Kathleen Poznick
and Christy Bellah at the Weatherford Public Library. Christy also went
above and beyond the usual responsibilities of any librarian to help me
piece together Martin's childhood and ancestry with colorful details. Barbara and Ted Flicker put me up at their glorious ranch in Santa Fe during
one extended weekend in 2010, when they opened up their hearts about
Larry Hagman and his mother Mary Martin, and introduced me to the
brilliant Joan Tewkesbury, who recalled working with Martin in both
Peter Pan and the revival of *Annie Get Your Gun*.

Having provided a good deal of behind-the-scenes help with my biography of Doris Day, both Ned Comstock and Jenny Romero rushed to
do the same for my biography of Mary Martin. Ned led me to the Pete
Martin and Andrew Stone collections at USC's Cinematic Arts Library,
as well as to three volumes of Constance McCormick's Mary Martin
scrapbooks, which were generously reproduced. Ned also provided in-
despensible guidance in helping me sort out Martin's seemingly endless involvement with television specials. Jenny drew my attention to all the
relevant documents at the Margaret Herrick Library, including the Paramount Studio archives, and the Michael Curtiz, Robert McCormick,
Sammy Cahn, Alan J. Pakula, and Ivan Kahn collections. The real treasure

trove at the Herrick are the Mary Martin and Hedda Hopper papers, all of which Jenny carefully prepared for my perusal.

There is, of course, far more involved in creating a book than research or interviews—or even writing. For his belief in me and in this project from the very beginning, I thank my agent, Mitchell Waters, of Curtis, Brown, Ltd. Ken Geist, my husband and partner for life, is also my first editor for everything I write (except my journals), and he saves me from any number of errors even as he improves my writing. Steven Samuels was also a behind-the-scenes editor, who brought his customary intelligence and care to helping me shape *Some Enchanted Evenings* during every step of the sometimes agonizing process. Steve particularly helped me through the thornier thickets of the first chapter, when various developments failed to make sense.

And for even making this book possible, I am especially indebted to my editor, Michael Flamini of St. Martin's Press. When we first met for lunch, Michael told me that this was the book he was "born to publish." He has remained true to his word, bringing his passionate enthusiasm to every aspect of making this book become a reality, with concern and perspicacity. Assistant editor Vicki Lame coordinated every aspect of readying this book with both grace and dispatch. Joel Breuklander copyedited the manuscript with a precision any author would envy, prompting me to dig still deeper and "say what I mean and mean what I say," as a high school English teacher once instructed. Attorney Elisa Rivlin came in at the last minute to read carefully and vet the manuscript, helping me make prudent cuts and paraphrases to all of the letters I quote.

I am also grateful to Luis Aristondo, of NBC, for his speedy and last-minute delivery of a link to the Barbara Walters *Today Show* interview with Martin in 1976; to Larry Verbit, for providing me with a copy of the Mary Martin *This Is Your Life* episode, courtesy of Ralph Edwards Productions; to Stacey Behlmer at the Margaret Herrick Library; to Doug Reside, the Lewis and Dorothy Cullman Curator for the Billy Rose Theatre Division of the New York Public Library; and to Amanda Rush of the Doss Heritage and Cultural Center.

NOTES

1 "A Star Is Born"

1 *"Robert H. Johnson: Tinner and Plumber"*: ads in the 1914 edition of the *Melon Vine Yearbook.*

1 *"splintery-floored barn of a place"*: Ellen Bowie Holland, *Gay as a Grig* 1963).

3 *"My father always insisted that they traded off a horse"*: Mary Martin, *My Heart Belongs,* 16.

3 *"I must have known that [mother] really wanted a boy"*: Ibid., 20.

4 *"It was all joy"*: Ibid.

4 *"Everyone loved her because she"*: Author interview with Harvey Schmidt.

4 *"Daddy had time for everyone"*: Martin, *My Heart Belongs,* 19.

4 *"It was a very wealthy community"*: Author interview with Joyce Hayes Gertz.

5 *"Mary was always pretty much of a tomboy"*: Ford White, *NBC Biography in Sound, 1955,* for the Armed Forces Radio and Television service, narrated by Frank Blair.

5 *"When Juanita Martin was teaching violin"*: Ronald L. Davis, *Mary Martin: Broadway Legend,* 8.

6 *"They were my babysitters"*: Martin, *My Heart Belongs,* 29.

6 *"My mother would tackle anything"*: Martin, *My Heart Belongs,* 49.

6 *"Her mother pushed her"*: Davis, 7.

7 *"Daddy I'm not sure ever made up his mind"*: Martin, *My Heart Belongs,* 27.

7 *"which finally had everything I was looking for: beauty, formality, pageantry, singing"*: Ibid., 23, 26–27.

7 *"attacked in several courtrooms"*: Jean Roberta, "Christian Martyr, Pagan Witness," *The Gay and Lesbian Review,* (January 2014), 20.

7 *"didn't have the remotest idea"*: Martin, *My Heart Belongs,* 18.

7 *"I wanted to be Peter Pan the first time"*: Gladwin Hill, "Mary Martin Arrives in Never-Never Land," *New York Times,* October 17, 1954.

8 *"She did all right by herself, too"*: John R. Franchey, "Her Heart Belongs to Hollywood," *Hollywood,* January 1940, 26+.

8 *"sent China Rose [her character]—in costume"*: Laurence Schwab, "Star from Texas," *McCall's,* November 1949, 78.

9 *"That girl"*: Ibid.

9 *"I was never known as a good student"*: Mary Martin, *Mary Martin's Needlepoint,* 106.

9 *"With this show [Marilyn Miller] became Broadway's"*: Gerald Bordman, *American Musical Theatre,* 356.

9 *"This is the play in which Ruth Chatterton"*: *Daily Herald,* May 17, 1929.

10 *"landed on a broken Mentholatum"*: Martin, *My Heart Belongs,* 31.

10 *"That may have been one reason why my parents"*: Martin, *My Heart Belongs,* 35.

10 *"Ward-Belmont still reflected the values of a traditional girls' school"*: Pethel, *All-Girls Education,* 65.

10 *"For Nashville's young women, behavioral expectations"*: Ibid., 78-79.

11 *"She made them a box-office smash"*: Hendon Holmes, "Heartbreak Behind—Happiness Ahead," *Radio and Television Mirror,* (March 1940), 18+.

11 *"Mary kept the story of that marriage a secret"*: Ibid., 65.

11 *"When her best friend [Bessie Mae] wriggled out of writing"*: Jeanne Perkins, "Mary Martin," *Life,* December 27, 1943, 101.

12 *"They were married in a church"*: *Hollywood Citizen News,* 1939, Constance Mc-Cormick Collection, vol. 1.

13 *"How hillbilly can you get?"*: Martin, *My Heart Belongs,* 36.

13 *"Ben and I talked Mother into letting us get married"*: Ibid.

13 *"Our marriage was not consummated for a week or so"*: Davis, 17.

14 *"For some reason, my grandmother brought Ben"*: Hagman, *Hello Darlin',* 17, 15.

14 *"big Ben Hagman, a football player from her"*: Schwab, "Star from Texas," 78.

14 *"we married much too soon"*: Pete Martin, *Saturday Evening Post,* March 28, 1959.

14 *"Mr. Martin didn't want the marriage at all"*: Author interview with Gertz.

15 *"doing legal work for an insurance company"*: Holmes, 65.

15 *"Mary had a watermelon party for me in her yard"*: Davis, 18.

15 *"when I wasn't throwing up"*: Martin, *My Heart Belongs,* 39

15 *"Mary just bore him"*: Davis, 19.

15 *"She was a kid herself"*: Hagman, *Hello Darlin',* 17.

16 *"It was perhaps the most perceptive statement"*: Davis, 20–21.

16 *"I think that for my grandmother, sex was"*: Author interview with Kristina Hagman.

16 *"She said to her father"*: Author interview with Gertz.

16 *"It was enormous and drafty"*: Martin, *My Heart Belongs,* 43.

16 *"The grocer would give me four dollars"*: Ibid., 44.

17 *"I began to make up ballet steps"*: Ibid., 43.

17 *"Mary told her father"*: Author interview with Gertz.

17 *"Usually they put me in the front row"*: Pete Martin, 116.

17 *"It was a redbrick house, with mirrors"*: Author interview with Gertz.

17 *"I was called the Crazy Girl"*: Schwab, "Star from Texas," 78.

17 *"To begin with, I had five pupils"*: Pete Martin, 115.

18 *" friend, companion, chaperon, boss"*: Martin, *My Heart Belongs,* 47.

18 *"That's how it is in small towns"*: Francey, "Her Heart Belongs to Hollywood," *Hollywood,* January, 1940, 26+.

18 *"When I first started teaching"*: this and other quotations in the next few paragraphs are from Pete Martin, 116.

19 *"Then, in 1936, they had the Texas Centennial"*: Author interview with Gertz.

19 *"So I went to father and told him I wanted to go back"*: Pete Martin, 116.

2   Finding a Voice

20 *With great expectations*: Hopper, *Whole Truth,* 154.

20 *"When I think of it now I shudder"*: Helen Weller, "Mary Martin—Fairy Godmother," *Hollywood* (April 1942).

20 *According to Hopper, Frank Whitbeck at MGM*: Hedda Hopper, "Columnist's Dinner Honors Mary Martin," *Los Angeles Times* (June 23, 1954).

21 *Juanita made another visit to LA*: Robert McIlwaine, "Mother Knew Best," *Silver Screen* March 1940.

21 *Martin had no idea that Juanita*: Ibid.

22 *"One black day I heard in central casting"*: Schwab, "Star from Texas," 82.

22 *Preston Martin . . . arranged for his daughter's divorce*: Martin, *My Heart Belongs*, 63.

22 *"From the Casanova I went back to another bar"*: Ibid.

22 *In her memoir, Martin would claim"*: Ibid., 62.

23 *It was probably on May 8 when Ivan Kahn*: Kahn papers, Margaret Herrick Library.

23 *"The Trocadero always showed off"*: Author interview with Marge Champion.

23 *"I'd prepared two encores"*: McIlwaine, "Mother Knew Best."

23 *"For half a chorus she poured out her golden, dramatic soprano"*: John R. Franchey, "Her Heart Belongs to Hollywood," *Hollywood* (January 1940) 29:1.

23 *As Martin explained some years later*: Peter Martin, "I Call on Mary Martin," *Saturday Evening Post* (March 28, 1959), 115.

23 *"I started it straight"*: Ibid., 116.

24 *"It felt completely natural"*: Mary Martin, "The Day I Found Me," *Parade*, October 21, 1956, 2.

24 *"You see, it was one of those nights"*: McIlwaine, "Mother Knew Best."

24 *In her memoir, Martin would erroneously claim*: Martin, *My Heart Belongs*, 68.

25 *"For the rest of the afternoon"*: Schwab, "Star from Texas," 16.

25 *According to Martin, her first substantial contract*: Martin, *My Heart Belongs*, 69.

25 *It was her surprising rendition of "Il Bacio"*: Schwab, "Star from Texas," 82.

25 *"In Hollywood I discovered drive-ins"*: Martin, *My Heart Belongs*, 61.

25 *"Oscar had rented a studio for her audition"*: Fordin, *Getting to Know Him*, 155.

25 *As Martin recalled, she sang for Kern "Les Filles de Cadix"*: Martin, *My Heart Belongs*, 60.

26 *The young Larry Hagman developed a lasting friendship*: Hagman, *Hello Darlin'*, 20.

26 *"We were living in Houston temporarily at that point"*: Author interview with Gertz.

26 *Martin felt like she was speaking a foreign language*: Schwab, "Star from Texas," 83.

26 *"When I was in Texas"*: Lydia Lane, "Mary Martin Says Correct Breathing Secret of Vitality," *Los Angeles Times* (October 3, 1954).

26 *"I remember Mary Martin when she came to call on me"*: Radie Harris, "Just Leave it to Mary," *Modern Screen*, May 1940.

27 *Shortly after she arrived in New York*: This paragraph and the five following drawn from Martin, "I Call on Mary Martin," and Schwab, "Star from Texas."

28 *The Spewacks based their libretto for* Leave It to Me! *on their own 1932 play*: Bordman, *American Musical Theatre*, 59.

28 *"a once elegant Moscow"*: the rest of the paragraph taken from Martin, "I Call on Mary Martin," and Schwab, "Star from Texas."

29 *In the number, Martin was surrounded*: Quotes in this paragraph from Martin, *My Heart Belongs*, 76.

29 *"the most starry overnight debut"*: Morley, *Gene Kelly*, 38.

30 *"Mary Martin, you know, is probably the most basically naïve person I've ever met"*: McBrien, *Cole Porter*, 221.

30 *"People don't realize now what a major hit it was"*: Author interview with Schmidt.

30 *According to Kristina Hagman*: Author interview with Hagman.

30 *talent scout Ivan Kahn wrote a memo*: Kahn papers at Herrick Library.

30 *an NBC radio program devoted to Martin's life*: *Biographies in Sound: Meet Mary Martin* (October 16, 1956).

31 *"It took Mary a while"*: Joe McCarthy, "Her Heart Belongs," *Cosmopolitan* (January 1956) 30–31.

31 *Martin also realized that she still required vocal training*: This paragraph and the two following drawn from Schwab, "Star from Texas," 84.

32 *appearance on the cover of* Life *magazine*: "Mary Martin Is Broadway's Newest Star," *Life* (December 19, 1938) 29.

32 *"The cover of* Life *in fur coat and underwear"*: Schwab, "Star from Texas," 83.

33 *Martin decided not to attend the funeral*: Harry Ferguson, "Song Becomes Dad's Requiem," *Hollywood Citizen News* (December 21, 1938).

33 *According to Hedda Hopper*: Hopper, *Whole Truth,* 155.

33 *"working with a mike [as] a defense mechanism to preserve her voice"*: *Variety* (January 18, 1939), and Rivadue, *Mary Martin,* 5.

33 *"officially, if not emotionally, engaged"*: Martin, *My Heart Belongs,* 94.

33 *"masses of flowers"*: Ibid., 83.

3   The Unlikely Movie Star

35 *"When I was sixteen and seventeen"*: Mary Martin, "The Day I Found Me," *Parade,* October 21, 1956, 2.

36 *"dearest friend in all the world" and "my closest most special friend"*: Martin, *My Heart Belongs,* 89, 106.

36 *In her memoir, Martin would recall turning on the television*: Ibid., 89.

36 *"Just how close Arthur and Martin became"*: Oller, *Jean Arthur,* 128.

37 *As theater scholar Ethan Mordden would claim*: Mordden, *Broadway Babies,* 119.

37 *Martin herself was extremely dismissive of her film career*: Martin, *My Heart Belongs,* 89.

37 *"I couldn't stand the pictures I was in"*: Peter Martin, "I Call on Mary Martin," *Saturday Evening Post* (March 28, 1959), 118.

37 *part of Freeman's mission was to make "fewer but better movies"*: Eames, *Paramount Story,* 123.

38 *"long before the picture went into production"*: Radie Harris, "Just Leave It to Mary," *Modern Screen* (May 1940), 50–51.

38 *an interview prepared for the studio pressbook*: *The Great Victor Herbert* pressbook.

39 *"She rode into town behind a whooping parade"*: "Texas Town Hails Its Favorite Daughter on Her Cinema Debut," *Life,* n.d., and Constance McCormick Scrapbook.

39 *"It was a really big deal with its premiere in Weatherford"*: Author interview with Gertz.

40 *"With arc lights flooding the streets"*: Harris.

40 *The review in the* New York Times *by Bosley Crowther*: *New York Times* December 7, 1939.

40 *"Martin, as we knew"*: Richard Holman to Y. Frank Freeman (February 5, 1940), Paramount archives at Margaret Herrick Library.

40 *As another new contract player at the studio*: Author interview with Morison.

41 *"Strange to say, I was the only executive there who voted against signing Mary"*: Hedda Hopper, "Mary Martin," *Woman's Home Companion* (January 1956).

41 *It was later, in Hollywood, that agent John McCormick*: All quotes in this paragraph are from Hopper, "Mary Martin."

41 *Several years later, Martin claimed that Halliday*: Katherine Albert, "She's Different," *Movies* (November 1943) 81.

42 *Following a lunch some days after Elsa Maxwell's party*: Hopper, "Mary Martin."

42 *"When Mary finishes work in the film"*: *Hollywood Citizen News,* n.d., and Constance McCormick Scrapbook.

42 *"The first night we began our love life together"*: Martin, *My Heart Belongs,* 100.

43 *A movie magazine described him as resembling "a monk out of the Middle Ages"*: Jeane Karr, "Happy Ending," *Modern Screen,* (April 1941), 39.

43 *"Halliday's becoming Martin's manager masculinized him"*: Stacy Wolf, "Washin' That Man Right Outta Her Hair," in *Passing Performances: Queer Readings of Leading Players in American Theater History,* ed. Robert A. Schanke and Kim Marra, 287.

43 *"My parents attracted creative people," recalled Halliday*: Irving Stone, "Mary Martin's Marriage," *American Weekly* (January 8, 1956).

43 *When Hope Harvey left her husband*: Elliott Sirkin, "My Son, Larry Hagman," *Good Housekeeping* (July 1987), 262.

44 *But as Halliday also told Stone, he was "crazy about movies"*: Quotes in this paragraph drawn from Stone, "Mary Martin's Marriage," 9.

44 *Larry had a rather indifferent reaction*: Martin, *My Heart Belongs,* 99.

44 *"Earned my first check at sixty-three"*: Karr, "Happy Ending."

45 *the new bride would seek Hope Harvey's advice*: Stone, "Mary Martin's Marriage," 11.

45 *"Wouldn't you just know"*: Elizabeth Wilson, "MM's Honeymoon Home," *Screenland* (February 1941).

45 *"The only thing I knew how to do when I got married was to buy a piano"*: Martin, "I Call on Mary Martin," 114.

45 *"As soon as I got six dining room chairs"*: Wilson, "MM's Honeymoon Home."

46 *"Making movies with Bing almost made Hollywood worthwhile"*: Martin, *My Heart Belongs,* 87.

47 *"possibly [the] worst of [Allen's] screen efforts"*: Taylor, *Fred Allen,* 244.

47 *Martin conversely wrote*: Martin, *My Heart Belongs,* 89.

48 *"The combination of the title"*: Richard Holman to Y. Frank Freeman (February 5, 1940), Paramount papers at Margaret Herrick Library.

49 *Wally Westmore, makeup man at Paramount, would recall*: *Biographies in Sound: Meet Mary Martin* (October 16, 1956).

50 *According to an internal memo*: Jacob N. Karp (September 7, 1940), Paramount papers at Margaret Herrick Library.

50 *"mob of five hundred extras"*: Stone, "Mary Martin's Marriage."

51 *"We shot [the scene] on a studio set but under real rain"*: Martin, *My Heart Belongs,* 103.

51 *"You see, Mammy . . . now my taste"*: Peter Martin, unpublished manuscript for *Saturday Evening Post,* n.d.

52 *"I don't remember what all the letter said," claimed Martin*: Martin, *My Heart Belongs,* 104.

52 *"I almost lost her every month, because of my blood type"*: Ibid., 106.

52 *A cover story on Martin*: Evans Plummer, "Mary Martin's Plans for Motherhood," *Movie-Radio Guide* (August 16, 1941), 3.

53 *"Mary Martin, I notice with some alarm, is playing Jean Arthur"*: Agee, *Agee on Film,* 54.

53 *"Mary is a big favorite with the boys in service"*: Helen Hover, "Hollywood's War Effort," *Hollywood* (November 1942), 14.

54 *Martin would ostensibly sign autographs*: Ibid.

54 *Martin took first aid classes—"like dozens of other movie stars"*: "Liza," "Mary Ties a Bandage," *Screenland* (July 1942).

54 *"Like Mary, Rosemary was a dancing instructor"*: Helen Weller, "Mary Martin—Fairy Godmother," *Hollywood* (April 1942).

4 A Little Touch of Mary in the Night

55 *"The professional climate [in Hollywood] was too frigid"*: Hedda Hopper, "Mary Martin," *Women's Home Companion* (January 1956), 91.

55 *"go back to Broadway"*: Martin, *My Heart Belongs,* 108.

56 *Martin would tell Rex Reed . . . "that she made the decision"*: *Daily News* (January 8, 1978), and Martin, *Mary Martin's Needlepoint,* 48.

56 *According to Lawrence Langner, head of the Theatre Guild*: Block, *Richard Rodgers Reader,* 119.

56 *The review in* Variety *was hopeful*: Quotations in this paragraph from Leonard, *Broadway Bound,* 112.

57 *"I cannot play this play [because] it is too sexy and profane"*: Barranger, *Gambler's Instinct,* 72.

57 *Weill's music for* One Touch of Venus: Hirsch, *Kurt Weill on Stage,* 210.

57 *"was very much a Broadway musical comedy of the wartime 1940s"*: Mordden, *Broadway Babies,* 228.

57 *"Crawford's lesbian friendships were commonly known"*: Barranger, *Margaret Webster,* 160.

58 *"original, meaningful, and entertaining material"*: Barranger, *Gambler's Instinct,* 68.

58 *"That skinny thing with a Texas accent to play Venus?"*: Hirsch, *Kurt Weill on Stage,* 216.

58 *"When I first saw Mainbocher I couldn't believe it"*: Martin, *My Heart Belongs,* 109.

59 *"I will do your clothes for the show"*: Barranger, *Gambler's Instinct,* 75–76.

59 *"directly to every man and woman in the audience"*: Irving Stone, "Mary Martin's Marriage," *American Weekly* (January 15, 1956).

59 *"In Hollywood the studio had draped me with hair"*: Peter Martin, "I Call on Mary Martin," *Saturday Evening Post* (March 28, 1959), 118.

59 *"a concession to the fact that after all, Venus is never a clothed lady"*: Constance McCormick Scrapbook, and *Life,* n.d.

59 *Martin was somewhat "green"*: Osato, *Distant Dances,* 211.

60 *"grew tremendously in the show"*: Crawford, *One Naked Individual,* 129.

60 *"It must have been in Venus"*: Schwab, "Star from Texas," 85.

60 *As far as Kazan was concerned*: Kazan, *Elia Kazan,* 234–35.

60 "How do you think . . . won't have to direct you really," Crawford, *One Naked Individual,* 128.

61 *"I met Mary at Vinton and Mary Freedley's"*: All Paula Laurence quotes from author interview with Laurence.

63 *"just too vulgar"*: Crawford, *One Naked Individual,* 131.

64 *Mary McCarthy was even more emphatic in the* Partisan Review: *Mary McCarthy's Theatre Chronicles, 1937–1962,* 72.

64 *"Martin is still no singer"*: Suskin, *Opening Night on Broadway,* 526.

64 *"She turns in such an engaging job of acting and warbling"*: Harry Evans, "Broadway Diary," *Family Circle* (December 17, 1943), 10.

64 *A day or two after the opening*: Lucy Greenbaum, "One Touch of Mary," *New York Times* (October 10, 1943).

64 *A cover story in* Life *proclaimed Martin*: "One Touch of Venus," *Life* (October 25, 1943), 61.

65 *Still another, more extensive story in* Life: Jeanne Perkins, "Mary Martin," *Life* (December 27, 1943), 101.

65 *Richard Rodgers wrote Cheryl Crawford a fawning note*: Farneth, *Kurt Weill*, 228.

66 *"Later, in Miss Martin's dressing room"*: Harry Evans, "Broadway Diary," *Family Circle* (December 17, 1943), 11.

66 *According to Sono Osato, the highlight"*: Osato, *Distant Dances*, 224.

66 *"112 degrees . . . sweltered"*: Crawford, *One Naked Individual*, 140.

67 *"Venus must be happy"*: Shirlee P. Newman, "Mary Martin on Stage," *New York Herald Tribune*, n.d.

67 *"16 young . . . exceed three"*: Charlotte and Denis Plimmer, "Her Heart Belongs to Broadway," *Coronet* (March 1954), 71.

67 *As documented by a two-page spread in* Mademoiselle: James Pendleton, "Venus Lives Here," *Mademoiselle* (April 1944).

68 *"Mother and everyone else expected"*: Hagman, *Hello Darlin'*, 25.

68 *Her funeral in Weatherford*: documents from Weatherford Public Library.

68 *"On Saturday, a matinee day, she slept till eleven"*: Hagman, *Hello Darlin'*, 26.

68 *"[Larry] came from a household"*: Elliott Sirkin, "My Son, Larry Hagman," *Good Housekeeping* (July 1987), 166.

69 *"hell . . . at the table"*: Hagman, *Hello Darlin'*, 26.

69 *"One night, as Richard was taking Mother to the theater"*: Ibid., 28.

69 *"Mother most likely wouldn't have had such a brilliant career"*: Ibid., 29.

70 *"He said that after a week, he was taken out of the part"*: Author interview with Warren's friend Robert Ray.

70 *Following a performance one night in Cleveland*: Martin, *Mary Martin's Needlepoint*, 89.

70 *"after they got back to the hotel"*: Davis, *Mary Martin*, 88.

70 *Martin had advised Sono Osata*: Osata, *Distance Dances*, 246–47.

70 *"Some of the audiences have been the best we've ever had"*: Davis, *Mary Martin*, 88.

71 *"By that time . . . for that episode"*: Crawford, *One Naked Individual*, 143.

71 *"Martin's excellence [and future unavailability] may be the reason"*: Mordden, *Broadway Babies*, 119.

71 *"As soon as the show"*: Mary Martin, "The Lights in the Halliday Home," *Coronet* (November 1955), 128.

71 *"We bought the place in Norwalk because of Heller"*: Peter Martin, unpublished manuscript for *Saturday Evening Post*, n.d.

72 *"It's two years"*: Mary Martin to Hedda Hopper, March 16, 1945, Martin papers at Margaret Herrick Library.

72 *It was the first time that Bessie Mae met Halliday*: Davis, *Mary Martin*, 92.

72 *"all the reviewers" had particular praise*: McBrien, *Cole Porter*, 297.

73 *"Hedda Hopper apparently did not see . . . insisted on Doris Day"*: Hopper papers at Margaret Herrick Library.

5 From the Far East to . . . the Far East

75 *"That part scared me out of my wits"*: Davis, *Mary Martin*, 91.

75 *Schwab recalled visiting the Hallidays*: Laurence Schwab, "Star from Texas," *McCall's* (November 1949), 87.

76 *Martin would spend several years embroidering the proverb*: Martin, "The Lights in the Halliday Home," *Coronet* (November 1955), 126–27.

76 *Martin . . . took complete responsibility for discovering Brynner*: Martin, *My Heart Belongs*, 120.

76 *Director John Houseman put his finger on*: Houseman, *Front and Center*, 162.

77 *"As a couple they were fretful and insecure"*: Ibid., 167.

77 *"The Hallidays decided that sharing a man"*: Ibid., 168.

77 *"Whenever Mother's best friend, Jean Arthur, visited"*: Hagman, *Hello Darlin'*, 31.

78 *"My parents wanted me to go to Putney"*: Author interview with Phillips.

78 *In his memoir, Hagman relays Martin's awkward attempt*: Hagman, *Hello Darlin'*, 31.

78 *Phillips recalled Larry's mother returning to Woodstock that fall*: Author interview with Phillips.

79 *"in a lighter . . . unhappiness"*: Houseman, *Front and Center*, 167.

79 Lute Song *would become*: Pendleton, *The Theatre of Robert Edmond Jones*, 133–34.

79 *"melt scene into scene"*: Ibid., 138.

79 *"Mary was able to achieve"*: Houseman, *Front and Center*, 171.

80 *"a pink-cheeked"*: Ibid., 165.

80 *"tried hard to get rid of Nancy Davis"*: Ibid., 172.

80 *"I'm not right for this"*: Davis, *Mary Martin*, 97.

80 *"Mary and I will always remember your kindness"*: Houseman, *Front and Center*, 175.

81 *"More and more"*: Nathan, *The Theatre Book of the Year: 1945–1946*, 307, 310.

81 *"the season's loveliest production and most charming failure"*: *Time* (February 18, 1946).

81 *As emphasized by Lewis Nichols in his review*: Bordman, *American Musical Theatre*, 551.

81 *as Burton Rascoe wrote*: Suskin, *Opening Night on Broadway*, 410.

81 *Alan Jay Lerner would come to feel*: Lerner, *Musical Theatre*, 161.

82 *"Her sister actresses were unanimous"*: Courtney, *Laurette*, 365.

82 *"Afterward she gave a party"*: John S. Wilson, "The Life of *Jennie*," *New York Times* (October 13, 1963).

82 *According to her daughter, Marguerite Courtney*: Courtney, *Laurette*, 365.

82 *Taylor's son, Dwight Taylor*: Kear, *Laurette Taylor, American Stage Legend*, 223.

82 *Yul Brynner would blame*: Davis, *Mary Martin*, 94.

83 *"It wasn't at all that Dolly was a better actress"*: Ibid., 100.

83 *"Cut your throat"*: Martin, *My Heart Belongs*, 145.

83 *Noël Coward sent Mary Martin a telegram*: Coward, *Letters of Noël Coward*, 516.

83 *All three of the principals*: Barranger, *Margaret Webster*, 164.

83 *Martin told them that she "wasn't an actor"*: Author interview with Elliott Sirkin.

84 *To increase the show's chances*: Morley and Leon, *Gene Kelly*, 108–09.

84 *"worried sick"*: Coward, *Letters of Noël Coward*, 518.

84 *Coward received an "irritating cable"*: Payn, *Noël Coward Diaries*, 62.

85 *"They were madly enthusiastic"*: Ibid., 64.

85 *Coward scribbled in his diary*: Ibid., 67.

85 *As late as November 14*: Ibid., 69.

85 *But by December 11*: Ibid.

85 *"They were well rewarded"*: Hoare, *Noël Coward*, 368.

86 *"Alice was really at it"*: Martin, *My Heart Belongs*, 133.

86 *Martin seemed particularly "nervous"*: Vickers, *Vivien Leigh*, 170.

86 *"From the first week of rehearsal onward"*: Morley and Leon, *Gene Kelley*, 109.

86 *At the end of the rehearsal*: Payn, *Noël Coward Diaries,* 70.

86 *Coward even wrote a "private" verse*: Coward, *Letters of Noël Coward,* 521.

86 *Sheridan Morley further noted*: Morley and Leon, *Gene Kelley,* 110.

87 *"Gladys rather took"*: Hoare, *Noël Coward,* 369.

87 *"Gladys's bows"*: Payn, *My Life with Noël Coward,* 41.

87 *In the end*: Morley and Leon, *Gene Kelley,* 110.

87 *Martin found something worthwhile*: Martin, *My Heart Belongs,* 134.

87 *"Realizing her technical limitations"*: Payn, *My Life with Noël Coward,* 41.

87 *"In Noël Coward's show I had to slap a man"*: Schwab, "Star from Texas," 85.

88 *"There is plenty of honest dullness"*: Rivadue, *Mary Martin,* 38.

88 *"The evening flowed mildly on"*: Ibid.

88 *"Pseudo-Viennese sentimentality*: Payn, *My Life with Noël Coward,* 44.

88 *After the opening*: Martin, *My Heart Belongs,* 140.

88 *Payn acknowledged that he and Martin never connected*: Payn, *My Life with Noël Coward,* 44.

88 *Martin "played on doggedly"*: Morley and Leon, *Gene Kelly,* 111.

88 *"Everybody thought it was a telephone number"*: Peter Martin, "I Call on Mary Martin," *Saturday Evening Post* (March 28, 1959).

89 *"report of the opening . . . something called taxes"*: Mary Martin letters to Hedda Hopper (undated), Hopper papers at Margaret Herrick Library.

89 *"WE WANT TO COME HOME"*: Peter Martin, "I Call on Mary Martin," *Saturday Evening Post* (March 28, 1959).

6   Mary Got Her Gun

90 *"I wouldn't have played it"*: Martin, *My Heart Belongs,* 147.

90 *Martin also recalled*: Ibid., 220.

90 *"Richard and I were so heartsick"*: Ibid., 146.

90 *"During a working weekend that summer"*: Fordin, *Getting to Know Him,* 251.

91 *"Logan took a break"*: Maslon, *The* South Pacific *Companion,* 99.

91 *"I went numb"*: Hagman, *Hello Darlin',* 34.

92 *Roger Phillips recalled having dinner with Larry and his mother*: Author interview with Phillips.

92 *Looking back, Hagman realized*: Hagman, *Hello Darlin',* 35.

92 *Hagman would only tell part of the story*: Further details from author interview with Ted Flicker.

92 *wrote about shooting*: Hagman, *Hello Darlin',*

92 *During the same trip*: Hagman, *Hello Darlin',* 39; further details from author interview with Ted Flicker.

93 *Heller said the worst aspect*: Author interview with Heller Halliday Weir.

93 *Logan would point out years later*: Logan, *Josh,* 206–07.

93 *"I don't think anybody can be a better Annie"*: Peter Martin, "I Call on Mary Martin," *Saturday Evening Post* (March 28, 1959), 118.

93 *"She has a pure, honest, God-given voice"*: Martin, *My Heart Belongs,* 149.

93 *Mordden would weigh in*: Mordden, *Broadway Babies,* 114.

94 *"Everything about the national company"*: Davis, *Mary Martin,* 115.

94 *"There's no business"*: Lyrics from Laurence Schwab, "Star from Texas," *McCall's* (November 1949).

94 *a story in the* Dallas Morning News: Newman, *Mary Martin on Stage,* 59.

95 *"Even though Mummy"*: Ibid., 59–60.

95 *"It was agony"*: Davis, *Mary Martin,* 116.

95 *reviewer in the* Pittsburgh Post: Rivadue, *Mary Martin,* 42.

95 *Martin was presented with the key to the city*: Schwab, "Star from Texas," 89.

95 *Tommy Wonder . . . left the tour*: Author interview with Wonder's longtime partner Don Dellair.

96 *"In Kansas City"*: Schwab, "Star from Texas," 89.

96 *racist whims of Lloyd Binford*: Whitney Strub, "Black and White and Banned All Over," *Journal of Social History* (Spring 2007), 690–91.

96 *a letter dated October 28*: John Montague to Hedda Hopper (October 28, 1947), Hedda Hopper papers at Margaret Herrick Library.

96 *"Movie producers, directors, top stars scrambled to get tickets"*: Louis Berg, "Her Heart Belongs to Broadway," *This Week* (May 1, 1949), 20.

97 *"Richard and Mary sat in her* Annie *dressing room"*: Schwab, "Star from Texas," 89.

97 *According to Sidney*: Davis, *Mary Martin,* 123.

97 *"Mary seemed ideal"*: Crawford, *One Naked Individual,* 169.

7 "Some Enchanted Evenings"

98 *Hedda Hopper wrote in her column*: Los Angeles Times (May 10, 1949).

99 *"What was blocking Oscar was the GI talk"*: Ross Drake, "South Pacific," *TV Guide* (November 20, 1971), 20.

100 *According to Logan*: Logan, *Josh,* 249.

100 *"[Rodgers] pretends to hate business"*: Ibid.

100 *"Something in them needed to work"*: Author interview with Chapin.

100 *Logan described his leading man*: Logan, *Josh,* 252.

101 *"She was scared to death"*: Cosmopolitan (April 1950).

101 *Rodgers assured Martin*: Rodgers, *My Favorite Things,* 260.

101 *Pinza's contract included a clause*: Maslon, Sound of Music *Companion,* 112.

101 *"She and Dick [Halliday] announced"*: Author interview with Rodgers.

101 *"One day while Mary"*: Fordin, *Getting to Know Him,* 268–69.

102 *With Rodgers himself at the piano*: Martin, *Mary Martin's Needlepoint,* 47.

102 *"It was written in about two minutes"*: Author interview with Bernice Saunders.

102 *"For all its integral specificity"*: Maslon, Sound of Music *Companion,* 78.

102 *Mary discovered a photo of herself*: Martin, *My Heart Belongs,* 163.

103 *"That was the song I always hummed"*: Ibid., 169.

103 *"Logan had foregone"*: Mielziner, *Designing for the Theater,* 23.

103 *"He had insisted"*: Ibid., 50–51.

103 *"We had been within inches of terminal disaster"*: Logan, *Josh,* 256.

103 *But Logan introduced problems*: Author interview with Saunders.

104 *"This was one of the first concrete signs"*: Martin, *Mary Martin's Needlepoint,* 25.

104 *One of the innovations of* South Pacific: Rodgers, *My Favorite Things,* 261.

104 *"Dances were not choreographed"*: Fordin, *Getting to Know Him,* 277.

105 *Rodgers told a reporter for the* Los Angeles Times: Maslon, Sound of Music *Companion,* 123.

105 *As Martin told Radie Harris for a radio interview*: March 3, 1950, WOR radio interview: transcript from the Radie Harris papers at Margaret Herrick Library.

105 *As Logan recalled*: Logan, *Josh,* 251.

105 *"Everyone loved [Pinza]"*: Ibid., 252.

105 *Martin readily agreed*: Martin, *My Heart Belongs,* 171.

105 *Alan Jay Lerner would claim*: Lerner, *The Musical Theatre,* 172.

105 *Don Fellows, who played Lieutenant Buzz Adams, recalled*: Secrest, *Somewhere for Me,* 292.

106 *Martin would tell Hector Arce*: *Women's Wear Daily* (December 11, 1970).

106 *Rodgers . . . quipped about them in a letter to Logan*: Secrest, *Somewhere for Me,* 292.

106 *According to Ted Chapin*: Author interview with Chapin.

106 *"There was no concentration in the crowd"*: Logan, *Josh,* 257.

106 *"The next night"*: Maslon, South Pacific *Companion,* 93.

107 *Logan also had Hammerstein turn "A Wonderful Guy" into a soliloquy*: Logan, *Josh,* 262.

107 *According to one story*: Maslon, South Pacific *Companion,* 149.

107 *Winthrop Rockefeller*: Schwab, "Star from Texas," 90.

107 *"Hayward and his colleagues"*: Maslon, South Pacific *Companion,* 129.

107 *"For human interest"*: Rose, "Preview," *Variety* (March 9, 1949).

108 *Years later it would be reported*: Maslon, South Pacific *Companion,* 129.

108 *Martin attended in a striking outfit designed by Mainbocher*: Martin, *My Heart Belongs,* 170.

108 *Socialite and patron Mildred Hunter Green*: Secrest, *Somewhere for Me,* 356

108 *recalled Don Murray*: Murray, letter to author, August 19, 2011.

109 *The anonymous reviewer in* Newsweek: "Theater," *Newsweek* (April 11, 1949), 78.

109 *yet another cover story in* Life *magazine*: "South Pacific," *Life* (April 18, 1949), 93.

109 *Ethel Merman famously quipped*: Schwab, "Star from Texas," 90.

109 *Richard Rodgers recognized that he had a gold mine*: Laurence Maslon, *American Musicals: The Complete Books and Lyrics of Eight Broadway Classics, 1927–1949* (Library of America, 2014), 704.

109 *Helen Hayes would include Martin's Nellie Forbush in her list*: Helen Hayes, "Helen Hayes Picks the 10 Most Memorable Stage Performances," *Collier's* (September 22, 1951).

109 *Brooks Atkinson would claim*: Atkinson, *Lively Years,* 208.

110 *"even fake ticket stubs"*: Maslon, South Pacific *Companion,* 153.

110 *"Heat literally made me sick"*: Martin, *My Heart Belongs,* 171.

110 *"By this time Richard and I were pretty expert on hair"*: Ibid., 167.

110 *"When she was working, there was nothing else"*: Author interview with Saunders.

111 *Don Fellows, who had a problem with stuttering*: Secrest, *Somewhere for Me,* 290–91.

111 *"It was awful," reported Saunders*: Author interview with Saunders.

111 *The cast's close-knit feeling*: Rodgers, *My Favorite Things,* 230.

111 *a cover story by Louis Berg in* This Week: Louis Berg, "Her Heart Belongs to Broadway, *This Week* (May 1, 1949), 21.

112 *Columnists had a field day*: Secrest, *Somewhere for Me,* 291–92.

112 *Saunders recalled that news of her own forthcoming marriage*: Author interview with Saunders.

112 *"He loved basking in the adulation"*: Rodgers, *My Favorite Things,* 263.

112 *Hedda Hopper would echo Rodgers's opinion*: Hedda Hopper to Colonel McCormick (circa 1954), Margaret Herrick Library collection.

112 *"From the beginning, Mary was wonderful"*: Author interview with Saunders.

112 *"One of the girls"*: Ibid.

113 *According to Richard Rodgers's wife*: Rodgers, *My Favorite Things,* 55.

113 *Martin had taken up needlepoint*: *New York Times* (April 1950; as reprinted in Reader's Digest).

113 *"It will illustrate our home life"*: Ibid.

113 *Decades later, Martin would tell a reporter*: Connie Berman, "Mary Martin . . . She's a Star at Needlepoint, Too!" *Needlecraft* (Spring/Summer 1980), 40.

114 *Hopper sent Luce a letter*: Hedda Hopper to Clare Boothe Luce (undated), Hopper papers at Margaret Herrick Library.

114 *Martin wrote in a subsequent letter to Hopper*: Mary Martin to Hedda Hopper (May 9, 1949), Mary Martin papers at Margaret Herrick Library.

114 *Another illustrious backstage visitor was Hellen Keller*: Hedda Hopper, "Mary Martin," *Woman's Home Companion* (January 1956), 23.

114 *"Mary was really enchanting"*: Payn, *Noël Coward Diaries,* 128.

115 *"Everyone in the world came to see it"*: Davis, *Mary Martin,* 141.

115 *Nearly three decades later, Martin would recall*: Elliott Sirkin, *Peter Pan Recruits a Lost Boy* (unpublished manuscript, 1976).

115 *In an article for the* New York Times: Mary Martin, "My One Year of *South Pacific,*" *New York Times* (April 2, 1950).

115 *Martin sent Ethel Merman*: Kellow, *Ethel Merman,* 129.

115 *There was almost another flare-up with Coward*: Schwab, "Star from Texas," 88.

116 *Given Larry's "total dislike"*: Martin, *My Heart Belongs,* 177.

116 *"Larry called and said, 'Hey Rog'"*: Author interview with Phillips.

116 *"My first memory of Larry"*: Author interview with Flicker.

116 *"Honestly, as long as I live"*: Elliott Sirkin, "My Son, Larry Hagman," *Good Housekeeping* (July 1987), 166.

116 The American Magazine *ran a story*: Wayne Amos, "A Day in the Life of Mary Martin," *American Magazine* (June 1950), 43.

117 *Martin was visited in her dressing room*: March 4, 1950, transcript from the Radie Harris papers at Margaret Herrick Library.

117 *a follow-up story in* Time *magazine*: *Time* (December 18, 1950).

117 *"We had never so much as sung 'Silent Night' together"*: Davis, *Mary Martin,* 173.

118 *The four men who were responsible for the character*: Martin, *Mary Martin's Needlepoint,* 45–46.

118 *a well-circulated anecdote*: Secrest, *Somewhere for Me,* 296.

119 *It was here that Halliday became irate*: Hagman, *Hello Darlin',* 67.

119 *During rehearsals, Larry was impressed by*: Ibid.

120 *But friction quickly escalated*: Ibid.

120 *"We invited Mary and Richard"*: Author interview with Flicker.

120 *From Logan's perspective, the problems stemmed from Martin*: Logan, *Josh,* 287.

121 *"I decided to face Mary Martin"*: Logan, *Josh,* 287–88.

121 *As Logan also pointed out it's difficult*: Logan, *Josh,* 289.

121 *As Martin herself recalled*: Martin, *Mary Martin's Needlepoint,* 52.

121 *Broadway musical performer Walter Willison recalled*: Author interview with Willison.

122 *Rodgers was "shocked"*: Richard Rodgers, *Musical Stages* (De Capo Press: 2002), 264.

122 *"I would come out of the shower"*: Martin, *Mary Martin's Needlepoint,* 176.

122 *"Show incredibly slow"*: Payn, *Noël Coward Diaries,* 179.

123 *Larry flubbed his single line*: Hagman, *Hello Darlin',* 68–69.

123 *"I'm not important"*: Charlotte and Denis Plimmer, "Her Heart Belongs to Broadway," *Coronet* (March 1954), 72.

123 *"I remember Jinx saying to me"*: Martin, *My Heart Belongs,* 178.

123 *"In America,* not *to have seen* South Pacific *is a social gaffe"*: David Mitchell, "South Pacific," *Picture Post* (December 1, 1951), 31–33.

123 *begrudging the "vast publicity campaign"*: Wright, *West End Broadway,* 74.

124 *"For Mary Martin's sake"*: Ibid., 75.

124 *As Martin summarized the response*: Martin, *My Heart Belongs,* 178.

124 *Tynan went so far*: Tynan, *Curtains,* 245–46.

124 *As Martin characterized the British critics' responses*: Martin, *My Heart Belongs,* 178.

124 *In December, Martin sent a handwritten letter*: Mary Martin to Hedda Hopper, from the Mary Martin papers at Margaret Herrick Library.

125 *"And that was the [very] night"*: Martin, *Mary Martin's Needlepoint,* 6.

125 *"She gave a superb performance"*: Payn, *Noël Coward Diaries,* 201.

126 *"Really a triumph"*: Ibid., 188.

126 *a well-crafted survey of her life appeared in* Coronet: Charlotte and Denis Plimmer, "Her Heart Belongs," 71.

126 *"During the last months of the run"*: Harry Evans, "At Home with Mary Martin," *Family Circle* (September 1956), 66.

126 *in a letter to Ray Walston*: Davis, *Mary Martin,* 154.

126 *They sailed on the freighter*: Corrales, AP photo caption.

126 *"flat attempt to show"*: Halliwell, *Film Guide 2008,* 735.

126 *With Martin's work on* Main Street *completed*: *Newsweek* (November 9, 1953), 58.

127 *"They, the hosts, left early"*: Payn, *Noël Coward Diaries,* 204.

8   A New Direction

128 *As documented in his diary*: Payn, *Noël Coward Diaries,* 196.

128 *"Mary is obviously the greatest star"*: McHugh, *Loverly,* 9.

129 *"those dear boys"*: Lerner, *Musical Theatre,* 51.

129 *When Halliday approached her with the idea*: Whitney Bolton, "Even Without a Song, Mary Martin Is Tops," *Quick* (December 9, 1953), 7.

129 *As Crawford told Logan and Krasna*: Logan, *Josh,* 313–14.

129 *"our favorite way . . . compulsive needlepointer is something new"*: Martin, *Mary Martin's Needlepoint,* 17–18.

130 *As Martin also recalled, "The only thing I knew"*: Peter Martin, "I Call on Mary Martin," *Saturday Evening Post* (March 28, 1959), 119.

130 *"I had never done television"*: Martin, *My Heart Belongs,* 197.

130 *"You get a feeling of timing"*: Joe McCarthy, "Her Heart Belongs," *Cosmopolitan* (January 1956), 32.

130 *"If television and radio"*: *This Fabulous Century: Volume VI* (Time-Life Books, 1972), 250.

131 *a "TV show which would evoke the spirit of the past half century"*: "Fabulous Ford Birthday Show," *Life* (June 29, 1953).

131 *Once he learned the Hallidays were stopping in Cuba on their way home to the States*: Joe McCarthy, "Her Heart Belongs," *Cosmopolitan* (January 1956), 32.

131 *"I know how fond you are"*: Peter Martin, "I Call on Mary Martin," *Saturday Evening Post* (March 28, 1959), 119.

132 *the editors of Time-Life Books*: *This Fabulous Century: Volume VI*, 264.

132 *"The duet was destined"*: Kellow, *Ethel Merman*, 150.

132 *"It was Jerry"*: Vaill, *Somewhere*, 225.

132 *Having rehearsed "our heads off"*: Martin, *My Heart Belongs*, 199.

132 *"Both women were in superb voice"*: Kellow, *Ethel Merman*, 150.

132 *"Spontaneous it may have seemed"*: Vaill, *Somewhere*, 226.

132 *Martin gave full credit to Robbins*: Martin, *My Heart Belongs*, 198.

133 *According to Martin, it was only when they were well into rehearsals*: Peter Martin, "I Call on Mary Martin," *Saturday Evening Post* (March 28, 1959), 118.

133 *But in spite of Martin's claim*: Martin, *My Heart Belongs*, 198.

133 *Lawrence White recalled, "they hardly spoke to each other"*: Lawrence, *Dance with Demons*, 215.

133 *"Television, which already has brought about a small revolution"*: "2 Girls, 4 Notes," *TV Guide* (November 13, 1953), 11.

134 *Decca sold 200,000 copies*: *Newsweek* (November 9, 1953), 60.

134 *As Hedda Hopper wrote about the inauguration*: Hedda Hopper, syndicated column (July 24, 1953).

134 *"Mary was hesitant"*: "Bull Wins . . ." *Look* (July 9, 1957), 26–27.

134 *Martin sent Hedda Hopper a Western Union telegram*: Mary Martin to Hedda Hopper, Hopper papers at Margaret Herrick Library.

134 *"The city was so in awe"*: Logan, *Josh*, 319.

135 Life *magazine ran a five-page photo spread*: "New Orleans Dolls Up for *Kind Sir*," *Life* (October 12, 1953), 161.

135 *According to Hopper, Martin "poured out her gratitude"*: Hopper, *Whole Truth*, 156.

135 Kind Sir *proved a "fiasco"*: Hopper, "Mary Martin," *Woman's Home Companion* (January 1956), 21.

135 *"In the seat next to me, Mainbocher"*: Davis, *Mary Martin*, 178.

135 *Martin herself would declare* Kind Sir *a "disaster"*: Martin, *My Heart Belongs*, 183.

135 *"We never knew what Josh was going to say next"*: Davis, *Mary Martin*, 176.

136 *"Although I have no memory"*: Logan, *Josh*, 323.

136 *a cover story in* Newsweek: "Martin, Boyer, and *Kind* Sir," *Newsweek* (November 9, 1953).

136 *"My great idea"*: Logan, *Josh*, 336.

136 *As the anonymous writer in* Newsweek *wrote*: "Martin, Boyer, and *Kind* Sir," *Newsweek* (November 9, 1953), 56.

136 *As described in an issue of* Pageant: *Pageant* (April 1956), 133.

137 *Martin put it succinctly: "When they review the clothes"*: Martin, *My Heart Belongs*, 187.

137 *Wallis Windsor's autobiography would be excerpted*: Wallis Windsor, "Mary Martin and 'The Shape,'" *McCall's* (March 1956).

137 *managing his wife's business affairs*: "Martin, Boyer, and *Kind* Sir," *Newsweek* (November 9, 1953), 60.

137 *"The Hallidays have found that the fewer outside jobs Mary accepts, the greater is the demand for her services"*: Ibid.

9 "The First Lady of Television"

139 *"Like Peter Pan, Mary flies untouched"*: Hedda Hopper, "Mary Martin," *Women's Home Companion* (January 1956).

139 *"One of our bonds"*: Martin, *My Heart Belongs,* 202.

139 *"That was my happiest role"*: Oller, *Jean Arthur,* 195.

139 *"It's the shortest I've ever worn [my hair]"*: Edwin Schallert, "Mary Martin's Dream Comes True with *Peter Pan* Role," *Los Angeles Times* (June 27, 1954).

140 *"According to Mother, Peter Pan is the most important thing"*: Hagman, *Hello Darlin',* 82.

140 *"The role, although that of a boy, traditionally is feminine"*: Gladwinn Hill, "Mary Martin Arrives in Never-Never Land," *New York Times* (October 17, 1954).

140 *"I hate to admit it"*: Martin, *My Heart Belongs,* 202.

140 *one critic responded*: Bordman, *American Musical Theatre,* 290.

141 *According to Jean Arthur biographer John Oller*: Oller, *Jean Arthur,* 180–81.

141 *As early as 1944 . . . the Hallidays had approached Kurt Weill*: Davis, *Mary Martin,* 180.

141 *Assuming his wife's voice in a letter*: Richard Halliday to Sam Zolotow, Lee Tuft collection (April/May 1970).

141 *The Hallidays were also at the time considering*: Sam Zolotow, "Musical Line Up for Mary Martin," *New York Times* (December 18, 1953).

142 *"Richard and I discovered Carolyn Leigh"*: Hanson, *Peter Pan Chronicles,* 177.

143 *"Jerry had a fit"*: Lawrence, *Dance with Demons,* 224.

143 *"Peter Pan was my first chance to sing"*: Heller Halliday Weir, "My Mother Mary Martin," *Good Housekeeping* (January 1963), 108.

143 *Martin would also take credit*: Martin, *My Heart Belongs,* 203.

144 *"I was eliminated because I was too tall"*: Here and throughout author interview with Joan Tewkesbury.

144 *"The Texas-born singer-actress has been away"*: "Mary martin Returns with Peter Pan Hairdo," *Los Angeles Times* (June 17, 1954).

144 *"When I first saw [Mary Martin]"*: Here and throughout author interview with Sondra Lee.

145 *Hedda Hopper gave an all-star dinner*: Hedda Hopper, "Columnist's Dinner Honors Mary Martin," *Los Angeles Times,* June 23, 1954.

146 *"No Peter Pan had ever flown very far"*: Martin, *My Heart Belongs,* 204.

146 *"There may have been Peter Pans who could fly better"*: Albert Goldberg, Constance McCormick Scrapbook.

146 *"It was all piano wires"*: Martin, *My Heart Belongs,* 205.

146 *"I was stunned and dangling"*: Martin, *My Heart Belongs,* 208.

146 *Heller would recall a problem with her own wiring*: Heller Halliday Weir, "My Mother Mary Martin," *Good Housekeeping* (January 1963).

147 *The* Variety *critic*: Hanson, *Peter Pan Chronicles,* 195–96.

149 *Kathleen Nolan succinctly summarized the problem*: Hanson, *Peter Pan Chronicles,* 196.

149 *According to Comden, they thought*: Ibid., 199.

150 *"Miss Martin's Peter Pan is one of the great events of theatredom"*: Hanson, *Peter Pan Chronicles,* 208.

150 *"Mary didn't know the girl"*: Hopper papers, Margaret Herrick Library.

150 *"Maj had serious reservations"*: Hagman, *Hello Darlin',* 77.

150 *Hagman claimed that "Mother" . . . gave them an Austin-Healey*: Ibid., 78.

150 *"He married Maj because she is very shrewd"*: Author interview with Flicker.

151 *Though probably apocryphal, one of the more delightful theatrical anecdotes*: These two paragraphs from Suskin, *Opening Night on Broadway: 1943 to 1964,* 548–51.

151 Time *magazine claimed*: *Time* (November 1, 1954).

151 *"I'm one of the ones who did see Maude Adams"*: Biographies in Sound: Meet Mary Martin (October 16, 1955).

151 *After attending the show, Coward wrote in his diary*: Payn, Noël Coward Diaries, 245.

152 *Sandy Wilson (*The Boy Friend*) wrote in a letter*: Sandy Wilson to Elliott Sirkin (October 31, 1976).

152 *the* Los Angeles Times *named Martin Woman of the Year*: Los Angeles Times (December 5, 1954).

152 *Robbins described some nearly harrowing accidents*: Lawrence, Dance with Demons, 227.

152 *"After the show Martin received children of friends"*: Bach, Dazzler, 325.

153 *Declaring "NBC's* Peter Pan . . . *the biggest news of the week"*: "Radio and Television," Time (n.d.).

153 *given the number of other television specials she would appear in for them*: As evidenced by TV Guide during March–November 1955.

154 *"This television medium is fantastic"*: Joe McCarthy, "Her Heart Belongs," Cosmopolitan (January 1956), 32.

154 *"My honest desire," Martin told a reporter*: Gladwinn Hill, "MM Arrives in Never-Never Land," New York Times (October 17, 1954).

154 *According to Harvey Schmidt when they finally arrived*: Author interview with Schmidt.

154 *"To get there we had to fly in a small plane"*: Joe McCarthy, "Her Heart Belongs," Cosmopolitan (January 1956), 29.

155 *Their palatial house was "a dream in marble"*: Harry Evans, "At Home with Mary Martin," Family Circle (September 1956), 66.

155 *a king-size bed, which "was big enough for the four of us"*: Martin, My Heart Belongs, 257.

155 *"Why didn't you build over there?"*: Joe McCarthy, "Her Heart Belongs," Cosmopolitan (January 1956), 29.

10   By the Skin of Her Teeth

157 *Martin sent her intimate friend a letter*: Mary Martin to Hedda Hopper (March 16, 1955), Mary Martin papers at Margaret Herrick Library.

157 *"At our final run-through"*: Schneider, Entrances, 213.

157 *"Heller was a lovely young girl"*: Author interview with Murray.

157 *"Offstage, for the first time in my memory"*: Hagman, Hello Darlin', 80.

157 *"The whole place went gaga"*: Ibid.

158 *"Your dad sure didn't play it like that"*: Duchin, Ghost of a Chance, 151–52.

158 *Martin sent Chambers a follow-up letter in October*: Ibid., 152.

158 *"Everyone was always a bit late"*: Schneider, Entrances, 214.

158 *"Mary kissed me warmly"*: Ibid., 215.

159 *"Suddenly I felt a hand clutching my left shoulder"*: Ibid.

159 *"French stagehands, mostly Socialists or even Communists"*: Ibid., 214.

160 *"I knew I wasn't good in it"*: Martin, My Heart Belongs, 190.

160 *"Alan Schneider's method of direction was very personal"*: Abbott, Mister Abbott, 256.

160 *Martin "asked for extra time"*: Schneider, Entrances, 213.

160 *"We rehearsed in New York and then in Paris"*: Author interview with Murray.

160 *"In playing the part of the seductress"*: Ibid.

160 *"I went round afterwards to the Sarah Bernhardt Theatre"*: Sandy Wilson, letter to Elliott Sirkin (October 31, 1976).

161 *"'Vinnie' was the kindest"*: Martin, My Heart Belongs, 190–91.

161 *Schneider was embarrassed by the situation*: Schneider, *Entrances,* 217.
161 *Martin was also, according to Don Murray, "a great audience" . . . "magnanimous of her"*: Author interview with Murray.
162 *"She scared the shit out of me," said Heller*: Author interview with Heller Halliday.
162 *After pointing out that the "gala" opening*: Robert Coleman, *New York Mirror* (August 19, 1955).
162 *Richard Watts Jr. was even more emphatic*: *New York Post* (August 18, 1955).
162 *"If Miss Martin is more wonderful at one time than another"*: Walter Kerr, *New York Herald Tribune* (n.d.).
163 *"Miss Martin gives a brilliant comedy performance"*: Brooks Atkinson, *New York Times* (August 18, 1918).
163 *"From the moment that Mary Martin comes tripping onstage"*: William Peper, *New York World-Telegram and Sun* (August 18, 1955).
163 *"Suddenly, all the bright lights"*: Heller Halliday Weir, "My Mother Mary Martin," *Good Housekeeping* (January 1963).
164 *Martin would tell an interviewer*: Harry Evans, "At Home with Mary Martin," *Family Circle* (September 1956), 32.
164 *"This is what is so crazy"*: Peter Martin, "I Call on Mary Martin," *Saturday Evening Post* (March 28, 1959), 114.
164 *When Martin reminded Heller of their "dream"*: Martin, *My Heart Belongs,* 210.
164 *when Heller "changed her mind"*: Paul Rosenfeld, "Mary Martin: A Video First," *Los Angeles Times* (April 12, 1979).
164 *"Do you know the first time I talked on the phone"*: Mary Martin to Hedda Hopper (March 16, 1955), Mary Martin papers at Margaret Herrick Library.

11 "Together with Music"
165 *"I don't know of one enemy Mary has"*: Hopper, "Mary Martin," *Women's Home Companion* (January 1956), 91.
165 *"This is, of course, enormous money"*: Payn, *Noël Coward Diaries,* 258.
165 *As early as March 19, 1955, Coward wrote in his Diary*: Ibid., 259.
165 *In July, Martin sent a letter to Coward*: Day, *The Letters of Noël Coward,* 592.
166 *Coward's US agents were also in Jamaica*: Ibid., 591.
166 *"To my horror"*: Payn, *The Noël Coward Diaries,* 282.
167 *"The other evening at dinner"*: Ibid., 282–83.
167 *The night before the Hallidays' departure*: Ibid., 284.
167 *"Mary is a great performer"*: Ibid., 285–86.
169 *"The Press notices are unqualified raves"*: Ibid., 287.
169 *The raves included*: All taken from record liner notes.
169 *Gould, in fact, seized the special*: Jack Gould, "Nice and Naughty," *New York Times* (October 30, 1955), xii.
169 *"someone should have noticed during the camera rehearsals"*: Hal Humphrey, "It Can't Happen After," *Los Angeles Mirror-News* (October 25, 1955), II.6.
170 *Martin became one of Murrow's guests*: *Person to Person: Mary Martin* (1954), 31.
170 *It was "both an honor and an ordeal"*: Tim Brooks and Earle Marsh, *The Complete Directory to Prime Time Network TV Shows* (Ballantine Books, 2007), 486.
170 *"During the run of South Pacific"*: Peter Martin, "I Call on Mary Martin," *Saturday Evening Post* (March 28, 1959), 118.

171 *The* Women's Home Companion *ran a cover story*: Hopper, "Mary Martin," *Women's Home Companion* (January 1956), 90.

171 *"There is a lot of sunlight"*: Ibid.

172 *"Heller's baby dresses are framed"*: Joe McCarthy, "Her Heart Belongs," *Cosmopolitan* (January 1956), 28.

172 *"From the entrance hall"*: Harry Evans, "At Home with Mary Martin," *Family Circle* (September 1956), 71.

172 *Martin intended her 1956 version to be her final incarnation*: Kathy Pedell, "Farewell to Peter Pan," *TV Guide* (January 7, 1956), 14–15.

173 *"I had just been hired by NBC at that point"*: Author interview with Schmidt.

173 *"about 300 children from settlement houses"*: *Sarasota Herald-Tribune* (January 8, 1956).

174 *they paid "$16,000 to an American woman"*: Hopper, *Whole Truth,* 157.

174 *"After months and months of delay"*: Martin, *Mary Martin's Needlepoint,* 29.

174 *Joshua Logan . . . described this last leg*: Logan, *Movie Stars, Real People, and Me,* 457–58.

175 *"Mary Martin and Dick are at last on their farm"*: Adrian to Hedda Hopper (March 11, 1956), Hopper papers at Margaret Herrick Library.

175 *"They are like children . . . they have no shame"*: Maria Holanda Cavalcante, *Hollywood no Cerrado* (documentary, 2011).

175 *In her gossip-ridden response*: Hedda Hopper to Adrian (April 18, 1956), Hopper papers at Margaret Herrick Library.

176 *"Mom and Richard weren't there"*: Hagman, *Hello Darlin',* 82.

176 *"Larry intends to turn the property into a self-supporting coffee plantation"*: Joe McCarthy, "Her Heart Belongs," *Cosmopolitan* (January 1956), 29.

176 *As Hagman confirmed decades later, in his memoir*: Hagman, *Hello Darlin',* 85–86.

177 *"It was a disaster"*: Davis, *Mary Martin,* 200.

177 *[Kanin's] involvement was cited by Val Adams*: Adams, "Credit Up in Air for Comedy on TV," *New York Times* (October 24, 1956).

178 *"It just doesn't play too amusingly when Billie's a lady"*: Rivadue, *Mary Martin,* 122.

178 *Hal Humphrey shared his surprise*: Davis, *Mary Martin,* 200.

178 *Critic Humphrey also appreciated*: Hal Humphrey, "Two Fine Plays Boost TV," *Los Angeles Mirror-News* (October 30, 1956), III.6.

12   "Everything Old Is New Again"

179 *"My dear Main," she wrote*: Hedda Hopper to Mainbocher (December 6, 1956), Hopper papers at Margaret Herrick Library.

179 *"The twenty playing weeks"*: *Los Angeles Times* (January 28, 1957).

180 *Shortly after the Eisenhower inauguration, Martin wrote Hedda Hopper*: Mary Martin to Hedda Hopper, Mary Martin papers at Margaret Herrick Library.

180 *Mary Martin made some unusual demands*: Author interview with Erman.

180 *"My daughter has no interest in the stage now"*: Edwin Schallert, "Mary Martin to Open in *South Pacific*," *Los Angeles Times* (July 8, 1957).

181 *"Mary's relationship with her daughter"*: Hopper, "Mary Martin," *Women's Home Companion* (January 1956), 91.

181 *Martin claimed she slipped "right back into the show"*: Schallert, "Mary Martin to Open in *South Pacific*," *Los Angeles Times* (July 8, 1957).

181 *"We had a director [Albert Marre] who was as inept as anybody"*: Author interview with Erman.

181 *a puff piece in the* Los Angeles Times: "Surf Provides Realism for *South Pacific Cast,*" *Los Angeles Times* (May 27, 1957).

181 *According to Erman, "Richard Halliday was always present . . . Here she goes again"*: Author interview with Erman.

182 *"You fall in love with her at once"*: Albert Goldberg, "*South Pacific* Triumph for Star Mary Martin," *Los Angeles Times* (July 9, 1957).

183 *Logan acknowledged that casting*: Ross Drake, "*South Pacific,*" *TV Guide* (November 20, 1971), 21.

183 *"Outside of my own family, I love Mary"*: Shipman, *Great Movie Stars,* 382.

184 *Hedda Hopper sent a conciliatory letter to Martin*: Hedda Hopper to Mary Martin (February 7, 1957), Hedda Hopper papers at Margaret Herrick Library.

184 *Martin's revival of* Annie Get Your Gun *for the Civic Light Opera*: Edwin Schallert, "Mary Martin Dazzling in *Annie Get Your Gun,*" *Los Angeles Times* (October 8, 1957).

184 *"She was a force of nature"*: Author interview with Tewkesbury.

185 *"I resorted to a form of sign language"*: Vincent J. Donehue, "A Man in Three Mediums," *Theatre Arts* (n.d.).

185 *When Martin showed up at the studio*: "Mary Gets Her Gun," *TV Guide* (November 23, 1957), 25–26.

185 *Nor was Martin the only one*: Cecil Smith, "Mary Martin Set to Fly Again on TV," *Los Angeles Times* (November 24, 1957).

186 *During a final rehearsal, Martin slipped a bit in his arms*: *Life* (December 9, 1957), 124.

186 *"I'd never wanted to do television"*: Peter Martin, "I Call on Mary Martin," *Saturday Evening Post* (March 28, 1959), 118.

186 *"Just how much income [they gave up] is not known"*: Val Adams, "News of TV and Radio," *New York Times* (December 15, 1957), 141.

187 *"Richard . . . and I have had twenty-two homes"*: Peter Martin, "I Call on Mary Martin," *Saturday Evening Post* (March 28, 1959), 32.

187 *"It has been more trouble to us than anything"*: Ibid., 114.

187 *Hagman recalled being on the verge of getting small parts*: Hagman, *Hello Darlin',* 88.

188 *Martin also had an ulterior motive*: Author interview with Heidi Kristina Mary Hagman.

188 *When Heidi was only a year old*: Ibid.

13 Hail Mary

190 *Initially viewing the material*: Block, *Richard Rodgers Reader,* 319.

190 *"No way am I competing with Mozart"*: Wilk, *Overture and Finale,* 127.

190 *"The German picture had very little singing"*: Block, *Richard Rodgers Reader,* 319.

190 *"We had to explain"*: Rodgers, *My Favorite Things,* 299.

190 *Baroness von Trapp was ultimately tracked down*: Skinner, *Life with Lindsay and Crouse,* 221.

190 *the Hallidays themselves confronted Maria von Trapp*: Maslon, Sound of Music *Companion,* 60.

190 *"Dick was a very shrewd businessman"*: Wilk, *Overture and Finale,* 125.

191 *"My mother asked me to start writing lyrics for my sister"*: Author interview with Mary Rodgers.

192 *Martin would later term her "favorite tour"*: Martin, *My Heart Belongs*, 225.

193 *Hedda Hopper sent a cautionary letter*: Hedda Hopper to Mary Martin and Richard Halliday (August 26, 1958), Hedda Hopper papers at Margaret Herrick Library.

193 *In an undated letter to public relations agent Joseph Bleeden*: Richard Halliday to Joseph Bleeden of Bleeden, Morhaim and Switzer, Hedda Hopper papers at Margaret Herrick Library.

193 *"Staying overnight in hotels"*: Nelson Landsdale, "Her Heart Belongs to the Road," *Theatre Arts* (September 1958), 17.

193 *They were also eased by the constant ministrations of Ernest . . . and Nena Smith*: Martin, *My Heart Belongs,* 227–28.

193 *"a musical resume of my life"*: Peter Martin, "I Call on Mary Martin," *Saturday Evening Post* (March 28, 1959), 114–15.

194 *"Mary and Richard came in yesterday"*: Mainbocher to Hedda Hopper, Hedda Hopper papers at Margaret Herrick Library.

194 *"I had a hard time choking back my tears"*: Peter Martin, "I Call on Mary Martin," *Saturday Evening Post* (March 28, 1959), 114.

194 *The Hallidays opted for traversing the vast expanse of Texas in a commuter plane*: Rivadue, *Mary Martin*, B261.200.

194 *Martin recalled a mishap when she was performing in Lubbock*: John P. Shanley, "Immune from Fatigue," *New York Times* (March 29, 1959).

194 *the "regular dressing room" at Constitution Hall*: Martin, "I Call on Mary Martin," 114.

194 *"Dick [Halliday] was so drunk and out of control"*: Author interview with Mary Rodgers.

195 *"Both productions show one of the world's great show women"*: Jack Moffitt, "Television Review," *Hollywood Reporter* (March 31, 1959).

195 *much of the company was battling a "severe virus"*: Jack Gould, "TV: Mary Martin," *New York Times* (March 30, 1959).

195 *"Mary got sick"*: Author interview with Mary Rodgers.

195 *As Halliday told a columnist for the* New York Post: *New York Post* (March 30, 1959).

196 *"Working with Mary Martin again made me appreciate"*: Rodgers, *My Favorite Things*, 301.

196 *"It was one of the most disciplined shows"*: Martin, *My Heart Belongs,* 239.

196 *a ten-page cover story in* Life: "Tuneful Blend of Religion, Romance," *Life* (November 23, 1959).

196 *"She led us upstairs"*: Charles D. Rice, "Mary Martin Punches Out a Song," *This Week* (October 25, 1959).

196 *"everyone concerned agreed that we needed Sister Gregory's advice"*: Martin, *My Heart Belongs,* 245.

197 *Sister Gregory was but the first*: Ibid., 245–46.

197 *her "own religious belief"*: Ibid., 246.

197 *"It drove me to the chapel"*: Wilk, *Overture and Finale,* 133.

197 *Sister Gregory became an "unofficial technical advisor"*: Maslon, Sound of Music *Companion,* 67.

197 *This was the "closest Rodgers ever got"*: Ibid., 68.

198 *Haliday . . . "did whatever he could"*: Ibid.

198 *According to casting advisor Eddie Blub*: Secrest, *Somewhere for Me,* 347–48.

198 *After performing two Frank Loesser songs*: Wilk, *Overture and Finale,* 138.

198 *"I was a very good friend of Larry"*: Author interview with Bikel.

199 *"We interviewed more than 300"*: "Tuneful Blend of Religion, Romance," *Life* (November 23, 1959), 146.

199 *"The first day of rehearsals, Mary was so sweet"*: Author interview with Saunders.

199 *"[Fontanne] and Mary Martin were considered the best makeup artists"*: Peters, *Design for Living*, 278 and 237.

199 *He had just learned he requires surgery*: Fordin, *Getting to Know Him*, 351.

200 *Hammerstein received a reassuring cable*: Maslon, Sound of Music *Companion*, 69.

200 *"Stefan spent a lot of time with us"*: Author interview with Saunders.

200 *"They had a big fight over the drawers"*: Davis, *Mary Martin*, 210.

200 *"Richard Rodgers knew more about the theater"*: Secrest, *Somewhere for Me*, 349–50.

201 *"I remember he sat in a box"*: Wilk, *Overture and Finale*, 144.

201 *"The Broadway book had not served him well"*: Plummer, *Christopher Plummer*, 394.

201 *"I sent her opening night flowers every time"*: Arthur Unger, "Mary Martin," *Christian Science Monitor* (December 6, 1979).

201 *But what always worked like a good luck charm*: Davis, *Mary Martin*, 212.

201 *Lucinda Ballard recalled another funny offstage episode*: Nolan, *Sound of Their Music*, 218.

202 *there was a bizarre incident following a matinee*: Ibid.

202 *Referring to the "silliness, stiffness and corny operetta falseness"*: Maslon, Sound of Music *Companion*, 71.

202 *Upon her entrance*: Rivadue, *Mary Martin*, B195.188.

202 *"They were all 'Oh, how boring'"*: Richard Lee, "It's a New Life," *New York Post* (October 29, 1977).

202 *"The scenario," Brooks Atkinson wrote*: Suskin, *Opening Night on Broadway: 1943 to 1964*, 637–38.

203 *Henry Hewes emphasized the show's sentimentality*: Hewes, "Stalemates in the Broadway Musical Theatre," *Saturday Review* (December 5, 1959), 28–29.

203 *Kenneth Tynan was less sanguine*: Tynan, *Curtains*, 331–33.

203 *Even a puff piece in* Life: "Tuneful Blend of Religion, Romance," *Life* (November 23, 1959), 140.

203 *"Sentiment has never been unpopular"*: Skinner, *Life with Lindsay & Crouse*, 220.

203 *Most of the critics' "carping"*: Rodgers, *My Favorite Things*, 300, 302.

203 *"Although it's a true story"*: Skinner, *Life with Lindsay & Crouse*, 220–21.

204 *The eldest of the Trapp children was not*: Secrest, *Somewhere for Me*, 345.

204 *Ethan Mordden would call it*: Mordden, *Rodgers and Hammerstein*, 207.

205 *"by 1959 Martin was a phenomenally popular star"*: Ibid., 297.

205 *"It felt like she was talking directly to me"*: Author interview with Schulman.

205 *"She picked up two pieces of Melba toast"*: Martin, *My Heart Belongs*, 143.

206 *"Bea was very fond of Mary Martin"*: Laffey, *Beatrice Lillie*, 232.

206 *"The whole terrace at Monte Carlo was in hysterics"*: Martin, *My Heart Belongs*, 143.

206 *"When he died it was a matinee day"*: Nolan, *Sound of Their Music*, 221.

206 *A sedative Martin had taken*: Michael Mok, "Mary Martin Sings through the Tears," *New York World-Telegram* (August 24, 1960), quoted in Rivadue, *Mary Martin*, B196.188.

206 *"I had just returned from a tour of Europe"*: Heller Halliday Weir, "My Mother Mary Martin," *Good Housekeeping* (January 1963), 113.

206 *Doris Day attended* The Sound of Music: David Kaufman, *Doris Day* (Virgin Books, 2010), 282.

206 *Following a lunch Hedda Hopper had with Mrs. Eisenhower*: Hedda Hopper to Mary Martin (February 9, 1962), Hopper papers at Margaret Herrick Library.

207 *"I had no political discussions"*: Author interview with Bikel.

207 *"It was hysterical," recalled Bernice Saunders*: Author interview with Saunders.

207 *As Bikel would also point out*: Wilk, *Overture and Finale,* 136.

207 *"I don't think she really liked him"*: Author interview with Saunders.

207 *Bikel came to feel that "it wasn't her choice"*: Author interview with Bikel.

207 *As Lucinda Ballard observed, Halliday had been "drunk all the time"*: Davis, *Mary Martin,* 209.

207 *"In addition to being domineering"*: Author interview with Bikel.

208 *Bikel has certin memories*: Ibid.

208 *"I remember that the night before the company left"*: Wilk, *Overture and Finale,* 159.

209 *"And because I was low man on the totem pole"*: Author interview with Rothenberg.

209 *"Ben Washer was living with a guy"*: Author interview with Tuft.

209 *"I had a separate room"*: Ibid.

210 *According to a feature in* TV Guide: "What Makes Mary Fly?" *TV Guide* (December 3, 1960), 1.

210 *"There was a sound like a rifle shot"*: Martin, *My Heart Belongs*, 210.

210 *"It was feared at first that she had broken her arm"*: "What Makes Mary Fly?" *TV Guide* (December 3, 1960), 1.

210 *"As the postulant my arms were folded meekly"*: Martin, *My Heart Belongs,* 249.

211 *It became a bigger problem*: Wilk, *Overture and Finale,* 155.

211 *she discovered a sign that read*: "Mary Martin *slapped* here": from promotional material for the show.

211 *"NBC was smart enough"*: TV Guide (December 3, 1960), 49.

211 *"The sound stage in Brooklyn"*: Author interview with Tewkesbury.

211 *Sondra Lee, for one, felt that it didn't entirely work*: Author interview with Lee.

211 *"Everything was pretty much done in one take"*: Undated 2012 radio interview with Gaynes.

212 *Hedda Hopper followed up with a letter*: Hedda Hopper to Mary Martin (December 20, 1960), Hedda Hopper papers at Margaret Herrick Library.

212 *NBC was also "smart enough" to invest $20,000*: Val Adams, "2 TV Roles Slated for Mary Martin," *New York Times* (August 18, 1959), 59.

212 *The "authors' royalties" for the December 1960 telecast*: Edwin Lester letter to Dan O'Shea (August 17, 1961).

213 *the "current 'classic' version of her Peter Pan"*: Press release (January 10, 1963).

213 *"We couldn't wait to be free"*: Author interview with Bikel.

213 *"I was still an apprentice"*: Author interview with Rothenberg.

214 *"Whenever Bikel's name came up"*: Ibid.

214 *"She loves to paint with oil colors"*: Heller Halliday Weir, "My Mother Mary Martin," *Good Housekeeping* (January 1963), 113.

214 *"This chapter in my"*: Hedda Hopper, "Heller Lived Up to Name—She Elopes!" *Los Angeles Times* (February 13, 1962), and Hopper, *Whole Truth,* 158.

215 *"Mummy loved the whole trip"*: Heller Halliday Weir, "My Mother Mary Martin," *Good Housekeeping* (January 1963), 113.

215 *"What started as a quiet little elopement"*: Martin, *My Heart Belongs,* 263.

215 *"I modeled at Elizabeth Arden"*: Author interview with Heller Halliday.

14 "Poor Jenny, Bright as a Penny"

216 *"Technique, which is always composed of skill and instinct"*: Young, *Immortal Shadows,* 249–50

216 *"A luminous confusion composer her aura"*: Loggia, *Collected Works of Harold Clurman,* 101.

217 *Martin told a reporter for* Look *magazine that Taylor had been a friend*: Virginia Kelly, "Mary Martin: Perpetual Motion," *Look* (September 10, 1963), 67.

217 *"she was really an amateur at serious acting"*: Schwab, "Star from Texas," *McCall's* (November 1949), 87.

217 *"Laurette Taylor would rather share this with Mary Martin"*: John S. Wilson, "The Life of 'Jennie,'" *New York Times* (October 13, 1963).

218 *"Holliday's insecurity"*: Leonard, *Broadway Bound,* 262.

218 *Pakula approached Cheryl Crawford with his idea . . . "to begin working on dialogue"*: Pakula papers at Margaret Herrick Library.

219 *"Then I saw something in the* New York Times Book Review*"*: John S. Wilson, "The Life of 'Jennie,'" *New York Times* (October 13, 1963).

219 *"Jennie turned into the toughest production I ever tackled"*: Crawford, *One Naked Individual,* 181.

219 *"Richard and I believed in it passionately"*: Martin, *My Heart Belongs,* 193.

219 *"It all got very tacky"*: Ibid., 196.

220 *"Casey," claimed Hal Humphrey in his TV column, "can't kick"*: Hal Humphrey, "Bing Will Have a Merry Christmas," *Los Angeles Times* (December 24, 1962).

220 *"Bing Crosby seemed subdued"*: Cynthia Lowry, *Hartford Courant* (December 26, 1962).

221 *"They asked me if I wanted to be in the new show"*: Author interview with Saunders.

221 *the rotating wheel was "tall as a room"*: Martin, *My Heart Belongs,* 193.

222 *According to musical scholar Ken Mandelbaum*: Mandelbaum, *Not Since Carrie,* 54.

222 *"Today we had the day off"*: Author interview with Saunders.

224 *"Tonight we put in a new number"*: Bernice Saunders to her husband (August 21, 1963).

224 *the company "limped" its way to Detroit*: Crawford, *One Naked Individual,* 181.

226 *"Donehue was sitting in the front row"*: Author interview with Gregory.

226 *"we were told we would be sued for $2 million"*: Mary Martin, "The Healing in Solitude," *Guideposts* (June 1969), 5.

226 *Dietz and Schwartz's "lawyers told us"*: Martin, *My Heart Belongs,* 196.

227 *"The author said he was writing a serious play"*: Mary Martin, "The Healing in Solitude," *Guideposts* (June 1969), 4–5.

227 *According to Howard Dietz, the show's biggest problem*: Dietz, *Dancing in the Dark,* 273–74.

227 *"Mary's nun had triumphed"*: Ibid., 337.

227 *Schwartz took an even more dire position*: Mandelbaum, *Not Since Carrie,* 53.

228 *"Imagine having Mary Martin play an entire show"*: Suskin, *Opening Night on Broadway: 1943 to 1964,* 350–51.

228 *"The only way to walk out of* Jennie *in a satisfied frame of mind"*: *Newsweek* (October 28, 1963), 91.

228 Jennie *"seemed like a terrible self-indulgence"*: Sandy Wilson to Elliott Sirkin (October 31, 1976).

229 *"We in show business are schooled"*: Rich, *Ghost Light,* 191.

15   "The Real Theater of War"

230 *"Miss Martin learned to her dismay"*: Bordman, *American Musical Theatre,* 632.

230 *"I slept 10, 12, even 13 hours a night"*: Mary Martin, "The Healing in Solitude," *Guideposts* (June 1969), 5.

230 *her husband's drinking problems were exacerbated*: Hagman, *Hello Darlin',* 86.

231 *Rodgers felt Martin was too old for the part*: Zadan, *Sondheim and Co.,* 100.

231 *they had already seen Channing "knock Manhattan on its left ear"*: Martin, *My Heart Belongs,* 267.

232 *Jerry "loves everybody"*: Martin, *My Heart Belongs,* 268.

232 *"We opened in Minneapolis [on April 17]"*: Author interview with Sheridan.

233 *"Gower's secretary called me"*: Author interview with Carpenter.

233 *"She had been told that I was from Oklahoma"*: Author interview with Drake.

234 *"We had no audience rehearsal-staging"*: Author interview with Shaffer.

234 *John Sheridan got food poisoning*: Here and throughout, author interview with Sheridan.

235 *"From the same stage where Tebaldi and Kirsten were bravoed"*: Pericles Alexander to Hedda Hopper (May 21, 1965), Hopper papers at Margaret Herrick Library.

235 *"During her curtain speech in Dallas"*: Author interview with Sabinson.

235 *"There's a number where I pick up a gun"*: Author interview with Drake.

236 *"I was the first woman producer"*: Author interview with Jarvis.

239 *"We have to do this for our country"*: Author interview with Sheridan.

239 *"Marilyn Lovell and Coco Ramirez"*: Author interview with Drake.

239 *"Mary Martin and Richard took a liking to me"*: Author interview with Shaffer.

239 *"I remember going to a bar when we were in New Orleans"*: Author interview with Sheridan.

240 *The company was flown to Tokyo in "a drab, windowless troop transport"*: Shana Alexander, "Broadway Show in a Theater of War," *Life* (October 22, 1965), 30.

241 *"'Opening night' came at high noon"*: Ruben Salazar, "4,000 Troops Cheer Mary Martin as *Hello, Dolly!* Opens in Vietnam," *Los Angeles Times* (October 10, 1965).

241 *"The footlights may be dimmed after the show . . . PROUD OF YOU"*: "President Hails *Dolly* in Saigon," *New York Times* (October 11, 1965).

241 *"[This] meant we had to follow the music"*: Ruben Salazar, "4,000 Troops Cheer."

241 *"They had built a four-story building in Saigon"*: Author interview with Shaffer.

242 *"Dolly Levi is a matchmaker, after all"*: Alexander, "Broadway Show," *Life* (October 22, 1965), 30.

242 *"My face was bloated like a cream puff"*: Martin, *My Heart Belongs,* 277–78.

242 *US Ambassador Henry Cabot Lodge honored the visit*: Associated Press (October 14, 1965).

243 *"Mary was not a great beauty . . . rewrote the speech for her"* Author interview with Jarvis.

245 *the room was filled "practically from floor to ceiling with plants"*: Mary Martin to Geraldine Martin (December 10, 1965), from Hopper papers at Margaret Herrick Library.

245 *Roddy McDowell had sent her a "huge print of your photograph"*: Mary Martin to Hedda Hopper (December 13, 1965), from the Hopper papers at Margaret Herrick Library.
245 *"That eye was on this sparrow for many a year"*: McDowell, *Double Exposure,* 87.
245 *"I didn't realize it was a raked stage"*: Author interview with Carpenter.
246 *"You can really get tired from too much glamour!"*: Mary Martin to Geraldine Martin (December 10, 1965), from the Martin papers at Margaret Herrick Library.
246 *"They say it's the first time in history"*: Hedda Hopper, "Mary Martin's *Dolly* Draws Royalty," *Los Angeles Times* (Constance McCormick Scrapbook).
247 *"single-mindedly bent on mobilizing public enthusiasm"*: quoted in Wright, *West End Broadway,* 222.
247 *"It is the show-stopper of all time"*: Ibid., 223.
247 *"Imagine, me a girl from Weatherford"*: Sheila Graham, *New York World Telegram and Sun* (December 1965?).
247 *"when the album finally came out"*: Author interview with Sheridan.

16 "Love Isn't Everything"
250 *"Richard did not interfere with* I Do! I Do!*"*: Author interview with Schmidt.
250 *"It was discovered that NBC's contract was with one union"*: Aleene MacMinn, "Mary Martin—in her Easter Bonnet," *Seattle Post-Intelligencer* (April 3, 1966), 3.
250 *"the creeping squareness"*: Rivadue, *Mary Martin,* 127.
251 *Marge Champion felt that Martin's involvement with* Hello, Dolly!: Author interview with Champion.
251 *the producer's "longest creative partnership"*: Kissel, *David Merrick,* 209.
251 *"Gower had always wanted to do something with us . . . very pleased to get it"*: Author interview with Schmidt.
253 *"We finally got Mary to agree"*: Gilvey, *Before the Parade Passes By,* 160.
253 *As far as Tom Jones was concerned*: Ibid., 162.
253 *"a low hanging tree branch"*: Tony Mastroianni, "A Contract Named Mary Keeps Preston 'I-Do-ing' " *Cleveland Press* (May 10, 1967).
254 *"But I also think he was just tired"*: Author interview with Schmidt.
254 *"Mary was very disappointed"*: Ibid.
254 *"David Merrick asked us to fly to New York"*: Martin, *My Heart Belongs,* 284.
254 *"I didn't even know that I was going to go to Brazil"*: Author interview with Schmidt.
257 *"Gower was at his best as a director"*: Author interview with Marge Champion.
257 *"Our entire rehearsal time"*: Martin, *My Heart Belongs,* 286.
257 *"I may never work for anyone else as long as I live"*: Gilvey, *Before the Parade Passes By,* 166.
257 *Halliday would bring his wife's lunch*: McGovern, *Sing Out, Louise!,* 162.
257 *"I wrote to Mary and said I had been standby"*: Author interview with Withers.
257 *"Merrick would secretly have people dropping in on rehearsals . . . plane and go home"*: Author interview with Shaffer.
258 *While claiming in her memoir that it was "a lovely number"*: Martin, *My Heart Belongs,* 286.
258 *"Every show we ever did with Gower Champion"*: Author interview with Shaffer.
258 *"Whenever Gower visited her in the hospital"*: Gilvey, *Before the Parade Passes By,* 177.
259 *"I made a bad lighting mistake"*: Author interview with Shaffer.

259 *"Mary was a very, very slow study"*: Gilvey, *Before the Parade Passes By,* 178.

259 *"She never had an 'up' or a 'down' performance"*: Author interview with Shaffer.

260 *Schmidt and Jones "were able to withstand Merrick"*: Suskin, *More Opening Nights on Broadway,* 456.

260 *"after an enchanting first act"*: Cecil Smith, "Musical Taking Long Way to N.Y.," *Los Angeles Times* (October 27, 1966).

261 *Martin would claim that* I Do! I Do! *"seemed a culmination"*: Martin, *My Heart Belongs,* 282.

261 *"Just as the subject matter . . . was a culmination of my life"*: Ibid., 283.

261 *"Gower plotted the production like a wartime invasion"*: Ibid., 289.

261 *Walter Kerr in the* New York Times *centered his review*: Suskin, *More Opening Nights on Broadway,* 454–55.

261 *"Both of them superb"*: Payn, *Noël Coward Diaries,* 642.

262 *"We had a gentleman's agreement"*: Martin, *My Heart Belongs,* 287.

263 *"I bet you can't wait to take your Award home to London"*: Author interview with Marion Seldes.

263 *"We had house seats"*: Author interview with Drake.

263 *"Because I always threw the bouquet from the same spot"*: Martin, *My Heart Belongs,* 286.

263 *"Mary said that he absolutely loved the show"*: Author interview with Shaffer.

264 *In a story in the April issue of* Esquire: Mary Martin, "My Ranch in Brazil," *Esquire* (April 1968).

265 *"Robert Preston and Gower would walk around"*: Author interview with Shaffer.

265 *"The Road," Martin told Aleene MacMinn*: Aleene MacMinn, "Mary Martin's Love Affair with the Road," *Los Angeles Times* (June 16, 1968).

265 *"I first met Mary Martin at Dorothy Rodgers's gorgeous apartment"*: Author interview with Ullman.

266 *"Bob and I were both coming apart at the seams"*: Martin, *My Heart Belongs,* 290.

266 *"As soon as the Hallidays arrived in Dallas"*: Davis, *Mary Martin,* 242.

266 *"We were all spared the sight of a burst abscess"*: Martin, *My Heart Belongs,* 290.

266 *"If you want to live"*: Ibid.

266 *She was treated for six weeks for a bleeding ulcer*: Helen Rosenblum, "Everyone's Heart Belongs to Mary," *Motion Picture* (October 1973).

17   Deep in the Heart of . . . Brazil

267 *"We are deeply unhappy"*: Richard Halliday to Lee Tuft (August 30, 1970).

268 *"Customs were marvelous"*: Richard Halliday to Lee Tuft (July 24, 1969).

268 *"Dona Maria found the changes too thrilling"*: Richard Halliday to Lee Tuft (August 8, 1969).

268 *Halliday was "up at 5:30 a.m."*: Richard Halliday to Lee Tuft (January 24, 1970).

268 *"I don't know how to design, but I'm having a ball"*: *Jack Paar Tonight: Three Remarkable Women,* ABC (January 20, 1973).

269 *In addition to collecting "three or four dozens of roses"*: Richard Halliday to Lee Tuft (January 12, 1970).

269 *"Bergdorf's will have a window display"*: Lee Tuft to Mary Martin and Richard Halliday (July 31, 1970).

269 *"The book is doing very well"*: Lee Tuft to Mary Martin and Richard Halliday (September 18, 1970).

271 *"Your wife's letter got here in six days"*: Lee Tuft to Richard Halliday (September 25, 1969).

272 *"That sick man who thinks he's still a boy"*: Richard Halliday to Lee Tuft (November 22, 1969).

272 *"She says she has learned a lot"*: Lee Tuft to Mary Martin and Richard Halliday (December 22, 1969).

272 an *"IRON BRIDGE," she wrote*: Mary Martin to family (December 2, 1969).

272 *"Between you and Rick we know 99% more"*: Richard Halliday to Lee Tuft (January 23, 1970).

273 *"Sure wish you wouldn't be so unhappy about Heller"*: Lee Tuft to Richard Halliday (February 6, 1970).

273 *"We are gradually realizing it's Heller who has been too dependent"*: Richard Halliday to Lee Tuft (February 28, 1970).

273 *"We are having more joy than we even ever dared dream"*: Richard Halliday to David Warsham (February 3, 1970).

273 *"As M. M. said recently*: Richard Halliday to David Warsham (November 26, 1969).

273 *"It's hard to know . . . which is more painful"*: Richard Halliday to Lee Tuft (February 16, 1970).

274 she admired *"the complete freedom of amateurs"*: Rivadue, *Mary Martin,* 152, B7.

274 In a letter addressed to *"Dear Mr. Nicotine-less"*: Lee Tuft to Richard Halliday (June 15, 1970).

274 *"we have bitten off more than either of us realized"*: Richard Halliday to Lee Tuft (September 1, 1970).

275 *"There is so much curiosity about the building"*: Richard Halliday to Lee Tuft (September 23, 1970).

275 *"For the beauty shop, I got together with a Japanese ironmonger"*: Dennis Redmont, "Mary Martin, Resting Busily, Brings the Boutique to Brazil," *Los Angeles Times* (April 4, 1971).

275 *"[The store] really is the most hysterical success"*: Handwritten note on a letter from Lee Tuft to Richard Halliday (October 28, 1970).

275 Hector Arce ran a feature on his experience: *Women's Wear Daily* (December 11, 1970).

276 a three-hour operation ultimately consumed seven: Richard Halliday to Lee Tuft (March 27, 1971).

276 *"We were told there are ten different kinds"*: Richard Halliday to Lee Tuft (June 19 and 22, 1971).

277 *"The authors could not have been more ideal guests"*: Richard Halliday to Lee Tuft (May 27, 1971).

277 *"two composers from N.Y. were just here"*: Mary Martin to John Sheridan (May 25, 1971).

277 *"Jack Paar has been here after eight years"*: Richard Halliday to Edwin Lester (September 10, 1971).

278 *"The subway fare has gone up to 35 cents"*: Lee Tuft to Mary Martin and Richard Halliday (January 5, 1972).

279 Gloria Swanson, who phoned to say: Lee Tuft to Mary Martin and Richard Halliday (May 8, 1972).

279 *Tennessee Williams, "who did the weather on Channel 7 news"*: Lee Tuft to Mary Martin and Richard Halliday (April 25, 1972).

279 *Rodgers had exclaimed, in a comradely fashion*: Davis, *Mary Martin*, 250.

279 *Rodgers told him, "Let the lawyers fight"*: Sam Zolotow, "Rodgers Loses Bid in Royalties Case," *New York Times* (November 22, 1968).

280 *Rodgers and Hammerstein "asked to have their names first"*: Davis, *Mary Martin*, 250.

280 *Hayward and Halliday received an arbitration award*: "Royalties Awarded on 'Sound of Music,'" *New York Times* (April 18, 1968).

280 *"I think we kissed in about 1,000 pictures"*: Davis, *Mary Martin*, 251.

281 *"They're talking about you"*: Author interview with Willison.

281 *Cohen "also speculated on whether you would be interested, I mean MM"*: Lee Tuft to Mary Martin and Richard Halliday (February 15, 1972).

281 *which may or may not have been a TV version of* Do I Hear a Waltz?: Richard Halliday to Lee Tuft (July 15, 1972).

282 *"I just thought Mary treated Richard so badly"*: Author interview with Gregory.

282 *"Had five nurses out here!"*: Richard Halliday to Lee Tuft (August 13, 1972).

282 *"Yes, M.M. was really surprised re the TV show"*: Richard Halliday to Lee Tuft (August 21, 1972).

283 *"You must understand, Mr. Halliday"*: Lee Tuft to Richard Halliday (September 8, 1972).

283 *"Gee, Mr. Halliday, being an interior decorator"*: Lee Tuft to Richard Halliday (September 21, 1972).

284 *she got "a sense that there's not quite enough"*: Lee Tuft to Richard Halliday (January 5, 1972).

284 *"find something for Mary"*: Logan, *Movie Stars*, 453.

285 *Dinner was served by "three of their twenty-nine servants"*: Ibid., 458–60.

285 *"We would like you to go on working on it"*: Ibid., 461.

286 *"He just has to hold his breath"*: Ibid., 461–62.

18 An Icon Speaks

288 *"You keep dating all your letters October"*: Lee Tuft to Richard Halliday (November 16, 1972).

288 *"Saw a note that the Champions are getting a divorce"*: Lee Tuft to Richard Halliday (December 29, 1972).

289 *"In the end it was pneumonia that took him away"*: Davis, *Mary Martin*, 253.

289 *"When Richard was dying, I was told he kept asking for Bibi"*: Author interview with Kristina Hagman.

289 *"He told us that Richard had died"*: Hagman, *Hello Darlin'*, 161.

289 *"They looked so serious and solemn"*: Author interview with Schmidt.

289 *"Mary decided to bury Richard in Weatherford"*: Author interview with Gertz.

289 *his "$650,000 estate will be used"*: "Mary Martin Gets Estate," *New York Times* (March 10, 1973).

289 *"As soon as possible I went away"*: Martin, *My Heart Belongs*, 304–05.

290 *"It is just almost impossible for me to imagine life without Richard"*: Davis, *Mary Martin*, 254.

290 *"For thirty-four years it was* our *career"*: Paul Rosenfield, "Mary Martin: A Video First," *Los Angeles Times* (April 12, 1979).

291 *"she took the first place the Realtor showed her"*: Author interview with Gertz.

292 *"The first day I moved in, he came out to get his mail"*: Elliott Sirkin, unpublished manuscript for *After Dark* magazine (1977).

292 *"Ben Washer was really Halliday's friend"*: Author interview with Gertz.

292 *"Before then, his roommate"*: Author interview with Tuft.

292 *"I just never moved out," Washer would say*: Cathleen Decker, "Actresses Survive Fatal Auto Crash," *Los Angeles Times* (September 7, 1982).

292 *"Baby-sitter for the oldest baby in captivity"*: Martin, *My Heart Belongs*, 324.

292 *"Every morning and night when Ben and I go in the pool"*: Davis, *Mary Martin*, 257.

292 *"The why of her authorship"*: Allen Macaulay, *Bergen Record* (n.d.).

292 *"But that was a little early . . . fault but my own"*: Aleene MacMinn, "Mary Martin Back on Road—as Mary Martin," *Los Angeles Times* (April 20, 1976).

293 *"This is not only good. It is very, very good"*: Allen MaCaulay, *Bergen Record* (n.d.).

293 *"When I got to the part about Richard"*: Aleene MacMinn, "Mary Martin Back on Road."

294 *"How this dear lady by the name of Dodie Hamblin"*: Davis, *Mary Martin*, 256.

294 *"It will be like the old Paramount days"*: Eugenia Sheppard, *New York Post* (April 23, 1976).

294 *"When they sent out the itinerary, I'd never seen anything like it"*: Aleene MacMinn, "Mary Martin Back on Road."

295 *"I looked at that Monday schedule and said"*: Ibid.

297 *"He almost might as well not have been there"*: Author interview with Sirkin.

297 *In his review of* My Heart Belongs: Seymour Peck, "Mary Martin Amid the Alian [*sic*] Corn," *Los Angeles Times* (May 2, 1976).

297 *Foster Hirsch was somewhat more critical*: Foster Hirsch, *Chicago Tribune* (April 11, 1976).

298 *"Though the memoir avoids being a fully honest purge"*: Rivadue, *Mary Martin*, 180.

298 *"I always thought this lady was too sweet"*: Author interview with Shaffer.

299 *"cockeyed optimist . . . The avocadoes were the size of footballs"*: Aljean Harmetz, "Still the 'Cockeyed Optimist'?" *New York Times* (September 8, 1977).

299 *"I love it, but it's so far"*: Aleene MacMinn, "Mary Martin Back on Road—as Mary Martin," *Los Angeles Times* (April 20, 1976).

299 *"I'll do anything with Merman!"*: Radie Harris, "Broadway Ballyhoo," *Hollywood Reporter* (May 19, 1977).

300 *"They could have sold tickets for a thousand dollars a seat"*: Author interview with Saddler.

300 *various celebrities who weren't in the show tried to serve as* "ushers and usherettes": Enid Nemy, "Two Stars Bait a Better Mousetrap," *New York Times* (May 16, 1977).

300 *"They came through to such applause"*: Here and throughout, author interview with Saddler.

301 *Martin was, however, understandably nervous*: Kellow, *Ethel Merman*, 242.

302 *Radie Harris pronounced* Together on Broadway *"one of the greatest shows"*: Harris, "Broadway Ballyhoo."

302 *"There were two Dollys and two staircases"*: Author interview with Sheridan.

302 *According to Bob Ullman*: Author interview with Ullman.

302 *"Ethel Merman is the bonfire and Mary Martin is the smoke"*: Kerr, "The Merman-Martin Magic Blazes in Benefit 2-Alarm Fire of Genius," *New York Times* (May 17, 1977).

303 *"Ethel was raring to go and in great shape"*: Author interview with Ellis.

303 *When Radie Harris asked Larry Hagman if Martin was really his mother*: Radie Harris, "Broadway Ballyhoo."

303 *"Jesus," said Merman*: Kellow, *Ethel Merman*, 243.

304 *"I think what's happened to Broadway is devastating"*: Davis, *Mary Martin*, 262.

304 *Tisha Browne, for one, found it "riotously funny"*: Tisha Browne, "There Is Nothing Like a Dame," *Tidbits* (February 17, 1977), 17.

305 *Martin thought it might be reset in Boston and Cape Cod*: Michael Ryan, "Miss Martin Makes an Entrance," *Newsday* (January 8, 1978).

305 *"This play is about age and loneliness"*: Aljean Harmetz, "Still the 'Cockeyed Optimist'?" *New York Times* (September 8, 1977).

305 *"When I fell off the platform"*: Ibid.

306 *"I'm happy in this part," Martin told Sirkin*: Elliott Sirkin, unpublished manuscript for *After Dark* magazine (1977).

306 *She complained to Rex Reed*: Rex Reed, *Daily News* (January 8, 1978).

306 *"one of those defenseless Southern belles"*: Ibid.

307 *"This kind of bittersweet old folks' romance"*: John Simon, *New York* (January 23, 1978), 69.

307 *why Martin had chosen such a "dreary and vapid" work*: Rex Reed, *Daily News* (January 11, 1978), 55.

307 *its two stars "souffleed [it] into an amusing and often touching entertainment"*: Frank Trippet, *Time* (September 5, 1977).

307 *it was geared "for an audience"*: Sylvie Drake, *Los Angeles Times* (January 11, 1978).

307 *"Mary is a great lady of the theatre"*: Logan, *Movie Stars*, 486.

308 *"If they are too good I get a little nervous"*: Richard Lee, *New York Post* (January 17, 1978).

308 *"I have entered into a deal with Fieldcrest"*: Mary Martin to Elliott Sirkin (March 9, 1978).

308 *"I don't quite understand how we're going to manage singing sheets"*: "A Family Christmas with Mary Martin," *Harper's Bazaar* (December 1978).

309 *"Colors are soft and muted"*: Victoria Erin Towns, "Some of Her Favorite Things," *House Beautiful* (November 1978), 110.

309 *"I was appearing at a mall on a Sunday"*: Carol Wallace, *Sunday News Magazine* (May 24, 1981), 4.

309 *"What's it like to have an icon for a son?"*: Hagman, *Hello Darlin'*, 211.

309 *"Larry had T-shirts made"*: Author interview with Schulman.

309 *"Joel Grey, a close friend of Larry's"*: Crawford, *One Naked Individual*, 249.

310 *"As she rose and waved, people went nuts"*: Hagman, *Hello Darlin'*, 205.

310 *"While Miss Martin is delightful in the role"*: Arthur Unger, *Christian Science Monitor* (December 6, 1979), 18.

311 *"I missed a lot"*: Ibid.

311 *"One of the reasons Larry had been so mad at Richard"*: Author interview with Flicker.

311 *"After Richard died, Maj and Larry really took care of her"*: Author interview with Phillips.

19   "Sunnyside Up"

312 *"It was originally to star Glynis Johns as Maude"*: Author interview with Ellis.

313 *She spent much of the summer of 1980*: Author interview with Joan Yellen.

313 *"Walking off with the whole show were Mary"*: Kellow, *Ethel Merman*, 255–56.

313 *Martin was "tucked into his dressing room"*: Martin, *My Heart Belongs*, 317.

313 *"talking and appearing on TV and in department stores*: Ibid., 321.

314 *"Looks like I'm going to get top billing"*: *Time* (September 21, 1981).

315 *"Here is a woman who's got life"*: Aleene MacMinn, "Martin: Life Has Her Flying High," *Los Angeles Times* (September 25, 1981).

315 *According to Kristina Hagman, her grandmother "used 'Ephraim'"*: Author interview with Hagman.

315 *Hugh Downs had called, wanting her to cohost "a PBS talk show"*: "Mary Martin: Flying High Again," *Possibilities* (November/December 1983), 8.

315 *she recalled having to be prompted by Hartz*: Davis, *Mary Martin*, 268.

315 *"I did it because I thought I could be helpful"*: Judy Klemesrud, "Mary Martin's Newest Role," *New York Times* (September 30, 1981), C1.

316 *When Aleene MacMinn asked Martin*: Aleene MacMinn, "Martin: Life Has Her Flying High," *Los Angeles Times* (September 25, 1981).

317 *"The impact sent the cab skidding"*: Cathleen Decker, "Actresses Survive Fatal Auto Crash," *Los Angeles Times* (September 7, 1982).

317 *"Jules and I were already in bed"*: Author interview with Dorothy Powers.

317 *"They were still working on Mary when I saw her"*: Terrence O'Flaherty, "A Bouquet for Mary," *San Francisco Chronicle* (September 8, 1982).

318 *"Maj and I flew to be with her immediately"*: Hagman, *Hello Darlin'*, 210–11.

318 *Paul Gregory's negative views of Martin have calcified*: Author interview with Gregory.

318 *Gregory even came to blame Martin directly*: Ibid.

318 *"The cab driver had the longest hair"*: Nancy Faber, "After a Tragic Auto Accident, Mary Martin Heals Wounds of the Body and the Heart," *People* (October 11, 1982).

319 *"Paul Gregory asked her to testify in court"*: Author interview with Grushkin.

319 *superior court judge, Raymond Arata, admonished him*: "Driver Gets 3 Yrs. in Martin Crash," *Daily News* (March 16, 1983), and *The Globe and Mail* (March 18, 1983).

319 *"I started by raising myself to a sitting position"*: Mary Martin, "We're Tougher Than You Think," *Guideposts* (May 1983), 3.

319 *"Millions of people will miss seeing us on the Emmys"*: Kellow, *Ethel Merman*, 261.

320 *"I've never known anything in my career to equal it"*: Victor Merina, "After Accident, Martin's Back Where She Belongs," *Los Angeles Times* (September 30, 1982).

320 *"Her return [episode] is a homecoming"*: Ed Bark, "Mary Martin Comes Back," *Spokane Chronicle* (October 9, 1982).

320 *"He always thought it was one of the prettiest words"*: Nancy Faber, "After a Tragic Auto Accident, Mary Martin Heals Wounds of the Body and the Heart," *People* (October 11, 1982).

321 *"The house was in a new development"*: Author interview with Magor.

321 *"As Mary said later, 'Well, I just felt like going home'"*: Author interview with Mintun.

322 *"The worst comes around 3:30 in the morning"*: Bob Thomas, "Mary Martin Remains Strong and Optimistic Despite Her Injuries," *Philadelphia Inquirer* (January 2, 1983), quoted in Rivadue, *Mary Martin*, B288.

322 *"I received a package in the mail including a lovely letter"*: Author interview with Levin.

323 *"Burgess Meredith, out of the blue"*: Ibid.

323 *"When I saw her last week, she had pneumonia"*: Bob Thomas, "Mary Martin Remains Strong and Optimistic Despite Her Injuries," *Philadelphia Inquirer* (January 2, 1983), quoted in Rivadue, *Mary Martin,* B288.

324 *"I have stayed out of politics as much as I could"*: Martin, *My Heart Belongs,* 319.

325 *"She and I are very much alike"*: *New York Times* (January 13, 1984).

325 *"The apartment had wonderful bay windows"*: Author interview with Mintun.

325 *"I live four flights up"*: Stack, "Mary Martin Lends a Hand," *San Francisco Chronicle* (September 13, 1984).

326 *"My assignment on the program"*: Author interview with Mintun.

326 *"When the glee club started singing"*: Miriam Nelson, *My Life Dancing with the Stars* (BearManor Lane, 2009), 279.

326 *"As soon as she sang it"*: Gerald Nachman, "A High-Flying Affair at Davies," *San Francisco Chronicle* (October 24, 1984).

327 *"both she and John Raitt had problems"*: Author interview with Mintun.

327 *"had a hell of a time trading lines"*: Author interview with Magor.

20   What Becomes a Legend Least?

328 *"I have never been so happily busy"*: Martin, *My Heart Belongs,* 315–16.

329 *"Mary Martin was so incredibly gracious"*: Author interview with Magor.

331 *"Because of the fact that she was such a wealthy woman"*: Author interview with Marky Quayle.

331 *"As smart as you can get, in London"*: Author interview with Kyd.

331 *"Mary took a picture"*: Author interview with Marky Quayle.

331 *"I remember, when I had to pick her up"*: Author interview with Kyd.

332 Our Hearts Belong to Mary *cost $300 a ticket*: Details in this paragraph from Kirkwood, *Diary of a Mad Playwright,* 56.

332 *"I was very frightened," Hayes recounted*: Samuel G. Freedman, *New York Times* (October 21, 1985).

333 *"We had to keep her from Mary"*: Author interview with Magor.

333 Claiming *"there's a huge difference"*: Here and throughout, author interview with Grushkin.

334 *"I don't think Suzy knew what should happen"*: Author interview with Kabel.

335 *"I really think it's funny," he told Martin*: David Wallace, "Mary Martin and Carol Channing Are Bitchy Superstars in *Legends!*" *People* (December 16, 1985).

336 *"one thing Mr. Larry Hagman is very careful about"*: Elliott Sirkin, "My Son, Larry Hagman," *Good Housekeeping* (July 1987), 164.

336 *"She didn't know it was fake blood"*: Author interview with Sirkin.

336 *"If Claudette could do it"*: Aleene MacMinn, "Mary Martin: Being a Legend Agrees with Her," *Los Angeles Times* (January 30, 1986).

336 *"I'd want to be in top form"*: Connie Berman, "Mary Martin . . . She's a Star at Needlepoint, Too!" *Needlecraft* (Spring/Summer 1980), 46.

336 there was *"talk that her character might be expanded"*: Bob Thomas, "Mary Martin Remains Strong and Optimistic Despite Her Injuries," *Philadelphia Inquirer* (January 2, 1983).

336 *"My mother always told me, 'Let your conscience be your guide'"*: Arthur Unger, "Mary Martin," *Christian Science Monitor* (December 6, 1979).

337 she assumed she would be playing Sylvia: Kirkwood, *Diary of a Mad Playwright,* 24.

337 *"Mary struck me as being down to earth"*: Ibid., 25.

337 *"They kept sending me the play"*: Janice Arkatov, "Two Old Pals Play Old Rivals in *Legends*!" *Los Angeles Times* (December 13, 1985).

337 *"Sunday, while being honored by the city of Dallas"*: Kirkwood, *Diary of a Mad Playwright*, 184.

338 *"She called the minute she found out*: Elliott Sirkin, "My Son, Larry Hagman," *Good Housekeeping* (July 1987), 164.

338 *"Gossip about Legends was everywhere"*: Kirkwood, *Diary of a Mad Playwright*, xvi.

338 *"It was Nancy Reagan who recommended the ear bug"*: Author interview with Kabel.

338 *"her ear bug cut out"*: Kirkwood, *Diary of a Mad Playwright*, 181.

338 *"Mary started receiving taxicab dispatch calls"*: Ibid., 248.

339 *"Yes, she heard the taxi calls one night"*: Author interview with Grushkin.

339 *"Sure enough, Mary was getting those taxi calls"*: Author interview with Kabel.

340 *"Larry Hagman was suddenly around a lot"*: Author interview with Kabel.

340 *"In rehearsal we had an English director"*: Channing, *Just Lucky I Guess*, 241.

340 *"San Francisco was a crucial opening"*: Author interview with Kabel.

340 *"Gerald Nachman said the show had improved"*: Kirkwood, *Diary of a Mad Playwright*, 242.

341 he began *"hearing rumors that Mary and Larry Hagman were grumbling"*: Ibid., 241.

341 "I don't need to work": Ibid., 266.

341 *"Mary essentially said, 'If the speech is cut, I'm cut'"*: Author interview with Kabel.

342 *Martin and Channing "had two very different techniques"*: Author interview with Kabel.

342 *"Toward the end of August"*: Kirkwood, *Diary of a Mad Playwright*, 280–81.

342 *"So they were not only not coming"*: Ibid., 275.

342 *"Legends was a very* Rashomon *experience"*: Author interview with Ellis.

343 *"Basically, I told her"*: Author interview with Sirkin.

343 *"Everybody I talk to in the theatrical community here"*: Kirkwood, *Diary of a Mad Playwright*, 305.

344 *"Miss Martin and Miss Channing admit their stylistic differences"*: Dena Kleiman, "Legends Turns a Profit Without Broadway," *New York Times* (December 9, 1986).

344 *Kirkwood would put the blame on Martin*: Kirkwood, *Diary of a Mad Playwright*, 335.

344 Legends *had grossed nearly $10 million*: *New York Times* (December 22, 1986).

345 *"For all the talk of their not getting along"*: Author interview with Ellis.

345 *he observed Martin cover her ears*: Ibid.

21 Benefit Mary

348 *"A startlingly spry 74"*: Leslie Bennetts, "And Now, the International Festival of the Arts," *New York Times* (June 10, 1988).

348 *"After she finished her introduction to the screening"*: Author interview with Klain.

348 *"The person who got up in the audience"*: Author interview with Schulman.

349 *"It is news that Mary Martin still"*: Dan Sullivan, "Stage Review: That Was Some Enchanted Evening at the Hollywood Bowl," *Los Angeles Times* (August 31, 1988).

349 it *"seemed a natural to become a TV perennial"*: Aleene MacMinn, "Mary Martin's Return From Never-Never Land," *Los Angeles Times* (March 19, 1989).

350 *"It is Miss Martin's conviction"*: Jeremy Gerard, "TV Notes," *New York Times* (January 19, 1989).

350 *"I don't feel seventy-five"*: Jeanne Wright, *USA Today* (March 22, 1989), quoted in Rivadue, *Mary Martin*, B312.

350 *"She said yes, she said no"*: Davis, *Mary Martin*, 279.

350 *"It worked very well in Chicago"*: Author interview with Schmidt.

350 *Grushkin arranged for Schmidt to introduce Martin*: Author interview with Grushkin.

351 *"We went out to Mary's in Palm Springs"*: Author interview with Schmidt.

351 *"Before the cruise"*: Author interview with Grushkin.

351 *Grushkin also recalled a "large storm"*: Ibid.

351 *Schmidt recalled showing the ad to Martin*: Author interview with Schmidt.

352 *"Mother's prognosis wasn't good"*: Hagman, *Hello Darlin'*, 225.

352 *"She was and is and always will be Peter Pan"*: Kevin Davis, "Kennedy Center Gala: A Five-Star Tribute for Living Legends," *Los Angeles* (December 4, 1989), and Miles Beller, "Kennedy Center Honors," *Hollywood Reporter* (December 29, 1989).

353 *"The day before, I noticed something didn't feel quite right"*: Author interview with Grushkin.

353 *"She had no professional commitments to fulfill"*: Ibid.

354 *"He came only once, which meant a lot to Mary"*: Ibid.

354 *He was dismayed to discover that a "prominent television pastor was sitting on her bed"*: Hagman, *Hello Darlin'*, 226.

354 *"She didn't follow any one religion"*: Author interview with Grushkin.

355 *"Mary's dying wish"*: Rivadue, *Mary Martin*, 21, 207.

355 *"She'd never liked Bach"*: Hagman, *Hello Darlin'*, 226.

355 *"I was living in Houston at that point"*: Author interview with Heller Halliday.

356 *Carol Channing was one of the last to see her alive*: Rivadue, *Mary Martin*, 21.

356 *"I remember calling Heller"*: Author interview with Grushkin.

356 *"We're not going to dwell on this illness"*: Ibid.

22   "What a Way to Go!"

357 *"I'll keep living until it's time"*: Rivadue, *Mary Martin*, 196.

357 *"More than any of her peers"*: Mel Gussow, "Mary Martin, 76, First Lady of Musicals, Dies," *New York Times* (November 5, 1990).

358 *"If Martin . . . was the most airborne"*: *New York Times* (November 11, 1990).

358 *"Her special charm was an innocence"*: Rivadue, *Mary Martin*, 21.

358 *Hagman also forgot which particular Palm Springs mortuary*: Hagman, *Hello Darlin'*, 226.

359 *According to Susan Grushkin, Hagman next contacted her*: Author interview with Grushkin.

359 *In his memoir, Larry Hagman described the "whole family" congregating*: Hagman, *Hello Darlin'*, 227–28.

360 *"The memorial was a spectacular event"*: Author interview with Kristina Hagman.

361 *"My dream is to fly in Madison Square Garden"*: Leslie Bennetts, "And Now, the International Festival of the Arts," *New York Times* (June 10, 1988).

SELECTED BIBLIOGRAPHY

Abbott, George. *Mister Abbott*. New York: Random House, 1963.

Agee, James. *Agee on Film*. Vol. 1. New York: Grosset & Dunlap, 1969.

Atkinson, Brooks, and Albert Hirschfeld. *The Lively Years: 1920–1973*. New York: Association Press, 1973.

Bach, Steven. *Dazzler: The Life and Times of Moss Hart*. New York: Alfred A. Knopf, 2001.

Barranger, Milly S. *A Gambler's Instinct: The Story of Broadway Producer Cheryl Crawford*. Carbondale: Southern Illinois University Press, 2010.

———. *Margaret Webster: A Life in the Theater*. Ann Arbor: University of Michigan Press, 2004.

Bergreen, Laurence. *As Thousands Cheer: The Life of Irving Berlin*. New York: Viking, 1990.

Block, Geoffrey. *The Richard Rodgers Reader*. New York: Oxford University Press, 2002.

Bordman, Gerald. *American Musical Theatre: A Chronicle*. New York: Oxford University Press, 1978.

———. *American Musical Theatre: A Chronicle of Comedy and Drama, 1930–1969*. New York: Oxford University Press, 1996.

Bray, Christopher. *Sean Connery: A Biography*. New York: Pegasus Books, 2011.

Channing, Carol. *Just Lucky I Guess: A Memoir of Sorts*. New York: Simon & Schuster, 2002.

Clurman, Harold. *Lies Like Truth*. New York: Macmillan, 1958.

Colacello, Bob. *Ronnie and Nancy: The Path to the White House*. New York: Warner Books, 2004.

Courtney, Marguerite. *Laurette*. New York: Rinehart, 1955.

Crawford, Cheryl. *One Naked Individual*. Indianapolis: Bobbs-Merrill, 1977.

Davis, Ronald L. *Mary Martin: Broadway Legend*. Norman: University of Oklahoma Press, 2008.

Day, Barry. *The Letters of Noël Coward*. New York: Alfred A. Knopf, 2007.

Dietz, Howard. *Dancing in the Dark*. New York: Quadrangle, 1974.

Duchin, Peter. *Ghost of a Chance: A Memoir*. New York: Random House, 1996.

Eames, John Douglas. *The Paramount Story*. New York: Simon & Schuster, 2002.

Farneth, David, with Elmar Juchem and Dave Stein. *Kurt Weill: A Life in Pictures and Documents*. Woodstock, NY: Overlook Press, 2000.

Feuer, Cy. *I Got the Show Right Here*. New York: Simon & Schuster, 2003.

Fordin, Hugh. *Getting to Know Him: Oscar Hammerstein II*. New York: Ungar Publishing, 1986.

Gilvey, John Anthony. *Before the Parade Passes By: Gower Champion and the Glorious American Musical*. New York: St. Martin's Press, 2005.

Goldman, William. *The Season: A Candid Look at Broadway*. New York: Harcourt, Brace & World, 1969.

Green, Stanley. *The Rodgers and Hammerstein Story*. New York: Da Capo Press, 1963.

Grissom, James. *Follies of God: Tennessee Williams and the Women of the Fog*. New York: Alfred A. Knopf, 2015.

Hadleigh, Boze. *Hollywood Lesbians*. New York: Barricade Books, 1994.

Hagman, Larry. *Hello Darlin'*. New York: Simon & Schuster, 2001.

Hanson, Bruce K. *The Peter Pan Chronicles*. New York: Birch Lane Press, 1993.

Harding, James. *Emlyn Williams: A Life*. London: Weidenfeld & Nicolson, 1993.

Hirsch, Foster. *Kurt Weill on Stage: From Berlin to Broadway*. New York: Alfred A. Knopf, 2002.

Hoare, Philip. *Noël Coward*. New York: Simon & Schuster, 1995.

Hopper, Hedda. *The Whole Truth and Nothing But*. New York: Doubleday, 1963.

Houseman, John. *Front and Center*. New York: Simon & Schuster, 1979.

Jacobson, Stuart E. *Only the Best: A Celebration of Gift Giving in America*. New York: Harry N. Abrams, 1985.

Kazan, Elia. *Elia Kazan: A Life*. New York: Alfred A. Knopf, 1988.

Kear, Lynn. *Laurette Taylor, American Stage Legend*. Jefferson, NC: McFarland, 2010.

Kellow, Brian. *Ethel Merman: A Life*. New York: Viking, 2007.

Kirkwood, James. *Diary of a Mad Playwright*. New York: E. P. Dutton, 1989.

Kissel, Howard. *David Merrick: The Abominable Showman*. New York: Applause, 1993.

Laffey, Bruce. *Beatrice Lillie: The Funniest Woman in the World*. New York: Wynwood Press, 1989.

Lawrence, Greg. *Dance with Demons: The Life of Jerome Robbins*. New York: Putnam, 2001.

Leonard, William Torbert. *Broadway Bound: A Guide to Shows that Died Aborning*. Metuchen, NJ: Scarecrow Press, 1983.

Lerner, Alan Jay. *The Musical Theatre: A Celebration*. New York: McGraw-Hill, 1986.

———. *The Street Where I Live*. New York: Norton, 1978.

Logan, Joshua. *Josh: My Up and Down, In and Out Life*. New York: Dell, 1976.

———. *Movie Stars, Real People, and Me*. New York: Dell, 1978.

Loggia, Marjorie, and Glenn Young. *The Collected Works of Harold Clurman*. New York: Applause, 1994.

Mandelbaum, Ken. *Not Since Carrie*. New York: St. Martin's Press, 1991.

Mann, William J. *Behind the Screen*. New York: Penguin Books, 2001.

Martin, Mary. *Mary Martin's Needlepoint*. New York: Galahad Books, 1969.

———. *My Heart Belongs*. New York: Quill, 1984.

Maslon, Laurence. *The Sound of Music Companion*. New York: Simon & Schuster, 2007.

———. *The South Pacific Companion*. New York: Simon & Schuster, 2008.

McBrien, William. *Cole Porter: A Biography*. New York: Alfred A. Knopf, 1998.

McCarthy, Mary. *Mary McCarthy's Theatre Chronicles, 1937–1962*. New York: Farrar, Straus, 1963.

McDowell, Roddy. *Double Exposure*. New York: Delacorte Press, 1966.

McGovern, Dennis, and Deborah Grace Winer. *Sing Out, Louise!* New York: Schirmer Books, 1996.

McHugh, Dominic. *Loverly: The Life and Times of My Fair Lady*. New York: Oxford University Press, 2012.

Mielziner, Jo. *Designing for the Theatre*. New York: Atheneum, 1965.

Mordden, Ethan. *Broadway Babies: The People Who Made the American Musical*. New York: Oxford University Press, 1983.

——. *Love Song: The Lives of Kurt Weill and Lotte Lenya*. New York: St. Martin's Press, 2012.

——. *Rodgers & Hammerstein*. New York: Harry N. Abrams, 1992.

Morley, Sheridan, and Ruth Leon. *Gene Kelly: A Celebration*. London: Pavilion Books, 1996.

Nathan, George Jean. *The Theatre Book of the Year: 1945–1946*. New York: Alfred A. Knopf, 1946.

Newman, Shirlee P. *Mary Martin on Stage*. Philadelphia: Westminster Press, 1969.

Nolan, Frederick. *The Sound of Their Music: The Story of Rodgers and Hammerstein*. New York: Walker, 1978.

Oller, John. *Jean Arthur: The Actress Nobody Knew*. New York: Limelight Editions, 2004.

Osato, Sono. *Distant Dances*. New York: Alfred A. Knopf, 1980.

Payn, Graham, with Barry Day. *My Life with Noël Coward*. New York: Applause, 1994.

——, and Sheridan Morley. *The Noël Coward Diaries*. Boston: Little, Brown, 1982.

Pendleton, Ralph, ed. *The Theatre of Robert Edmond Jones*. Middletown, CT: Wesleyan University Press, 1958.

Peters, Margot. *Design for Living: Alfred Lunt and Lynn Fontanne*. New York: Alfred A. Knopf, 2003.

Pethel, Mary Ellen. *All-Girls Education from Ward Seminary to Harpeth Hall, 1865–2015*. Charleston, SC: History Press, 2015.

Plummer, Christopher. *Christopher Plummer: In Spite of Myself: A Memoir*. New York: Alfred A. Knopf, 2008.

Rich, Frank. *Ghost Light*. New York: Random House, 2000.

Rivadue, Barry. *Mary Martin: A Bio-Bibliography*. New York: Greenwood Press, 1991.

Rodgers, Dorothy. *My Favorite Things: A Personal Guide to Decorating and Entertaining*. New York: Atheneum, 1964.

Sanders, Ronald. *The Days Grow Short: The Life and Music of Kurt Weill*. New York: Holt, Rinehart and Winston, 1980.

Santopietro, Tom. *The Sound of Music Story*. New York: St. Martin's Press, 2015.

Schanke, Robert A., and Kim Marra. *Passing Performances: Queer Readings of Leading Players in American Theater History*. Ann Arbor: University of Michigan Press, 1998.

Schneider, Alan. *Entrances: An American Director's Journey*. New York: Viking, 1986.

Schulman, Susan L. *Backstage Pass to Broadway*. New York: Heliotrope Books, 2013.

Secrest, Meryle. *Somewhere for Me: A Biography of Richard Rodgers*. New York: Alfred A. Knopf, 2001.

Shipman, David. *The Great Movie Stars: The Golden Years*. New York: Hill and Wang, 1979.

Skinner, Cornelia Otis. *Life with Lindsay and Crouse*. Boston: Houghton Mifflin, 1976.

Steyn, Mark. *Broadway Babies Say Goodnight: Musicals Then and Now*. New York: Routledge, 1999.

Suskin, Steven. *More Opening Nights on Broadway*. New York: Schirmer Books, 1997.

——. *Opening Nights on Broadway*. New York: Schirmer Books, 1990.

Taylor, Robert. *Fred Allen: His Life and Wit*. Boston: Little, Brown, 1989.

This Fabulous Century: Volume VI, 1950–1960. New York: Time-Life Books, 1970.

Tynan, Kenneth. *Curtains*. New York: Atheneum, 1961.

Vaill, Amanda. *Somewhere: The Life of Jerome Robbins*. New York: Broadway Books, 2006.

Vickers, Hugo. *Vivien Leigh*. Boston: Little, Brown, 1988.

Wallace, David. *A City Comes Out: How Celebrities Made Palm Springs a Gay and Lesbian Paradise*. Fort Lee, NJ: Barricade, 2008.

Wilk, Max. *Overture and Finale: Rodgers and Hammerstein and the Creation of Their Two Greatest Hits*. New York: Back Stage Books, 1999.

Winer, Deborah Grace. *On the Sunny Side of the Street: The Life and Lyrics of Dorothy Fields*. New York: Schirmer Books, 1997.

Wright, Adrian. *West End Broadway: The Golden Age of the American Musical in London*. Woodbridge, UK: Boydell Press, 2012.

Young, Stark. *Immortal Shadows*. New York: Charles Scribner's Sons, 1948.

Yule, Andrew. *Sean Connery: Neither Shaken Nor Stirred*. London: Little, Brown, 1993.

Zadan, Craig. *Sondheim and Co.* 2nd ed. New York: Harper & Row, 1986.

INDEX

MM stands for Mary Martin.